GLOBAL ENGAGEMENT

JANNE E. NOLAN
Editor

GLOBAL ENGAGEMENT

Cooperation and Security in the 21st Century

THE BROOKINGS INSTITUTION
Washington, D.C.

THE BROOKINGS INSTITUTION
1775 Massachusetts Avenue, N.W., Washington, D.C. 20036

Library of Congress Cataloging-in-Publication data:
Global engagement: cooperation and security in the 21st century / Janne E. Nolan, editor.
p. cm.
Includes bibliographical references and index.
ISBN 0-8157-6098-1 (cloth) — ISBN 0-8157-6097-3 (paper)
1. Nuclear disarmament. 2. Security, International. 3. International cooperation. I. Nolan, Janne E.
JX1974.7.G54 1994
327.1'74—dc20 93-39464
CIP

9 8 7 6 5 4 3 2 1

The paper used in this publication meets the minimum requirements of the American National Standard for Information Sciences—Permanence of Paper for Printed Library Materials, ANSI Z39.48-1984

THE BROOKINGS INSTITUTION

The Brookings Institution is an independent organization devoted to nonpartisan research, education, and publication in economics, government, foreign policy, and the social sciences generally. Its principal purposes are to aid in the development of sound public policies and to promote public understanding of issues of national importance.

The Institution was founded on December 8, 1927, to merge the activities of the Institute for Government Research, founded in 1916, the Institute of Economics, founded in 1922, and the Robert Brookings Graduate School of Economics and Government, founded in 1924.

The Board of Trustees is responsible for the general administration of the Institution, while the immediate direction of the policies, program, and staff is vested in the President, assisted by an advisory committee of the officers and staff. The by-laws of the Institution state: "It is the function of the Trustees to make possible the conduct of scientific research, and publication, under the most favorable conditions, and to safeguard the independence of the research staff in the pursuit of their studies and in the publication of the results of such studies. It is not a part of their function to determine, control, or influence the conduct of particular investigations or the conclusions reached."

The President bears final responsibility for the decision to publish a manuscript as a Brookings book. In reaching his judgment on the competence, accuracy, and objectivity of each study, the President is advised by the director of the appropriate research program and weighs the views of a panel of expert outside readers who report to him in confidence on the quality of the work. Publication of a work signifies that it is deemed a competent treatment worthy of public consideration but does not imply endorsement of conclusions or recommendations.

The Institution maintains its position of neutrality on issues of public policy in order to safeguard the intellectual freedom of the staff. Hence interpretations or conclusions in Brookings publications should be understood to be solely those of the authors and should not be attributed to the Institution, to its trustees, officers, or other staff members, or to the organizations that support its research.

Foreword

In the past few years the character of international security has changed markedly, so that the foundations of past strategy, based on the preparation for massive military confrontation, are no longer adequate or appropriate for the challenges ahead. In analyzing that change, the authors of this volume focus on an alternative form of security that emphasizes cooperative strategies. These include practical steps for moving away from the accumulation of the means for mass, deliberate, and organized aggression, such as the seizure of sovereign territory by force or the destruction of vital assets by remote bombardment for unilateral gain.

In the face of an altered security environment, it is argued, cooperation has become the new strategic imperative. To be usable and effective against new security contingencies, even military force demands internationally agreed-upon norms to guide the composition and objectives of force postures. In essence, cooperative security renders explicit the existing commitment among most states to regulate the size, technical composition, investment patterns, and operational practices of all military forces by mutual consent for mutual benefit.

Security based on cooperation and the prevention of conflict will probably remain an aspiration that can only be incompletely fulfilled. But even aspirations give coherence to security policy. They define what is desirable and at least partly achievable. Organizing principles like deterrence, nuclear stability, and containment embodied the aspirations of the cold war, and they were invaluable in guiding thought and action. For many practical and inescapable reasons discussed in the book, cooperative security is the corresponding principle for international security in the post–cold war era.

Yet, however compelling a prescription for future security, any cooperative approach invariably provokes skepticism about its achievability. Many people believe, with ample historical support, that sovereign nations will always have an inherent propensity for armed conflict and will not conform to cooperative standards that renounce the unilateral projection of power as the leading instrument of security. As with containment and deterrence, therefore, the usefulness of the cooperative security principle demands that we recognize its constraints and limits as well as its promises. Individual chapters in this collection gauge the prospects for cooperation against current regional and global political realities that may complicate its realization.

A diverse group of experts, including legal scholars, political scientists, technical analysts, and regional specialists contributed to this volume. It grew out of a series of meetings and discussions on cooperative security held over the course of a year and a half, with the collaboration of the Carnegie Corporation of New York, the Brookings Institution, the Carnegie Endowment of International Peace, and Harvard and Stanford Universities. The authors were guided by the conceptual work initiated by John D. Steinbruner, in an occasional paper, *A New Concept of Cooperative Security,* coauthored with Ashton B. Carter and William J. Perry and published by Brookings in late 1992. Building on that paper, and incorporating portions of its text, this book develops and refines the basic ideas of cooperative security, and analyzes their implications for specific policy challenges and regional realities. The book is therefore not intended to reflect a unanimity of views, nor is it a blueprint for comprehensive action. Rather its aim is to provoke a wider debate about the utility of cooperative engagement for future strategy. Three of the chapters—1, 2, and 16—are composites from several authors, whose names are listed. The published content of these chapters, however, is the responsibility of the volume editor.

Janne E. Nolan, a senior fellow in the Brookings Foreign Policy Studies program, wishes to thank all the contributors to the volume, including those who did not write chapters. Their participation in the workshops and as commentators was invaluable. A list of the people who assisted in the project appears at the back of the book. Several members of the group, however, deserve special mention here: David Hamburg, Jane Wales, and Alexander George, for their intellectual inspiration; and Michael B. Levin, for his guidance in supervising the logistics of the project and overseeing it from its inception to completion.

The editor is also grateful to Rachel Epstein for her research assistance; to Adrianne Goins, Charlotte Hebebrand, Alexander Ratz, Susan Sherwin, and Dan Turner for verifying the factual content of the chapters; and Louise Skillings for preparing the manuscripts for editing. Princeton Editorial Associates edited the manuscript and compiled the index. Brookings is grateful to the Carnegie Corporation of New York for initiating and supporting the Cooperative Security consortium, and to the W. Alton Jones Foundation, Inc., and the John D. and Catherine T. MacArthur Foundation for their financial support.

The views expressed in this book are solely those of the authors and should not be attributed to the Brookings Institution, to its trustees, officers, or other staff members, or to the organizations that support its research. Despite the number of individual contributors who have assumed positions in government since their participation in this project, no views expressed here should be construed as representing official policy.

BRUCE K. MACLAURY
President

January 1994
Washington, D.C.

Contents

Part Three: Applications of Cooperative Security

Part Four: Near-Term and Other Challenges

Part Five: Conclusion

Tables

Figure

Abbreviations and Acronyms

ABM	antiballistic missile
	Anti-Ballistic Missile (Treaty)
ACE	Allied Command Europe
APEC	Asia-Pacific Economic Cooperation Group
ARF	Association of South East Asian Nations Regional Forum
ARRC	Allied Command Europe Rapid Reaction Corps
ASEAN	Association of South East Asian Nations
ATTR	Automated Technology Transfer Registry
ATTU	Atlantic-to-the-Urals region (CSCE)
AWACS	airborne warning and control system
BCCI	Bank of Credit and Commerce International
BSA	Bank Secrecy Act
BWC	Biological Weapons Convention
CBM	Confidence-building measure
CD	Conference on Disarmament
CENTO	Central Treaty Organization
CFE	Conventional Armed Forces in Europe (Treaty)
CFE 1A	A follow-on agreement to CFE, on personnel ceiling
CIS	Commonwealth of Independent States
CITES	Convention on International Trade in Endangered Species
COCOM	Coordinating Committee on Multilateral Export Controls
CPC	Conflict Prevention Centre (CSCE)
CSBM	Confidence- and security-building measure
CSCA	Conference on Security and Cooperation in Asia
CSCAP	Council for Security and Cooperation in the Asia-Pacific
CSCE	Conference on Security and Cooperation in Europe
CSO	Committee of Senior Officials (CSCE)
CWC	Chemical Weapons Convention
EBRD	European Bank for Reconstruction and Development
EC	European Community

ECAFE	Economic Commission for Asia and the Far East
EDC	European Defense Community
EEA	Export Administration Act
EEZ	exclusive economic zone
EFA	European Fighter Aircraft, also known as the Eurofighter 2000
EFTA	European Free Trade Association
EPC	European Political Community
EPCI	Enhanced Proliferation Control Initiative
ESCAP	Economic and Social Commission for Asia and the Pacific (formerly ECAFE)
EURATOM	European Atomic Energy Community
FSC	Forum on Security and Cooperation
FSU	former Soviet Union
GA	General Assembly
GAO	General Accounting Office
GATT	General Agreement on Tariffs and Trade
GCC	Gulf Cooperation Council
IAEA	International Atomic Energy Agency
ICCA	International Currency Control Agency
ICJ	International Court of Justice
IEPG	Independent European Program Group (NATO)
IFI	International financial institutions
ILO	International Labor Organization
IMF	International Monetary Fund
INF	Intermediate-Range Nuclear Forces (Treaty)
IRRC	Investor Responsibility Research Center
JCG	Joint Consultative Group (CFE)
JVP	Jatika Vimukthi Peramuna (Sri Lankan political party)
KOBRA	Kontrolle bei der Ausfuhr
MBFR	mutual and balanced force reductions
MFO	Multinational Force and Observers
MSC	Military Staff Committee
MTCR	Missle Technology Control Regime
MTM	multinational technical means
NACC	North Atlantic Cooperation Council (NATO)
NASD	National Association of Securities Dealers
NASDAQ	National Association of Securities Dealers Automated Quotation system
NATO	North Atlantic Treaty Organization
NIS	newly independent states (FSU)
NMP	net material product
NNA	nonaligned and neutral states
NPT	Treaty on the Non-Proliferation of Nuclear Weapons
NSG	Nuclear Suppliers Group
NSWTO	Non-Soviet Warsaw Treaty Organization states
NTM	national technical means (of verification)

NWFZSA	nuclear weapon–free zone in south Asia
OAS	Organization of American States
OAU	Organization of African Unity
ODIHR	Office of Democratic Institutions and Human Rights (CSCE)
OECD	Organization for Economic Cooperation and Development
OEEC	Organization for European Economic Cooperation
OSI	on-site inspection
OSIA	On Site Inspection Agency
PDK	Party of Democratic Kampuchea
PECC	Pacific Economic Cooperation Council
PKO	peacekeeping operation
PLC	prelicense checks
PSV	postshipment verification
R&D	research and development
RCD	regional cooperation for development
SAARC	South Asian Association for Regional Cooperation
SALT	Strategic Arms Limitation Talks
SCC	Standing Consultative Commission
SDI	Strategic Defense Initiative
SEATO	South East Asia Treaty Organization
SEC	Securities and Exchange Commission
SHAPE	Supreme Headquarters Allied Powers, Europe (NATO)
START	Strategic Arms Reduction Talks
SWAT	Stock Watch Automated Tracking
TLE	treaty-limited equipment
UNDOF	United Nations Disengagement Observation Force
UNEP	United Nations Environmental Program
UNITAF	United Nations Task Force
UNOSOM	United Nations Operation in Somalia
UNPROFOR	United Nations Protection Force
UNSCOM	United Nations Special Commission
UNTAC	United Nations Transitional Authority in Cambodia
WEU	Western European Union
WTO	Warsaw Treaty Organization

Part One

INTRODUCTION

ONE

The Concept of Cooperative Security

THE END of the cold war and the dissolution of the Soviet Union have transformed the familiar imperatives of international security. The possibilities of massive ground assault or deliberate nuclear attack are no longer the dominant problems to be considered in defense planning.

These traditional security preoccupations have been replaced by burdens of an entirely different character. With economic performance emerging as the overriding concern of the major industrial powers, their military establishments must now undertake a dramatic demobilization of the assets they had accumulated in preparing for large-scale war on short notice. They must reduce active deployments to lower, more sustainable levels and must restructure their activities to support the preventive management of security conditions, a task significantly different from responding to a specific attack. The longer-term consequences of technical diffusion, weapons proliferation, and political disintegration are a greater source of danger than is any immediate threat of deliberately calculated aggression.

In undertaking this restructuring, the major military establishments face planning problems that are conceptually more sophisticated and emotionally more difficult than those encountered during the cold war mobilization. They must safely dispose of large stocks of conventional and nuclear weapons and must strengthen managerial controls over those that remain. They must redirect a significant portion of their military personnel and supporting industrial organizations to other productive purposes. They must fashion their doctrines and deployments to distinguish between legitimate and illegitimate military purposes under conditions of evolving technology that make some illegitimate

This chapter, drafted by Janne E. Nolan, is based on contributions by other authors in this volume, especially Ashton B. Carter, William J. Perry, Wolfgang H. Reinicke, and John D. Steinbruner.

activities increasingly more feasible. And in accomplishing all these tasks, they must collaborate across the residual fault lines of confrontation.

The context of immediate events gives urgency to many of these new problems. A problem of deep historic significance is unfolding as the destiny of the nuclear arsenal of the former USSR is debated among its successor states and as these states face the very real prospect of further disintegration, a process into which the nuclear arsenal could be swept. Threats that in the past were not considered central to U.S. security, including civil disorder in Europe, other regional tensions, and the proliferation of destructive technologies to hostile states, now cast a shadow over future U.S. security in a way that cannot be directly addressed by the assertion of unilaterally superior force or readiness.

The political crises in the former Soviet bloc, not least the struggle for control of nuclear weapons in Ukraine, Kazakhstan, and Belarus, and the widening conflict in Yugoslavia are just two manifestations of the resistance of new security challenges to resolution via traditional security instruments. Similarly serious economic and environmental problems point to an inescapable interdependence of U.S. interests and the interests of other nations. And even when U.S. interests are not directly at risk, as in Somalia, the United States bears an unavoidable responsibility for political leadership in the world order.

Together these challenges amount to a transformed agenda for the international system, altering the formative conditions of security planning. It is clear that new principles are needed to ensure that the pending reconfiguration of military establishments and commensurate security policies are steered toward safe and stable outcomes that minimize any adverse effects on international and regional politics. It is only logical that radical transformations in the nature of security threats compel commensurately dramatic revisions in security concepts. If it is acknowledged that these threats cannot be met effectively with traditional forms of readiness and deterrence, then more constructive and sophisticated forms of influence and intervention will obviously be required.

To date, however, attempts to redefine security objectives and to restructure forces accordingly have consisted largely of redefinitions of old threats; for example, a reconstituted superpower Russia is viewed in terms of its implications for the maintenance of nuclear forces, or one or several implicit replays of the Gulf War are seen as the basis for gauging requirements for conventional forces. That U.S. security policy might be based on the prevention of threats by cooperative means is not an idea that has as yet fully taken hold at either the official or the expert level.

It is the purpose of this volume to explore the proposition that cooperative engagement is the appropriate principle for security relations under the new international circumstances that have emerged. Cooperative engagement is a strategic principle that seeks to accomplish its purposes through institutionalized consent rather than through threats of material or physical coercion. It presupposes fundamentally compatible security objectives and seeks to establish collaborative rather than confrontational relationships among national military establishments. The basis for such collaboration is mutual acceptance of and support for the defense of home territory as the exclusive national military objective and the subordination of power projection to the constraints of international consensus. A fully developed cooperative security arrangement embodying these principles would set and enforce appropriate standards for the size, concentration, technical configuration, and operational practices of deployed forces. Reassurance would be the principal objective, as distinct from deterrence and containment, although as a practical matter both of the latter objectives would be securely accomplished.

Cooperative security is not a description of the inexorability of a peaceful world system, a prediction about how the future will actually be formed, or a theory of international relations. The central purpose of cooperative security is to recognize and articulate how the character of security has changed in recent years and to demonstrate how this change has rendered the foundations of past strategy—based on the preparation for military confrontation—no longer an adequate or appropriate emphasis for meeting the challenges ahead.

At the practical level cooperative security seeks to devise agreed-upon measures to prevent war and to do so primarily by preventing the means for successful aggression from being assembled. By eliminating the material basis for organized aggression, such arrangements would also reduce or even obviate the need for states otherwise threatened to make their own counterpreparations.

Thus cooperative security replaces preparations to counter threats with the prevention of such threats in the first place and replaces the deterring of aggression with actions to make preparation for it more difficult. In the process the potential destructiveness of military conflict—especially incentives for the use of weapons of mass destruction—would also be reduced.

Cooperative security is a model of intrastate relations in which disputes are expected to occur, but they are expected to do so within the limits of agreed-upon norms and established procedures. While tolerating diversity and even animosity among disparate governments and cultures, this kind of international system allows for conflicts to be resolved without recourse to mass violence. In a system in which economic and political interdependence is explicitly recognized as both an objective and a deepening reality, armed aggression can become as futile as it is self-destructive.

Cooperative security differs from the traditional idea of collective security much as preventive medicine differs from acute care. Cooperative security is designed to ensure that organized aggression cannot start or be prosecuted on any large scale. By contrast, collective security is an arrangement for deterring aggression through military preparation and defeating it if it occurs.

Clearly the one strategy does not preclude the other and both are, in fact, mutually reinforcing. A fully developed cooperative security framework would include provisions for collective security as a residual guarantee to its members in the event of aggression. Systematic prevention of dangerous or aggressive military postures would make these guarantees easier to convey because they would be less likely to be required and, in the event, easier to underwrite. But the cooperative security concept assumes that war is not inevitable and that a commitment to the prevention of conflict is actually a more accurate reflection of states' pragmatic security interests in the 1990s than the assumption that power will always derive from the ability to wage war successfully.

A systematically developed cooperative security arrangement would be a dramatic revision of explicit policy but less so of actual practice. The sharp change in conceptualization would not be as radical a departure from the past as some may imagine, but more a conscious recognition and elaboration of existing trends. A cooperative form of security is already being practiced in many areas of the world, not least in the struggle to promote the denuclearization of the former Soviet Union and to define appropriate responses to the threat of continued disintegration of political order in eastern Europe. The enduring challenge in both these cases is not deterrence or force projection but the need to craft consensus for a cooperative intervention strategy that is seen as both effective and legitimate.

With the advent of protracted civil conflict in the former Yugoslavia and even in Somalia and Haiti, the international community has discovered that it has yet to define either the principles or the mechanisms for establishing order when it has collapsed within a sovereign state. On the contrary, governments are discovering that traditional security policies have reinforced the violent disintegration that has been the practical result of external sanctions, intervention constrained under humanitarian rules, and porous regulation of the distribution of arms to factions engaged in conflict. Efforts to forge cooperative responses to contain these kinds of risks are not random events; they are responses to changing political conditions that make cooperation the only practical alternative.

The demise of a dualistic global security system based on confrontation between the superpowers has already allowed a distinctly more pronounced habit of cooperation to emerge among former military rivals in NATO and the former Warsaw Pact. Decades of intense enmity are beginning to be replaced by a sense of shared destiny. The pattern of relations is not yet close to the Western alliance model, nor is it even guaranteed to survive, but it has already progressed far beyond what would have been considered a reasonable prediction just one or two years ago.

While political mutation is taking place on the most dramatic scale in the East-West context, moreover, the passing of the bipolar international security order is having an impact globally. International agreements and norms restricting the acquisition or use of unconventional weapons, including biological, chemical, and nuclear technologies and ballistic missiles, are the subject of renewed international attention and support. Efforts to strengthen codes of conduct guiding conventional weapon sales are being discussed in the UN and within the governments of industrial and some nonindustrial countries. The need to contain and redress the causes of regional and subregional conflict, from Yugoslavia to the Middle East to the horn of Africa, is challenging policymakers to examine new instruments of international mediation, peacekeeping, and collective intervention.

A greater emphasis on cooperation is also emerging among countries where military tensions have traditionally been and may remain severe. The preparation for interstate conflict is still very much embedded in the security policies of many regional powers, as it is indeed among the advanced countries. Regional antagonisms aside, however, there are signs of a growing perception of common threats among some regional actors, including the risks posed by weapons of mass destruction, ecological destruction, and the ravages of economic recession for domestic or regional stability. For some countries the spread of chemical or crude nuclear capabilities in volatile areas—systems that are for now effective only against unprotected populations or poorly equipped forces—really contributes to the making of the "poor man's bomb," since it is undeveloped countries that may face its gravest threats. Partly as a result of prompting from the advanced countries, there is evidence of a distinctly higher level of interest in confidence- and security-building measures (CSBMs) being expressed in key conflict areas such as the Middle East and South Asia. In time these might lead to greater political accommodation and limitations on certain military capabilities.

Cooperative security is initially a matter of making such arrangements a more conscious, central objective of international security policy. A cooperative security order need not take the form of a single, all-encompassing legal regime or arms control agreement, but would probably begin with a set of overlapping, mutually reinforcing arrangements derived from agreements already in force. In fact, a look at the rich fabric of constraints that have already grown up in more or less unconnected fashion indicates that existing ingredients of cooperative security are not hard to find on the international landscape. These constraints include limits on military operations, such as various CSBMs in place in Europe and the Middle East; agreements for averting war, such as measures covering accidents, hot lines, and crisis centers between the superpowers; limits on force size, weapon types, and operational practices, such as those contained in the Strategic Arms Reduction Talks (START), Conventional Armed Forces in Europe (CFE), and Intermediate-Range Nuclear Forces (INF) agreements; and the nuclear, biological, and chemical weapons and ballistic missile nonproliferation regimes. They extend to cooperative verification and transparency measures, such as the data exchanges and on-site inspections required by various arms control agreements, the UN arms sale registry, and the 1990 Open Skies agreement.

They are embodied in formal agreements, such as START, and in informal regimes, such as the London Suppliers and Australia groups working to stem global commerce in nuclear and chemical weapons. And they are embodied in tacit but firmly established norms of international behavior, such as those condemning the use of weapons of mass destruction or changing international borders by force. Since many existing arrangements emerged exclusively among industrial countries and have been subject to violation by developing states, building on these foundations will require adaptation to the unique security dilemmas of different regions and should seek to encompass all regions in a more representative international security system.

But however compelling a prescription for future security, the discussion of cooperative approaches to security invariably provokes skepticism about their achievability. It is widely believed, with ample historical support, that sovereign nations will always have an inherent propensity for armed conflict and that they cannot be expected to conform to cooperative standards that renounce the projection of power as a way of promoting state interest. Therefore the usefulness of the cooperative security principle, like that of containment and deterrence, is predicated on a recognition of its constraints and limits as well as its promises.

Cooperative security does not aspire to create an international government, to eliminate all weapons, to prevent all forms of violence, to resolve all conflicts, or to harmonize all political values. The focus is on preventing the accumulation of the means for mass, deliberate, and organized aggression, such as the seizure of territory by force or the destruction of vital assets by remote bombardment for unilateral gain. Cooperative security does not pretend to have easy answers for the underlying causes of conflict, including those currently fueling civil disorder around the world. But cooperative security may help provide a framework for the international community to organize responses to conflict, including civil violence. Indeed it may be the essential framework for preventing and containing such dangers in the future.

Developing a regime for cooperative engagement that has broad international support is not a normative aspiration or a messianic venture. In the face of the changing character of security threats, it is the new strategic imperative. To be usable and effective against new security contingencies, even military force will require internationally agreed-upon norms to guide the composition and objectives of force postures. In essence this requirement means that participants must embrace a commitment to regulate the size, technical composition, investment patterns, and operational practices of all military forces by mutual consent for mutual benefit.

In the world of practical politics, however, even the most powerful imperatives are not recognized immediately or fully if they involve departures from past practice. Redirecting the thoughts and emotions of large numbers of people usually requires much time and often a crystallizing crisis. In the United

States, in particular, fundamental changes in security policy can occur and be persuasively promoted internationally only if a new consensus is formed first at the domestic level.

How a new security agenda will be articulated and implemented is still uncertain. Thus security based on cooperation and on the prevention of conflict is now and probably will remain an aspiration only incompletely fulfilled. But even aspirations can give coherence to security policy. They define what is desirable and at least partly achievable. Organizing principles such as deterrence, nuclear stability, and containment embodied the aspirations of the cold war, and they were invaluable in guiding thought and action. For many practical and inescapable reasons, discussed in the following chapters, cooperative security is the corresponding principle for international security in the post–cold war era.

The effort to recast the foundations of security will stretch the minds of all those whose thinking about security continues to be premised on the immutability of international relations based on the threat of mass confrontation. Such a conceptual evolution is unavoidable if they are to understand and address the powerful forces reshaping the entire international security climate. As analyzed in this volume, the challenges ahead impose starkly different requirements from those encountered in the past and are likely to be resistant to the influence of even the most overwhelming demonstrations of traditional military capacity.

The eventual outcome of any effort to redefine a security regime turns upon political debates yet to be held, consensus judgments yet to form, and events yet to unfold. However, a reconceptualization of security policy is a necessary step in the right direction. The process must include defining the concept of cooperative security, identifying the trends that would motivate movement toward such a posture, analyzing the implications of the concept for practical policy action, and acknowledging its constraints. These are the tasks we have set for ourselves in this volume.

The following chapters explore various means by which cooperative approaches to security would alter and improve the formulation of policies guiding defense planning, military investment, and the use of force; other forms of international intervention; the design of regimes to control the diffusion of destabilizing technologies; and possible legal, trade, and financial inducements for promoting international standards of military behavior. They also explore the prospects and constraints that should be considered in adapting new norms and guidelines for cooperation in various regions, including the former Soviet bloc, western and eastern Europe, the Middle East, and South and Northeast Asia. The volume concludes with a discussion of the near-term challenges posed by an attempt to recast the foundations of security in the United States and the Commonwealth of Independent States (CIS).[1]

The cooperative security arrangements envisioned and analyzed in this volume consist of five major elements: (1) the establishment of strict controls and security measures for nuclear forces, building on agreements of the recent past; (2) a regime for the conversion of defense industries whose excess capacity could lead to unwarranted global weapons proliferation and thus exacerbate international instability; (3) cooperative agreements regulating the size and composition of forces to emphasize defensive configurations and also to restrict the flow of dangerous technologies; (4) articulation of an internationally supported concept of effective and legitimate intervention, in which the use of force is always multilateral and elected only as a last resort; and (5) the promotion of transparency and mutual interest as the basis for monitoring agreed-upon constraints, including those on the diffusion of advanced technologies.

As a practical matter cooperative approaches to security planning would first focus on the regulation of force postures that accord offensive capabilities, including constraints on the size and character of nuclear arsenals, ground forces, and tactical air assets. However imprecise judgments about offensive and defensive postures may seem, common sense and long-standing security planning principles dictate that there exist guidelines about force configurations that could aid such an effort. The important first step is to acknowledge that the national deployment of military capability must be governed by a strict principle of nonprovocation and be reflected in force postures accordingly.

As is discussed in chapters 6 and 15, by William J. Perry and by Ashton B. Carter and Steven E. Miller, such a regime would thus put strong constraints on nuclear weapons and seek to severely devalue nuclear forces as a currency of statecraft or a tool of power projection. Among the established nuclear powers, forces would be declared to have at most residual deterrent functions, bolstered by common arrangements to ensure high standards of safety for their security and control. The expressed desire on the part of Russian officials to remove all nuclear weapons from alert status and to extract the target instructions from the memories of the guidance computers on nuclear missiles signals a transformation in nuclear doctrine that is already occurring.

This transformation is motivated not only by a desire to demonstrate concretely that the dangerous cold war standoff is a political relic. A key objective guiding the recomposition of remaining nuclear forces would be to eliminate any perception of vulnerability to nuclear attack among all states, thereby also helping to discourage further production or deployment of nuclear weapons globally. Constraints on the nuclear arsenals of the established nuclear powers are a necessary, if not sufficient, condition to help persuade other states that nuclear weapons have little compelling utility. As a corollary the regime would seek the elimination of all weapons of mass destruction. Most members of the international system already agree that forces that are so obviously destabilizing and that pose high risks to noncombatants and civilians should not be sanctioned.

The fear that nuclear weapons might be used deliberately in a global war or in a calculated surprise attack of decisive proportion is no longer a guiding principle for the formulation of defense doctrine in any case. It is now acknowledged that virtually all plausible varieties of deterrence against nuclear attack could be underwritten with a fraction of the existing nuclear arsenals. The focus of the nuclear agenda has shifted from securing core deterrence to the safe management of nuclear weapons—from ensuring their security and safety in the established nuclear powers, to preventing the flow of nuclear technologies to other states, to creating conditions to discourage their deployment or use in regional conflict.

New nations created out of the former Soviet Union—as well as emerging powers in what has long been called the third world—are struggling to conceptualize their place in the security order and to define their military policies accordingly. They look to the rest of the international community to indicate how they should relate to emerging security structures and norms. The success of the heirs of the cold war in safely managing and reducing their arsenals and in relegating nuclear weapons to a background role in security affairs will have a powerful effect on efforts to stem nuclear proliferation in other regions of the world.

But it is not only nuclear forces that must be considered. After the Persian Gulf War the United States was generally conceded to possess a power projection capability, based on highly advanced conventional forces, that no other military establishment could match, at least not without also matching the lengthy and intense investment that created it.[2] For more than a decade to come, therefore, no other military establishment will be able to contemplate any major offensive without acknowledging that the United States is capable of decisive retaliation. That inevitably makes the United States, in the estimation of most countries, the ultimate answer to acts of aggression; for some, it also makes the United States a potential problem.

It is somewhat ironic that this new type of conventional capability successfully resolved the enduring challenge that had plagued NATO doctrine for decades—assembling the capacity to field effective conventional forces that could counter any conceivable military threat—at the same time that its intended opponents had disappeared. It is equally ironic that this long-sought and formidable array of advanced technology now poses new kinds of security dilemmas for which it has no ready answers.

Prominent among these dilemmas are the effects of this force posture on the security perceptions of regional powers, including nations that were not direct participants in the cold war or even in the Gulf War. After witnessing the performance of U.S. technology and military forces during Operation Desert Storm, some countries have clearly become concerned about potential future domination by a great-power coalition armed with long-range, highly precise, and readily usable military capabilities. Given their own access to weapons technology and growing technical capacities, some of these powers may already be seeking ways to contain such a threat by acquiring countermeasures, including nonconventional arsenals. In the future the security judgments of regional powers, as such, will inevitably affect the evolution of international security conditions, in turn impinging directly on choices made by the larger security establishments.

As Perry argues, the central objective served in redefining the composition, character, and utility of forces cooperatively is not only to reassure states that they will not be threatened by larger military establishments seeking unilateral advantage, but also to make the threat of collective force against potential aggressors credible if the need arises. Thus a cooperative approach to force projection is aimed at reducing the threat perceptions that drive states to acquire destabilizing arsenals and ensuring the ability of the international system to protect states credibly against the resurgence of aggression, by force if necessary.

Although a comprehensive set of restraints on conventional forces has never been established on a global basis, a precursor of such a regime for ground and air forces can, as noted earlier, be found in Europe. The CFE agreement imposes national ceilings on ground force equipment (tanks, armored personnel carriers, and artillery pieces) and tactical aircraft and helicopters. These ceilings are not derived from a requirement to make all national arsenals strictly defensive in character, but they nonetheless go a long way toward establishing the principle of defensive postures within recognized sovereign borders.

The extensive CSBMs established by the Conference on Security and Cooperation in Europe in 1990, which restrict the peacetime movement and concentration of the armies limited by the CFE agreement, also further constrain offensive potential. The Open Skies agreement, together with the inspections that are part of the CFE agreement and their accompanying CSBMs, establishes a standard of transparency for military deployments. Finally, negotiations are under way to provide integrated air traffic control over the whole of Europe, a potential foundation for regulating military operations more widely in the future.

Major ingredients of a cooperative security regime therefore already exist in western Europe and are discussed further in chapter 8, by Catherine McArdle Kelleher. This evolving regime provides all states with a reassuring cap on the threat posed by their neighbors. It furnishes an internationally shared rationale for the economically and socially disruptive process of rapid military demobilization faced by all European governments. It establishes a cooperative benchmark for the size and structure of their military establishments for new states emerging from the former Soviet Union that are defining their security postures, as well as for old states realigning their postures to their post–cold war situations. The regime is struggling with, but nevertheless actively confronting, the need to establish a framework in which violators of the rules or the peace are sanctioned and contained effectively.

In many cases cooperative standards for the overall size of ground forces and tactical air forces would be a political convenience rather than an imposed burden for military establishments in the industrial world and parts of the industrializing world. Most are already affected by competing economic priorities and by a growing realization that the preparation for and projection of military power cannot be the dominant instrument of policy. The dissolution of an immediate sense of threat and corresponding domestic budget restrictions are likely to shrink the major military establishments to levels more compatible with standards of cooperative security. That prospect gives the establishments an incentive to formalize those standards and to induce compliance by others, for their mutual benefit.

A cooperative security regime may appropriately begin by formalizing the tacitly cooperative security postures that already exist in Europe. But the types of threats that imperil international security require a more comprehensive arrangement that encompasses all like-minded states. As is argued from a legal standpoint by Antonia Handler Chayes and Abram Chayes in chapter 3 and in chapter 4 on international restraint regimes by Leonard S. Spector and Jonathan Dean, it is presumed that cooperation would ideally be comprehensively consensual, including all significant features of military capability as well as all the major military establishments.

Mutual restraint would be verified and reassurances given among cooperating parties through extensive transparency in force deployment and operations and in production, sale, and purchase of weapons. Such an international regime of transparency would mean greater sharing of national intelligence, as well as cooperatively established "international technical means" of monitoring in areas such as missile warning, air traffic surveillance, satellite photography, and cooperatively emplaced ground sensors on national territory for monitoring significant military operations.

The purpose of promoting transparency is to ensure that all military establishments are informed of the military preparations of others and that significant violations of agreed-upon constraints cannot be concealed. In turn this would require broadly supported international agreement that the deliberate concealment of suspect military activities denotes hostile intent, subject to the same response as overt violations. Thus such an arrangement would be based on enforceable sanctions and positive incentives to induce compliance and to manage the consequences of violations. The resulting limits on equipping and operating military forces would be consensual and aspire to be universally shared.

A cooperative security system involving extensive constraints on military preparations would have to require all parties to accept a level of intrusive monitoring of key defense programs, a challenge discussed in chapters 3 and 4 and by James A. Schear in chapter 7. First, such transparency would apply to force size and equipment, as in the START and CFE agreements. It would extend to major exercises and selected military operations, as in the European system of CSBMs, certain superpower agreements covering accidents and potentially hazardous military activities, and elements of peacekeeping efforts of the kind found in the Camp David accords. Second, it would cover certain development, test, and manufacturing activities, as in the START, INF, and Anti-Ballistic Missile (ABM) treaties, as well as in the Nuclear Non-Proliferation and Chemical Weapons treaties. Third, it would constrain sales and purchases of particular military-related technologies, as in START, the ABM treaty (forbidding transfer of weapons to other states), efforts among the permanent five members of the UN Security Council to forge guidelines for conventional arms sales, and the nuclear, biological, and chemical weapons and missile regimes.

For the control of nuclear, biological, and chemical weapons especially, a cooperative regime permitting regular inspection, including challenge inspections, would strengthen all three sets of limits in a mutually reinforcing way. Analyzed in greater detail in chapters 4 and 7, the integration of policies to monitor and enforce such limits is already under way at a practical level in several spheres, notably in the conduct of the UN Special Commission's activities in Iraq.

Control strategies for exports, especially for dual-use technology and for certain aspects of nuclear, biological, and chemical weapons proliferation, are currently based on denial of access to advanced technology. In a cooperative system that promoted transparency, the emphasis on supply controls and protectionism would give way on a selective basis to a control strategy stressing much freer availability of technology to all states if such states agreed to free disclosure of technology's disposition and application. This strategy would in turn require agreements to restrict particular forms of military investment and production for proscribed military capabilities.

As is elaborated in the analysis presented in chapter 5 by Wolfgang H. Reinicke, states that cooperated would in principle enjoy relatively unencumbered access to the technology of the advanced industrial states, including advanced dual-use technologies for civilian development and weapons systems consistent with the principle of defensive configuration. In this regard the radical advances in the processing and transmission of information that are a prime factor driving the problem of weapons proliferation also offer some significant opportunities for devising responses. Both Reinicke and Chayes and Chayes argue that, if disclosure is made the primary basis for regulation, some very effective measures could be introduced to facilitate monitoring and enforcement without disrupting normal trade flows.

An international registry could be established to record the manufacturer, the user, and the end use of all weapons products, major components, and sensitive technologies.[3] Such a registry would enforce disclosure of weapons manufacturers and transfers, embody agreed-upon restrictions on weapons deployments, set requirements for arms sales and other types of transfers to be consistent with norms, and monitor categorical prohibition of weapons of mass destruction. As a first step, if the principal producers and suppliers of advanced technologies—primarily the United States, the United Kingdom, Germany, France, Russia, China, and Japan—used such a registry to coordinate their arms deployments, transfers, and technical trade, the core of an international transparency arrangement would be formed. This proposal is elaborated in chapter 2, by Janne E. Nolan and others.

There are, in turn, powerful and as yet largely undeveloped inducements that could be offered to all countries to encourage them to comply with such an arrangement. Monitoring the registry and selectively inspecting products would make it much more difficult to conceal clandestine national weapons programs or international transfers. It would also provide the basis for bringing effective sanctions to bear should the need arise. As Reinicke and Chayes and Chayes emphasize, access to trade credits and other sources of international capital could be made contingent on participation in such agreements and compliance with their rules. A key premise underlying this approach is that countries participating in the cooperative security arrangement and complying with its rules not only would face lessened physical threat from other nations but also could gain access to extremely valuable security information, advanced technology for domestic modernization, and ultimately collective security guarantees from all the other members. Countries not participating would not gain any offsetting benefits and, even more significantly, would risk costly isolation within the international community.

Only countries in compliance with the arrangement would be guaranteed access to the international lending institutions or to any form of publicly subsidized credit, for example. With a systematic pattern of disclosure established as an internationally accepted norm and intelligence assets brought to bear to monitor compliance, systematic violation would be a great risk for defiant individuals, organizations, or states. National governments trying to develop proscribed military capabilities outside the cooperative regime would face real penalties, forcing decisionmakers and other actors who favor violations to contend with competing domestic interests, such as their own economic ministers and civilian industries, before subjecting the nation to the risk of economic loss and even pariah status in the international arena.

A key element of this argument, elaborated by Perry and by Nolan, is that an international arrangement that incorporates a concept of cooperative security and accepts its consequent constraints must also accept the central principle that the only legitimate purpose of national military forces is the defense of national territory or the participation in multinational forces that enforce internationally supported sanctions to create or maintain peace. That principle is consistent with the declared military doctrines of the major military establishments and is now believed to be consistent with their real expectations as well. Since it requires that any effort to change recognized borders by force be disavowed, there will be political difficulties with it in some parts of the world, particularly in areas where sovereign borders remain in dispute, such as the Middle East and South Asia. Nonetheless, this principle is accepted broadly and seriously enough in the international community to be a promising foundation for enhancing international consensus.

Still, even the most exacting rules could be too ambiguous to carry the full burden of international security. Exploitation of the common rules, variations in geography that make defensive policies more difficult for some countries than others, and the possibility of a rogue nation secretly developing an offensive capability in violation of the norm may always provide the rationale for aggression. Therefore an integral part of any cooperative security regime must be the capability to organize multinational forces to defeat aggression should it occur. This capacity would provide a background deterrent effect as well as physical protection to targeted states.[4]

In a cooperative security regime the use of military force would be a last resort, to be invoked only after the full range of other instruments of influence or coercion had been exhausted. The threat of force would be maximally effective in discouraging aggression if military forces were configured in a broadly based coalition equipped with modern weapons and born of political consensus. This broad international support would make the threat of military action politically credible.

It is central to Perry's argument that the threat of force of this kind would also be most credible militarily if the coalition was organized around the capabilities contained in a reconnaissance strike complex, as employed by the United States in Operation Desert Storm. Trying to organize such a coalition around more traditional configurations, such as conventional armored combined forces, could result in protracted and costly engagements. The absence of public support for such forms of intervention within the industrial countries alone in and of itself suggests that this kind of interventionary force would be unlikely to provide an effective deterrent.

Organizing the threat of military force around nuclear weapons would also not be credible or legitimate, whether or not a potential aggressor had nuclear weapons. Nations in a cooperative security regime may choose to maintain a nuclear capability sufficient to keep any aggressor nation from ever seeing an advantage in initiating a nuclear attack. However, they cannot regard nuclear weapons as a deterrent to aggression with conventional weapons if they also hope to dissuade nuclear ambitions globally.

Since cooperative security arrangements are to be established by consent rather than imposed by threat of force, they must be based on premises that can be widely accepted as politically legitimate, a key theme developed by Chayes and Chayes. Such arrangements should also be inclusive in the sense that all countries are eligible to belong to the regime as long as they conform to its rules. Indeed the spirit of cooperative security is to ensure that all countries do belong and do conform. This inclusiveness requires incentives to induce voluntary compliance and also careful construction of the rules to be sure they can be reasonably judged to be equitable from a universal perspective.

In order to calibrate cooperative strategies with regional realities and thus maximize the prospects for eliciting support, it is necessary to identify the heterogeneous security objectives of key countries and adapt policies accordingly. Chapters 8 through 12 and chapter 14 focus on the security conditions in six major cases, encompassing the United States, the former Soviet Union, western and eastern Europe, the Middle East, Northeast Asia, and South Asia. The challenge is to identify instruments that might best promote global standards in a way that is most consonant with domestic conditions and, conversely, to avoid the promotion of policies that are seen as antagonistic or discriminatory.

A growing number of security risks are emerging in contexts in which central authority and even basic order are weakening; therefore it is also vital to explore how cooperative security might be used to promote conflict resolution and other forms of positive intervention. As Alex Rondos argues in chapter 13, the devolution of authority from governments to substate actors has been a progressive trend in many of the poorer third world countries for more than a decade. Lessons from these contexts, especially about nonmilitary forms of intervention, have compelling importance for the design of policies for containing risks in the former Soviet bloc.

However, uncoiling the old habits of security planning, even such modest steps as altering the readiness posture of strategic nuclear forces, is very much an unfinished task. It will require dedicated leadership and innovative policies. To date the ingrained habits of military organizations and their associated political systems militate against much-needed innovations. The volume concludes with some suggestions for near-term strategies for the United States and the CIS to address current and future challenges.

Notes

1. The Commonwealth of Independent States comprises all the republics of the former Soviet Union except the three Baltic states.

2. William J. Perry discusses reconnaissance strike capability in greater detail in chapter 6. There are three basic elements: (1) command, control, communications and intelligence (C^3I), (2) precision-guided munitions, and (3) defense suppression. In Operation Desert Storm the United States was the first nation to use reconnaissance strike capabilities. For more information on the origins, definition, employment, and potential deterrent value of these technologies, see William J. Perry, "Desert Storm and

Deterrence," *Foreign Affairs*, vol. 70 (Fall 1991), pp. 66–82. For more detailed analysis of the difficulties associated with the regulation and proliferation of reconnaisance strike capability technologies, see chapter 2 of this volume.

3. For example, encoded labels could be attached to each of the items included in the registry, supplying the information needed to monitor its destination and application. The labels could be designed to be updated according to changing circumstances and not to be successfully manipulated or detached without giving reliable evidence of that fact. (Direct labeling of chemical and biological agents would be technically more demanding but not inconceivable.) If full disclosure was the norm, unregistered products or products without labels would be regarded as illegal. Individuals, firms, and supplier networks involved with such products would be subject to criminal proceedings, and states in violation would be subject to international sanctions. This is discussed further in chapter 5.

4. As Perry and Schear argue, the UN Security Council can authorize multinational military forces for this purpose. Indeed, the UN is authorized to form its own military force. However, it is more immediately realistic to focus on UN authorization of multinational forces to deal with major acts of aggression, for now on an ad hoc basis.

TWO

The Imperatives for Cooperation

Janne E. Nolan, John D. Steinbruner, Kenneth Flamm, Steven E. Miller, David Mussington, William J. Perry, and Ashton B. Carter

IF THE PRINCIPLE of cooperative engagement depended primarily on trends in political opinion or on the natural inclination of sovereign governments to collaborate, its practical significance would presumably be very meager indeed. Prevailing judgment in virtually all parts of the world is clearly skeptical about the reliability of international cooperation. Conflict is widely believed to be the dominant impulse and national military capacity the more effective means of protection.

The chief imperatives for cooperation do not emerge from trends of opinion, however, but rather from the pressure of events. The cold war did not end by organized vote or by any strategic design. It was terminated by diffuse, spontaneous historical forces powerful enough to override the prescriptions of established policies, powerful enough also to induce massive social transformation. Those same forces are revising the axioms of international politics. They generate strong incentives to form a cooperative security arrangement to replace the cold war confrontation whether or not the idea itself is immediately evident.

Such forces are felt and their consequences experienced long before they are explicitly understood. It is reasonable to presume that observers are still in the early stages of full comprehension. Nonetheless it is also reasonably apparent that specific changes in the international economy have occurred that radically alter the context of security, and from these changes the incentives for cooperation arise. The diffusion of technology and the internationalization of eco-

Although this chapter is a composite of the work of seven authors, the final contents are the responsibility of the volume editor.

nomic activity have changed the conditions for making military investments. They have also altered the reasons for doing so. It has become extremely difficult to sustain national technical advantage over the longer term, and the longer term is what matters. Meanwhile political disintegration has replaced imperialist aggression as the principal source of immediate danger. In reaction to these changes governments have begun to develop elaborate mechanisms for collaboration even as they may have preached the need to prepare for unilateral forms of intervention.

The Diffusion of Civil and Military Technology

The rise of a world economy driven by large-scale increases in the international flows of information has already profoundly altered the conditions for making technical investments in security. Besides the five formally acknowledged nuclear weapon states, perhaps as many as ten other countries have the technical ability or potential to deploy nuclear weapons if they choose to do so. Four—Israel, Pakistan, India, and South Africa—are already considered de facto nuclear powers, although the latter decided to terminate its nuclear program in 1992. Well over a dozen countries, including many with nuclear potential, also have capacities to produce ballistic or cruise missiles and have growing access to the advanced sensing and information-processing technologies that are the chief ingredients of advanced conventional munitions.

Thirty years ago it was possible to formulate the proliferation control problem by reference to three blocs of suppliers: the United States, the Western industrialized nations, and the Soviet Union. In the intervening years an expanded base of supply has taken root and altered the conditions of control. The expanded base includes China, India, Pakistan, newly industrialized nations of the Pacific rim, North Korea, Israel, and the states of the former Soviet bloc, including the new states emerging from the former Soviet Union (FSU). A number of these states are themselves active in promoting proliferation.

Many new suppliers began their weapons programs through cooperative developments with defense firms in the industrialized world, gradually increasing their own technological capabilities until they could produce weapons indigenously. The expansion of the global supplier base has been accompanied by the emergence of joint development programs among new suppliers and truly global networks of supply for weapons technology. Cooperative weapon development programs are becoming more commonplace in the industrializing world, exemplified in the celebrated (though now defunct) Condor missile collaboration effort among Argentina, Iraq, and Egypt and in China's provision of weapons production technology to countries like Syria and Pakistan.

In many cases the establishment of a military technology base and the capacity to export arms have served as an integral part of countries' strategies for civil, economic, and technological development. Countries are now seeking a fair market share in the international arms trade, commensurate with their capabilities. Though most nations of the world support nonproliferation objectives, many resist joining in regimes based on technological denial orchestrated by the advanced nations, which they perceive as discriminatory.

The traditional policies of controlling the diffusion of weapons of mass destruction, advanced delivery vehicles, and their necessary support services by denying access to materials and information have thus been decisively undermined by technical diffusion and changed political imperatives. National choice, not technical access, has become the decisive factor in many areas of proliferation. But the regimes established to control military trade have yet to formally acknowledge or adapt to these new realities.

In the United States alone, there are currently at least six separate arrangements to constrain the spread of nuclear weapons, chemical weapons, biological agents, ballistic missile technology, standard conventional munitions, and other dual-use technologies. In each case there are substantial differences in the legislative basis for control, the administrative apparatus that executes control, the operational practices that have evolved over time, the arrangements for international collaboration, and the effectiveness achieved. To date there has been no systematic attempt to rationalize and integrate these separate activities into a comprehensive control program. It is clear that integration could strengthen all six regimes by unifying control bureaucracies and procedures for efficiency, sharing verification and transparency measures synergistically, and depoliticizing individual applications of the controls. But for now these goals remain a distant prospect.

The nuclear nonproliferation regime has proved the most enduring of control efforts, although it is being severely tested by recent developments. Most of the major industrial countries have made their choices about nuclear weapons as well as about chemical weapons. The number of states that maintain overtly deployed nuclear weapons has held at five for almost three decades. Several other industrial states, such as Germany, Japan, Canada, Sweden, and Italy, could readily produce deployable nuclear forces but have shown no inclination to do so. They support the Nuclear Non-Proliferation Treaty and other restraints on destabilizing forces, such as the Chemical Weapons Convention, designed to remove all existing stocks of chemical weapons. The four states that are assumed to have acquired nuclear weapons capabilities of minimal to modest size have so far not engaged in actively displayed deployments, and, as mentioned, South Africa has recently pledged to abandon its nuclear program.[1] These latter states' measured steps beyond the threshold of acquiring nuclear technology have been recognized for some years, but thus far these steps have strained though not destroyed the prevailing structure of nuclear control.

It is unlikely that this equilibrium will be sustained, however, without significantly strengthening and formalizing the arrangements for international restraint. A nuclear weapons program in North Korea and a potential one in Iran are not under reliable control. Active nuclear weapon deployments by either or both of these countries would probably shatter the political accommodation that has evolved so far and might trigger the development of nuclear weapons programs in inherently more capable countries that have so far desisted. Even if that reaction could be prevented, uncontrolled programs of this sort in radical states are likely to stimulate assertive development of advanced conventional forces by their neighbors.

Advanced conventional weapons capability is based on the integrated combination of several basic functions: frequent wide-area surveillance, rapid extraction of relevant information from ample surveillance data, rapid dissemination of this information and its integration into operational plans, and extremely precise navigation to designated targets of vehicles that are difficult to detect. Most of these capabilities are the product of commercial innovations and are likely to spread over time through international trade channels.

Once this combination of functions has been fully mastered, a military organization could in principle identify and attack any visible target more than a few square meters in size anywhere in the world in less than one hour. This can provide a highly intrusive type of force projection capability that has never before been available: extremely efficient violence with exact precision in time and place at long range. Fully competitive international development of this capability would enable an array of coercive actions that would pose security problems of an entirely new character. Military installations, economic targets, and even political leaders would not be secure from a highly precise and potentially devastating surprise attack using forces unencumbered by the constraints and taboos of nuclear or chemical weapons.

Fortunately time, in combination with active initiatives, can still offer meaningful protection from this situation. After fifteen years of intense investment, the United States alone has entered the initial stages of this type of capability, and even U.S. achievements so far fall short of full technical potential. Because it requires the integration of many functions and technical components, the development of an advanced reconnaissance strike capability cannot emerge as quickly as the underlying revolution in technology that enables it. No other military organization is within a decade of matching the United States in this respect, and the United States itself is more than a decade away from complete realization of the development it has pioneered.

The problem of regulating reconnaissance strike capability has nonetheless been posed. A security nightmare looms on the horizon, and its prevention creates a powerful incentive for cooperative arrangements. The current lead the United States enjoys in reconnaissance strike capability creates a temptation to neglect the longer-term imperative and to rely on the immediate national comparative advantage conferred. But there are some strong incentives to discipline this tendency.

If there is no military organization in position to match the United States quickly, there are many in position to undercut it, at least in local areas, by targeting critical assets. Aircraft carriers or airborne warning and control system aircraft and satellites, for example, which are critical ingredients of the U.S. capability, are exceedingly vulnerable to intrusion or negation by far less sophisticated capabilities in the hands of an opponent. A lesser power can aspire to attack the information sensors in the reconnaissance strike complex fairly readily, even if it cannot field full-fledged countermeasures of equal capacity. Countries that may feel threatened by an intrusive reconnaissance strike capability they cannot match can contemplate use of even crude chemical weapons as a strategic counterweight. The United States is highly exposed to chemical destructive agents delivered by small aircraft or through clandestine means. Despite its advantages in both nuclear and conventional weapons operations, therefore, the United States faces problems of weapons proliferation strong enough to motivate fundamental changes in its own security planning.

As argued earlier, for the United States to have any reasonable hope of inducing restraint among countries that have the inherent capacity and potential incentive to acquire advanced weapons, the major military establishments may have to subordinate their own national forces to international coalitions that are seen as nonprovocative. To do so, they would also have to reduce their own forces and development activities and adopt deployment restrictions to reflect their commitment to defensive configurations, especially with respect to weapons of mass destruction. Fortuitously, historic contractions in military forces and investment are taking place throughout North America, Europe, and the FSU. If carried out cooperatively, this process of contraction could set the standard for reduced military preparedness and for force and investment cuts that could be emulated in other regions. Contraction of defense industries and control of export sales, in turn, could be recast from politically unpopular national burdens into internationally shared obligations in pursuit of the benefit of lower levels of militarization everywhere.

Perhaps the most compelling case for this kind of cooperation is emerging from recent advances in biotechnology and biological warfare, a microcosm of the overall problem of modern technical diffusion. Despite the close comparison to chemical agents that is frequently assumed, biotechnology in fact presents a unique threat and a fundamentally different problem of control. The distinction begins with the obvious and important fact that biological agents can regenerate themselves and spread from one person to another. That simple feature creates the theoretical possibility of tremendously destructive consequences. An agent that could defeat the human immune system and spread efficiently could threaten a significant portion of the entire world population.

Fortunately in the long process of evolution human defenses have dominated the various offensive strategies of the organisms that attack them, and so far that balance has been quite robust. Though many biological agents have been identified that are capable of producing life-threatening infections in human hosts, they all reflect a basic trade-off that has enabled human survival. The most rapid and efficient killers—anthrax, for example, whose potential use was feared during the Persian Gulf War—spread so inefficiently that they give ample time for natural or organized containment. The most efficient spreaders—influenza, for example—generally do not have lethal effects. Mutant agents produced by genetic engineering techniques have so far tended to be less vigorous in their effects than naturally evolved organisms and to be subject to the same trade-off between lethality and efficiency of propagation.

There is no reason to believe, however, that this trade-off is an immutable law of nature, and there is every reason to believe that rapidly progressing understanding of the genetic code will deliver tremendous power over biological interactions. That power will almost certainly confer the ability to produce major, indeed massive, consequences—for good and for ill. Power of that magnitude will compel commensurately effective management.[2]

Because neither known nor projected biological agents are competitive with explosives or with chemical agents in tactical military applications, their development has not been a central commitment of military organizations. Even the most virulent biological agents require too much time to work for their lethal effects to be of use in immediate battles, and the major military establishments have focused on immediate battles rather than on wanton strategic destruction. Moreover, any temptations to biological warfare have been checked by the obvious danger of falling victim to one's own actions.

The Biological Weapons Convention of 1972 prohibits the development, production, storage, or use of biological agents as weapons but allows research for defense or prophylactic purposes. Since the distinction between legitimate and prohibited activities was not specified beyond those general formulations, there has been legal ambiguity and intense suspicion about research activities on biological agents conducted by military organizations. That suspicion has been strengthened since the dissolution of the Soviet Union by allegations from Russian sources that preparations were made during the Soviet period for producing biological agents on a scale that would unambiguously contradict the 1972 convention.

However, the development of biotechnology has been primarily conducted not by military organizations but by national medical establishments whose basic purposes are legitimate and compelling. Virtually all the relevant information and materials have necessarily been made widely accessible. There is no prospect whatsoever of denying access in the manner that has been used to protect nuclear materials and weapons design information. Thus managerial control of the dangers and opportunities of biotechnology must rest on complete transparency of relevant activity and active international monitoring. These imperatives will eventually be powerful enough to overwhelm embedded resistance. The practical question is whether international cooperation will be accepted on the basis of reasonable prediction or whether some disastrous experience will be necessary to make the point.

Current trends in the spread of dangerous technology thus compel a decisive shift in policy. The pursuit of national comparative advantage through technological development must be tempered and eventually subordinated to considerations of the risks of proliferation. Accompanying this shift should be a change in the principal mechanisms of control from denial of access to technology to cooperatively induced restraint. Controlling access to information and materials remains feasible and important for some of the critical components of nuclear weapons, which can be segregated from commercial markets. But for chemical and biological agents, conventional munitions, and advanced delivery system technology and for the command and control systems that make the difference in modern warfare, basic access to the underlying technology and components cannot be controlled in this manner. As is discussed later in this chapter, a control regime will therefore focus on ways to restrict the application of technology, rather than on the increasingly futile effort to choke off supply.

Shrinking Military Budgets and Export Markets

The recent political transformations in East-West relations have brought about major reductions in military forces and military budgets for most of the nations of the world. These changes imply a reduced capability to pay for new weapons coupled with a reduced need for such weapons. But during the cold war many nations established large defense industries to produce the weapons then needed, and these industries have become an important part of their economy and social structure. As defense budgets decrease in most nations of the world, governments are faced with the problem of downsizing their defense industries while minimizing adverse economic impact and social disruption.

Today the defense industries in most of the industrial countries are trying to convert their excess capacity to the production of civilian products; but for a variety of reasons this conversion has proved to be very difficult. Alternatively, many of these nations are trying to cushion the economic and social impact of this excess capacity either by continuing to order unneeded weapons (the "pork barrel" approach to defense management) or by trying to increase their sales of weapons to other nations. The latter approach has often involved selling arms to nations in politically troubled parts of the world, as suppliers let domestic economic considerations override longer-term security considerations.

The savings from reduced defense budgets made possible by the end of the cold war could in principle allow governments to reallocate spending to other

Table 2-1. *Arms Transfer Agreements with Developing Countries, 1985–91*
Millions of U.S. dollars

Country	*1985*	*1986*	*1987*	*1988*	*1989*	*1990*	*1991*
United States	5,903	4,113	6,095	9,815	8,225	19,109	14,161
Soviet Union	21,095	29,818	23,771	14,048	12,430	11,754	5,000
France	1,850	1,563	3,729	1,461	4,107	3,253	400
United Kingdom	23,810	1,082	583	1,011	1,189	1,784	2,000
China	1,727	2,164	5,477	2,360	1,729	2,204	300
Germany	247	601	932	225	973	315	400
Total	54,632	39,341	40,587	28,920	28,653	38,419	22,261

Source: Richard Grimmett, *Conventional Arms Transfers to the Third World, 1984–91*, CRS Report (Washington: Congressional Research Service, July 20, 1992), p. 50.

purposes, but the timing of these changes continues to present special problems for defense industries and for those who rely on their products for employment. Besides drastic cuts in domestic procurement, a decade-long decline in international weapons sales has reduced the export markets available to defense firms throughout the world. Arms exports are no longer reliable supports for economical domestic weapons production (see table 2-1).

The response to recessionary trends among many weapons producers has been to try to buy time by seeking a larger share of the export market. The technology transfer implications of unregulated foreign sales by defense enterprises will of necessity be a continuing target of international diplomacy.[3] Left unconstrained, transfers of weapons production technologies to developing states may increase the sophistication of second-tier defense producers in a way that poses new risks to U.S. and international security.

As table 2-1 suggests, traditional markets in developing countries have been in decline for at least five years, and the end of the Iran-Iraq war eliminated the most significant arms export market of the 1980s. Competition among arms exporters has actually had a downward effect on revenues gained from international arms markets.[4] The use of countertrade and offset measures in arms transfers has increased in importance, with the benefits to the purchaser frequently exceeding the value of the weapons transferred.[5] Similarly changes within the defense industries of Western arms-exporting nations are promoted by the decline in domestic and international orders.

The restructuring of these industries has profound implications for future technology transfer patterns. The rise of large dual-use technology firms in western Europe means that industrial competitiveness concerns will now be an increasing part of policies designed to preserve defense industries.[6] This trend may exacerbate problems in trade relations between the United States and other industrial nations, which wish to see open-market policies enter the defense sector during the current period of recession and conversion.

The most significant event in the global arms trade, however, is the loss of Soviet control over arms sales from the region. The main arms production facilities of the Commonwealth of Independent States (CIS) are in Russia, Ukraine, Kazakhstan, and Belarus. Other small manufacturing facilities are scattered throughout the rest of the FSU. Weakening central authority in these countries has given defense enterprise managers considerable *theoretical* autonomy in arms exports. As discussed further in a later section, plans for the privatization and conversion of much of the Russian defense-industrial base add to the uncertainty regarding CIS arms production. The weakness of the CIS's traditional markets means that exports are unlikely to be adequate to underwrite conversion efforts, but export promotion programs are nevertheless actively under way.

As table 2-1 makes clear, Soviet—and now CIS—arms exports have been in decline for many years. The weakening of central authority in the CIS may offset this trend marginally if it leads to illegal transfers of arms. Unfortunately individual defense enterprise managers have incentives to violate weak governmental regulations, in part as a response to the reduction of subsidies to defense producers that are part of the defense conversion programs in Russia and elsewhere. Exports are also viewed by some Russian government officials as a source of foreign exchange to finance other economic activities, including defense conversion.[7] The export picture confronting Russia makes these efforts dubious at best. However, such intentions are a warning sign about the challenges posed to efforts for agreements for international arms transfer restraint.[8]

The increasingly competitive arms market is contributing some interesting side effects to Russia's defense conversion problem. First, more sophisticated technologies are likely to become available to hard currency customers. To compete with Western and second-tier (developing country) arms producers, Russian defense enterprises are trying to increase the quality of the technology included in their export weapons systems. Indications of this trend were visible at recent international arms expositions, where previously unknown systems were on display. Some, though not many, of these weapons contain technology that may be competitive with that of advanced arms available in the West.[9]

An especially alarming prospect is the combination of advanced Russian technologies with the weapons development efforts of potential proliferators. The recent sale of aircraft production factories to China as a part of a longer-term coproduction arrangement with that country is indicative of this potentiality.[10] Process (production) technology sharing may lead to the more rapid diffusion of advanced weapons. It is also possible that such coproduction arrangements—broadened to include dual-use technologies—could undercut the feasibility of international arms transfer regulation as currently conceived.

The decline in export outlets is only a small element of the overall recessionary trend brought about by changing political circumstances. Far more significant is the massive decline in levels of domestic procurement. Table 2-2

Table 2-2. *Defense Expenditures for Selected NATO Countries and NATO Total, 1985, 1989, 1990*
Millions of U.S. dollars

Country	*1985*	*1989*	*1990*
Italy	9,733	9,690	9,320
Germany	19,922	17,122	16,940
Canada	7,566	6,996	7,064
United States	258,165	260,024	249,149
United Kingdom	23,791	20,451	19,574
Total	319,177	314,283	302,047
Total NATO	357,966	349,398	337,341

Source: International Institute for Strategic Studies, *The Military Balance, 1991–1992* (London: Brassey's, 1992), p. 212.

provides an overview of broad trends in future defense expenditures, all of which are markedly downward.

For the future, defense spending increases are highly unlikely in both Europe and North America. Within declining defense budgets there will continue to be competition for resources among military services to preserve core military capabilities.[11] In this area the fluidity of international threat perceptions and the new types of security challenges that have emerged in Somalia, Bosnia-Herzegovina, and Iraq are shifting the pattern of procurement of weapons and military equipment in the leading industrial nations to favor flexible, multipurpose forces, supported by airpower and naval units.[12]

Firms in North America and western Europe are adjusting to recessionary pressures in part by restructuring their operations and through the sale of less profitable businesses.[13] In Europe the process of adjustment has gained more momentum because of the smaller national markets, at least compared with the domestic market of the United States. In Europe in the late 1980s there began a rapid series of mergers and acquisitions by firms that sought economies of scale and a broader international base for their operations.[14] These developments were originally designed to make European firms more competitive with their U.S. counterparts. The end of the cold war has reduced this focus considerably, because the larger firms are confronted by many of the same problems as their North American competitors.

The defense sector has also seen the establishment of industrial consortia to bid for particular weapons and infrastructure projects. In Europe these teaming arrangements are common, and the Panavia Tornado strike aircraft, the European Fighter Aircraft (EFA) project, and the Airbus consortium are merely the most prominent examples. These consortia are involved not only in collaborative work on a system or application but also on *precompetitive research*, which will have great significance for future government access to research and development (R&D) projects. In Europe defense firms are more frequently *dual-use technology* firms, with their most profitable operations often lying in the civil sector. This bias in markets affects the distribution of their R&D expenditures, perhaps reducing the amount of independent research and development in defense-related applications, as is discussed further in the subsequent section on the globalization of the international economy.

In the United States, however, the pace of mergers and acquisitions was not appreciably linked to the shrinkage of defense markets until recently. The sale by General Dynamics of its aircraft unit to Lockheed in 1992 and the pursuit by McDonnell Douglas of a buyer for its helicopter division both signify a shift in the future prospects for defense producers. In the United States, the reduction in orders seems to be promoting two dominant strategies: (1) increased concentration of defense firms in areas of core competence and (2) the sale of profitable subsidiaries, with the earnings from the sales passing directly to shareholders.[15] These strategies are clearly not mutually exclusive but serve to demonstrate the already significant impact of shrinking domestic orders on the industries making up the defense industrial base in the United States.

An export orientation of remaining defense-dependent firms is encouraging the extension of offset benefits and the provision of production technology in arms transfer arrangements. This trend will, as it has in the past, help accelerate the development of defense industries in recipient countries, pointing to a greater international dispersal of the weapons production system and the diffusion of intellectual property associated with weapons research.[16] These developments may lead to a paradoxical integration of second-tier defense producers with systems integration firms in the core of the global defense economy. This possibility may be particularly likely in the case of the FSU, where the foreign licensing of weapons technologies may greatly hasten the secular trend toward defense industrialization in the periphery. The globalization phenomenon at work is thus twofold. Firms in western Europe are becoming rationalized on a continental basis, through merger and acquisition activities in the defense sector. These consortia are sometimes launched at the initiative of governments, frequently with the calculation that it is better to have a small part of a strategic industry than no industry at all. This process is producing a varied and geographically dispersed production system in which firms make decisions that may run counter to the defense industrial and security interests (that is, the state's interest in autonomy or nonproliferation) of particular nations.[17]

However, in North America the globalization of the defense sector is an artifact of trends in the civilian economy, in which dual-use technologies are increasingly supplied by foreign firms. In areas where these technologies have multiple foreign sources, security of supply is less problematic. In areas where potential or actual monopoly exists, however, state autonomy may require remedial measures, such as the maintenance of special stockpiles and support for "uneconomic" domestic production.[18] In these cases globalization is an effect of differential technological progress, with "spin-on" to the defense sector of civil technology developments replacing "spin-off" as the predominant fact in the dual-use area.[19]

The performance of Western arms in the 1991 Gulf War has reconfirmed the superiority of U.S. defense technologies. Since the war a number of large arms transfer agreements have been signed, with the major Western suppliers—the United States and the United Kingdom—receiving most of the orders. These particular transactions may never be completed, because the hard currency difficulties of some of the oil-rich nations that are the major intended recipients may make their absorption of existing weapons into their arsenals increasingly difficult.[20] Nevertheless, a new technical standard has been set for weapons and warfare, one that may well be imitated by developing states in their attempted design of more advanced armed forces and military postures in the future.

The expansion of global arms industries and the increasing use of industrial offsets in arms transfer arrangements mean that Western standards are likely to be extended into production processes as well. Aside from increasing efficiency in second-tier defense production, this expansion is likely to exacerbate the problem of proliferation, for technologies not deemed inherently "destabilizing" may contribute to the development of proscribed technologies because they add to the autonomous capacity of already existing infrastructures in a particular locale.[21] Globalized methods of production and imitation in the design and integration of weapons technologies, as such, may significantly increase the sophistication of second-tier defense products.

The more highly proliferated world to which these trends may lead will create new challenges for arms and technology transfer regulations, as already discussed. Paradoxically, however, the integration of global arms industries may increase the efficacy of technology export controls if it is pursued as part of a conscious cooperative strategy. Linked technological and production centers can operate only in a regulated political and economic context. Thus the framework that overarches arms production can have great influence over the incentives for both producers and consumers in this area.

In the context of a shrinking arms market, competitive pressures are creating new types of arms transfer relationships. These ties are integrating arms recipients into the technological and industrial policies of the leading suppliers. The extension of offset benefits and codevelopment arrangements are actively promoting exchanges of intellectual property at both the manufacturing and systems integration stages of a procurement program. This development exemplifies the shrinking technology gap separating developed and developing countries. Centers of innovation are still, however, overwhelmingly concentrated in the developed world. The emerging globalization of defense industries will thus create, or exacerbate, various forms of technology dependence when developing countries face single suppliers for essential weapons and spare parts. The linking of developed world defense manufacturers in joint ventures and precompetitive consortia means that governments may increasingly confront a monopoly supplier for key technologies and R&D functions.[22]

The regulation of a globalized defense production sector that could be brought about in these changed conditions will require careful international cooperation among governments. Proposals for collaboration in weapons development, such as the EFA project and other smaller interoperability arrangements within NATO, could help to fulfill this function. Balancing the different defense-industrial interests of European and North American countries will necessitate the resolution of trade disputes in dual-use technologies, a process that has thus far proved difficult. But the shared interest in preventing the proliferation of dangerous conventional and unconventional weapons is already fostering cooperation through regimes such as the Missile Technology Control Regime (MTCR) and the Coordinating Committee on Multilateral Export Controls (COCOM), and so far without success, in the so-called P-5 forum consisting of the five permanent members of the UN Security Council. Reconciling competing economic interests with shared security concerns is a central task facing political leaders in the emerging defense industrial climate.

Thus developing codependencies in weapons and dual-use technologies create a paradoxical situation for policymaking. On the one hand, the desire for economic growth counsels the removal of all barriers to free trade in technology. One of the side benefits of COCOM was the establishment among its members of more or less free trade in items that were proscribed to nonmembers. Extending this kind of benefit to new countries is itself a difficult thing to reconcile with near-term concerns about proliferation. Developing states can increasingly use multiple sources for the acquisition of sensitive technical capabilities, even without such an arrangement. Iraq's success before Operation Desert Storm in using an elaborate international supply network to obtain legal technologies for an illegal program provides a powerful example of the dangers of a world in which proliferation can proceed largely unchecked. The critical lesson of Iraq's achievement is that the established supplier-led regimes for regulating technology transfer were vulnerable to opaque circumvention. The lack of transparency and enforcement capabilities among the Treaty on the Non-Proliferation of Nuclear Weapons (NPT), the MTCR, and the various national export control systems was easily exploited by Iraq to achieve nuclear and chemical weapons as well as ballistic missile capabilities.

The increasing competitive pressures to transfer advanced technologies, as well as pressure to increase the industrial offsets included in arms transfer arrangements brought about by recessionary trends in the supplier countries, obviously present additional problems for these technology transfer regimes. Under these new conditions supplier controls are no longer adequate for the restriction of trade, prompting the necessity for a cooperative system based on transparency and disclosure.

The sharing of information and intelligence among supplying countries is key to preventing circumvention of established rules of behavior. An opportunity also exists for transfer regimes to be converted into permissive zones for technology transfer. In return for access to sensitive technologies, countries could be required to provide evidence of established end use. End-use certification of this type, along with the continuing surveillance of transfer arrangements, could do much to allay fears of the proliferation of advanced weapons and military equipment. Such a set of guidelines could also assist governments to police the sales activities of transnational dual-use technology firms, which may otherwise violate politically agreed-upon guidelines intended to restrict the transfer of certain systems. At this stage of development of the global weapons transfer system, new restraint arrangements of this kind would help the governments of the CIS to minimize the proliferation risks of their arms sales and could encourage the coordination of defense-industrial policies. These policies could help reduce the long-term pressures on defense industries to export, thus contributing to a less militarized and proliferated world.

However, the more significant challenge ahead is to accelerate the process of defense conversion so as to reduce the pressures of excess capacity that fuel proliferation. The excess arms capacity in the world today provides the strongest motivation for the arms-producing nations to promote the diffusion of technology globally. It is the key barrier to achieving constraints on the regulation of military commerce among suppliers and an important reason that diplomatic efforts for arms restraint have historically proved ineffective.

Thus there is a broad international interest, though not yet fully articulated, in helping countries find solutions to the problems caused by excess dependence on military industry. These problems vary from nation to nation, and the attempted solutions must therefore also vary. In particular, the solutions being implemented in the market economy nations (primarily NATO nations) are very different from the solutions appropriate for nations with a command economy (primarily the People's Republic of China) or nations in transition from a command to a market economy (primarily nations of the former Warsaw Pact).

Linked to the looming contraction of the military establishment of the FSU are not only the potential loss of control over the diffusion of technology but also an enormous internal problem of social dislocation that could have security implications. Millions of soldiers and their dependents will need housing and new jobs. Even more catastrophic in many ways is the plight of the military industry in the FSU, where the number of wage earners and their dependents threatened by the steep downturn in state orders for weapons systems figures in the tens of millions. Success in converting defense industries to civil production is essential to stem the risks of potential social upheaval as well as to promote the success of overall economic and political reform.

Along with the problems of social welfare, a restive technical and managerial elite in the previously privileged military-industrial complex poses the greatest threat to the new democratic spirit in the FSU, a threat greater than any consumer revolt or backlash. Thus political leaders in these countries will be strengthened if they can claim that these painful restructurings are part of an international cooperative design, if they can point to active assistance from Western countries, and if they can point to analogous processes of difficult retrenchment in Western military industries.

Indeed, in Western nations as well, massive demobilization is politically contentious. The process is much less significant economically than it is in the FSU, since it affects a much smaller share of the gross national product and is taking place in large, flexible market economies. Nevertheless, demobilization has its political opponents in Western countries. A natural place for threatened defense industries to look for new markets is in the international arms trade. A cooperative security arrangement that relates these politically difficult defense restructurings to a larger international purpose and makes clear that all countries are sharing in the pain is essential for allowing the desired post–cold war contraction to take place and for preventing proliferation through increased arms exports.

In industrializing countries as well there are analogous trade-offs between military investment and civil investment necessary for economic development. These trade-offs have political salience as economic and military officials contend for the ear of national leaders. From India to Brazil and Egypt, emerging suppliers are finding their fledgling defense industries in dire straits as the worldwide market for arms declines. They too will face their own conversion dilemmas.

Governments are increasingly being held accountable for their nations' economic performance, directly where democracy has taken root but indirectly even where dictatorship prevails. In many of these countries the sophistication of economic policymaking is increasing rapidly. Thus in a growing number of countries the influence of economic entrepreneurs who can challenge the military for a share of the nation's technology investment is increasing. Their case would be strengthened if a system of international security cooperation could demonstrate that defense spending can be safely and efficiently reduced. Therefore a cooperative approach to defense conversion and regulation of military trade could help promote and give international legitimacy to demilitarization efforts throughout the world.

The Internationalization of Economic Activity

The internationalization of the global economy is by far the most obvious driving force helping to break down national and ideological barriers and forcing a high degree of conformity among governments and private actors to a common set of operating rules. An integrated international economy is well along in formation, although its evolution has been largely spontaneous. Its logic and policy requirements have yet to be fully mastered, but almost certainly its management challenges will transcend the capacity of national governments. It is safe to say today that the condition of the emerging economy already compels more pervasive international coordination than that to which nations have ordinarily been accustomed.

Since World War II the extraordinary and disproportionate growth of a loosely defined complex of high-technology ("high-tech") industries has transformed the global economy. New technologies commercialized by these industries have altered the channels linking national economies to one another through flows of goods, services, and information. The new technology brings countries closer together and makes it impossible for them to ignore their neighbors. In a smaller world they are also forced to cooperatively work out economic conflicts that might in the past have been ignored, when distances more truly separated them from their neighbors. The basic fabric of economic life, the infrastructure of exchange, grows every day more global and less local.

This change is crystallized in the explosive growth of global computer and communications networks. Electronic arteries throb with information, data vital to trade, finance, investment, and the international flow of technology. Maintaining and improving connections to these global networks, and the flows of goods and information they support, is a critically important task for a modern industrial state. Sever the connections, and access—to goods, information, and technology—is immediately lost.

The globalization of the basic infrastructure required by a modern industrial economy has been accelerated by a complementary shift in the fundamentals driving competition in advanced, technology-intensive industries. High-tech industries are characterized by large investments in research and development. Temporary monopoly on new technology flowing from these investments finances further investments in R&D, which creates a further cycle of technological advantage, even as the initial monopoly dissipates with the inevitable diffusion of ideas and proliferation of imitators.

Because R&D costs are approximately fixed (whether one produces one unit or ten thousand, the costs of developing the product are the same), economies of scale are important in R&D-intensive industries. To maximize the return on the relatively fixed investment in a new technology, firms have been forced to reach out to the widest possible market, the greatest number of possible customers. For this reason all high-tech industries are intrinsically global, seeking to expand across national boundaries virtually from their moment of birth.

Matters are further complicated by the fact that much R&D, particularly more basic research, has a "public good" character. Not all the knowledge created by investments in research can be appropriated, captured by investors for their exclusive use. New knowledge tends to diffuse to others. Once it is released, exclusive possession can never be recaptured. Ironically the growth of the global communications infrastructure and the cheapening of information transmission have probably worked to further break down the appropriability of new technology. Although it was once reasonable to suppose that new information created at least a local, temporary regional advantage for some period, the existence of cheap, high-speed, global information networks means that everyone plugged in, around the world, is filled in on new developments ever more quickly.

Increasingly, then, investments in research that may once have seemed a national public good are more appropriately described as an international public good.[23] This change has three significant implications for the economic environment in which any security regime must function. First, connections to the networks making up the global economic infrastructure are increasingly important—for both economic and security reasons—as a tap into an international pool of knowledge, as well as a vital means of international economic exchange. Second, the well-known problems of paying for a public good—in particular, the temptation of individual economic actors to act as free riders, to enjoy the benefits while shirking any share of the costs—can no longer be addressed by national policy and instead may require international cooperation. Third, as more and more national firms crowd into an increasingly global marketplace, management of international economic conflicts in high-technology sectors will demand increasing attention. As a result forces that seem likely to push the international economic regime—the "rules of the game" for trade, investment, and information flow—in new directions have already been set in motion. Together with the growing economic importance of access to technology-intensive international infrastructure, the crucial role of connections enabling firms and nations to tap into the networks making high technology an increasingly international public good, those forces seem likely to promote forms of cooperation in the economic sphere that complement movement toward cooperation in the international security regime.

Broad debates about the principles regulating trade and investment flows between the United States and its international competitors are now taking place in the United States. Because a significant degree of intervention by national governments in high-tech industries seems inevitable, what is likely to emerge from a process just now being set into motion is a new international framework designed to harmonize rules for competition and intervention in high-tech industries. Such international rules are necessitated by powerful forces driving intervention by government in high-tech industries.

First, high-tech products require investments in R&D accounting for a much greater than average fraction of sales. Because of problems associated with the public good aspect of investments in technology, particularly the inability of a private firm to capture the full social value of the technological advance resulting from that R&D, there is a solid economic argument for government to subsidize or otherwise stimulate investments in research. Indeed, governments around the world are heavily involved in supporting investment, both public and private, in technology. Pure market forces alone are therefore less likely to determine outcomes in high-tech industries, and thus some international negotiation process is required to determine what constitutes an acceptable intervention in high-tech industries.

Second, because a high-tech company must have at least a temporary monopoly on the outcome of its R&D investments (otherwise it would be unable to earn a return on its R&D), high-tech companies often have some degree of monopoly power in particular industry segments. Many high-tech products are key inputs to other sectors of an economy, and the potential for these companies to maximize their returns by integrating forward into downstream sectors must be considered. The potential exercise of technology-based monopoly power to collect rents in high-tech and associated downstream sectors of the economy raises interesting questions about whether government intervention in that market might be appropriate. Small numbers of firms in leading-edge sectors and the not infrequent encouragement by government of coordination of R&D activity among rival firms make ground rules for what constitutes unreasonable departures from an acceptable degree of "competition" among national firms all the more important.

Third, high-tech industries typically display economies of scale (some of which are derived from R&D cost) and their dynamic analogue, learning economies. It is now well established that so-called strategic trade policy interventions by government can under certain circumstances raise national welfare. Such interventions, or policies to respond to such interventions, pose a real danger of setting off cycles of action and response resembling trade wars.

Finally, high-tech industries frequently have direct links to defense technologies. Even when no economic rationale may be persuasive, national defense may provide a justification for national policies to promote high-tech industries, especially in the area of advanced technologies needed for a reconnaissance-strike capability.

It is already clear that intensifying regional rivalries in high-tech industries are pushing national governments to cooperate in constructing a new system of rules regulating global competition in technology-intensive industries. The resolution of current frictions will be critically dependent on the ability of national governments not to focus on narrow and ultimately futile attempts to defend some parochial conception of national interest. Instead, what is required is the cooperative formulation of an international system that preserves the open international market so essential to fostering maximal technological investment and favors particular companies and countries only on the basis of superior innovative performance. The construction of that new cooperative economic system is as much a political challenge as an economic one. Initial steps toward this new world economic order can already be discerned in ongoing discussions in multilateral forums such as the Organization for Economic Cooperation and Development and bilateral negotiations such as the U.S.-Japan structural impediments initiative. Some broad principles likely to emerge can be enumerated.

The argument thus far is that rapid growth in high-tech industries, globalization of world markets for high-tech products, and the collateral effects of new technology on the structure of the markets themselves have set in motion a process that has already begun to construct a new set of rules regulating international flows of technology-intensive goods and services. The advanced industrial countries are leading this effort, but it seems likely that the framework will ultimately include most of the world's economies in a new set of rule-making and enforcing institutions.

One nagging problem troubling this incipient effort is that national security issues are inevitably posed as an exception to the rules being formulated. A troublesome loophole to demands for transparency and reciprocity in national R&D efforts, for example, is an exception to these requirements for defense R&D. This seemingly inevitable exception creates problems for the entire enterprise. How can one demand termination of closed programs to finance commercial aircraft R&D in one region, for example, when military resources can be used to finance related developments in another region and be exempted from both reporting and open access requirements? Since suitable definitions of national security can move virtually any high-tech investment from the commercial to the defense side of the ledger book, this kind of exception would seem to create a loophole one could drive a tank (or more appropriately, a supercomputer) through.

Creating a cooperative security regime along the general lines outlined in this volume, however, would seem to go a long way toward solving this problem. Such a cooperative security regime would create a set of constraints on military investments that largely parallels and complements the constraints placed on commercially oriented investments by the developing high-tech trade regime. The requirement for transparency in the use of public resources for R&D and other investment projects, for example, would be made more credible by a similar requirement for transparency in reporting military investments. Negotiated limits on commercially oriented subsidies would be more effective with a system of limits on military investments.

Similarly, the principle of multilaterally supervised, rule-based resolution of territorial and political disputes is a new sphere of application of the idea of rule-based resolution of commercial disputes now widely accepted in the economic domain. Just as strengthened international institutions will be required to enforce a more comprehensive high-tech trade regime, more powerful international institutions, with significant enforcement powers, are implicit in proposals for a meaningful cooperative security regime.

The free flow of goods and services within the boundaries of a trading area is both an objective and an incentive for nations to commit themselves to the emergent new rules for high-tech trade. Free-trade flows would play an identical role for countries considering membership in the cooperative security enterprise. Thus there are many conceptual parallels between the principles and institutional requirements for the emerging rules of the game for international trade and investment and the proposals contained in this volume for a new international security regime. Indeed, one can only wonder whether the parallels could profitably be extended into a common institutional framework for the two.

The complementarities in principles and purpose are already evident. The need for new enforcement mechanisms for both economic and security regimes has also been mentioned. Given the essential harmony between the purposes of the two, it might seem reasonable to suggest that both would gain in stature and authority by being set up as the economic and military sides of a single new international framework, into which some existing international institutions with related functions might be absorbed. Nowhere does the potential value of the economies of scope to be reaped by combining the two seem more evident than in the workings of the reporting systems tracking flows of economic and military goods across international borders.

This development is being driven by a revolution in the processing and transmission of information. In recent decades the handling of information has undergone the most radical gains in raw capacity and efficiency in economic history, and the consequences of that progress are just beginning to unfold. Among other trends access to advanced technology is widening, and that reality is altering the technical circumstances in which defense investments are made.

Moreover, as information, technology, and economic activity diffuse, so do formative attitudes. In countries with wide differences in history and culture, an imperative to establish political authority more on the basis of social consensus than from coercion seems to be emerging. Compliance with this imperative is probably a necessary condition for operating an economy that can compete internationally. Conversely, economic performance is probably a necessary condition for viable political authority. This interaction appears to establish a powerful connection between national politics and international circumstance for virtually all countries of the world. However strong the impulse to project a separate national or ethnic identity and however pressing domestic priorities may be, it does not appear that international detachment can be achieved or that deviation from international economic standards can be sustained. Some international collaboration has become a presumed requirement for operating an economy that prospers. Conversely, standing at odds with the international community through some transgression of its established norms can be made to have very serious economic consequences for pariah nations, as is argued in subsequent chapters.[24]

The Demise of the Soviet Union and Implications for Regional and International Security

Transnational economic organization is breaking down the barriers that governments constructed around their national economies, collapsing in particular the efforts to operate centrally planned economies. The same trend has undermined authoritarian governments as well. The flexibility, decentralized control, and dispersed competence necessary to conduct economic operations at world standards do not appear compatible with rigid political rule. The sheer inefficiency of attempting to coerce political loyalty and to enforce dictated standards of behavior so weakens economic performance that such efforts seem destined to be eventually caught in a self-liquidating spiral. The greater the effort to resist, the more dramatic the ultimate failure.

The Soviet Union was a primary test case for the preceding propositions. The precipitous disintegration of its entire economic and political structure offers confirmation of the synergism between impeded economic performance and the lack of legitimate government. In the Soviet case the effort to sustain a gradual centrally managed economic reform program was itself overwhelmed by a radical, spontaneous dispersion of effective control. The political system has lost legitimacy to the extent that its coherence at any level is in question. Legitimacy is the binding power that enables organized activity to occur. If it is mysterious in its origins and impossible to measure directly, it is nonetheless as vital to the operations of a political system as its physical equivalent, gravity, is to a stellar constellation.

The old Soviet Union is irretrievably gone. The replacement Commonwealth is but a declaratory shell. The successor states are all struggling to establish viable authority within their new borders. None has yet succeeded to the extent that it can reliably enforce basic laws, let alone formulate and implement policies of the inherent difficulty that its circumstances require.

The implications for immediate economic performance have been very stark. Published figures record extremely sharp declines in the economic output of Russia since 1990—a 9 percent drop in gross domestic product and an 11 percent drop in net material product in 1991, with a further 19 percent drop in GDP and a 20 percent drop in NMP in 1992.[25] Western projections indicate that between 1990 and 1993 the Russian economy, which includes the leading 60 percent of the former Soviet economy, will decline by as much as 40 percent.[26] If so, this would be an economic depression of unprecedented magnitude for a large industrial economy, substantially exceeding that which struck the United States in the 1930s.

For a time Soviet economic practices buffered the work force from the direct consequences of this decline. In 1991 employment fell by only 1.1 percent and wage increases exceeded controlled price increases, thereby imposing large reductions in average labor productivity. This policy, combined with falling tax revenues as governmental functions disintegrated, produced large fiscal deficits, estimated to have reached approximately 20 percent of GDP by the time the Soviet Union was dissolved.[27] Although the monthly rate of inflation declined slightly after the jump in prices caused by the liberalization of pricing policies at the begining of 1992, by the middle of the year inflation was again running at 20 to 30 percent a month. Overall consumer prices rose by more than 2,300 percent in 1992.[28]

This was the legacy inherited by the Yeltsin government and the background against which its conceptually more radical reform efforts were initiated. It began a progressive decontrol of prices, instituted a new tax system based on the value-added tax, passed a budget nominally designed to cut the fiscal deficit to manageable levels, and committed itself in principle to privatizing economic assets. This combination of stabilization and reform gave credible evidence of the intention to align with international economic standards, but the most resolute of intentions could not immediately arrest the momentum of decline or deflect the political pressures it generated. Tax receipts fell short of projections, and the drastic cut in government subsidies embodied in the budget could not be completely implemented in the more democratic political process. As a consequence, the fiscal deficit reached an estimated 22 percent of GDP for 1992[29] and threatened the intended stabilization effect. The legal intricacies of privatization bogged down in disputes over who was to benefit and in the ominous implications for unemployment. Very few existing enterprises are likely to be viable if they have to absorb all their existing labor forces under existing labor rules.

Regardless of the textbook reform intentions at the center of the Yeltsin government, therefore, the main hope for escape from the spiral of decline rests with the process of spontaneous regeneration that is occurring outside the bounds of government policy and even legal control. Though this process is difficult to observe systematically, anecdotal and indirect evidence suggests that there is a surge of initiative at lower levels of the economy with sufficiently productive results to prevent the degree of abject misery that would normally accompany the officially measured decline. In the absence of coherent agricultural reform, private farming is nonetheless believed to be growing, particularly in the countryside surrounding the smaller cities. With their traditional institutions stagnating under fiscal austerity, professionals are scrambling to market their skills. Without central direction or legal clarity, enterprise managers are acting as if they were validated owners of their assets, and at least some of them are maneuvering to make the enterprise as a whole profitable. Among the many things that remain as yet unmeasured and unknown about the situation, this dispersed process of spontaneous regeneration is sufficiently constructive and potentially important enough to be a major consideration in attempting to devise responsive policy.

The process of internal reform and economic regeneration is clearly the dominant context of policy in Russia as well as in the other Soviet successor states, and all security issues are primarily embedded in that context. That fact inevitably imposes a reversal of priorities from the cold war period. Resource investment in military forces will necessarily be determined far more by the larger objectives of economic performance and far less by military doctrine. The inherited military establishment will have to be reduced drastically in order to meet fiscal constraints, and internal control will almost certainly be the principal consideration affecting the process of reduction. Russia's ability to conduct external military operations will unavoidably decline in comparison with that of the other major military establishments, to a degree that reverses traditional international security concerns. Potential weakness rather than excessive strength is emerging as the driving problem.

The early stages of this evolution are already quite visible. The Yeltsin stabilization budget reduces Russian defense spending to half of what it was under the Soviet Union. Since Russia inherits more than half of Soviet assets, that reduction projects a disproportionate decline in the military establishment. The reduction must be managed, moreover, simultaneously with a major relocation. Several hundred thousand former Soviet military personnel stationed in eastern Europe and the Baltic states must be moved to Russian territory.

The budget allocation clearly reflects dominant social and economic priorities. Weapons procurement accounts have been reduced by 70 percent, and reports of drastic reductions in state orders for military equipment indicate that this portion of the stabilization plan appears to be holding. The design of economic reform envisages the conversion of a large part of the privileged defense industry to civilian production, and there appears to be little inclination to constrain that process to protect residual defense needs. Joint ventures are being sought in virtually all areas of technical effort, including by the individuals and institutions involved in nuclear weapons design and ballistic missile defense. These activities were highly protected under the old system.

As discussed in a preceding section, domestic weapons producers are being encouraged to export in order to earn hard currency to finance conversion. Although basic proliferation controls remain in effect, there appears to be no reluctance to deal with the peer military establishments that were considered enemies until just recently. The military planning system in place is directing the resources it can command to preserving military personnel, and its top priority appears to be that of providing adequate housing for military officers being relocated and alternative training for those who will have to be released from duty.

This radical shift in circumstances and in policy priorities imposes immense problems of planning and implementation. The imperatives of economic regeneration seem to require and may well spontaneously force a rapid release of assets from the military establishment and therefore a rapid process of reduction and relocation of existing forces. The initially formulated intention of Russian military planners to scale their establishment down gradually to a level of 1.5 million or so military personnel over a five- to ten-year period is unrealistic; actual reductions are likely to be deeper and more rapid than that. If they are to be orderly and coherent, however, rapid reductions are costly. Because there are no resources to spend on the process of transition, it is difficult to see how a coherent outcome can be designed and produced even if all those involved are unequivocally dedicated to carrying it out.

Similarly it is well known that the conversion to viable commercial purposes of plants that have long been exclusively devoted to weapons production is very difficult to accomplish. Western experience records only a very small number of successful efforts, most of which benefited from special conditions.[30] The conversion of an entire industrial sector involving hundreds of producers under peacetime conditions is entirely unprecedented. Even assuming that the myriad problems of product design and market strategy are mastered, large sums of investment capital would be required—$150 billion, according to the Russian planners originally mandated to undertake the effort.[31] Since the process of conversion in nearly every instance is likely to consume more time than investment markets allow to establish competitive rates of return, macroeconomic stabilization and spontaneous regeneration will not be sufficient to generate an investment program of this magnitude. Without a systematically directed and adequately financed investment program, which does not yet exist, the industrial enterprises that constructed the Soviet military establishment will disintegrate, and their most marketable skills and knowledge will disperse into the international economy.

These general observations do not enable any exact prediction of the eventual outcome, but they do establish an important presumption: the military command systems of the Russian Federation and other Soviet successor states will not be able to manage the problems that currently confront them. The combination of weak internal authority, severe economic austerity, and continuing international isolation denies them the ability to ensure a safe and stable configuration for the military forces they inherit. Therefore, unless these systems are strengthened by some appropriate action of the international community, they are likely to lose control of their weapons inventories, technical support teams, and even some of their operational units. The unadjusted correlation of forces, to evoke the traditional Soviet conception, will produce disintegration.

The potential consequences of this disintegration are obviously threatening. It would undermine the safe operation of nuclear weapons. It would give an irreversible impulse to weapons proliferation. It could produce civil war. The imperative to prevent such disintegration is emerging as a major focus of international security.

Whatever outcome the internal transformation of the FSU might ultimately produce, the military establishment the Soviet Union created will be profoundly altered. The successor states of the Commonwealth are gripped by an extended economic crisis that is imposing large reductions on defense expenditures. They cannot sustain the forces they have inherited at anything like their size of recent decades. Those forces and the defense industry that supplied them will necessarily undergo a precipitous contraction. Moreover, the planning mechanisms needed to design a coherent outcome and to control the process of transition have been severely disrupted by the collapse of the central government. Reconstituting the capacity for managing the military establishment depends on settling fundamental constitutional and economic issues that cannot readily be made to march to the schedule required by force structure planning.

This situation has several stark implications for international security. Not only does it preclude any invasion of western Europe, but it reverses the physical basis for that conception of threat. Unless the major military powers in Europe and Asia reduce their forces in tandem, the states of the Commonwealth will not be able to remain convinced of the safety of the path they are on, nor will the smaller members of the Commonwealth be able to do so with respect to neighboring Russia. Moreover, management of the process of demobilization is a prime internal security consideration. The integrity of political authority in these states bears more directly on their security than does any traditional measure of external threat they might theoretically postulate. For the CIS and for the international community as well, responsible management of the large existing inventories of conventional and nuclear weapons is the most immediately compelling security issue. That fact dictates that all must cooperate in subordinating traditional military considerations to the interests of secure managerial control.

This new imperative of internal control has been recognized as it applies to nuclear weapons. The Nunn-Lugar legislation initiated a process of engagement between the United States and the Commonwealth states for consolidating control over nuclear weapons. That compelling focus provided political impetus and a practical context for working out the details of cooperation. But this initial, narrowly defined objective cannot be achieved unless the process of cooperation is extended to conventional forces as well. Despite the special organizational arrangements for handling nuclear weapons that developed in both the United States and the FSU, their operations have been so integrated into overall military activity that an effective approach to consolidating control cannot exclude conventional forces. This condition is especially true for the ground forces that have been the larger part and the organizational core of the traditional Soviet establishment. They are most seriously affected by the impending demobilization, and their fate has a stronger effect on most of the issues endemic to internal security. It is extremely unlikely that secure control of nuclear weapons could be maintained while the Red Army disintegrates.

Neither the CIS itself nor its constituent states can be expected to handle the necessary reconfiguration of their conventional military forces without substantial international collaboration. Without the cover of international restraints on conventional forces, they might not believe themselves able to match the legitimate requirements of territorial defense with their available forces, and they might be driven to rely primarily on nuclear weapons. Such a development would burden the integrated nuclear control that has been agreed upon among the successor states but that cannot be taken for granted. The graceful apportionment of inherited conventional forces by members of the Commonwealth is an issue that could easily trigger internal conflict dangerous to economic and political reform.

Substate and Civil Violence

The four decades of confrontation between two major alliances succeeded in preventing aggression of the kind that had twice engulfed the world during the previous four decades. It did not succeed in preventing violence, however. Some 22 million people died in conflicts that were categorized as civil wars and internal insurgencies during the forty years of armed peace. A principle for guiding organized international approaches to this type of violence is badly needed.

Cooperative security contributes to, and indeed may be indispensable to, the development of appropriate principles for organizing international approaches to substate violence. Many substate conflicts have reflected the politics of alliance confrontation in Europe and were fueled by the supply of arms that emanated from it. Many conflicts have now moved dramatically toward political resolution as the global confrontation has dissolved, in turn allowing the international community to begin to turn its energies to mediation and conflict management, most notably in Cambodia, in Somalia, and, so far with little success, in Yugoslavia.

Clearly international political accommodation has not removed the indigenous causes of violence, however, and in some cases it seems to have removed important restraints. As authoritarian political structures have crumbled under circumstances of severe economic austerity and as ethnic assertion and religious fundamentalism have surged into the vacuum created, spontaneous civil violence has emerged as an endemic problem in many parts of the world. Yugoslavia and Somalia are particularly destructive examples, but similar potential clearly exists in many other areas, perhaps most ominously in the successor states of the FSU.

As the bloodshed in the former Yugoslavia has sadly revealed, the international community does not yet possess security mechanisms adequate to control serious civil violence. The available apparatus of diplomatic mediation backed by the imposition of economic sanctions or even by threatened or actual military intervention requires a corresponding political structure to have any constructive effect. But it is precisely the disintegration of internal political structures that lies at the core of the problem. It does no good to persuade or to coerce leaders who cannot implement decisions. If civil order has broken down to the extent that it cannot be internally reconstituted, the only choice is either to tolerate violence until it produces some self-limiting outcome or to intervene with sufficient strength to impose civil order. To date tolerance has been the dominant choice by default. In Bosnia, intervention has been excluded as a practical matter, not for want of raw capability but because no coalition of countries has been willing or able to construct the necessary consensus to intervene significantly.

In light of emerging international circumstances, no national government can or should assume the primary responsibility for imposing basic civil order when it has broken down in another sovereign or even substate entity. The implications of attempted hegemony and the consequent risks of stimulating decisive international opposition will dominate any calculus of national interest. This judgment is particularly true for the United States, whose relative advantage in capacity for military intervention can provoke proportionate international and domestic sensitivity. The failure to restore stability in Somalia is a case in point.

To continue tolerance by default could become exceedingly costly, however. The combination of economic austerity, ethnic conflict, and political disintegration is now so widespread that civil violence could become a general conflagration if tolerance remains the only realistic international option.

Since the control of civil violence is more a matter of national than of international interest, refined collaboration is almost certainly a necessary condition for dealing with it. For any intervention of the size and character necessary to impose civil order, it is prudent to assume that the costs, political risks, and operational burdens will have to be shared. A cooperative security arrangement focused systematically on preventing aggression could provide the context for creating effective interventionary instruments when they were required. Therefore the threat of widespread civil violence gives significant indirect incentive to embark on such a course.

Emerging Support for Cooperative Approaches

As noted in chapter 1, cooperative approaches to security are already embedded in the international system, if not yet clearly articulated as an explicit objective for global application. An overview of existing and emerging bilateral and multinational cooperative security initiatives aimed at containing the consequences of technical diffusion, offensive force configurations, and military rivalry provides ample examples of the habit of cooperation in the international system.

These initiatives include the political ascendance and increasing salience of multinational conflict-resolution and mediation institutions such as the UN; multinational efforts to craft new approaches to force planning and technology export controls, including transparency measures and linkages of financial inducements and military restraint; and regional confidence- and security-building measures (CSBMs), including new consultative mechanisms among military rivals.

The amelioration of relations between East and West should not be misinterpreted as a sufficient catalyst to promote more cooperative approaches among regional antagonists, but it is clearly a necessary condition. In the past superpower rivalry reached into regional relations by helping to encourage the perception of national security as derivative of a state's relationship to one or both of the rival power blocs, reinforcing the notion of security as inherently threat-based. The degree to which the great powers perceived a stake in the outcome of a country's local conflicts was a vital determinant of that country's military and political status, manifested through membership in international alliances, the granting of security guarantees, and access to superpower economic assistance and military technology.

Now that regional conflicts are no longer serving as surrogates for superpower competition, an overarching rationale used to justify direct or indirect engagement of the large powers in regional matters has disappeared. This change can be expected to affect decisions about the character and purpose of security commitments, overseas troop presence, extended deterrence, and the pace and nature of military sales to allies and clients.

Regional tensions persist, as does the diffusion of weapons and weapons technology. The prospect of intervention by advanced countries in regional contingencies may continue, but the politics have obviously changed. Instead of subsuming all other security objectives under the rubric of containment, the industrial world is now focusing on the consequences of its past policies for global security, including the effects of its technological largesse extended to clients that are now seen as potential threats.

The unprecedented stature currently being accorded international organizations and regimes, especially the UN, could not have been anticipated even five years ago. Most U.S. policymakers have traditionally viewed multilateral mechanisms as little more than symbolic, often a nuisance, and certainly powerless to effect significant change. Without these international arrangements to help guide diplomatic and military collaboration, however, the chaotic international conditions that governments are now confronting would be far more difficult to manage.

In eastern Europe and in the CIS, the central challenge for the international community is to try to forge peaceful coexistence between the unleashed forces of nationalism and the rights of religious, ethnic, and subnational minorities within fledgling democratic structures. As discussed earlier, the ability to maintain military order in the midst of sweeping political changes has, however imperfectly, been helped by preexisting agreed-upon restraints on military forces, including the Strategic Arms Reduction Talks (START) and Conventional Armed Forces in Europe (CFE) treaties and the various nonproliferation regimes.

The completion of the START treaty has helped to guide the process by which contentious issues regarding the size, location, and command of former Soviet strategic nuclear forces will be decided. The West has also been able to promote initiatives for the security, transfer, or dismantling of the former Soviet nuclear arsenal and to encourage the removal of tactical nuclear weapons. The East-West nuclear arms control agenda has shifted from incremental technical limits on forces to exchanges of unilateral proposals to render the threat of deliberate nuclear conflict close to moot.

By providing definitive ceilings on and standards for conventional forces and by devising a system of CSBMs, the various elements of the CFE treaty together make up a framework of transparency and predictability that helps to underpin military stability. Further provisions for additional information exchanges, prior notification of military activities, and other CSBMs continue to be added, including the successful conclusion of the Vienna Document and an Open Skies Treaty in mid-1992.

A multiplicity of European security organizations have been playing a role in the management of the region's political transitions, but the Conference on Security and Cooperation in Europe (CSCE) has emerged as the primary institutional vehicle. It has developed a growing record of success in devising norms for and monitoring the military behavior of states in the region. Under its auspices, member nations have set forward a series of verification and arms control arrangements that set high standards of transparency and compliance. It also continues to evolve into a mechanism through which the United States and its European allies could undertake more effective efforts toward peaceful resolution of nationalist tensions, the prevention of mass violations of human rights, and diffusion of conflicts.

The regimes guiding the trade and possession of nuclear, chemical, and ballistic missile technologies, in turn, have provided an international standard to guide new states' policy formation. In the future the recently established CSCE Forum on Security Cooperation could provide a foundation for even more ambitious undertakings, such as further arms reductions and verification, mediation and early warning, and crisis management.[32] The CSCE has certain well-recognized limitations, including limits on its power and authority resulting from its nontreaty status and the difficulty of making decisions in an organization that has long depended on unanimous decisions among a large number of members. Greater use of the North Atlantic Cooperation Council (NACC), formed in 1991 and composed of the sixteen NATO nations and nineteen states that once made up the territory of the Warsaw Pact, is being discussed as one way to help strengthen the process of military collaboration between former enemies. Members of NACC, together with other CSCE countries, could earmark national forces for cooperative security, including peacekeeping missions under CSCE auspices, for example. Membership in these organizations could also be a way to set standards of state performance and behavior, which might include a democratic form of government, adherence to the rule of law, renunciation of territorial claims, and compliance with existing treaties and agreements limiting sale or purchase of technology related to weapons of mass destruction.

Beyond Europe the series of UN Security Council resolutions mandating the disarmament of Iraq and their subsequent implementation through the United Nations Special Commission (UNSCOM) has lent renewed credibility to the use of multilateral efforts on behalf of commonly shared disarmament objectives. Despite the continued intransigence of the Iraqi government and the logistical problems faced by the inspection teams in the early stages, this mission to date has been largely successful. UNSCOM is the first independent organ established by the Security Council that bears the specific task of eliminating the arsenal of a sovereign country. Whether it proves to be an experiment or a "pilot plan," as one commissioner has put it, there are lessons and precedents to be drawn from this initiative.

If nothing else the experience with Iraq has prompted an international consensus that existing instruments for enforcing controls on nuclear, chemical, biological, and missile technology diffusion are far too weak. As the director of UNSCOM put it, "If there is anything to learn from the Iraq experience, it is that only intrusive, short-notice, non-refusal inspections of declared or non-declared locations of the type which the United Nations Special Commission has carried out would be effective against deliberate concealment and deter potential violators."[33] A series of proposals to reform and strengthen the global nonproliferation regime, including granting greater authority and resources to the International Atomic Energy Agency (IAEA) to carry out challenge inspections, is among the first steps being undertaken that will bring this regime closely into line with the full concept of cooperative security.

UN peacekeeping forces are increasingly being called upon to end armed conflicts between and within states that the United States or its allies were not prepared to take on alone. Peacekeeping forces now monitor disengagement agreements, supervise elections, disarm hostile factions, and even administer territories in dispute. UN guards are being sent in fairly significant numbers to protect humanitarian relief workers in volatile areas. Special UN envoys are being dispatched more often to mediate disputes and, if necessary, to consider collective intervention to forge peaceful settlements.

There are obvious limits to the use of multilateral force, and most countries still insist on reserving the right and capability to act unilaterally if necessary. There is, however, growing international recognition that multilateral security initiatives, if organized effectively, are likely to enhance rather than constrain legitimate and effective uses of military power. The UN's ability to enforce security will nevertheless require reforms in the structure of the Security Council, the roles of UN agencies, the powers and resources of the secretary-general, and the organization and practices of the Secretariat.

In early 1992 Secretary-General Boutros Boutros-Ghali issued a report detailing recommendations on how to strengthen the UN's ability to engage in more effective enforcement activities. At a minimum the UN's mandate and obligations to carry out peacekeeping operations need to be clarified, he argued, and its resources increased accordingly.[34] The demand for peacekeeping operations is rapidly outstripping existing financial and organizational assets. The definition of peacekeeping is being stretched as well. UN peacekeepers are now being asked to move into territory where war is being waged, territory not subject to a peace agreement or even a durable cease-fire. If UN peacekeepers are to become instruments of military intervention, the international community must explicitly grant legitimacy to these kinds of operations, backed by forces that are adequately trained and equipped and imbued with commensurate authority.

After a series of negotiations beginning in 1991, a majority of members of the General Assembly approved a proposal in December 1991 to establish an international registry of arms exports and imports, under the auspices of the UN secretary-general.[35] The permanent five members of the Security Council (the United States, Russia, China, the United Kingdom, and France) also began discussions of procedures and guidelines for prior notification of arms contracts, an initiative that so far has not been successful.[36] For all of their limitations these negotiations represent the first efforts to formally coordinate North-South technical diffusion by multinational agreement in many years. They may presage a renewed commitment to managing and possibly eventually reducing the global trade in conventional weapons. At a minimum the arms registry, if it succeeds, will represent an important move toward greater transparency in the international defense trade system.

Within the international lending institutions such as the World Bank, the International Monetary Fund, and the more recently established European Bank for Reconstruction and Development, interest is growing in linking international financial assistance to various norms of military behavior, including defense expenditures and, more ambitiously, compliance with treaties. This interest represents a marked shift in attitude among institutions that for decades promulgated the formal fiction that a country's defense sector should not be included in evaluations of its economic performance, political stability, and other variables that go into decisions about credit or aid eligibility.

Bilateral aid agencies, such as the Agency for International Development in the United States and Japan's Ministry of Foreign Affairs, have made it explicit that they will consider military behavior a consideration in granting aid.[37] Further examples of this linkage abound from various Western arrangements to provide financial and material assistance to the countries of the former Soviet bloc. The founding president of the European Bank for Reconstruction and Development, for example, argued that preventing the escalation of civil war across Europe can come about only if the West opens its markets and provides substantial short- and long-term aid.[38] That aid, in turn, could help provide the West with leverage to induce the newly emancipated countries of the former Soviet bloc to support and to join a cooperative international system of military and technology restraint.

Direct financial inducements are being used currently to achieve several nonproliferation goals, including constraining former Soviet weapon designers and engineers from lending their expertise to defense industries in third world countries. The United States, Germany, and Russia agreed to establish an international science and technology institute to employ former Soviet weapon scientists and engineers. Its purpose, clearly stated in its charter, is to minimize any "incentives to engage in activities that would result in proliferation of nuclear, biological, and chemical weapons and missile delivery systems."[39] The recognition by the international community of new interrelationships between economic instruments and the promotion of security objectives is an important development for cooperative security. These spheres are obviously mutually reinforcing. Conditionality is not a new phenomenon in international trade relations or private commerce, although it is being promoted far more actively both by governments and international organizations today than ever before. Such linkages are critical for the design of a credible system of incentives that can effectively elicit countries' support for international military regulations.

As discussed earlier, it is already recognized that the various regimes for regulating the commerce in or use of proscribed weapons technology need reform. It is the weaknesses in the various arrangements, including the lack of effective enforcement of the NPT and the absence of controls on the sale of conventional weapons and dual-use technologies to states such as Iraq, that have focused international attention on the global diffusion of technologies. The current attitude among a large number of countries is not to give in to fatalism about the futility of military controls, however, but rather to find ways to try to redress systemic weaknesses.

Regarding the NPT, in particular, the majority view seems to be that it should be given greater powers and should emerge from its final review conference in 1995 with renewed legitimacy and international support. In addition to the agreement by the IAEA in early 1992 to invoke its powers to conduct challenge on-site inspections at suspect sites, the twenty-seven-country Nuclear Suppliers Group devised new guidelines in 1992 for controlling dozens of commercial and dual-use technologies, including stricter end-use provisions for transferred technology.[40] The international community seems to favor granting additional resources to the nuclear nonproliferation regime, although there is still a reluctance to increase funding on the scale believed necessary.

For all the controversy that now surrounds the regime, several examples of greater international acceptance of the NPT nevertheless exist. In the last few years previously recalcitrant states such as France and China have agreed to join. The French government also announced a unilateral nuclear test moratorium in 1992, joining the Russians in a test ban in which they both hope to elicit international participation. In the developing world there is a roster of new NPT adherents, including Algeria, China, South Africa, Tanzania, Zambia, and Zimbabwe, along with several of the former Soviet republics.[41]

There has been considerable effort to advance the cause of chemical and biological disarmament, and some are optimistic that ratification of the Chemical Weapons Convention may be imminent in many countries. The Australia Group, which monitors dual-use technologies for chemical weapon development, recently placed more stringent restrictions on the list of chemicals it monitors and added biological weapon technologies to its monitoring obligations. Poland, Hungary, Czechoslovakia, Romania, and Bulgaria all recently agreed to apply export controls to chemical and biological agents and components, as did Israel. Russian President Boris Yeltsin disclosed in mid-1992 that the Soviet Union had been conducting significant biological weapon research in past years but that all such efforts and associated facilities would now be terminated.[42] There are even signs of interest in chemical and biological weapons limits being expressed in India.[43]

Similarly the more modest cartel-like agreement to regulate trade in ballistic and cruise missile technologies, the MTCR, has elicited support from unexpected sources. It grew from an initial membership of seven in 1987 to twenty-three members as of late 1993. New adherents include Israel, several of the neutral countries in Europe and Scandinavia, and numerous former Soviet states, including Russia.[44]

Perhaps the most significant trend in the nonproliferation area is the growing willingness of the industrial countries to exert leadership on behalf of military restraints, including lending assistance to states interested in joining in such arrangements. In the future technical and financial assistance of the kind being granted to the CIS for weapon destruction or dismantling could become a far more significant instrument of international diplomacy.

Chemical demilitarization is already a multinational enterprise. Among many initiatives the U.S. Army is conducting standardized training programs for foreign-national chemical weapons inspectors and exchanging site visits with representatives of the former Soviet Union to discuss the handling and destruction of chemical weapon stocks. This effort parallels programs in Germany, Norway, and Finland, all of which are providing courses in Chemical Weapons Convention verification to, among others, specialists from the third world.[45] Many countries are also applying new and more stringent codes of conduct to their own industries and bureaucracies to enforce technology trade laws. In the aftermath of the adverse publicity about German participation in Iraqi weapon development programs, for example, the German government began instituting sweeping reforms of its arms export control apparatus.[46] In the United States the so-called enhanced proliferation control initiative was devised by the Bush administration in early 1991 to impose more rigorous criteria for licenses involving technologies or components that could pertain to nuclear, chemical, or ballistic missile development, including punitive sanctions imposed on violators. With the assistance of Western specialists, the Russian government also announced plans to set up a special body for exercising political control over arms exports, comprising senior officials from departments in the foreign policy, industry, economics, finance, and security ministries.[47]

There are also signs of greater interest in at least selective export controls among companies whose products include technologies that may be subject to international restrictions. Facing continued conflicts over the permissibility of exports of supercomputers and associated software, in 1990 IBM set about helping to devise credible end-use assurances that would prevent the diversion of civilian computers to military uses. Similarly there has been considerable industry interest in proposals put forward by a National Academy of Sciences study group in 1990 that argued for shifting the emphasis of export restrictions from controls on supply to end-use controls on applications.[48]

Significant obstacles remain to the development of an effective, integrated, and politically legitimate nonproliferation regime that would reflect cooperative security. Aside from the challenges posed by dedicated outlier states such as Iraq and North Korea, a serious impediment to progress is the reluctance of some advanced countries to renounce certain aspects of their military sovereignty on behalf of nonproliferation goals. In the chemical area, for instance, although finally agreeing to renounce its chemical arsenal two years ago, the United States continued to oppose rigorous on-site verification in the global ban because of concerns that such inspections could compromise highly classified U.S. military modernization programs. As an opponent of this position has put it, "At a time when the tendency towards transparency in military matters is obvious, and when the principle of absolute noninterference in internal matters has to be modified everywhere in favor of international responsibility and cooperation, the reluctance to accept the only effective tool against treaty violations seems strangely outmoded."[49]

Most of the existing nonproliferation arrangements are maintained by the major weapons-producing countries, and the political legitimacy of these arrangements is questioned by key regional powers. The history of past efforts to limit armaments shows that restraints that depend solely on supplier cartels are doomed to failure, as are policies that appear discriminatory. Like the effort to control drug trafficking or other illicit forms of trade, control agreements must ultimately focus on the demand side and at least aspire to universality. It is in regional contexts that cooperative security deserves the most attention and where it has the least developed political infrastructure. For cooperative security to be considered seriously outside the advanced countries, new mechanisms must be devised for regional security consultations that can help enfranchise new states in a broader security partnership.

The interest in cooperative approaches to security is receiving some attention in countries and regions where the tradition of military antagonism and conflict has tended to dominate political conditions. The enduring rivalry between Argentina and Brazil, for example, recently gave way to several joint efforts to ameliorate bilateral relations, including an agreement to permit inspections of each other's nuclear facilities and inspections by the IAEA, to become parties to the 1967 Treaty for Prohibition of Nuclear Weapons in Latin America (Treaty of Tlatelolco), and to jointly renounce indigenous nuclear and missile development programs. These decisions were motivated by the gravity of the two states' economic situations, changes in their respective governments, and important national defense decisions, such as Argentina suspending its Condor intermediate-range missile program. In Central America, the UN has helped to craft political agreements to end the conflict in El Salvador, among other initiatives.

China has been exhibiting some movement toward international accommodation in return for continued access to Western trade and technology. For all its recalcitrance, China acceded to the NPT, agreed in principle to adhere to MTCR guidelines, and, although it currently remains the stumbling block to progress, initially joined in the permanent five discussions to consult about the international arms trade. China is not fully complying with some of these arrangements, however, in part because of a perception that the regimes are discriminatory.

Although North Korea's nuclear program has dominated the news about the Korean Peninsula, negotiations between North and South Korea in 1992 resulted in the two sides signing a joint declaration for the denuclearization of the region, and until early 1993 made it possible to open a dialogue to discuss a system of CSBMs. There is still great concern about the North's nuclear arsenal, but it is not ruled out that Pyongyang may eventually agree to abide by international nonproliferation norms as it faces the costs of noncompliance, including greater economic isolation or even military sanctions. In Cambodia, the most extensive peacekeeping operation ever organized by the UN was organized in March 1991, initially with mixed success, but helped make it possible to hold the first elections in many years in that country in mid-1993.

In South Asia, several CSBMs have been under active consideration by India and Pakistan, including continued efforts to conclude agreements prohibiting targeting of their respective nuclear installations in wartime and allowing for bilateral inspections of nuclear facilities. While still not successful, a proposal for five-power talks in 1991 (including Russia, China, the United States, Pakistan, and India) might provide a potential vehicle to discuss nuclear weapons in the region, although the Indian government continues to oppose their legitimacy. There may still be some possibility of bilateral agreements on nuclear forces over time, a possibility suggested in mid-1992 by Pakistan announcing unilaterally that it was freezing production of highly enriched uranium and weapons cores and halting its overall nuclear development program. India and Pakistan may also have interest in negotiating a bilateral chemical weapons ban.

The legacy of Iraq's invasion of Kuwait, along with the promises of accommodation implied in the signing of a Palestinian-Israeli accord in September 1993, has lent renewed vigor to the prospects for CSBMs and bilateral discussions among antagonists in the Middle East. An unprecedented level of debate about arms restraint measures is occurring at least in the nonofficial expert communities of several countries, especially in Israel. Serious consideration is being given to a regional ballistic missile freeze, and discussion continues in the UN General Assembly, the Committee on Disarmament, and the IAEA of measures that could lead to a regional nuclear weapon–free zone or a phased agreement to ban all weapons of mass destruction, as proposed by Egyptian president Hosni Mubarak, among others.

Several of the more traditionally belligerent countries in the region have shown modest signs of interest in nonproliferation. In 1992 Syria agreed to negotiate an accord with the IAEA for inspections of its territory. Libya allowed UN inspectors to investigate its chemical facilities, and the IAEA was allowed to inspect Iranian nuclear facilities, although grave doubts remain about Iran's nuclear ambitions. In general, the combination of military insecurities and recessionary economic trends could be propitious for encouraging military restraint in some of the more politically stable countries with large military establishments, including Saudi Arabia, Jordan, and Israel.

In most of Africa, by contrast, conditions for cooperative security may remain dismal. Vicious and bloody conflicts have become endemic in many parts of the African continent, and no other region of the world has suffered more from war in recent years. Tragically, no other region can afford to delay the implementation of a cooperative security regime less. The Organization of African Unity notwithstanding, the region lacks even the basic instruments to mediate disputes credibly or to contain the consequences of regional or local wars that exacerbate the problems of mass starvation, disease, and social chaos. The advanced countries, including the

United States, have been reluctant to become involved, with the exception of intervention in Somalia, and only the UN and private organizations can be said to have demonstrated any commitment to humanitarian relief or other forms of intervention in this region for the last several decades.

The problems of Africa are instructive for cooperative security globally, whether or not the region for now possesses the ability to project war or misery beyond its own borders. There are important parallels between the conflicts among African states and the resurgence of ethnic, religious, and other minority disputes in the countries of the former Soviet bloc. The two regions share the problems of sudden impoverishment, mass migrations, disintegration of central authority and territorial boundaries, and a history of weak domestic institutions resulting from hegemonic relations with outside powers.

The ongoing conflicts in the former Yugoslavia and Somalia underscore the urgency of new approaches to securing peace that transcend old definitions of security. The traditional notion of war defined as organized aggression between sovereign militaries is equally irrelevant in both of these otherwise disparate cases. But the policy apparatus currently available to the international community to redress new threats is conceptually adrift, hampered by old ideologies and a lack of international resolve. A regime that attempts to ignore substate conflicts because their effects are not believed to warrant international action not only misses important dimensions of the security challenge but is also likely to be ridiculed as a vision for a future world order.

Conclusion

The diffusion of technology, the internationalization of economic activity, the collapse of the Soviet Union, the surge of civil violence, and the extensive evolution of practical collaboration have clearly created a new context for international security, generating strong pressures for corresponding changes in policy. The circumstances do not dictate specific outcomes and certainly do not guarantee the eventual emergence of a fully developed cooperative security arrangement. Nonetheless they do give powerful practical relevance to the principle of cooperative engagement. It is increasingly difficult to meet the requirements of security by confrontational means. The imperatives of the new era are driving even the most recalcitrant national governments into more sophisticated forms of collaboration.

Notes

1. For a comprehensive survey of potential nuclear states, see Leonard S. Spector, *Nuclear Ambitions* (Boulder, Colo.: Westview Press, 1990). For more information about

South Africa's nuclear program and subsequent renunciation of nuclear weapons and accession to the Nuclear Non-proliferation Treaty, see Leonard S. Spector, "Repentant Nuclear Proliferants," *Foreign Affairs,* no. 88 (Fall 1992), pp. 21–37.

2. This prospect has already descended from the level of informed speculation to immediate practical significance. In recent years techniques for manipulating the influenza virus have been identified. Influenza has the most effective mechanism of transmission of all known biological organisms. Some strains have demonstrated the ability to infect 80 percent of the total human world population within a six-month period. Influenza can also be highly lethal. Some strains, which happen to infect birds rather than humans, have killed almost all the infected population. The immune resistance to influenza infection of the current world population is sensitive to differences in strain type, that is, to the range of mutations that regularly occur. These facts suggest that a highly efficient and highly lethal influenza virus could be deliberately created; indeed, such a strain could emerge naturally. The world at the moment is very poorly organized for prevention or for effective reaction. Cooperation is an essential element in managing biotechnology for this or for any other purpose.

3. Western diplomacy has focused on the accommodation of the CIS and the states of eastern Europe within an expanded COCOM framework. In this regard, on November 23–24, 1992, a meeting of the COCOM Cooperation Forum, a body involving the Western member states of COCOM as well as the nations of eastern Europe and the CIS, reached tentative agreement on an assistance package whereby the former Warsaw Treaty Organization countries would receive assistance in setting up export control structures of their own and a reduction in barriers to technology trade with Western countries.

COCOM has agreed to drop most of the remaining controls on technology transfer for these countries if the following measures are taken:

—A demonstrated national intent must be made to ensure only civilian use of sensitive technologies and the setup of agencies to apply international standards of export control to sensitive technologies.

—A system of prelicense checks must be established for potential customers and suppliers of sensitive technology to ensure their ability and willingness to comply with export control regulations.

—A system of postdelivery checks must be established to maintain consistent surveillance on the proscribed use of exported technologies.

—A competent bureaucracy must be created to enforce controls, and it must be reinforced with an increase in the effectiveness of border controls to cope with increased levels of illegal diversion.

This agreement may help strengthen political forces inside the CIS that are concerned with the illicit sale of arms and the proliferation dangers therein. See Roger Cohen, "West Will Expand High-Tech Sales," *New York Times,* November 25, 1992, p. A9; and Carol Reed, "COCOM opens up to ex-WP Nations," *Jane's Defence Weekly,* December 5, 1992, p. 9.

4. An example of increasing price competition was the United Arab Emirates' acquisition of Russian BMP armored fighting vehicles in 1992. These vehicles were purchased from inventories of the former Warsaw Treaty Organization. Unit prices were reported to be a fraction of the cost of the United Kingdom's comparable GKN Warrior armored fighting vehicle. See Philip Finnegan, "Russia Extends Mideast Arms Sales Hunt," *Defense News,* June 15–21, 1992, p. 1.

5. One aspect of this phenomenon is the growth of global supplier networks supporting defense production because of the establishment of foreign production sites via offset agreements. As a part of the globalization of defense industries, this trend is

particularly novel, since it parallels a similar one in the civil sector. See Ian Anthony and others, "The Trade in Major Conventional Weapons," in *SIPRI Yearbook 1992: World Armaments and Disarmament* (Oxford University Press, 1992), p. 278.

6. Large-scale unemployment and firm restructuring are just two results of the decline in global arms markets. The Stockholm International Peace Research Institute reports that the transnationalization of firms for reasons of market access and technology sharing is further undermining national economies. Some defense firms have avoided these problems because of large orders placed during the cold war. Once these contracts are filled, however, they are unlikely to be replaced by new business. Economic prospects vary across industrial sectors, but the decline in defense sector employment is present in both western Europe and the United States. See Paolo Miggiano and others, "Arms Production," *SIPRI Yearbook 1992,* pp. 361–69.

7. Mikhail Maley commented on this issue at length. As Russian president Boris Yeltsin's counselor for defense conversion, Maley's views carry some weight in Moscow. As he puts it, the Russian government "will take all measures necessary to eliminate unfair quotas and restrictions on Russian arms trade and high-technology export in the international markets." Sergio Rossi, "Russia to Fight Weapons Sales Curbs," *Defense News,* May 18–24, 1992, p. 1.

8. Proposals for export restraints among the five permanent members of the UN Security Council have surfaced in the aftermath of the 1991 Persian Gulf War; however, they have failed to garner a significant degree of international consensus, and China has ceased to paticipate in response to a U.S. decision to sell F-16 fighters to Taiwan in 1992. The P-5 process (as it has come to be called) has reached agreement on an informal code of conduct regarding arms transfers. This code proscribes *destabilizing* arms transfers to regions with ongoing conflicts. It also fails to define stability in varying security situations. More fundamentally the code does not contain provisions for the prior notification of major arms transfer agreements. See "Bum's Rush," *Aviation Week and Space Technology,* June 15, 1992, p. 31.

9. See "Russian AMRAAM Details Disclosed," *Jane's Defence Weekly,* August 29, 1992, p. 23.

10. The integration of Western technologies into Chinese systems is taking place on an ad hoc, subcomponent replacement basis. Technologies such as those involved in the Patriot antiballistic missile system are finding their way into reengineered Soviet and Chinese weapons. An expanded discussion of this standardization trend is given in David A. Fulghum, "China Exploiting US Patriot Secrets," *Aviation Week and Space Technology,* January 18, 1993, p. 20.

11. In the United States, these conflicts are already under way. See Tom Philpott, "Defense Hardliners Shift Support from Bush to Clinton," *Defense News,* October 12–18, 1992, p. 68; and Neil Munro and Barbara Opall, "Army, Navy Challenge USAF Strike Mission," *Defense News,* November 23–39, 1992, p. 4.

12. Proposals for some form of permanent force under the control of the UN would undermine this source of "roles and missions" for national armed forces. One can guess what national defense establishments will argue if these proposals should move forward more aggressively. It is already clear that defense establishments will claim that peacekeeping and peacemaking functions are *their* area of expertise, and thus do not require a UN military agency. These claims would certainly complicate the "permanent" assignment of military forces for the use of the UN in its cease-fire surveillance duties.

13. Louis Uchitelle, "Business Scene—Weapons Makers Thinking Small," *New York Times,* August 11, 1992, p. D2.

14. Philip Finnegan, "US Girds for Wave of Mergers," *Defense News,* November 30–December 6, 1992, p. 1.

15. This pattern is visible in a number of different mergers and divestitures in the defense industrial sector. The abortive Taiwan-Aerospace–McDonnell Douglas co-development plan for the MD-12 airliner illustrated the political and economic effects of an increasingly globalized aerospace industry. This arrangement also raised important issues of technology security and defense industrial-base weakness. A subsequent attempted acquisition of LTV Corporation's aerospace units by Thomson-CSF of France and the Carlyle Group of Washington, D.C., ran into some of the same problems. See Elisabeth Sköns, "Western Europe: Internationalization of the Arms Industry," in Herbert Wulf, ed., *Arms Industry Limited* (Oxford University Press, 1993), p. 169; Mark Tapscott, "Thomson-CSF, LTV Deal Facing Serious Political Hurdles," *Defense Electronics,* July 1992, p. 8; Jeff Cole and Andy Pasztor, "McDonnell Faces Major New Setbacks in MD-12 Airliner, Fighter Jet Projects," *Wall Street Journal,* June 15, 1992, p. A3; and Jeff Cole and Jeremy Mark, "McDonnell Seals $1.2 Billion China Job, but Taiwan Venture Seems to Be Fading," *Wall Street Journal,* June 29, 1993, p. A3.

16. This point should not be overstated. What is at work is an expansion in production facilities, not an inevitable expansion in the number of centers of weapons innovation. A longer-term process does exist, however, which is the diminishment of technological gaps separating developed and developing countries.

17. See Andrew Moravcsik, "Arms and Autarky in Modern European History," *Daedalus,* vol. 120 (Fall 1991), pp. 23–46.

18. The distinctive institutional and economic signals operating in the defense and civil sectors are outlined in John A. Alic and others, *Beyond Spinoff: Military and Commercial Technologies in a Changing World* (Harvard Business School Press, 1992), pp. 28–53. There is little reason to assume that governmental concerns with security of supply will be respected in an increasingly globalized technology diffusion setting. Much of the diffusion dynamic itself stems from the exchange of intellectual property in mergers and consortia negotiations.

19. For a detailed discussion of these issues, see ibid.

20. States as wealthy as Saudi Arabia and Kuwait have been forced to delay the delivery of weapons because of temporary hard-currency shortages. Although this situation was an outgrowth of expenditures during the Gulf War, the absorption of previously ordered systems is a continuing drag on the deployment of new acquisitions. For more information, see Yahya M. Sadowski, *Scuds or Butter? The Political Economy of Arms Control in the Middle East* (Brookings, 1993).

21. The technologies imported by Iraq are a case in point. That country was able to put together a comprehensive nuclear weapons program from a wide variety of sources. Individual technologies acquired by Iraq were frequently dismissed as "normal," possessing conventional applications. In hindsight the acquisitions were part of a highly imaginative program to circumvent existing international regulations on technology transfer.

22. Again the United States will escape many of the harsher implications of this situation because of the dominance of U.S. companies in defense technology. Even there, however, there is still political concern that spot dependencies upon foreign technologies may create vulnerabilities to pressure and embargo in the distant future.

23. The issue of public goods and its implications for the management of military trade is discussed in detail in chapter 5.

24. See chapters 3 and 5 in this volume.

25. International Monetary Fund (IMF), *Economic Review of the Russian Federation* (Washington, June 1993), pp. 85–86; Keith Bush, "An Overview of the Russian Economy," *RFE/RL Research Report,* vol. 1 (June 19, 1992), p. 50. The IMF report

suggests that the output figures published by Goskomstat of the Russian Federation understate the output decline.

26. Bush, "An Overview of the Russian Economy."

27. Ibid., p. 49.

28. IMF, *Economic Review of the Russian Federation,* p. 1.

29. Ibid., p. 8.

30. In the course of World War II, for example, the United States successfully converted its automobile industry to defense production and then back again. The companies and specific plants involved had evolved in the private market and left it only temporarily. There are at most only a few documented cases—less than five—in which a plant that had been developed for defense production switched successfully to consumer product production under normal market conditions.

31. The $150 billion figure is frequently cited by Russian officials as the amount required to convert the Rusisan defense industries. See, for example, "Yeltsin Aid Cited on Conversion Program," *Rossiyskiye vesti,* May 22, 1992, p. 3, in Foreign Broadcast Information Service, *Daily Report: Central Eurasia,* June 1, 1992, pp. 28–30. (Hereafter FBIS, *Central Eurasia.*)

32. The CSCE has certain well-recognized limitations, including limits on its power and authority resulting from its nontreaty status and the difficulty of making decisions in an organization that has long depended on unanimous decisions among a large number of members. Greater use of the North Atlantic Cooperation Council (NACC), formed in 1991 and composed of the sixteen NATO nations and nineteen states that once made up the territory of the Warsaw Pact, is being discussed as one way to help strengthen the process of military collaboration between former enemies. Members of NACC, together with other CSCE countries, could earmark national forces for cooperative security, including peacekeeping missions under CSCE auspices, for example. Membership in these organizations could also be a way to set standards of state performance and behavior, which might include a democratic form of government, adherence to the rule of law, renunciation of territorial claims, and compliance with existing treaties and agreements limiting sale or purchase of technology related to weapons of mass destruction.

33. Rolf Ekeus, "Chemical Weapons and the New Global Security Structures, *Chemical Weapons Convention Bulletin,* no. 16 (June 1992), p. 4.

34. Boutros Boutros-Ghali, *An Agenda for Peace: Preventive Diplomacy, Peacemaking and Peace-keeping,* report of the secretary-general pursuant to the statement adopted by the Summit Meeting of the Security Council on January 31, 1992 (United Nations, 1992).

35. See, for instance, Lee Feinstein, "'Big Five' Weapons Exporters: More Talk, More Sales," *Arms Control Today,* vol. 21 (November 1991), p. 22.

36. The major disagreement among the five results from China's insistence that notification of contracts occur only after transfers have actually taken place. See Lee Feinstein, "Big Five Accomplish Little during Washington Talks," *Arms Control Today,* vol. 22 (March 1992), p. 23.

37. See, for example, Steve Coll and David Hoffman, "Shipments to Pakistan Questioned; Commercial Sales of War Materiel May Break US Law," *Washington Post,* March 7, 1992, p. A1; and Jim Hoagland, "Will Kim Blink," *Washington Post,* April 21, 1992, p. A19.

38. See David Marsh, "The French Referendum: EC Urged to Renegotiate Trade Deals with Eastern Europe," *Financial Times,* September 8, 1992, p. 2; and "Attali Attacks Leading G7 Industrial Nations," *Financial Times,* October 26, 1992, p. 3.

39. George Leopold, "US, Russians Push Joint Efforts in Defense Cooperation," *Defense News,* vol. 7 (February 24, 1992), p. 56.

40. Eduardo Lachica, "U.S., 26 Other Nations to Control Exports That Could Be Used in Nuclear Bombs," *Wall Street Journal,* April 3, 1992, p. C10.

41. Ukraine and Belarus pledged to join the NPT as nonnuclear states as part of the Alma-Ata agreement signed in December 1991. Kazakhstan pledged to join in 1992 pending clarification of its status under the agreement. See, for instance, "Agreement on Joint Measures on Nuclear Weapons," *Pravda,* December 23, 1991, p. 2, in FBIS, *JPRS Report: Proliferation Issues,* January 16, 1992, pp. 35–36; and "Official Visit to Pakistan," ITAR-TASS, February 24, 1992, in *JPRS Report: Proliferation Issues,* March 3, 1992, p. 13. More recently, however, the Ukrainian parliament has rejected NPT for the time being, and many deputies now argue that Ukraine should not accede to the NPT until the 1995 review. Kazakhstan has also neglected to fulfill the terms of the Alma-Ata agreement by failing to respond to Russian requests for negotiations over transferring the control of Kazakhstan's nuclear weapons to Russia. In July 1993 Belarus acceded to the NPT by formally depositing its instrument of ratification. See John Lepingwell, "Or Lisbon without Article Five?" *RFE/RL Daily Report,* no. 221 (November 18, 1993); John Lepingwell, "Russia Concerned over Nukes in Kazakhstan," *RFE/RL Daily Report,* no. 232 (December 6, 1993); and Institute for Defense and Disarmament Studies, "Chronology 1993," *Arms Control Reporter 1993,* pp. 602.B.239–52.

42. N. Urakov, the general director of one of the FSU's biomedical research institutes, has said, "Many kinds of bacteriological weapons are known that are based on pathogens of particularly dangerous infections. . . This does not mean that our country . . . must develop weapons of mass destruction. But we are obligated to have effective biological medicines and vaccines against them." V. Kaysyn, "Visiting a Caged Beast," *Pravda,* February 4, 1992, p. 6, in FBIS, *JPRS Report: Arms Control,* March 9, 1992, pp. 47–49.

43. Although India has supported the idea of worldwide negotiations to ban chemical weapons, India is also suspected of exporting chemical technologies to other states. See Michael R. Gordon, "U.S. Accuses India on Chemical Arms," *New York Times,* September 21, 1992, p. A1. For more information on the Committee on Disarmament agreement to ban the production and stockpiling of chemical weapons, see Michael R. Gordon, "Hopes and Fears; Negotiators Propose Treaty to Ban Chemical Weapons by the Year 2005," *New York Times,* September 6, 1992, sec. 4, p. 2.

44. More recently, however, the U.S. government determined that China has violated the MTCR standards by selling M-11 missile-related technology to Pakistan. The U.S. government then imposed a category 2 sanction against China. For more information, see the statement by the department spokesman Michael McCurry, "China and Pakistan: M-11 Missile Sanctions," *US Department of State Dispatch,* vol. 4 (August 30, 1991), p. 607. For recent changes in MTCR standards and regulations, see "US Broadens Missiles Controls," *Export Control News,* vol. 7 (January 28, 1993), p. 2; and Tom Lewis, "North Atlantic Assembly: Ballistic Missile Proliferation," Draft Special Report, AK256STC(93) 11 (October 1993).

45. U.S. Army chief of staff General Gordon R. Sullivan testified in early 1992 that the U.S. Army was dedicated to fostering cooperative efforts with other nations to join the United States in reducing chemical arsenals and pursuing "the US goal of achieving a global and effectively verifiable CW ban." *National Defense Authorization Act for Fiscal Year 1993–H.R. 5006 and Oversight of Previously Authorized Programs,* House Committee on Armed Services, 102 Cong. 2 sess. (Government Printing Office, 1992), p. 319.

46. See, for instance, "Germany Sets Up Export Control Data Base," in *Mednews,* vol. 5 (July 6, 1992), pp. 4–5.

47. "Group to Control Arms Exports," *Radio Rossi,* February 3, 1992, in FBIS, *Central Eurasia,* February 4, 1992, p. 36.

48. See National Academy of Sciences, Committee on Science, Engineering, and Public Policy, *Finding Common Ground: U.S. Export Controls in a Changed Global Environment* (Washington: National Academy Press, 1991).

49. Ekeus, "Chemical Weapons and the New Global Security Regime," p. 4. He went on to say, "It is incomprehensible that procedures could not be outlined which would make it possible for international chemical weapons inspectors, dispatched by a multilateral verification agency, to carry out their tasks in full without in any way compromising non-chemical weapons activities and items. Modern chemical weapons verification methods and means as applied by Special Commission, for instance, are sophisticated enough to discriminate between what is chemical weapons relevant and what is not."

Part Two

THEMES OF A POTENTIAL COOPERATIVE ORDER

THREE

Regime Architecture: Elements and Principles

Antonia Handler Chayes and Abram Chayes

THE CENTRAL strategic problem for a cooperative security regime is not deterrence, as in the cold war, but reassurance. For deterrence to be effective, the actors must be convinced that any attack will be met by a response sufficient to erase any potential gains to the aggressor. In a cooperative security system, by contrast, the actors must have confidence that the other participants are abiding by the applicable restrictions on force structures and capabilities. Unlike deterrence, which relies on strategic interactions between opposed states, the key to reassurance is a reliable normative and institutional structure.[1]

The intellectual and political problems of deterrence relate primarily to the details of force structures, command and control, and alliance politics. Arms control and other cooperative measures are secondary. The problem of reassurance is more complex. It requires an ability to initiate and maintain cooperation among sovereign states on matters that have been traditionally conceived of as the heart of sovereignty: decisions about what is needed to maintain and preserve national security.

Cooperative security contemplates an expanding network of generally applicable limitations on weapons systems and force structures. The limits will be defined primarily by agreement rather than strategic interaction, that is, unilateral responses to the moves of other actors. Although sanctions have a place in such a system, the absence of any central political authority and the practical limits on resort to force mean that substantial compliance with these strictures cannot be achieved by the threat of military retaliation. Compliance must be induced by the continuing sense that the limits imposed on military capabilities

We are grateful to the Pew Charitable Trust for a grant that has enabled us to do research and writing across many international regulatory regimes and permitted us to develop a more comprehensive view of the experience and prospects of regime architecture.

are consistent with the security requirements of the participants and that they are being generally observed.

These parameters are the challenge for designers of a cooperative security regime. It is true, as emphasized earlier, that "cooperative security is, and probably will remain, an aspiration that will be only incompletely fulfilled. It is not a description of the world system, a prediction about the future, or a theory of international relations. But aspirations give coherence to security policy."[2]

Given this evolutionary framework, the fundamental design elements and principles needed to achieve a functioning security system based on reassurance can be identified as a strong normative base, inclusiveness and nondiscrimination, transparency, regime management, and sanctions.

A strong normative base. The basic conception of cooperative security implies general acceptance of and compliance with binding commitments limiting military capabilities and actions. The key to compliance with such a system of norms is that it be seen as legitimate. Legitimacy, in turn, requires that the norms be promulgated by fair and accepted procedures, applied equally and without invidious discrimination, and reflect minimum substantive standards of fairness and equity.

Inclusiveness and nondiscrimination. Inclusiveness is a requirement both for effectiveness and for legitimacy. A cooperative security regime that requires reductions and reconfiguration of force structures must be broadly inclusive to be effective. Although significant holdouts would undermine the enterprise, the regime cannot be imposed. It must be accepted by the participants, and, when power is relatively diffused among the actors, no system is acceptable unless its constraints are widely applicable without invidious discrimination.

More broadly, cooperative security cannot be achieved if more than half the world feels threatened and victimized by perceived inequities or discriminatory policies. Without an effort to accommodate the concerns of the "have not" countries, it would be impossible to create the norms that an effective regime requires.

Inclusiveness does not mean a single, overarching, integrated structure. There is room, even at an advanced stage, for regional arrangements and organizations devoted to specific issues or problems. But, at a minimum, avoidance of overlapping and duplication requires some linkages between the constituent elements. Moreover, each participant needs a clear picture, not only of separate elements of the military posture of potentially threatening adversaries, such as weapons of mass destruction, but of the overall military capability it might have to face.

Transparency. In modern international regulatory regimes, the key to compliance is transparency: the availability and accessibility of information about the regime and the performance of parties under it. Transparency induces compliance in a variety of ways. It serves the functions of coordination, reassurance, and deterrence. More important, to the extent that the system is open to scrutiny, it gains legitimacy, for participants can see that it is not being subverted. The main source of information will necessarily be the self-reporting of the parties, subject to evaluation, checking, and independent verification, using all the techniques in the arms control inventory as well as new types of measures that become available as a result of technological or political developments.

Regime management. The administration of a complex enterprise of international cooperation requires a significant institutional capability. Collection, evaluation, verification, and analysis of information is itself a huge organizational task. Using this information stream to reassure the parties that undertakings are being complied with increases the organizational burden. The design of such an organization and the distribution of functions among new and existing institutional components is itself one of the most difficult tasks involved in the construction of a cooperative security regime. In addition to information management, the other main organizational functions are as follows:

—Review, assessment, and response. Information indicating a possible violation of regime requirements must be acted upon promptly and effectively. Responses must be graduated to clarify the issues, to give the party an opportunity to explain and justify its actions, and to correct suspect conduct that is attributable to a mistake or misunderstanding. The regime must provide the forum for jawboning and the gradual escalation of pressures to move the offender back into compliance. Exposure and disapproval from the other parties to the agreement, linkage to other economic and political issues, and domestic political pressures can all be marshaled to this end.

—Capacity building. Security regimes have been traditionally directed to state behavior. But many of the objectives of a cooperative security regime, as is the case with nonproliferation agreements, also require regulation of behavior of private actors—primarily companies producing, exporting, and transporting materiel subject to treaty regulation. Assurance that states have the capability and will to perform this regulatory function is a crucial part of regime management.

—Interpretation and dispute settlement. Treaty ambiguity and differences of interpretation often underlie apparent noncompliance. Binding adjudication of such disputes will likely remain out of reach for a long time, perhaps indefinitely. Nevertheless, other mechanisms for authoritative interpretation and dispute resolution are available to resolve issues of contested behavior and are essential for effective administration of the regime.

—Adaptation and flexibility. Any enduring international regime must be able to maintain itself in the face of frequent and often quite disjunctive changes in the technological, economic, political, and scientific context. The treaty amendment process is often too cumbersome and time consuming to adapt readily to such changes. The institutions of the regime should have powers of interpretation and quasi-rule-making authority to respond more flexibly to changing circumstances.

Sanctions. If the regime is well constructed, taking adequate account of the legitimate interests of all its members, the likelihood of outright defiance that threatens the viability of the system is very low. Yet, as the case of Iraq shows, it is not zero. Some prospect of sanctions must be available to deter and if necessary redress egregious and obdurate violations. Unilateral military action for this purpose is inconsistent with the postulates of cooperative security. Unilateral economic sanctions may be available, but are of doubtful efficacy, particularly in situations in which prompt response is needed. The ultimate recourse in such cases must be for the UN Security Council or some other legitimate collective organ to authorize concerted economic or military response. Marshaling the necessary consensus for such action will always be difficult, but recent experience gives hope that this alternative may be depended on in a regime-threatening crisis.

We elaborate on these requirements in the remainder of this chapter.

The Normative Base

The success of the cooperative security regime will depend centrally on the strength of the structure of norms that the regime establishes. Work in a wide range of disciplines is converging on the notion that the possibility of cooperative action, whether among individuals or organized groups, as well as the solution to collective choice problems, is to be found in the operation of norms.[3] If so, the very possibility of cooperative security depends upon the ability to generate, adapt, and enforce a system of governing norms.

Norms, as used here, in a generic sense, include a broad class of generalized prescriptive statements—rules, standards, principles, and so forth—both procedural and substantive.[4] All of these statements are *prescriptions for action in situations of choice,* carrying a sense of obligation, a sense that they *ought* to be followed. It is not necessary here to explore the source of obligation, whether pure utilitarian calculation, social conditioning, or belief in God. Contemporary academic discussion tends to emphasize the importance of tradition and, more important, of belief (grounded in historical and cultural experience) that social life would be impossible unless there were some kind of obligation to follow prescriptions of the general types here involved.[5]

In any case, norms are social artifacts. They arise out of conduct or activity in a social context, and they are interpreted, applied, and enforced by social practice and interaction, with official coercion playing a secondary role at most. Thus, the sense of obligation to obey normative prescriptions operates within the social setting that produced them. The area of interest for this analysis is international relations, and the relevant prescriptions operate among states, international organizations, and other actors in the international system.

Norms are not predictive. Since they are prescriptions for action in situations of choice, the actor may or may not choose to obey them. It follows, further, that departure from a norm, even frequent or persistent departure, does not necessarily invalidate it. That there have been many instances since 1945 of the use of force in violation of Article 2(4) of the UN Charter does not disprove the continuing existence, validity, or even operational effect of the norm. Unlike a scientific or predictive rule, a norm is not falsified by counter-examples.[6]

Nevertheless, actors in general *do* comply with prescriptions to which they are subject. Again, it is not necessary to identify the causes of this phenomenon. Utility, stasis, internalization, and moral compulsion doubtless all contribute. An important consequence is that an actor whose conduct appears to deviate from the norm can be called upon to justify or explain.

Not all norms carry *legal* obligation. The Conference on Security and Cooperation in Europe (CSCE) negotiators specified that their highly articulated agreement would not "affect their rights and obligations."[7] Nevertheless, international legal norms form the core of most international regulatory regimes.[8] International relations is in large part a matter of explanation and justification, persuasion and dissuasion, approval and condemnation. In this discourse, legal norms have a prominent role. It is almost always an adequate explanation for an action, at least prima facie, that it follows the legal rule. It is almost always a good argument for an action that it conforms to the applicable legal norms and against one that it departs from them. The arguments may not persuade, but there is no doubt where the burden of proof lies. It is almost always a basis for disapproval that an action violates the norms.

Most important in terms of enforcement of norms is that deviant action calls for explanation and justification. The actor when challenged must show that the facts are not as they seem to be, that the rule, properly interpreted, does not cover the conduct in question, or that some other matter excuses the failure to fulfill the normative requirement. It may be true, as Hans Morgenthau said, that states can always find a legal argument to justify their position.[9] But within some limits, good legal arguments can generally be distinguished from bad.[10] For example, in defense of its Strategic Defense Initiative, the Reagan administration advanced a "new interpretation" of the Anti-Ballistic Missile (ABM) Treaty, exempting exotic technologies from its scope.[11] Again, the Soviet Union sought to justify the Krasnoyarsk radar by claiming it was a space-tracking installation rather than an early warning radar that was prohibited by the treaty. In neither case was it hard to discredit the asserted defense. In both, the treaty norm prevailed against powerful internal political forces pressing for departure from the treaty.[12]

All attempts at a general definition of *law*—let alone of *international law*—on the basis of one or even a few factors have been abject failures. However, legal norms have some identifiable characteristic attributes. In contrast to other types of norms that operate in international regimes, legal norms have a relatively high degree of formality. They are often authoritatively stated in formal instruments. The norm system is operated by a set of professionals using techniques and practices that specify what counts as probative, persuasive, or relevant.[13] The production of legal norms is linked to the apparatus of government and in domestic legal systems commonly involves its coercive force. Still, as does any other basic cultural manifestation, law, whether domestic or international, has an enormously complex derivation that stubbornly resists specification.[14]

Treaties are the most unproblematic source of international law. A treaty is "an international agreement concluded between states in written form and governed by international law."[15] Treaties are subject to the universally acknowledged norm of *pacta sunt servanda:* "Every treaty in force is binding on the parties to it and must be performed in good faith."[16] Thus, treaties embody rules that are legally binding on states that ratify them.

The existing international security regime is based in large part on a network of treaties: the UN Charter, treaties of alliance, arms control agreements, and treaties governing the acquisition and use of weapons. There is no single, overarching comprehensive constitutional document, but the constituent elements are linked in important and complicated ways. The International Atomic Energy Agency (IAEA), for example, is not operationally "subordinate" to the United Nations, but the two are linked, not only by the agreement defining the IAEA's position as a specialized agency but also because it depends on the Security Council to take action in case of violations. But institutional linkages are not always either so explicit or so formal.

International law is not limited to treaty prescriptions, however. *Pacta sunt servanda* itself, from which treaties "derive" their force, is a background norm of general international law. An important contemporary development in international law is that treaties, which according to the rules noted previously are consensual instruments obligatory only on states that agree to them, can sometimes be transmuted into general international law and thus become binding on nonsignatories. The Exclusive Economic Zone (EEZ), which extends the jurisdiction of coastal states 200 miles seaward, was agreed to in the Law of the Sea Convention.[17] Although that convention has not come into force, there is now general agreement that the EEZ is in fact an obligatory rule of general international law.[18] The rule allocates control over both regulatory jurisdiction and resources and has enormous economic and political consequences. Yet the rights and obligations incident to the EEZ, which did not exist at all twenty years ago, are universally acknowledged.

A similar development occurred with the Nuclear Non-Proliferation Treaty (NPT). Although in the technical sense it is binding only on signers, it has helped to create a more general norm against acquisition of nuclear weapons. The pressure of this norm has been a significant (though not exclusive) factor in a number of situations. Some earlier recalcitrants have signed up or, as in the case of Brazil and Argentina, have submitted themselves to the norm without ratifying the NPT (discussed further in the next section). All the republics of the former Soviet Union have announced that they will adhere to the treaty, although some have yet to follow through on their promise.[19] Even holdouts not bound by the treaty, such as India, Pakistan, and Israel, explain and justify their policies in ways that acknowledge the existence of a recognized nonproliferation norm. Except for the original five nuclear weapon states, no state, whether or not a party to the NPT, is prepared to acknowledge that it has a nuclear weapons program.[20]

In this case, norm formation has been immensely helped by the universal dread of nuclear war both among ordinary people and political leaders and by a general sense that proliferation contributes to the danger. This extratreaty norm lent impetus to the negotiation of the treaty in the first place, to its relatively successful implementation, and to the extension of the norm, at least in some degree, to nonsigners.

The opposite dynamic may be operating with respect to chemical warfare. The popular horror that led to the 1924 Protocol after World War I[21] seems to have dissipated to some extent in recent years. The use of chemical weapons in the Iran-Iraq war and elsewhere failed to mobilize overwhelming public outrage. The drafters now look to the new Chemical Weapons Convention (CWC) to reinvigorate the norm. One of the main difficulties in developing a system of control for ballistic missiles, in turn, is the almost complete absence of any such extratreaty sentiment.

International law addresses the question of how treaty provisions may transmute themselves into general obligations, applicable to nonsigners. The classic formula is that "the acts concerned [must] amount to a settled practice, but they must also be such, or be carried out in such a way, as to be evidence of a belief that this practice is rendered obligatory by the existence of a rule of law requiring it."[22] In this, the legal principle is consistent with institutional and social theory, which holds that norms are products of discursive social interaction—not just repetitive practice but practice that generates reciprocal expectations of performance and ultimately the acceptance of an obligation.[23]

To be durable, international legal norms, whether or not treaty based, must meet broad tests of legitimacy. They must be the product of regular and accepted procedures, be applicable equally and without invidious discrimination, and satisfy minimal notions of substantive fairness.[24] These criteria are admittedly nebulous and admittedly aspirational. No existing legal system fully meets them. Yet the members of a regime are continually assessing it against these standards (as well as calculating costs and benefits). If law is at the heart of international regimes, then constructing or strengthening a regime entails constructing and maintaining a legal framework that meets these tests of legitimacy.

The elements of a compliance system, discussed in the following section, derive their effectiveness from the strength of the normative base of the cooperative security regime. At the same time, these elements contribute reciprocally to the legitimacy of the norms and thus to the durability of the regime.

Inclusiveness and Nondiscrimination

A regime is inclusive to the extent that the states affected by it have reasonable opportunity to participate in its processes and it does not unfairly discriminate against any of its members. This section examines, in the light of this standard, the nonproliferation regimes now in existence and in near prospect. These existing components are among the most important in the cooperative security system, and experience with them illustrates many of the problems of inclusiveness and discrimination in national security regimes.

Formal nonproliferation treaties—the CWC, the Biological Weapons Convention (BWC), and the NPT[25]—aspire not only to inclusive but to universal membership. The first two are also nondiscriminatory. The NPT, however, sets up two classes of members: nuclear weapon states, which manufactured and tested weapons before 1967 and are permitted to keep them, and non–nuclear weapon states, which under the treaty must forego nuclear weapons.

Adjunct to these formal treaties are informal export restraint agreements among supplier states, backed by the domestic export control regulations of the members.[26] This study concludes that technological denial will become increasingly ineffective.[27] From the perspective of nondiscrimination, however, the denial strategy has an additional flaw. Conceptually, supplier controls represent an attempt by a self-selected group of "have" nations, meeting in private, to develop and impose their own views of appropriate security policy by virtue of their technological and economic superiority. The inherently discriminatory character of supplier regimes is exacerbated by restrictions that are overinclusive and methods of control that are overreaching. They are easy targets for resentment,[28] which contributes to the persistence and all too often the success of attempts to circumvent them, both by private exporters in supplier states and by recipient governments (discussed in the section "Inclusiveness and the Role of Supplier Groups"). Although all the groups are seeking to expand their membership to include new suppliers, to do so will not necessarily cure these defects.[29]

Evolution toward a comprehensive cooperative security regime calls for a different approach for each of these two types of agreements. As to the formal treaties, it is important to put the NPT on a broader and more inclusive basis and to intensify efforts to obtain treaties for weapons not now covered. For the supplier regimes, the task is to moderate their discriminatory features, by linking them more closely to existing treaties and making them more inclusive.

Formal Nonproliferation Agreements

The agreements cover four categories of weapons: nuclear, biological and toxin, chemical, and conventional.

NUCLEAR NONPROLIFERATION. The oldest and most fully developed of all the nonproliferation regimes is the one governing nuclear weapons. It is a complex edifice of formal and informal arrangements. Its centerpiece is the NPT, in force since 1970. It includes as well the statute of the IAEA, regional instruments like the Treaty of Tlatleloco, and the South Pacific Nuclear Free Zone,[30] safeguards agreements between non–nuclear weapon states and the IAEA, and the informal guidelines drawn up by the Nuclear Suppliers Group and Zangger Committee of nuclear supplier states.[31] Taken together, these instruments constitute an international regulatory regime that even its detractors admit has had a distinct measure of success.

Yet, as Hans Blix, director general of the IAEA, states, "Universalization of binding non-proliferation commitments and nuclear disarmament should help to reduce the risk of violation of non-proliferation commitments. So long as some states remain outside the non-proliferation regime and the nuclear weapon States have not taken decisive steps towards nuclear disarmament, non-proliferation can still be subject to some strain."[32] Significant progress has been made on both fronts in the past decade.

Universalization. China and France, the two nuclear weapon states that were nonsigners, have now indicated that they will adhere to the treaty.[33] In a further reassuring gesture, all the republics of the former Soviet Union have announced their intention to sign the treaty. The three republics with nuclear weapons on their territory, Ukraine, Belarus, and Kazakhstan, have agreed to join as nonnuclear states, although as yet only the last two have done so.[34]

Of the nations traditionally said to be on the nuclear threshold, three—Argentina, Brazil, and South Africa—have agreed to comprehensive restraints. South Africa signed the NPT on July 8, 1991, and has since agreed to full scope inspections and safeguards.[35] On December 1, 1991, Argentina and Brazil signed an agreement for international safeguards on all material involved in nuclear activity in the two countries to be administered with the assistance of the IAEA.[36]

It appears that Iraq, the NPT member thought to be the most serious proliferation threat, no longer has a nuclear capacity, as a result of the Gulf War and the efforts of the UN Special Commission and the IAEA to detect and destroy any capability that remained, as mandated by UN Security Resolution 687.[37]

In terms of formal nonproliferation commitments, India, Pakistan, and Israel, all weapons-capable states, remain holdouts. The one retrograde development is North Korea, which became a party to the treaty in 1985, but in March 1993 became the first state ever to give notice of withdrawal from the NPT after refusing an IAEA demand for a "special inspection." As of this writing, the situation remains unresolved, although North Korea agreed in June 1993 to suspend its withdrawl and to negotiate the terms for its accession in the future.[38]

Progress toward nuclear disarmament. The division between weapons states and nonweapons states was built into the treaty. Short of the abolition of nuclear weapons, nobody expects this distinction to be eliminated. The quid pro quo for the non–nuclear weapon states, however, was Article 6 of the treaty, in which the nuclear powers undertook "to pursue negotiations in good faith on effective measures relating to cessation of the nuclear arms race at an early date." The preamble, in a passage that is often linked to Article 6, also emphasizes the need to achieve a comprehensive ban on nuclear testing.

Increasing dissatisfaction on the part of the non–nuclear weapon states with the performance of the nuclear weapon states under Article 6 reached a climax at the 1990 NPT review conference, at which Mexico led a demand by many nonaligned countries that the United States at least signal its willingness to enter into negotiations for a Comprehensive Test Ban Treaty. In the end, Mexico blocked a consensus on a compromise resolution, and the conference ended without adopting a final act.[39] By the terms of the NPT, the next review conference in 1995 must decide "whether the Treaty shall continue in force indefinitely, or shall be extended for an additional fixed period or periods."[40] Thus the future of the treaty is at some risk and the first step toward dealing with the problem of discrimination under the NPT is full compliance by the nuclear weapon states with their undertakings outlined in Article 6.[41]

The completion of the Strategic Arms Reduction Treaty and the subsequent agreement between President Bush and President Yeltsin signed in December 1993 to reduce their nuclear weapons arsenals to between 3,000 and 3,500 warheads each by no later than the year 2003 are major steps toward Article 6 goals.[42]

The issue that currently looms large for the 1995 conference is the comprehensive test ban. U.S. objections that a ban on underground testing could not be verified prevented agreement in earlier years. Now that these have disappeared, there are the beginnings of movement on this issue. In 1990 the United States finally ratified the Threshold Test Ban Treaty, limiting underground tests to 150 kilotons,[43] but this parameter provides only limited assurance against proliferation, since states can test well below it. Russia declared a unilateral twelve-month testing moratorium in October 1991, and France has announced the cessation of its test program.[44] In response to these developments, on

September 24, 1992, the U.S. Congress, over President Bush's objection, imposed an immediate nine-month test moratorium and mandated a total cutoff in late 1995 unless another nation is still conducting tests.[45]

If the nuclear powers would now take the final step and negotiate a Comprehensive Test Ban Treaty, it would go far to erase the basis for continuing resentment of discrimination in the NPT, especially given the progress in strategic arms control. The U.S. decision in July 1993 to extend a moratorium on nuclear tests and seek international support for this initiative is encouraging.[46]

BIOLOGICAL AND TOXIN WEAPONS. As was noted, the BWC, which entered into force in 1975, is a nondiscriminatory regime. It prohibits the development, production, or stockpiling of biological or toxin agents "that have no justification for prophylactic, protective, or other peaceful purposes" and of weapons or delivery systems designed to use such agents "for hostile purposes or in armed conflict."[47] The treaty does not discriminate among parties. There are no exceptions to its prohibitions.

Unlike the NPT, however, it has no provisions for verification, and no permanent organizational framework to ensure its implementation. When the BWC was negotiated, there had been little effort to develop verification techniques and there was as yet no tolerance for the kind of intrusive inspections that became acceptable in the late 1980s. The moral stigma of biological weapons as well as their questionable military value seemed sufficient to ensure its effectiveness.

Such constraints do not seem to be as strong as they once appeared. According to U.S. intelligence estimates, at least ten nations are working to produce both previously known and futuristic biological weapons.[48] Reports that several countries had used chemical, biological, or toxin weapons led the UN General Assembly, in December 1982, to adopt a resolution requesting the secretary-general to investigate. Because of opposition from the Soviet Union and several eastern European countries, however, he was unable to invoke this authority when Iran formally requested an investigation in March 1984.[49]

Several review conferences have been held over the years in an effort to correct the deficiencies in the BWC. In 1986, the parties agreed to exchange data, to report on unusual outbreaks of infectious disease or toxification, and to publish research findings.[50] At the Third Review Conference in September 1991, the parties began to address the issue of verification seriously. They undertook to establish a group of experts to identify and examine potential verification measures from a scientific and technical standpoint. This group is to complete its work by the end of 1993.[51] Many nongovernmental experts, including a Federation of American Scientists Working Group, propose the CWC as a model for treaty-based verification of prohibitions on biological and toxin weapons, emphasizing on-site inspections, including challenge inspections of private research and manufacturing facilities.[52] The procedures would need to be tailored to the special problems created by production that is almost entirely dual-use in nature. It would also have to be sensitive to the problems of proprietary information and would have to include special health precautions.

Because biological weapons are low cost and easily produced, universal adherence to the BWC seems especially important. However, several countries have not ratified the treaty, among them Egypt, Syria, and Israel.[53] As in other cases, parties to the treaty, singly or in concert, can bring political pressures to bear on nations that have thus far failed to join. In this one area, initiative and pressure by a combination of industrial and developing nations could make a difference.

CHEMICAL WEAPONS. The CWC is intended to correct the shortcomings of the Geneva Protocol banning the use of chemical weapons in warfare, signed in 1925 after the experience of the First World War.[54] The new convention includes prohibitions against development, manufacture, and stockpiling of prohibited weapons as well as an elaborate verification system. The subject matter is extraordinarily difficult, and the convention was under negotiation for more than ten years in the UN Disarmament Commission.[55] An agreed treaty text was approved by the United Nations General Assembly in 1992 and was opened for signature in Paris on January 13, 1993.[56] More than 120 states, but not Iraq, North Korea, or Vietnam, were at the signing ceremony. The convention will come into force when it is ratified by 65 states,[57] but the goal of inclusiveness dictates a much wider membership. This near-term action item is urgent for progress toward cooperative security.

CONVENTIONAL WEAPONS. Advanced conventional weapons pose recognized threats in the hands of potential aggressors, but as yet, with the exception of the treaty on Conventional Armed Forces in Europe (CFE), there is no prospect of a treaty limiting conventional force sizes or acquisitions. The lack of serious steps to restrain such weapons in part reflects ambivalence by the major suppliers in the United States, Europe, and the former Soviet Union. Despite rhetorical commitments to restraint, they continue to permit and even stimulate escalation in geographic areas of tension by their military assistance and arms sales policies.[58] Between the end of the Gulf War and January 1993, the United States had approved up to $23.8 billion in military sales to the Middle East.[59]

In all these cases, economic motivations are at work. But the United States is also influenced by a delicate web of diplomatic relations, particularly in the Middle East. It is not an easy matter for the United States to refuse Saudi Arabia sophisticated fighter aircraft given the perceived threats from neighboring Iraq and Iran and the fulsome Saudi cooperation in the Gulf War.[60] Moreover, the availability of oil dollars has always permitted Saudi Arabia to look elsewhere if the United States refuses.

In spite of these incentives for continuing the status quo, an important first step toward controlling conventional arms transfers was taken with the establishment on a voluntary basis of a UN Register of Conventional Arms Sales. First proposed in mid-1990 by Soviet foreign minister Eduard Shevardnadze, it was formally authorized by General Assembly Resolution 46/36-L on December 9, 1991.[61] Under the Transparency in Armaments resolution, member states are requested to provide data voluntarily on an annual basis with respect to all imports and exports covered by the register. The secretary-general formally created the register on January 1, 1992, and appointed a panel of technical experts who produced a consensus report on procedures for operation of the register.[62] The first registration was scheduled for submission by April 30, 1993.[63]

Potentially, the UN Register has exactly the attributes of inclusiveness and nondiscrimination needed for widespread acceptability. To the extent that reporting requirements become universal in fact, it will represent a crucial new initiative in alerting the international community to potentially threatening conventional arms buildups, particularly of technologically advanced weapons.

Inclusiveness and the Role of Supplier Groups

There are three principal supplier control groups, each operating in one of the areas of proliferation concern: the Nuclear Suppliers Group (NSG), dealing with nuclear exports, the Australia Group, concerned with chemical and biological weapons, and the Missile Technology Control Regime (MTCR).[64] The members are primarily advanced industrial states, and there is considerable overlap in membership.

The NSG is the oldest of these groups and set the general pattern for the others. It was established by informal agreement, initially among a relatively few supplier states. It does not purport to be legally binding and does not "ban" the export of any item. The agreement reiterates the commitment of the parties not to export nuclear material without IAEA safeguards and added a list of nuclear-specific technology that should also be exported only if subject to safeguards. The parties further agreed to "exercise restraint" on exports of enrichment and reprocessing technology. The agreement is implemented through the domestic export control machinery of the participating states. The parties consult on issues related to the regime, but there is no systematic reporting requirement.[65]

Like the NSG, other supplier groups depend on national export control systems to carry out the undertakings of the parties. These systems are far from impermeable. In the first place, the decision to grant an export license is made by a complex national bureaucratic process in which nonproliferation considerations do not always dominate. In the United States, the Department of Commerce, which issues the licenses, has an institutional bias in favor of exporters. The State and Defense Departments also have a say, but, in both the Iraq and the Pakistan cases, for example, it appears that political considerations overrode nonproliferation concerns.[66] Similar bureaucratic infighting often has similar outcomes in other states.[67] A high proportion of the materials and equipment purchased by Iraq for its nuclear program were entirely legal and met the licensing requirements of the exporting country.[68]

In addition, the history of the Pakistani and Iraqi nuclear programs shows that a determined state can often evade the laws even of states that are strongly committed to nonproliferation objectives and have significant enforcement capability. Only after scandals emerged involving exports of chemical weapons technology to Libya, did Germany finally tighten its export control laws and substantially increase the penalties for violation.[69] In January 1992, despite considerable controversy, the Bundestag acted again, giving officials the authority to conduct wiretaps to detect illegal commerce.[70]

The supplier groups pose a special dilemma. In the short run, it may be necessary to maintain and even strengthen these arrangements in order to control the spread of nuclear and chemical weapons and ballistic missiles. To eliminate them would probably contribute to proliferation of dangerous technologies at a time when the goal of cooperative security is far from realized. But the persistence of the supplier groups in their current form threatens to deepen perceptions of discrimination and separation between "haves" and "have nots," compromising, perhaps fatally, the ultimate goal of a universal cooperative security regime.

Ideally, the divergence between suppliers and recipients would disappear under a fully comprehensive treaty. This fate seems likely for the Australia Group, at least for chemicals, when the CWC comes into force. The CWC contains its own list of prohibited transfers of chemical weapons precursors and machinery, applicable to parties and nonparties alike, to be administered by an Executive Council, based on information provided by the Technical Secretariat.[71]

The NPT, however, includes no such prohibitions. A non–nuclear weapon state must declare imports of items subject to safeguards, but the treaty contains no reporting requirement. Between 1971 and 1974, before the formation of the NSG, a committee of IAEA supplier and potential supplier members (called the Zangger Committee after its chairman) identified a "trigger list" of items that the members of the committee agreed would only be exported subject to IAEA safeguards in the importing country.[72] There is no formal verification mechanism and no central evaluation, and each exporting government undertakes to satisfy itself that safeguards are applied.[73] As noted, the NSG agreement extended the trigger list to nuclear technology and called for "restraint" in exports of technologies connected with uranium enrichment or nuclear fuel reprocessing.[74] The members sent similar letters to the IAEA, notifying it that they proposed to act in accordance with the principles embodied in the NSG agreement.[75] This is the only *formal* connection between the NSG and the IAEA.

The NSG subsided into relative dormancy during most of the 1980s, but began meeting again in March 1991.[76] At a meeting in Warsaw in 1992 the NSG, at the instance of the United States, finally agreed that exports of items covered by the agreement should be contingent on the recipient's acceptance of "full-scope" safeguards covering all its peaceful nuclear activities, not just the particular import. At the same meeting, for the first time, dual-use items were added to the list of items subject to control.[77]

The result of twenty years of NSG activity is a fragmentary and erratic control system that provides no comprehensive picture of the nuclear exports or imports of any country. The NSG suffers from the reputation of a discriminatory denial regime of industrial states, without achieving effective denial of nuclear-capable technology.

At its February 1992 meeting, the IAEA Board of Governors endorsed in principle a far-reaching change in the current situation whereby all members would be required to report their imports, exports, and domestic production of nuclear materials and nuclear-capable equipment and facilities. The board asked the staff to prepare a draft instrument embodying this proposal.[78] These reforms would stop short of internationally mandated export controls, but the increased visibility, both of the suppliers' export activities and the recipients' import programs, is designed to enhance the prospects for restraint.

The MTCR, in contrast to the NSG and the Australia Group, is not an adjunct of a treaty in being or in contemplation. The only relevant formal international instrument is the UN Register of Conventional Weapons. Missiles, which are regarded as one of the most dangerous platforms for conventional weapons as well as weapons of mass destruction, will surely be subject to reporting requirements under the resolution. It is important, therefore, to focus first upon making that effort more effective.

In recent years, the MTCR has expanded to include more suppliers.[79] Russia has agreed to abide by its terms. In a bilateral agreement with the United States, China has committed to abide by the guidelines in the MTCR,[80] after complaining for some time that aircraft are left unconstrained even though they are equally potent delivery systems. These commitments have yet to be fulfilled in practice.[81]

On the other hand, the United States has enacted legislation prescribing mandatory sanctions against states and enterprises for exports of items on the MTCR list. As a result, the United States imposed sanctions against a Russian enterprise that sold equipment to India, assertedly for use in India's peaceful space program, and against the Indian purchaser.[82] Such unilateral coercive measures are not likely to be effective, and they increase the resentments and resistance of the importing countries.

End-use commitments with respect to dual-use technology, adequately verified, provide an alternative that would eliminate some of the arbitrary and restrictive aspects of the present strategy of technology denial. Under these arrangements, the recipient would certify that the import is to be used for specified peaceful purposes and would agree to permit the exporter or, in some cases, its government to inspect for the purpose of verifying that the undertaking was being fulfilled. Thus, direct restrictions on transfer of technology and materials could be relaxed and the supplier regimes could be administered on a more rational basis. End-use assurances also introduce an element of consent by the recipients that has been lacking in supplier regimes. If the complaint is that technology restrictions are too broad and crippling to industrial growth, then acceptance of seriously monitored end-use restrictions should remove some of the burden of prohibition. The supplier groups should agree to require such commitments, perhaps on a limited trial basis, and arrange for reporting on the results.

Despite their deficiencies, all the supplier regimes are serving an important nonproliferation function. To dismantle them would be as unwise as it is unlikely. As Janne Nolan concludes, "The MTCR . . . should be seen as a triumph of unusual technical consensus. Those who devised the regime have gone a long way in identifying technologies that can contribute to missile development and securing agreement from [fifteen] countries about guidelines to control dissemination. The MTCR has also helped pinpoint the most difficult aspects of missile design, such as guidance technology, and target these for special scrutiny."[83] The conclusion holds for the other regimes as well.

It has been suggested that the supplier arrangements could be enhanced if recast in treaty form.[84] There is little doubt that creating binding legal obligations would strengthen the regimes. But it would do so at the price of giving permanence to what are admittedly discriminatory entities that may become increasingly incapable of performing their functions. The trade-off is between a more reliable supplier regime now and the long-term effort to achieve universality and legitimacy.

There is a critical need to enhance the legitimacy of the existing arrangements during the period of evolution toward a cooperative security system. This enhancement will require modification of the most discriminatory and exclusive features of the existing arrangements. Two approaches to this end may be pursued simultaneously. The first is to take inclusiveness seriously and open up the membership, not only to new supplier states, which must be included if export restraint is to be effective, but to recipient states as well. These countries should be given an opportunity to air their views, particularly their concerns about the broad scope of the restraints and about arbitrary decisions. To be sure, a larger group may be unwieldy. But meetings can be consultative, with nonbinding decisions, so there is little risk of veto.

The second approach is to insist on wider disclosure, opening trade in listed items to general scrutiny, subject to limitations to protect classified and proprietary information. As argued in the next section, transparency in itself will help legitimize the activity and help protect against arbitrary or discriminatory application of the rules.

Assurance of Compliance: Creating Transparency

Transparency is much talked about, but not often defined. We use it here to mean the availability and accessibility of knowledge and information, generated through the processes of the regime about (1) the policies and activities of parties to the treaty and of the central organizations established by it as to matters relevant to treaty compliance and regime effectiveness and (2) the operation of the norms, rules, and procedures established by the treaty.

So defined, transparency is a matter of degree. There is no ideal level of transparency applicable to all treaties. But increased access to relevant information sets up a powerful dynamic that helps ensure that a treaty will work as intended.

The Functions of Transparency

Economics, game theory, and other disciplines have turned increasing attention to how the availability of information affects action, and particularly to how it helps elicit cooperative action. Transparency—that is, conditions under which the relevant information is available to all participants—allows three important functions to work to create a compliance dynamic:

—It permits *coordination* between actors making independent decisions.

—It provides *reassurance* to actors cooperating or complying with the norms of the regime that they are not being taken advantage of.

—It exercises *deterrence* on actors contemplating noncompliance or defection.

These three functions may be treated separately for analytic purposes, but in practice they interact and reinforce each other. In many instances, the independent strategic responses of the parties to these forces will be sufficient to ensure compliance.[85] But when such interaction is insufficient by itself to avoid or correct defection, the information revealed provides a basis for using management tools that can deal with suspect behavior. The power of transparency in such cases is that deviations from prescribed conduct can be observed by the other members of the regime and must be accounted for and justified (further discussed in the section "The Response to Suspect Conduct").

COORDINATION. In the simplest case, transparency reduces transaction costs by providing information that the participating states would otherwise have to assemble with their own resources, often at high or prohibitive cost. The system of reporting on infectious diseases established by the World Health Organization, for example, enables members to adjust their own policies to the epidemiological threat.[86]

Coordination is one of the animating ideas behind the IAEA's call for full reporting of nuclear exports, imports, and production by IAEA members.[87] No formal regulation of purchase and sales of nuclear materials is contemplated, but they would be subject to the scrutiny of other interested parties. Since both buyers and sellers are bound by the NPT not to assist non–nuclear weapon states to obtain nuclear weapons, suppliers acting independently will be less likely to sell to a state where the data suggest the possibility of a weapons program. Decisions under conditions of transparency will tend to converge around the norm.

The same conception underlies the UN Register of Conventional Arms. If a reliable, systematic, and public data base on arms transfers had been in existence after the Gulf War, for example, the United States and other arms suppliers would have faced a requirement to account systematically for the divergence between their actions and their repeated commitments to restraint. Such exposure conceivably could have dampened the escalation of post–Gulf War arms sales to the Middle East.

Confidence- and security-building measures (CSBMs) perform a similar function by permitting nations to carry out military exercises and other security activities in ways that do not appear threatening to their neighbors. Provisions for advance notification and mutual observation of potentially threatening activities are the hallmarks of a transparent regime. In Europe, during the early 1980s, these CSBMs, negotiated meticulously at Stockholm, helped to moderate severe political tensions.[88]

REASSURANCE. The example of CSBMs shows the close relationship between coordination and reassurance. There is no doubt that in the European theater these measures served an important reassurance function by preventing misunderstanding about deployments and other military activities of neighboring states.

In a cooperative security regime, the reassurance function would assume increasing importance. A party that is prepared to limit its military capability in accordance with the dictates of the regime would want to be assured that the other parties are complying as well. Classically, mutual arms reduction is thought of as a "prisoner's dilemma" in which the incentives for defection dominate. But one reason it is a dilemma is the lack of transparency. The conditions of the game specify that the parties cannot communicate with each other.[89] Conversely, if each had reliable information that the others were complying, all could proceed in confidence that the benefits of cooperation would not be expropriated.

The U.S. domestic debates on verification of arms control agreements stressed the need for certainty that the other side was not "cheating," often raising verification requirements to increasingly unattainable levels.[90] In the Reagan era, controversies about elevating verification standards from "adequate" to "effective" became exercises in scholasticism, more rhetorical than real.[91] The verification systems in the treaties that were actually concluded, however, never achieved these levels of certainty. Their main function, even during the cold war, was to provide reassurance that the Soviet Union was substantially complying with the obligations it had undertaken so that the

United States could continue to adhere to existing treaties and to try to negotiate new ones.[92] Compliance problems were uncovered in the verification process, but they were contained, if not resolved, in the Standing Consultative Commission (SCC) and other diplomatic forums. Even the case of the Krasnoyarsk radar, in which there seemed to be a "smoking gun" violation, did not precipitate a break. What counted was that none of these violations threatened U.S. security or the basic function of the treaty.[93]

Elinor Ostrom, in her pathbreaking study, *Governing the Commons,* finds that reassurance about compliance is central to the successful management of "common pool resources" such as irrigation systems and fishing areas. Such systems, similar to arms limitation arrangements, are frequently portrayed as prisoners' dilemmas. She argues, however, that the participants can pursue a "contingent strategy" and make safe, advantageous, and credible commitments to follow the rules so long as most similarly situated individuals adopt the same commitment. But "making a contingent rule-following commitment requires that individuals obtain information about the rates of rule conformance adopted by others."[94] In other words, transparency is critical to the success of the cooperative arrangement.[95]

DETERRENCE. Deterrence is in a sense the obverse of reassurance. Each acts at the opposite end of the transaction. A party disposed to comply needs reassurance. A party contemplating violation needs to be deterred. Transparency supplies both. The probability that conduct departing from treaty requirements will be discovered operates to reassure the first and to deter the second, and that probability increases with the transparency of the treaty regime.

In the standard analysis, deterrence works if the costs incurred by being caught in a violation outweigh the expected gains from the defection. Costs can take various forms. The most obvious is loss of the anticipated benefits of the agreement itself. In bilateral treaties, or in treaties in which the impact of the violation is sharply focused on one of the parties, the aggrieved party may retaliate in kind or renounce the treaty, and in serious cases the response may infect other aspects of the relationship between the parties.[96] In a multilateral setting, the delinquent may suffer more diffuse negative reactions from states and other groups with a stake in the treaty regime. Still less tangible, but not to be discounted in a world of increasing interdependence, is the impact on the reputation of the defector as a reliable partner in cooperative enterprises.[97] Finally, at least in democratic states, the disclosure of breach may trigger domestic political reaction against the government. As explained further on, regularized procedures within the treaty regime can be structured to mobilize and intensify these negative reactions. The foreknowledge of these processes will itself serve as a deterrent.

Arms control treaties operate on the benefit, as well as the cost side of the violator's equation. The main purpose of the ABM treaty, for example, is to prevent either party from deploying a nationwide ABM system. It accomplishes this goal by prohibiting precursor activities: development and testing of defensive systems and components. If one party discovered that the other was engaged in these activities, it would have ample time for an offsetting response. Thus the treaty created "a buffer zone so that neither party could come close enough to deployment to be worrisome to the other."[98] Since the prohibited activities were clearly visible to each side's national technical means of verification (NTM), the likelihood of discovery was high, and the possibility of obtaining a unilateral advantage through deployment of an ABM system was correspondingly low. The high probability of discovery operated to reduce the expected benefits of a contemplated violation in addition to increasing the costs of defection, as is the usual case.[99] Prohibition of testing and other precursor activities in other arms control contexts is designed to have a similar effect.

Assembling the Data Base

The transparency dynamic depends on the effectiveness of the systems used to provide and disseminate information about the regime. Independent data collection by a central organization is costly, intrusive, and by no means error-free, as the U.S. experience with the decennial census shows. Military affairs are at the heart of traditional sovereign prerogatives, and secrecy is an almost universal proclivity of military establishments. So, in the field of arms limitation, even more than in other international regulatory endeavors, assembling needed information will almost necessarily depend in the first instance on self-reporting by the parties to the arrangements.

A fully developed cooperative security regime will require a broad range of general statistical information, including the size and distribution of budgets, force structures and deployments, available armament, and the like.[100] In existing arms control treaties, however, reporting is tied closely to the needs of the particular agreement.

Self-reported baseline data has been the starting point for the verification system in all contemporary arms control treaties. Thus, under the Strategic Arms Limitation Talks (SALT) II agreement, the parties established an "agreed data base," to be updated regularly, on the number of strategic weapons each party deployed in categories covered by the treaty.[101] It consisted of a one-page Memorandum of Understanding appended to the treaty. It is said that when the Soviet negotiator turned over his report disclosing the numbers of Soviet weapons he remarked, "You realize, you have just repealed 900 years of Russian history."[102] The agreed-upon data base accompanying the Intermediate-Range Nuclear Forces Treaty, concluded less than ten years later, had swelled to fifty-six printed pages, to be updated every six months.[103]

Similarly, states subject to IAEA safeguards are required to declare their peaceful nuclear facilities. It is this declaration that provides the starting point for the IAEA's work.

It is not a simple matter to obtain and maintain an adequate and reliable data base, and earlier arms control treaties never fully met this challenge. The Soviet Union did not begin to shed its reluctance to supply data until the Gorbachev years. Even then, there were questions of accuracy and completeness in the reports made under the CFE.[104] For developing nations, lack of sophisticated information infrastructures and overall lack of relevant technical capacity become important considerations. In many such states, the military may have considerable independence from the civil government.[105] The data requirements of a more comprehensive cooperative security regime, running to many thousands of items, portend staggering reporting and management problems.

Two principal issues arise in a system that relies on self-reporting: (1) inaccuracy of reporting and (2) failure to report at all. Why would a state report—or report accurately—information that is to be used in appraising its performance under an arms limitation agreement?

NONREPORTING. Most international experience with self-reporting is found outside the national security area. There, the failure to report seems to be a greater problem than deliberate falsification of reports. A recent General Accounting Office (GAO) study found that reporting under environmental treaties is less than satisfactory.[106] The principal problems seem to be not deliberate flouting of reporting requirements but limitations of capacity and the constraints and priorities of the bureaucratic setting in which reports are generated.[107]

The International Labor Organization (ILO) emphasizes the importance of compliance with its reporting requirements, although the obligation is complex and burdensome. Failure to report is reviewed by the ILO Conference Committee on Compliance, and four of the seven offenses for which a party can be blacklisted are reporting failures. In 1979, there was a proposal to end this practice and list reporting failures separately, since they were likely to be caused by administrative and technical difficulties, personnel changes, or the outbreak of armed conflict. The suggestion was accepted with reservations, and the parties agreed to distinguish among reporting failures but with the understanding that reporting was so essential to the compliance process that it would be unwise to diminish the significance of reporting failures.[108] As a result, the record of reporting compliance is good, coming to well over 80 percent in every year of the organization's existence, except for the World War II years.[109]

For bilateral arms control treaties, as would be expected, the parties insist on strict fulfillment of the reporting obligation. A rare instance of nonreporting under the NPT occurred when North Korea delayed the filing of its initial declaration of peaceful nuclear facilities.[110] Intense pressures, both by the IAEA and important member states, ultimately elicited a lengthy and detailed report.[111] Nevertheless, the IAEA suspected that two sites had not been declared and demanded a special inspection. The action led to North Korea's notice of withdrawal from the NPT on March 12, 1993.[112] Its subsequent decision not to withdraw in June 1993 notwithstanding, as of the present writing, it is not clear how the impasse will be resolved.[113]

RELIABILITY. Self-reporting is only the beginning, not the end of the data-gathering process. External checks and balances are needed, even in regulatory areas unconcerned with security and military policy.[114]

In the bilateral East-West arms control treaties, if a party challenges the accuracy of the data submitted by its treaty partner, the information is not accepted until discrepancies are resolved to the satisfaction of the objecting party. This formal provision simply codifies the formidable incentives to report accurately that already exist in any case. Each side knows that the other has detailed knowledge about its deployments, based on intense and continuous surveillance by NTM and other sources of intelligence. An inaccurate report could sour the whole treaty process.[115] One side cannot be sure what gaps there are, if any, in the other's knowledge. In these circumstances, the incentives for telling the truth are high and the possible gains from misreporting are small.

A dramatic example of this checking process is seen in the IAEA/UN Special Commission (UNSCOM) inspections of Iraq pursuant to the 1991 cease-fire resolution of the Security Council.[116] The resolution, like the bilateral arms control agreements discussed above, requires Iraq to declare all of its nuclear, chemical, biological, and missile weapons and facilities, providing the starting point for the inspection process. The first Iraqi declarations pursuant to this obligation were checked against information supplied by U.S. and other Western intelligence services and found wanting. A series of increasingly intense exchanges with Iraq produced much improved disclosures. Indeed, an iterative process of interchange leading to increasingly complete and detailed Iraqi disclosure has continued throughout the inspection period.[117]

Similarly, the IAEA apparently made use of U.S. satellite observation in verifying North Korea's declaration as to its peaceful nuclear materials. Although it seems likely that the declaration was more voluminous and complete than it would otherwise have been because North Korea expected it would be subject to such scrutiny, as noted, two sites remained undisclosed.[118] Again it seems likely that U.S. intelligence was the key in identifying the discrepancy.

Verification

The model for increasingly elaborate and costly verification schemes was a creation of the U.S.-Soviet bilateral arms process control of the cold war era. In a relationship characterized by extreme mistrust, suspicion, and often hostility, verification was critical in providing sufficient information to permit arms control agreements to proceed. Verification was performed unilaterally, principally by NTM, because neither party was willing to rely on the cooperation of the other.[119]

Cold war verification philosophy was dominated by the need to ensure the continued viability of deterrence. American participants in the process might say that the United States had to proceed on the assumption that the Soviet Union would take advantage of any loopholes or ambiguities and "salami slice" to see what the United States would permit. The result was U.S. insistence on detailed accountability for every provision and time line. During the 1980s, this led to public confrontation on alleged violations that were often ambiguous and, even if true, quite trivial.[120]

The confrontational style of cold war verification is not appropriate for a security system in which reassurance is the primary objective. A more cooperative approach is already apparent in the baseline verification procedures under the Intermediate-Range Nuclear Forces (INF) Treaty. This shift to a reassurance mode, however, does not imply less exacting standards for verification. The parties have continued to insist on meticulous compliance with a very complex verification protocol. Discrepancies are for the most part worked out on the ground between the members of the inspection teams. The few "ambiguities" that are not resolved in the field have been dealt with in a low key, businesslike manner by the bipartite Special Verification Commission constituted by the treaty.[121]

For the future, NTM will continue to play an important role, particularly for large treaty-limited items, visible to overhead surveillance, and for troop movements. In the future, however, increasing reliance will be placed on on-site inspection (OSI). The breakthrough in the INF treaty, extended in the more complex CFE and Strategic Arms Reduction Talks (START) agreements, was itself a product of more cooperative and less adversarial U.S.-Soviet relations. It added flexibility and precision to the verification process. It was the model for the CWC and has been strongly urged for the BWC.[122] However, two problems, intrusiveness and cost, suggest limits to the potential utility of OSI.

—Intrusiveness. Contrary to what the United States maintained during the cold war, resistance to highly intrusive verification, it seems, is not necessarily proof of guilty intent. After nearly 30 years of pressuring the Soviet Union to agree to on-site inspections, the United States, in both the INF and START negotiations, found itself rejecting the "anytime-anywhere" challenge inspections, citing concerns about its own military and commercial security.

Similarly, in the CWC negotiations, this newfound caution led the United States to withdraw its approval of a draft convention providing for no-notice challenge inspections directed at private research and manufacturing facilities. It proposed instead a notice period before challenge inspections as well as other limitations on the scope of inspection of "sensitive sites" to protect highly classified information unrelated to chemical warfare.[123] Lengthy behind-the-scenes negotiations led to a compromise in which some of the surprise element in the inspections is retained.[124]

—Cost. Issues of both absolute cost and relative cost-effectiveness would affect the completeness and intrusiveness of any OSI system. According to GAO calculations, INF inspection alone cost the United States about $105 million a year in the first four years of operation, including equipment, travel, and personnel.[125] The annual expenditure will drop as baseline inspections are completed. But some estimates of the On Site Inspection Agency's (OSIA) likely budget increases have suggested that START verification costs will add in the range of $200 million to $300 million annually. CFE and CWC could increase OSI outlays to $1 billion.[126] The magnitude of the likely costs of a more highly regulated world is staggering. It suggests that the value of exhaustive inspections, particularly on a routine basis, must be reassessed. There is need to begin a search for economies of scale and alternative methods of verification.

One possibility is the use of national intelligence facilities to supplement international verification. The potential for pooling national intelligence efforts emerged in the aftermath of the Gulf War and the efforts of the UNSCOM/IAEA under Resolution 687 to locate all Iraqi facilities for and stockpiles of weapons of mass destruction.

The use of national intelligence sources in verifying international agreements presents special problems, however, largely because of the fear that the information could be manipulated by the supplying state for its own purposes. The effort to secure approval for the use of information provided by national intelligence establishments for IAEA "special inspections" has run into resistance on this ground.[127] Any authorization to rely on such information will have to provide for careful, neutral evaluation. A small (two-person) intelligence evaluation unit has already been established in the Office of the Director General for this purpose.[128] Despite these caveats, it seems likely that national intelligence will play a role in the verification activities not only of the IAEA but of other nonproliferation regimes as well.

The Open Skies Treaty, signed by twenty-five states in March of 1992 and covering the territory from the Atlantic to the Urals, establishes substantial quotas of overflights for aerial surveillance to provide reassurance about items regulated by a number of treaties.[129] International air traffic control has also been suggested as a possible method for extending transparency, while reaping nonmilitary benefits and cost reductions (see chapter 6).

To try to solve these two problems, it has been suggested that the United Nations or a subsidiary multinational arms control agency might establish an independent observation and intelligence capability, leading to independent assessment.[130] Some kind of internationalized intelligence capability will doubtless be a necessary component of a full-fledged cooperative security regime. Over time, a track record of neutrality and fairness in the use of national intelligence by the IAEA and other nonproliferation organizations might help to overcome some of the concerns that make such a proposal politically unrealistic now.

The demands of equity can also be costly. In an inclusive regime, it is politically difficult to concentrate verification resources on "suspect countries." The IAEA considers itself bound to conduct inspections on all safeguarded facilities worldwide every six months. As a result, about 89 percent of its safeguards budget is expended on Japan, Germany, Canada, Holland, Belgium, and Sweden even though there is no real concern about those states' compliance. The IAEA believes that greater reliance on "special inspections," not necessarily involving suspect activity, would permit it to reduce the number of routine inspections that now exhaust its budget.[131]

It is equally important to cast the limitations of the treaty in a form that reduces the cost and intrusiveness of verification. For example, *prohibitions* on trade in dual-use items would be costly and intrusive to verify. Requiring *end-use assurances* with evidence of compliance, perhaps monitored by the industry, would achieve verification without burdensome governmental intrusion. The inclusion of many items in addition to the list of conventional weapons now contemplated would enhance the value of the UN Registry, once the system is well established. Technology is also becoming available to tag or label items of particular concern in a way that reveals their location. There are, of course, many practical problems with such a scheme, and its feasibility and cost for monitoring large numbers of dual-use items have yet to be fully examined. Definitional problems will continue to be controversial, and enforcement by governments against domestic violators will need to be improved to ensure effectiveness.[132]

On any view of this matter, cooperative security will require the commitment of significantly larger resources to verification. Ultimately, however, no system of verification, no matter how well funded, can be adequate to verify completely all the activities subject to regulation. Too heavy a burden is placed on the verification aspect of transparency, in large part as a legacy of cold war arms control. The basic assumptions and motivations of a cooperative security regime imply that compliance with its prescriptions will be the norm, and incentives to defect will be limited. If these assumptions are correct, a shift to more cooperative approaches to verification, including emphasis on exacting and detailed reporting requirements, will give states and the international institutions charged with managing treaty regimes greater and less costly ways of creating transparency and thus providing reassurance.

Regime Management: The Response to Suspect Conduct

The principal functions of transparency are to reassure and to deter. But in order to accomplish these ends, the regime must be able to deal successfully with instances of inadvertent or deliberate departures from treaty norms.

The assumption that every such case reflects a deliberate decision to violate is not borne out by experience. Apparent departures may derive from factual misunderstandings or differing interpretations of treaty provisions. Lack of internal capacity to enforce the international rules, bureaucratic failure, or other relatively innocuous causes may also account for seemingly noncomplying behavior. Moreover, deviations from treaty requirements range from trivial technicalities to those that threaten the viability of the regime. In dealing with the Soviet Union, the United States usually acted with proportionality in responding to suspect conduct, but its rhetoric, even as to minor offenses, was often heated. Since 1985, U.S. presidents have been required to present annual "noncompliance reports" to Congress. Initiated by critics of arms control, this requirement has generated reports decrying numerous asserted Soviet violations of arms control agreements.[133] Still, the United States was content to remain a party to all the treaties involved and to engage in almost continuous negotiations with the USSR for new ones.

Review and Assessment of Performance

The foregoing analysis of the potential sources of suspect conduct suggests the utility of a managerial approach to compliance in a cooperative security regime. The production and review of information about performance is a standard management tool in private enterprise and public bureaucracies, as well as in international organizations. One of the most important functions of transparency, then, is to generate information that helps assess party performance and overall treaty effectiveness.

As in other managerial settings, the assessment process in international organizations is not primarily accusatory or adversarial, at least in the first instance. It begins by accepting that all the participants are engaged in a common enterprise and that the objective is to discover how individual and system performance might be improved.

Experience from actively managed regulatory regimes, new and old, indicates that early intervention—not always gentle—helps to keep the treaty going in the right direction.[134] The first step is to clarify the issues involved. States are given ample—sometimes excessive—opportunity to explain and justify their conduct. Technical and (less often) financial assistance may be provided to help correct deficiencies. Promises of improvement take the form of commitments to increasingly concrete, detailed, and measurable performance. If resistance persists, however, the process assumes a more confrontational tone and pressures for compliance can intensify. The purpose and often the effect is to correct suspect conduct that is attributable to mistake, misunderstanding, or inattention and to identify, expose, and isolate the deliberate offender.[135] The procedure is not an arbitrary application of power, because the challenged conduct is evaluated against norms that were accepted by all, including the offending state.

This perhaps idealized version of the managerial approach is most fully and elaborately exemplified in the practice of the ILO, which, as the oldest of the modern international organizations, pioneered an approach to inducing compliance that has been followed by many successors. As discussed, required reporting from members on the implementation of ILO Conventions and Recommendations triggers an elaborate set of procedures to identify cases of noncompliance, with a finely calibrated series of responses to correct them. The country reports are first examined in a committee of experts. It transmits "observations" on unsatisfactory implementation, together with suggestions for corrective action, directly to the states concerned. Beginning as an advisory body, the committee has grown in authority and now makes critical observations, acknowledges, refutes, or comments on government responses, and makes suggestions to reporting governments.[136]

The annual report of the committee of experts to a conference committee (made up of delegates to the ILO Conference) includes specific "observations" on serious or persistent cases of failure to implement treaties that the party has ratified.[137] The conference committee in turn "discusses" these observations with the representative of the country involved. The conference committee's ultimate sanction is to recommend in its annual report to the International Labor Conference that the noncomplying state be blacklisted.

There are two intermediate steps between reporting a country for nonimplementation by the committee of experts and the recommendation of blacklisting by the conference committee. First, the state may request "direct contacts," a site visit by ILO staff to try to work out the problem on the ground.[138] Second, the conference committee may list the country in a "special paragraph," identifying steps that must be taken to avoid blacklisting.[139] The "special paragraph" is in effect a notice to the delinquent country that it will be blacklisted if it does not take the indicated actions. At one time or another in the 1980s, twenty-three states were listed in special paragraphs, but only three—Iran, Guatemala, and the USSR—were ultimately blacklisted for continued failure to implement.[140]

A similar managerial approach to compliance is standard in economic organizations such as the International Monetary Fund (IMF), the Organization for Economic Cooperation and Development (OECD), and more recently the General Agreement on Tariffs and Trade (GATT), as well as the newly emerging environmental organizations.[141] Nor is the idea wholly foreign to the security field. This approach has been adopted by both the U.S.-Soviet dyad and nonproliferation regimes in response to troublesome information. We have elsewhere described the experience of living under the ABM treaty and the Interim Agreement (SALT I) as "an on-going negotiation."[142] Like the managerial model, this process worked best when it was facilitative in tone, when intervention occurred at an early stage before the issue had become politically salient, and when there was concern about assuring continuing mutual understanding of obligations and preventing breakdown.

The SCC, the mechanism created to resolve disputes under SALT I, seems to have worked in the early years; the parties were able to defuse or resolve some serious questions. In 1973, for example, the Americans observed that the Soviets appeared to have more missile silos than permitted by the Interim Agreement of SALT I. The commissioners discussed the issue, and the Soviets produced blueprints to demonstrate that what had appeared to be missile launchers were in fact launch control centers. The additional information supplied enabled American NTM to verify that the explanation was true.[143] In the 1980s, conversely, the SCC became one of the arenas for heightened confrontation between the two superpowers and its managerial role diminished accordingly.[144] Even so, two agreements were worked out clarifying one of the most contentious issues in the ABM treaty, the meaning of "testing in an ABM mode" as applied to air defense systems.[145]

Multilateral settings provide greater opportunities for the managerial approach because they are not inherently adversarial. The secretariat or parties that are not directly involved in the particular issue can often serve as mediators. Moreover, in a transparent treaty organization, the suspect conduct will be publicly exposed, not least to the other members of the organization. As noted, this places the onus of public defense and justification of its conduct on the party. What ensues is a process of jawboning—a mixture of persuasion, argument, and pressure, operating both on the state and its representatives as individuals—in which the occasions and possibilities for unpleasant consequences—diplomatic, economic, and otherwise—increase with the recalcitrance of the offending party.

As Oran Young argues,

> There are . . . many situations in which those contemplating violations will refrain from breaking the rules if they expect their non-compliant behavior to be exposed, even if they know that the probability that their violations will be met with sanctions is low. Policy-makers, like private individuals, are sensitive to the social opprobrium that accompanies violations of widely accepted behavioral prescriptions. They are, in short, motivated by a desire to avoid the sense of shame or social disgrace that commonly befalls those who break widely accepted rules.[146]

This may seem a slender reed on which to rest the fate of cooperative security, but there are certainly instances where shame, embarrassment, and fear of ostracism seems to have tipped state behavior in favor of compliance. Japan accepted a ban on ivory imports when the parties to the Convention on International Trade in Endangered Species (CITES) said that otherwise they would refuse to hold a scheduled treaty conference in Kyoto.[147] And the constant reference to the United Kingdom as "the dirty old man of Europe" ultimately helped bring it into line with the sulfur dioxide emissions standards of the Long Range Transboundary Air Pollution Treaty.[148]

Even nondemocratic states may not be immune to the impact of ostracism. The Final Act of the Helsinki Conference endorses fundamental human rights norms, although it expressly stipulates that it is without legally binding effect.[149] Nevertheless, periodic review sessions discussed and debated the conduct of the parties in light of the provisions of the act. During the 1980s, these review sessions became a major platform for systematic public exposure, review, and critique of Soviet and eastern European human rights policies. Preparation for the conferences was a high priority for all parties, East and West. The conferences themselves were the subject of intense media attention. In particular, Helsinki provided a semiprotected focus for dissident activity. Helsinki Watch Committees were formed in all the communist states to prepare reports on human rights violations for the use of the review conferences.[150] It would obviously be too much to credit the Helsinki process with the change in attitudes toward human rights in eastern Europe, although the Soviets and others made concessions on specific issues.[151] Nevertheless, the public shaming fed into and reinforced the deep fissures that ultimately led to the fall of the communist governments.[152]

Shaming, of course, was not the only form of pressure. The Soviet human rights record was a principal target of U.S. diplomacy across the board. Indeed, the first sign of the fading of the détente of the early 1970s was the Jackson-Vanick amendment, prohibiting most favored nations treatment for the Soviet Union until it allowed Jews to emigrate freely.[153] Threats of economic action also bolstered the pressure on Japan to accept the ivory ban.[154]

The case of the Krasnoyarsk radar illustrates the interplay of more diffuse instruments of pressure. Although the United States was convinced that the radar represented a clear breach of the ABM treaty, it was unwilling to withdraw from the treaty or take any other specific retaliatory action. Nevertheless, it kept the issue alive in all forums: the SCC, the media, the academic community, other private persons with contacts in the Soviet Union, and the highest diplomatic and political levels. Ultimately the United States made resolution of the problem a condition of the conclusion of a START treaty. In response, the Soviets first acknowledged the existence of the radar (claiming it complied with the treaty), then permitted inspection by a group of U.S. senators and representatives. Finally it admitted formally that the radar was a violation of the ABM treaty and agreed to destroy it.[155]

IAEA "special inspections" are intended precisely for situations in which there is specific suspicious behavior.[156] As exemplified in the North Korea case, when credible evidence of suspicious activity at an undeclared site comes to the attention of the director general, an explanation is first requested. If not satisfied with the response, the director general requests permission for a special inspection. In the event of refusal, the director general reports the matter to the Board of Governors, which may decide to call the party before it to explain. If the explanation is unsatisfactory, the Board may take such action as it deems appropriate, including, in an egregious case, reporting the matter to the UN Security Council with a recommendation for action. The Security Council may also decide on its own to address the problem. Although the procedure may seem slow and stylized, it provides the opportunity for persuasion and escalating pressure at every stage. North Korea has played out this string to the very end. Although the denouement is unknown at the moment of writing, it is hard to believe that North Korea will be able to hold out indefinitely.

It is true that an extended exchange may provide the opportunity to conceal the violation, but unless the inspection team is in the country with extraordinary rights of access, it will always have to rely to some extent on the cooperation of the state to conduct an inspection, and so the state can delay or thwart it, as the experience with North Korea shows. Refusal to cooperate, unless adequately explained, will itself be treated by the IAEA members and organs as noncompliance warranting corrective action.

Capacity Building and Second-Level Enforcement

In the traditional conception, a treaty governs the actions of states. Compliance with the treaty means bringing state behavior into conformity with treaty norms. In some areas, however, notably international environmental regulation, achieving the objectives of the international agreement requires change in the behavior of private entities and individuals. The security area has both these characteristics. Agreements concerned with force structure and weapons reduction operate on the state-to-state plane. But to control exports or other activities conducted by private enterprise, the state must take steps within its borders to ensure that the relevant private behavior is consistent with the obligations it has undertaken. In the current nonproliferation context, this means adherence to limitations on exports of designated weapons, materials, and technology.

The first step is for the state to enact legislation regulating the conduct of its corporate and individual citizens in accordance with the stipulations of the treaty. Even this legislative capability may be deficient in some states, particularly in those in transition to democracy. In such instances, countries may need outside technical assistance in drafting workable and comprehensible legislation and administrative regulations.

The second step is harder. The state must be able to mobilize an effective administrative and political effort to translate the legislation on the books into effective action by national enforcement authorities.[157] This problem of administrative capacity is not unique to developing countries. The United States and other industrialized countries have experienced difficulties in enforcing their export control laws. An analysis of the Pakistani nuclear weapons program, for example, concludes that it was heavily based on foreign suppliers, including manufacturers in Switzerland, Germany, the Netherlands, France, and Great Britain. Some of the exported items were not included on the formal control lists or were licensed on the false representation that they were to be used for nonnuclear purposes. Others were sold to Pakistani agents or front companies within the originating country and exported under false papers or simply smuggled to Pakistan, sometimes via one or more intermediate destinations.[158]

A National Academy of Sciences study of U.S. export control policy reported that "export controls are issued under a multiplicity of statutes with differing objectives and criteria. . . . The statutes themselves were not coordinated at the time they were written and come under the supervision of different congressional committees. Over a dozen agencies, plus the military services, are engaged in administering controls and apply distinct regulatory provisions that often overlap and conflict. The lead agencies in constructing export control policy hold strongly diverse positions corresponding to their separate interests."[159] Thus, it is hardly surprising that, although the United States has probably the most stringent export control laws and enforcement in the world, U.S. suppliers have contributed to Iraqi and other third world programs for sophisticated weaponry, nuclear and otherwise.

With the breakup of the Soviet Union and the entry of "second-tier" suppliers like Brazil, China, and Korea into the market, the problem of regulatory capacity has assumed even greater importance and poses a more serious challenge. The desperate economies of eastern Europe and the former Soviet Union are increasingly relying on arms exports to generate hard currency. A new entrepreneurial breed in these countries may be prepared to challenge weakened administrative and enforcement systems.[160] Among the newly industrializing suppliers, the capacity to administer export controls is far less than their technical capability to produce weapons or components that other countries want.[161]

In the developing countries, as experience under environmental treaties shows, the problem of compliance capacity may take many forms: inadequate bureaucratic structure, limited trained manpower, absence of record-keeping and statistical procedures, low enforcement priority, or insufficient financial resources.[162] Systematic policy review and assessment can help address these problems. For example, the IMF makes periodic intensive reviews of members' economic performance in close cooperation with the responsible local officials. These exercises have contributed to the development of the expertise and sophistication of national fiscal and monetary authorities. In the security area, in which military establishments are often protected from ordinary political and bureaucratic controls, such review and assessment activities may provide leverage for civilian officials to begin to bring military programs under control.[163]

Finally, capacity to elicit compliance from domestic actors is related to the form that the treaty rules take. For example, initially the International Maritime Organization imposed treaty limitations on the quantity of oil to be discharged into the sea in oil tanker cleaning and deballasting operations. These limitations proved unenforceable, because, although aerial observation could detect oil slicks on the surface of the sea indicating that a violation had occurred, the observation could not be linked to any particular ship with sufficient certainty to support enforcement in court. Later, the standard was changed to require new oil tankers to be built with separate tanks for oil and ballast. This rule could be verified visually in port, and compliance is substantially 100 percent.[164] In the field of export controls, the KOBRA on-line data collection system for customs documents may enhance the enforcement of German laws by simplifying the processing and analysis of documentation.[165]

Dispute Resolution

Treaties, like all legal instruments, are rarely self-defining. Language is unable to capture meaning with precision. Drafters do not foresee many of the possible applications of the treaty language, let alone the contexts in which it may be used. Issues actually foreseen often cannot be resolved in the negotiation and are sometimes swept under the rug with a formula that can mean what each party wants it to. Underlying circumstances affecting the treaty may change, but the language does not. These are unavoidable incidents of the effort to formulate legal rules to govern future conduct. Thus the management of compliance requires a procedure for resolving disputes about the interpretation and application of the governing text.

The canonical sequence of methods recognized by international law for the peaceful settlement of disputes is found in Article 33 of the UN Charter: "negotiation, enquiry, mediation, conciliation, arbitration, judicial settlement." Of course, treaties do not usually incorporate this stepladder of techniques. The CSCE flirted for a considerable period with an effort to require resort to the traditional modes in strict sequence, but at the insistence of the United States, it seems to have decided that this requirement is too rigid and to be moving toward a more flexible approach.[166]

As noted, ongoing negotiation in the SCC has served as the official forum for resolving disputes under the ABM/SALT I agreements, with only mixed success.[167] The INF treaty established a similar bilateral body, the Special Verification Commission, with which the experience so far is better, in part no doubt because of the overall improvement in the relations between the parties. As indicated, most of the problems of interpretation are worked out in the field between the leaders of the inspection teams, with the SCC acting as a kind of appellate body when they cannot reach agreement. In reaching agreements the security area is not so different from most other fields of regulation. Negotiation remains the primary method for settling disputes, legal or otherwise, in international affairs.[168]

But negotiation involves the inherent possibility of irreconcilable impasse, and in a world increasingly dependent on the reliable performance of international regimes, states and their citizens are less willing to accept that kind of uncertainty. It will surely not be enough for a cooperative security regime. At the opposite end of the spectrum, however, binding adjudication by arbitration or by an international judicial tribunal has rarely been used in international regulatory regimes, and hardly at all in the security area. Many treaty provisions for binding third-party determination require subsequent agreement of the parties before submission to the tribunal. In any case, resort to provisions for judicial settlement of treaty disputes is vanishingly small. The International Court of Justice (ICJ) has decided only thirty or so treaty disputes in its entire fifty-year history.[169] In the United States, the Constitution requires the consent of the Senate for submission to binding arbitral or judicial determination, which has only rarely been forthcoming.[170]

A number of ICJ cases have dealt directly or peripherally with national security issues, not always in the context of a treaty: the *Corfu Channel* case, French nuclear testing in the Pacific, the *Iran Hostages* case, *Nicaragua* v. *United States*, and the Iran airbus shootdown.[171] Whatever one thinks of the law the court made in those cases, in practice the outcomes were not very satisfactory for any of the parties. In most of them, the respondent state did not participate fully and ignored the judgment of the court against it. As a result of the *Nicaragua* case, the United States withdrew its acceptance of the compulsory jurisdiction of the court. Of the fifty-three states that have submitted to the court's jurisdiction, eight have imposed reservations as to cases involving national security or the use of force.[172] Although opinions like those in the *Corfu Channel* and *Nicaragua* cases contribute to the elaboration of international norms on the use of force, the process remains too episodic for a satisfactory mode of dispute resolution. Sovereignty may be eroding in today's interdependent world, but states still try to retain as much control as they can over decisions on fundamental issues of national security, and they are thus unprepared to submit them to regularized, binding third-party determination.

Contemporary interest in more reliable dispute settlement has concentrated on procedures that fall somewhere between negotiation and adjudication. One method, in particular, is compulsory reference to nonbinding third-party mediation or conciliation. An example with considerable pertinence for a cooperative security regime is the Vienna Convention on the Protection of the Ozone Layer, which provides for mandatory submission to a conciliation commission that must, in the absence of agreement, "render a final and recommendatory award, which the parties shall consider in good faith."[173] The 1990 Amendments to the Montreal Protocol add a "non-compliance procedure." "Reservations" regarding a party's performance of its obligations are brought before a five-member implementation committee that hears the case "with a view to securing an amicable resolution." The committee reports to a meeting of the parties, which may, "taking into consideration the circumstances of the case, decide upon and call for steps to bring about full compliance with the Protocol."[174]

These provisions and others like them draw generally on past practice under the GATT. A GATT member's complaint that its expected benefits under the agreement are being "nullified or impaired" is submitted to an ad hoc panel, usually of five persons, acting in their individual capacities.[175] The panels have operated with varying degrees of formality during the forty years of GATT history, sometimes seeking to bring the parties to agreement in a conciliation process, sometimes acting more judicially.[176]

In recent years, the balance has swung toward the judicial side in GATT dispute resolution. Before the recent changes made in the Uruguay Round, however, panel opinions were not binding until adopted by the GATT Council. Since the council acts by consensus, the losing party in effect had a veto. Although, in practice, it was not always easy to exercise this right, it was used to delay decisions and to gain other tactical advantages. The Uruguay Round draft removes the veto and other possibilities for delay. Panel decisions are now to be automatically adopted, subject to an appeal to a special tribunal on questions of law.[177] The panel is now, in effect, a court, or at least a specialized arbitral tribunal. It remains to be seen whether this procedure will be flexible enough to deal with trade disputes of high political visibility.

A less contentious method for resolving disputes over the meaning of treaty provisions is to give the power of interpretation to a particular organ established by the treaty. The IMF Agreement gives such power to the executive directors, subject to an appeal to the governing board.[178] The key question of whether drawings against the IMF's resources (analogous to loans to a member) could be made conditional on the economic performance of the borrower—a hotly contested but unresolved question in the negotiation of the agreement—was decided by an interpretation of the executive directors.[179] The International Coffee Agreement lodges the power to resolve disputes concerning interpretation or application with the Coffee Council, the highest body of the organization.[180] In some cases, the organization's governing board exercises the power as a matter of practice.[181]

Almost all international disputes have a legal component. In disposing of these questions, it is not important whether the decision is technically binding, but whether it is rendered by a procedure that is accepted as fair and authoritative.

Adaptability

If a cooperative security regime is to endure and serve its intended purpose over time, it must be adaptable to inevitable changes in technology, substantive problems, and economic, social, and political developments. The traditional way of changing treaty obligations is by amendment or by the addition of a protocol. The ABM treaty, for example, originally provided that each party could deploy a limited number of missiles at two sites. Later, the parties concluded that two sites were unnecessary, and the allowable number was reduced to one by a protocol signed at the Moscow summit in 1974.[182]

Many environmental agreements have adopted a "framework and protocol" approach. The Vienna Convention on the Protection of the Ozone Layer, for example, contains no substantive limitations on the use of ozone depleting substances. It provides only that the parties will cooperate in research and in the exchange of information on legal, technical, and scientific matters concerning the ozone layer.[183] Controls on the production and use of specific substances were to be dealt with in subsequent protocols. Two years later, in 1987, the Montreal Protocol providing for cutbacks in consumption of chlorofluorocarbons was signed. And in 1990, the protocol was amended to add additional controlled substances and to mandate a rapid phaseout.[184] A similar "framework and protocol" approach might be adapted to an evolving control regime governing the size and character of conventional military establishments or the technologies to be included in a nonproliferation regime.[185]

But formal amendment or the adoption of a protocol, like the process of amending the U.S. Constitution, remains slow, uncertain, and cumbersome. The ABM protocol, a comparatively simple exercise, was signed in May 1974 and did not come into force until almost two years later. Treaty amendments are subject to the same ratification process as the original treaty. In the United States, this process entails the political pitfalls of submission to the Senate for advice and consent. Similar, if not always as formidable, political obstacles exist in other parliamentary governments. Moreover, parties that do not ratify the amendment are not bound by it, so there is a possibility that the members of the regime would be subject to differing sets of obligations.

As a result, treaty lawyers have devised a number of ways to deal with the problem of adaptability short of seeking formal amendment. The easiest is the device already discussed of vesting the power to "interpret" the agreement in some governing organ. The U.S. Constitution has kept up with the times, not primarily by the amending process, but by the Supreme Court's interpretation of its broad clauses.

A number of international organizations have authority to make regulations on technical matters by vote, usually of a special majority. The decisions are binding on all, though in some cases dissenters have the right to opt out. The International Civil Aeronautics Organization has such power with respect to operational and safety matters in international air transport.[186] In many regulatory treaties, "technical" matters may be relegated to an annex that can be altered by vote of the parties. The Montreal Protocol permits changes in the schedule for reduction in consumption of controlled substances to be made by this process.[187] A new development in recent U.S-Russian arms control treaties is the authorization to make changes and modifications on "technical matters" by executive agreement without reference to the legislative bodies.[188]

Finally, as shown by the Helsinki Final Act, "soft law"—recommendations, guidelines, resolutions, joint policy declarations, and other instruments that do not purport to be legally binding—play an important part in the evolution of treaty obligations in response to new developments. The parties to the CFE, for example, established "politically binding" troop ceilings for the area covered by the treaty through parallel unilateral declarations, although the treaty proper deals only with weapons deployments and deliberately avoided imposing limits on personnel.[189] This form of undertaking is thought by U.S. executive branch lawyers to avoid the requirement of Section 33 of the U.S. Arms Control and Disarmament Act prohibiting any action "that will obligate the United States to . . . limit the armed forces of the United States, except pursuant to the treaty making power of the President under the Constitution or unless authorized by further affirmative legislation by the Congress of the United States."[190]

Creating Consensus for Coercive Measures

International treaties, like other legal rules, are able to accommodate a significant amount of noncompliance as long as the basic objectives are not threatened.[191] Not all violations, even persistent ones, threaten the life of the regime, even of a security regime. At some point, the trade-off between the benefits of obtaining improved compliance and the costs of the necessary effort tips in favor of accepting the situation as it is.

On the other hand, it remains true that some defections are so serious that failure to deal with them would mean collapse of the regime, which may explain the case of Japan and the CITES ivory ban. Overall levels of compliance with that treaty are by no means extraordinary. However, the defection of a major importer from a proscription widely publicized as crucial to the survival of the African elephant would have destroyed the credibility of the regime and reduced the treaty to a charade.[192]

In security regimes, the problem of the obdurate violator is of particular concern. Because the members rely on the regime in matters that may involve their very survival, they must have assurance at the outset that the system can respond effectively to dangerous defections. What is needed, it is said, is "a treaty with teeth." But coercive sanctions require the commitment of large economic, political, and, on occasion, military resources. Equally important, they require close to universal consensus in support of the chosen action if it is to be successful. These necessary conditions are extremely hard to meet in what is still a world of independent states.[193] Thus far, as in the invasions of South Korea and Kuwait, the international consensus has been catalyzed by the

United States, after an ad hoc decision that concerted enforcement action was the solution to a U.S. foreign policy problem. As the unfolding of the Yugoslav wars shows, this means is not a very reliable foundation for consensus building.

Our contention is that regime transparency and the systematic management process described in this chapter can be used to help identify the truly obdurate defector and generate the consensus necessary for concerted response. In the face of persisting resistance, management shades into enforcement. At some point, the reassurance game turns into a game of chicken.[194]

Coercive action in support of treaty norms is likely to be taken only where the violator is isolated and shown to be in deliberate defiance of a clear-cut obligation. Except in cases like the Gulf crisis in which the situation is obvious, these conditions typically have to be realized by a preparatory process. Disputes over interpretation, obfuscations, excuses, and evasions by the recalcitrant state must be definitively exposed. The issues must be progressively narrowed and focused, so that the question is reduced to whether the recalcitrant state will fulfill its undertaking to perform a single, well-defined act: permit access to *this* building; destroy *that* facility. The collective stake in the outcome is escalated and the probability of concerted enforcement action increases correspondingly.

The pattern can be seen in the work of the UN Special Commission and IAEA team in enforcing the terms of Security Council Resolution 687, requiring Iraq to disclose and then destroy its weapons of mass destruction and missiles as well as the facilities for manufacturing them. Of course, UNSCOM/IAEA had unusual advantages. Iraq had been defeated in a war waged under UN auspices, and international economic sanctions were already in place. On the other hand, Saddam Hussein was stubbornly determined to resist, the consensus in the Security Council was not unshakable, there was increasing concern over the hardships of the civilian population, and the options for renewed military action were doubtful.[195]

There were eight major confrontations over violations of the cease-fire resolution between its adoption on April 3, 1991, and April 1, 1993:

—On June 23 and 25, 1991, Iraqi military authorities denied an inspection team access to facilities at the Abu Ghraib Army Barracks.

—Several days later, Iraqi soldiers fired small arms into the air when members of the same team attempted to photograph loaded vehicles leaving a military transportation facility east of Fallujah.

—In September 1991, Iraq refused to allow UN inspectors to use helicopters as provided in Resolution 707.

—On September 23, Iraq detained about forty UN inspectors for almost twelve hours in a Baghdad parking lot and seized documents the team had discovered in an adjacent building.

—Also in September, forty-four inspectors from the same team were detained for three days in another parking lot when they refused to hand over documents that, as it turned out, provided definitive proof of the existence and scope of Iraq's nuclear weapons program.

—In February and March of 1992, Iraq refused to destroy or permit the destruction of particular weapons-related facilities as required by Resolution 715.

—In July 1992, Iraq prevented the inspection of its Ministry of Agriculture building, thought to contain documents relating to Iraq's missile program, for a period of three weeks during which UN inspectors were harassed by crowds of demonstrators and ultimately forced to withdraw from the area.

—In December 1992 and January 1993, Iraq refused to let UN inspection planes land, initially insisting that the inspectors travel on Iraqi Airways and later asserting that they could only fly from Jordan and not through the no-fly zone in the south. At the same time, Iraq announced that it would no longer recognize the no-fly zone in the south. Iraq reversed its stand on both issues in January after a week of limited U.S. air strikes, primarily on active antiaircraft positions in or near the no-fly zones.[196]

In each case, Saddam Hussein blinked. The skillful maneuvering of UNSCOM/IAEA, applying pressure on the ground and adroitly shifting the forum back and forth between Baghdad and New York, seems to have succeeded at least as of the current writing.[197] Despite repeated efforts to thwart the UN, it now seems probable that any significant capacity of Iraq in nuclear, chemical, and biological weapons and in ballistic missiles will be eliminated, as required by the Security Council resolutions.[198]

Not many violators will have the will and absolute control over the domestic situation that Saddam Hussein has. Yet the Iraq experience offers considerable hope that a determined enforcement effort backed by a solid international consensus can succeed even against such an opponent.

Organizational Implications

What has been described to this point is a complex, sophisticated, and active information and management process. The gathering, verification, and analysis of information and the carefully calibrated steps to ensure that the regime continues to function as intended over time require substantial and effective organizational resources. It is premature to attempt the detailed design of one or more international organizations, even for the transition to cooperative security, much less its final incarnation. It is clear, however, that a robust and vigorous institutional base will be necessary to accomplish the many tasks discussed in this chapter.

There has been considerable debate in recent years about how to achieve organizational effectiveness in implementing international regulatory regimes. Negative reaction to what was perceived as the bloated bureaucratic structure of UN agencies was only partly a product of cold war paralysis. The conventional wisdom is that large international bureaucracies become increasingly autonomous and preoccupied with their own agendas and are at the same time increasingly wasteful and inefficient. According to this view, they tend to become entrenched and remote from the concerns of the parties that created the treaty regime in the first place. It is argued that the cure for international bureaucratic bloat is for the parties to become reinvolved in continuing management, in place of the traditional large permanent secretariat.[199]

Recent environmental treaties, for example, have moved away from reliance on well-staffed and well-funded central secretariats and toward less formal arrangements involving much more participation by the parties themselves. Thus, each environmental treaty has its own conference of the parties, sometimes with an executive council that meets occasionally between conferences, a small secretariat not capable of performing much beyond housekeeping tasks, and a series of ad hoc committees or working groups, staffed by national experts and foreign office representatives, to do the substantive work. This type of arrangement is also the pattern in the various suppliers' groups.

It is becoming evident from the experience in the environmental area, however, that an implementation process without a strong and effective secretariat at its core, as it is repeated over the vast range of international substantive regulation, soon exhausts the limited national resources of personnel, time, and energy, particularly of small and developing countries. Perhaps as a reflection of these developments, the Rio Summit in June 1992 mandated a new umbrella organization, the Commission on Sustainable Development,[200] although the UN Environment Programme, created for that purpose in 1972, had been a target of criticism for traditional bureaucratic failings.

There are, however, established international institutions capable of assuming tasks of the magnitude implied by a cooperative security regime. The common characteristic of these institutions is that they have both an expert management and staff and extensive party involvement at a high level. The most obvious examples of this formula are the major international financial institutions. The IMF and the World Bank have a history of distinguished senior management, professional staffs of high quality, and large-scale involvement of responsible officials of the member states. The IAEA—for all its limitations a major policy actor in the field of nuclear nonproliferation—also has a record of outstanding directors general, highly qualified technical staff, and continuous involvement of influential officials from national nuclear energy programs. The ILO jawboning process works both because of staff continuity and expertise *and* because of the weight of the tripartite government-labor-business conference that is responsible for the blacklisting process. It too has had distinguished and dedicated directors general. And there are other examples.

The case for institutional strength together with continuing party involvement is even stronger in the context of a cooperative security regime. The starting point—and perhaps the end point—of such a regime is a network of arms control, nonproliferation, and regional security treaties. Coordination among a number of organizations addressing particular facets of the overall problem of cooperative security will be essential. The costs of duplication and lack of coordination in the area of verification alone might strain the available resources. If countries are to be assured not just that threats from a particular source or weapons system have been eliminated but that their security needs overall will not be compromised, the implementing organizations must be capable of cooperation at a technical and expert as well as at a policy level.

Although the experience with UN bureaucracies in the 1960s and 1970s gave considerable ground for complaint, it is also true that the major financial contributors have since organized to assert greater financial and policy discipline. It should not be beyond the abilities of the international community, based on the lessons of the earlier experience, to create new organizational arrangements that are lean, effective, and politically responsive. The UN system itself, for all its shortcomings, has persisted through fifty years and has established an impetus and a community that has helped to promote continuing international cooperation even in times of enormous difference and division.

Sanctions

> Sanctions are . . . required not as the normal motive for obedience, but as a *guarantee* that those who would voluntarily obey shall not be sacrificed to those who would not. —H. L. A. Hart, *The Concept of Law* (Oxford University Press, 1961), p. 193.

In a functioning cooperative security regime, some combination or clarification of obligations, assistance, persuasion, and pressures will usually suffice to bring a defector into compliance, although this may take both art and collective muscle. Pressures and expressions of disapproval are the stock in trade of political and diplomatic intercourse among states. They are directed not only at treaty violations but at all kinds of state behavior that the sanctioning state may disapprove. The gamut includes the withholding of courtesies or amenities (such as state visits), protest notes and tongue lashings at various diplomatic levels, deferral or cancellation of desired actions, and suspension or interruption of diplomatic relations. The ordinary experience of diplomatic life teaches a state and its leaders to expect embarrassment, political isolation, and subtler diplomatic signals of displeasure if they violate an important treaty commitment, and that anticipation, in turn, serves to help deter unwanted behavior.

In this section, we go beyond these conventional expressions of disapproval and consider the availability and effect of explicitly coercive sanctions.[201] We distinguish between unilateral or concerted action outside the treaty framework, on the one hand, and enforcement action carried out under the authority and according to the procedures of the regime, on the other.

Unilateral or Concerted Action outside the Treaty

A perennial topic of academic and journalistic discussion is unilateral military and economic sanctions. In our judgment, these expedients are much overrated as methods of inducing states to behave in accordance with the wishes of the sanctioner.

MILITARY AND ECONOMIC MEASURES. Unilateral military action, except in self-defense, has been prohibited in international law since 1945. Article 2(4) of the UN Charter forbids "the threat or use of force against the territorial integrity or political independence of any state," and in the *Nicaragua* case the World Court held, not surprisingly, that this prescription has become a rule of general international law, binding on all states, whether or not they subscribe to the charter.[202] The norm has been disparaged as more honored in the breach than in the observance.[203] And it cannot be denied that, under the conditions of the cold war, major powers and their clients have been able to disregard the charter prohibition, although not always with impunity.[204] Still, when states have used force, they have not denied the applicability of the rule but sought to justify their actions as within some exception, usually self-defense.

Be that as it may, a cooperative security regime will, by definition, have to place stringent limits on the freedom of states to employ military force except when authorized or approved by the procedures of the regime. It is doubtful that the regime could survive many episodes like Hungary, Czechoslovakia, Afghanistan, Panama, Grenada, or Osirak. Thus the role of unilateral military sanctions must decline to the vanishing point.

The status of unilateral economic measures is more problematic. In the flush of post–World War II enthusiasm, the Organization of American States (OAS) Charter prohibited "not only armed force but also any other form of interference or attempted threat against the personality of the State or against its political, economic or cultural elements."[205]

Whether because of the difficulty of defining the proscribed conduct or because economic pressure is so endemic in international relations, this position has not found many takers. Even the broad UN Resolutions on the Definition of Aggression or the Principles of Friendly Relations among States do not address the issue of economic coercion.[206]

On the other hand, unilateral economic measures have not been particularly effective in achieving their objectives. The most extensive recent study examined 116 cases of economic sanctions since World War I (most of them not involving treaty violations) and rated only 34 percent of them as successful. In the period since 1973, accounting for about half the cases, the success rate dropped to 25 percent.[207] Although one might quarrel with the methodology, few critics would disagree with the gross conclusions.[208] In the overwhelming majority of the cases, the sole or leading sanctioner was the United States, with the Soviet Union a distant second, suggesting that economic sanctions were mainly instruments of hegemonic discipline. The declining position of the cold war superpowers, the more general diffusion of economic power, the diversification of trade and financial patterns, and the drying up of resources for bilateral military and economic assistance portend a much smaller role for such measures in the future. Indeed, it is now often argued that economic sanctions are imposed not primarily with the instrumental purpose of changing the policy of the target state but for "domestic political or other rhetorical purposes."[209]

THE INTERNATIONAL FINANCIAL INSTITUTIONS. As Wolfgang Reinicke shows in chapter 5, the international financial institutions (IFIs)—the World Bank family, the regional investment banks, and the IMF—deploy enormous resources, far exceeding all the bilateral economic assistance programs put together. They are governed by a weighted voting formula that ensures a dominant position for the United States and absolute control by the industrialized countries. It is tempting to think that denial of access to these resources might be converted into a powerful tool to secure compliance with a cooperative security regime.

When the norms of the regime coincide with the mission of the IFIs, there is little difficulty with this approach. Thus, if the issue is the aggregate level of military expenditures, it seems perfectly appropriate that the IMF and the banks should take this into account in funding decisions. Military budgets are an important aspect of the overall economic situation of drawers and borrowers and should be evaluated accordingly. Nor need the approach be only negative. By making the level of military expenditure an issue for discussion, the IFIs may provide a positive incentive for shifts in national financial priorities away from excessive military expenditures.

This approach has been followed in the area of human rights policy and "governance" issues, and it is already being extended to the field of military policy. Beginning in 1989, IMF managing director Michel Camdessus and World Bank president Barber Conable began speaking out publicly on the impact of military expenditures on economic development and stability. In September 1989 Conable said, "It is important to place military spending decisions on the same footing as other fiscal decisions, to examine possible trade-offs more systematically, and to explore ways to bring military spending into better balance with development priorities."[210]

This was clear notice that the old rules of the game were changing. The staff of the IMF was instructed to include a review of military expenditures in its periodic consultations with members under Article 6 of the Fund Agreement.[211] Bank lending officers were to consider them in connection with structural adjustment loans. The IFIs insist that they will not make reductions in military budgets a "condition" of assistance. But even without addressing military expenditures directly, they can set targets in other sectors that would require squeezing the military. In 1991 the IMF may have gone further and linked support for India and Pakistan more directly to reductions in military spending.[212]

Indeed, there are possibilities for direct interaction between the IFIs and the cooperative security regime. They could assist one another in gathering and verifying information about military budgets and programs.[213] The IFIs have understandably found it awkward to appear to be dictating how much spending is too much for national security. The norms established by the regime could help supply the measure.

When it comes to denial or cancellation of support as a means of enforcing security prescriptions unrelated to economic performance, however, the situation is somewhat different. The IFIs are adamant that their charters require them to make decisions exclusively on economic grounds.[214] The legal department of the World Bank takes the position that these provisions are binding not only on the management and the staff, but also on the executive directors, who are elected by and represent the members.[215]

In the 1960s the issue was tested when the UN General Assembly adopted resolutions calling on the Bank to refrain from lending to Rhodesia, South Africa, and Portugal. In an extended exchange, the Bank maintained that it would be improper for it to accept these resolutions in view of the requirement of its articles that it take only economic considerations into account in granting loans.[216] This continues to be the Bank's position. Then and now, however, it has acknowledged that it would be bound by an action of the Security Council under Chapter 7 imposing economic sanctions.[217] The Bank's current view, expressed in the context of human rights violations, is that "the degree of respect paid by a government to political and civil rights . . . has not been considered in itself a basis for the Bank's decision to make loans to that government. Violation of political rights may, however, reach such proportion as to become a Bank concern either due to significant direct economic effects or if it results in international obligations relevant to the Bank such as those mandated by binding decisions of the UN Security Council."[218]

That statement does not conclude the matter, however. Presumably, the IFI charters could be amended to permit denial of access in case of specific violations, for example, of nonproliferation obligations, without regard to their overall economic impact. At present, it is not likely that such a move would succeed.[219] Nations have many foreign policy goals, sometimes inconsistent, and they are hesitant to bind themselves to give absolute priority to any one of them. Apart from feasibility, the question remains whether it would be wise to accord this authority to the Bank, short of action by the Security Council or some similarly superior political body. Such a rule could distort the economic development mission of the IFIs when development is also a high international priority. And, although neutral on its face, such an arrangement would be deeply discriminatory in application, since it would affect only poorer nations that depend on international financial resources.

TRADE RESTRAINTS. We touched earlier on unilateral trade restrictions as a general coercive measure. In addition, a treaty may itself contain prohibitions against production or trade in certain items. One of the first great modern international agreements is the treaty banning the slave trade.[220] CITES prohibits commercial imports and exports of certain endangered species. It is, after all, a treaty to regulate international trade in endangered species. Likewise, chemicals listed in Schedule 1 of the draft CWC have no civil use, and trade in these items is prohibited.[221]

A somewhat more subtle instance is the International Coffee Agreement, which authorizes the Coffee Council to require importing members to prohibit or restrict imports from nonmember countries under certain circumstances. The purpose is to protect the market for exporting member states and the quota system on which the treaty depends. The GATT provides a special exemption for restrictions imposed in support of recognized commodity agreements.[222]

The Montreal Protocol also prohibits trade in controlled substances to nonmembers. The trade ban does not affect the computation of emissions in the member countries, however, since imports, whatever their source, are charged to a country's allowable consumption, and exports to nonparties are not deducted.[223] The object was primarily to preserve the export markets of the existing producers, all of which were located in member states, during the phaseout period. Presumably, the provision is within the exception of GATT Article 22(b) covering restrictions "necessary to protect human, animal or plant life or health."

In the cooperative security context, a special problem arises if an importing state fails to satisfy end-use assurances for items or technologies with dual-use potential. A trade ban in such circumstances could also be reconciled with the GATT under the national security exception.[224] Despite the logical appeal of this approach, the outcome in the CWC negotiations shows that neither the adoption of such trade sanctions nor their implementation will be without problems. As early as 1988 President François Mitterrand proposed a broad ban on the use of poison gas or other chemical weapons and the technology needed to produce them and perhaps an embargo on all arms sales to offending nations.[225] Later in the negotiations, it was proposed that if a party diverted dual-use items to weapons purposes, members should cut off further exports of that item to the offender. Yet it was argued in opposition that automatic denial would not have survived the Iran-Iraq war, because of the reluctance of many of the parties to support Iran.[226] In the end, the treaty omits any specific reference to trade sanctions, although "the Conference may recommend collective measures to States Parties" in cases of serious violation.[227]

Enforcement Action under the Authority of the Regime

MEMBERSHIP SANCTIONS. Membership sanctions encompass expulsion, suspension, or limiting the privileges of membership on a temporary or conditional basis. Many treaties, particularly the constitutions of UN organizations, explicitly provide for some kind of membership sanctions,[228] but they have seldom been invoked as a means of ensuring compliance with the treaty.[229]

It seems anomalous to consider the use of membership sanctions in a security regime that seeks to reduce proliferation and curb arms buildup, since it depends on inclusivity for strength. Expulsion would seem to punish the regime more than the defecting state, which by its action has already placed itself outside the community. The UN Charter provision for suspension of a member "against which preventive or enforcement action has been taken by the Security Council" was not invoked against either South Africa, Iraq, or Yugoslavia, the only members ever to qualify.[230]

On the other hand, in January 1962 Cuba was prohibited from further "participation in the Inter-American system."[231] More recently the CSCE suspended Yugoslavia's voting rights for the duration of hostilities and later suspended it from the organization for three months.[232] In turn, the General Assembly on September 22, 1992, stated that Yugoslavia (Serbia and Montenegro) cannot participate in the General Assembly.[233] And although South Africa was not formally suspended from the UN, it was drummed out of the UN specialized agencies one after another and has not participated in the General Assembly since 1974.[234]

It is noteworthy that in all these cases the action was something less than outright expulsion, and in none of them did it have any immediate effect. Its importance was as a part of a broader political campaign to isolate the offender.

ENFORCEMENT ACTION. The only treaties that provide for formal economic and military sanctions are the UN Charter and its regional counterpart, the OAS Charter, formed in the same era.[235] Chapter 7 of the UN Charter empowers the Security Council, after determining the existence of "a threat to the peace, breach of the peace, or act of aggression," to decide what measures shall be taken to maintain or restore international peace and security. The possibilities include "complete or partial interruption of economic relations and of rail, sea, air, postal telegraphic, radio, and other means of communication, and the severance of diplomatic relations" (Article 41). If these measures should prove inadequate, the Security Council "may take such action by air, sea, or land forces as may be necessary to maintain or restore international peace and security" (Article 42). Decisions under Chapter 7 are binding on members of the UN by virtue of Article 25 of the charter.

These powers to order economic and military sanctions were regarded as the great breakthrough that distinguished the United Nations from its impotent predecessor, the League of Nations. Yet, if membership sanctions have proved difficult to apply, the political and economic costs entailed in the use of formal military and economic sanctions have proved greater still. A rueful observer, looking back over the events of 1950, said, "The Korean War . . . has shown us that an international enforcement action is, for all practical purposes, a war."[236]

In all, the Security Council has invoked its extraordinary powers to authorize military action only twice, in Korea and Kuwait. And it has ordered economic sanctions only against Rhodesia, South Africa, Libya, Iraq, and the former Yugoslavia.[237] The OAS, which does not operate under the threat of veto, has been similarly circumspect. It authorized the use of force once—in the Cuban Missile Crisis—and economic sanctions twice—against the Trujillo regime in the Dominican Republic in 1960 and against Haiti in 1991. All of the instances involving the use of force were extraordinary situations of high political valance, where the basic foreign policy requirements of the United States and its allies, which bore the brunt of the burden, coincided with deep-seated and comprehensive disapproval of the target of the sanctions.

Concerted economic sanctions would seem to be irresistible in an increasingly interdependent world economy. They comprise not only trade sanctions and termination of bilateral and multilateral foreign assistance but also the blocking of assets, prohibition of fund transfers, and severance of transportation links. But for all their implicit power, they need time to take effect. The administration and its allies thought them too slow in Kuwait, and a similar judgment is likely in serious crises that might beset a cooperative security regime.

Military sanctions raise questions beyond the most obvious ones of cost in money, political will, and perhaps blood. Technically, the Security Council has never acted under Article 42 because it has had no forces at its disposal, as had been contemplated by Article 43 of the charter. Instead, in both Korea and Kuwait, it *authorized* UN members to come to the assistance of the party under attack with their own forces. Secretary-General Boutros Boutros-Ghali recently proposed that Article 43 be activated at last.[238] He seemed to be contemplating that relatively small contingents of battalion size would be placed at the disposal of the council. Although these may be appropriate for interposition in civil wars or to protect against systematic violation of human rights, they may not be adequate to respond to a determined and willful violator of the central precepts of the cooperative security regime (see chapter 6). It seems unlikely that forces of that magnitude will be committed to the control of the Security Council, or any other international body, in advance of the occasion for their use. Thus the application of serious military sanctions will continue to depend on states that volunteer, and they will make the decision in the light of their own national interests and policies.

A second important issue is the relation of the Security Council to other bodies in the regime. It is possible to envision that military action would be taken under the auspices of regional bodies rather than by the UN itself. In the

Cuban Missile Crisis, the United States acted under the mantle of the OAS, and more recently the Economic Organization of West African States provided the authorization for primarily Nigerian intervention in Liberia.[239] The CSCE has been touted for such a role in Europe, although its performance in the Yugoslav crisis, while no worse than any other organization's, has cast doubt on its capability.

Under existing rules, such organizations are not free to act on their own. Article 53 of the UN Charter provides that "no action shall be taken under regional arrangements or by regional agencies without the authorization of the Security Council." In the Cuban Missile Crisis, the United States took the position that this requirement was satisfied by the tacit approval of the council, evidenced by its failure to act on a resolution disapproving the OAS quarantine. Whatever the legal force of this argument, as a practical matter it is unlikely to appeal to states that do not wield a veto in the Security Council.

Similarly, the IAEA depends ultimately on the Security Council to act in cases of violation of the NPT or safeguards agreements. The Board of Governors must refer cases of violation to the parties or to the Security Council for action. The same is true of the CWC.[240] Whether or not the Security Council retains its monopoly on military sanctions, it seems unlikely that states will wish to delegate final power to use force to subordinate organizations, either regional or functional, without some form of oversight by a universal organization operating at the highest political level.

The UN Charter imposes requirements of consensus among the five permanent members of the Security Council that could rarely be met during the cold war. There is much talk in its wake that conclusions based on an experience dominated by the U.S.-USSR confrontation must be reconsidered. The actions against Libya, Yugoslavia, and Haiti provide some support for this thesis, at least for economic sanctions, but the jury is still out. The aftermath of the Gulf War and events since then have done little to dissipate the skepticism about the efficacy and viability of military enforcement action in all but the most egregious cases.

Conclusion

Although the stakes may not seem as high as during the cold war, when the world faced the possibility of nuclear extinction, the containment of violence in a cooperative security regime will be a much more complex and demanding problem. The superpowers will no longer enforce hegemonic discipline in their respective camps. Formal military sanctions, if not a paper tiger, cannot be relied on for routine enforcement of ordinary obligations of the regime or even the run of serious violations. They are available, if at all, only in response to egregious violation of Article 2(4) of the UN Charter or in cases of extreme civil violence with international ramifications. Economic sanctions, though perhaps easier to organize, are costly, slow to take effect, and difficult to maintain.

Thus a cooperative security regime cannot rely for enforcement on external penalties. If it is to survive, it must be a reassurance regime. The incentives for compliance must be built in—inherent in the regime itself, so that each party will continue to conform to regime norms and can do so in confidence as long as it can be assured that the others are also conforming. We cannot overemphasize the importance of transparency, which is not an orthodox military virtue, in undergirding that confidence.

A priori, it does not seem implausible that, under these conditions, the protection from military threat and the savings in military expenditures would be more than enough to induce most countries to comply with a regime that ensured these benefits. In practice, a number of circumstances may introduce significant ambiguities into the balance. Despite these difficulties, the goal of a system based on cooperation and reassurance is not unattainable.

This chapter suggests that the key to a sturdy regime is legitimacy. Legitimacy in turn depends on widespread acceptance by members that the military constraints of the regime in fact substantially ensure their security. That acceptance requires equally widespread participation in formulating these norms. Like the command and control system for nuclear weapons developed by both antagonists in the cold war, cooperative security "is a social and political matter as well as a technical matter."[241]

The substantive limits cannot be rigid and unbending, however. The level of military capability a country needs to defend against external threats is obviously not a matter of precise calculation but of judgment, made the more difficult because, in many countries, the chief mission for the armed forces is to maintain internal security. The regime will have to adapt to changes in the technological and political context over time. Most important, the problem is not to maintain an existing system in steady state but, in a sense, to bring the cooperative security regime into being. The boat will have to be built while it is sailing. Thus legitimacy also requires a fair procedure of governance over time, and again transparency and participation will be crucial.

The existing nuclear nonproliferation regime, despite serious imperfections, begins to approximate a reassurance regime. For the vast majority of its 149 parties,[242] the regime offers sufficient reassurance against nuclear threat that they have little or no incentive to pursue a nuclear weapons option, and they have not done so. A handful of holdouts remain, but to date the regime seems to have operated to reduce their number. The remaining intransigents are increasingly identified and isolated as targets for a range of focused pressures by the international community. The challenge is to maintain and extend these successes within the field of nuclear nonproliferation and to expand the zone of cooperation over the whole range of security issues.

Notes

1. See Amartya K. Sen, "Isolation, Assurance and the Social Rate of Discount," *Quarterly Journal of Economics,* vol. 81 (1967), p. 112; and Carlisle Ford Runge, "Institutions and the Free Rider: The Assurance Problem in Collective Action," *Journal of Politics,* vol. 46 (1984), p. 154.

2. Ashton B. Carter, William J. Perry, and John D. Steinbruner, *A New Concept of Cooperative Security,* Brookings Occasional Papers (1992), p. 9.

3. See, for example, Margaret Levi and others, "Introduction: The Limits of Rationality," in Karen Schweers Cook and Margaret Levi, eds., *The Limits of Rationality* (University of Chicago Press, 1990), p. 1; Russell Hardin, "The Social Evolution of Cooperation," in ibid., pp. 358, 377–78; Douglass C. North, "Institutions and Their Consequences for Economic Performance," in ibid., pp. 383, 395; Margaret Levi, "A Logic of Institutional Change," in ibid., pp. 402, 406–10; Jon Elster, The Cement of Society: A Study of Social Order (Cambridge University Press, 1989), p. 15; and Elinor Ostrom, *Governing the Commons: The Evolution of Institutions for Collective Action* (Cambridge University Press, 1990), pp. 204–07.

4. The standard definition of an international regime is principles, norms, rules, and decisionmaking procedures around which actor expectations converge in a given issue area. Stephen D. Krasner, "Structural Causes and Regime Consequences: Regimes as Intervening Variables," in Krasner, ed., *International Regimes* (Cornell University Press, 1983), p. 1. In this formula, the elements seem to be ranked in order of decreasing generality, but there is not much concern with precise distinctions between them. The arrangement is not hierarchical, however, in the sense that the more general statement does not always trump the more specific. In practice, all the elements interact in complex ways.

5. See, for example, Friedrich V. Kratochwil, *Rules, Norms, Decisions: On the Conditions of Practical and Legal Reasoning in International Relations and Domestic Affairs* (Cambridge University Press, 1989), pp. 128–29; Alexander Wendt, "Anarchy Is What States Make of It: The Social Construction of Power Politics," *International Organization,* vol. 46 (Spring 1992), pp. 391, 399; and Elster, *Cement of Society,* pp. 97–107.

6. Norms also differ from rules of games, in which the rules define the activity. Moral precepts and codes of etiquette, although they are also prescriptions for action in situations of choice carrying a sense of obligation to obey, are distinguished in other ways from norms that are the components of regimes.

7. "Conference on Security and Cooperation in Europe, Final Act," August 1, 1975, Article 10, *International Legal Materials,* vol. 14 (September 1975), p. 1296. See also Charles Lipson, "Why Are Some International Agreements Informal?" *International Organization,* vol. 45 (Autumn 1991), pp. 533–34.

8. That is not to say that law is the exclusive source of regime prescriptions. Many informal, tacit, or practice-based elements are necessary to turn the legal structure into an organic functioning institution. See *Missouri* v. *Holland,* 252 U.S. 416, 433 (1920) (Holmes, J.). On the other hand, the legal system is not confined to the particular regime but is linked to and shares elements with the broader international legal system.

9. Hans Morgenthau, *Politics among Nations* (Knopf, 1978), p. 282.

10. See Oscar Schachter, "The Invisible College of International Lawyers," *Northwestern University Law Review,* vol. 72, no. 2 (1977), p. 217.

11. Bill Keller, "Pentagon Asserts 'Star Wars' Tests Won't Break Pact," *New York Times,* April 21, 1985, p. A1; and Abram Chayes and Antonia Handler Chayes, "Testing

and Development of 'Exotic' Systems under the ABM Treaty: The Great Reinterpretation Caper," *Harvard Law Review,* vol. 99 (June 1986), p. 1956.

12. Harald Muller, "The Internalization of Principles, Norms and Rules by Governments: The Case of Security Regimes," prepared for the conference The Study of Regimes in International Relations, Tübingen, Germany, July 14–18, 1991, pp. 14–25.

13. Ronald Dworkin, *Law's Empire* (Belknap Press of Harvard University Press, 1986), pp. 62–67, 88, 91.

14. Ibid., p. 413.

15. "Vienna Convention on the Law of Treaties," May 23, 1969, Article 2(1)(a), in *International Legal Materials,* vol. 8 (July 1969), p. 681 (hereafter "Vienna Convention"). *Treaties* as defined in Article 2, section 2 of the United States Constitution are only a relatively small subset of the broad class of agreements giving rise to international obligation—those that are submitted to the Senate for advice and consent to ratification. In recent years this practice has been used in only a small fraction of U.S. international agreements. See Barry E. Carter and Phillip R. Trimble, *International Law* (Little, Brown, 1991), pp. 79, 169–172.

16. "Vienna Convention," Article 26, p. 690.

17. "1982 United Nations Convention on the Law of the Sea," part 5, Articles 55–75, *International Legal Materials,* vol. 21 (November 1982), pp. 1261, 1279–86.

18. White House, "Proclamation of an Exclusive Economic Base," March 10, 1983, *International Legal Materials,* vol. 22 (March 1983), p. 463.

19. Barbara Crosette, "4 Ex-Soviet States and U.S. in Accord on 1991 Arms Pact," *New York Times,* May 24, 1992, p. A1.

20. The foreign secretary of Pakistan, however, admitted in a February 7, 1992, *Washington Post* interview that his country had the components to assemble at least one nuclear bomb. R. Jeffrey Smith, "Pakistan Official Affirms Capacity for Nuclear Device; Foreign Minister Vows to Contain Technology," *Washington Post,* February 7, 1992, p. A18. Although on March 24, 1993, South African president F. W. de Klerk announced in parliament that its nuclear weapons program, begun in 1974, had yielded six crude atomic bombs, he stated that the weapons were destroyed and the means of production dismantled upon his taking office in 1989. Bill Keller, "South Africa Says It Built 6 Atomic Bombs," *New York Times,* March 25, 1993, p. A1. In turn, North Korea has indicated its intention to withdraw from the NPT but has not admitted having a nuclear weapons program. David Sanger, "North Korea, Fighting Inspection, Renounces Nuclear Arms Treaty," *New York Times,* March 12, 1993, p. A1.

21. "The Geneva Protocol for the Prohibition of the Use in War of Asphyxiating, Poisonous or Other Gases, and of Bacteriological Methods of Warfare," *Arms Control and Disarmament Agreements* (Washington: U.S. Arms Control and Disarmament Agency, 1990), p. 15.

22. "North Sea Continental Shelf," Judgment, in International Court of Justice, *Report of Judgements, Advisory Opinions, and Orders* (Hague, 1969), pp. 3, 44. Hereafter *ICJ Reports.*

23. See, for example, Kratochwil, *Rules, Norms, Decisions,* pp. 74–81; Wendt, "Anarchy Is What States Make of It," pp. 391–92; and Edna Ullman-Margalit, *The Emergence of Norms* (Oxford: Clarendon Press, 1977), p. 87.

24. See Thomas M. Franck, *The Power of Legitimacy among Nations* (Oxford University Press, 1990), p. 19; and Lon L. Fuller, "A Reply to Professors Cohen and Dworkin: The Morality of Law," *Villanova Law Review,* vol. 10 (Summer 1965), p. 655.

25. "United Nations Convention on the Prohibition of the Development, Production Stockpiling and Use of Chemical Weapons and on Their Destruction" (Paris, January 13, 1993), *International Legal Materials,* vol. 32 (May 1993), p. 800 (hereafter

"CWC"); "Convention on the Prohibition of the Development, Production and Stockpiling of Bacteriological (Biological) and Toxin Weapons and on Their Destruction," (Washington, London, and Moscow, April 10, 1972, entered into force, March 26, 1975), *United Nations Treaty Series,* vol. 1015 (New York, 1984) p. 163 (hereafter "BWC"); and "Treaty on the Non-Proliferation of Nuclear Weapons" (July 1, 1968, entered into force March 5, 1970) *United Nations Treaty Series,* vol. 729 (1974), p. 161 (hereafter "NPT").

26. For the Nuclear Suppliers Group (NSG), see Office of Technology Assessment, *Nuclear Proliferation and Safeguards* (Praeger, 1977), p. 220–21; for the Zangger Committee, see IAEA Documents INFCIRC/209/Mod.2, Vienna, February 1984, INFCIRC/209/Mod.3, Vienna, August 1985, and INFCIRC/209/Mod.4, Vienna, February 1990; for the Australia Group, dealing with chemical weapons, see J. P. Perry Robinson, "The Australia Group: A Description and Assessment," in Hans Günter Brauch and others, eds., *Controlling the Development and Spread of Military Technology: Lessons From the Past and Challenges for the 1990s* (Amsterdam: Vu University Press, 1992), pp. 157–76; and for the Missile Technology Control Regime (MTCR), see Department of Defense, "Missile Technology Control Regime: Fact Sheet to Accompany Public Announcement," April 16, 1987.

27. Carter and others, *New Concept of Cooperative Security,* p. 49.

28. Janne E. Nolan, *Trappings of Power: Ballistic Missiles in the Third World* (Brookings, 1991), p. 60.

29. Ibid., p. 18.

30. "Statute of the International Atomic Energy Agency," October 26, 1956, *United Nations Treaty Series,* vol. 276 (1957), p. 4; and "Tlatleloco Treaty for the Prohibition of Nuclear Weapons in Latin America," April 22, 1968, *United Nations Treaty Series,* vol. 634 (1968), pp. 326–56, 362–66, 419–21; and "South Pacific Nuclear Free Zone Treaty," August 6, 1985, *International Legal Materials,* vol. 24 (September 1985), p. 1442.

31. See Office of Technology Assistance (OTA), *Nuclear Proliferation and Safeguards,* pp. 220–21.

32. Hans Blix, "Statement of the Director General to the Board of Governors of the IAEA," Vienna, February 24, 1992, p. 14.

33. See "NPC Decides to Join Nuclear Arms Pact," *Beijing Review,* vol. 35 (January 13–19, 1992), p. 9; and Tom A. Zamora, "Moruroa-torium," *Bulletin of the Atomic Scientists,* vol. 48, no. 5 (1992), p. 11.

34. Barbara Crossette, "4 Ex-Soviet States and U.S. in Accord on 1991 Arms Pact," *New York Times,* May 24, 1992, p. A1; and "Belarus Ratifies START I Pact; Ukraine Remains Last Holdout," *Arms Control Today,* vol. 23 (March 1993), p. 20. For more information on Kazakhstan's ratification of the NPT, see John Lepingwell, "Kazakhstan Ratifies Non-Proliferation Treaty," *RFE/RFL Daily Report,* no. 238 (December 14, 1993). At the present writing, the prospect that Ukraine will sign the NPT in the near future seems somewhat doubtful, although it has made no announcement contradicting its earlier expressed intention.

35. "South Africa Signs a Treaty Allowing Nuclear Inspection," *New York Times,* July 9, 1991, p. A11. South Africa signed a safeguards agreement with the IAEA on September 16, 1991. See Richard L. Williamson, Jr., "Using Law to Impede Advanced Proliferation: An Urgent Task for the Non-proliferation Regime" (forthcoming).

36. "Argentina and Brazil Sign Nuclear Accord," *New York Times,* December 14, 1991, p. A7; and "Statement by State Department Spokesman Margaret Tutwiler, Dec. 13, 1991," in *US Department of State Dispatch,* vol. 2 (December 23, 1991), p. 907.

37. Interview with Ambassador Rolf Ekeus, chairman of the United Nations Special Commission in Vienna, February 1992. See "UN Says Iraqi Atom Arms Industry Is Gone," *New York Times,* September 4, 1992, p. A2; and John H. Cushman, Jr., "Iraq

Accepts Radiation Tests to Water," *New York Times,* September 8, 1992, p. A8. The cease-fire resolution and its implementing measures are designed to ensure that Iraq will not "use, retain, possess, develop, construct or otherwise acquire" chemical, biological, or nuclear weapons or ballistic missiles with a range greater than 150 kilometers. The prohibition extends to stocks of agents, related subsystems and components, and all research, development, support, and manufacturing facilities. United Nations Security Council Resolution 687 (1991), adopted by the Security Council at its 2981st meeting on April 3, 1991, UN Doc. S/RES/687 (1991). The implementation of the Security Council resolution and the conduct of the inspections under it are discussed later in this chapter.

38. Steven A. Holmes, "U.S. Rebukes North Koreans for Scrapping Nuclear Pact," *New York Times,* March 18, 1993, p. A6. South Korea and Japan invoked economic sanctions on North Korea. North Korea withdrew its notice of withdrawal hours before the expiration of the ninety-day notice period. "North Korea Suspends Nuclear Treaty Withdrawal," *Facts on File,* June 17, 1993, vol. 53, p. 442.

39. Douglas Roche, "Nuclear Build-Up Continues; Western Intransigence Angers Non-Aligned Nations," *Toronto Star,* September 27, 1990, p. A17.

40. "NPT," Article 10(2). See George Bunn, Charles N. van Doren, and David Fisher, *Options and Opportunities: The NPT Extension Conference of 1995,* PPNN Study 2 (University of Southampton, England: Programme for Promoting Nuclear Non-Proliferation, November 1991), p. 28.

41. Ibid., p. 31.

42. Michael Wines, "Summit in Washington: Bush and Yeltsin Agree to Cut Long-Range Atomic Warheads," *New York Times,* June 17, 1992, p. A1. The reductions would come in two stages: first, to within a range of 3,800 to 4,250 each, and second to between 3,000 and 3,500 warheads. Both stages could be completed as early as the year 2000 if the United States assists Russia in the required destruction of ballistic missile systems.

43. "Protocol to the Treaty between the United States of America and the Union of Soviet Socialist Republics on the Limitation of Underground Nuclear Weapon Tests," July 3, 1974, Articles 1, 2, and 3, *Arms Control and Disarmaments Agreements* (U.S. Arms Control and Disarmament Agency, 1990), p. 189.

44. "Gorbachev's Remarks on Arms Cuts," *New York Times,* October 6, 1991, p. A12; Zamora, "Moruroa-torium"; and Alan Hiding, "France Suspends Its Testing of Nuclear Weapons," *New York Times,* April 9, 1992, p. A5.

45. Michael R. Gordon, "U.S. Tightens Limit on Nuclear Tests," *New York Times,* July 15, 1992, p. A5; "The Politics of Testing," *National Journal,* vol. 24 (October 3, 1992), p. 2264; "U.S. Stops Nuclear Testing; Test Ban Group Praises Initiative," U.S. Newswire, October 2, 1992; and "Moratorium Extended on U.S. Nuclear Testing," *US Department of State Dispatch,* vol. 4 (July 12, 1993), p. 501.

46. See Paul Doty, "A Nuclear Test Ban," *Foreign Affairs,* vol. 65 (Spring 1987), pp. 750, 766–69; *Congressional Quarterly,* vol. 50 (September 26, 1992), p. 2932; and "Moratorium Extended on U.S. Nuclear Testing."

47. "BWC," Article 1, pp. 164, 166.

48. "Speech by Ronald F. Lehman II, Director of the U.S. Arms Control and Disarmament Agency," at the World Affairs Council, Riverside, California, March 1, 1991, p. 4.

49. Elisa Harris, "Towards a Comprehensive Strategy for Halting Chemical and Biological Weapons Proliferation," *Arms Control,* vol. 12 (September 1991), pp. 143–44. In November 1987, with the changing political climate in the Soviet Union, the General Assembly adopted by consensus a resolution authorizing the secretary-general

to develop additional technical guidelines for subsequent investigations. UN Resolution 42/37 C, "Measures to Uphold the Authority of the 1925 Geneva Protocol and to Support the Conclusion of a Chemical Weapons Convention," November 30, 1987. In December 1989 the new guidelines were adopted by the General Assembly, again by consensus. UN Resolution 44/115 B, "Chemical and Bacteriological (Biological) Weapons: Measures to Uphold the Authority of the 1925 Geneva Protocol and to Support the Conclusion of a Chemical Weapons Convention," December 15, 1989.

50. Harris, "Towards a Comprehensive Strategy," p. 146.

51. Ibid., p. 147.

52. "Implementation of the Proposals for a Verification Protocol to the Biological Weapons Convention," Report of the Federation of American Scientists Working Group on Biological and Toxin Weapons Verification, February 1991.

53. Harris, "Towards a Comprehensive Strategy," p. 150; and U.S. Department of State, Office of the Legal Advisor, *Treaties in Force* (January 1992), pp. 295–96.

54. The Geneva Protocol for the Prohibition of the Use in War of Asphyxiating, Poisonous or Other Gases, and of Bacteriological Methods of Warfare. See R. R. Baxter and Thomas Buergenthal, "Legal Aspects of the Geneva Protocol of 1925," *American Journal of International Law,* vol. 64 (October 1970), p. 853.

55. In a speech to the United Nations in September 1989, President Bush proposed a complicated arrangement that would have permitted the United States and the Soviet Union to retain 2 percent of their chemical weapons until "all nations capable of building chemical weapons sign that total-ban treaty." Michael Gordon, "Neutralizing Poison Gas," *New York Times,* September 26, 1989, p. A1. The effect would have been to introduce into the CWC the same discriminatory structure that plagues the NPT and thus generate bitter resentment among developing countries. After two years, in recognition that the proposal could not be reconciled with the nondiscrimination principles on which the convention was conceived, the United States withdrew the proposal.

56. See Sid Balman, Jr., "U.S. Hails Chemical Weapons Agreement," United Press International, September 2, 1992; and Alan Riding, "Signing of Chemical Arms Pact Begins," *New York Times,* January 14, 1993, p. A16.

57. "CWC," Article 21, p. 821.

58. Amy Borrus and James E. Ellis, "Crying 'Jobs' to Sell Weapons Abroad," *Business Week,* March 16, 1992, p. 37; and OTA, *Global Arms Trade: Commerce in Advanced Military Technology and Weapons* (June 1991), pp. 12–16.

59. "F-15 Sale: Wrong New World Order," *New York Times,* March 8, 1992, sec. 4, p. 14; "George Bush, in The Arms Bazaar," ibid., June 6, 1992, sec. 1, p. 1; Calvin Sims, "Market Place; Seeking Bargains in Military Stocks," ibid., September 24, 1992, p. D10; "Mr. Bush Sells Out Arms Control," ibid., September 29, 1992, p. A22; Eric Schmitt, "Arms Makers' Latest Tune: 'Over There, Over There,'" ibid., October 4, 1992, sec. 3, p. 5; and "U.S. To Sell to Kuwait $4.5 Billion in Arms," ibid., January 6, 1993, p. A5.

60. "F-15 Sale: Wrong New World Order"; "Saudis Seeking McDonnell Jets," *New York Times,* November 6, 1991, p. D4; Borrus and Ellis, "Crying 'Jobs' to Sell Weapons Abroad," March 16, 1992, p. 37; and Andrew Rosenthal, "Jet Sale to Saudis Approved by Bush, Saving Jobs in U.S.," *New York Times,* September 12, 1992, sec. 1, p. 1.

61. "The Rebirth of the U.N.," speech by Eduard Shervardnadze, Foreign Minister of the Soviet Union, to the United Nations General Assembly, New York, September 25, 1990, p. 10, in *Vital Speeches of the Day,* vol. 57 (October 15, 1990), p. 10. "UN Resolution 46/36," which contains Resolutions A through L, *International Legal Mate-*

rials, vol. 31 (March 1992), p. 469. Resolution L calls for the establishment of the arms register.

62. "UN Resolution 46/36," pp. 482, 485; and Edward J. Laurance, "The UN Register of Conventional Arms: Rationales and Prospects for Compliance and Effectiveness," *Washington Quarterly,* vol. 16 (Spring 1993), pp. 163–66.

63. "UN Resolution 46/36," pp. 486–87. As of early May 1993, more than forty reports had been submitted. Interview with Silvana Dasilva, Manager for Treaty Status, UN Office for Disarmament Affairs, Washington, May 10, 1993.

64. See OTA, *Nuclear Proliferation and Safeguards,* pp. 220–221.

65. Ibid.

66. Export Administration Act of 1979, 50 App. U.S.C. sec. 2401–2420, 2404; Clyde H. Farnsworth, "Official Reported to Face Ouster after His Dissent on Iraq Exports," *New York Times,* April 10, 1991, p. A1; and Seymour M. Hersh, "On the Nuclear Edge," *New Yorker,* March 29, 1993, p. 56 (describing Pakistani purchases of nuclear equipment in the United States).

67. David Goodhart, "German Companies Sold Arms to Iraq," *Financial Times,* March 25, 1991, p. 1. (As of this writing, German suppliers are still concealed.)

68. Interview with Jon Jennekens, deputy director general for safeguards, IAEA, Vienna, January 23 and 24, 1992.

69. Giovanni de Briganti, "European Governments Take Steps to Tighten Military Export Controls," *Defense News,* April 1, 1991, p. 20.

70. Ramesh Jaura, "Germany: Businessmen Anxious about New Third World Export Controls," Inter Press Service, March 19, 1992. See also the chapter by Wolfgang Reinicke in this volume.

71. "CWC," Article 23, p. 821.

72. Appendix to IAEA Doc. INFCIRC/209/Rev.1, Vienna, November 1990, pp. 1–3.

73. Ashok Kapur, *International Nuclear Proliferation: Multilateral Diplomacy and Regional Aspects* (Praeger, 1979), p. 73.

74. Ibid., pp. 9–11.

75. *Communications Received from Certain Member States Regarding Guidelines for the Export of Nuclear Material, Equipment or Technology,* IAEA Doc. INFCIRC/254, Article 7, Vienna, February 28, 1978, pp. 1–7.

76. "NSG to Explore Dual-Use Controls, May Meet in Eastern Europe in 1992," *Nuclear Fuel,* vol. 16 (March 18, 1991), p. 5.

77. Michael Knapik, "Nuclear Suppliers Reach Agreement on Control of Dual-Use Items," *Nucleonics Week,* vol. 33 (April 9, 1992), p. 1. As a practical matter, the action on full-scope safeguards affects only India, Pakistan, and Israel, since NPT parties are already subject to safeguards on all peaceful nuclear activities under Article 3 of the treaty. But it also eliminated the anomaly that NPT parties had a more onerous safeguards obligation than nonsigners, which had been a source of considerable irritation to NPT non–nuclear weapon states.

78. IAEA Press Release, PR 92/12 (February 26, 1992).

79. Nolan, *Trappings of Power,* p. 121.

80. "Senate Approves Bill Setting Conditions on China MFN, but Veto Override Unlikely," *International Trade Reporter* (Bureau of National Affairs), vol. 9 (September 16, 1992), p. 1582.

81. David A. Bitzinger, "Arms to Go," *International Security,* vol. 17 (Fall 1992), pp. 85, 108.

82. Michael R. Gordon, "U.S. Accuses India on Chemical Arms," *New York Times,* September 21, 1992, p. A1.

83. Nolan, *Trappings of Power,* p. 146.

84. Abram Chayes and Antonia Handler Chayes, "To Catch a Thief: A Re-examination of Arms Control Verification and Compliance," in Aspen Strategy Group, *Balancing National Security Objectives in an Uncertain World* (Aspen, Colo., 1989).

85 A similar argument is developed in Kenneth W. Abbot, "'Trust but Verify': The Production of Information in Arms Control Treaties and Other International Agreements," *Cornell International Law Journal,* vol. 26 (Winter 1993), pp. 1–58. We are grateful for the opportunity to have discussed these issues with Abbot.

86. "Constitution of the World Health Organization," Articles 2 and 64, *United Nations Treaty Series,* vol. 14 (1948), pp. 185–285.

87. Of course, reporting would serve other functions as well as coordination. See the discussion in the section "Regime Management."

88. Timothy E. Wirth, "Confidence- and Security-Building Measures," and Adam-Daniel Rotfeld "CSBMs in Europe: A Future-Oriented Concept," in Robert E. Blackwill and F. Stephen Larrabee, eds., *Conventional Arms Control and East-West Security* (Duke University Press, 1989), p. 342–78. See the chapter by Leonard S. Spector and Jonathan Dean in this volume.

89. For a definition of prisoner's dilemma, see Ostrom, *Governing the Commons,* pp. 3–5, and also p. 39, where Ostrom notes that, in the true prisoner's dilemma, "acting independently in this situation is the result of coercion, not its absence." As to the problem of credible communication, see Thomas C. Schelling, *Strategy of Conflict* (Harvard University Press, 1980), pp. 39, 214.

90. Kosta Tsipis, David W. Hafemeister, and Penny Janeway, eds., *Arms Control Verification: The Technologies That Make It Possible* (Washington: Pergamon-Brassey's, 1986); see especially Ralph Earle II, "Verification Issues from the Point of View of the Negotiator," pp. 14–19. Both CTBT and Salt II were victims of unrealistic verification requirements.

91. Michael Krepon, "The Politics of Treaty Verification and Compliance," in Tsipis and others, *Arms Control Verification,* pp. 20–32.

92. See Abram Chayes and Antonia Handler Chayes, "Living under a Treaty Regime: Compliance, Interpretation, and Adaptation," in Antonia Handler Chayes and Paul Doty, eds., *Defending Deterrence: Managing the ABM Treaty Regime into the 21st Century* (Washington: Pergamon-Brassey's, 1989), pp. 198, 215. Indeed, there was a broader kind of assurance that the overall relationship had not descended to a level of unbounded hostility.

93. Ibid., p. 214. The experience with the Standing Consultative Commission is discussed later in this chapter.

94. Ostrom, *Governing the Commons,* pp. 186, 187.

95. Commentators have pointed out that the success of the tit-for-tat strategy in Axelrod's model depends on the assumption of perfect information about the past plays of participants. See, for example, Runge, "Institutions and the Free Rider, p. 154. See also Robert Axelrod, *The Evolution of Cooperation* (Basic Books, 1984).

96. Robert O. Keohane, "Reciprocity in International Relations," *International Organization,* vol. 40 (Winter 1986), pp. 1, 19–24.

97. See David Charny, "Nonlegal Sanctions in Commercial Relationships," *Harvard Law Review,* vol. 104 (December 1990), pp. 375, 392 ff., for economic literature on reputation effects.

98. Paul Doty and Antonia Handler Chayes, "Introduction and Scope of Study," in Chayes and Doty, *Defending Deterrence,* p. 3; and Ashton B. Carter, "Underlying Military Objectives," in ibid., p. 18.

99. Abram Chayes, "An Inquiry into the Working of Arms Control Agreements," *Harvard Law Review,* vol. 85 (March 1972), pp. 905, 946; and Carter, "Underlying Military Objectives."

100. Reporting of relevant statistical information is a common feature of regulatory treaties. See, for example, "Montreal Protocol on Substances That Deplete the Ozone Layer," September 16, 1987, Article 7, *International Legal Materials,* vol. 26 (November 1987), p. 1556; and "Articles of Agreement of the International Monetary Fund," December 27, 1945, Article 8, sec. 5, *United Nations Treaty Series,* vol. 2 (1947), pp. 40, 70 (hereafter "IMF Agreement").

101. "Treaty between the United States of America and the Union of Soviet Socialist Republics on the Limitation of Strategic Offensive Arms (SALT II)," June 18, 1979, Article 17(3), and "Memorandum of Understanding between the United States of America and the Union of Soviet Socialist Republics Regarding the Establishment of a Data Base on the Numbers of Strategic Offensive Arms, June 18, 1979," *Arms Control and Disarmaments Agreements* (U.S. Arms Control and Disarmament Agency, 1990), pp. 290, 295–97.

102. Strobe Talbott, *Endgame* (Harper, 1979), p. 98.

103. See "Treaty between the United States of America and the Union of Soviet Socialist Republics on the Elimination of Their Intermediate-Range and Shorter-Range Missiles," June 1, 1988, Article 9, and "Memorandum of Understanding Regarding the Establishment of a Data Base for the Treaty between the USSR and the United States on the Elimination of Their Intermediate-Range and Shorter-Range Missiles," *Arms Control and Disarmaments Agreements* (U.S. Arms Control and Disarmament Agency, 1990), pp. 356–58, 363–65.

104. U.S. Department of State, Bureau of Public Affairs, "Soviet Noncompliance with Arms Control Agreements," March 30, 1992, pp. 2–10.

105. Nicole Ball, "Pressing for Peace: Can Aid Induce Reform?" Overseas Development Council Policy Essay 6 (Washington, 1992), pp. 17–23, 62–63, 115–17.

106. GAO Report, "International Environment: International Agreements Are Not Well Monitored," GAO/RCED-92–43 (January 1992), pp. 23–28.

107. Occasionally, a country will simply skip its report to avoid revealing a serious violation, as was apparently the case with Panama and the whaling convention. P. Birnie, *International Regulation of Whaling: From Conservation of Whaling to Conservation of Whales and Regulation of Whale Watching* (Dobbs Ferry, N.Y.: Oceana Publications, 1985).

108. International Labor Conference, *Provisional Record,* Sixty-sixth Session (Geneva, 1980), pp. 37/4–10, 19–22.

109. International Labor Conference, *Report of the Committee of Experts on the Application of Conventions and Recommendations,* app. 2 (Geneva, 1992), pp. 530–31.

110. Strictly speaking, the reporting requirement is in the safeguards agreement and does not come into play until the party has signed such an agreement. The IAEA takes the position that all NPT parties should sign safeguards agreements, but a number have yet to do so. Since none of these have any nuclear program, the IAEA does not regard them as in violation of their obligations. In contrast, North Korea did not sign a safeguards agreement until 1992, although it adhered to the NPT in 1985. Since it certainly had some kind of a nuclear program during that period, it was in violation of its treaty obligation. The incident is unique in the history of the NPT. Interview with Hans Blix, director-general of the International Atomic Energy Agency, Vienna, January 22, 1992.

111. David E. Sanger, "North Korea Reveals More about Its Nuclear Sites," *New York Times,* May 7, 1992, p. A8.

112. David E. Sanger, "North Korea, Fighting Inspection, Renounces Nuclear Arms Treaty," *New York Times,* March 12, 1993, p. A1.

113. "North Korea Suspends Nuclear Treaty Withdrawal," *Facts on File,* vol. 53 (June 17, 1993), p. 442.

114. J. H. Ausubel and David G. Victor, "Verification of International Environmental Agreements," *Annual Review of Energy and Environment,* vol. 17 (1992), pp. 21–23.

115. In 1990 a dispute over the designation and disposition of Soviet tanks under the CFE threatened the implementation of the agreement. First, the Soviets removed some 20,000 tanks from the areas specified in the treaty before the signing of the agreement, thereby avoiding having to destroy them. Second, they redesignated several army divisions, including tanks, as naval infantry, which they subsequently claimed were exempt from the treaty. Michael R. Gordon, "Soviets Shift Many Tanks to Siberia," *New York Times,* November 15, 1990, p. A3; "The Tank War Continues, on Paper," *New York Times,* January 12, 1991, sec. 1, p. 24; and "U.S. Soviet Accord on Issue of Armies," *New York Times,* April 26, 1991, p. A7.

116. United Nations Security Council Resolution 687, UN Doc. S/RES/687, pp. 4–6. The resolution, according to its terms, did not go into effect until it was "accepted" by Iraq.

117. See Sean Côté, "A Narrative of the Implementation of Section C of United Nations Security Council Resolution 687," Occasional Paper, Harvard University, Center for Science and International Affairs, 1993. See also the discussion later in our chapter. As of this writing, Iraq has still not revealed a list of its nuclear technology suppliers. "U.N. Arms Inspectors Expect Iraq to Accept Surveillance by Copter," *New York Times,* February 17, 1993, p. A2. However, Maurizio Zifferero of the IAEA issued a statement on September 4, 1992, that "there is no longer any nuclear activity in Iraq . . . [the Iraqis] have no facilities [where they can] carry out this activity." "U.N. Says Iraqi Atom Arms Industry Is Gone," *New York Times,* September 4, 1992, p. A2; and "John H. Cushman, Jr., "Iraq Accepts Radiation Tests of Water," *New York Times,* September 8, 1992, p. A8.

118. Sanger, "North Korea Reveals Nuclear Sites."

119. There are some minor cooperative elements in the ABM treaty and SALT I. The parties undertake not to interfere with each other's NTM and not to take measures of deliberate concealment. "Limitation of Anti-Ballistic Missile Systems Treaty," October 3, 1972, Article 12 (2) and (3), 23 U.S.T. 3435; "Limitation of Strategic Offensive Arms, Interim Agreement and Protocol," October 3, 1972, Article 5 (2) and (3), 23 U.S.T. 3462. In addition, SALT II would have required advance notification of launches and "functionally related observable differences" to distinguish heavy bombers from air-launched cruise missile launchers. "Treaty between the United States and the Union of Soviet Socialist Republics on the Limitation of Strategic Offensive Arms," signed June 18, 1979, Fourth Agreed Statement, Articles 15 (2) and (3), 16 (1), and 2 (3), *Arms Control and Disarmament Agreements* (U.S. Arms Control and Disarmament Agency, 1990), pp. 159–60, 170, 269, 288–89.

120. Antonia Handler Chayes and Abram Chayes, "From Law Enforcement to Dispute Resolution: A New Approach to Arms Control Verification and Compliance," in *International Security,* vol. 14 (Spring 1990), pp. 152–54; and Chayes and Chayes, "Living under a Treaty Regime," pp. 200–01, 204–05. See also, for example, Assistant Secretary of Defense Richard Perle, "Responding to Soviet Violations Policy (RSVP) Study," Memorandum to the President, Secretary of Defense, December 1985; and "A Quarter Century of Soviet Compliance: Practices under Arms Control Commitments, 1958–1983," report prepared by the General Advisory Committee on Arms Control and Disarmament, October 1984.

121. Linda Netsch, "Fostering Compliance: The INF On-Site Inspection Experience," Harvard University Seminar on International Dispute Resolution, April 17, 1992, pp. 26–28. *Ambiguity* is the term of art for a questionable item that the teams cannot work out themselves.

122. Brad Roberts, "Chemical Disarmament and International Security," *Adelphi Papers,* vol. 267 (International Institute for Strategic Studies, 1992), pp. 22–29; and "CWC," part 4(D), pp. 840–43. See also our discussion of the BWC.

123. Roberts, "Chemical Disarmament and International Security," p. 25. See also Protocol on Inspections Procedures, in *Report of the Ad Hoc Committee on Chemical Weapons to the Conference on Disarmament,* CD 1033, August 10, 1990, p. 145. The U.S. move was criticized by, for example, William Colby and Elisa Harris, "Look Who's Barring Access to Weapons Sites," *Washington Post,* July 28, 1991, p. C7.

124. "CWC," Article 9, pp. 815–17.

125. "Intermediate-Range Nuclear Forces Treaty Implementation," in *Report to the Chairman, Committee on Governmental Affairs, U.S. Senate,* GAO/NSIAD-91–262 (September 1991), app. 4, pp. 1, 44; and Netsch, "Fostering Compliance," p. 61.

126. Netsch, "Fostering Compliance," p. 62. These are OSIA-specific costs and are additional to national intelligence costs.

127. Interview with Hans Blix, Vienna, January 22, 1992.

128. Brenda Fowler, "Atom Agency Seeks Stronger Safeguards System," *New York Times,* December 7, 1991, sec. 1, p. 3.

129. Stockholm International Peace Research Institute, *SIPRI Yearbook 1993* (Oxford University Press, 1993), p. 632. See also chapters 4 and 8 in this volume.

130. For a discussion of the role of the UN in arms control verification, see UN Group of Qualified Government Experts, *Verification and the United Nations* (New York: United Nations Department for Disarmament Affairs, 1991).

131. Interviews with Hans Blix, Vienna, January 22, 1992, and Ambassador Rolf Ekeus, Vienna, February 1992.

132. National Academy of Sciences, Panel on the Future Design and Implementation of U.S. National Security Export Controls, Panel on Science, Engineering, and Public Policy, *Finding Common Ground: U.S. Export Controls in a Changed Global Environment* (Washington: National Academy Press, 1991), pp. 61–105.

133. See, for example, U.S. Department of State, Bureau of Public Affairs, "Soviet Noncompliance with Arms Control Agreements," Special Report 136 (December 1985); "Soviet Noncompliance with Arms Control Agreements" (March 10, 1987); and "Soviet Noncompliance with Arms Control Agreements" (March 30, 1992).

134. See Michael Taylor, "Cooperation and Rationality: Notes on the Collective Action Problem and Its Solution," in Cook and Levi, eds., *Limits of Rationality,* pp. 222, 226, 234.

135. For the IMF experience, see Kendall W. Stiles, "IMF Conditionality: Coercion or Compromise," *World Development,* vol. 18 (1990) p. 959; Kendall W. Stiles, "Bargaining with Bureaucrats: Debt Negotiations in the International Monetary Fund," *International Journal of Public Administration,* vol. 9 (1987) p. 1; and A. Crockett, "Issues in the Use of Fund Resources," *Finance and Development,* vol. 19 (June 1982), p. 11. As to World Bank structural adjustment lending, see P. Mosely, "Conditionality as Bargaining Process: Structural Adjustment Lending, 1980–1986," Essays in International Finance 168 (Princeton University, Department of Economics, International Finance Section, October 1987); and R. S. Eckaus, "How the IMF Lives with Its Conditionality," *Policy Science,* vol. 19 (1986), pp. 237, 243.

136. Ernst B. Haas, *Beyond the Nation State: Functionalism and International Organization* (Stanford University Press, 1964), pp. 252, 256. However, this shift did

not come without controversy. Walter Galenson, *The International Labor Organization: An American View* (University of Wisconsin Press, 1981), p. 257. See also International Labor Conference, *Report of the Committee of Experts.*

137. Only about 30 percent of the infractions are listed in the committee of experts report. The remainder are notified directly to the country concerned with a request for information on corrective actions. A country is ordinarily given a two-year grace period before being reported by the committee of experts. Galenson, *International Labor Organization,* p. 204, n. 21.

138. Direct contacts were instituted in 1968 "in an effort to eliminate certain types of divergences," misunderstandings, and deadlocks. International Labor Conference, *Report of the Committee of Experts,* p. 675. Direct contacts are usually formally requested by a government, whose prior consent is requisite. The state has discretion over whether to invite worker and employer representatives to participate.

139. See, for example, International Labor Organization, *Report of the Committee of Experts.*

140. Poland was listed in a special paragraph in 1982 but avoided blacklisting for nonimplementation by the expedient of not appearing at the conference committee discussions. However, this resulted in an automatic blacklisting for absence, which is in some ways the most condemnatory of listings. Altogether there were more than eighty special paragraphs and blacklistings in the period, but the large majority were for reporting failures. Ibid.

141. See Abram Chayes, "Managing the Transition to a Global Warming Regime, or What to Do 'Til the Treaty Comes," in Jessica T. Matthews and others, eds., *Greenhouse Warming: Negotiating a Global Regime* (World Resources Institute, 1991), p. 61.

142. Chayes and Chayes, "Living under a Treaty Regime," p. 198.

143. "Compliance with SALT I Agreements," U.S. Department of State, July 1979; and Sidney Graybeal and Patricia Bliss McFate, "Assessing Verification & Compliance," in Chayes and Doty, *Defending Deterrence,* p. 178.

144. There has sometimes been a misconception that the SCC is an adjudicative, dispute settlement body rather than the negotiating forum that it was designed to be. See Chayes and Chayes, "Living under a Treaty Regime," pp. 204–08.

145. Ibid., p. 207.

146. Oran R. Young, "The Effectiveness of International Institutions: Hard Cases and Critical Variables," in James Rosenau and Ernst-Otto Czempiel, eds., *Governance without Government: Order and Change in World Politics* (Cambridge University Press, 1992), p. 177. See also Michael Taylor, "Cooperation and Rationality," in Karen Cook and Margaret Levi, eds., *The Limits of Rationality* (University of Chicago Press, 1990), pp. 222, 225.

147. David Swinbanks, "Japanese Importers Slide under the Wire," *Nature,* vol. 341 (September 28, 1989), p. 270; David Swinbanks, "Japan Agrees to Total Ban on Imports," *Nature,* vol. 342 (November 2, 1989), p. 7; and Michael J. Glennon, "Has International Law Failed the Elephant?" *American Journal of International Law,* vol. 84 (January 1990), pp. 1, 16.

148. Marc Levy, "The Greening of the United Kingdom: An Assessment of Competing Explanations," speech prepared for delivery at the 1991 Annual Meeting of the American Political Science Association, Washington Hilton, August 29–September 1, 1991, pp. 5–6.

149. "Conference on Security and Cooperation in Europe, Final Act," August 1, 1975, Article 10, *International Legal Materials,* vol. 14 (September 1975), p. 1296; and Max M. Kampelman, "Foreword," in Samuel F. Wells, ed., *The Helsinki Process and*

the Future of Europe, Woodrow Wilson Special Studies (Washington: Wilson Center Press, 1990), pp. xii–xv.

150. Interview with the head of the Polish Helsinki Watch Committee, 1991.

151. "Implementation of Helsinki Final Act, October 1, 1988–March 31, 1989," Special Report 182, U.S. Department of State, Bureau of Public Affairs (1989); "Fact Sheet: CSCE," *US Department of State Dispatch,* vol. 1 (October 8, 1990), p. 159; "Fact Sheet: CSCE," Summary of the President's CSCE Annual Implementation Report, *US Department of State Dispatch,* vol. 2 (June 24, 1991), p. 443; and "Helsinki Human Rights Day," *US Department of State Dispatch,* vol. 2 (August 12, 1991), p. 611.

152. See James E. Goodby, "The Diplomacy of Europe Whole and Free," in Wells, *Helsinki Process,* pp. 48–51; Joshua Muravchik, *Exporting Democracy: Fulfilling America's Destiny* (Washington: AEI Press, 1991).

153. U.S. Trade Act of 1974, subchapter 4, 19 U.S.C. 2432(a).

154. "Japan Decides to Join Ban on Trade of Ivory," *Boston Globe,* October 31, 1989, p. 7; and Jane Perlez, "Ivory Trading Ban Said to Force Factories Shut," *New York Times,* May 22, 1990, p. A14.

155. Muller, "Internalization of Principles," pp. 14–25.

156. The IAEA distinguishes between "special inspections" described in the text and "challenge inspections" provided for in the Tlatleloco Treaty, the CFE, INF, START, and the CWC. The principal difference is that the challenge inspection is initiated by a party to the treaty, as a matter of right; the special inspection is initiated by the organization, which would lead to some differences of detail in the subsequent steps. Interview with Hans Blix, Vienna, January 22, 1992.

157. See Andrew J. Pierre, *The Global Politics of Arms Sales* (Princeton University Press, 1982), pp. 275–311.

158. Matthias Dembinski, "Nonproliferation Strategies after the End of the East-West Conflict: Lessons and Perspectives," 1992.

159. National Academy of Sciences, *Finding Common Ground,* p. 86.

160. Kurt M. Campbell and others, *Soviet Nuclear Fission: Control of the Nuclear Arsenal in a Disintegrating Soviet Union* (Cambridge: Center for Science and International Affairs, CSIA Studies in International Security, November 1991), p. 41.

161. Nolan, *Trappings of Power,* p. 138.

162. For example, failure to report baseline and current consumption data of chlorofluorocarbons, as required by the Montreal Protocol, was attributed primarily to the inability of developing country parties to comply without technical and financial assistance. See *Report of the First Meeting of the Ad Hoc Group of Experts on Reporting of Data,* UNEP/OzL.Pro/WG.2/1/4 (Nairobi, December 7, 1990). Projects for these purposes are eligible for assistance under the Ozone Fund, established under the treaty to defray incremental costs of compliance for developing countries. "Montreal Protocol on Substances That Deplete the Ozone Layer, Final Act," Article 13 (Nairobi: UNEP, 1987), *International Legal Materials,* vol. 26 (November 1987), pp. 1541–61 (hereafter "Montreal Protocol"); and "London Amendments to the Montreal Protocol on Substances that Deplete the Ozone Layer, Report of the Second Meeting of the Parties to the Montreal Protocol on Substances That Deplete the Ozone Layer," Article 10, UNEP/OzL.Pro.2/3 (June 29, 1990), *International Legal Materials,* vol. 30 (March 1991), pp. 537–54 (hereafter "London Adjustments and Amendments to the Montreal Protocol").

163. Ball, "Pressing for Peace."

164. Ronald Bruce Mitchell, "From Paper to Practice: Improving Environmental Treaty Compliance," Ph.D. dissertation, Harvard University, 1992; and Ronald Bruce

Mitchell, "Intentional Oil Pollution of the Oceans: Crises," in Peter Haas, Robert Keohane, and Marc Levy, eds., *Institutions for the Earth: Sources of Effective International Environmental Protection* (MIT Press, 1993).

165. The KOBRA system is discussed more fully by Wolfgang H. Reinicke in chapter 5.

166. In its December 1992 meeting at Stockholm, the CSCE Council adopted a number of measures dealing with dispute settlement, including a convention establishing conciliation and arbitration procedures. Conciliation seems to be mandatory as between parties to the convention, but arbitration remains ad hoc unless the parties recognize compulsory jurisdiction by a separate declaration. A second decision establishes an optional conciliation procedure to be used when the parties to the dispute so agree. Finally, the council took a decision authorizing it to "direct" any two parties to seek conciliation when they have been unable to settle a dispute within a reasonable time. CSCE, "Decision on Peaceful Settlement of Disputes Including the Convention on Conciliation and Arbitration within the CSCE," *International Legal Materials,* vol. 32 (March 1993), pp. 551–71.

167. Chayes and Chayes, "From Law Enforcement to Dispute Settlement," *International Security,* vol. 14 (Spring 1990), p. 147; Gloria Duffy, project director, *Compliance and the Future of Arms Control,* Report of Project Sponsored by the Center for International Security and Arms Control, Stanford University, and Global Outlook, 1988, pp. 163–83; Graybeal and McFate, "Assessing Verification and Compliance," p. 193; and Michael Krepon, *Arms Control Verification and Compliance,* Foreign Policy Association Headline Series 270 (September–October 1984), pp. 37–45.

168. The same, of course, is true of disputes in the domestic legal system. More than 90 percent of cases actually filed in court are settled without trial, and the majority of disputes do not even reach the stage of formal filing.

169. Six of these were advisory opinions. Many others came before the court as a result of special submissions.

170. See Keith Highet, "Winning and Losing: The Commitment of the United States to the International Court—What Was It, What Is It, and Where Has It Gone?" *Transnational Law and Contemporary Problems,* vol. 1 (Spring 1991), pp. 157, 198–200.

171. "Corfu Channel," Merits, Judgment, *ICJ Reports* (1949), p. 4; "Nuclear Tests Case (*Australia* v. *France*)," Judgment, ibid. (1974), p. 253; "Nuclear Tests Case (*New Zealand* v. *France*)," Judgment, ibid. (1974), p. 457; "United States Diplomatic and Consular Staff in Teheran," ibid. (1980), p. 3; "Military and Paramilitary Activities in and against Nicaragua (*Nicaragua* v. *United States of America*)," Merits, ibid. (1986), p. 554; and "Aerial Incident of 3 July 1933, Order of 9 April 1991," ibid. (1991). There were also a number of cold war cases in which the United States and the United Kingdom sought to sue the Soviet Union or eastern European states in connection with aerial incidents, although none of the respondents had accepted the court's jurisdiction. See, for example, "Aerial Incident of 10 March 1953, Order of 14 March 1956," ibid. (1956), p. 6. The cases are summarized and discussed in Oscar Schachter, "Disputes Involving the Use of Force," in Lori Lisler Damrosch, ed., *The International Court of Justice at a Crossroads* (Dobbs Ferry, N.Y.: Transnational Publishers, 1987), pp. 223–27.

172. Leo Gross, "Compulsory Jurisdiction under the Optional Clause: History and Practice," in Damrosch, *International Court of Justice,* p. 26.

173. "UN Vienna Convention for the Protection of the Ozone Layer," March 22, 1985, Article 11(5), *International Legal Materials,* vol. 26 (November 1987), p. 1534. Other environmental agreements contain similar provisions. See "Antarctic Treaty Consultative Parties: Final Act of the Eleventh Antarctic Treaty Special Consultative Meeting and the Protocol on Environmental Protection to the Antarctic Treaty," Madrid,

Articles 11–12, *International Legal Materials,* vol. 30 (November 1991), pp. 1455–86; "UN Conference on Environment and Development Framework Convention on Climate Change," Article 14, *International Legal Materials,* vol. 31 (July 1992), pp. 849, 867; and "UN Conference on Environment and Development Convention on Biological Diversity," Article 27, and annex 2, part 2, *International Legal Materials,* vol. 31 (July 1992), pp. 818, 834, 841.

174. "London Adjustment and Amendments to the Montreal Protocol on Substances, annex 3," *Basic Documents of International Environmental Law,* vol. 3 (Boston: Graham and Trotman, 1992), pp. 1714, 1731.

175. "General Agreement on Tariffs and Trade, January 1, 1986," Article 23, *United Nations Treaty Series,* vol. 55 (1947), p. 194 (hereafter "GATT"). Originally the complaint was heard directly by the contracting parties, sitting as a group. The panel practice grew up as a way of helping the contracting parties to discharge their functions.

176. Robert E. Hudec, "GATT or GABB? The Future Design of the General Agreement on Tariffs and Trade," *Yale Law Journal,* vol. 80 (June 1971), p. 1299.

177. GATT Secretariat Trade Negotiations Committee, *Draft Final Act Embodying the Results of the Uruguay Round of Multilateral Trade Negotiations,* MTN.TNC/W/FA (Geneva, December 20, 1991).

178. "IMF Agreement," Article 18, pp. 40, 100.

179. "Decision 102-(52/11), Feb. 13, 1952," in International Monetary Fund, *Selected Decisions of the Executive Directors and Selected Documents* (Washington, September 1962), pp. 16–19.

180. "International Coffee Agreement, September 16, 1982," Article 58(1), cmnd. 9775, *Treaties and Other International Acts,* series 11095 (U.S. Department of State, 1986), pp. 1, 62–63.

181. The interpretation of the IAEA safeguards agreement to permit special inspections seems to have been made by an informal consensus of the Board of Governors. IAEA Press Release, PR 92/12 (Vienna, February 26, 1992).

182. "Protocol to the Treaty between the United States and the USSR on the Limitation of Anti-Ballistic Missile Systems," *Arms Control and Disarmaments Agreements* (U.S. Arms Control and Disarmament Agency, 1990), p. 182.

183. "UN Vienna Convention for the Protection of the Ozone Layer," Articles 2, 3, 4, 5, pp. 1529–31.

184. "Montreal Protocol" and "London Adjustments and Amendments to the Montreal Protocol," *International Legal Materials,* vol. 30 (March, 1991), p. 539.

185. See Antonia Handler Chayes and Abram Chayes, "Nonproliferation Regimes in the Aftermath of the Gulf War," in J. S. Nye, Jr. and R. K. Smith, eds., *After the Storm: Lessons from the Gulf War* (Lanham, Md.: Madison Books, 1992), pp. 49, 75.

186. "Convention on International Civil Aviation," signed at Chicago on December 7, 1944, Article 90, *United Nations Treaty Series,* vol. 15 (1948), pp. 295, 296, 356.

187. See "Montreal Protocol," Article 2(9) as amended, pp. 1541, 1553.

188. See David A. Koplow, "When Is an Amendment Not an Amendment?: Modification of Arms Control Agreements without the Senate," *University of Chicago Law Review,* vol. 59 (Summer 1992), pp. 981–1072.

189. "Concluding Act of the Negotiation on Personnel Strength of Conventional Armed Forces in Europe, CFE-1A," reported in *US Department of State Dispatch,* vol. 3 (July 13, 1992), pp. 560–61, and "25 Nations Sign CFE Follow-On," *Arms Control Today,* vol. 22 (July–August 1992), p. 29.

190. 22 U.S.C. sec. 2573. Upon the expiration of the SALT I Interim Agreement on Limitations of Strategic Offensive Arms in 1977, the United States and the Soviet Union made parallel unilateral statements declaring their intention not to take any action

inconsistent with the provisions of the agreement provided the other party exercised similar restraint. See Barry E. Carter and Phillip R. Trimble, *International Law* (Little, Brown, 1991), pp. 83–84. When it proved impossible to secure Senate approval for SALT II, a similar procedure was used. The World Court has held that unilateral declarations of this sort can give rise to international legal obligations, particularly if made in a reciprocal context. "Legal Status of Eastern Greenland, Judgment," PCIJ Series, *Judgements, Orders, and Advisory Opinions,* A/B (The Hague, 1933), no. 53, p. 22; "Nuclear Tests Case (*Australia* v. *France*)," and "Nuclear Tests Case (*New Zealand* v. *France*)."

191. Abram Chayes and Antonia Handler Chayes, "On Compliance," in *International Organization,* vol. 17 (Spring 1993), p. 1.

192. Glennon, "Has International Law Failed the Elephant?" p. 16.

193. The establishment of a coercive sanction system is itself a formidable collective action problem. See Taylor, "Cooperation and Rationality," pp. 222, 225; and Elster, *Cement of Society,* pp. 40–41.

194. Taylor, "Cooperation and Rationality," pp. 222, 225.

195. The following account is based on Côté, "Narrative of Implementation of Section C."

196. "U.N. Inspectors Fly to Iraq to Destroy Chemical Arms," *New York Times,* January 22, 1993, p. A6.

197. In the parking lot case, for example, Chief Inspector David Kay led a team in search of documents, reportedly cached in several buildings in downtown Baghdad, that would reveal the extent of Iraq's nuclear program. In its first attempt, on September 23, 1991, the team was successful in gaining entry to a building in which they found a number of documents. The accompanying Iraqis, seeing the volume of materials the team had uncovered, detained the forty inspectors for about twelve hours in a parking lot near the building and ultimately seized the documents.

In its next effort the following day, the team was again able to find a significant amount of documentation. This time, each of the members of the team kept some of the documents on his person, so that the Iraqis would have had to use physical violence to recover them. This the Iraqis were unwilling to do. Instead they detained the forty-four inspectors in the parking lot.

A coordinated campaign of pressure began with a Security Council resolution condemning Iraq's action and demanding the immediate release of the inspectors. Kay kept up the pressure from the parking lot with frequent telephone reports by satellite to the Security Council and the international press. The use of video cameras by members of the team seemed to intimidate Iraqi officers. Members of the Security Council made warning statements to Iraq's UN representative. Speculative stories in the U.S. press suggested that the administration was considering military action. Iraq made a formal protest, contesting the legality of the inspection, but the Security Council refuted this contention in a strongly worded statement.

On the morning of September 25, after the inspectors had been in the parking lot for two days, the secretary-general called in the Iraqi foreign minister to demand that they be set free immediately. That evening, Iraq sent a letter to the Security Council indicating that the inspectors would be permitted to leave after they and the Iraqi authorities prepared a joint inventory of the documents and photographs the team had taken. The next day, the UN stated that it "had no objections in this particular case to a joint inventory," and the crisis was over. The inspectors were released, and the documents they brought back provided the first evidence of the nature and extent of Iraq's clandestine nuclear weapons program and the international companies from which Iraq had procured equipment and materials.

198. As to nuclear weapons capability, see comments by Zifferero, reported in "U.N. Says Iraqi Atom Arms Industry Is Gone," *New York Times,* September 4, 1992, p. A8.

199. Peter Haas, Robert Keohane and Marc Levy, "Improving the Effectiveness of International Environmental Institutions," in Haas, Keohane, and Levy, eds., *Institutions for the Earth,* p. 397.

200. UN Conference on Environment and Development (Rio de Janeiro, Brazil, 1992), *Agenda 21* (Conches, Switzerland: UNCED, 1992), chap. 38, pp. 275–76, paras. 38.11–38.14.

201. We confine this discussion to the problems of applying sanctions and their efficacy if applied. In addition, the possibility that they might be applied, even if quite remote, no doubt has a deterrent effect.

202. "Military and Paramilitary Activities in and against Nicaragua (*Nicaragua* v. *United States of America*)," pp. 93–97. Most international lawyers regard the prohibition against the use of force as jus cogens, that is, not subject to derogation by consent or agreement.

203. See, for example, Thomas M. Franck, "Who Killed Article 2(4)? or: Changing Norms Governing the Use of Force by States," in *American Journal of International Law,* vol. 64 (October 1970), p. 809.

204. Every instance of transborder use of force since 1945, whether by the Soviet Union, the United States, China, India, or Vietnam, was overwhelmingly condemned at least in the General Assembly and was sometimes the object of economic sanctions or other forceful response. Oscar Schachter, "Self-Defense and the Rule of Law," *American Journal of International Law,* vol. 83 (April 1989), pp. 259, 263.

205. "Charter of the Organization of American States," April 30, 1948, entered into force December 13, 1951, Article 15, *United Nations Treaty Series,* vol. 119 (1952), pp. 48, 56 (hereafter "OAS Charter").

206. "Definition of Aggression," G.A. Resolution 599, UN GAOR, session 6, 368th meeting, U.N. Doc. A/2087, January 31, 1952; and "Consideration of Principles of International Law concerning Friendly Relations and Cooperation among States in Accordance with the Charter of the United Nations," G.A. Resolution 2181, UN GAOR, session 21, 1489th meeting, UN Doc. A/6547, December 12, 1966. But see "Helsinki Final Act," Article 6, *International Legal Materials,* vol. 31 (November 1992), pp. 1385, 1408–13.

207. G. C. Hufbauer, J. J. Schott, and K. A. Elliott, *Economic Sanctions Reconsidered,* 2d ed. (Washington: Institute for International Economics, 1990), pp. 92–93, 106, 111–14.

208. See San L. Lam, "Economic Sanctions and the Success of Foreign Policy Goals," *Japan and the World Economy,* vol. 2 (September 1990), pp. 239–47.

209. Hufbauer and others, *Economic Sanctions Reconsidered,* p. 93, citing M. F. Malloy, *Economic Sanctions and U.S. Trade* (Little, Brown, 1990), p. 626. A large number of Hufbauer's cases concerned human rights violations, property expropriations, or nuclear proliferation, in all of which economic sanctions are mandated by Congress, in each instance over the objection of the executive branch. A possible exception to the generally disappointing record of unilateral economic sanctions is the U.S. use of trade sanctions under Section 301 of the Trade Act of 1974. See Alan O. Sykes, "Constructive Unilateral Threats in International Commercial Relations: The Limited Case for Section 301," *Law and Policy in International Business,* vol. 23 (Spring 1992), pp. 263, 291.

210. Ball, "Pressing for Peace," pp. 75–76, quoting Barber Conable's Bank annual meeting speech, September 25, 1989. In his closing address to the 1991 IMF annual

meeting, Michel Camdessus said, "As regards military spending, I was impressed by the broad support for our aim to study more carefully the problem. An immediate priority must be to collect full and accurate information and analyze the economic implications." "Pressing for Peace," p. 46, citing IMF Press Release 64, October 17, 1991.

211. Ball, "Pressing for Peace," p. 63.

212. Ibid., p. 85 (Pakistan), p. 86 (India). See also "IMF-IBRD Assistance Conditional on 9 p.c. Defense Cut," *Dawn* (Karachi, Pakistan), September 14, 1991; "Defense Spending Freeze May Appease Creditors," *The Muslim,* April 1, 1992, in Foreign Broadcast Information Service, *Daily Report: Near East and South Asia,* April 2, 1992, pp. 39–40. These policies of the international institutions can be reinforced by coordinated actions of bilateral aid donors. Ball, "Pressing for Peace," pp. 87–89.

213. Ball, "Pressing for Peace," pp. 115–17.

214. "Articles of Agreement of the International Bank for Reconstruction and Development," Article 3, sec. 5(b), Article 4, sec. 10, *United Nations Treaty Series,* vol. 2 (1947), pp. 48, 134, 146. See also Ibrahim F. I. Shihata, *The World Bank in a Changing World: Selected Essays* (Boston: Martinus Nijhoff, 1991), pp. 62–79; "IMF Agreement," Article 4, sec. 3(b); and Joseph Gold, "Political Considerations Are Prohibited by the Articles of Agreement When the Fund Considers Requests for Use of Resources," *IMF Survey,* May 23, 1983, pp. 146–48.

215. Shihata, *World Bank in a Changing World,* pp. 106–07. The author suggests that this duty would not be "enforceable."

216. Ibid., pp. 99–104. Nevertheless, lending to these countries dropped off substantially in the following years. The World Bank lending handbook says it will not provide project financing for a project that violates a state's obligation under an environmental treaty by which it is bound, but the application of environmental standards more broadly to lending activities of the Bank is barely beginning, although the economic relevance is clear.

217. Ibid., pp. 76–77.

218. Ibid., p. 79.

219. Ball, "Pressing for Peace," p. 102.

220. "Suppression of African Slave Trade by the President [Lincoln] of the United States" (1862), 12 Stat. 1225, *U.S. Treaty Series,* vol. 126 (GPO, 1911), p. 3.

221. "CWC," p. 882.

222. "GATT," Article 20(h), p. 192.

223. "London Adjustments and Amendments to the Montreal Protocol," Article 4, p. 546.

224. "GATT," Article 21(b), p. 194.

225. Lewis A. Dunn and James A. Schear, "Combatting Chemical Weapons Proliferation: The Role of Sanctions," Henry L. Stimson Center Occasional Paper 3 (Washington, April 1991), p. 9.

226. Roberts, "Chemical Disarmament and International Security," p. 29.

227. "CWC," Article 12(3), p. 819.

228. Louis B. Sohn, "Expulsion or Forced Withdrawal from an International Organization," *Harvard Law Review,* vol. 77 (June 1964), p. 1381. Sohn classifies organizations into those (1) without express expulsion or suspension provisions, (2) in which expulsion is tied to expulsion from the UN, and (3) providing for expulsion or suspension for failure to fulfill the obligations of membership. Sohn notes that "of the more than one hundred organizations [that are not specialized agencies of the UN, most] do not have provisions on the subject" (p. 1409).

229. See Mark F. Imber, *The USA, ILO, UNESCO, and IAEA: Politicization and Withdrawal in the Specialized Agencies* (St. Martin's, 1989).

230. "Letter Dated September 29, 1992, from the Under-Secretary-General, the Legal Counsel, Addressed to the Permanent Representatives of Bosnia and Herzegovina and Croatia to the United Nations," Annex to Note by the Secretary-General on Agenda Item 8 of the 47th Session of the UN General Assembly, A/47/485 (September 30, 1992), states: "While the General Assembly has stated unequivocably that the Federal Republic of Yugoslavia (Serbia and Montenegro) cannot automatically continue the membership of the former Socialist Federal Republic of Yugoslavia . . . the only practical consequence that the Resolution draws is that the Federal Republic of Yugoslavia (Serbia and Montenegro) shall not participate (emphasis in original) in the work of the General Assembly . . . its subsidiary organs, nor conferences and meetings convened by it. On the other hand, the Resolution neither terminates nor suspends Yugoslavia's membership in the Organization. Consequently, the seat and nameplate remain as before, but in Assembly bodies, representatives of the Federal Republic of Yugoslavia (Serbia and Montenegro) cannot sit behind the sign 'Yugoslavia.'"

231. "Resolution 6, Eighth Meeting of Consultation of Ministers of Foreign Affairs," January 31, 1962, Pan American Union, Department of Legal Affairs, *Inter-American Treaty of Reciprocal Assistance Applications,* vol. 2, annex (OAS, 1964), p. 239.

232. Craig R. Whitney, "Belgrade Suspended by European Security Group," *New York Times,* July 9, 1992, p. A13.

233. *Recommendation of the Security Council of 19 September 1992,* UN Doc. A47/1, September 22, 1992; and "Letter Dated 29 September 1992 from the Under-Secretary-General."

234. John H. Spence, "Africa at the UN: Some Observations," *International Organizations,* vol. 16 (Summer 1962), pp. 375, 378; and Richard Bissell, *Apartheid and International Organizations* (Boulder, Colo.: Westview Press, 1977).

235. "OAS Charter," Article 25, incorporates by reference the "Inter-American Treaty of Reciprocal Assistance (Rio Treaty)," which contains the sanctioning authority. Articles 3, 6, 8, 20, 62, *United Nations Treaty Series,* vol. 119 (1952), pp. 48, 52–58, 60, 72.

236. J. L. Kunz, "Legality of the Security Council Resolutions of June 25 and 27, 1950," *American Journal of International Law,* vol. 45 (January 1951), p. 137.

237. "Rhodesia: UN Security Council Resolution 232" (December 16, 1966), *International Legal Materials,* vol. 6 (January 1969), pp. 141–43; "South Africa: UN Security Council Resolution 418" (November 4, 1977), ibid., vol. 16 (November 1977), pp. 1548–49; "Libya: UN Security Council Resolution 748" (March 31, 1992), ibid., vol. 31 (May 1992), pp. 749–52; and "Yugoslavia: UN Security Council Resolution 713" (September 25, 1991), ibid., vol. 31 (November 1992), pp. 1427–32.

238. Boutros Boutros-Ghali, "An Agenda for Peace: Preventative Diplomacy, Peacemaking and Peace-keeping," Report of the secretary-general pursuant to the statement adopted by the summit meeting of the Security Council on January 31, 1992, in *International Legal Materials,* vol. 31 (July 1992), pp. 953, 966.

239. Kenneth B. Noble, "Liberian Conflict Engulfs Neighbor," *New York Times,* April 16, 1991, p. A7.

240. "CWC," Article 12, p. 819.

241. Campbell and others, "Soviet Nuclear Fission," p. 3.

242. U.S. Department of State, Office of Legal Advisor, *Treaties in Force as of January 1, 1993* (March 1992), p. 364.

FOUR

Cooperative Security: Assessing the Tools of the Trade

Leonard S. Spector and Jonathan Dean

BY LATE 1993 an extensive and diverse array of international arrangements that reflect the concept of cooperative security were in evidence globally, regionally, or bilaterally—and important new arrangements were being implemented. In this chapter we provide a framework for visualizing a comprehensive cooperative security system, paying particular attention to the impact on states at different levels of military capability, and we examine in detail three key nodes of such a cooperative security system that are now emerging. In undertaking this analysis, we also highlight the limitations of existing arrangements when viewed against the criteria outlined by Antonia and Abram Chayes in chapter 3.

A Conceptual Framework

We first examine the range of threats that a cooperative security system must confront. We then describe the international arrangements that are encompassed by cooperative security.

Threats of Concern

Cooperative security has been defined as "in essence, a commitment to regulate the size, technical composition, investment patterns, and operational practices of all military forces by mutual consent for mutual benefit."[1] This concept refers to the armed forces of nation states, not to some future force of genuine international character. The application of the concept today must therefore

We wish to acknowledge the valuable contribution of James Macdonald Baker, whose skilled research greatly assisted us in completing the chapter.

take account of the extraordinary disparity in existing levels of military power among nations. This disparity runs the gamut from the ability of the United States to strike targets virtually anywhere on earth with nuclear-armed missiles in a matter of minutes to the inability of Somalia to muster the military force necessary even to maintain order within its own territory. Cooperative security seeks the harmonization and regulation of military capabilities among all states as an idealized norm, although, in reality, the concept must be applied in a world where radical differences in military power of states are likely to endure indefinitely.

TRADITIONAL THREATS FROM PEERS AND SUPERIORS. To enjoy the mutual benefits of regulated military establishments, states must believe that they are not threatened by their "peers"—that is, by their proximate or traditional adversaries, which possess roughly comparable military might. In addition, however, they must perceive that they are not threatened by their intra- and extraregional "superiors" in the global military pecking order. In other words, small states, such as Grenada and Panama, that might participate in a carefully calibrated agreement harmonizing forces in their region might also demand that the United States and other large powers also accept restraints limiting their global power-projection capabilities, including nuclear armaments.

Even if they do not eliminate the military advantages of superior powers, cooperative security arrangements among peers can be effective as long as the participants in the arrangements do not perceive themselves to be threatened by more powerful states. For example, the elaborate structures of reassurance provided by the Conventional Armed Forces in Europe (CFE) Treaty and the Conference on Security and Cooperation in Europe (CSCE) have been embraced with enthusiasm by their nonnuclear participants, even though they do not eliminate the potential nuclear threats posed by Britain, France, Russia, and the United States. This anomalous situation emerged originally because the nonnuclear parties to these accords believed that any nuclear threats to them would be effectively neutralized by the mutual deterrence projected by the nuclear weapon state participants. Today East-West nuclear deterrence is no longer the central principle, but the CFE and CSCE continue to enjoy support because the nonnuclear participants believe that, with the end of the cold war and the collapse of the Soviet Union, the likelihood of nuclear threats from the now more cooperative successor states has greatly lessened or that these potential threats continue to be neutralized by U.S., British, and French forces.

Thus, an initial premise that must be kept in mind in understanding the concept of cooperative security is that for the objectives of such a system to be achieved, it must address, either by formal or informal means, the threats from both peers and superior powers.

NEW THREATS FROM PEERS AND INFERIORS. The spread of nuclear, biological, and chemical weapons and associated missile delivery systems to additional states introduces new complexities to this scheme. Acquisition of these capabilities may enable a state to vault to a significantly higher military stratum than the one it formerly occupied. Such shifts could allow states in inferior ranks to challenge those that were long considered their military betters, or they can pose new threats to former equals. A newly nuclear-capable Pakistan, for example, was able to confront India during the South Asian war scare of 1990 in a manner that would have been unthinkable a decade earlier, when India enjoyed overwhelming conventional and nuclear superiority.[2]

Similarly, American concerns about the possible acquisition of nuclear arms by Iran and North Korea reflect the fears of a global power about potential new threats from "below." The acquisition of weapons of mass destruction or dramatically improved delivery systems can also unsettle military balances among rough equals by propelling a party in such a system to a significantly higher tier of strategic capability. This occurred, for example, when the Soviet Union found in 1945 that the United States had acquired nuclear arms and when the United States experienced comparable concerns in the early 1960s, as the result of the scare over the supposed missile gap with Moscow.[3]

Finally, states that have pledged to defend less powerful allies or that must protect territories or other vital interests at great distance must also be concerned about new challenges from nations that may be weaker on a global scale than the protector state but that may be quite strong locally. Great Britain confronted such a threat, for example, when Argentina occupied the Falklands in 1982, as did the United States when Iraq invaded Kuwait in 1990.

These factors—in particular the spread of weapons of mass destruction—extend the range of threats that a cooperative security system must confront. As such, a second premise for understanding the concept is that a cooperative security system must help avert new challenges from traditionally weaker states, as well as the sudden emergence of new superior powers from among the state's current rough equals.

In highly simplified terms, a successful cooperative security regime would have to offer reassurance to states at each level of military capability: first, that they were not threatened by nations at the same level (usually also in the same region) or at higher levels on the chart; and second, that new threats from states of lower or equal rank were unlikely to emerge. Finally, without an effective mechanism for collective enforcement of cooperative security norms, no state could feel safe from more potent nations that are able to project power in its vicinity.

A ranking of national military capabilities will help make this analysis more concrete and assist in evaluating the extent to which certain existing cooperative security arrangements have begun to address this complex of threats. Table 4-1 provides such a ranking.

Arrangements of Interest

A host of international arrangements are in place today that foster cooperative relations among states and seek to reduce the risk or intensity of interstate

Table 4-1. *Tiers of Military Capability*

Category and states	*Capabilities*
Superpower United States	Able to project massive advanced conventional and nuclear military power globally.
Major powers France, China, Russia, United Kingdom	Able to project substantial nuclear power globally and, except for China, able to project some conventional power globally.
Advanced industrialized powers Nonnuclear members of NATO and former Warsaw Pact; Australia; Japan; Sweden; Switzerland; Ukraine	Advanced conventional forces but projection capabilities largely limited to immediate region.
Nuclear regional powers India, Israel, Pakistan	Able to use nuclear weapons and project conventional power in immediate region. (Pakistani conventional capabilities more limited.)
Heavily armed regional powers seeking nuclear weapons Iran, Iraq, Libya, North Korea, Syria	Able to project conventional power regionally (including ballistic missiles and chemical weapons); potential challenge to "superior" powers and regional rivals, if nuclear weapons obtained.
Heavily armed regional powers Egypt, Saudi Arabia, South Africa (nuclear-capable), South Korea, Taiwan, Thailand, Vietnam	Limited regional power projection capabilities; not seeking nuclear arms; some possess ballistic missiles, chemical weapons.
Other regional states Other states in Africa, Asia, Europe, Latin America	Varying degrees of armaments and localized conventional force projection capabilities.

conflict. Of concern here are those that specifically seek to constrain the organization, armaments, deployment, operation, and investment patterns of national military establishments to make them less threatening; those that focus on the prevention and management of interstate crises; and those that provide for collective enforcement of cooperative security norms in the event of violations. Cooperative security, as it is used here, does not encompass international initiatives to deal with domestic conflicts, ethnic strife, forced migrations, and other intrastate events, even though these sometimes lead to interstate conflict.[4]

Figure 4-1. *Basic Objectives and Arrangements of a Cooperative Security Regime*

For states at each tier of military power, ideal cooperative security arrangements would	• Constrain threatening military establishments. • Help prevent and manage crises with potential adversaries. • Provide for collective enforcement of regime norms.	*vis-à-vis*	• Militarily superior states and existing peer states, so as to reduce prevailing threats. • Weaker states and peer states, so as to avert potential new threats from their development of weapons of mass destruction, acquisition of dramatic new conventional capabilities, or aggression against distant territories or interests of the state to be reassured.

As to the hierarchy of military capabilities sketched in table 4-1, in an idealized, comprehensive cooperative security system, all states at all levels of military capability would enjoy the benefits of each type of cooperative security arrangement with respect to every potential adversary that they might confront. Figure 4-1 summarizes these relationships.

In practice, arrangements that attempt to constrain military establishments take a variety of forms that include unilateral policies of restraint, confidence-building measures, arms control agreements, and nonproliferation regimes (including supplier country–sponsored efforts to control transfers of various military technologies or equipment). Provisions for crisis prevention and management are sometimes included in such arrangements, but these objectives have in the past been most successfully advanced in separate international undertakings or through multilateral organizations, such as the United Nations and various regional bodies. Collective security is provided for in the UN Charter, in the charter of many regional organizations, and in various military alliances.

The Three Key Nodes of Cooperative Security Today

The cooperative security measures that are in place or on the horizon in the international system today are, of course, far from achieving universal coverage, and as a practical matter, constitute a multidimensional patchwork. Many specific arrangements, for example, have a limited geographic ambit or are narrowly focused on particular types of weaponry. Some emerging arrangements, such as a universally accepted ban on the possession of chemical weapons, will affect virtually every state more or less equally. Other arrangements, such as the Treaty on the Non-Proliferation of Nuclear Weapons (NPT), enhance the security of states differentially, with the nuclear weapon states, in the case of this treaty, enjoying a separate preferred status. Disparities in transparency provisions, review and assessment capabilities, and enforcement mechanisms—among the key criteria outlined in chapter 3—also mean that some cooperative security arrangements are likely to prove more effective in reassuring participants than other such arrangements.

Force reductions by the major powers, such as those under the CFE treaty or the parallel decisions of the United States and the Soviet Union to withdraw land- and sea-launched tactical nuclear weapons, affect the global military map according to yet a different pattern, enhancing the security of other major powers as well as that of lesser powers. Still another reflection of the patchwork nature of current cooperative security arrangements is that, in some regions, there are so many cooperative security measures in place that together they approximate an idealized system, whereas in other regions key adversaries have yet to take even the most basic step toward cooperative security, even refusing to grant each other diplomatic recognition.

Despite this uneveness and diversity, it is possible today to discern three major hubs or "nodes" of cooperative security that are growing and that may provide a basis for an eventual global cooperative security system. Each of these nodes is important in its own right, but it is where the three intersect that an especially potent cooperative security system is being created.

The first node is the cooperative security apparatus emerging in Europe, which has become closely intertwined with U.S-Russian arms control measures in a mutually reinforcing structure. The central elements of this node are the CSCE process and the CFE, Open Skies, and nonproliferation treaties; initiatives toward European economic, political, and military integration; and with respect to U.S.-Russian nuclear weapons, the Intermediate-Range Nuclear Forces (INF) Treaty, and when ratified, the two Strategic Arms Reduction Talks treaties (START I and II).

The second node is the global network of restraints aimed at curbing the spread of weapons of mass destruction, a network that appears to be expanding and gaining strength. The central elements of this regime are the NPT and other components of the nuclear nonproliferation regime, such as the International Atomic Energy Agency (IAEA) and the Nuclear Suppliers Group (NSG); the 1925 Geneva Protocol prohibiting the first use of chemical and the actual use of biological weapons, the Australia Group, and the Chemical Weapons Convention (CWC), which, when it enters into force, will include a verification organization and export control system; the Biological Weapons Convention (BWC); and the Missile Technology Control Regime (MTCR).

The third node, which is slowly increasing in acceptance by the international community and, in particular, by the United States, is a broad rule of military self-restraint. In simplified terms it provides that, except in self-defense, military force may be used against nations only under multilateral auspices. The central elements of this node are the formal and informal restrictions on the unilateral use of force adopted by individual states, stated codes of conduct for multilateral military intervention "to maintain international peace and security" contained in the UN Charter,[5] and a number of regional pacts. These have been reinforced by the recent actions and declarations of the United States and other major powers to implement such strictures. This node remains the most inchoate of the three, but because it is so essential to a global cooperative security regime, its emergence, even in its current rudimentary state, is of great significance.

As discussed elsewhere in this volume, many other valuable cooperative security arrangements are emerging at the regional level, including such unexpectedly hopeful initiatives as the Middle East Peace Talks and the nuclear nonproliferation accords between Argentina and Brazil and between North and South Korea. Such regional arrangements could emerge as significant additional nodes of cooperative security, on the model seen in Europe. These arrangements are highlighted in the appendix to this chapter. At the present time, however, none possess the complexity or geographic scope of the three major cooperative nodes and, accordingly, are not discussed further in this analysis.

The remainder of this chapter describes in detail and then assesses each of these three major nodes, first by using the five design criteria set out in chapter 3 and second by evaluating them from the perspective of participating states.

The First Node: Cooperative Security in Europe

Today Europe enjoys an unusually comprehensive regional system of interlocking cooperative institutions and agreements. Europe is a particularly useful model for cooperative security because its security problems are at the same time probably more acute while its peacemaking institutions are more fully developed than elsewhere in the world. Europe is a good test case too, because the governments participating in these institutions, which include the governments of the United States and Canada (with the exception of Japan, all the major industrial states of the world), are determined to make multilateral cooperative security arrangements succeed. Consequently, the relative success or failure of the European peacemaking experiment over the next several years will have a decisive impact on the pattern of multilateral cooperative security at the global level.

After two world wars, a cold war, and two totalitarian dictatorships that together took more than 100 million human lives, the states of Europe and the

North American states that have been involved in these crises want to do everything in their power to prevent the repetition of tragedies like these. The result has been a series of confidence-building measures and arms control agreements, new institutions for multilateral peacemaking, and the expansion of existing institutions of a multiplicity and scope unparalleled in human history.

KEY ELEMENTS. Since France joined the nuclear club in 1960, there have been no additional nuclear weapon states in Europe, and all European countries, except for a number of the successor states of the Soviet Union whose status is discussed below, are non–nuclear weapon state parties to the NPT. Thus they have formally renounced nuclear arms and permit comprehensive inspections by the IAEA of their nuclear activities.[6] Britain, France, and Russia (as successor to the USSR) are nuclear weapon state parties to the pact, which prohibits their transferring nuclear weapons to any non–nuclear weapon state or otherwise assisting such states to acquire nuclear arms. The NATO alliance and, during its life, the Warsaw Pact, provided nuclear deterrent umbrellas to the states of Europe that reduced incentives for the acquisition of nuclear arms.

Against this stable nuclear backdrop and the rudimentary beginnings in the 1975 Helsinki Accords, a major expansion of cooperative measures for Europe began in the period of Soviet president Mikhail Gorbachev's rule and is continuing. The CSCE is the most comprehensive of the European security institutions, both in scope and membership. Its membership expanded to fifty-two states from the original thirty-five states after the collapse of the Soviet Union and Yugoslavia. Besides NATO member states, European neutral states, and those of eastern Europe, the CSCE now includes the three Baltic states, the twelve Soviet successor states, Slovenia, Croatia, and Bosnia-Herzegovina. (The membership of rump Yugoslavia—Serbia and Montenegro—has been suspended.)[7]

Starting with a provision in the Helsinki Accords for voluntary advance notification of military maneuvers exceeding a total of 25,000 military personnel,[8] three successive rounds of confidence-building negotiations organized by the CSCE produced agreements in 1986, 1990, and 1992. The program of CSCE confidence-building measures now provides for advance notification of ground and air forces maneuvers involving more than 9,000 troops, and for observations of activities involving 13,000 troops or more and 3,500 amphibious and parachute troops by other CSCE member states, and for restriction of the maximum size of these activities.[9] This complex of measures eliminates most possibilities of preparing for surprise attack under the guise of maneuvers or of using military maneuvers for the purpose of political intimidation.

The program of CSCE confidence-building measures also provides for exchange and discussion of data on armed forces, production of arms, and defense budgets; for advance notice of field deployment of new models of tanks, artillery, and aircraft; and for some verification of these obligations. The Open Skies Treaty (signed in March 1992) provides for an annual quota of low-altitude overflights by aircraft equipped with standard cameras and sensors over the territory of twenty-seven signatory states, including Russia, Canada, and the United States (as the largest countries, Russia and Belarus combined and the United States must each accept up to forty-two overflights a year), as well as for sharing the information generated. These overflights, which will also be used to verify the CFE, can provide timely warning of unannounced large force concentrations and other unusual military activities. The information is provided in a form accessible to all member states, particularly those that, unlike the United States and Russia, do not have their own developed capabilities for satellite imaging. The treaty is open for participation by all CSCE member states and by states in other parts of the world.[10]

The INF treaty, signed in 1987 between the United States and the Soviet Union, provides for the destruction and prohibition of further production of all surface-to-surface missiles of ranges between 500 and 5,500 kilometers deployed by the two countries in Europe.[11] Both countries have reported that the verified missile destruction required by the treaty has been satisfactorily completed.[12] In September and October 1991 Presidents George Bush and Gorbachev agreed to augment the treaty by withdrawing from ground deployment and naval vessels throughout the world, including Europe, all nuclear warheads designed for delivery by tactical range missiles, artillery, and land mines, leaving only some U.S. air-delivered tactical range nuclear weapons deployed outside national borders.[13] In July 1992 the United States announced the completion of the withdrawal of its tactical weapons from Europe except for air-delivered weapons.[14]

The CFE treaty was signed in November 1990 and entered into effect in July 1992 after the Soviet successor states had agreed on allocating among themselves the weapons permitted under the treaty to the armed forces of the former Soviet Union. The treaty eliminated the large numerical preponderance of the former Warsaw Pact states over the NATO states in tanks, artillery, armored combat vehicles, attack helicopters, and combat aircraft and established a numerical ceiling on the holding of these arms by each of the signatory states, including the Soviet successor states.[15] An executive agreement among CFE participating states concluded in July 1992 also placed a ceiling on their active duty military manpower and on reserve personnel called to active duty.[16] The collapse of the Soviet Union and the elimination of its communist regime dissolved the political antagonism underlying the NATO–Warsaw Pact military confrontation. Nonetheless, the CFE treaty still has great value in establishing force levels for all signatory states, levels that can be verified by all of these nations. It is therefore an indispensable framework for security, political, and economic cooperation in Europe.

And the cooperative process is ongoing. The Helsinki summit meeting of leaders of governments participating in the CSCE, held in July 1992, established a Forum on Security Cooperation, a new channel of negotiation for further confidence-building and arms control measures. This forum is focusing on extending CFE-style limits to the European neutral states ("harmonizing"); organizing discussion of the long-term defense planning and budgets of member states; developing stabilization measures for localized crises; and providing data exchanges covering all territory of member states, including Russia and the United States, to include naval vessels.[17]

While one group of CSCE negotiators was developing new confidence-building measures, a second group was developing permanent institutions for the CSCE. As approved at the Paris summit (November 1990) and at the Helsinki summit (July 1992), these institutions include (1) regular summit meetings at two-year intervals; (2) annual meetings of foreign ministers; (3) a Committee of Senior Officials from participating governments meeting every three months (in practice, it has been much more frequent); (4) a secretary-general and a permanent secretariat to service these meetings; (5) an Office for Democratic Institutions and Human Rights, whose goal is to promote both objectives, especially in the former communist states of eastern Europe and the Soviet Union;[18] (6) the Forum on Security Cooperation just discussed; (7) a Conflict Prevention Centre, where military information is exchanged and unusual military activities can be investigated at the request of a participating government; (8) a high commissioner for national minorities, whose job is to investigate, mediate, and warn of minority frictions that could lead to conflict; and (9) a common communications system.[19]

In addition, the CSCE has adopted procedures for fact finding in human rights cases and for convening umpires or arbitrators in persistent interstate disputes (participants are obligated to call on umpires or arbitrators, though not to accept their verdict). It has also established a conciliation and arbitration court for those members that wish to subscribe to it (the United States and the United Kingdom do not). And the CSCE has exercised the capacity to send observers, fact finders, and mediators to trouble spots.

The CSCE is a consensus-based organization, but it can depart from consensus to convene emergency sessions, summon a participating state to account for unusual military activities among its armed forces, oblige a state to accept a fact-finding mission in cases of alleged human rights violations, and condemn the actions of a member state or suspend it from membership in the organization, as was done with Yugoslavia by the leaders meeting at the Helsinki summit. The CSCE also has an assembly of parliamentarians from member states, which held its first full-scale meeting in Budapest in July 1992.

In response to outbreaks of ethnic and nationalistic violence in Yugoslavia, and in Moldova, Nagorno-Karabakh, and other Soviet successor states, the 1992 Helsinki summit approved a procedure for the CSCE to organize peacekeeping actions and for calling on NATO, the Western European Union (WEU), or the post-Soviet Commonwealth of Independent States (CIS) to furnish the troops for the mission. It also assumed status as a regional organization for peacekeeping under Article 52 of the UN Charter.[20] This action places the UN Security Council in a position to call on the CSCE and, through it, on NATO, WEU, or the CIS for peacekeeping services. This capability may at a later time extend to peace enforcement operations, but the CSCE decided at Helsinki not to undertake peace enforcement actions. Moreover, the CSCE lacks a permanent steering committee or "security council" that could take charge in crisis situations. Nonetheless, it is highly probable that the further expansion of CSCE institutions and crisis management measures will come in time.

A revised NATO, with a new strategy and military organization, is an important institution for European security. NATO remains essential as assurance against the possible emergence of noncooperative policies in the two strongest European states, Russia and Germany. However unlikely such developments may appear at this time, the absence of this assurance could seriously undermine the willingness of the European states to cooperate among themselves. With its integrated staff, logistics, and intelligence capability, NATO has the highest capability in Europe for conducting peacekeeping and peace enforcement actions and could be used for peacekeeping in Bosnia. NATO's capabilities have led to repeated expressions of interest by Poland, the Czech Republic, and Hungary in joining NATO, a possibility that NATO governments are endorsing in general terms for the long run.

In the meanwhile, to meet these interests and to keep NATO alive through adding new functions, the NATO governments in late 1991 created the North Atlantic Cooperation Council (NACC), an organization for discussion and coordination on mutual security problems, with membership including all NATO member states, eastern European states, and all of the Soviet successor states, including the Baltics (but not the twelve European neutral states, such as Sweden and Austria, that are members of the CSCE). With an agenda that covers conversion of military industry to civilian production, civilian control of armed forces, and coordination of efforts to cope with natural disasters, the NACC to some extent duplicates the work of CSCE committees and institutions, but it provides a channel for military-to-military liaison not greatly developed in the CSCE.[21] In mid-1993 the NACC decided on an extensive program of cooperation in peacekeeping.[22] In the long run, if this experiment develops positively, the NACC might slowly become the military arm of the CSCE.

Finally, the European Community (EC) is one of the most important institutions concerned with European security. In the draft treaty agreed at Maastricht in December 1991, which entered into force on November 1, 1993, the EC took the first steps toward a common foreign and security policy and designated

WEU as its future defense arm. Although ensuing events, including negative trends in European public opinion toward further integration and the near collapse in mid-1993 of the exchange rate mechanism, raise doubts about the speed of further development, in the long term these arrangements will probably be enlarged, and EC membership will expand to include many neutral states and perhaps, ultimately, some of the states of eastern Europe. Given its role as the coordinating center of a unified European economy and given expanding capability in the area of security, over a period of decades the EC may become the most important of the institutions dealing with European security.

The European security system has some capacity for geographic expansion. In some respects—exchange of information on armed forces and defense budgets, human rights obligations, the beginnings of coordination of policy on nuclear proliferation and arms transfers, and the Open Skies Treaty—CSCE institutions cover not only Europe but all the territory of Russia and other CIS states and of Canada and the United States. Moreover, at the July 1992 Helsinki CSCE summit, Japan entered into a loose working association with the CSCE. If this relationship develops further, the CSCE could be on its way to becoming an organization that covers most of the Northern Hemisphere.

Since the collapse of the Soviet Union, there has been a vigorous expansion of subregional organizations in central and eastern Europe and in the former USSR, some of them with peacemaking roles or the potential for such a role. The most important of these is the Commonwealth of Independent States (1991), which now links all of the independent republics that constituted the Soviet Union (except the Baltic states). Although CIS members in June 1993 abandoned the effort to integrate their armed forces, several remain allied to Russia, and, at Russian initiative, many are moving to reestablish economic links severed in the dissolution of the USSR.[23] In mid-1992 Russia brought about a cease-fire in the secessionist trans-Dniester area of Moldova and began a peacekeeping mission (in collaboration with Romania, Moldova, and Bulgaria) and undertook a second mission in South Ossetia in collaboration with Georgia.[24] In actions that led to more criticism, Russian troops intervened in 1993 in fighting in Tajikistan and in Georgia.[25]

Other subregional groups are the Council of the Baltic Sea States; the Central European Initiative (formerly the Pentagonale), with Italy, Austria, the Czech Republic, Hungary, Slovakia, Poland, Slovenia, and Croatia; the Visegrad Group (Poland, the Czech Republic, Slovakia, and Hungary); and Danubian, Balkan, and Black Sea groupings.

ASSESSMENT: OPERATIVE CRITERIA. In chapter 3, Antonia and Abram Chayes set out five fundamental "design" elements and principles that are needed to satisfy the reassurance requirements of a cooperative security regime. The five are the necessity for a strong normative base, maximal inclusiveness and nondiscrimination of regime elements, maximal transparency regarding compliance with regime requirements, flexible and extensive mechanisms for regime management, and a system of sanctions to enforce regime rules.

Analyzing the cooperative security arrangements now in place in Europe from the standpoint of these criteria, it is clear that structures within Europe meet these standards quite well. The very existence of such a wealth of arrangements reflects the *strong normative base* behind them, and the wide and increasing participation of regional states in these arrangements also gives them high marks in the area of *inclusiveness and nondiscrimination*. Mechanisms for *transparency* are unparalleled; those for *regime management* are good.

However, the system has shown clear management weaknesses in the continuing frictions between Russia and some of the surrounding republics, including Georgia, Azerbaijan, and especially Ukraine, where the frictions in part reflect domestic divisions in Ukraine and sometimes domineering Russian tactics. Despite U.S. and European efforts to mediate, these problems have caused Ukraine to delay a long time in ratifying the START I treaty and adhering to the NPT, with Kazakhstan also delaying its signature of the NPT.[26]

What remains even less clear, however, is whether a *sanctioning system* for enforcing regime norms can be implemented. From 1991 through 1993, the European security system was unable to meet the serious tests it was facing in the form of ethnic conflicts in Yugoslavia and the former Soviet Union. Although the cooperative security arrangements that are the focus of this chapter are not primarily designed to deal with intrastate turmoil of the kind seen in these settings, all of the European institutions concerned with European security—the EC, WEU, NATO, the CSCE, and even the UN—have become deeply involved in the former Yugoslavia, and all have to some extent been discredited.

If these institutions continue to fail to contain or at least damp down these conflicts, more basic elements of cooperative security in Europe might well be called into doubt. This shortcoming has become apparent in Slovenia, Croatia, and Bosnia. Kosovo and Macedonia are, for now, still in the wings. Development of these conflicts into interstate war with Serbia, Albania, Greece, Bulgaria, or Turkey as participants is quite possible. The weakness of the European cooperative security system has also become apparent in Nagorno-Karabakh, where fighting has gone on for five years even though it could have been blocked by a peacekeeping buffer force, and in Moldova and Georgia. These are all situations that could easily develop into interstate conflict. If the undeclared war now in progress between Armenia and Azerbaijan over Nagorno-Karabakh should spread, Turkey, a NATO ally, might take the side of the Azeris against Russia, now an ally of Armenia. The fighting in Tajikistan involves Russia, Uzbekistan, and Afghanistan, as well as the Tajikistan government and dissident factions. Both Russia and Ukraine have pressed for a relaxation of zonal limits on CFE-limited arms to permit more concentration of forces vis-à-vis each other, and in the case of Russia in the Transcaucasus region.[27]

Although some American and European leaders have claimed that these conflicts do not involve their national interests, this conclusion does not withstand analysis. The negative consequences of the conflicts include deaths in the tens of thousands, with hundreds of thousands of refugees; economic disaster for the areas of conflict; the continuing possibility of interstate war; serious discrediting of the institutions involved in security in Europe; zero progress toward functioning democracy and free markets in the affected areas; the hostility and suspicion of Muslim countries toward the West; an enormous burden of economic rehabilitation that will have to be borne by Western states; a growing feeling of insecurity among member states of the European system, including Germany; and an emerging conviction that the system of cooperative security is not functioning and that more reliance has to be placed on individual defense efforts. If these conflicts continue unchecked, the European security system could unravel, with extremely negative effects on the international system as a whole.

ASSESSMENT: PARTICIPANT PERSPECTIVE. Despite these serious shortcomings, seen from the standpoint of individual participant states, the structures outlined in the preceding section do provide significant reassurance about the conventional military establishments of potential regional adversaries. Under the CFE, CSCE, and Open Skies agreements, each participating state is able to carry out many direct inspections, ground and air, of a neighboring state; receive information about inspections carried out against the target country by other participants; and summon a neighboring state to account for unusual military activities before a committee of all CSCE member states.

The European security arrangements do not provide safeguards against the threats that could arise from the nuclear capabilities of the nuclear weapon states. To some degree, however, any underlying dangers to nonnuclear parties that are seen to be posed by the British, French, Russian, or U.S. nuclear capabilities are being reduced because of the political changes brought about by the end of the cold war.

In addition, a number of U.S.-Soviet and U.S.-Russian nuclear arms control agreements have also reduced the risk of a nuclear conflict that might engulf Europe. Besides the INF treaty, this complex of agreements includes the Treaty on the Limitation of Anti-Ballistic Missile Systems (ABM treaty) and the Strategic Arms Limitation Talks (SALT) I agreement (1972), which froze the number of strategic ballistic missile launchers. SALT II (1979), not ratified but nonetheless largely observed by both countries, placed an equal aggregate limit on the number of strategic nuclear delivery vehicles, including ground- and submarine-based strategic range missiles and heavy bombers, and on the numbers of launchers for multiple-warhead missiles and of heavy bombers with long-range cruise missiles.[28] The START treaty (1991) provides for a roughly

30 percent reduction in deployed strategic nuclear delivery vehicles (ground- and submarine-launched strategic range missiles and heavy bombers) and in the nuclear warheads they carry.[29] Ratification of the treaty was placed in some jeopardy by the collapse of the Soviet Union, but on May 23, 1992, the four successor states with strategic nuclear weapons on their territory—Russia, Belarus, Ukraine, and Kazakhstan—together with the United States signed the Lisbon Protocol to the treaty, which provides for the participation of all five states in the implementation and verification of the treaty.[30]

Two important related agreements carried U.S.-Russian nuclear arms reduction forward. In an initiative set forth on September 27, 1991, President Bush not only proposed worldwide withdrawal of tactical range nuclear weapons, both ground-based and deployed on naval vessels (surface and submarine), including cruise missiles, but also unilaterally canceled three proposed new U.S. nuclear missiles: the rail-based version of the MX missile, a projected single-warhead missile, and the new short-range attack air-to-surface missile. Bush also proposed cooperation with the Soviet Union on nuclear command and control, warhead security and safety, secure transport, storage, and dismantling. President Gorbachev accepted these proposals in early October 1991 and also said the Soviet Union would cut its strategic warheads to 5,000 instead of 6,000 during the seven-year implementation of START.[31]

In January 1992 President Bush proposed that both Russia and the United States cut to a level of about 4,700 warheads (a 50 percent cut from pre-START levels), eliminate all land-based multiple-warhead missiles, cut U.S. submarine-based missiles by roughly one-third, and cut off B-2 bomber production at 20 airplanes. President Boris Yeltsin responded with a proposal of still deeper warhead cuts to a level of 2,000 to 2,500.[32] These proposals culminated in the START II treaty, signed in January 1993. The treaty provides for a ten-year reduction to a maximum level of 3,000 to 3,500 warheads on each side, with complete elimination of multiple warheads (MIRVs) from ground-based intercontinental missiles. There would be a limit of 1,750 warheads deployed on submarine-launched ballistic missiles. The end point would be a level about 60 percent below the post-START level by 2003.[33] (In reaction to the initial U.S. and Soviet moves, the United Kingdom announced the withdrawal of tactical nuclear weapons from its naval vessels, and the French government canceled the production of the HADES tactical-range surface-to-surface missile.)[34]

In addition to these measures, in October 1992 the United States and Russia signed an agreement for the purchase by the United States of up to 500 metric tons of Russian weapon-grade uranium.[35] The United States has also made available $1.2 billion to assist in the transport and storage of warheads and fissile material in Russia, improve systems of export control in all of the successor republics, and provide alternative employment for former Soviet experts on the production of nuclear weapons.[36] In mid-1993 the United States also proposed negotiations on a comprehensive nuclear test ban; an international convention to ban the production of fissile material for nuclear weapons; and, ultimately, an international regime to monitor the storage of weapons-grade plutonium and uranium.[37]

As of late 1993 Russia and the United States had effectively ratified START I, but their legislatures had imposed conditions that made its implementation dependent on ratification by Belarus, Kazakhstan, and Ukraine and the adhesion of these three states to the NPT.[38] Belarus had carried out both actions, as had Kazakhstan, but Ukraine, enmeshed in its quarrel with Russia and a constitutional crisis of its own, ratified START I with conditions that restrict the value of ratification and had not moved on NPT.[39] Unless resolved, the Ukraine impasse could threaten the implementation of both START I and START II and weaken prospects for the indefinite extension of the NPT in 1995, when the duration of that accord must be decided.

Moreover, there is still no bilateral U.S.-Russian obligation under either the START treaty to dismantle the warheads or destroy the missiles of reduced strategic weapons, to place fissile material from dismantled warheads in monitored storage, or to agree bilaterally to stop production of fissile material for weapons—steps needed to move toward an irreversible reduction of the strategic arsenals of the two countries. If new agreements are not concluded successfully, a very large arsenal of nuclear warheads, missiles, and fissile material could remain in Belarus, Kazakhstan, and Ukraine during the next few years and indefinitely in Russia, with a continuing possibility of forcible seizure, theft, illegal sale, or even, in the event of a nationalist regime, use of these stocks to rapidly raise the level of still deployed nuclear weapons. This remains a highly disquieting prospect in view of the continuing political instability of the area, which threatens to continue for some decades.

Given continued good U.S.-Russian relations (which are not assured), it is possible that within the next decade the U.S.-Russian regime could expand to cover these areas: still further warhead reductions, agreed destruction of reduced strategic warheads and missiles, along with agreed restrictions on the production of fissile materials and long-range missiles and on the testing of nuclear warheads.[40] Even so, for the foreseeable future, while European security structures continue to evolve, European states will have to continue to live in a nuclear-armed environment (to which, of course, the British and French nuclear arsenals also contribute). As a practical matter, however, the end of the cold war has meant that the actual nuclear threat posed by any of these nuclear weapon states to the nonnuclear nations of Europe has been vastly reduced.

The member states of the CSCE and of the NACC have also pledged to coordinate information and action against proliferation of weapons of mass destruction within the CSCE area and outside it. However, this cooperation is still in its beginning stages and not fully developed. These threats are being addressed more directly by the nonproliferation regimes discussed in the next section.

Finally, European security structures have done relatively little to address the potential threats to the territories or other vital interests of the participating states that are outside the region. Although NATO has begun to discuss joint out-of-area military actions for this purpose, these measures for now amount to little more than traditional coordination among allies for potential military action rather than cooperative initiatives undertaken with potential adversaries to increase mutual reassurance. However, with continual prompting from Spain, France, and Italy, the CSCE has organized an ongoing series of Mediterranean conferences with the participation of Arab states and Israel. On September 13, 1993, the ongoing dialogue between Israel and neighboring Arab states, promoted by the United States for many years, brought a potentially historic agreement between Israel and the Palestine Liberation Organization for Palestinian administration of Jericho and the Gaza Strip.[41] This agreement could have a considerable impact on European relations with Arab states in the Middle East and northern Africa, as well as on Arab-Israeli relations.

European security institutions, especially the CSCE, with its highly developed repertory of confidence-building measures, have already had a strong intellectual effect elsewhere. They have been used as a model for the parallel discussion of political, economic, and security issues in the Middle East talks between the Arab states and Israel, restarted by the United States in Madrid in October 1991. And they have been used as a model by the two Korean states in their own security dialogue. The United States is seeking to start a similar round of multitopic parallel talks between India and Pakistan, with the participation of China and Russia, and there is recurrent discussion of a CSCE-type structure for the whole Asian-Pacific area.[42]

The Second Node: The Nonproliferation Regimes

Several worldwide networks of treaties, agreements, export controls, inspection systems, and other international undertakings currently exist for curbing the proliferation of weapons of mass destruction and missile delivery systems for them.

KEY ELEMENTS. Efforts to stem the spread of nuclear weapons have led to the development of the most comprehensive and widely accepted arms control regime in force today. The centerpiece of the regime is the 1970 NPT treaty. Under the pact, nearly 150 non–nuclear weapon state parties have formally renounced nuclear weapons and accepted inspection by the IAEA of all their nuclear materials to verify that they are not being used for nuclear arms. With the accession of China (1992) and France (1992), all the nuclear weapon states (states that had manufactured and detonated a nuclear explosive device by January 1, 1967) are now also parties to the treaty, greatly enhancing its stature and normative force. The weapon states are not obliged to give up nuclear weapons, but they are required to pursue negotiations on ending the nuclear arms race, negotiations that are today making greater progress.[43]

In July 1991, after more than a decade as a de facto nuclear state, South Africa acceded to the NPT, thus becoming the first nation in history to give up an existing nuclear arsenal voluntarily. Since all of the states of Europe (except France and Great Britain) are also non–nuclear weapon state parties to the accord, the NPT can help to prevent the emergence of new nuclear powers in this region, providing an essential complement to the CFE treaty and CSCE process, as suggested above.

The treaty is also playing an important role in North Korea and in the former Soviet Union. In May 1992 North Korea, which acceded to the accord in 1985, permitted comprehensive IAEA inspections to begin, after more than six years of delay. This was an important step that promised to check North Korea's apparent quest for nuclear weapons. In early 1993, however, Pyongyang barred inspection of two suspected nuclear sites demanded by the IAEA, and in March, after the IAEA had referred the issue to the UN Security Council, North Korea announced its intention to withdraw from the NPT as of mid-June. At the last moment, however, it suspended its withdrawal from the pact, while continuing its refusal to allow the inspections sought by the IAEA.[44] The matter, which remained unresolved in late 1993, raised questions about the effectiveness of the NPT in this case, but the widespread international support at the IAEA and Security Council for enforcing the accord also underscored the NPT's underlying vitality.

The treaty is also playing a critically important role in efforts to ensure the denuclearization of three of the four Soviet successor states that have nuclear weapons on their territory, Belarus, Kazakhstan, and Ukraine. Belarus has ratified the treaty and appears prepared to permit the removal to Russia of all Soviet nuclear weapons on its territory. Ukraine has pledged to join the NPT and allow the withdrawal of all Soviet nuclear arms to Russia, but the Ukrainian parliament has prevented the implementation of these undertakings and appears increasingly to favor retaining the weapons. Kazakhstan has recently ratified the NPT but has not yet carried out the terms of the treaty. Nonetheless, the NPT has provided a normative and legal basis for international efforts to press Ukraine and Kazakhstan to accept nonnuclear status and will provide the mechanisms for verifying compliance if they can be brought to implement their respective pledges.

Algeria (which hinted in January 1992 that it might join the treaty), India, Israel, and Pakistan remain the only major regional states that reject on principle the comprehensive controls embodied in the treaty.[45]

In the aftermath of the 1991 Gulf War, the IAEA, carrying out inspections in Iraq under the direction of the UN Security Council, found that during the 1980s Iraq had repeatedly violated the NPT by building undeclared nuclear facilities. This discovery led the agency in February 1992 to strengthen its inspection regime under the NPT by activating its long-dormant authority to conduct "special inspections," that is, inspections of suspected, undeclared nuclear sites in non–nuclear weapon states that are parties to the NPT.[46] Unfortunately, although the IAEA has performed well in pressing North Korea for access to all of its nuclear facilities, as noted earlier, it has been prevented by Pyongyang from implementing the inspections it seeks.

The nuclear nonproliferation regime also contains a multilateral system to limit transfers of equipment, materials, and technology relevant to the production of nuclear arms, a system implemented by the Nuclear Suppliers Group (1974).[47] Twenty-eight countries, including four of the five nuclear weapon states—the United States, France, the United Kingdom, and Russia—are members of the group. In an important meeting in Warsaw in April 1992, the group adopted new guidelines to extend controls to sixty-seven dual-use items with nuclear applications. In Warsaw the group also agreed on a common policy requiring full-scope IAEA safeguards (opening all national nuclear installations to IAEA inspection) as a necessary condition for all significant new nuclear exports to non–nuclear weapon states, in effect imposing an economic sanction (denying sales of such matériel) against states refusing comprehensive inspections.[48]

The biological weapons nonproliferation regime, like its nuclear weapon counterpart, also has as its centerpiece a treaty prohibiting the development, production, or stockpiling of this weapon of mass destruction, namely the Biological Weapons Convention, signed in 1972 and entered into force in 1975. The BWC is nondiscriminatory in that it does not exempt any class of states from its prohibitions the way the NPT exempts the nuclear weapon states. This strength is offset, however, by the fact that the convention does not provide mechanisms for verifying that its members are adhering to its prohibitions.[49] Indeed, Russia has since confirmed long-standing U.S. charges that the Soviet Union had violated the pact for many years by manufacturing biological arms at a number of locations, and it did agree to destroy illegal stocks of such weapons and to cease any further production. Nonetheless, member states are making serious efforts to develop cooperative verification methods to include extensive information exchange and inspection visits.[50]

The second element of the biological weapons nonproliferation system consists of controls on transfers of materials, equipment, and technology related to the manufacture of these arms administered by the Australia Group, which comprises twenty-five member states plus the European Commission. Finally, the Geneva Protocol of 1925 prohibits the use of biological (and the first use of chemical) weapons, a restraint relevant to states that have ratified this instrument but not the BWC.

A new chemical weapons regime will be introduced in 1995. The Geneva Protocol of 1925 prohibits the use of chemical weapons, but not their manufacture or stockpiling. Thus, currently, the principal tool for combatting the spread of these arms has been the Australia Group. However, the Chemical Weapons Convention, signed in January 1993, will enter into force in two years after sixty-five ratifications.[51] The pending CWC will prohibit the production, possession, testing, transfer, or use of chemical weapons; require the destruction of production facilities and of existing stocks;[52] identify lethal chemicals and those "precursor chemicals" that can be used to produce them, including dual-use chemicals also used for legitimate non–weapon purposes; and establish a central inspection and verification authority similar to the IAEA.[53] Moreover, unlike the NPT, which exempts nuclear weapon states, the CWC will not exempt any class of states from its prohibitions. The convention has provisions for verification, including challenge inspections that failed to satisfy some Western verification experts but that were considered barely acceptable by more secretive negotiating participants such as China, Pakistan, and Iran. Inspections can also be carried out in the event that the use of chemical weapons is claimed. Thus there is promise for a chemical weapons nonproliferation regime that will rival and may, in some respects, ultimately surpass that for nuclear weapons.

The regime for controlling the spread of ballistic and cruise missiles is less developed than any of the nonproliferation efforts already described. It consists solely of the Missile Technology Control Regime (1987), a system of parallel export controls, which in late 1993 had been adopted by twenty-three Western industrialized states to restrict the spread of missile technology. In addition, Argentina and Hungary were applying the regime's export control rules and have been invited to join the group; China, Israel, and Russia have also agreed to apply its standards but have not been invited to become full participants.[54]

On the assumption that rudimentary nuclear warheads that might be manufactured by regional powers would weigh at least 1,100 pounds (500 kilograms) and that the regime should not attempt to regulate widely available short-range battlefield missiles, the MTCR was originally designed to restrict transfers of unmanned delivery systems, including both ballistic and cruise missile systems, able to carry payloads of 1,100 pounds to a range of 186 miles (300 kilometers).[55] The 1991 Gulf War, however, heightened concern that missiles might be used to deliver chemical or biological weapons. This concern led the MTCR members to agree in January 1993 to broaden the scope of the regime to include less powerful systems.

The new MTCR guidelines regulate technology for all missiles capable of delivering *any* payload to a distance of 300 kilometers or more. In addition, they provide that members will exercise "particular restraint" in considering exports of any missile (regardless of range) and any missile technology if there is convincing information that these are "intended to be used for the delivery of weapons of mass destruction," in which case there will be "a strong presumption to deny such transfers."[56]

In contrast to the other regimes, there is no international treaty providing for parties to renounce the possession of MTCR-covered missile delivery systems, nor any related verification system. (The U.S.-Russian INF treaty might arguably be thought of as an adjunct to the MTCR, although it was adopted as a bilateral nuclear arms control measure.)

Table 4-2 summarizes some of the principal features of these various nonproliferation regimes and highlights the states thought to possess or to be seeking the weapons of concern to each system.

ASSESSMENT: OPERATIONAL CRITERIA. Before examining the impact of these regimes on reducing threats to states at different ranks of military capability, it is useful to assess the regimes against the criteria of performance highlighted in chapter 3. Such an assessment underscores the fact that basic limitations in some of these regimes greatly reduce their value as cooperative security measures, at least at present.

The NPT and BWC enjoy strong *normative bases*,[57] and this is true as well for the emerging CWC. Stated simply, all of these initiatives are based on a widespread abhorrence of these armaments. Support is less widespread for the supplier country–dominated technology transfer controls adopted in each of these spheres, particularly when targets of the control regimes fear that the restrictions will interfere with their legitimate efforts to modernize their economies or militaries. This complaint may be most pronounced with respect to chemical weapon– or missile-related controls but is more muted today with respect to nuclear technology, since the enthusiasm for nuclear energy has waned in the developing world. Moreover, as noted, a number of emerging nuclear suppliers, recognizing the dangers of nuclear proliferation, have adopted the export control guidelines of the NSG—and even India and Pakistan, though they have rejected nonproliferation controls on their own nuclear programs, have agreed to restrict transfers of nuclear commodities to others.[58]

The normative base of the missile technology control regime is considerably weaker, an assessment reflected most clearly in the fact that no global treaty exists under which states have agreed to renounce MTCR-class missiles. Contributing to its weakness is the fact that the regime emerged quite recently and after missile delivery capabilities had spread to many states. Moreover, the use of such systems has never evoked the same revulsion as that associated with the use of nuclear, chemical, and biological arms. Nonetheless, the MTCR has been gaining new adherents, and as of late 1993, only two nations—North Korea and China—were continuing to supply MTCR-class missiles or related technology on the international market, which demonstrated that among supplier countries, at least, the norm against the spread of these systems was taking hold.[59] Growing supplier country support for the MTCR has also been demonstrated by the decision, noted earlier, to tighten the MTCR's standards to restrict transfers not only of missiles able to deliver nuclear warheads to

Table 4-2. *Nonproliferation Regimes*[a]

Item	*Nuclear weapons*	*Biological*	*Chemical*	*Missile*
Treaty prohibiting possession and classes of states exempted	Yes (NPT) Nuclear weapon states exempted 150 NNWS parties 5 NWS parties	Yes (BWC) No classes of states exempted 122 parties	?1995 (CWC) No classes of states exempted 152 signatories (4 ratifications)	No
Verification agency or system	IAEA	None	1995 (Organization for the Prohibition of Chemical Weapons)	None
Countries of continuing concern	All NWSs retain nuclear arms Not NPT parties and possessing nuclear weapon capabilities: Israel, India, Pakistan NPT parties but future compliance in doubt: Iran, Iraq, Libya, North Korea	Said by U.S. to have BW programs: China, Iran, Iraq, Libya, North Korea, Russia, Syria, Taiwan	Said by U.S. to have CW programs: China, Egypt, France, India, Iran, Iraq, Israel, Libya, Myanmar, North Korea, Pakistan, Russia, South Korea, Syria, Taiwan, U.S., Vietnam	States with MTCR-range missiles or space launchers or development programs: Brazil, China, Egypt, European Space Agency, France, India, Indonesia, Iran, Iraq, Israel, Japan, Libya, North Korea, Pakistan, Russia, Saudi Arabia, South Korea, Syria, Taiwan, Ukraine, U.K., U.S., Yemen

Multilateral export control system	NSG, NPT Exporters' Committee	Australia Group	Australia Group; CWC system, in 1995	MTCR
Members of suppliers' group	Australia, Austria, Belgium, Bulgaria, Canada, Czech Rep., Denmark, Finland, France, Germany, Greece, Hungary, Ireland, Italy, Japan, Luxembourg, Netherlands, Norway, Poland, Portugal, Romania, Russia, Slovakia, Spain, Sweden, Switzerland, U.K., U.S. (28)	Argentina, Australia, Austria, Belgium, Canada, Denmark, EC, Finland, France, Germany, Greece, Hungary, Iceland, Ireland, Italy, Japan, Luxembourg, Netherlands, New Zealand, Norway, Portugal, Spain, Sweden, Switzerland, U.K., U.S. (25 + EC)	Same as for biological weapons	Australia, Austria, Belgium, Canada, Denmark, Finland, France, Germany, Greece, Iceland, Ireland, Italy, Japan, Luxembourg, Netherlands, New Zealand, Norway, Portugal, Spain, Sweden, Switzerland, U.K., U.S. (23)
	Other states applying some NSG standards: all NPT parties require IAEA safeguards on exports; Argentina, South Africa apply some additional NSG rules		Others applying Australia Group CW standards: Bulgaria, China, Czech Rep., India, Israel, Pakistan, Poland, Romania, Russia., Slovakia	Others applying standards: Argentina, China(?), Hungary, Israel, Russia

Sources: For NPT, *Arms Control Reporter 1993,* pp. 602.A.7–10; for NSG, ibid., pp. 602.A.2–3; for Australia Group, ibid., pp. 704.B.549, 552; for states with MTCR-range missiles, Robert Shuey, "Missile Proliferation: A Discussion of U.S. Objectives and Policy Options," CRS Report 90-120F (February 21, 1990), p. 3; for states said to have BW or CW programs, Elisa D. Harris, "Towards a Comprehensive Strategy for Halting Chemical and Biological Weapons Proliferation," *Arms Control,* vol. 12 (September 1991), pp. 129–60, especially p. 129.

a. NWS, nuclear weapon state; NNWS, non–nuclear weapon state; BW, biological weapons; CW, chemical weapons; MTCR, Missile Control Technology regime.

300 kilometers or more but also of those able to carry lighter chemical and biological weapon payloads.

Although some states, such as India, have rejected the very principle of controls over the spread of missiles, at least one supposed "target" of the MTCR, Argentina, has embraced its objectives by both canceling domestic missile production programs and adopting the regime's guidelines. If the United States and Russia were to agree at some point to restrict production of their long-range missiles, this action could give greater authority to the MTCR.[60]

The various nonproliferation regimes also differ markedly in terms of *inclusiveness and nondiscrimination*. The BWC and emergent CWC contain universal prohibitions on the possession of these weapons, prohibitions applicable to all states joining these treaties without distinction, a factor that enhances their legitimacy. In addition, the BWC, with 122 parties, enjoys wide membership. Unfortunately, there is some doubt whether the CWC will gain similarly wide support, particularly in the Middle East and South and East Asia.

In contrast to the BWC and CWC, the NPT, as was noted, is explicitly discriminatory, permitting the nuclear weapon states to retain their nuclear arsenals, while requiring all other parties to renounce such arms. Despite this fact and despite the fact that three de facto nuclear weapon states, India, Israel, and Pakistan, remain outside the accord, the NPT enjoys great legitimacy, demonstrated most obviously by its growing and near-universal membership.[61] Finally, once again, the MTCR stands apart, with only twenty-three supplier-state participants and only limited support among the remaining members of the international community.

The various nonproliferation regimes also obviously differ markedly in terms of *transparency,* given the great disparities in their respective verification systems. It must also be stressed that even the pervasive inspections of the IAEA, which may be the most intrusive of all the verification arrangements among the various regimes now in effect, have been shown to have serious weaknesses.[62] Thus, where they are applied, comprehensive IAEA inspections may not offer complete reassurance to potential adversaries of the inspected state that it is complying with its treaty obligations, and therefore additional measures, such as the bilateral inspections contemplated between North and South Korea, might be required. Moreover, a number of states are not subject to such comprehensive monitoring because they are not parties to the NPT or, as nuclear weapon states, are exempted from inspections under it. This privileged status could be diminished, however, if the nuclear weapon states adopt the Clinton administration's proposal for an international convention banning the production of fissile material for nuclear arms. The advent of the CWC will introduce a second intrusive and wide-ranging inspection system, but one that will also have a number of limitations.[63] When applied in tandem, however, the NPT and CWC systems will create a high degree of transparency, and synergies between them may increase the underlying effectiveness of each. Indeed, even though the BWC and MTCR contain no verification provisions, states that are simultaneously inspected under both the CWC and full-scope IAEA systems may also be deterred from developing biological weapons or ballistic missiles, for fear that a nuclear or chemical weapon inspection might discover prohibited BW- or missile-related work. Still greater transparency, verging on an ideal system, will emerge in states subject to CWC and full-scope IAEA inspections that are also participating in the wide-range confidence-building and verification measures of the CSCE process and the CFE and Open Skies treaties.

The nuclear nonproliferation system has extensive *regime management* mechanisms, including jawboning and diplomatic pressure by individual participants, interpretation and dispute settlement operations by the IAEA safeguards directorate, diplomacy at the level of the IAEA Board of Governors and General Conference, and referral of apparent IAEA inspection violations to the UN Security Council. Links between the IAEA and the Security Council have been strengthened in the aftermath of the Gulf War through the workings of the UN Special Commission on Iraq, which called upon the IAEA to expose and dismantle Iraq's clandestine nuclear weapons program; moreover, both organs have indicated their intent to work closely together in the future.[64]

The CWC will also incorporate elaborate regime management arrangements, including the conference of state parties of the Organization for the Prohibition of Chemical Weapons, the agency's Executive Council, and its Technical Secretariat, headed by the director general. The Executive Council will engage in fact finding on request, can demand clarification from a member state of ambiguous situations, can convene special sessions of the conference of members in cases of no compliance, can pass on requests for challenge inspections, and can determine whether any noncompliance has occurred. The Technical Secretariat will carry out inspections; provide information on chemical weapons, detection devices, and decontamination and medical assistance for victims of chemical attacks; and offer staff support for the deliberations of the organization's Executive Council and general conferences.[65]

The BWC provides for the Security Council to investigate charges of violations of the treaty and requires states accused of such violations to cooperate in these inquiries. The recent acknowledgment by Russia that the Soviet Union had violated the treaty for many years,[66] as the United States had charged, highlights the difficulties that have been experienced in settling disputes under the pact. In distinction, disputes arising under the MTCR have been handled on an ad hoc basis among the participants and between participants and outsiders, with varying degrees of success.

Sanctions under the various nonproliferation regimes present a complex picture. Those under the nuclear regime are the most elaborate and have the longest history. They include unilateral sanctions, such as the withholding of

Table 4-3. *Assessment of Existing Nonproliferation Regimes under Cooperative Security Design Criteria*

Item	*Nuclear*	*Biological*	*Chemical*	*Missile*
Normative base	*Strong* (NPT) *to moderate* (NSG).	*Strong* (Geneva Protocol, BWC) *to moderate* (Australia Group).	*Strong* (Geneva Protocol, CWC) *to moderate* (Australia Group).	*Moderate*. Improving somewhat as additional suppliers and some "targets" of regime accept its norms and export controls.
Inclusiveness and nondiscrimination	*Moderate*. Near-universal and growing membership in NPT, but five NWSs exempted and three de facto nuclear weapon states not party.	*Strong*. Widespread membership in Geneva Protocol and BWC. No class of states exempted.	*Potentially strong*. Widespread membership in Geneva Protocol; breadth of CWC membership still uncertain; no class of states exempted from CWC.	*Moderate*. Limited membership (Western supplier states only); improving somewhat as some other suppliers and "targets" of regime accept its norms and export controls.
Transparency	*Strong*. IAEA safeguards widely applied and improving; also new adjunct measures (e.g., those between Argentina and Brazil).	*Very weak*. No verification measures.	*Potentially strong* under CWC's intrusive inspection system in member states.	*Very weak*. No verification measures.
Regime management	*Strong*. NPT and IAEA system provide wide range of mechanisms for interpretation, resolution of apparent violations, and so on.	*Moderate*. BWC provides for investigations of alleged violations by UN Security Council.	*Potentially strong*. CWC provides wide range of mechanisms for interpretation, resolution of apparent violations, and so on.	*Weak*. Limited principally to supplier state negotiations.
Sanctions	*Strong*. Extensive unilateral sanctions (principally U.S.) and growing multilateral sanctions for violation of regime norms; explicit mechanisms for referral to UN Security Council.	*Moderate to strong*. BWC provides for referral of violations to UN Security Council; U.S. legislation imposes sanctions for use on entities that assist foreign BW programs.	*Potentially strong*. CWC provides for suspension of membership, unspecified collective actions against offenders, and referral to UN Security Council. U.S. legislation imposes sanctions for use and on entities that assist foreign CW programs.	*Weak to moderate*. No sanctions provided in MTCR; U.S. legislation imposes sanctions on entities assisting development of MTCR-class missiles abroad.

peaceful nuclear cooperation or economic and military aid—measures that have been imposed principally by the United States against states that have rejected or violated various regime norms; and multilateral sanctions, such as the termination of IAEA technical assistance and the NSG's withholding of major nuclear transfers from states refusing to accept comprehensive IAEA inspections. Multilateral sanctions here also include the prospect of referral of NPT violations to the Security Council, which could result in the imposition of wide-ranging economic or even military sanctions by that body. Unilateral military action, such as Israel's destruction of the Osiraq reactor outside Baghdad, has been another, more controversial aspect of efforts to curb proliferation, and though it is not a recognized element of any nonproliferation regime, it is receiving increasing attention.[67]

In the area of biological weapons, sanctions have never been imposed for the use of such arms, nor specifically for violations of the BWC ban on the possession or production of such weapons. Since the BWC calls on the Security Council to investigate violations, it implicitly anticipates that the organization would consider the imposition of sanctions in the event a violation was found to have occurred. U.S. legislation calls for unilateral economic penalties against states that use such weapons and on entities helping foreign states to develop them.

With respect to chemical weapons, sanctions have yet to be imposed for the use, possession, or development of such armaments. The CWC does not provide for specific penalties for noncompliance despite much discussion of the subject during the negotiations. The Executive Council can restrict or suspend a member state's participation, call on other states to take unspecified collective measures against offenders, or refer the case to the UN Security Council. In addition, U.S. legislation imposes unilateral sanctions against foreign states that use chemical weapons and on U.S. and foreign entities that provide assistance in the development of chemical weapon capabilities abroad.

With regard to the MTCR, finally, sanctions have, once again, never been imposed for the use of MTCR-class missiles, and no nation has been the target of sanctions (other than export controls) for developing such systems. U.S. legislation similar to that adopted in the chemical and biological weapons area, however, imposes economic sanctions—which can include the denial of export licenses, import licenses, and U.S. government contracts—on firms, corporations, or governmental organizations that assist foreign states to develop such missiles or that receive such assistance. Under this legislation, in 1993 the United States imposed sanctions against firms and governmental organizations in China and Pakistan because of China's transfer of missile components to Pakistan in violation of the MTCR guidelines. In 1993 the United States also briefly imposed sanctions against the Russian firm Glavkosmos for the transfer of cryogenic rocket engine technology to India, but these were lifted after agreement was reached on restricting the scope of the transfer.[68]

Table 4-3 summarizes the preceding analysis.

ASSESSMENT: PARTICIPANT PERSPECTIVE. Under a global cooperative security system, all states would, presumably, be confident that they would not become the subject of nuclear, chemical, or biological weapon threats. Today, however, few states enjoy such comfort, in part because of the uneven application and effectiveness of the regimes for curbing the spread of proscribed weapons, which have left what may be termed serious reassurance gaps.

Most obviously, the five nuclear powers remain able to threaten one another and to threaten all nonnuclear states with their nuclear forces. The three de facto nuclear states can also do so regionally.[69] The nuclear threats among the five major nuclear powers in the past were managed through alliances and an architecture of nuclear deterrence. Some of the same tools have been used to manage the more limited threat to the five from the three de facto nuclear powers. These latter powers, in turn, have tended to rely on friendly relations, alliances, and, possibly, deterrence (Israel-USSR, India-China) to keep potential threat from the declared nuclear states—and, where relevant, from each other—in check. Formal cooperative security or nonproliferation arrangements have become a central feature of nuclear relations between the United States and Russia (as they became between the United States and the Soviet Union), but as yet, with limited exceptions such as the Partial Test Ban Treaty, not among the remaining declared and de facto nuclear states.[70]

In theory, all nuclear states also pose a threat to nonnuclear states. If most nonnuclear states have shrugged off this threat, it is again not because of formal cooperative security or nonproliferation arrangements. Rather it is because the potentially endangered states have had credible alliances with one or more nuclear weapon states to deter the threat of nuclear attack by others or because the nonnuclear states happen to enjoy cordial relations, for the moment, with all the nuclear powers relevant to their geostrategic situation. The nearly fifty-year-long taboo against using nuclear weapons and unilateral "negative security declarations" by the nuclear powers (usually pledging not to use nuclear arms against nonnuclear states) may also contribute to reducing the threat perceptions of the nonnuclear nations. For nonnuclear states, such as Algeria, Bangladesh, Cuba, Iran, Iraq, Libya, Saudi Arabia, Sri Lanka, Syria, Taiwan, Thailand, and Vietnam, that perceive threats from some nuclear states but lack credible countervailing alliances with others, the current situation remains fraught with anxiety and, in many cases, has created pressures for members of this group to seek nuclear arms of their own.

Similarly, states at virtually every tier of military capability, including the nuclear powers, remain apprehensive about the risk that new states may be able to develop threatening nuclear capabilities. The nuclear weapon ambitions of Iran, Iraq, Libya, and North Korea are sources of particular concern in this regard, given their radical foreign policies and propensity for aggression.

The important recent initiatives of the United States and Russia to reduce their nuclear forces, the U.S. proposal for a ban on the production of fissile materials for nuclear weapons, the growing support (now including the support of the United States) for a Comprehensive Test Ban treaty, the strengthening of the IAEA safeguards system, and the growing international political support for the NPT are muting these concerns to some degree but have by no means eliminated them. Moreover, even if, as some optimists hope, the nonproliferation regime someday brings India, Israel, or Pakistan to renounce nuclear arms as South Africa has, the regime would still tolerate the continued existence of five nuclear-armed major powers as a given in the international order, a given that many states will continue to perceive as threatening.

The threat from the proliferation of biological weapons presents a different picture and one that is more difficult to assess. Since biological weapons have never been used on a wide scale, some question remains about their ability to inflict mass casualties. The consensus seems to be, however, that biological weapons should indeed be treated as weapons of enormous destructive potential, more akin to nuclear weapons. If this view is correct, the risk to different states along the spectrum of military capability would be much like that posed by nuclear arms. All states, including those with nuclear weapons, would thus have reason to be fearful about the proliferation of biological arms. The BWC's currently inadequate verification and enforcement mechanisms mean that the convention offers little protection against the spread of these weapons.

The dangers from the spread and potential use of chemical armaments also remain widespread. These arms have inherently less lethal capability than nuclear weapons, however, and their effect is far more dependent on weather and battlefield conditions. Thus, it is probably fair to state that countries with nuclear arms have had less reason to fear a chemically armed adversary than have states lacking such more potent weapons.[71] Massive conventional military force may also be able to offset an adversary's chemical weapon capability, as the United States believed during the 1991 Gulf War, and of course the development of a countervailing chemical weapon capability is another means for answering such a threat.[72] States lacking such military counters, however, remain vulnerable to an adversary's acquisition of a chemical weapon capability. Thus, generally speaking, the threat posed by the proliferation of chemical arms is likely to affect states at the lower echelons of the global military hierarchy far more severely than those at the higher levels, in contrast to the more widespread impact arising from the spread of nuclear and biological weapons. The CWC, with its powerful verification mechanisms, is likely to go far toward reducing the remaining threat posed by chemical arms. The chemical weapon peril is likely to continue in a number of regions, however, if, as expected, the pact is rejected by a number of key regional powers.

The spread of missile delivery systems, finally, poses a threat that is even more differentiated. The threat posed by missiles depends on several variables, including the type of warhead with which they are equipped, their range, and their accuracy. Because of their particular usefulness for preemptive operations

Table 4-4. *Continuing Threats from Weapons of Mass Destruction and Missile Delivery Systems*

Category of states[a]	*Nuclear threats*	*Chemical weapon threats*	*Biological weapon threats*	*Missile threat*
Superpower	All states potentially threatened by declared and de facto nuclear states and by emergence of new radical nuclear powers.	States with nuclear weapons or powerful conventional capabilities able to deter, respond; lesser powers more vulnerable.	All states potentially at risk. States with nuclear arms or BW capabilities may be able to deter; lesser powers more vulnerable.	Dependent on warhead and ranges; potential threat to all states. MTCR slowing spread of missiles, but existing systems remain.
Major (nuclear) powers	Nuclear states able to manage threats via deterrence and alliances; nonnuclear states principally via alliances and in some cases by seeking nuclear weapons.	CWC should greatly reduce threat, but important regional states may refuse to sign.	BWC not sufficient to address problem because of lack of verification and past cheating.	
Advanced industrialized powers	Nonproliferation regime helpful, but key threats remain.			
Nuclear regional powers				
Heavily armed regional powers seeking nuclear weapons				
Heavily armed regional powers				
Other regional states				

a. See table 4-1 for the military capabilities of each category and the states included.

and ability to penetrate existing antimissile defenses, missiles intensify the underlying threats posed by nuclear, chemical, and biological weapons. They can serve as a powerful conventional weapon as well.

The MTCR appears likely to slow the spread of missile delivery systems somewhat, but it will probably be less effective in states with strong industrial bases and will not, in any event, eliminate existing systems.

Table 4-4 highlights the many threats from weapons of mass destruction and missile delivery systems that states at various echelons of military capability continue to face today.

The unavoidable conclusion from the preceding analysis is that despite the important progress that has been made in recent years toward strengthening the various nonproliferation regimes, building a global cooperative security system that could reassure all states against the threats posed by these weapons remains an enormous challenge. Indeed, some elements of this challenge, such as eliminating the nuclear arsenals of the five nuclear weapon states, may not be achievable within the next decades or in the absence of a functioning system of world security with a convincing track record of actual success.

The Third Node: The Rule of Restraint

Ultimately, the cornerstone of a global cooperative security regime must therefore be the institutionalization of a global prohibition against the unilateral use of force to advance national objectives. Except for self-defense, admittedly a broad exception, the use of force would be limited to multilateral actions to enforce cooperative security norms, a stricture akin to that contained in the UN Charter.

Though the rule of restraint may be codified in that document and in the statutes of such regional organizations as the Organization of American States, the rule has been honored only rarely in the past. Nonetheless, the end of the cold war has opened a new era in international relations, and in the past several years the rule has been applied in a number of important instances.

The Bush administration's insistence on working through a broad, UN-sanctioned coalition in liberating Kuwait from Iraqi occupation is the most notable case in point. U.S. reluctance to act unilaterally to restore parliamentary government in Haiti or to stand alone in challenging Serbian aggression in Bosnia are additional examples. They reflect not only military prudence and the reality of resource constraints but also the judgment that, to gain legitimacy, such actions should be undertaken in conjunction with others, and with the approval of a wide segment of interested states. A modest step toward the codification of this norm is the 1992 U.S. "Defense Planning Guidance" document, which, after considerable debate within the Bush administration, expressed the U.S. support for the use of multilateral mechanisms to meet challenges to U.S. security interests whenever feasible.[73] The Clinton administration has continued this pattern, and its senior policymakers have underscored the administration's commitment to this approach.[74] With the added factor that the United States, the countries of western Europe, Russia, Japan, and China are increasingly preoccupied with domestic issues, the post–cold war environment presents favorable conditions for strengthening a code of restraint.

Many other states around the globe have also declared their support for military restraint and are participating in multilateral cooperative security arrangements. But commitments by the major powers, especially the nuclear powers, are the most critical element of a viable cooperative security regime. These are the states against whom the weaker members of the global military hierarchy most often have no recourse. To reassure these weaker states that their security can be preserved without the need to acquire their own weapons of mass destruction or extensive conventional capabilities, they must be convinced that they will neither be the targets of major-power aggression nor be left isolated in the event of aggression by regional adversaries.

The unwillingness of the declared nuclear weapon states to use nuclear arms in military conflicts, despite the involvement of all these states over the years in numerous, often bloody and protracted conflicts with a range of lesser powers, is an important factor. If a similar pattern of major-power restraint in the unilateral use of force (except in self-defense) were to emerge in the decades ahead, an international taboo of immeasurable value to a cooperative security system might develop. And if this taboo were, in turn, accompanied by a consistent pattern of multilateral intervention to block unilateral aggression on the part of lesser states, such a global cooperative system would appear increasingly achievable.

The key point is that as long as the global military hierarchy endures, the weak will feel threatened by the strong and will inevitably seek countervailing military capabilities. To break this cycle, less powerful states must be convinced that their more powerful counterparts will not take advantage of the military edge they possess and that, if aggression does occur, the international community will intervene on the side of the aggrieved party. As far as the smaller European states are concerned, this confidence has been severely shaken by the failure of the United States and the EC countries to intervene effectively in Yugoslavia. It is a central point that the existence of an effective multilateral peacemaking system ultimately depends on the willingness of its member states to use military force, risking the lives of their own soldiers, to prevent or contain organized violence. Without this willingness, states cannot entrust their security with confidence to the mulitlateral system. Ultimately, of course, such a global system rests on the maintenance of peace among the major guarantor states.

Conclusion

Drawing upon each of the three cooperative security nodes discussed in this chapter, it is possible to sketch the outline of a global cooperative network. In an idealized system, a state and its regional neighbors would be enmeshed in an elaborate set of reassurance arrangements like those found in Europe today, which focus on eliminating the threat posed by each other's conventional forces and which move the parties toward greater economic and political cooperation. Superimposed on these arrangements would be the various nonproliferation regimes, which, if adopted universally within the region, would significantly reduce the risk of new nuclear or chemical weapon states emerging and would constrain the further development of missile delivery systems—steps that, in effect, would help preserve the stable military status quo, which the first set of cooperative security arrangements had addressed.

These steps would nonetheless leave some of the participating states at some risk, since these measures would not address the remaining nuclear threat from the existing nuclear powers nor necessarily eliminate the threat of intervention by extraregional states with superior conventional capabilities. These threats must be dealt with through the institutionalization of the rule of restraint.

The residual risk to all states from biological weapons would, regrettably, remain, as would the possible threats to out-of-area territories and interests, unless these various cooperative security arrangements were truly globalized and took such distant defense concerns into account.

In many ways the model may be reflected in Europe several years hence, assuming that the CWC is in force there, that Kazakhstan and Ukraine join the NPT, and that Russia remains in its current pacific posture (not, for example, intervening unilaterally in the struggles of the other Soviet successor states to protect Russian interests). At that point, any threat to Europe from Russian (or U.S.) nuclear and conventional forces would be outweighed by amity and self-restraint.

In ten years' time the model may also obtain in Latin America, where significant confidence-building, regional integration, and nonproliferation initiatives are under way. Gradually, a rule of self-restraint is also emerging in U.S. policy toward Latin America, which may be further entrenched over time, particularly if there are no repetitions of recent U.S. unilateral interventions in the Caribbean Basin.

If the current nuclear impasse in North Korea is successfully resolved, and North and South Korea implement previously adopted normalization, nonaggression, and nonproliferation agreements, Northeast Asia may become another regional locus of cooperative security, overlain with global nonproliferation measures. A posture of restraint on the part of China, Japan, Russia, and the United States has also emerged and will probably be strengthened if North Korea ultimately relinquishes its intemperate foreign policy.

Prospects for a fully elaborated cooperative security system in the Middle East and South Asia may take longer to fulfill, but if the recent breakthrough in Palestinian-Israeli relations can be implemented, there may be hope for progress in the former setting. The India-Pakistan rivalry seems less promising, but with the passage of time tensions between the two may subside, and even today a process of limited confidence building is under way. As progress toward cooperative security is made elsewhere, moreover, pressures for the settlement of Indo-Pakistani differences will increase.

In sum, major building blocks of a global cooperative security regime are taking shape in terms of both global and regional understandings, and it is possible to visualize their slow but steady extension. Although the disparity in military capabilities among the nations of the world entails serious challenges for such a regime, these challenges are not insurmountable. They must, however, be acknowledged, and attempts must be made to address them directly.

Appendix: Principal Existing Regional Cooperative Security Arrangements outside Europe

Regional Organizations

There are several other regional security organizations besides those in Europe. The oldest is the Organization of American States (OAS), established in 1948 as a successor to the International Union of American Republics (1890). The OAS has often been hamstrung because of disputes between the most powerful member, the United States, and the Latin American member states; for example, with regard to the treatment of Cuba, Nicaragua, Grenada, and the Falklands war of 1982. The OAS's cohesion has improved with the fading of the cold war; a peacekeeping function was agreed on in principle in 1985. The OAS has been active in attempting to restore parliamentary government to Haiti after the eviction of President Jean-Bertrand Aristide (September 1991). In 1984 the Contadora Group (Colombia, Mexico, Panama, and Venezuela) initiated consultations with five Central American governments (Costa Rica, Guatemala, El Salvador, Honduras, and Nicaragua) to seek a political solution to Central American problems, which led to the "Arias Plan" and eventually to political settlements in Nicaragua and El Salvador.

The Organization of African Unity (OAU, 1963) has been preoccupied for most of its existence with the problem of South Africa and more recently with disputes over the status of the Polisario Front guerrillas in the Western Sahara, and it has been only moderately successful in mediating regional disputes. Nevertheless, the OAU has contributed to the settlement of several regional disputes, including the Algerian-Moroccan border dispute (1963), the Nigerian Civil War (1967–70), and the trouble in Chad, where in 1979 and again in 1981, the OAU sent a pan-African peacekeeping force to separate the warring factions (the force was disbanded in 1982). The OAU has been trying since 1964 to get agreement on establishing permanent peacekeeping forces. In July 1992, encouraged by the post–cold war increase in UN peacekeeping activity, the OAU agreed in principle that it should have such a force. The sixteen-member Economic Community of West African States, founded in 1975, has peacekeeping and security as an explicit objective. It mounted a peacekeeping force in Liberia in 1990.

The Association of South East Asian Nations (ASEAN) was founded in 1967. Its six member states (Indonesia is the largest) cooperate mainly in economic and social issues, but it also has a security function, with a long-discussed program for confidence-building measures and a project for establishing a nuclear weapon–free zone in the member states. In 1971 ASEAN declared Southeast Asia a zone of peace, freedom, and military neutrality. ASEAN contributed to the settlement of the ongoing conflict in Cambodia, convening the first meeting of the Cambodian parties involved in the conflict (informally held in Jakarta in 1988). The South Asian Association for Regional Cooperation (1985), which includes Bangladesh, Pakistan, India, Sri Lanka, Bhutan, Maldives, and Nepal, has focused mainly on economic cooperation but has also handled issues with security connotations, like terrorism.

Several other regional organizations have undertaken mediation and conciliation activity in security issues. These include the Arab League (1945), with a current membership of twenty-one states; the larger Islamic Conference (1972), which extends east to Indonesia; the Cooperation Council for the Arab States of the Gulf (1981); and the Nordic Council (1952). On a worldwide scale the Commonwealth of Nations (formerly the British Commonwealth) with fifty member states, and the Non-Aligned Movement (1961), which at its cold war peak had more than 100 members, have undertaken regional mediation and conciliation.

Regional Arms Control Agreements

Besides the regional arms control agreements in Europe already reviewed, there are several agreements in effect in other regions, and the network of such agreements appears likely to expand. The Antarctic Treaty (signed in 1959) declares that "Antarctica shall be used for peaceful purposes only" and prohibits "any measures of a military nature."[75] The Latin America Nuclear-Weapon-Free Zone Treaty (Treaty of Tlatelolco, 1967), which has a permanent council charged with verification, prohibits the testing, production, and possession of nuclear weapons by the participating Latin American states; it has entered into force for twenty-three of the twenty-eight signatory states. Five eligible states are not yet bound by the treaty, but Brazil and Argentina have committed themselves to apply the treaty to their territories in the near future. The South Pacific Nuclear Free Zone Treaty (Rarotonga Treaty, entered into force 1986; signatories, Australia, the Cook Islands, Fiji, Kiribati, Nauru, New Zealand, the Solomon Islands, Vanuatu, and Western Samoa) prohibits the manufacture, testing, or possession of nuclear weapons by the parties. The Mendoza Accord (1991) commits the participating states (Argentina, Brazil, Chile, Bolivia, Ecuador, Paraguay, and Uruguay) to not produce or possess chemical or biological weapons. The Cartagena Declaration (1991) commits the Andean signatory states (Bolivia, Colombia, Ecuador, Peru, and Venezuela) to not produce, possess, or test any weapon of mass destruction. The Joint Declaration on the Denuclearization of the Korean Peninsula between North Korea and South Korea (ratified in 1992) prohibits the deployment, production, possession, or testing of nuclear weapons.

Several further projects for nuclear-free zones include the proposed Middle East nuclear weapon–free zone; the South Asian nuclear weapon–free zone proposed by Pakistan; the project for the Indian Ocean as a zone of peace; the Arctic-Nordic nuclear weapon–free zone; the Southeast Asia nuclear weapon–free zone proposed by Indonesia for application to the member states of ASEAN; the South Pacific nuclear-free zone; and the OAU draft treaty making all of Africa a nuclear-free zone. A number of these appear to have some prospect of ultimate adoption.

There is a network of bilateral arms control arrangements in the Middle East arising from wars between Israel and the Arab states, including the Israeli-Egyptian Cease-Fire Agreement (1973), the Egyptian-Israeli Peace Treaty of 1979; and the Israeli-Syrian Disengagement of Forces Agreement (1974). These agreements establish verified zones of disengagement.

Notes

1. Ashton B. Carter, William J. Perry, and John D. Steinbruner, *A New Concept of Cooperative Security,* Brookings Occasional Papers (Brookings, 1992), p. 6. Elaborating on this definition, in chapter 3 Antonia and Abram Chayes offer the following useful conceptualization: "Cooperative security contemplates an expanding network of generally applicable limitations on [permissible] weapons systems and force structures. The limits will be defined primarily by agreement rather than strategic interaction. . . . Although sanctions have a place in such a system, the absence of any central political authority and the practical limits on resort to force mean that substantial compliance with these strictures cannot be achieved by the threat of military retaliation. Compliance must be induced by the continuing sense that the limits imposed on military capabilities are consistent with the security requirements of the participants and that they are being generally observed."

2. See Seymour M. Hersh, "A Reporter at Large: On the Nuclear Edge," *New Yorker,* March 29, 1993, pp. 56–73.

3. The rapid buildup of conventional forces, as seen in Iraq during the late 1980s, or the intensive application of new conventional military technologies, exemplified by Israel's decimation of the Syrian air force in 1982, can have a major impact on local military balances, but is unlikely to have a global impact as is possible with the spread of weapons of mass destruction, whose acquisition can affect states at all levels of military attainment. Moreover, efforts to constrain this form of proliferation have yet to reach what might be termed a regime, being limited principally to talks among the five permanent members of the UN Security Council and the UN arms transfer registry. For these reasons and because of constraints of space, the discussion of nonproliferation regimes in this chapter is confined to those relevant to the spread of nuclear, biological, and chemical weapons and missile delivery systems for them.

4. The distinction we draw here between interstate conflict and large-scale organized violence inside the borders of states is viewed by many as increasingly artificial. Established views of state sovereignty are weakening in the face of increasingly strong international norms for preserving human life and human rights. Moreover, because of the clear possibility that organized violence inside a state could trigger interstate war, governments and multilateral organizations interested in conflict prevention are also becoming more active in traditional domestic realms. Somalia and Yugoslavia are excluded here, however, because our study focuses on nation-states as still the main participants of the international system. We do not include domestic conflicts in our analysis.

5. See Chapter 1 of the UN Charter, in Francis O. Wilcox and Carl L. Marcy, *Proposals for Changes in the United Nations* (Brookings, 1955), p. 482.

6. Germany has also formally renounced nuclear weapons under Article 3 of the final settlement treaty providing for the reunification of the country. See "Treaty of 12 September 1990 on the Final Settlement with Respect to Germany," *The Unification of Germany in 1990: A Documentation* (Bonn: Press and Information Office of the Federal Government, April 1991), pp. 99–102; Article 3 on p. 100.

7. For a chronology and brief description of the agreement, see *Arms Control Reporter 1993* (Cambridge: Institute for Defense and Disarmament Studies, 1993), pp. 402.A.1–5.

8. See "Document on Confidence-Building Measures and Certain Aspects of Security and Disarmament, Included in the Final Act of the Conference on Security and Cooperation in Europe, 1 August 1975," in Stockholm International Peace Institute, *SIPRI Yearbook 1976* (Stockholm, 1976), pp. 359–62, especially p. 360.

9. See the agreement of CSBM Negotiators on February 21, 1992, *Arms Control Reporter 1992,* p. 402.B.297; and "Vienna Document 1992," in *SIPRI Yearbook 1993* (Oxford University Press, 1993), pp. 635–53.

10. *Arms Control Reporter 1992,* pp. 409.3–4. The entire text of the Open Skies Treaty can be found in *SIPRI Yearbook 1993,* pp. 653–71.

11. *Arms Control Reporter 1993,* pp. 403.A.3–6.

12. Ibid., pp. 403.A.1–2.

13. Ann Devroy and R. Jeffrey Smith, "President Orders Sweeping Reductions in Strategic and Tactical Nuclear Arms," *Washington Post,* September 28, 1991, p. A1; and Serge Schmemann, "Gorbachev Matches U.S. on Nuclear Cuts and Goes Further on Strategic Warheads," *New York Times,* October 6, 1991, p. A1.

14. George Leopold, "U.S. Nukes Leave Europe," *Defense News,* vol. 7 (July 6–12, 1992), p. 2.

15. See "Outline of the CFE-Treaty," *Arms Control Reporter 1992,* pp. 407.A.4–8. For more information on the treaty, see Catherine Guicherd, "Treaty on Conventional

Armed Forces in Europe (CFE): A Primer," CRS Report (Congressional Research Service, July 5, 1991).

16. This was a follow-on agreement to the CFE, both of which went into effect on July 17, 1992. Unlike the CFE, the CFE 1A does not require ratification and exists as a politically, not legally, binding document. *Arms Control Reporter 1992,* pp. 410.B.22–24.

17. On the Helsinki summit meeting, see *Arms Control Reporter 1992,* p. 402.B.308–09. See also the document on the CSCE Forum for Security Cooperation, ibid., pp. 402.D.69–74.

18. This aspect of the CSCE process and the establishment of a high commissioner for national minorities, noted below, extend beyond the core of cooperative security as the term is being used here, which speaks to arrangements for the regulation of national military establishments.

19. See "The Charter of Paris for a New Europe," *SIPRI Yearbook 1991,* pp. 603–10; and "Helsinki Document 1992," *SIPRI Yearbook 1993,* pp. 190–209.

20. Wilcox and Marcy, *Proposals for Changes in the United Nations,* p. 490.

21. Frederick Kempe, "NATO Leaders Prepare to Expand Ties to Ex–Warsaw Pact Countries," *Wall Street Journal,* November 4, 1991, p. 14. See also "North Atlantic Cooperation Council Statement on Dialogue, Partnership and Cooperation, 20th December 1991," NATO Press Service, Communiqué M-NACC-1(91)111 (Brussels, December 20, 1991).

22. Bruce George, *European and Transatlantic Security in a Revolutionary Age,* Report of the North Atlantic Assembly (October 1993), p. 11.

23. Fred Hiatt, "Ex-Soviet States End Joint Forces," *Washington Post,* June 16, 1993, p. A24.

24. Serge Schmemann, "Yeltsin Plans Peacekeepers for Moldova," *New York Times,* July 7, 1992, p. A8. See also "Peacekeepers Occupy Former Soviet Region," ibid., July 15, 1992, p. A4; and "Russia and Moldova Reach Accord on Dniester Region," ibid., July 22, 1992, p. A9.

25. Serge Schmemann, "Yeltsin Suggests Russian Regional Role," *New York Times,* March 1, 1993, p. A7. See also "Russia Sends Troops to Protect Tajikistan's Border with Afghanistan," ibid., July 20, 1993, p. A6; and Lee Hockstader, "Georgians Rush Reinforcements to Key City," *Washington Post,* October 20, 1993, p. A31.

26. Robert Seely, "Ukrainian Retreats on A-Pledge," *Washington Post,* October 20, 1993, p. A31; Thomas W. Lippman, "Harried Christopher Buoyed by Kazakh Success," *Washington Post,* October 25, 1993, p. A14; and Doyle McManus, "Ukraine Chief Says He Wants to Dump A-Arms," *Los Angeles Times,* October 26, 1993, p. A2.

27. *Arms Control Reporter 1993,* pp. 407.B.493–94. See also *SIPRI Yearbook 1993,* pp. 594–96.

28. *SIPRI Yearbook 1980,* p. 211.

29. Over a period of seven years both countries will reduce to a maximum level of 6,000 accountable strategic warheads on no more than 1,600 deployed strategic delivery vehicles. Launchers reduced by agreement (silos, submarines, and bombers) will be destroyed, but reduced missiles and warheads may be retained. See "Excerpts from the 1991 START Treaty and Related Documents," in *SIPRI Yearbook 1992,* pp. 38–63.

30. Under the Lisbon Protocol, moreover, Belarus, Kazakhstan, and Ukraine agreed to join the Nuclear Non-Proliferation Treaty "in the shortest time possible," commitments that, if fulfilled, will reduce the risk that any of these countries might develop nuclear weapons in its own right. Don Oberdorfer, "3 Ex-Soviet States to Give Up A-Arms," *Washington Post,* May 24, 1993, p. A1.

31. *Arms Control Reporter 1991,* pp. 611.B.695–96, 699–701. See also Schmemann, "Gorbachev Matches U.S. on Nuclear Cuts."

32. *Arms Control Reporter 1992,* pp. 611.B.717–20. See also Don Oberdorfer and R. Jeffrey Smith, "New Era of Nuclear Disarmament," *Washington Post,* February 2, 1992, p. A26.

33. See "START II Treaty," *Arms Control Reporter 1993,* Article 1, p. 614.D.4. See also Michael R. Gordon, "A New Amity, a New Treaty," *New York Times,* December 30, 1992, p. A1. Final disposition of the nuclear weapons withdrawn from field deployment through the U.S.–Soviet successor state agreements has not been resolved. Russia has undertaken a commitment to dismantle all tactical nuclear warheads withdrawn from outside the former USSR and from the republics and apparently intends to carry it out in a ten-year period. It is unclear to what extent Russia has undertaken a commitment to dismantle the warheads of strategic range delivery systems that are withdrawn from Belarus, Ukraine, and Kazakhstan. Russia is reported to be still producing weapons-grade plutonium. *Arms Control Reporter 1993,* p. 611.E.03.

In announcing unilateral withdrawal of U.S. tactical nuclear weapons in September 1991, President Bush said an unspecified number of these weapons would be dismantled and their fissile material stored. He did not announce the dismantling of any strategic warheads to be reduced under START. In July 1992 he announced the unilateral cessation of U.S. production of fissile material for weapons. R. Jeffrey Smith, "Bush Formalizes Halt to Nuclear Production," *Washington Post,* July 14, 1992, p. A6.

34. Immediately after President Bush's decision to remove sea- and land-based tactical nuclear weapons from Europe, the British government announced the scrapping of its short-range nuclear missiles and the removal of nuclear depth charges from its naval vessels. See Craig R. Whitney, "German Leaders and Other Allies Welcome Plan for Weapons Cuts," *New York Times,* September 29, 1991, p. A14. In June 1992 the French government announced the cessation of the *Hades* program. It was predicted that the existing thirty missiles would become nonoperational. See Marc Dufresse, "Mitterrand Abandons Final Warning," *Quotidien de Paris,* in Foreign Broadcast Information Service, *Daily Report: Western Europe,* June 23, 1992, p. 29. Bush and Yeltsin also agreed to work on a global system providing protection against ballistic missiles. See Ann Devroy and R. Jeffrey Smith, "U.S., Russia Pledge New Partnership," *Washington Post,* February 2, 1992, p. A1. There are many uncertainties in this project. On the one hand, such a system, if genuinely global with access to all states, might offer some protection against nuclear- or chemically charged missiles launched by a rogue state. On the other hand, the project would be very expensive and full of uncertainties as regards its effectiveness and effects on the military balance among participants. It would consume large amounts of monetary, technical, and political resources that, if applied to tightening the nuclear nonproliferation regime, might well have greater and more rapid positive results.

35. Tariq Rauf, "Safeguard the Nuclear Plowshare," *Defense News,* vol. 7 (September 28–October 4, 1992), pp. 23–24.

36. The U.S. Congress authorized and appropriated $400 million for fiscal year 1994. Added to the existing $800 million provided by the Nunn-Lugar bill, this amounts to a total aid package of $1.2 billion. Dunbar Lockwood, "Congress Approves Defense Bill, Cuts Back B[allistic] M[issile] D[efense] Spending," *Arms Control Today,* vol. 23 (December 1993), pp. 24, 27.

37. Douglas Jehl, "Clinton Asks Nuclear Powers to Join Test Ban," *New York Times,* July 4, 1993, p. A9; and Michael R. Gordon, "U.S. Hopes to Curb A-Arms by Restricting Fuel Output," ibid., July 28, 1993, p. A2.

38. See *Arms Control Reporter 1992,* pp. 611.B.746–47, on limitations of the U.S. Senate; and ibid., p. 611.B.755, on the Supreme Soviet.

39. *Arms Control Reporter 1993,* p. 611.B.817; and Jill Barshay, "Ukraine Ratifies Nuclear Arms Reduction Treaty," *Financial Times,* November 19, 1993, p. 3.

40. It is also possible that the three other declared nuclear powers—the United Kingdom, France, and China—will be drawn into a regime of nuclear controls and that this circumstance, together with the discovery of Iraq's secret efforts to achieve nuclear weapons capability, will lead to a more determined effort to limit the capability of the undeclared nuclear weapon states—India, Pakistan, and Israel—perhaps through regional agreements to restrict and monitor the production of fissile materials that could be used for weapons.

An additional area of U.S.-Russian nuclear restraint is nuclear testing. The United States and the Soviet Union put into effect the Threshold Test Ban Treaty (signed 1974, entered into force December 1990), which limits underground testing to yields of 150 kilotons. For the text of the treaty, see *Arms Control and Disarmament Agreements* (Washington: U.S. Arms Control and Disarmament Agency, 1982), pp. 164–70. Although the treaty did not go into force until 1990, both sides claimed adherence to it from the date of signing. The United States has suspended negotiations on a comprehensive test ban, however, which Russia advocates. In January 1991, at the request of five signatories of the Limited (or Partial) Test Ban Treaty, an amendment conference was held with the objective of converting the treaty to a comprehensive test ban convention. No agreement was reached owing to opposition by the United States and United Kingdom, which also opposed a vote mandating the foreign minister of Indonesia to continue negotiation. The sponsors intended to call for resumption of negotiations in 1993. See *Arms Control Reporter 1993,* p. 601.A.1. In July 1992, after Russia and also France had announced suspension of warhead testing for 1992, President Bush backed Defense Secretary Richard B. Cheney in insisting on the continuation of tests by the United States. However, to head off more drastic action by Congress, he announced that the United States intended to restrict its own testing to six a year over the next five years, with three of these below 35 kilotons. See R. Jeffrey Smith, "Bush Rejects Proposed Limits on Underground Nuclear Tests," *Washington Post,* July 15, 1992, p. A16. In October 1992 President Bush signed a water and energy bill containing a congressionally mandated testing ban. It provides for a nine-month moratorium on all testing beginning in October 1992, to be followed in the period 1993–96 by a regime of up to five tests a year, and then by complete suspension of tests for an indefinite period unless another state undertakes a test. See Jonathan Medalia, "Nuclear Weapons Testing: Should There Be Further Restrictions?" CRS Issue Brief (Congressional Research Service, June 2, 1993), p. 3. In July 1993 the Clinton administration declared a fifteen-month moratorium on U.S. nuclear testing, providing no other state conducted a nuclear test, and announced that it would seek to initiate negotiations on a comprehensive test ban treaty. See R. Jeffrey Smith, "President Extends Moratorium on Underground Nuclear Tests," *Washington Post,* July 4, 1993, p. A9.

41. Ann Devroy and John M. Goshko, "Israel and PLO Sign Peace Pact," *Washington Post,* September 14, 1993, p. A1; and Thomas L. Friedman, "Dividing a Homeland," *New York Times,* September 15, 1993, p. A1.

42. Only India has declined to participate in five-party discussions, claiming that "proliferation in South Asia is primarily a regional problem and, in the end, will require a direct high-level dialogue between India and Pakistan and a regional solution." *Arms Control Reporter 1993,* p. 454.B.173. For a summary of an administration report to the U.S. Congress on progress toward regional nonproliferation in South Asia, released

May 6, 1993, see ibid., pp. 454.B.172–74. For details of recent attempts to create a CSCE-type structure for the Asian-Pacific area, see ibid., pp. 850.365–73.

43. See "Treaty on the Non-Proliferation of Nuclear Weapons," *Arms Control Reporter 1993*, pp. 602.A.1–10.

44. R. Jeffrey Smith, "N. Korea Won't Quit Nuclear Ban Treaty," *Washington Post*, June 12, 1993, p. A1. See also *Arms Control Reporter 1993*, pp. 457.B.129, 138–39.

45. In 1995 the NPT must be extended indefinitely, or for a fixed term or terms. Given the growing importance of the pact and the dramatic actions by the United States and Russia to cut their nuclear arsenals, together with new hopes for the adoption of a global, comprehensive nuclear test ban treaty, there is growing optimism that the treaty will be extended for a substantial term.

46. See *Arms Control Reporter 1992*, pp. 602.B.216–17. Previously, IAEA practice had been to confine its inspection exclusively to installations declared by the inspected country. U.S. intelligence capabilities, which have been the principal, if unannounced, mechanism for detecting treaty violations in the past, have also been expanded with the establishment of a Non-Proliferation Center within the Central Intelligence Agency.

In addition, the UN Security Council has become increasingly active on nonproliferation issues, as evidenced by its forceful actions to eliminate Iraq's weapons of mass destruction and ballistic missile capabilities. In January 1992, moreover, the leaders of the members of the Security Council (except for Indian prime minister Narasimha Rao, who qualified his statement) issued an unusually strong joint declaration that reaffirmed their commitment to stemming the proliferation of such armaments around the globe. The declaration stated that the spread of weapons of mass destruction was a "threat to international peace and security," alluding to Chapter 7 of the UN Charter, which authorizes the council to impose economic sanctions or to use military force to address such threats. See "Summit at the U.N.; Security Council Summit Declaration: 'New Risk for Stability and Security,'" *New York Times*, February 1, 1992, p. A4.

Agreements between Argentina and Brazil and between North and South Korea for the implementation of bilateral nuclear inspections are an additional strand of cooperative nuclear nonproliferation efforts. Finally, reciprocal or unilateral freezes on the production of fissile nuclear materials, essential for the manufacture of nuclear weapons, are growing in number. North and South Korea have agreed not to build the facilities needed to produce such materials; Argentina and Brazil have informally pledged not to improve uranium to weapons grade; South Africa and Pakistan have both ceased producing fissile materials; and the United States has announced a similar freeze, while Russia has indicated it may do so once a dual-purpose plant that produces both plutonium and electrical power can be closed down. In September 1993, moreover, President Clinton announced that the United States would seek the adoption of a global ban on the production of fissile material for nuclear arms. Thomas L. Friedman, "Clinton to Outline New U.S. Proposals for Limiting Arms," *New York Times*, September 27, 1993, p. A1.

47. A second suppliers' group composed solely of NPT parties and known as the NPT Exporters Committee was formed in 1970 to develop export controls covering nuclear materials and nuclear-unique equipment. *Arms Control Reporter 1993*, pp. 602.A.2–3. The Nuclear Suppliers Group (which included several states that were not NPT parties when the group was formed) extended controls to nuclear technology and adopted additional guidelines to limit the transfer of particularly sensitive nuclear goods.

48. See Eduardo Lachica, "U.S., Other Nations to Control Exports That Could Be Used in Nuclear Bombs," *Wall Street Journal*, April 3, 1992, p. C10. See also *SIPRI Yearbook 1993*, pp. 242–44. Argentina and South Africa are not members of the group

but apply its rules, and all of the 155 parties to the NPT, including China and the other nuclear weapon states, are bound by that treaty to make all exports of nuclear equipment or materials subject to IAEA inspection in the recipient state.

49. For the development and a summary of the BWC, see *Arms Control Reporter 1993*, pp. 701.A.1–4.

50. For the series of events that led to Russian confirmation of Soviet BWC violations and the ensuing efforts to strengthen verification measures, see *Arms Control Reporter 1992*, pp. 701.B.88–106. For the text of a Joint U.S.-U.K.-Russian statement on biological weapons, see ibid., pp. 701.D.1–2.

51. By October 1993, 152 states had signed and 4 had deposited their ratifications. *Arms Control Reporter, 1993*, pp. 704.A.13, B.559.

52. This problem is not an easy one, as shown by slow Russian progress in implementing the U.S.-Soviet bilateral agreement to destroy most of the two countries' existing stocks of chemical weapons.

53. It is far easier to make chemical weapons than nuclear weapons, and chemical installations capable of doing so are far more widespread than nuclear installations; they can be found in nearly all countries of the world. Consequently, verifying this agreement to the satisfaction of member states will be even harder than verifying adherence to the Non-Proliferation Treaty. The CWC establishes an Organization for the Prohibition of Chemical Weapons to be based in The Hague with a Technical Secretariat and an Executive Council that should be more agile than the IAEA Board of Governors. For the CWC Executive Summary and the text of the convention, see "The Chemical Weapons Convention: Banning the Poisons of War," *Arms Control Today*, vol. 22 (October 1992), Supplement, pp. 2–16.

54. For more information, see *Arms Control Reporter 1993*, pp. 706.A.1–3. In September 1993 Russia signed an agreement with the United States under which Russia agreed to apply the standards and guidelines of the MTCR. Ibid., pp. 706.B.145–46.

55. See "Summary of Terms of MTCR," ibid., p. 706.A.4.

56. *Arms Control Reporter*, p. 706.B.101; and Jon B. Wolfsthal, "MTCR Members Agree on New Export Restrictions," *Arms Control Today*, vol. 23 (January–February 1993), p. 22.

57. As noted later, the growing and near-universal participation in the NPT leaves no question about its strong normative base, notwithstanding its discriminatory nature. In this respect, we disagree with the Chayeses' assessment in chapter 3.

58. Interviews with U.S. and Indian officials. See also R. Jeffrey Smith, "Pakistan Warned on Nuclear Parts," *Washington Post*, January 14, 1992, p. A12.

59. During 1993 the United States successfully persuaded Russia to modify an agreement to sell India cryogenic rocket engines, gaining Russian agreement to block plans to sell technology for manufacturing the system. See Serge Schmemann, "Russian Gives U.S. Challenge on Aid," *New York Times*, March 7, 1993, p. A7; and Sanjoy Hazarika, "India Asserts It Will Develop Rocket Engines," *New York Times*, July 18, 1993, p. A17. Washington had less success in gaining Chinese compliance with its pledge to abide by the MTCR guidelines, however, and in August 1993 imposed sanctions against Beijing for the transfer of MTCR-regulated missile components to Pakistan. See Daniel Williams, "U.S. Weighs Trade Curbs against China," *Washington Post*, August 25, 1993, p. A1.

60. See William R. Long, "Argentina Abolishes Missile Program with Iraq," *Los Angeles Times*, September 26, 1993, p. A15. Proposals for a global ban on all ballistic missiles are also receiving renewed attention. See Alton Frye, "Zero Ballistic Missiles," *Foreign Policy*, no. 88 (Fall 1992), pp. 3–20.

61. Evidence of this can also be seen in the recent adhesion of South Africa, the Baltic states, Belarus, and Uzbekistan, in the pledges of Kazakhstan and Ukraine to join the treaty, in the reluctance of North Korea to effectuate its threatened withdrawal from the treaty in June 1993, and in the decisions of the Islamic Middle Eastern states to remain in the pact notwithstanding the Israeli nuclear threat. Although Argentina and Brazil continue to reject the treaty because of its discriminatory nature, they have adopted nonproliferation controls identical to those in the accord, demonstrating their underlying support for the norm it embodies. See the "Safeguards Agreement," signed by the two countries, the IAEA, and the Argentinian-Brazilian Agency for Accounting and Control of Nuclear Materials on December 13, 1991. *Arms Control Reporter 1991*, pp. 452.B.132–34.

62. Under the NPT and relevant IAEA charters, IAEA inspectors have authority to inspect any location in an NPT party to determine if nuclear material may be present. In practice, IAEA inspections have been more limited, but the agency, in fact, has wide-ranging inspection authority, which is not subject to the detailed time and place limitations that restrict inspections under the draft of the CWC.

As suggested earlier, IAEA inspections failed to detect key elements of Iraq's massive clandestine nuclear weapons effort and have been subsequently strengthened. Nonetheless, the system continues to suffer from important limitations, particularly in cases where comprehensive inspections must be applied in states such as South Africa, Brazil, and Kazakhstan that have engaged in unmonitored nuclear activities before coming under the IAEA inspection system. See Leonard S. Spector, "Repentant Nuclear Proliferants," *Foreign Policy*, no. 88 (Fall 1992), pp. 21–37.

63. In 1991 the United States took action to withdraw its demand for "anytime, anywhere" inspection access in the CWC. The actively debated outcome created an obligation on the part of signatory states to provide access and the right to protect confidential installations not related to the convention. See Article 11, sec. 11, of the CWC, in "Chemical Weapons Convention," p. 13. The apparent contradiction is resolved by the concept of "managed access," which permits inspected states to remove documents and shroud sensitive equipment. See Lee Feinstein, "Germany Proposes Chemical Weapons Compromise," *Arms Control Today*, vol. 22 (July–August 1992), pp. 25, 32.

64. For a description of the relationship between the Security Council and the IAEA, see the testimony of Lawrence Scheinman, in *Iraq's Nuclear Weapons Capability and IAEA Inspections in Iraq*, Joint Hearing before the Subcommittees on Europe and the Middle East, and International Security, International Organizations, and Human Rights of the House Committee on Foreign Affairs, 103 Cong. 1 sess. (Government Printing Office, 1993), pp. 33–45.

65. See Article 8 of the CWC in "Chemical Weapons Convention," pp. 10–12.

66. *SIPRI Yearbook 1993*, p. 288.

67. See, for example, Carnegie Endowment National Commission on America and the New World, *Changing Our Ways: America and the New World* (Washington: Carnegie Endowment for International Peace, 1992), p. 75.

68. R. Jeffrey Smith, "U.S., Russia Settle Dispute on Selling Rocket Engines, Technology to India," *Washington Post*, July 17, 1993, p. A12. See also Steven A. Holmes, "U.S. Determines China Violated Pact on Missiles," *New York Times*, August 25, 1993, p. A1.

69. These states could, in principle, also threaten more distant states by using unconventional means of nuclear delivery; for example, by smuggling a nuclear device into an adversary state that could be detonated remotely.

70. It may be noted that until the START treaty, most U.S.-Soviet arms control measures were intended to strengthen and stabilize the nuclear deterrence relationship between the superpowers and thus played an ancillary rather than central role in the nuclear relations of the two states.

71. Israel, with its small, geographically compressed population and special sensitivity to chemical arms because of the Holocaust, is a possible exception to this generalization.

72. Chemical arms are presumably less threatening than biological weapons, but because there is so little familiarity with the latter as instruments of strategic deterrence and because no state has acknowledged possessing them, it is difficult to assess whether a "chemical weapon state" would be deterred by a "biological weapon state."

73. Patrick E. Tyler, "U.S. Strategy Plan Calls for Insuring No Rivals Develop," *New York Times,* March 8, 1992, p. A1.

74. See, for example, "From Containment to Enlargement," address of National Security Adviser Anthony Lake, at the Johns Hopkins Paul Nitze School of Advanced International Studies, Washington, D.C., September 21, 1993; and "Use of Force in a Post–Cold War World," address of Ambassador to the United Nations Madeleine K. Albright, at the National War College, National Defense University, Fort McNair, Washington, D.C., September 23, 1993, in *US Department of State Dispatch,* vol. 4 (September 27, 1993), pp. 658–64, 665–68.

75. See Article 1 of the Antarctic Treaty, *Arms Control and Disarmament Agreements,* p. 22.

FIVE

Cooperative Security and the Political Economy of Nonproliferation

Wolfgang H. Reinicke

THIS CHAPTER elaborates on a fundamental building block of cooperative security—the design and implementation of an effective regime to control the diffusion of weapons and dual-use technologies. It also addresses the implications of two motivating trends for cooperative security—the progressing integration of national economies and the worldwide spread of technology.

The international arms and technology trade, its subsidization, and the associated proliferation of weapons and weapons-related technologies were until quite recently largely a reflection and an instrument of the global competition between the two superpowers and their respective military and economic alliances.[1] Although the end of the cold war does not mean that the supply of and demand for weapons will subside, it does imply that this relatively predictable and controllable environment no longer exists. In the future, policymakers may have to deal with a much more unstable international climate, dominated largely by economic and technological factors on the supply side and by the likely resurgence of regional instabilities and conflicts on the demand side.

Although not the focus of this chapter, it is important to note that the design of a cooperative security regime also depends on and is shaped by other motivating trends, including the decline of military budgets and arms markets, in both developed and less developed countries, and the unprecedented opportunity for new forms of international cooperation that has come about as a result of the end of the East-West conflict. Without adequate policy responses

I am grateful to John Steinbruner for helpful comments on a draft of this chapter, to Adrianne Goins for valuable suggestions throughout its writing, and to Charlotte Hebebrand, Audrey Shimomura, and Dan Turner for excellent research assistance.

to these new domestic and foreign policy challenges, the various proposals to control proliferation developed in this chapter will fail.

Addressing the problem of proliferation as a set of issues separable from the broader foreign, economic, and security agenda is no longer appropriate. On the supply side, for example, the excess capacity in global arms production and the economic pressure on industry that is emerging mean that, in addition to its role as one of the principal causes of traditional security concerns, proliferation is now also becoming a consequence of political considerations such as unemployment as the industry struggles to adjust through a search for new markets abroad. As a result, successful consolidation and downsizing of the military industrial base must be one of the primary foci of nonproliferation policy attention. This process will redefine the traditional relationship between the defense and high-technology industries and the governments in supplier countries. The industry is progressively being transformed from an instrument of foreign policy enjoying generous subsidies and protection to a national liability with the potential for doing political harm to elected officials.[2] The debate over proliferation, therefore, will no longer be restricted to matters of foreign or traditional security policy. Rather, it will penetrate deeply into the domestic political economy of each nation, encompassing aspects such as labor market policies, investment, productivity, industrial policy, and restructuring.

Similarly, on the demand side of the proliferation equation, the end of the cold war has opened up the possibility of addressing, in a more consistent and comprehensive way, other aspects of international security. These aspects have, for political reasons, traditionally been kept off the international political economy agenda, including the persistent underdevelopment and poverty of much of the Southern Hemisphere, the pollution of our global environment, and the destruction of the planet's biodiversity. The magnitude of these problems and the urgent need to stabilize this situation are likely to require an unprecedented degree of technology transfer to the less developed regions of the world.[3] Under these circumstances, the imperative of economic development and the protection of our environment are the principal policy objectives, and proliferation is becoming a possible consequence of these objectives, as on the supply side.

As such, the dynamics of proliferation in a post–cold war world are becoming more complex. They will be driven by economic, social, and technological factors, in addition to traditional politicomilitary security concerns. A successful regime, therefore, must be able to deal with these multiple and sometimes conflicting policy objectives. It must internalize the shifting policy priorities, interests, and incentives of the actors—private and public—on both the supply and demand sides.

In addition to the near-term changes that have arisen as an immediate consequence of the end of the cold war, the progressive internationalization of national economies and the worldwide spread of technology have also affected the defense industrial sectors of the industrial countries. The globalization of the defense industry and the resultant "internationalization of availability" have already transformed the external environment of proliferation and export controls.[4] A brief overview of these forces and a discussion of the implications for proliferation is therefore useful.

Turning first to the progressive globalization of the economy, it is helpful to distinguish between increasing flows of goods and services across borders in the form of trade and financial transactions and the internationalization of production reflected in rising foreign direct investment. For many years, the rapid expansion of international trade has been one of the primary factors behind the trend toward internationalization. This expansion has been accompanied by even faster growth in international financial transactions.[5] During the second half of the 1980s, however, foreign direct investment by transnational companies overtook foreign trade as the driving force behind globalization.[6] The increase in foreign direct investment outpaced the growth in exports by two and a half times, amounting to a total stock of $1.7 trillion, with an annual flow of $225 billion during 1990.[7] The emergence of a truly global manufacturing network is reflected by the fact that in 1990 almost 40 percent of merchandise trade represented trade among the largest 350 multinational companies.[8] As to the United States, more than one-third of its external trade arises from trade between U.S. companies and their overseas affiliates.[9]

This globalization of economic activities through trade and foreign direct investment has led to a globalization of technology.[10] The exchange of finished and semifinished products, as well as growth in licensed production agreements, codevelopment programs, subcontracting, joint ventures, mergers and acquisitions, and exchanges of data and personnel—occurring even in closely guarded industrial sectors such as the semiconductor industry—has increased the spread and exchange of military and dual-use technology in the international economy, which now also includes the nations of the former Soviet Union.[11] In addition, the economic crisis in central and eastern Europe and the successor states of the Soviet Union has forced many of these governments as well as their scientists and engineers to offer their technologies, weapons, and scientific knowledge to the world market to earn urgently needed foreign exchange.[12] Although Western nations have tried to respond to this new threat of proliferation by offering joint scientific projects, the proliferation of weapons, technology, data, and human capital is nonetheless likely to be considerable, and the full extent of it will probably never be known.[13]

The internationalization of production and trade, coupled with the global diffusion of technology, has led to a sharp increase in what is known as "foreign availability" and in turn has enabled an increasing number of countries to produce many proscribed items indigenously.[14] In numerous instances, U.S. foreign availability assessment procedures simply have not kept up with the actual spread of technology.[15] For example, in the case of supercomputers, considered to be vital tools in the design of nuclear weapons and advanced missiles, three (and possibly five) countries other than the United States and Japan are close to producing their own supercomputers. To maintain a level playing field, U.S. and Japanese industries have pressured their governments to include these other countries in any future agreement controlling the spread of supercomputers.[16] In many other instances, the diffusion of a particular technology has been so widespread, spreading even to proscribed destinations, that a traditional approach based on denial has become unrealistic. In the case of fiber optics, for example, the nations of the former Soviet Union are expected to have completed development of their own fiber-optic technology by the middle of 1993.[17] Moreover, at least ten countries outside the Western Coordinating Committee on Multilateral Trade (COCOM) regime are now producing fiber-optic cables, further undermining export controls and creating an uneven playing field in the global market for telecommunications equipment.[18]

The progressive integration of national economies and the global diffusion of technology, both of which have been accelerated by the end of the cold war, present a major challenge to traditional approaches to the control of weapons of mass destruction and modern technology, in particular export controls. The following sections discuss various ways to respond to this challenge. After a brief discussion of the analytical framework, the analysis first outlines a series of policy responses on the supply side of the proliferation equation. To a large degree, these responses are shaped by the fact that, as national economies become more integrated, national borders as instruments of control become increasingly ineffective. Subsequently, the analyses discuss policy instruments that address alternations emerging on the demand side in a post–cold war environment and an increasingly integrated international economy.

Analytical Framework

The preservation of national security and defense remains one of the primary interests of any state or alliance of states. Given national security's inclusive character, and a government's monopoly over the protection of military security, the field of political economy conceptualizes national security as a public good.[19] This concept implies that the state, rather than the market, is best suited to, and thus primarily responsible for, the provision of the good in adequate and preferably optimal levels.[20] Uncontrolled proliferation of weapons and the spread of dual-use technology, if applied toward military use, are a threat to national security and the provision of the public good. In both cases, the sale and purchase of arms and weapons-related technology abroad represent instances of external diseconomies, in which market forces fail to generate an optimal outcome for society, resulting in market failure.[21] The risks and high costs of proliferation, as well as the need to contain this externality, justify the control of arms sales and dual-use technology, both domestic and international.[22] From the perspective of political economy, in short, proliferation is seen as a problem of economic regulation, that is, an economic activity that, although permitted in general, must be transparent so that public authorities can monitor it and avoid the occurrence of market failure, providing a public good, in this case, a nation's security.

The objective of traditional national or international export and proliferation controls such as the Export Administration Act (EAA) or COCOM has been the denial of access to technology.[23] This denial was primarily directed at the former Warsaw Pact countries and their allies. An extensive set of lists identified numerous categories of goods whose export to any destination in a proscribed country was illegal. The early success of COCOM, which was implemented at the domestic level of member countries through national export legislation control, was based on the leaders' ability to form a supplier cartel involving a relatively small number of countries and gain broad agreement on the merits of a denial strategy as long as the bipolar conflict existed.[24]

The transformation of the international system has challenged and undermined the traditional form of proliferation control based on denial. The internationalization of availability has made the successful maintenance of a supplier cartel increasingly difficult. The process of system transformation in eastern Europe and the former Soviet Union and their eventual integration into the world economy no longer justifies the objective of denial. Moreover, world trade has increased in both absolute and relative terms. In absolute terms, the volume of trade has steadily risen as tariff barriers have been progressively removed.[25] In relative terms, the increasing application of high-technology components in the civilian sector has led to a steady growth in the number of product categories classified as dual use.[26] This growth is likely to accelerate as the integration of civilian and military production increases with the worldwide restructuring of defense industrial sectors.[27]

Lower and more permeable borders present a particular challenge to the supply side of the proliferation chain, since they have rendered export controls increasingly ineffective and inefficient. In the future, any comprehensive control effort could seriously obstruct the relatively uninhibited flow of international trade. This obstruction would hamper the continued economic expansion vital to world economic growth, as well as the integration of the former eastern bloc and the less-developed countries into the world economy. To allow, therefore, for continued integration and liberalization of the world economy as well as effective control, new regulations will have to be applied further "upstream" in the chain of proliferation, closer to or at the level of production and relying on the principle of disclosure, which allows regulators to gather the necessary information. But in moving away from the objective of denial to the principle of disclosure, it is important not to confuse the change with deregulation. The increasing reliance on disclosure as a policy instrument is a reflection of the changing external circumstances that have undermined the effectiveness of a strategy of denial. The ultimate policy goal, however, remains nonproliferation and a nation's security.

However, no supply-side regime alone can hope to stem the rising tide of proliferation. Any comprehensive regime must also focus on the demand side, which has benefited equally from the integration of the world economy and the failure of traditional regulatory instruments. The sharp rise in foreign direct investment and the associated internationalization of production and global sourcing have allowed states to acquire individual components of weapons in different countries from different suppliers. The organizational structure of transnational corporations and the division of production processes into multiple stages in different countries with different regulatory frameworks have enabled the demand side to purchase individual parts for weapons in different locations over a longer period—a strategy called piecemealing—and have complicated the regulatory effort on the supply side.[28] Thus, although the supplier-recipient relationship remains an important one, regulatory efforts must also be able to track industry-industry relationships on a regional and global level, as horizontal and vertical integration continues to deepen.

From a regulator's perspective, in a global arms market the externality is becoming global as well, and even the most effective domestic supply-side or demand-side regime is likely to fail. Because national authorities lack regulatory power in the global market, they are unable to provide this international public good.[29] Moreover, efforts by an individual country to implement new and more effective regulations will be strongly resisted by that country's private sector, that is, unless these regulations are reciprocated by other countries.

Unilateral impositions of tighter controls on these transfers in a single integrated market create an uneven playing field, distorting international competition. In the medium term, they will lead to a reallocation of investment flows to areas with a more lenient regulatory environment. In the long term, they could lead to a reallocation of production facilities, costing additional investment and employment. In order to avoid "free riding" by corporations or countries in the international political economy of proliferation, supply and demand regimes must therefore be global in scope. From a corporation's perspective, only an international regime will guarantee a harmonized regulatory framework within which companies can compete on a level playing field. From a state's perspective, a supply regime will only be effective in controlling proliferation if it includes all suppliers.[30] Similarly, a demand-side regime in a regional or global context is more likely to succeed if all members of that region subscribe to its norms and principles.

In developing new regulatory approaches, both domestic and international, this chapter distinguishes between two forms of regulation: ex-ante, or preventive regulation, and ex-post, or protective regulation. Preventive regulation aims to create an incentive structure on behalf of corporations and governments that will reduce, or even rule out, the occurrence of market failures. Setting conditions for entry into the market for a particular product category, for example, can contribute to such an environment. Most important, however, preventive regulation should be geared toward the reduction of the so-called information asymmetry characteristic of any market environment. Asymmetries in the information available on the nature and characteristics of goods and services exist not only between sellers and buyers (sellers usually have more information about a particular product) but also between regulators and regulatees.[31] This asymmetry between market actors and public authorities often develops into what is also referred to as the regulatory dialectic—an adaptive sequence of regulation, avoidance, and reregulation.[32]

The structural changes in the international economy described earlier have increased the information asymmetry in the markets for arms and dual-use goods and technologies and have consequently reduced the capacity of the authorities to regulate the activities of market actors. National borders—once the central element of information gathering—have become more permeable. Global piecemealing, the internationalization of availability, and the ever-increasing number of dual-use goods and technologies have made borders increasingly obsolete in anticipating or detecting illegal behavior by corporations.[33] In addition, rapid technological innovation and development and their use across a wide spectrum of industrial processes make it almost impossible for the authorities to keep up with their potential military application.

Information asymmetry is likely to grow as the international economy continues to adjust. Authorities must therefore impose their control and information-gathering efforts at a different stage in the life cycle of a product. For example, some of the information asymmetry can be overcome by acquiring information directly from the manufacturer. Another approach would be to gather data indirectly from other market participants, including banks and other investors, insurance companies, and competitors. The information asymmetry must be overcome at the international level as well. The lack of information and inefficient exchange of data have made the global sourcing of weapons components a particularly successful strategy of acquiring countries. If applied through international institutions, preventive regulation can be used to induce countries to comply with an international regulatory effort on both the demand and supply sides.

In developing preventive regulatory mechanisms, one option is to use a mixed model of regulation, which incorporates elements of self-regulation into the larger control effort.[34] Unlike government regulation, self-regulation exists when industry members jointly pursue regulatory activities even in the absence of legal requirements.[35] A mixed regulatory approach uses elements of private sector autonomy, often with respect to administrative aspects of the regulations. Or it may develop regulatory standards with a clear and unmistakable role for government in enforcement, information gathering, and the establishment of due process. This approach may be of particular value on the supply side of the proliferation process, where close industry cooperation will be required to reduce the information asymmetry. In addition, an industry effort to monitor the flow of a broad array of goods and technologies is likely to be opposed if the scheme is designed and administered solely by the government.

Protective regulation, as opposed to preventive regulation, assumes that proliferation has occurred, and it tries to protect society from the costs of this externality and to prevent its reoccurrence. Merely by virtue of its existence, protective regulation can act as a deterrent for corporations and governments. The mechanisms used can include monetary fines, the revocation of manufacturing and trading licenses, and criminal penalties on violators at the domestic level and sanctions or other forms of economic and political isolation at the international level. Protective regulation, therefore, is vital for maintaining the credibility of preventive regulation, and it must be implemented with vigor and consistency. As conceptualized by cooperative security, the ultimate form of protective regulation—the instrument of last resort—would be military action.

Policy Implications: Supply Side

To be effective, supply side controls for many goods, especially for dual-use goods, will have to be implemented at an earlier stage than at present in the proliferation chain. To reiterate, the principal purpose of these regulations is to overcome the information asymmetry that exists between market actors and government regulators. Ideally these controls should start at the level of origination. It is possible to distinguish between two forms of controls, direct and indirect. Direct controls apply to the producer and distributor of a product. Indirect controls apply to other market actors involved in the production or distribution process, who also have access to the privileged and timely information required for effective preventive regulation.

Direct Controls

With the exception of a few countries and a relatively small number of technologies and product groups, the regulatory implications of international economic integration, combined with the need to promote economic development in the Southern Hemisphere, and the threat of global environmental pollution requiring the diffusion of needed technologies make traditional export control arrangements based on technological denial—national (EEA) or international (COCOM)—increasingly less tenable. The principal challenge for public policy, therefore, is to develop a series of preventive safeguards that allow the uninhibited flow of dual-use items and technology, while at the same time ensuring its civilian application. Such a scheme combines the goals of providing the public good, while maintaining an open international economy.

First and foremost, such safeguards can be established by ensuring a high degree of transparency at the firm level and in the subsequent distribution process. This transparency should reduce the information asymmetry and allow regulators to collect important data. The data gathered should provide for an effective monitoring of the source, quantity, foreign destination, user, and purpose of dual-use items.

As of April 1991, the German government has implemented a new data collection system called *Kontrolle bei der Ausfuhr* (KOBRA), which may serve as one model.[36] KOBRA is an online system available to all customs offices in Germany. It centralizes in a single data base all documents filed with customs offices. KOBRA signals whether or not a stated end user for a given product is known to be involved in weapons development. It compares an export document against a checklist of known "bad" end users, as well as against a list of countries and particular products those countries may be seeking to further their weapons development programs. These lists have been developed by the Customs Criminological Institute, which investigates and prosecutes violations in conjunction with the intelligence services.

KOBRA covers a very broad array of products. In addition to arms and munitions, it includes all chemical products, all related written materials and plans, all steel and metal products, machinery and transport equipment, electrotechnical and electronic products, fine mechanics, and optical devices.[37] For 1990 and 1991 these product categories amounted to 71.6 percent and 71.1 percent of all German exports, respectively.[38]

As currently organized, the system does not necessarily fulfill all of the transparency requirements necessary for regulators to overcome their lack of information and thus to permit a more open flow of dual-use technology. The system has also been strongly criticized by German industrial associations for being too cumbersome and overly bureaucratic, and it will certainly require improvement in the next few years.[39] What is important in this context is that a country has already implemented such a central data base and that this experience may serve as a model for other countries.[40] Moreover, as more goods are regulated in some form, industry may actually profit from a more efficient scheme using a single procedure. Given that it is computerized, licensing or other requests may actually be expedited.

In addition, other preventive regulations could be designed to induce exporters to provide regulators with necessary information. For example, a company can be required to appoint an individual in senior management, a board member, an executive, or a partner as a "technology transfer officer," who would be made personally responsible for the company's compliance with all national and international regulations. In cases of proven violations, such an officer would be held accountable. The officer would be charged with developing a company's own internal control system. The agency responsible for issuing licenses would not accept any requests unless the application contained the signature of the designated export official.

Another preventive mechanism is a measure that can effectively deal with the increased splitting of procurement operations to focus on smaller items that are not registered on any control list. In recent revisions of their export control laws, German authorities now require that any dual-use item be licensed if, with the company's knowledge, it will be used in the construction of or used within a plant that produces, modernizes, or services weapons or it will be used in weapons, munitions, or any military-related products.[41] Apart from destination and customer, the license must also indicate the exact purpose of the item's application. If authorities can demonstrate ex-post that a license should have been requested for an exported item, the exporting company will be found guilty of a violation. These data could be stored electronically, enabling the relatively easy identification of a particular country or individual company engaging in piecemealing. A proposal submitted by the European Commission to the Council of Ministers, detailing the structure of a European export control regime, proposes the same regulation for all twelve countries.[42]

For regulators, this approach is yet another way of reducing information asymmetry. They can gain important information on dual-use items and how they contribute to proliferation, and on the identity of foreign countries and companies purchasing these items. This highly valuable and up-to-date information can also be incorporated into the data base. Exporters would be likely to provide this information so as to comply with the law, especially because the authorities would have wide latitude in presuming the presence of "knowledge."[43]

It is often argued that companies simply cannot know the exact nature of a particular contract and its intended uses. Such an assertion, however, is questionable. For their own economic self-interest, the marketing and sales divisions of companies usually have very good information about the activities of their customers. Long-established customer relationships often provide insider information about the purpose of a particular order. Large corporations have foreign offices that are in close contact with their customers. On the basis of a historical pattern, they can evaluate whether an order is in any way suspicious, either because of the quantity of goods requested or the order's timing. Referring to the recent revelations of German companies' involvement in supplying Iraq with dual-use items, for example, most of which were *not* on any control list, a department head at the German Export Control Office stated simply, "They [German companies] had to know."[44]

Trading companies and third parties should be treated with particular care in this system. New customers must be screened and a background check of their previous suppliers run through the data base.[45] Support personnel such as technicians will have to install and service equipment on a regular basis. Contracts for the replacement of spare parts will provide an opportunity for the company to check on the precise usage of the items in question. In the future, companies will have to reform and tighten their internal self-control mechanisms. Better personnel training and more efficient dissemination of information should be priorities and should start at the research and development stage, when the potential military application of a product is often already known to scientists.

An acknowledged obstacle to the establishment of these various procedures is that companies often lack adequate intelligence information about possible arms-related activities by foreign companies—an instance of reverse information asymmetry. To make their claim of "existing knowledge" more credible, authorities should, in conjunction with the intelligence community, provide companies with information enabling them to make better judgments about legitimate and illegitimate contracts. To facilitate such intelligence sharing, business associations could be briefed routinely, perhaps on a bimonthly basis, and information could be distributed to all interested companies. Such an early warning system would not only help authorities in their effort to control multiple sourcing but also help companies suspend suspect potential business deals at an early stage, saving the unnecessary time and expense of canceling contracts later.

Another form of preventive regulation would be to subject recurrent violators to a series of special and costly controls. Such controls could range from unannounced company audits to special reviews of license applications, which could harm a company's reputation as a prompt and reliable business partner, especially if violations are publicized in the press. Investigating authorities could even be given the authority to tap phone lines and open business correspondence, given reasonable suspicions about a company's compliance with the law.[46] These measures can be implemented quickly and could be particularly effective against so-called front companies, often established with the sole purpose of disguising illegal transfers.

By definition, protective regulation, which limits the cost of proliferation to society, cannot be applied on the supply side ex-post. Proliferation occurs when a proscribed item has left the country of origin, and supply-side authorities thus lack the power to intervene. Protective regulation, however, can serve to deter future violators from engaging in an illegal activity. At the same time, it should be considered as a vital supporting element giving credibility to the entire set of preventive regulations.

In addition, such regulation could alter the incentives of the private sector actors and thus perhaps induce behavior conforming with the norms and principles of nonproliferation. For example, regulators can set financial penalties that would almost certainly ensure financial ruin for a company, or regulators could revoke business licenses for a specified or unlimited period. Less severe penalties could include an export ban on violators for all arms and dual-use items, independent of end use and destination. Such a penalty not only would hurt the company for the duration of the ban but also would tarnish the company's reputation. In addition, an export ban would allow competitors to take over the company's share of international markets, which could be difficult to regain. Long-term prison sentences can serve as another deterrent and could provide for a stiff minimum penalty to preclude suspended sentences, adding to the deterrent value of criminal penalties.

A Mixed Regulatory Regime?

The broad mix of preventive and protective regulations that would have to be implemented at the industry level would require close industry cooperation and interaction with governments. Cooperation would be needed to set workable and enforceable standards to manage the scheme, as well as to keep data up to date as technological innovation continues to change the definition of pertinent dual-use technologies.

Acknowledging this need for cooperation raises the question of whether a more mixed regulatory regime would be better suited to cope with these concerns. Such a regime would combine elements of industry self-regulation, focusing in particular on the preventive aspects of the regime, with government regulations, focusing more on the protective aspects as well as on enforcement of preventive regulation.

A brief example of such a regime from another policy domain may be instructive, to show that mixed regulatory regimes already exist that can accommodate very large numbers of participants and transactions and that have developed highly sophisticated monitoring and warning systems.

In the United States, policymakers can rely on a long and mostly successful tradition of mixed regulation in financial markets, in particular in the securities markets.[47] One such mixed regulatory organization is the National Association of Securities Dealers (NASD).[48] The NASD was established for the purpose of cooperating with the government in its efforts to prevent improper transactions in the securities business.[49] Pursuant to the provisions of federal law, the organization adopts, administers, and enforces the rules governing the securities industry. These rules must be designed to promote just and equitable principles of trade and to meet other statutory requirements. The Securities and Exchange Commission (SEC) supervises the NASD's operations and is authorized to review all its disciplinary actions and decisions.[50] In addition, the SEC has the right to review applications for membership and to examine any changes that are made in the rules by the NASD Board of Governors.

Among its many provisions, the NASD requires the registration of all securities brokers and dealers, and it maintains a detailed file containing professional and personal data to protect the integrity of the organization.[51] Detailed records of all NASD-registered representatives are maintained in the

NASD's Central Registration Depository system, which the public can consult using a toll-free number.[52]

The National Association of Securities Dealers Automated Quotation (NASDAQ) system is a computerized system that provides price information on the stocks of thousands of companies to broker-dealers. Each trade is registered by the system, and between 1978 and 1989 the annual volume of shares traded through NASDAQ increased from 3.7 billion to 33.5 billion shares.[53] To prevent any unlawful activity, NASDAQ continuously monitors securities trading activity through its system. Using a sophisticated computer system and software, NASDAQ's monitoring system, Stock Watch Automated Tracking (SWAT), tracks about 150,000 trades and 40,000 price quotes generated daily across the country, identifying any unusual price and volume movements. SWAT knows the historical trading patterns of over 4,200 NASDAQ companies. If indicators such as volume, price, or quote spread cannot be explained by the model, it automatically triggers an alert. A team of five analysts subsequently determines whether trading in that security should be interrupted.[54] The automated surveillance software is essential for detecting possible insider trading or other instances of questionable trading patterns, and it continues to be refined.[55] In 1992, the market surveillance system triggered 5,839 online price and volume alerts, leading to 96 formal investigations and the referral of 28 cases to the SEC for further examination or prosecution.[56] In addition, in 1992 disciplinary action initiated and acted upon by the NASD's compliance and arbitration committees, which are composed of industry members, led to 62 firms being expelled, 11 firms being suspended from membership, and 491 individuals being barred from membership.[57]

Authorities responsible for a country's export control policy could consider establishing a similar institution that requires the registration of all companies involved in the production or transfer of sensitive dual-use goods and technology. Although more refined and sophisticated, in many ways it would resemble the KOBRA system. The principal function of such an institution would be to establish the Automated Technology Transfer Registry (ATTR). The ATTR would take advantage of the sophisticated and powerful technology available to monitor technology transfers both within a single country and abroad. In addition to registering and tracking the flow of technology, a specially designed computer program would trigger a warning if a planned transfer did not comply with the parameters set by the program.

Among other criteria, these parameters should stipulate that (1) transfers can only take place among companies that are registered with the ATTR; (2) transfers can only take place if all the required information, including the destination, recipient, and purpose of the end use, is furnished; (3) transfers must be checked against a proscribed product and destination list that includes countries and end users and is regularly updated; and (4) transfers must be checked for possible piecemealing by the same supplier or across several suppliers.[58] If the ATTR sends a warning, the transfer is interrupted and cannot proceed unless it has been cleared by the authorities.

In addition to monitoring the activities of its members, the NASD also provides a series of other services. The various forms of support include written materials, updated reports, and training seminars for securities firms to help them comply with the regulations and to keep them informed of any changes in regulations. The ATTR could provide similar services that would be tailored to the specific needs of suppliers and act as an information exchange. The registry could be responsible for updating and explaining new export control regulations to companies. It could alert suppliers to new techniques used by front companies and countries to circumvent regulations and disseminate intelligence information that would be shared by the authorities via its computer network.

Many small- and medium-size companies would resist the implementation of such a scheme since compliance with such a broad-based and technically sophisticated control effort is likely to present high fixed costs. To reduce that burden, companies could contract out to the ATTR for the implementation and execution of their internal control effort, which would be subject to a regular export control audit.[59] Because of the economies of scale involved, these services would be likely to result in lower costs for each individual business and at the same time generate some income for the ATTR to support its monitoring operations.

In 1992 costs for the NASD and the NASDAQ system amounted to $191 million. These costs were covered by a total income of $218 million, leaving the organization with a net profit of $27 million and increasing its equity to $196 million as of December 1992.[60] User service fees were the largest source of income (36 percent), closely followed by membership fees (27 percent).[61] The greatest expenses were salaries (48 percent) and office expenses and data processing and communications, accounting for 8 percent and 7 percent, respectively.[62] Given the ATTR's emphasis on monitoring market activities rather than on providing them, income derived from user service fees is likely to be much smaller. This income may rise, however, as the registry begins to offer new and innovative services. Moreover, unlike the NASD, the ATTR would provide a public good and could raise additional income from member countries to match its expenses.[63]

The computerized monitoring system developed and used by the NASD and the discussion of the ATTR demonstrate that a broad-based regime is feasible from a technical perspective. Like NASDAQ, the ATTR would be made up of a large number of members, on which the registry would maintain very detailed information, including a profile of previous violations. The ATTR would have to absorb, manage, and store a large amount of data on a daily basis and retain it over a long period. The experience of NASDAQ, however, shows that handling these data is no longer the problem it may have seemed to be in the past. Although it does present a challenge, the implementation of measures to control access to the proprietary information of its members and to any pending disciplinary actions has been successful in the case of NASDAQ. Finally, NASDAQ has developed a high level of cooperation with the federal government, which is vital to ensuring its credibility with policymakers and the public. A mixed regulatory regime that monitors and controls the transfer of technology must likewise enjoy such close interinstitutional cooperation.

Indirect Controls

Even if such a highly effective regulatory regime were implemented, it is unlikely that direct controls alone or government regulation would be sufficient to overcome the information asymmetry. Authorities should therefore also rely on other market participants on the supply side to induce behavior that promotes the public good. For example, a regulatory regime is likely to encourage competitors to notify authorities if they are aware of any unlawful activities. Specific regulations, such as revocation of licenses or severe financial penalties that would result in bankruptcies, are likely to help induce such behavior. Companies are usually very knowledgeable about the activities of their competitors, and the preventive regulatory potential of tapping into that information could be considerable.

Since the motivating factor for competitors to share information would not just be ethical or moral but also economic, there is a risk that regulators might be given misleading and false information that could damage the reputation of a business, and set off a spiral of false accusations behind which true offenders could hide. To avoid this possibility, the institution responsible for implementing the regulations should set up a special division that verifies information of this kind and ensures that it is treated with the utmost confidentiality.

Another group of market participants that might provide valuable information about corporate activities are financial intermediaries. Intermediaries that finance the production of weapons and dual-use items and channel the proceeds from their sales could be subject to tighter controls on lending for activities that pose implications for proliferation. Regulating deposits of profits from proliferation activities would be a useful protective measure, for it would deter banks from repeat violations. These controls must be applied uniformly across all financial institutions, including branches and subsidiaries of foreign banks.[64]

Many countries already have regulations in place that are designed to target illegal cash proceeds and wire transfers of funds. Although wire transfers are more difficult to regulate, it is vital that these be scrutinized as well. The U.S. Department of the Treasury, for example, is considering a requirement for "financial institutions to develop a 'suspicious international wire transfer profile' and to report suspicious transactions to the Treasury."[65] In the United

States, which has by far the most extensive set of financial regulations, a series of laws address this issue.[66] The Bank Secrecy Act of 1970 requires financial institutions to ensure that adequate records are maintained of transactions that have a "high degree of usefulness in criminal, tax or regulatory investigations or proceedings." In practice, this requirement means that all transactions of $10,000 or more must be reported.[67]

More recently the 1986 Money Laundering Control Act makes institutions and individuals criminally liable for knowingly participating in money laundering. In addition, it covers a broad range of conduct and financial transactions that might facilitate the knowing concealment of the source or the existence of illegally obtained proceeds and criminalizes use and expenditure of illegally obtained proceeds. The 1988 Money Laundering Prosecution Improvements Act further stiffened these penalties and lowered the amount that must be reported.[68]

An effective supply-side proliferation control regime must make full use of these provisions and enforce them rigorously. If such rigor cannot be applied, legislation should be passed that specifically addresses the relationship between proliferation and money laundering. The recent incidents involving the Bank of Credit and Commerce International (BCCI) and the Atlanta branch of the Banca Nazionale del Lavoro have revealed that money laundering is not restricted to the drug trade but is also a widespread practice in international arms sales.[69] Among other provisions, such legislation could require banks to inform regulatory authorities about transfers from "proscribed" destinations or to companies or other end users that have a history of violating export control laws. As intermediaries, banks are in a unique position to inform authorities about incoming and outgoing payments for possible illegal activities, notice which could prevent the transaction from being concluded.[70]

To comply with such requirements, banks must institute the necessary internal control mechanisms in their foreign trade and exchange departments. The history of the Bank Secrecy Act (BSA) suggests that its reporting requirements have proved highly useful for civil and criminal law enforcement purposes. As one Treasury official commented, "Unlike various forms of compulsory processes, such as grand jury subpoenas or judicial orders, which are used only after the initiation of a criminal investigation, the reports provide a constant stream of data on large domestic and international movements of cash and furnish the basis for either initiating or expanding an investigation."[71] Given that most of these payments are made electronically, the tagging of country, company, and even product codes need not be a very costly or elaborate procedure. Bank employees in the relevant divisions should be sensitized to the problem of proliferation through training seminars and be kept informed of new developments in regular meetings. If a mixed regulatory regime is in place, these seminars could also be conducted by a supervisory organization such as ATTR. Since many of these national and international payments are made via foreign branches or foreign correspondent banks, cooperation among financial institutions is an important element in determining success.[72]

To support these efforts by banks, regulatory authorities—as is the case for direct controls—should work with intelligence services to provide financial institutions with all the information necessary to detect possible cases of money laundering. At the same time, the data gathered by financial institutions on money laundering should be collected and processed by responsible authorities and should be made available to corporations in a manner that respects proprietary information. The U.S. Department of the Treasury has established a Financial Crimes Enforcement Network, which is a multisource data access, financial analysis, and data processing system using artificial intelligence. It links federal law agencies with state and local governments, foreign governments, and financial institutions to collect information on suspected illegal transactions.[73]

In addition to the extra cost imposed on financial institutions, banks are likely to criticize these regulations on the ground that they interfere with the traditional confidentiality covering relations between banks and their customers. However, the history of the implementation of the BSA and subsequent money laundering legislation suggests that, over time, new requirements to combat proliferation would be met with greater acceptance.

One reason for acceptance is the growing public awareness of the serious implications of proliferation. From a public relations perspective, banks are likely to become more careful to avoid participating knowingly or unknowingly in channeling the proceeds from illegal transfers of arms and dual-use technology. Concerns about damage to a bank's public image from involvement in proliferation can encourage the promulgation of corporate policy guidelines among financial intermediaries, with the aim of learning as much as they can about their customers and the conduct of their business. This result is confirmed by the history of the practice of laundering drug money: financial institutions have become more aware of their strategic position in this process and the government's need to tap into information acquired by them. As one former regulatory official from the Treasury stated,

> The role of the banker has changed and is changing. Financial privacy is not absolute. It is a Hobson's choice for the banker dealing with a customer that *may* be a bit shady; either report him to the IRS . . . or face the prospect of being personally involved . . . in a sensational drug money laundering case.
>
> It is clear that bankers can no longer act in complacent ignorance of the world around them. . . .
>
> I have been amazed at the changes in attitude in the industry since I first assumed the position as Deputy Assistant Treasury Secretary for Law Enforcement. At first, virtually all bankers were opposed to the intrusion of government regulation aimed at illegal money laundering activity. Today, either because of the enormity of the drug problem, or because of a greater sensitivity and awareness of the potential for

> abuse within the financial systems of this country, I have seen a much more active interest and participation in the drug war by bankers.[74]

Although the resistance by banks to such a scheme is likely to decline over time because of their own self-interest, regulators can also encourage this evolution. The BSA has often been criticized for setting up a power structure between the government and banks, giving the impression that banks by themselves are uninterested in curtailing illegal activities, and for being too costly and excessively bureaucratic. One way to mitigate this criticism would be to adopt a mixed regulatory approach, as suggested earlier, which would rely more directly on private initiative. Such an approach is currently being practiced in Canada, where banks have been remarkably successful in developing procedures for detection and prevention among financial institutions. This approach could become a model for other countries.[75]

Another criticism that is likely to arise is that new regulatory requirements may stigmatize potential clients of banks because of the fear of criminal liability. As one critique of the BSA stated, "The social cost of imposing such a stigma on individuals—especially those who have not been convicted of, let alone charged with, any crime—should present grave civil liberties concerns even for the most ardent law-and-order legislator."[76] To counter such criticism, regulators must develop clear and fair guidelines for recognizing and reporting any illegal activity. The information collected by public authorities that is made available to banks is one measure that would help. In addition, law enforcement officials should provide assistance to financial institutions to identify criminal activity, including the sharing of intelligence, as already suggested in the case of direct controls.[77]

Financial intermediaries can help protect society from corporations' misdealings not only through the interception of payments and profits gained from illegal arms and dual-use sales but also through other direct contributions to the authorities' preventive regulatory efforts. In preparing a loan or underwriting a stock or bond issue, for example, a bank obtains access to very detailed information about the issue's intended purpose. Regulators could establish specific guidelines for financial institutions that provide credit or underwrite bonds or equity for projects either in a particular country or of a specific nature. The guidelines would require the creditor to furnish authorities with specific data to allow them to assess a project's proliferation potential at a very early stage, and if necessary either to intervene even before production or delivery has started or to keep the project on a watch list until further information is available. To ensure the availability of adequate information, financial institutions could in turn request a study by the borrower that discusses the proliferation potential of the borrower's planned project.

To guarantee compliance by financial institutions, regulators could establish liability for creditors that have failed to provide the required information in case a company has been found guilty of violating the regime. This liability would result in the imposition of fines or criminal charges if a loan office knowingly concealed information that could have led to the prevention of the proliferation. In developing such a legal scheme, policymakers can rely on the considerable experience that has been gained in establishing corporate and lender liability for environmental pollution.[78] In a recent case, a court in the United States ruled that banks are liable if they participate in the financial management of a facility to a degree indicating a capacity to influence the corporation's treatment of hazardous wastes.[79]

As the history of environmental liability suggests, financial institutions and insurance companies initially may reject this role in supporting antiprolifera-tion efforts. They will argue that they are ill equipped to perform this function, and that impositions of liability would be likely to reduce their willingness to provide credit to prospective borrowers in any business or area in which there is a risk of proliferation liability.[80] At the same time the experience also shows that the institutions have learned to cope with the new and still emerging environment and have responded positively in various ways.[81]

To cope with potential liabilities emerging from environmental pollution, for example, financial institutions and insurance companies have begun to seek services from special advisers who coordinate and market pollution and environmental engineering programs, conduct environmental risk assessments, handle environmental claims, and provide feasibility studies for captive insurers.[82]

To ease implementation of proliferation controls, a large international bank should establish a technology transfer unit with a specialist who focuses on these issues. It should also establish a clear internal decisionmaking process that assigns responsibility to a senior management official. Clients should be informed of the information that will be required, including documented proof that the company itself has adhered to necessary licensing rules. Looking again at the experience of environmental liability, banks in the United States have already taken on a central role in this process. As one expert put it, "Lenders become essentially an enforcement agency. . . . Almost all U.S. property now goes through a site assessment."[83]

Finally, financial institutions can use their efforts to support nonprolifera-tion by advertising a socially responsible investment strategy. In fact, so-called screened investment portfolios that ensure that funds are not invested to produce weapons originated as far back as the 1960s.[84] This form of investor responsibility is another way by which other market participants can engage in preventive regulation and ensure regulatory compliance by corporations. During the last decade, investors have become increasingly interested in ascertaining the uses to which their funds will be applied and the activities of firms in which they invest.[85]

The Securities Act of 1933 and the Securities Exchange Act of 1934 provide the legal basis for such an interest. Companies that raise capital through publicly offered securities must file various reports that disclose to the SEC and to shareholders all "material" financial information and other data. The term *material* is in fact not clearly defined, a circumstance that has led to many prolonged disputes.[86] However, the SEC itself has stated that any information for which there exists "a substantial likelihood that a reasonable investor would attach importance in determining whether to buy or sell the securities registered" must be considered material.[87] In addition, in a recent case, the Supreme Court stated that "disclosure, and not paternalistic withholding of accurate information, is the policy chosen and expressed by Congress. We have recognized time and again, a 'fundamental purpose' of the various Securities Acts, 'was to substitute a philosophy of full disclosure for the philosophy of *caveat emptor* and thus to achieve a high standard of business ethics in the securities industry.'"[88]

Together, these two interpretations of the laws could enable investors to require that they be provided with information with respect to both companies' involvement in arms production and trade and their history of compliance with nonproliferation and export control regulations. Investors can make use of organizations that compile information about corporations' policies and businesses on a regular basis. The Investor Responsibility Research Center (IRRC) in Washington, D.C., for example, is a nonprofit research organization founded by and for institutional investors.[89] Among many other services, investors can subscribe to the so-called Social Issues Service, which follows social policy proxy issues and their economic impact, including information on military contracting and nuclear energy.[90]

Investment banks and brokerage houses can also set up special funds that do not invest in any companies engaged in the production or sales of arms.[91] Given proper regulation, companies that are careful to adhere to the regulations will not incur any penalties, financial or otherwise, and may therefore also provide sizeable and secure returns to shareholders. The popularity of such funds could easily be further increased by granting investors special tax treatment, for example, a reduced capital gains tax. For the dual-use area, this solution is obviously not practical, but institutional investors could implement a policy of withdrawing investments, domestic and international, from a company that has been found guilty of violating the proliferation regime.

Caveats

The preceding discussion has shown that direct and indirect controls can be implemented on the supply side that will enable authorities to overcome the information asymmetry that exists in any regulatory environment, even one that has increased sharply in recent years. Proliferation has increased as a result of the progressive integration of national economies and the spread of modern technology around the globe.

The internationalization of economic activity not only requires authorities to reform existing controls to adjust to a new external environment but also makes unilateral reform increasingly difficult. Given that institutional structures differ considerably across countries, reform will require a wide variety of policy responses. Although these problems cannot be discussed in detail here, they should be addressed at least briefly.

With respect to unilateral reform, market actors will reject the imposition of new direct and indirect controls unless they are applied to all suppliers.[92] From the perspective of a firm or industry in a particular country, unilateral regulations represent an additional cost that distorts competition in the global marketplace, and industry will strongly resist their imposition.[93] Moreover, as experience in other policy domains suggests, imposing unilateral regulations will not achieve the intended effect.[94] Unless a country has a complete monopoly over a particular product, customers will engage in regulatory arbitrage and orient their acquisition strategy to other countries. (Ironically, a different country does not necessarily mean a different supplier.) In the longer run, the experience suggests that policymakers charged with enforcing nonproliferation will come under increasing pressure to adjust regulatory standards downward as industry contracts or threatens to leave its national jurisdiction to relocate in a more lenient regulatory environment, thus threatening investments and jobs. Aside from political controversies this pressure could set off a process of competitive deregulation and undermine the entire regulatory effort.[95]

The success of implementing new supply-side controls will therefore depend very much on the ability to establish an international regime that is characterized by common regulatory and enforcement standards. The regime does not necessarily require a full-fledged global institution for implementation. In fact, national regulators are in many ways better suited to implement internationally agreed-upon rules.

But some form of international institutionalization seems necessary. An international body could serve as an information exchange and coordinating mechanism, sharing data on the experiences of national regulators in implementing the rules and suggestions about how the process could be improved.[96] Many of the participating countries would also need to strengthen their domestic institutional structure to ensure that they could participate in such a regime, and an international organization could serve as a training center.

For a regime to be effective and credible, it will also require constant maintenance. Given that regulation fundamentally interferes with the market, some market actors will try to circumvent regulations not only by violating the regime but also by finding legal loopholes or through innovation. This action creates a regulatory dialectic and forces public authorities to monitor constantly the activities of the private sector and to adjust a regime accordingly.[97] Changes in the external environment of the market (such as new suppliers or deeper integration) may also require adjustments.

Experience from the field of global financial regulation suggests that, although it can be difficult and often time consuming, the creation of such a comprehensive supplier regime is not impossible.[98] In fact, in one area related to proliferation—money laundering—extensive efforts to build a regime have been under way for some time at the Bank for International Settlements.[99] In June 1992 the Group of Ten endorsed the Basel Code, which established new minimum standards to regulate international banks in order to reduce banking malpractice. The Basel Code was a direct response to the collapse of BCCI and the related illegal activities.[100] A particularly sensitive issue in forming such a regime has been the willingness of national regulators to share information with their counterparts, providing an interesting parallel with intelligence sharing to achieve nonproliferation.[101] Similarly, the Financial Action Task Force, formed at the 1989 G-7 economic summit, which operates under the auspices of the Organization for Economic Cooperation and Development (OECD), is currently reviewing the results of cooperation already undertaken in order to prevent the utilization of the banking system and financial institutions for the purposes of money laundering and will consider additional preventive efforts.[102] The 1988 UN convention against illicit traffic in narcotic drugs and psychotropic substances has even addressed the issue of bank liability.[103]

In many cases, the United States has taken a leadership role in these multilateral efforts. But it has also acted on a bilateral basis and induced other countries to strengthen their own internal control mechanisms as well as to support an international collaborative effort.[104] The U.S. 1988 Anti-Drug Abuse Act, for example, calls for the establishment of an International Currency Control Agency (ICCA). The agency is envisaged "as a centralized source of information and database [to] collect and analyze currency transaction reports filed by the ICCA's member countries, and encourage the enactment of uniform cash transaction and money laundering statutes by member countries."[105] In addition, recent legislation has strengthened the ability of national regulators to force foreign banks that want to establish a branch or subsidiary in the United States to adopt U.S. regulatory standards.[106]

A second issue that will arise in trying to forge such international rules is that different countries have different domestic structures and thus require different responses. Considering again the role of financial intermediaries in nonproliferation, a system relying only on the disclosure requirements of capital markets would capture a very small share of the investment activity in countries such as Germany, where much financing is provided through bank loans and where individual shareholders have delegated their rights to the banks through proxy votes. These conditions do not imply that indirect control is not possible in Germany, but it will require a different approach, one that focuses primarily on the universal banks, which make loans and underwrite debt and equity, rather than on the stock market in order to achieve the same result.

Most important, successful international cooperation will also depend on the ability of national actors to demonstrate leadership in international forums and to implement internationally the norms and standards that have been agreed upon at the domestic level. A weak, decentralized domestic regulatory structure that is characterized by turf fights and conflicting goals will not achieve such a goal.[107] In the United States, this effort would require the streamlining and consolidation of the current regulatory structure by establishing an independent agency, as has been suggested on many occasions for other reasons.[108] In conjunction with its recent revisions of the export control laws, Germany has split off its export control department from the Ministry of Economics and created a new independent federal control agency.

The three caveats briefly discussed pose additional challenges to policymakers in their efforts to create effective supply-side regulations in the changed global environment. But even if they were able to respond to these challenges, it is possible to think of several instances in which efforts to move the control regime further upstream would not necessarily lead to any greater control of proliferation. First and most important, such a policy measure would rely on governments to cooperate actively in the establishment of the regime. In some cases, however, *states themselves* are the source of proliferation and cannot be counted on as reliable partners to provide the public good by containing proliferation. Once controlled goods have left national jurisdictions, a scheme that relies on the ability of national political actors to enforce internationally accepted rules will obviously fail if states do not comply with them. Some states will remain immune to a regime that focuses on the supply side alone.

Second, in some countries, market structures—real and financial—are insufficiently developed to rely on other market participants' strategies to rectify information asymmetries. Even the most effective scheme that monitors the domestic market may not be able to control proliferation decisively. One of the advantages of the new supply-side regulations is that they permit the free flow of many dual-use items. This flow is possible because the regulations are designed to achieve a high degree of transparency that allows authorities to collect sufficient information to ensure compliance. For the regime to work, this transparency has to reach beyond the supplier nation and allow similar access to information on the demand side.

Policy Implications: Demand Side

As indicated earlier, the progressive integration of national economies has created a situation that is characterized by the coexistence of an increasingly unified world economy and a political system of divided authority. The operational domain of corporations already exceeds the political domain of regulatory authorities and has led to a decline in the state's capacity to regulate economic activities. As the global market allocates resources on a global scale, it also generates externalities on a global scale. As a result, the institutions of government become increasingly conditioned by the very market they themselves originally set out to constrain.[109]

If the process of international economic integration generates externalities at the global level, the public goods that counteract those externalities must also be provided at the global level. However, on the demand side of proliferation, the sources of the externality are not only private corporations that violate regulations. They are also states that purchase arms or acquire dual-use technology with the goal of producing arms and potentially threatening other states.[110] What was economic market failure at the domestic level in this particular case has turned into political market failure in the international political economy.[111]

A global suprastate to provide an international public good—nonproliferation—does not exist. Nonproliferation can thus only be provided through collective action by national governments in order to enable existing international institutions to internalize the norms of a nonproliferation regime or by creating a new regime founded on such norms. Although the structural specifics of such an institution are discussed by other contributors to this volume, it is worth pointing out that its design should be seen as an extension of the supply-side regime. Indeed this approach is essential if success on the supply side is to be achieved. For example, the various data collection schemes suggested in this chapter will only be successful if data collection can extend beyond the supply-side controls so that export data can be matched with import data.[112] This transparency will reduce the information asymmetry that exists among the members of the collective and induce behavioral patterns that conform to the rules of the regime, that is, induce preventive regulation. Transparency, or lack thereof, allows or constrains the collective to enforce the rules, that is, it induces protective regulation. Both types of regulation are therefore also central instruments for the provision of the public good on the demand side.

Military intervention to ensure compliance is only considered as a last resort under the principles of cooperative security, and other policy measures must be made available to ensure the implementation of preventive and protective regulation. Since there is no global government, many of the traditional measures, in particular legal instruments, employed at the domestic level are unavailable in the near term. The collective will therefore have to rely on its combined political and economic power to ensure regime compliance. This power could be exercised through the United Nations, with the support of such international financial institutions (IFIs) as the World Bank, the International Monetary Fund (IMF), and the various regional development banks, including the European Bank for Reconstruction and Development (EBRD), as is discussed in chapter 3 of this volume.

Preventive Regulation

With the end of global superpower rivalry, what has for some time been an economic reality has now also become politically more feasible. Proposals to reduce military budgets, based on the notion that such measures would facilitate the disarmament process and help release resources for economic and social development, date back to the 1950s and 1960s and have recently regained their prominence, with two former World Bank presidents endorsing such a policy.[113] Both the World Bank and the IMF have publicly linked excessive military expenditure to a lack of economic development.[114] In addition, the likelihood of a global capital shortage and the tightening of the financial resources of most members as a result of increased budget deficits may force lenders to establish high-priority expenditures that do not include funds for military expenditures. According to the managing director of the IMF, "in a world of scarce resources, we would be derelict in our duty to our membership if we were to ignore the hemorrhage of financing from productive to unproductive sectors of national economies."[115] The IMF estimates that if the industrial countries cut military expenditures by 20 percent from their 1989 level, budgetary savings of about $90 billion a year would be possible, after the initial cost of the major reallocation of resources. Also, if countries—mostly developing ones—with high military expenditures (as a percent of GDP) reduced them to the level of the world average (4.5 percent of GDP), an additional $140 billion would be released for economic development purposes.[116]

These policy statements are based on research undertaken by the IMF.[117] This work shows that military expenditures divert resources from other areas, such as social and economic services. In addition, military spending has tended to exhibit resilience during the implementation of adjustment programs that have emphasized fiscal tightening. This finding implies that the share of military expenditures as a percentage of total expenditures has actually risen as a result of IMF policies.[118] Both of the above-mentioned facts have prompted the Fund to offer assistance to countries in understanding the scope and economic effects of their military spending. The Fund's expectation is that if the waste and inefficiency of this process are demonstrated to them, countries are likely to reduce their overall spending on military hardware and to reallocate these resources to productive expenditures. (Note, however, that this may not necessarily result in an actual decline of a country's military arsenal.) At the same time, countries may also provide some of the data needed to achieve the high degree of transparency required both to achieve a nonproliferation regime and to implement the overall concept of cooperative security.[119]

The World Bank also considers military expenditures unproductive. The Bank has estimated that military expenditures in many countries exceed the combined government expenditures on health and education, a level that contradicts the bank's new emphasis on poverty reduction and is in conflict with its framework for controlling public expenditures. Most certainly the issue will be raised during the Bank's public expenditure review process, which is part of its new emphasis on fighting poverty.[120] Furthermore the Bank is considering the inclusion of a category for military-related debt in its debt-reporting system. Several countries, including China and Czechoslovakia, have already sought assistance with conversion, and a number of African states are seeking advice on demobilization and demilitarization, approaches which are supported by the Bank. Thus the Bank too plans to influence the level of military expenditure and in turn indirectly free resources for economic development by pointing to the opportunity cost of this nonproductive expenditure.

In addition, both institutions have demonstrated their concern with proliferation. As Camdessus argued in 1991, "We must not ignore the international trade in armaments. It is most desirable to avoid a recurrence of a situation in which substantial holdings of offensive weapons—far beyond the justified needs for defense—can be readily accumulated and indeed financed on easy terms."[121] This policy statement is in congruence with the principles of cooperative security.

The evidence suggests that both institutions could contribute to the establishment of a nonproliferation regime. Their efforts with respect to the transparency of budgetary policies, just as a first step, would help to reduce some aspects of the information gap among the collective of states and within each individual country.

At the same time, both institutions have on many occasions emphasized that they have only limited ability to influence behavior by setting specific conditions that require compliance with a particular regime. Respecting each member country's sovereignty and its own long-standing tradition of noninterference in the domestic political affairs of member countries, the Fund has pledged not to introduce a new form of "military conditionality" as a condition for access to IMF resources.[122] According to Camdessus, countries "should be assured that the Fund does not intend to interfere with their sovereign decisions when dealing with their national security."[123] The Bank, in accordance with the Fund's position, has also indicated that it will not consider any direct linkage between military expenditure and economic aid. This position is based on the Bank's Articles of Agreement. According to Article 4, section 10, "the Bank and its officers shall not interfere in the political affairs of any member; nor shall they be influenced in their decisions by the political character of the member or members concerned."[124] At the same time, a group of developing countries, referring to the end of the cold war and the possibility of channeling additional resources for economic development, "cautioned against the involvement of the Fund and the Bank in issues beyond their strict economic and financial mandate."[125] Under the present circumstances, therefore, IFIs appear to be limited in their ability to contribute directly or indirectly to the establishment of strong preventive or protective nonproliferation-related regulatory mechanisms unless they can undergo some form of policy adjustment.

Several other possibilities do exist. First, a close review of its charter indicates that the Bank could exert a greater influence on the level of military spending than it currently exercises, even while remaining within the constraints on political activity stated in section 10 of Article 4. This article also states that "only economic considerations shall be relevant to their decisions, and these considerations shall be weighed impartially in order to achieve the purposes stated in Article 1."[126]

Article 1 lists the purposes of the Bank, which include "the reconversion of productive facilities to peacetime needs and the encouragement of the development of productive facilities and resources" and "encouraging international investment for the development of the productive resources of the members."[127] Given that the Bank and the Fund have classified military expenditure as unproductive, loans that finance military or military-related production or purchases could be interpreted as inconsistent with the standards set out in Article 1. On this basis, moreover, borrowers could be asked to furnish information that demonstrates compliance with Article 1. Unless this information is provided, the Loan Committee could deny a loan based on its inability to determine if it constitutes a violation of the Bank's charter.[128] Thus even while staying within the limits of the Articles of Agreement, by focusing on the economic dimension of military expenditure, both institutions could exert more pressure than might be expected based solely on their current advisory status on budgetary matters.

At the same time, it is unlikely that this policy alone provides sufficient grounds for the establishment of a broad-based preventive regulatory regime that could exert pressure on members to comply with given norms and principles and contribute to nonproliferation. Yet as one IMF study clearly states, the institutions should become more fully engaged since "the evidence indicates that military expenditures are quite reactive to financial constraints. Therefore, without controls or pressure, foreign financial assistance both enables and encourages a nation to spend more on the military."[129]

As discussed, the provision of a public good—at the domestic or international level—requires political intervention. For IFIs to breach their official policy of noninterference in the political affairs of any member country may be problematic. Whether the Bank and the Fund have in practice managed to maintain such a clear-cut separation between economics and politics in the past is beyond the scope of this discussion, but evidence exists that the Fund and in particular the Bank have become involved in the political affairs of their member countries in recent years.[130] With the rising interest in poverty reduction, the Fund no longer refuses to consider "the impact on poverty and income distribution of policy changes supported by Fund financial assistance."[131] In fact some recent letters of intent have dealt specifically with poverty issues.[132] Similarly, the IMF has become increasingly concerned about the linkage between environmental pollution—an externality—and development.[133] Although official statements stress that the Fund has not adopted any form of environmental conditionality, it has been suggested that if the Fund "feels strongly about the environmental aspect . . . it might show itself less than forthcoming with a credit arrangement unless the member undertakes to adopt adequate environmental safeguards."[134]

The Bank has also become increasingly involved in issues of environmental degradation and poverty reduction. With respect to the environment, the Bank now calls for "targeted policies to change [environmental] behavior."[135] These policies advocate government intervention via the regulatory system, thus recognizing the presence of externalities in conjunction with market failure. The Bank goes even further to point out that effective policies against environmental pollution have to counteract political pressures "taking rights away from people who may be politically powerful." The poor and the weak "may be less potent politically than the polluters whom governments must challenge."[136]

Poverty reduction has become one of the Bank's principal policy objectives.[137] It has issued a detailed handbook and an operational directive on poverty reduction, which in effect details its involvement in the domestic politics of a borrower.[138] This handbook goes so far as to establish a clear sociopolitical basis for conditionality. According to the Bank, "the volume of lending should be linked to country efforts to reduce poverty. Stronger government commitment to poverty reduction—as measured by the adequacy of the policy framework for growth plus human development and/or willingness to reform—warrants greater support; conversely, weaker commitment to poverty reduction warrants less support."[139]

However, nowhere has the Bank abandoned its formal separation of politics and economics more than in its new initiative to promote good governance. According to the Bank, "governance is defined as the manner in which power is exercised in the management of a country's economic and social resources."[140] On the basis of that definition, the Bank has closely linked good governance to the provision of public goods. As a result, it has pledged to support a country's efforts to provide public goods and engage in an intensive dialogue with the country to induce change so that they can be better provided. "When that dialogue is not fruitful," the mandate stipulates, "it inevitably affects the Bank's analysis of the country's overall development management and performance, and in turn the nature and extent of Bank support for the country."[141]

All of these cases point to the fact that the Fund, and even more so the Bank, no longer really maintain the artificial separation between politics and economics and are in fact already moving toward a more integrated approach to political economy. Such an approach, in turn, would allow them to become more active in the establishment of a nonproliferation regime.

As already demonstrated, the World Bank position on good governance has already established a conditionality premised on the provision of public goods. The Bank thus would be in a position to implement preventive regulatory mechanisms. By reducing the information asymmetry, the Bank can ensure that its resources are not misused for the purchase of military hardware or the application of dual-use technology for military purposes. In many ways such mechanisms must rely on the same techniques that must be employed on the supply side. If possible, the Bank could therefore also rely on indirect controls by engaging other market participants, especially in the case of project-related financing. Apart from ensuring that World Bank loans do not contribute to proliferation, the data provided can be compared against those on the supply side in order to detect any inconsistencies in reporting. To give this process credibility, the data would have to be verifiable, though not necessarily by the Bank itself.

Still, several problems are likely to arise from including nonproliferation in such an explicit form of conditionality. First, many countries will simply reject this linkage as discriminatory, especially since the majority of countries on the demand side belong to the developing world. No doubt this form of conditionality will run the risk of being categorized as just another form of Northern domination of the South.[142]

It is true that the traditional notion of conditionality has been the subject of many disputes and is even controversial among economists. But this does not imply that attaching conditionality to the issues of nonproliferation is equally controversial in every case. On the contrary, the universality of the goal of nonproliferation from both a moral and a technical perspective, if globally applied, makes it an ideal concept for inclusion as a criterion for conditionality. In fact, by including such notions as poverty reduction, environmental protection, and nonproliferation in the overall concept of conditionality, the Bank and the Fund would substantiate their own recent acknowledgments of the interdisciplinary and complex nature of economic development. Moreover, by challenging the monopoly of economic factors in defining the terms of conditionality and reducing the associated social hardship of adjustment, this notion of conditionality would be more acceptable to developing countries.

These new aspects of conditionality are all enabling factors for economic development, turning it into a positive notion. Given the security guarantees that would be extended by a cooperative security regime, the ability to divert resources to nonmilitary activities and to gain greater access to advanced technology would appear to be a highly attractive incentive for joining such a regime. Finally, the small number of countries that have been actively seeking to avoid proliferation controls form only a small minority within IFIs.

A second weakness may arise if other IFIs, such as regional development banks and even the IMF itself, do not participate in such a scheme; the Bank's efforts would be weakened. IFIs must therefore apply conditionality criteria across institutions. To some degree, this is already the case. Lending by the Bank and the Fund are linked to each other and also increasingly to lending by regional banks.[143] However, to achieve a significant preventive effect, IFIs could begin by issuing a joint policy statement regarding nonproliferation. Given the overlapping membership in those institutions, cooperation in this matter should not be too difficult to achieve. Even more effective would be a linkage to private sector banks, since countries rejected for funding by IFIs are likely to approach them as alternative sources of funds. This particular linkage could be created in the context of individual domestic supply-side regimes, as long as national regulators agree to respect the need for a level playing field.

A third problem that is likely to arise is the need for consistency among institutions and the principal donors in their policies toward recipient countries. For preventive regulation to be credible and to act as a deterrent, its scope must be universal and cannot be subjected to a trade-off against other foreign policy considerations of individual countries.[144] This universality will be difficult to achieve. One possible way to do so would be to delegate to IFIs greater independent decisionmaking power. Although some transfer of power may be possible, its effect will be limited, and individuals will resist it. Another strategy to ensure consistency among regime members would be to establish procedures for extensive consultations, in particular with the country that may be the target of conditionality. The purpose of such consultations would be to draw the country into the regime before any policy action. According to the UN *Human Development Report 1990,* aid donors "should also recognize that the recipients do have legitimate security needs and that changes take time—and will require considerable adjustment to a country's economic and social policy. More can be achieved by persuasion than by coercion, by a vigorous policy dialogue than by formal conditionality."[145] But unless formal conditionality remains a policy instrument and IFIs have the power to apply it, the regime and its aims will not be credible.

In the long run, the question arises whether IFIs might be prepared to change their charters in such a way that they could more actively contribute to preventive regulation, thus providing an international public good. To a considerable degree, IFIs are a reflection of their members' interests and positions on these issues—usually those of the more powerful members. Thus any pressure for change in the charter to include some form of conditionality to enhance the international public good, such as regulating excessive military expenditure, encouraging compliance with the norms and rules of a nonproliferation regime, or providing incentives to join such a regime, is likely to come from countries that already plan to adjust their policies to include such forms of conditionality. Change in national legislation of this kind was advocated by the managing director of the IMF when he proposed as a "very practical first step . . . to tighten the rules for granting export credits for arms sales."[146]

It is encouraging to note that numerous countries have moved in this direction recently, to consider national legislation that contains elements of conditionality and even sanctions. In the United States, for example, the Pressler amendment has conditioned U.S. aid to Pakistan on a written certification by the president to Congress that Pakistan does not "possess" a nuclear explosive device.[147] In 1990, the United States cut off $573 million in aid to Pakistan because Pakistan was attempting to produce components for a nuclear device.[148] More recently, Executive Order 12735, implemented through the International Emergency Economic Powers Act, imposed conditionality for bilateral and multilateral U.S. aid and mandated sanctions on countries that are engaged in the proliferation of chemical and biological weapons.[149]

As table 5-1 shows, several bills have recently been introduced in the U.S. Congress attaching conditionality to development aid, including some export credits.[150] Other bills have gone even further by threatening trade sanctions and freezing assets (see table 5-2). Some of the legislation introduced is probably too sweeping to be desirable. HR 4803, for example, would, among other things, deny U.S. funding to the World Bank and the IMF and other "multilateral development institutions until such institutions revoke the membership of countries not adhering to appropriate non-proliferation regimes."[151] This bill thus would penalize the majority of countries for the activities of a few others. Better ways can be found to isolate such countries.

Germany and Japan, two other increasingly influential IFI members, have also recently begun to introduce aid conditionality into their bilateral programs, including measures to encourage transparency and restraint in recipients' military programs. Japan, which is the world's largest donor of economic assistance, has stated that its aid will be based in part on a potential recipient's military expenditures, its human rights record, and its establishment of a market economy.[152] At the same time, the Japanese have indicated that the strategy is based on rewarding countries that follow these conditions rather than on punishing those that do not. One exception is North Korea, on which Japan has applied stronger pressure. It has linked diplomatic recognition, the payment of war indemnities, and the provision of economic aid to the country's willingness to open its nuclear installations to international inspections.[153]

Germany too has begun to consider a broad range of conditionality in its bilateral aid programs. According to Carl-Dieter Spranger, minister for economic cooperation, Germany will evaluate a country's military expenditure in its future development policies. In assessing the defense spending of a country the ministry will apply the following criteria: "the share of military expenditure and total expenditure as a percentage of GNP; the ratio of military spending to other public expenditures, in particular education and health; and the share of arms imports as a percentage of total imports."[154]

Table 5-1. *Weapons Nonproliferation Legislation Invoking Aid Conditionality: Selected Bills Introduced during the 102d U.S. Congress*

Bill and sponsor	*Date introduced*	*Objectives or directives of the legislation*
H.R. 4803, Gonzalez	4/8/92	To promote the nonproliferation of weapons of mass destruction by denying funding to the international financial institutions until such institutions revoke the membership of countries not adhering to appropriate nonproliferation regimes
H.R. 4581, Rinaldo S. 2162, Harkin	3/25/92 1/24/92	To amend the International Financial Institutions Act to advocate and promote policies to encourage developing countries to reduce military and military-related expenditures and to dedicate an equitable allocation of resources for health and education
S. 2157, Cranston	1/23/92	To limit the provision of United States foreign assistance, including security assistance, to developing countries whose military expenditures do not exceed more than 3.6 percent of their gross national product
S. 1128, Glenn	5/22/91	To instruct U.S. representatives to international financial institutions to oppose any use of the institutions' funds to promote the acquisition, development, or stockpiling of any unsafeguarded special nuclear material or explosive device by a non–nuclear weapon state
		To amend the Export-Import Bank Act of 1945 to narrow the circumstances under which the Export-Import Bank of the United States may participate in financing the sale of defense articles or services to foreign countries
H.R. 2175, Kleczka	5/1/91	To amend the Export-Import Bank Act of 1945 to narrow the circumstances under which the Export-Import Bank of the United States may participate in financing the sale of defense articles or services to foreign countries
H.R. 1635, Moody	3/22/91	To expand the limited prohibition against the financing, by the Export-Import Bank of the United States, of the export of defense articles or services
S. 552, Cranston	3/5/91	To amend the Foreign Assistance Act of 1961 to provide support for emerging democracies and civilian control of military and security establishments in central and eastern Europe
S. 156, Mitchell	1/14/91	To reform the international military education and training program so as to empower civilians in the oversight and management of foreign militaries

Source: Foreign Affairs and National Defense Division, "Weapons Nonproliferation Policy and Legislation: 102d Congress," *CRS Report* 92-429 F (Congressional Research Service, July 3, 1991; updated May 5, 1992).

Table 5-2. *Weapons Nonproliferation Legislation Invoking Sanctions: Selected Bills Introduced during the 102d U.S. Congress*

	Nuclear nonproliferation		*Nuclear-chemical-missile nonproliferation, conventional arms transfers, dual-use commodities, and technology export legislation policy*	
Item	*(1)*	*(2)*	*(1)*	*(2)*
Bill and sponsor	H.R. 830, Stark	S. 1128, Glenn	H.R. 669, Rinaldo H.R. 868, Hunter S. 309, McCain	H.R. 3489, Gejdenson H.R. 3527, Schumer H.R. 2755, Markey S. 1601, Wirth
Targeted activity	Foreign "proliferation profiteers" violating U.S. and international standards for nuclear transfers	Foreign or U.S. persons who assist foreign countries in acquiring a nuclear explosive device or unsafeguarded special nuclear material	Acquisition or use of weapons of mass destruction or the transfer of illegal or dual-use goods and technology	Restrictions on nuclear and dual-use exports
Sanctions[a]				
Import ban	Two-year minimum	Yes	Yes	Two-year minimum
Export ban	No	Yes[b]	Yes	Two-year minimum
Forfeiture of property and assets	n.s.	n.s.	Yes	n.s.

Source: Foreign Affairs and National Defense Division, "Weapons Nonproliferation Policy and Legislation."

n.s. Not specified.

a. Under each bill the Office of the President is responsible for the identification of infractions. In addition, there are provisions requiring annual compliance reports, as well as a requirement that Congress be notified of all infractions subject to sanctions.

b. Ban on U.S. arms sales.

Other factors that will influence policy decisions are "arms production as a share of industrial output, military spending as a share of domestic savings, and soldiers as a share of the total population."[155] If a German aid recipient exceeds the regional average for one or more of these indicators, further studies will be undertaken that "focus on possession of or efforts to obtain weapons of mass destruction, long-ranged delivery systems and other technologically sophisticated weapon systems, the nature of the domestic arms industry, the role of the military in politics and in domestic social or ethnic conflicts. Of special importance are the recipient's attitudes toward international arms control negotiations and treaties."[156]

These indicators provide the basis for a constructive policy dialogue that, although it does focus on actual levels, attaches great importance to changing trends in the indicators. The new policy that includes other political and social criteria has already had practical implications for the 1992 budget. The aid budgets for India, China, Indonesia, Pakistan, Cameroon, and Zaire were reduced whereas those for Benin, Namibia, Nepal, Nicaragua, and Tanzania were increased. As for India, the initial reduction amounted to as much as 25 percent, although after further intensive dialogue with India and sincere efforts by the Rao government to reduce military expenditure, the figure was revised downward to 10 percent.[157]

The European Community has also used political conditionality in its relations with other countries. For example, the association agreements concluded between the EC and Czechoslovakia, Poland, and Hungary in late 1991 and early 1992 set specific political criteria.[158] In November 1991, the EC passed a resolution concerning development policies, policies understood to provide the policy framework for national decisions as well. In addition to stressing the importance of human rights and good governance, "the Council attaches very great importance to the question of military spending. Excessive military expenditure not only reduces the funds available for other purposes, but can also contribute to increased regional tensions and violations of international law, as well as often being meant and used for purposes of internal repression and denial of universally recognized human rights."[159]

The resolution stresses that at a time when donor countries themselves are attempting to reduce levels of armaments, development cooperation with governments that maintain excessively ambitious military structures will become increasingly difficult to justify. Accordingly EC members "may consider increasing support for countries which achieve substantial reductions in their military expenditure, or reducing support for countries which fail to do so."[160] Moreover the resolution also states that the Community will request countries that do receive development aid to cooperate voluntarily with the UN arms registry, an initiative that is supported by the EC and its member countries.[161] This resolution creates a clear linkage between the provision of aid and membership in a nonproliferation regime. In addition, if the Maastricht Treaty is ratified by the members of the Community, it will move the EC further down the road toward a common foreign policy, which will also include political conditionality.[162]

The EC approach suggests that it will make little sense for donor countries to impose conditions on their bilateral aid but not insist that their contributions to intergovernmental or multilateral organizations be subject to similar conditions. According to Germany's minister for economic cooperation, the "initiative with regard to taking defense spending on the part of recipient countries into account in connection with the provision of development assistance has found broad support among our bilateral and multilateral partners."[163] In fact, the World Bank's changing position on development issues and its new emphasis on the positive role of government in economic development can be traced to the increasing influence of some of its members.

Whether these developments will ultimately result in an amended charter is an open question, but it is important for the Bank and its members to internalize the dramatic changes that have occurred in the international political economy. It is significant, however, that the first international financial institution created after the cold war clearly reflects that change. Article 1 of the charter of the EBRD establishes a clear linkage between economic progress and political condition by stating that it will promote economic progress and reconstruction only in countries that are "committed to and applying the principles of multiparty democracy, pluralism and market economics."[164]

Several problems are still likely to arise when implementing conditionality measures at the national level. First, as in the case of the IFIs, tying developmental aid to low levels of military expenditure or to compliance with nonproliferation regimes runs the risk of being compromised on other foreign policy grounds. This situation can arise among different internal government institutions, as in the recent case of Germany and its foreign aid for Syria,[165] or as a result of different foreign policy objectives among countries, as in the recent disagreement among the United States, Europe, and Japan over the delivery of dual-use goods to Iran.[166] To make conditioned aid equitable and credible, clear policy priorities must be established and fully adhered to by the foreign policy establishments of participating countries. Similarly countries will have to come to agreement about the potential threats that may arise from the transfer of technology or from the sale of weapons to a particular region.

Finally, the OECD has been engaged in an effort to stop the practice by its members of tying aid or credits to the purchase of goods from the donor/creditor country. In February 1992, new rules on export credits came into force.[167] Officials must ensure that a policy that links aid and credits to regime compliance is not also used to tie these guarantees to the purchase of goods and services, thus undermining the efforts of the OECD.

Protective Regulation

As mentioned earlier, protective regulation is designed to serve as a last resort in the provision of the international public good and in limiting the costs of market failure. As is the case on the supply side, the principal function of this set of measures should be to act as a deterrent and to induce states to comply with the preventive regulatory regime. However, to achieve effective deterrence, regulations must be credible and applied in a consistent manner. The regime must be able to minimize the costs to other states in the collective if proliferation occurs.[168] Protective regulation in the international political economy relies on such instruments as sanctions in the area of trade and finance and the freezing of a country's physical and financial assets abroad.

Many have argued in the past that the success of sanctions has been at best mixed, although more recent evidence suggests a somewhat improved record.[169] Countries are often unable to reach a consensus on whether to impose sanctions, and effective sanctions are difficult to implement given the large number of supplier countries. Profits can be obtained from sanction busting by sidestepping an embargo, a violation that is difficult to verify. Sanctions also can backfire and, instead of improving a target country's behavior, can end up making it worse as the country grows more determined to fight back. This situation can arise particularly if the target country succeeds in gaining self-sufficiency and is able to circumvent the effects of sanctions. Often the harshest impact of sanctions falls not on the governing elite or the military, but on innocent civilians, and in particular on the poor.

Moreover, rather than prevent the use of force, sanctions may precipitate it since "military action is almost always required to make economic sanctions even somewhat effective. . . . Such military action . . . risks the combat that economic sanctions were meant to avoid."[170] Finally, sanctions also are often resisted by economic interests in the sanctioning countries since they hurt exporters and possibly even importers.

Two policy implications follow from the preceding analysis. First, given the difficulties of implementing sanctions, protective regulations should be applied only when *all* other possibilities have been exhausted. This implication puts the burden back on preventive regulations. These regulations must be prominent, well developed, and systematically structured, essentially establishing a norm that justifies subsequent enforcement actions. A failure to comply with these preventive mechanisms can thus only be interpreted as an open and deliberate rejection of the cooperative security regime, which threatens the security of members of the regime.

From an institutional perspective, the role of IFIs in applying international economic sanctions should be indirect. The decision to impose sanctions should be made by a recognized international authority, such as the UN. A decision of this kind made by the Security Council "create[s] a mandatory obligation for all states to comply, and afford[s] complying states complete justification for their actions."[171] This decision can help ensure institutional continuity during the implementation of protective regulations, avoiding unnecessary bureaucratic overlap among several institutions. But the UN can rely on IFIs to support its actions. Although both the World Bank and the IMF are autonomous international institutions, the UN recognizes them as two of its specialized agencies. The Bank and the Fund have signed an agreement with the UN in which they pledge to pay due regard to resolutions of the Security Council declaring sanctions against a country.[172]

Institutional Implications: A Primer

It follows from the preceding analysis that preventive regulations should be administered and monitored by the UN as well. The biggest challenge for the UN would be to institute a control mechanism that is able to verify the accuracy of information provided by recipient countries or companies, ranging from data about military expenditures and weapon production to information about the end uses of dual-use technologies.[173] Although the UN arms registry agreed upon in December 1991 could be seen as a first step in that direction, it will require a much more comprehensive effort to achieve concrete results. Some aspects of that effort are outlined in this section.[174]

The issue of verification has long been among the most challenging aspects of any technology control regime, and it is vital for sustaining effectiveness and credibility. The debate over effective end-use controls, on dual-use technologies in particular, has been given renewed impetus with the end of the cold war and the urgent need for technology transfer to former Warsaw Pact states. Technology is needed not only to support their reintegration into the international economy but also to combat high levels of environmental pollution, to reduce the risk of nuclear accidents in central and eastern Europe and in the former Soviet Union, and to discourage the migration of technology and expertise associated with the production of weapons of mass destruction.[175]

The degree to which end-use monitoring and in particular on-site inspections represent an intrusion on national sovereignty or could be used for illicit purposes such as industrial espionage makes this a very politically sensitive subject. Since most of the technology subject to control is still transferred from the developed to the less-developed world, such monitoring also runs the risk of being perceived as an instrument of commercial control and domination of the South by the North.

Several elements of a monitoring regime could help to avoid these negative consequences. First, the burden of proof in enforcing end-use controls should not fall only on technology recipients. Much of the needed information gathering can take place on the supply side. This arrangement would not only help allocate some of the costs of monitoring more equitably but also would allow the collection of important data early in a transaction. The data could be verified against information obtained on the demand side.

This approach is already being taken in the Enhanced Proliferation Control Initiative (EPCI) in the United States, a policy directed at the spread of chemical and biological weapons and implemented by the Bush administration in the wake of the Iraqi invasion of Kuwait.[176] It requires exporters when filing an application to consider "1. the specific nature of the end-use; 2. the significance of the export in terms of its contribution to the design, development, production, stockpiling, or use of chemical or biological weapons; 3. the non-proliferation credentials of the importing country; and 4. the types of assurances or guarantees against the design, development, production, stockpiling, or use of chemical or biological weapons that are given in a particular case."[177]

In another example the Department of State has initiated the so-called Blue Lantern program, which is designed to determine the destinations and end uses of defense articles and services originating in the United States.[178] Besides eliciting the cooperation of foreign governments, the program also enlists the support of U.S. diplomatic posts in the conduct of prelicense checks (PLCs) and postshipment verification (PSVs) of defense exports.[179] A PLC is an effort to predetermine the reliability of overseas recipients and to ensure that the proposed use of the commodity or technical data in question is consistent with the normal business of the recipient and that the transaction serves U.S. foreign policy and security interests. A PSV is employed to confirm that the exports have in fact been received by the designated end user and that they are being used in accordance with the terms and provisions of the approved license.

In Germany too new export control laws introduced in 1991 and 1992 place greater emphasis on supply-side controls in providing information about the end uses of technology. As described earlier, companies are required to ensure that the items transferred are for civilian use only. Firms can be held accountable for failing to do so. Authorities in turn support the private sector by providing intelligence information about violations of end-use requirements by the importing country or private company.

Another way to mitigate the appearance of the North infringing upon the South is to ensure that the monitoring of end-use compliance with proliferation controls is conducted on a multinational basis through an international institution or body. The executive council of the recently concluded Chemical Weapons Convention (CWC), which has jurisdiction for end-use monitoring procedures, represents such a multinational body. It is composed of forty-one states whose representation is based on geographic distribution as well as on the relative importance of chemical industries in particular countries. Although membership is decided on a rotating basis, countries with the most significant national chemical industries will always serve as permanent members.[180]

Many aspects of the end-use monitoring procedures of the CWC can serve as a model for a UN-administered technology transfer control system. The CWC contains extensive and detailed provisions for end-use monitoring.

To comply with the principal provision of the convention, a prohibition on the development, production, acquisition, stockpiling, transfer, and use of chemical weapons, the agreement provides for inspections to monitor the destruction of chemical weapons and dismantling of chemical weapons production sites. Given that many chemicals have a dual-use character, the convention also provides for the inspection of permitted chemical production. Inspectors may be notified only forty-eight hours before they are required to call in. The agreement also limits the quantity of certain chemicals that a country can possess at any time and requires detailed declarations about a country's production activities.[181]

Finally, Article 9, sections 8–25, of the CWC details the workings of so-called challenge inspections, which permit teams of inspectors, at the request of another country, to visit sites of potential treaty violations within as little as twelve hours of a request.[182] The access is "managed," permitting the inspected nation to take measures to protect sensitive installations and to prevent disclosure of confidential information and data not related to chemical weapons.[183] To avoid potential misuse of the convention for commercial or competitive reasons, "the Executive Council may . . . decide by a three-quarter majority of all its members against carrying out the challenge inspection, if it considers the inspection request to be frivolous, abusive, or clearly beyond the scope of this Convention."[184] The CWC convention demonstrates that, at least in principle, it is possible to design a regime that contains credible end-use control procedures and that is also able to deal with the sensitive issue of proprietary information.[185]

Politically, it is likely to be more difficult to establish such a regime for dual-use goods and technology, given that this area covers a much wider spectrum of industry. From a technical standpoint, only an electronic registry could manage the enormous variety and volume of transfers that would have to be recorded.[186] To process the data, members of the regime might consider a common coding scheme that makes the information for product specification, geographic origin and destination, end-use purpose, and other data comparable.[187]

Ideally, the UN would act as an umbrella organization that would allow national systems such as the ATTR, outlined earlier, to link up across states. Such a system would facilitate the detection of global piecemealing across supplier nations; it would allow recipient countries or companies to register licensed imports with an international body that could match these data with the information received on the supply side, and it would permit much tighter control of reexport violations since items would essentially be equipped with an electronic tag. In addition, the national systems could share data about previous violations and current inquiries and create a wealth of information in support of the nonproliferation effort.

Specially designed software could facilitate evaluation of the incoming information. Suspicious transfers—because of their origin (individual or multiple), their destination (country or company), their volume (either in a single shipment or over a period of time), the type of product, certain combinations of products or other selected indicators—would send a warning signal and initiate an investigation.

The investigation could start with a mere inquiry about the alleged violation but could escalate to a request for a detailed inspection of a plant under conditions similar to those provided for under the CWC convention.[188] National control authorities would be informed about the inquiry and, if it were deemed necessary, asked to stop any transfers until further notice. To deter competitors from abusing the system for commercial or competitive reasons, a procedure for not going ahead with an inspection, as in the CWC convention, could also be instituted. In addition, those violating the regime could be asked to carry the entire cost of an inspection.

Competitive concerns may also be a major stumbling block to the initial implementation of a regime. As discussed, industry in any country is likely to resist membership unless its competitors also join the regime.[189] End-use monitoring procedures are costly to implement, may create delays in deliveries, and can create confrontation between suppliers and their customers. These factors could create a competitive advantage for those that do not subscribe to the regime.

Great efforts must therefore be made to encourage a large number of countries to adhere to the regime and to ensure that the rules and principles of the regime are applied with equal rigor in each member's home market. To increase such an incentive, the regime could provide additional benefits or services to its subscribers. Limited but not direct access to the data base could provide valuable information intended to help companies avoid conflict with national legislation containing liability provisions. The regime could provide training seminars and other logistical help for countries that need to improve their national control systems in order to meet the international standards. In this context, the current experience by the EC in implementing its own control regime across different national structures and resources offers some valuable insights.[190]

In some cases the central registry could be a temporary substitute for those countries that do not have sophisticated registration systems in place and could save the high costs of implementing such a registry at the national level. Many developing countries do not possess adequate financial resources or the expertise needed to collect the required data. The regime should consider giving financial support to those countries that are willing to join but do not have the resources to create an adequate system of controls.

In the longer run, secondary or spillover benefits are also likely to arise from membership in such a regime. The risk that a participant in the regime will become involved in illegal activities is low, which enhances the participant's status as an attractive and reliable business partner.[191] Members of the regime may share additional commercial or other information that is beneficial to them through the network. Once a standardized coding system such as the unique identification code methodology (UNIC) is implemented, participants no longer would have to service different references created at each stage of a transaction. In international trade, these references range from the placement of the order to the delivery of goods. This coding system could avoid unnecessary errors and save time and resources, helping in turn to link shipping marks on the goods to references shown on documents and thus creating a competitive advantage for those that subscribe to it.

Members of the regime could also apply economic and political pressure on others to join. In the case of international bank regulation, for example, the United States requested that foreign banks that wanted to set up branches or subsidiaries in the United States adhere to internationally agreed-upon regulatory standards.[192]

The role of IFIs in such a structure would be similar to that of financial institutions at the domestic level: to require documentation by borrowers of regime compliance and to register these data with the UN. If it were deemed necessary, the regime could also share a selected amount of intelligence information with the IFIs, a process that would not only facilitate their efforts but also serve to reinforce them.

Conclusion

From a political perspective, the establishment of a global regime is likely to find increasing support among regulators. The last two years have demonstrated the inability of national authorities to provide the public good at the national level. To maintain their legitimacy, they will have to exercise their power collectively at the international level. As the experience of the globalization of financial markets has shown, the threat posed by an international financial crisis to the legitimacy of regulators will draw states, acting out of self-interest, into seeking cooperation within the international political economy.

From an economic perspective, the regime should gain the support of corporations. Given the general acceptance of some form of regulation of proliferation, it is a necessary condition for the continued liberalization of world trade, finance, and technology transfer. The alternative faced by companies is a resurrection of the type of barriers to international trade and finance that allow for more traditional controls. Though not entirely impossible, this forced disintegration of the international economy would be very difficult to realize and extremely costly.

From a social perspective, a global nonproliferation regime should gain the support of the people on both the demand and the supply sides. It would free badly needed resources for productive purposes, furthering economic development. It would allow for a more open and safer transfer of technology and would enhance a country's national security.

Finally, from an institutional perspective, a single regulatory framework that encompasses both demand and supply sides would allow for a truly globally integrated approach to proliferation since many, if not all, countries are likely to be subject to both supply- and demand-side regulations. A single institution would be essential for carrying out an evaluation of the intelligence information and data collected on both sides of the proliferation equation. Such an evaluation would be central to determining the success or failure of the regime. A single institutional framework would also facilitate the observance of level playing field conditions and provide a forum for the resolution of the disputes that almost certainly will arise on this issue. The UN arms registry and the P-5 process are policy innovations that both take place in a single institutional framework and contain elements of the proposals made in this chapter. Over time, both could develop into core elements of the regime.

If implemented, a regime that regulates the flow of arms and dual-use technology could broaden its scope to other areas of trade in the future. Trade in the chemical precursors required for the production of cocaine, heroin, and synthetic drugs can no longer be controlled nationally and has facilitated the work of international drug cartels; nor can individual countries monitor illegal trade in hazardous materials and waste, which has emerged as a highly profitable but largely unregulated industry, threatening people and the environment alike.

Notes

1. For a summary of the global arms trade, see Norman S. Fieleke, "A Primer on the Arms Trade," *New England Economic Review,* November–December 1991, pp. 47–63.

2. For example, in the United States alone, defense industry cutbacks in the period from late 1990 to mid-1992 accounted for over 25 percent of the nation's unemployment in July 1992. Furthermore, it is estimated that "the combined effect of direct and indirect defense private sector employment could well exceed 1.8 million jobs lost by 1996." Jacques S. Gansler, "The Changing Economics of Arms Production and Sales (in Advanced Industrialized Countries)," July 1992.

3. See World Bank, *World Development Report 1992: Development and the Environment* (Oxford University Press for the World Bank, 1992); and Clive Cookson, "Technology Alone Is Not Enough," *Financial Times,* June 2, 1992, p. 8. See also United Nations Conference on Trade and Development, *Periodic Report 1990: Policies, Laws and Regulations on Transfer, Application and Development of Technology,* UNCTAD/ITP/TEC/16, 1992 (New York, 1992); and UN General Assembly Resolution 44/228, adopted December 22, 1989.

4. On the internationalization of the defense industry, see Theodore H. Moran, "The Globalization of America's Defense Industries: Managing the Threat of Foreign Dependence," *International Security,* vol. 15 (Summer 1990), pp. 57–99; Ethan Barnaby Kapstein, "International Collaboration in Armaments Production: A Second-Best Solution," *Political Science Quarterly,* vol. 106 (Winter 1991–92), pp. 657–75; and Aaron L.

Friedberg, "The End of Autonomy: The United States after Five Decades," *Daedalus*, vol. 120 (Fall 1991), pp. 69–90.

5. On the internationalization of banking, see, for example, Ralph C. Bryant, *International Financial Intermediation* (Brookings, 1987); G. Bröker, *Competition in Banking*, Trends in Banking Structure and Regulation in OECD Countries (Paris: Organization for Cooperation and Development, 1989); Richard Portes and Alexander K. Swoboda, eds., *Threats to International Financial Stability* (Cambridge University Press, 1987); Shijuro Ogata, Richard N. Cooper, and Horst Schulmann, *International Financial Integration: The Policy Challenges: A Task Force Report to the Trilateral Commission*, Triangle Papers 37 (New York: Trilateral Commission, 1989); and Stephen Axilrod, *Interdependence of Capital Markets and Policy Implications*, Occasional Papers 32 (Washington: Group of Thirty, 1990). On securities markets, see Kevin F. Winch, Edward Knight, and Mark Jickling, "Globalization of Securities Markets," CRS Report, 89-363 E (Congressional Research Service, June 7, 1989); Joseph A. Grundfest, "Internationalization of the World's Securities Markets: Economic Causes and Regulatory Consequences," *Journal of Financial Services Research*, vol. 4 (December 1990), pp. 349–78; and Organization for Economic Cooperation and Development (OECD), *Systemic Risks in Securities Markets* (Paris, 1991).

6. This trend was facilitated by a gradual removal of regulatory barriers to both inward and outward investment in many countries. In addition to these liberalizations, foreign direct investment has also benefited from the innovations and liberalizations in major financial markets, including the lifting of exchange controls and the lifting of barriers to market entry.

7. The bulk of this investment originates in developed countries, which also attract more than four-fifths of total outflows, with the European Community, the United States, and Japan together accounting for 70 percent of world inflows. United Nations, Department of Economic and Social Development, Transnational Corporations and Management Division, *World Investment Report 1992: Transnational Corporations as Engines of Growth* (New York, 1992), pp. 1, 11–17. See also OECD, *International Direct Investment: Policies and Trends in the 1980s* (Paris, 1992).

8. World Bank, *Global Economic Prospects and the Developing Countries* (Washington, 1992).

9. Ibid.

10. See, for example, Janet H. Muroyama and H. Guyford Stever, eds., *Globalization of Technology: International Perspectives*, Proceedings of the Sixth Convocation of the Council of Academies of Engineering and Technical Sciences (Washington: National Academy Press, 1988).

11. For an overview of the issues, see John D. Moleff, "The Commercial Implications of Exporting and Importing Military Technology: A Review of the Issues," CRS Report, 90-409 SPR (Congressional Research Service, August 24, 1990). On the semiconductor industry, see OECD, *Globalisation of Industrial Activities, Four Case Studies: Auto Parts, Chemicals, Construction and Semiconductors* (Paris, 1992), pp. 133–60. The most recent wave of global strategic alliances took place in the semiconductor market. See Steven Butler and Louise Kehoe, "Partners Thank Each Other for the Memory," *Financial Times*, July 14, 1992, p. 17; and Paul Blustein and John Burgess, "High-Tech's Global Links: Costs Unite Former Rivals," *Washington Post*, July 16, 1992, p. A4. On scientific exchange with the former Soviet Union, see George Graham, "US to Buy New Russian Reactor," *Financial Times*, March 28–29, 1992, p. A1; Thomas W. Lippman, "Russian Purchases Approved," *Washington Post*, March 28, 1992, p. A1; and John Burgess, "The Search for Soviet Science Is Well on Its Way," *Washington Post*, February 23, 1992, p. H1.

12. On the former Soviet Union see, for example, Robert Mauthner, "The Arms Bazaar Fragments," *Financial Times,* January 15, 1992, p. 13; Doug Clarke, "Arms for Sale," *RFE/RL Daily Report* 55, March 19, 1992, p. 2; Chrystia Freeland, "Foreign Headhunters Lure Ukraine Missile Scientists," *Financial Times,* January 24, 1992, pp. 1, 14; "Former Soviet Borders Prove Easy Target for International Gun-Runners," *Financial Times,* April 29, 1992, p. 2; R. Jeffrey Smith, "Facing a 'Messy' Nuclear Scenario," *Washington Post,* November 26, 1991, p. A17; and Gary Milhollin and Gerard White, "Explosive Disunion: The Trade in Soviet Nuclear Know-how," *Washington Post,* December 8, 1991, p. C4. On eastern Europe, see "Klondike: Czechoslovak Trade in Arms," *Respekt* (Prague), no. 4 (January 27–February 2, 1992), pp. 5–7, reprinted as "Arms Trade Operates 'Uninhibited by Any Controls,'" in Foreign Broadcast Information Service, *Daily Report: East Europe* (hereafter FBIS, *East Europe*), February 4, 1992, pp. 10–16; "A Stop to Nuclear Projects," *Hospodarske Noviny* (Prague), February 5, 1992, p. 2, reprinted as "Carnogursky Does Not Rule Out More Arms Exports," in FBIS, *East Europe,* February 10, 1992, p. 6; Michael S. Lelyveld, "E. European Arms Exports Raise Concerns at US Agency," *Journal of Commerce,* August 6, 1991, p. 5A; "Corruption Discovered among Custom Officials," SOFIA BTA, January 14, 1992, in FBIS *East Europe,* January 16, 1992, pp. 14–15; and Paul Richter, "Ex-Officials of Poland Nabbed in Arms Sting," *Washington Post,* March 28, 1992, p. A17.

13. On the West's efforts to engage in scientific cooperation, see David Buchan, "West Urged to Hire Soviet N-Experts," *Financial Times,* January 29, 1992, p. 2; William Dawkins and David Buchan, "West Takes Steps to Plug Soviet Brain Drain," *Financial Times,* March 12, 1992, p. 2; and "EC Supports Establishment of Scientific and Technological Center in CIS," *The Week in Germany,* February 21, 1992, p. 1.

14. According to section 5 of the Export Administration Act (EAA) of 1979, foreign availability exists when any good or technology is available from a non-U.S. source "in sufficient quantity and sufficient quality so that the requirement of a validated license for the export of such goods or technology is or would be ineffective." 93 STAT. 509. However, recent experience in the case of weapons of mass destruction—in particular in the area of chemical and biological weapons—suggests that the quality condition imposed in the EAA is flawed. Chemical weapons can be and have been produced with technology far less sophisticated than that used in the West, making current foreign availability provisions ineffective.

15. See National Academy of Sciences, *Finding Common Ground: U.S. Export Controls in a Changed Global Environment* (Washington: National Academy Press, 1991), pp. 255–56. The diffusion of modern technology also presents a challenge to traditional efforts at arms control and containment of proliferation, since countries will try to compensate for quantitative restrictions with improved technological innovations.

16. John Markoff, "U.S. Seeks Broad Ban on Computers," *New York Times,* March 11, 1992, p. D1. The countries that are believed to be able to manufacture supercomputers are Britain, Germany, France, and possibly the Netherlands and Italy. The U.S.-Japanese agreement does not prohibit outright the sale of these computers, and the United States has sold such equipment to some developing countries, including India and Brazil, but attached stringent safeguards limiting their use to such nonmilitary applications as weather forecasting, scientific research, and engineering. See also "Supercomputer Export Controls Are Streamlined by Commerce," *Journal of Commerce,* May 15, 1992, p. 2A.

17. John Maggs, "Soviets Developing Fiber-Optic System despite Western Restrictions on Exports," *Journal of Commerce,* July 17, 1991, p. 5A.

18. Michael S. Lelyveld, "New Sources Peril Fiber-Optics Ban," *Journal of Commerce,* February 27, 1992, pp. 1A, 2A. The countries are Austria, Brazil, China, Finland, India, Israel, South Korea, Sweden, Switzerland, and Taiwan. Among them there are six "Section 5k" countries that cooperate voluntarily with COCOM, which leaves Brazil, China, India, and Israel. See also Michael S. Lelyveld, "US Official Denies Shipment to Russia of Fiber-Optic Cable," *Journal of Commerce,* February 28, 1992, p. 10A.

19. For some of the original work in this field, see Thomas C. Schelling, *The Strategy of Conflict* (Oxford University Press, 1960), and *Arms and Influence* (Yale University Press, 1966); Mancur Olson, Jr., and Richard Zeckhauser, "An Economic Theory of Alliances," *Review of Economics and Statistics,* vol. 48 (August 1966), pp. 266–79; Bruce M. Russett, *What Price Vigilance? The Burdens of National Defense* (Yale University Press, 1970); John D. Sullivan, "International Alliances," in Michael Haas, ed., *International Systems: A Behavioral Approach* (Chandler Publishing, 1974), pp. 99–122; Bruce M. Russett and John D. Sullivan, "Collective Goods and International Organization," *International Organization,* vol. 25 (Autumn 1971), pp. 845–65; and Duncan Snidal, "Public Goods, Property Rights, and Political Organizations," *International Studies Quarterly,* vol. 23 (December 1979), pp. 532–66.

20. For the seminal articles on public goods, see three articles by Paul A. Samuelson: "The Pure Theory of Public Expenditure," *Review of Economics and Statistics,* vol. 36 (November 1954), pp. 387–89; "Diagrammatic Exposition of a Theory of Public Expenditure," *Review of Economics and Statistics,* vol. 37 (November 1955), pp. 350–56; and "Aspects of Public Expenditure Theories," *Review of Economics and Statistics,* vol. 40 (November 1958), pp. 332–38. For an excellent summary of the issues, see J. G. Head, "Public Goods and Public Policy," *Public Finance,* vol. 17, no. 3 (1962), pp. 197–219. Note that it is not the production of these goods in and of itself that is considered an externality but rather their distribution by private sector actors, which are likely to have a different set of interests and thus have developed a different set of criteria for distribution (short-term economic gain) from that of their public counterparts (long-term national security).

21. For a useful summary account of externalities, see Francis M. Bator, "The Anatomy of Market Failure," *Quarterly Journal of Economics,* vol. 72 (August 1958), pp. 351–79; and E. J. Mishan, "The Postwar Literature on Externalities: An Interpretative Essay," *Journal of Economic Literature,* vol. 9 (March 1971), pp. 1–28. See also Tibor Scitovsky, "Two Concepts of External Economies," *Journal of Political Economy,* vol. 62 (April 1954), pp. 143–51; and Howard R. Bowen, *Toward Social Economy* (Rinehart and Company, 1948).

22. For a recent overview of some domestic control regimes, see Ian Anthony, ed., *Arms Export Regulations* (Oxford University Press, 1991); for developments at the international level, see International Institute for Strategic Studies, *Strategic Survey 1991–1992* (London: Brassey's for the IISS, May 1992), pp. 195–211.

23. For some background on the EAA, see Glennon J. Harrison and George Holliday, "Export Controls," CRS Issue Brief IB91064 (Congressional Research Service, March 2, 1993). For the history and workings of COCOM, see Michael Mastanduno, *Economic Containment: CoCom and the Politics of East-West Trade* (Cornell University Press, 1992); National Academy of Sciences, *Finding Common Ground;* Gary K. Bertsch, ed., *Controlling East-West Trade and Technology Transfer: Power, Politics, and Policies* (Duke University Press, 1988); and Ian Anthony, "The Co-ordinating Committee on Multilateral Export Controls," in Anthony, ed., *Arms Export Regulations,* pp. 207–11.

24. It must be noted, however, that the consensus over this strategy broke down long before the end of the cold war. Since the mid-1970s the United States and some European allies have differed over the merits of technology denial.

25. It is true that many tariff barriers have been replaced with nontariff barriers and thus that the degree of trade liberalization is often exaggerated. However, from the perspective of proliferation, this does not affect the argument, which is solely concerned with the disappearance or lowering of national borders.

26. The most striking evidence of this fact is that a comparison of the lists of the technologies most important for designing future weapons and the lists of critical emerging technologies required for international competitiveness in the twenty-first century overlap by about 80 percent. See Department of Defense, *Critical Technologies Plan,* prepared for the Committees on Armed Services, U.S. Congress (May 1, 1991); and Department of Commerce, *Emerging Technologies: A Survey of Technological and Economic Opportunities* (Spring 1990). See also Statement of Donald J. Atwood, Deputy Secretary of Defense, before the Senate Armed Services Committee, June 4, 1992, in *Department of Defense Authorization for Appropriations for Fiscal Year 1993 and the Future Years Defense Program,* 102 Cong. 2 sess., pt. 5 (Government Printing Office, 1992), pp. 483–84.

27. On civilian-military integration, see Gansler, "Changing Economics of Arms Production and Sales"; and U.S. Congress, Office of Technology Assessment, *Building Future Security,* OTA-ISC-530 (June 1992).

28. Take, for example, recent German arms exports to India and Iraq. A total of about 20,000 "Hot" antitank missiles as well as "Milan" and "Roland" surface-to-air missiles were exported to these countries by the French manufacturer Euromissile. See "Knacker für Kaschmir," *Der Spiegel,* no. 8 (1991), pp. 114–15; and "Nachschub für Saddam," *Der Spiegel,* no. 15 (1991), pp. 28–29. These missiles are jointly produced by Euromissile and MBB, which holds a 50 percent stake in the French manufacturer. These exports, forbidden under German law, are subject to a Franco-German treaty of 1971 that stipulates that neither of the two governments will obstruct one country's export of arms that have been jointly produced to third countries.

29. Wolfgang H. Reinicke, "Rethinking Contemporary Approaches to International Cooperation: International Public Goods and the Prisoner's Dilemma Reconsidered," Brookings, 1990.

30. As will be shown, however, this requirement does not imply that the building of a regime cannot start with a smaller number of countries. Similarly, the number of countries that belong to a regime may vary over time as more countries are classified as suppliers or others may renounce the production of a particular weapon, subject to inspection, indefinitely.

31. For the classic article on this subject, see George A. Akerlof, "The Market for 'Lemons': Quality Uncertainty and the Market Mechanism," *Quarterly Journal of Economics,* vol. 84 (August 1970), pp. 488–500. See also Richard O. Zerbe, Jr., and Nicole Urban, "Including the Public Interest in Theories of Regulation," *Research in Law and Economics,* vol. 11 (1988), pp. 4–5.

32. Edward J. Kane, "Policy Implications of Structural Changes in Financial Markets," *American Economic Review,* vol. 73 (May 1983, *Papers and Proceedings, 1982*), pp. 96–100; and Edward J. Kane "Interaction of Financial and Regulatory Innovation," *American Economic Review,* vol. 78 (May 1988, *Papers and Proceedings, 1982),* pp. 328–34. In financial markets the emergence of so-called financial derivatives is a recent case of regulatory dialectic. Those regulated will constantly try to avoid existing regulatory constraints. They can do this through innovation and the creation of loopholes in the legislative framework or they can take advantage of structural changes in

markets that open the possibility of avoiding existing regulations. The information asymmetry allows them to gain some advantage over the authorities. Regulators will eventually catch up with such market developments and reregulate, but not before a period has elapsed during which the potential for market failure is high.

33. Several countries are now actively trying to promote the integration of military and civilian technologies—especially in electronics and software—to dampen the economic consequences of cuts in their military budgets by creating a larger customer base; they also anticipate savings because regulations governing the military procurement process would have to be eliminated.

34. For some background, see Harvey J. Levin, "The Limits of Self-Regulation," *Columbia Law Review*, vol. 67 (April 1967), pp. 603–44; Jerrold G. Van Cise, "Regulation—by Business or Government?" *Harvard Business Review*, vol. 44 (March–April 1966), pp. 53–63; Ian Maitland, "The Limits of Business Self-Regulation," *California Management Review*, vol. 27 (Spring 1985), pp. 132–47; and David A. Garvin, "Can Industry Self-Regulation Work?" *California Management Review*, vol. 25 (Summer 1983), pp. 37–52.

35. Self-regulation includes such practices as the disclosure of product information, the establishment of minimum standards of safety and quality, the grading of products, and the creation of industry or professional codes of conduct.

36. *VSF-Nachrichten*, Vorschriftensammlung Bundesfinanzverwaltung N 1391, March 13, 1991.

37. According to a confidential industry document, it is expected that the system eventually will cover all products.

38. Statistisches Bundesamt, *Aussenhandel*, Fachserie 7, Reihe 2, "Aussenhandel nach Waren und Ländern," Dezember und Jahr 1991 (Wiesbaden: Statistisches Bundesamt, 1992), pp. 6–13.

39. One improvement would be to allow companies to register their intended exports directly with customs authorities from company offices. The authorities in turn would be required to respond to the registration request within a specified time period. As both regulators and regulatees gain experience, many other improvements are likely to be made. However, so far no complaints have been voiced that the system would leak proprietary information to competitors, an issue that is often brought up in discussions on such central data collection systems.

40. The Congressional Budget Office is also considering the creation of a data base for registration of weapons transfers. See Congressional Budget Office, *Limiting Conventional Arms Exports to the Middle East* (September 1992), pp. 42–44.

41. See, for example, "Bericht der Bundesregierung über die Verschärfung der Kontrolle des Exports von zivil und militärisch verwendbaren Gütern," Bundesministerium für Wirtschaft, *Dokumentation*, no. 318 (Bonn, March 11, 1992); "Massnahmen der Budersregierung zur Verbesserung der Exportkontrollen," *Bulletin*, no. 15 (February 1991); and Ministry of Economics, "Subject: Tightening of the Foreign Trade and Payments Controls since the Beginning of 1989," V B 2-48 03 00/5 (Bonn, August 6, 1991). The regulation has been implemented through Article 5c of the new Foreign Trade and Payments Act, which went into effect on February 14, 1992. See "Germany Sets Up Export Control Data Base," *Mednews*, July 6, 1992, pp. 4–5.

42. Commission of the European Communities (CEC), "Proposal for a Council Regulation (EEC) on the Control of Exports of Certain Dual-Use Goods and Technologies and of Certain Nuclear Products and Technologies," COM(92)317 final (Brussels, August 31, 1992); and CEC, "Export Controls on Dual-Use Goods and Technologies and the Completion of the Internal Market," communication from the Commission to the Council and the Parliament, SEC(92)85 final (Brussels, January 31, 1992).

43. According to a conversation in spring 1992 with a German official in the Ministry of Economics who is involved in shaping the regulation, the difficult aspect is to determine when knowledge was present. According to the official the government is likely to interpret this clause very broadly—that is, not "must have known" but "could have known."

44. R. Jeffrey Smith and Marc Fisher, "German Firms Primed Iraq's War Machine," *Washington Post,* July 23, 1992, p. A1.

45. The German chemical firm BASF has an extensive internal control mechanism that includes many more such controls and safeguards. If the customer is not known, for example, the company simply does not deliver. See "Industrie und Verbände warnen eindringlich vor einem übereilten 'Aktionismus' der Bonner Politiker," *Handelsblatt,* January 28, 1991.

46. The last of these provisions has now been introduced in Germany. Under a court order customs agents can infringe this right of privacy if there is prima facie evidence that the company plans a criminal offense. See paragraph 39 of the Gezetz zur Änderung des Aussenwirtschaftsgesetzes des Strafbuchgesetzes und anderer Gesetze, February 28, 1992, in *Bundesgesetzblatt,* 1992, pt. 1. See also "Der Bundestag beschliesst verschärfung der Exportkontrollen," January 24, 1992, pp. 1, 2.

47. See for example Franklin R. Edwards, "Futures Markets in Transition: The Uneasy Balance between Government and Self-Regulation," *Journal of Futures Markets,* vol. 3, no. 2 (1983), pp. 191–206; and Todd E. Petzel, "Self-Regulation and Futures Markets: Benefits from Technology Gains," in Anthony Saunders and Lawrence J. White, eds., *Technology and the Regulation of Financial Markets: Securities, Futures, and Banking* (Lexington: Heath, 1986), pp. 73–77.

48. For some background material, see Leo M. Loll and Julian G. Buckley, *The Over-the-Counter Securities Markets,* 4th ed. (Prentice-Hall, 1981).

49. The NASD was created in 1939 under the Maloney Act, as an amendment to the Securities Exchange Act of 1934. See ibid., p. 410.

50. Garvin, "Can Industry Self-Regulation Work?" pp. 46–47; and Marianne K. Smythe, "Government Supervised Self-Regulation in the Securities Industry and the Antitrust Laws: Suggestions for an Accommodation," *North Carolina Law Review,* vol. 62 (March 1984), p. 503.

51. These data include a record of any denial of membership or registration and of any disciplinary action taken or sanction imposed on a broker; a record of any denial, suspension, expulsion, or revocation of membership or registration of any member, broker, or dealer with whom the broker was associated; and a record of any arrests, indictments, or convictions for any other misdemeanor. *NASD Manual,* Official Publication of the National Association of Securities Dealers, Schedule C of the By-Laws, paragraphs 1782 through 1792 (Chicago: Commerce Clearing House, 1990) (continuously updated).

52. See John F. Wasik, "How to Check Out a Broker: Just Tap into Central Registration Depository," *Barron's,* January 14, 1991, pp. 24, 51; Elyse Tanouye, "Investigating Brokers' Histories Is Easier, but Not Foolproof Yet," *Wall Street Journal,* October 4, 1991, p. C1. The data base maintains files on more than 5,700 firms and 417,000 individuals that are currently active. See Anne Newman, "NASD Slaps Increasingly Stiff Penalties on Stockbrokers Who Cheat Customers," *Wall Street Journal,* February 4, 1991, p. C6.

53. See Gary H. Anthes, "Computer Cop Stakes Out OTC Trading," *Computer World,* June 11, 1990, p. 25. The system has been under development for more than twenty years, with an almost continuous mandate to improve and expand its capacity. John Desmond, "Mapping the Ideal, Comparing to Real," *Software Magazine,* January

1992, pp. 46–47; and Wayne Eckerson, "Network Security Lacking at Major Stock Exchanges," *Network World,* September 16, 1991, pp. 23–24.

54. Each day the model issues as many as eighty to ninety alerts. The system will then rank the alerts, assigning priority according to how suspicious any given activity appears. At the same time news stories appear on the analysts' screens, fed to their workstations by a subsystem monitoring the news stories from four commercial wire services. The subsystem automatically picks out news stories mentioning NASDAQ companies. Relevant news stories are automatically downloaded to a data base from which analysts can retrieve current and past news stories or headlines using a NASDAQ company symbol. See Anthes, "Computer Cop Stakes Out OTC Trading," p. 25.

55. By measuring the relationship between set parameter values and case outcomes through logistic regression analysis, it is possible to do the following: "(1) Identify which indicators are the most significant, (2) Suggest parameter settings that best discriminate between true exceptions and reasonable activity patterns, and (3) Reflect the composite effect of a set of indicators to ensure that a critical mixture of smaller effects is duly detected." See Samuel G. Davis, and J. Keith Ord, "Improving and Measuring the Performance of a Securities Industry Surveillance System," *Interface,* vol. 20 (September–October 1990), p. 40.

56. National Association of Securities Dealers (NASD), "1992 Annual Report: Uniting Creativity of Growth Companies, Vision of Investors, Commitment from Member Firms," Washington, 1993, p. 2. See also Davis and Ord, "Improving and Measuring the Performance," p. 33.

57. NASD, "1992 Annual Report," p. 2.

58. This check would allow suppliers to track piecemealing over long periods. Obviously this scheme cannot prevent international piecemealing. More discussion on international piecemealing appears later in this chapter.

59. Thomas H. Truitt and others, *Environmental Audit Handbook: Basic Principles of Environmental Compliance Auditing,* 2d ed. (New York: Executive Enterprises Publications Co., 1983); I. M. J. Bins-Hoefnagels and G. C. Molenkamp, "Environmental Auditing," KPMG Milieu, (n.d.), translated from *Tijdschrift voor Milieuaansprakelijkheid* (Journal for Economic Liability), no. 3 (September 1988); Nigel Haigh and Alastair Baillie, "Development of a Community Policy on Environmental Auditing," Final Report, vol. 1 (Bonn: Institute for European Environmental Policy, October 1991); "Industrial Environmental Auditing Update: Environmental Performance Evaluation," supplement to *Environment Business,* November 1991; and Hannes Pflug, ed., *Checkliste Umweltschutz* (Berlin: Erich Schmidt, 1992).

60. NASD, "1992 Annual Report," p. 41.

61. Ibid., p. 38. Membership fees consist of an application fee of $5,000, $3,000, or $1,500, depending on the nature of the business. In addition, companies pay an annual fixed membership fee of $500 plus an annual amount equal to whichever is greater: $350, or the total of 0.21 percent of annual gross income from state and municipal securities transactions, 0.25 percent of annual gross income from over-the-counter securities transactions, and 0.25 percent of annual gross income from U.S. government securities transactions if books and records are examined by the NASD. *NASD Manual,* Schedule A, paragraphs 1752, 1753.

62. NASD, "1992 Annual Report," p. 38.

63. For fairness individual contributions should be weighted by the per capita gross national product of the member.

64. The activities of the Bank of Credit and Commerce International and the Atlanta branch of the Banca Nazionale del Lavoro have raised some doubts about whether existing legislation in the United States, in particular the Foreign Bank Supervision

Enhancement Act of 1991, is sufficient to monitor foreign banks, even though the Fed has taken the position that existing legislation is sufficient. See Statement of John P. LaWare, Member, Board of Governors of the Federal Reserve System, in *The Non-Proliferation of Weapons of Mass Destruction and Regulatory Improvement Act of 1992,* Hearing before the House Committee on Banking, Finance and Urban Affairs, May 8, 1992, 102 Cong. 2 sess. (GPO, 1992), pp. 31–34. The regulations mandated by the act were approved by the Federal Reserve Board in the fall of 1992. Claudia Cummins, "Fed Oversight of Foreign Banks Formalized," *American Banker,* vol. 157 (November 5, 1992), p. 2.

65. M. Maureen Murphy, "Money Laundering: Federal Law and Current Legislative Proposals," CRS Report 90-157A (Congressional Research Service, March 22, 1990), p. 5.

66. For some background, ibid., pp. 12–13; W. John Moore, "Nixing the Cash Injection," *National Journal,* no. 48 (December 2, 1989), pp. 2924–29; Peter E. Meltzer, "Keeping Drug Money from Reaching the Wash Cycle: A Guide to the Bank Secrecy Act," *Banking Law Journal,* vol. 108 (May–June 1991), pp. 230–55; Lara W. Short, Robert G. Colvard, and John T. Lee, "The Liability of Financial Institutions for Money Laundering," *Banking Law Journal,* vol. 109 (January–February 1992), pp. 46–70; and Gerald L. Hilsher, "Money Laundering: The Banker's Role as Watchdog," *Issues in Bank Regulation,* vol. 13 (Fall 1989), pp. 11–16.

67. Jonathan J. Rusch, "Hue and Cry in the Counting-House: Some Observations on the Bank Secrecy Act," *Catholic University Law Review,* vol. 37 (Winter 1988), p. 467.

68. Bruce Zagaris, "Dollar Diplomacy: International Enforcement of Money Movement and Related Matters—a United States Perspective," *George Washington Journal of International Law and Economics,* vol. 22, no. 3 (1989), pp. 469–71.

69. See, for example, Kenneth Katzman, "Iraq's Campaign to Acquire and Develop High Technology," CRS Report 92-611 F (Congressional Research Service, August 3, 1992); Robert E. Powis, *The Money Launderers* (Chicago: Probus Publishing Company, 1992), pp. 191–237; Peter Truell and Larry Gurwin, *False Profits: The Inside Story of BCCI, the World's Most Corrupt Financial Empire* (Houghton Mifflin, 1992); and David Lascelles and others, "BCCI: Behind Closed Doors," *Financial Times,* seven-article series, November 9–10 through November 16–17, 1991.

70. See, for example, Matthew C. Gruskin, "Invading the Private Sector," in *Bank Secrecy Act,* Corporate Law and Practice Course Handbook Series 202 (New York: Practicing Law Institute, 1976), pp. 61–70.

71. Rusch, "Hue and Cry in the Counting-House," p. 471.

72. More discussion on this subject and the role of international cooperation appears later in this chapter.

73. See, for example, Statement of Peter K. Nunez, in *Money Laundering Legislation,* Hearing before the Subcommittee on Financial Institutions Supervision, Regulation and Insurance of the House Committee on Banking, Finance and Urban Affairs, March 8, 1990, 101 Cong. 2 sess. (GPO, 1990), pp. 10–12; and "Treasury to Seek Comment on Proposal Requiring Electronic Filing of CTRs," *BNA's Banking Report,* vol. 53 (November 20, 1990), pp. 729–30.

74. Hilsher, "Money Laundering," p. 16.

75. R. D. Fullerton, "Clearing Out the Money Launderers," *World of Banking,* September–October 1990, pp. 6–7.

76. John K. Villa, "A Critical View of Bank Secrecy Act Enforcement and the Money Laundering Statutes," *Catholic University Law Review,* vol. 37 (Winter 1988), p. 501.

77. See Murphy, "Money Laundering." A series of other recommendations have been made by the American Bankers' Association's Task Force on Money Laundering:

> 1. Government-Industry cooperation is essential for any successful national drug policy. Establishment of a formal financial industry advisory board will greatly enhance communications between these two critical groups.
>
> 2. The government should establish a mechanism for prompt dissemination of money laundering activities and trends to the financial industry.
>
> 3. There should be a thorough review of all recordkeeping and reporting regulations designed to attack the drug money laundering problem. There is a need for a study addressing the law enforcement utility of the Bank Secrecy Act.
>
> 4. Successful prosecutions resulting from active support from the banking industry should be publicized by the government whenever possible.
>
> 5. The problem with tracking possible laundering schemes through the use of wire transfers and other complex transactions should be addressed.

See "Toward a New National Drug Policy—the Banking Industry Strategy: Task Force Recommendations," in *Congressional Record,* May 18, 1989, pp. S 5555–56.

78. The most relevant legislation is the Comprehensive Environmental Response, Compensation, and Liability Act of 1980 (CERCLA), also known as the Superfund Act. For some background, see Eleanor H. Erdevig, "Lenders and Environmental Policies," *Economic Perspectives* (Federal Reserve Bank of Chicago), November–December, 1991, pp. 2–12; Peter Reuter, "The Economic Consequences of Expanded Corporate Liability: An Exploratory Study," A RAND Note, Institute for Civil Justice (Santa Monica, Calif.: RAND Corporation, November 1988); and Peter Huber, "Environmental Hazards and Liability Law," in Robert E. Litan and Clifford Winston, eds., *Liability: Perspectives and Policy* (Brookings, 1988), pp. 128–54. See also J. Dexter Peach, "Superfund: Actions Needed to Correct Long-Standing Contract Management Problems," GAO/T-RCED-92-78 (General Accounting Office, July 8, 1992).

79. David Lascelles, "Only Clean and Green Borrowers Need Apply," *Financial Times,* March 27, 1992, p. 15.

80. Stephen Labaton, "Business and the Law: Bank Liability for Toxic Sites," *New York Times,* April 18, 1991, p. D2. For this argument with respect to environmental liability, see, for example, the statement by Oliver Ireland, in "Statements to the Congress," *Federal Reserve Bulletin,* vol. 77 (September 1991), pp. 706–08. This problem has been especially acute for small businesses dealing with chemicals, which claim that it has become increasingly difficult to receive a loan. Bill Atkinson, "Banks' Caution Hurts Small Business," *American Banker,* April 27, 1992, p. 6A.

81. See, for example, Bruce Smart, ed., *Beyond Compliance: A New Industry View of the Environment* (Washington: World Resources Institute, April 1992). For a different perspective on the industry, see Kenny Bruno, *The Greenpeace Book of Greenwash* (Washington, 1991).

82. The firm Environmental Compliance Services, in Exton, Pennsylvania, provides such services. See "ECS, Underwriting: Proven Protection in a Changing Environment," information package, 1992; and Stephen Kleege, "'Clean' Lending," *American Banker,* April 27, 1992, pp. 2A, 3A.

83. Lascelles, "Only Clean and Green Borrowers Need Apply," p. 15.

84. Jacqueline Emigh, "Vermont National Taps Social Concern," *American Banker,* April 27, 1992, p. 6A.

85. Capital currently invested in socially screened fund amounts to about $7.2 billion; "The growth in options for mutual fund investors parallels the growth in social investing in general, and represents an increasing willingness on the part of both

investors and financial professionals to screen potential investments using social as well as financial criteria." Trex Proffitt, "Ethical Investment Funds Proliferate; Set Tenor for Social Investing in the 1990s," *IRRC News for Investors,* December 1990, p. 234.

Among the many guides to socially responsible investing are Amy L. Domini and Peter D. Kinder, *Ethical Investing* (Reading, Mass.: Addison-Wesley, 1986); and Myra Alperson and others, *The Better World Investment Guide,* a publication of the Council on Economic Priorities (Prentice Hall, 1991).

86. Michael V. Seitzinger, "Securities Law: Environmental Disclosures," CRS Report 91-422 A (Congressional Research Service, May 12, 1991).

87. 17 C.F.R. 240.12b-2 (1992).

88. *Basic Inc. et al.* v. *Levinson et al.,* 485 S. Ct. 234 (1988).

89. They include banks and trust companies, investment managers and advisers, insurance companies, pension funds, foundations, educational institutions, church groups, corporations, and law firms. IRRC, *Annual Report 1991* (Washington, April 1992).

90. The IRRC is registered as an investment adviser with the SEC. Other services it provides include the Corporate Governance Service, which tracks corporate governance and financial performance; the Global Shareholder Service, which provides information on corporate practices, shareholder issues, and shareholder rights in other countries; and the Environmental Information Service, which tracks business and the environment. In addition, the IRRC will conduct research on more specific topics as requested by clients. See IRRC, *Annual Report 1991.*

93. So-called ethical funds became more popular in the early 1980s. A British fund called Stewardship Unit Trust with £105 million under management is the largest ethical fund and, among other criteria, avoids companies dealing in armaments. Since the late 1980s "green funds," such as NPI Global Care and Sovereign Ethical, have begun to emerge and are becoming increasingly popular. Scheherazade Daneshkhu, "Why This May Be the Time to Turn Green," *Financial Times,* May 30–31, 1992, p. 3. In 1991 OPIC set up the International Environmental Investment Fund to attract investors for Third World projects that have sound environmental purposes. Paula L. Green, "Investors Mixing with Environment," *Journal of Commerce,* September 6, 1991, p. 3A. See also Jamie Heard, "Investor Responsibility: An Idea Whose Time Has Come?" *Journal of Portfolio Management,* vol. 4 (Spring 1978), pp. 12–14.

92. The strongest criticism by German companies against the new stringent export control laws was directed at the fact that they do not apply to their European competitors in light of the creation of a single market by the end of 1992. See Wolfgang H. Reinicke, "Arms Sales Abroad: European Community Export Controls beyond 1992," *Brookings Review,* vol. 10 (Summer 1992), pp. 22–25.

93. It is interesting to note, however, that with respect to environmental regulations that there appears to be "little evidence that pollution-control measures have exerted a systematic effect on international trade and investment," as well as "little force to the argument that we need to relax environmental policies to preserve international competitiveness." Maureen L. Cropper and Wallace E. Oates, "Environmental Economics: A Survey," *Journal of Economic Literature,* vol. 30 (June 1992), pp. 698, 699. Similarly, "there is surprisingly little evidence suggesting that liability currently hinders international competitiveness." Reuter, "Economic Consequences of Expanded Corporate Liability," p. 37.

94. For a discussion of these dynamics in global financial markets, see Wolfgang H. Reinicke, *Banking, Politics and Global Finance: American Commercial Banks and Regulatory Change* (Cheltenham, U.K.: Edward Elgar, forthcoming).

95. Ibid.

96. For more on this subject see the section "Institutional Implications: A Primer."

97. See Kane, "Policy Implications," and "Interaction of Financial and Regulatory Innovation."

98. Reinicke, *Banking, Politics and Global Finance;* and Statement of Paul A. Volcker, *Risk-Based Capital Requirements for Banks and Bank Holding Companies,* Hearing before the Subcommittee on General Oversight and Investigations of the House Committee on Banking, Finance and Urban Affairs, April 30, 1987, 100 Cong. 1 sess. (GPO, 1987), pp. 14, 22. See also Jeffrey Bardos, "The Risk-based Capital Agreement: A Further Step towards Policy Convergence," Federal Reserve Bank of New York, *Quarterly Review,* vol. 12 (Winter 1987–88), pp. 26–34.

99. Committee on Banking Regulations and Supervisory Practices, "Prevention of Criminal Use of the Banking System for the Purpose of Money-Laundering," Basle Committee on Banking Supervision, Bank for International Settlements, Basle, December 1988.

100. Robert Peston, "Basle Code to Avoid Repeat of BCCI Case," *Financial Times,* July 7, 1992, p. 3. Entitled "Minimum Standards for the Supervision of International Banking Groups and Their Cross-Border Establishments," the code is a revision of the 1975 and 1983 Concordats that were established in response to the failure of the Herstatt Bank and the Banco Ambrosiano and deal with the issue of host versus home country responsibility in a global financial market. See Richard Dale, *The Regulation of International Banking* (Cambridge: Woodhead-Faulkner, 1984).

101. According to the code, supervisory authorities should cooperate on "all prudential matters pertaining to international banks, and, in particular, in respect of the investigation of documented allegations of fraud, criminal activity, or violations of banking laws. In addition, both the Committee and its members will continue their efforts to reduce impediments to the sharing of information among supervisory authorities." Federal Reserve Board, "Basel Minimum Standards," Press release, July 6, 1992, p. 2. For more on information sharing, see Basel Committee on Banking Supervision, "Exchanges of Information between Banking and Securities Supervisors," April 1990, and Basel Committee on Banking Supervision, "Exchanges of Information between Supervisors of Participants in the Financial Markets," April 1990.

102. "Summit Participants Agree to Set Up Task Force to Curb Money Laundering," *BNA's Banking Report,* vol. 53 (July 24, 1989), pp. 145–46. See also Financial Action Task Force on Money Laundering, "Report," Paris, February 7, 1990; Financial Action Task Force on Money Laundering, "Report, 1990–1991," Paris, May 13, 1991; and Financial Action Task Force on Money Laundering, "Annual Report, 1991–1992," FATF-III, June 25, 1992.

103. David E. Spencer, "Bank Liability under the UN Drug Trafficking Convention," *International Financial Law Review,* vol. 9 (March 1990), p. 16.

104. Colin Jones, "What's in the Suitcase?" *The Banker,* vol. 140 (April 1990), pp. 12, 14; Alan Riding, "New Rule Reduces Swiss Banking Secrecy," *New York Times,* May 6, 1991, p. D1; and "Government to Act Against Money Laundering," *Der Spiegel,* March 2, 1992, p. 152, in FBIS, *Daily Report: West Europe,* March 2, 1992, p. 10.

105. Zagaris, "Dollar Diplomacy," pp. 470–79.

106. The 1991 Foreign Bank Supervision Enhancement Act has "expanded the [Federal Reserve Board's] powers to include approving and terminating licenses of foreign banks doing business in the [U.S.]." State of New York, Banking Department, *Report of the Superintendent's Advisory Committee on Transnational Banking Institutions* (March 1992), p. 2.

107. For a discussion of these problems in the U.S. bank regulatory system, see Wolfgang H. Reinicke, "A European Perspective on Bank Regulation in the United

States," in *Strengthening the Supervision and Regulation of the Depository Institutions,* Hearings before the Senate Committee on Banking, Housing, and Urban Affairs, 102 Cong. 1 sess. (GPO, 1991), vol. 1, pp. 1127–61. See also Wolfgang H. Reinicke, "Turf Fights in Regulatory Reform," *Challenge,* vol. 34 (November–December 1991), pp. 42–50.

108. The most recent proposal has been made by Senator Jake Garn. See "Export Administration Act" S.2519, *Congressional Record,* April 2, 1992, S 4826. See also *Strengthening the Export Licensing System,* H. Rept. 102–137, 102 Cong. 1 sess. (GPO, 1991); Glennon J. Harrison and George Holliday, "Export Controls," CRS Issue Brief, IB91064 (Congressional Research Service, March 27, 1992); National Academy of Sciences, *Finding Common Ground: U.S. Export Controls in Changed Modern Environment* (Washington: National Academy Press, 1991); and chapter 4 in this volume.

109. Wolfgang H. Reinicke, "Rethinking Contemporary Approaches to International Cooperation: International Public Goods and the Prisoner's Dilemma Reconsidered," Brookings, 1988.

110. As the Matrix Churchill incident shows, however, governments can also be the source of proliferation on the supply side. See, for example, John Mason, "Tory Ex-Minister Knew Exports Could Make Iraq Arms," *Financial Times,* November 5, 1992, p. 11; Daniel Green and Alan Friedman, "The Matrix Churchill Scandal: Whitehall Knew of Chemical Weapons Link," *Financial Times,* November 12, 1992, p. 10; and David Donkin and David Owen, "Matrix Churchill: How UK Helped the Iraqi War Effort," *Financial Times,* November 11, 1992, p. 8. See also Alan Friedman, "Matrix Churchill: Bush Administration 'Knew about Arms Network,'" ibid.

111. See Robert O. Keohane, *After Hegemony: Cooperation and Discord in the World Political Economy* (Princeton University Press, 1984).

112. In addition, the institution could also house those activities that are required to bring about a harmonization of national supply-side regimes that were discussed in this chapter.

113. United Nations, Department of Political and Security Council Affairs, *The United Nations and Disarmament, 1945–1970* (New York, 1970); Barber B. Conable, Jr., "Growth—Not Guns," *Washington Post,* December 24, 1991, p. 13; and Nicole Ball and Robert S. McNamara, "Link Economic Aid to Military Limits," *New York Times,* January 11, 1992, p. 19. See also Joseph A. Yager, "Influencing Incentives and Capabilities," in Yager, ed., *Nonproliferation and U.S. Foreign Policy* (Brookings 1980), pp. 407–25.

114. Paul Blustein, "World Bank and IMF to Press Defense Cuts," *Washington Post,* October 18, 1991, p. B1. See also chapter 3 in this volume.

115. "Reflections on the IMF," interview with Michael Camdessus, *Finance and Development,* vol. 29 (March 1992), p. 3.

116. "Address by M. Camdessus, Managing Director of the International Monetary Fund," Annual Meetings of the International Monetary Fund and the World Bank, Bangkok, October 15, 1991, in Deutsche Bundesbank, *Auszüge Aus Presseartikeln,* no. 79 (October 21, 1991), p. 8.

117. Daniel P. Hewitt, "Military Expenditure: International Comparison of Trends," IMF Working Paper, WP/91/54 (May 1991); and Hewitt, "Econometric Testing of Economic and Political Influences," IMF Working Paper, WP/91/53 (May 1991).

118. Paula De Masi and Henri Lorie, "How Resilient Are Military Expenditures?" *Staff Papers* (IMF), vol. 36 (March 1989), pp. 130–65.

119. In many countries disclosing the unpublished military data is illegal. In addition, the Fund's or the Bank's negotiating partner (in most cases the finance ministry) often has no access to these data. However, the Fund's managing director has stated that

"the major global powers have already announced plans to cut back their military spending. In the context of the increased need for global savings, this is a welcome move. The Interim Committee has placed this concern on our agenda and we will pursue it with all members—borrowers and creditors alike—for example, during our routine Article IV consultations." "Reflections on the IMF," interview, p. 3.

120. World Bank, *Poverty Reduction Handbook and Operational Directive* (Washington, 1992), especially chapter 3. See also Michael Prowse, "Mr. Preston Makes Poverty His Judge," *Financial Times,* May 11, 1992, p. 32.

121. "Address by M. Camdessus, Managing Director of the International Monetary Fund," p. 8.

122. "Reflections on the IMF," interview, pp. 3–4; and Blustein, "World Bank and IMF to Press Defense Cuts."

123. "Concluding Remarks by M. Camdessus, Managing Director of the International Monetary Fund," Annual Meetings of the International Monetary Fund and the World Bank, Bangkok, October 7, 1991, in Deutsche Bundesbank, *Auszüge Aus Presseartikeln,* no. 79 (October 21, 1991), p. 14.

124. International Bank for Reconstruction and Development (IBRD), *Articles of Agreement* (as amended effective February 16, 1989) (Washington: World Bank/IBRD, August 1991), p. 13.

125. Intergovernmental Group of Twenty-Four on International Monetary Affairs, Forty-fifty Meeting of Ministers, "Communiqué," October 12, 1991, p. 5. See also Blustein, "World Bank, IMF to Press Defense Cuts."

126. IBRD, *Articles of Agreement,* p. 13.

127. Ibid. Similarly, one of the Fund's purposes is defined as contributing to "the development of the productive resources of all members as primary objectives of economic policy." IMF, *Articles of Agreement of the International Monetary Fund* (Washington, 1982), article 1, section 2, p. 2.

128. Obviously the country can rearrange its domestic expenditures to meet the requests.

129. Hewitt, "Military Expenditure," p. 20.

130. For some background, see Kendall W. Stiles, "IMF Conditionality: Coercion or Compromise?" *World Development,* vol. 18, no. 7 (1990), pp. 959–74; Paul Mosley, Jane Harrigan, and John Toye, *Aid and Power: The World Bank and Policy-Based Lending,* vol. 1: *Analysis and Policy Proposals* (London: Routledge, 1991). See also P. Streeten, "Conditionality: A Double Paradox," in C. J. Jepma, ed., *North South: Co-operation in Retrospect and Prospect* (London: Routledge, 1988), pp. 107–19. For an excellent review of the Fund's changing position, see Jacques J. Polak, "The Changing Nature of IMF Conditionality," Essays in International Finance 184 (Princeton University, International Finance Section, September 1991).

131. International Monetary Fund, *Annual Report 1990* (Washington, 1990), p. 42.

132. Polak, "Changing Nature of IMF Conditionality," p. 27. See also "Appendix G: Poverty (IMF)," in *International Finance,* Annual Report of the Chairman of the National Advisory Council on International Monetary and Financial Policies to the President and to the Congress for Fiscal Year 1990 (Department of the Treasury, May 1992), p. 201.

133. "Appendix D: The IMF and the Environment," in *International Finance,* p. 175.

134. Polak, "Changing Nature of IMF Conditionality," p. 29.

135. World Bank, *World Development Report 1992: Development and the Environment,* p. 12.

136. Ibid., p. 14.

137. Prowse, "Mr. Preston Makes Poverty his Judge."

138. World Bank, *Poverty Reduction Handbook and Operational Directive.*

139. World Bank, *Poverty Reduction Operational Directive* (Washington, 1992), p. 6.

140. World Bank, *Governance and Development* (Washington, 1992), p. 1.

141. Ibid.

142. For an excellent discussion of these issues, see Nicole Ball, *Pressing for Peace: Can Aid Induce Reform?* Policy Essay 6 (Washington: Overseas Development Council, 1992); and Joan M. Nelson with Stephanie J. Eglinton, *Encouraging Democracy: What Role for Conditioned Aid?* Policy Essay 4 (Washington: Overseas Development Council, 1992). See also chapter 3 in this volume.

143. Sidney Dell, "The Question of Cross Conditionality," *World Development,* vol. 16 (May 1988), pp. 557–68.

144. For a more detailed discussion of this issue, see chapter 3 in this volume.

145. Quoted in United Nations, *Disarmament Newsletter,* vol. 10 (June 1992), p. 11. A country could be under severe domestic pressure from its military establishment not to give in to the conditions set out in the regime. Swift action by the IFI could precipitate a military coup that in most cases would worsen the situation. Similarly, even if the country agrees to a program of demobilization, it will take a long time to reintegrate the army into the society and economy.

146. "Address by M. Camdessus," p. 8.

147. The 1985 Pressler amendment added a new subsection (e) to Section 620E of the Foreign Assistance Act. Richard P. Cronin, "Pakistan Aid Cutoff: U.S. Nonproliferation and Foreign Policy Considerations," CRS Issue Brief IB90149 (Congressional Research Service, February 16, 1993).

148. R. Jeffrey Smith, "Pakistan Warned on Nuclear Parts," *Washington Post,* January 14, 1992, p. A18. See also R. Jeffrey Smith, "Pakistan Official Affirms Capacity for Nuclear Device," *Washington Post,* February 7, 1992, p. A18.

149. George Bush, "Executive Order 12735—Chemical and Biological Weapons Proliferation," *Weekly Compilation of Presidential Documents,* vol. 26 (November 19, 1990), pp. 1835–37. Note, however, that Executive Order 12735 resulted from the president's veto of legislation reauthorizing the Export Administration Act, which expired on September 30, 1990, a bill that would have imposed even stricter sanctions on violators.

150. In the United States the institutional structure of export promotion is highly fragmented. As many as ten different agencies are involved in this process, and thus considerable coordination among them would be required. However, there have been several proposals to reform the system. See, for example, Allan I. Merdelowitz, "Export Promotion, Federal Approach Is Fragmented," GAO/T-GGD-92-68 (General Accounting Office, August 10, 1992).

151. Opening statement of Chairman Henry B. Gonzalez, in *H.R. 4803, The Non-Proliferation of Weapons of Mass Destruction and Regulatory Improvement Act of 1992,* Hearing, p. 1.

152. "Japan to Link Aid to Arms Trade," *Wall Street Journal,* April 11, 1991, p. A10. During 1990 Japan donated $9,222 million. Ministry of Foreign Affairs, *Japan's Official Development Assistance: ODA 1990 Annual* (Tokyo: Association for Promotion of International Cooperation, 1991), p. 16.

153. Leslie H. Gelb, "More Arms, Less Aid," *New York Times,* May 8, 1992, p. A31.

154. "Rede von Bundesminister Carl-Dieter Spranger vor der Bundespressekonferenz über 'Neue politische Kriterien des BMZ,'" Bundesminister für wirtschaftliche Zusammenarbeit, Pressereferat, Bonn, October 10, 1991, p. 3 (translated by author).

155. Klemens van de Sand, "New Political Criteria: The German Concept," Federal Ministry for Economic Cooperation, Bonn, February 1992, p. 3.

156. Ibid.

157. Ibid. See also Stephen Kinzer, "Germany to Cut Aid to Countries That Spend Heavily on Weapons," *New York Times*, August 3, 1991, p. A2.

158. Commission des Communautés Européennes, "Accords d'association avec les pays d'Europe centrale et orientale: cadre général," Communication de la Commission au conseil et au Parlement, COM(90) 398 final (Brussels, August 27, 1990). For the European Parliament's position see the report by Christa Randzio-Plath, "Report of the Committee on External Economic Relations on a General Outline for Association Agreements with the Countries of Central and Eastern Europe," European Parliament, Session Documents, DOC EN/RR/105815 (March 13, 1991).

159. "Resolution on Human Rights, Democracy and Development," Council and Member States, meeting within the Council, November 28, 1991, in Christiane Duparc, *The European Community and Human Rights* (Luxembourg: Office for Official Publications of the European Communities, 1993), p. 53. See also Gerd Langguth, "Aussenpolitische Chancen der Europäischen Integration. Die Europäische Gemeinschaft und die Dritte Welt," *Europa Archiv*, vol. 47 (April 25, 1992), pp. 222–30.

160. "Resolution on Human Rights," pp. 53–54.

161. On the EC's support, see Forty-Seventh Session of the UN General Assembly, "Statement by Ambassador Sir Michael Weston, Representative of the United Kingdom of Great Britain and Northern Ireland, on Behalf of the European Community and Its Member States, on the Subject of Transparency in Armaments," United Kingdom Mission to the United Nations, New York, November 4, 1992.

162. Commission of the European Communities, Communication from the Commission to the Council and Parliament, *Development Cooperation Policy in the Run-Up to 2000: The Consequences of the Maastricht Treaty*, SEC(92) 915 final (Brussels, May 15, 1992). See also "Human Rights, Democracy and Development," *Bulletin of the European Communities* (Brussels), vol. 24, no. 11 (1991), pp. 81–82; and "Press Statement on the Activity of the Community and Its Member States in the Field of Human Rights in 1991," Press Release—European Political Cooperation, P. 127/91, Brussels, December 10, 1991.

163. "Rede von Bundesminister," Pressereferat, p. 3 (translated by author).

164. "Agreement Establishing the European Bank for Reconstruction and Development," Article 1. See also EBRD, "Operational Challenges and Priorities: Initial Orientations," April 1991.

165. In this particular case the Foreign Ministry opposed any reduction in aid to Syria. The ministry believed such action would undermine Germany's efforts to support the Middle East peace process. "Ressortstreit um Entwicklungshilfe," *Die Welt*, August 2, 1991.

166. Leslie Helm, "Japan Reluctant to Back Embargo on Iran," *Washington Post*, November 14, 1992, p. A21.

167. William Dawkins, "OECD Chief Warns on Tied-Aid Restrictions," *Financial Times*, February 21, 1992, p. 5; and David Dodwell, "Compromise on Tied-Aid Rules," *Financial Times*, March 9, 1992, p. 2.

168. For further discussion, see chapter 3 in this volume.

169. For some background, see Gary Clyde Hufbauer and Jeffrey Schott, assisted by Kimberly Ann Elliott, *Economic Sanctions Reconsidered: History and Current Policy* (Washington: Institute for International Economics, 1985); Gunnar Adler-Karlsson, "Instruments of Economic Coercion and Their Use," in Frans A. M. Alting von Geusau and Jacques Pelkmans, eds., *National Economic Security: Perceptions Threats and Policies* (Tilburg, The Netherlands: John F. Kennedy Institute, 1982), pp. 160–82; James M. Lindsay, "Trade Sanctions as Policy Instruments: A Re-examination," *International Studies Quarterly,* vol. 30 (June 1986), pp. 153–73; and chapter 3 in this volume. For more recent evidence, see Peter A. G. van Bergeijk, "Success and Failure of Economic Sanctions," *Kyklos,* vol. 42, Fasc. 3 (1989), pp. 385–404.

170. Daniel N. Nelson, "Seeking International Consensus," *Foreign Service Journal,* vol. 67 (November 1990), p. 26.

171. James O. C. Jonah, "Sanctions and the UN," *International Review,* June–July 1988, p. 12.

172. Jonathan E. Sanford, "World Bank: Answers to 26 Frequent Questions," CRS Report 91-847 (Congressional Research Service, November 25, 1991), p. 8; and "Agreement between the United Nations and the International Monetary Fund," in IMF, *Selected Decisions and Selected Documents of the International Monetary Fund,* 17th Issue (Washington, May 31, 1992), p. 545.

173. For a recent discussion of some verification agreements, see Serge Sur, ed., *Verification of Current Disarmament and Arms Limitation Agreements: Ways, Means and Practices* (Aldershot, U.K.: Dartmouth for United Nations Institute for Disarmament Research, 1991); and Department for Disarmament Affairs, *The United Nations Disarmament Yearbook,* vol. 15 (New York, 1991), pp. 60–84.

174. See United Nations, General Assembly, *General and Complete Disarmament: Transparency in Armaments, Report on the Register of Conventional Arms, Report of the Secretary-General,* A/47/342 (New York, August 14, 1992). See also Paul Lewis, "U.N. Passes Voluntary Register to Curb Arms Sales," *New York Times,* December 10, 1991, p. A11.

175. In the case of COCOM, for example, this need has led to proposals to move away from the traditional denial regime to an approval regime. See Wolfgang H. Reinicke, "Political and Economic Changes in the Eastern Bloc and Their Implications for CoCom: West-German and European Community Perspectives," study prepared for the National Academy of Sciences' Panel on the Future Design and Implementation of National Security Export Controls, May 29, 1990; National Academy of Sciences, *Finding Common Ground;* and *The New Era in U.S. Export Controls,* Report of a Workshop, September 24–25, 1991 (Washington: National Academy Press, 1992).

176. EPCI was strongly criticized by U.S. exporters as the administration's way to disguise the failure of its foreign policy toward Iraq. See, for example, Walter S. Mussberg and Rick Wartzman, "Back to the Race," *Wall Street Journal,* March 4, 1991, p. A1; and "President's Advisory Group Calls for Easing of Export Controls," *Inside U.S. Trade,* vol. 10 (April 3, 1992), pp. 7, 9.

177. Frederick P. Waite and M. Roy Goldberg, "Responsible Export Controls or 'Nets to Catch the Wind'? The Commerce Department's New U.S. Controls on Exports of Chemical Precursors, Equipment and Technical Data Intended to Prevent Development of Chemical and Biological Weapons," *California Western International Law Journal,* vol. 22, no. 2 (1991–92), pp. 202–03.

178. "Blue Lantern Program: End-Use Checks in the Licensing Process," *Defense Trade News,* vol. 3 (July 1992), pp. 10–11. For a checklist of warning flags geared toward the customer, the end-user, and the shipment, see "Indications of Questionable

Exports: A Checklist of Warning Flags," *Defense Trade News,* vol. 2 (January 1991), pp. 12–13.

179. End-use inquiries by U.S. diplomatic personnel are coordinated with the host government. Depending on the item and the standing of the private entity receiving the export, an inquiry might range from simple oral or written contact to verify the bona fides of a a proposed transaction to physical inspection of the export.

180. For more information, see "Convention on the Prohibition of the Development, Production, Stockpiling, and Use of Chemical Weapons and on Their Destruction," reprinted in *Arms Control Today,* vol. 22 (October 1992), CWC Supplement, pp. 11–12.

181. Plants for inspection are selected on a random basis while ensuring equitable geographic distribution and considering the type of production carried out in a plant. On the dual-use character of chemicals, see, for example, S. J. Lundin, ed., *Verification of Dual-Use Chemicals under the Chemical Weapons Convention: The Use of Thiodiglycol,* SIPRI Chemical and Biological Warfare Studies 13 (Oxford University Press, 1992); and Ralph Trapp, *Möglichkeiten und Grenzen der Proliferationskontrolle bei Chemischen Waffen,* SWP–376 (Ebenhausen: Haus Eggenberg, June 1992).

182. "Convention on the Prohibition . . . Chemical Weapons and on Their Destruction," CWC Supplement, pp. 13–14. For a more detailed description of the challenge inspection, see "Challenge Inspections Pursuant to Article IX," in *Report of the Conference on Disarmament to the General Assembly of the United Nations,* CD/1173 (September 3, 1992), app. 1, annex 2, pp. 153–63.

183. For a detailed list of the measures, see "Challenge Inspections Pursuant to Article IX," app. 1, annex 2, p. 161.

184. "Convention on the Prohibition . . . Chemical Weapons," CWC Supplement, p. 13.

185. As such it goes far beyond previous verification procedures in other nonproliferation regimes. For a critique of the verification procedures in the Non-Proliferation Treaty and current efforts to improve them see Harald Müller, "Das nukleare Nichtverbreitungsregime im Wandel: Konsequenzen aus einem stürmischen Jahr," *Europa Archiv,* vol. 47, no. 2 (1992), pp. 51–58.

186. In early 1992 the Vienna Conflict Prevention Center decided to install a data base in which military data from CSCE member states will be stored. It is currently being tested, and there will be efforts to improve its performance. See "CSCE Military Database in Vienna," *Die Presse,* February 19, 1992, p. 2, reprinted as "CSCE Military Database to Be Installed," FBIS, *Daily Report: West Europe,* February 19, 1992, p. 2.

187. Efforts to simplify and harmonize the references that are shown on documents required in international trade are currently undertaken by the UN Working Party on Facilitation of International Trade Procedures. See, for example, United Nations, Economic Commission for Europe, "Unique Identification Code Methodology–UNIC," Recommendation no. 8/rev. 1 (Geneva, March 1992).

188. For more information on the need for the UN to implement challenge inspections, see George Leopold, "U.N. Inspections Lift Verification Role," *Defense News,* vol. 7 (May 4–10, 1992), p. 4.

189. For example, resistance by industry to unilateral tightening of end-use controls was present in the United States in the case of EPCI and in Germany in conjunction with the implementation of new export control laws during 1990 and 1991. For more information on EPCI, see, for example, "President's Advisory Group Calls for Easing of Export Controls," *Inside U.S. Trade,* vol. 10 (April 3, 1992), pp. 7–9; and Waite and Goldberg, "Responsible Export Controls."

190. Reinicke, "Arms Sales Abroad."

191. This diffusion effect can be observed in the area of international bank regulation, where an increasing number of countries or individual institutions outside the members of the Committee on Bank Regulation at the Bank for International Settlements adhere to the standards established there.

192. This pressure was applied to Japan, whose participation in the regime was essential given the importance of Japan's financial markets but who initially refused to join a such a regime. See Reinicke, *Banking, Politics and Global Finance*.

SIX

Military Action: When to Use It and How to Ensure Its Effectiveness

William J. Perry

A FUNDAMENTAL PRINCIPLE of a cooperative security regime is that each member agrees to limit its military forces to what is necessary for defense of its territory. However, a small number of nations, including the United States, must maintain certain elements of their armed forces beyond that required for territorial defense and make these elements available to multinational forces when needed. The objective of limiting national military forces to a defensive capability is to create a situation in which aggression cannot succeed, and therefore is not likely to occur. But there are great ambiguities in what constitutes defensive capability, great variations in geography that make defense more difficult for some countries than for others, and the ever-present possibility of a rogue nation developing an offensive capability, possibly in secret. Thus an exact balance of opposing forces in a region could never be achieved in practice, so a necessary constraint against aggression would be the aggressor's belief that it would face not only the military forces of its neighbor but a multinational force formed to defeat the aggression, as well as severe economic sanctions.

An integral part of any cooperative security regime must therefore be the capability to organize multinational forces to defeat aggression should it occur. The UN Security Council can authorize multinational military forces for this purpose; indeed, the United Nations is authorized to form its own military force, but here the focus is on UN authorization of multinational forces to deal with major acts of aggression on an ad hoc basis. The UN must give special priority to preventing the proliferation of weapons of mass destruction, especially nuclear weapons, because such weapons in the hands of a rogue nation can greatly complicate the ability of the regime to deter aggression and can lead to vastly greater casualties if deterrence fails.

A cooperative security regime is not intended to prevent violence of all kinds. In particular, although civil wars (as in Yugoslavia) and insurrections (as in Peru) could involve UN peacekeeping forces, they are not the subject of this chapter. Instead, this chapter focuses on means of preventing one specific form of military conflict, namely, that caused by an aggressor nation attacking its neighbor. A cooperative security regime is designed to minimize any underlying military causes for such conflicts, to deter rogue nations from initiating such conflicts, and if deterrence fails, to provide a multinational military force to defeat any aggressor nation. In a cooperative security regime, the use of military force by the UN—or any nation—is a last resort, to be invoked only after political pressure and economic sanctions have failed.

The threat of military force should be sufficient to obviate the need to use it if the right military and political conditions are met. The threat will be maximally effective when political conditions permit the military force to be a broadly based coalition. This broad international support makes the UN threat of military action politically credible. The threat will also be militarily credible if the coalition military force is organized around the reconnaissance strike capability used by the United States in Desert Storm. Such a reconnaissance strike force is, of course, not optimal for all military conflicts, but it is ideally suited to defeat an attack by combined armored forces—precisely the kind of military force likely to be used by a nation invading a weaker neighbor.

The alternative to having a reconnaissance strike force is organizing the coalition around combined armored forces or around tactical nuclear weapons. Basing the coalition military forces on combined armored forces could lead to a long and bloody ground war, and an aggressor might believe it could wear down the resolve of the coalition governments (as Saddam Hussein believed at the beginning of the Gulf War). Basing the coalition military force on nuclear weapons would lack credibility, particularly if the aggressor had some nuclear weapons of its own. Thus nuclear nations in a cooperative security regime must maintain sufficient nuclear capability to prevent an aggressor nation from ever thinking it advantageous to initiate a nuclear attack. On the other hand, they should not regard their nuclear weapons as a deterrent to aggression with conventional weapons.

In any multinational military force organized around a reconnaissance strike capability, the U.S. military would have a special role to play. It would provide most of the airlift required to quickly transport coalition military forces to the theater, most of the tactical intelligence data required to support the precision strike weapons, and most of the stealth aircraft used to suppress enemy air defenses. Coalition partners would participate on an equal basis in achieving air and naval superiority in the theater and would play a dominant role in the ground forces of the coalition. In this view of cooperative security, the special military capability of the United States would be used to give coalition forces an advantage that not only would ensure a military victory but that could be achieved with minimal losses to coalition forces. Therefore, it should provide maximum deterrent to any potential aggressor.

Precisely because of the great deterrent effect of this military capability, any potential aggressor would be seeking ways to defeat it. We should thus expect to see efforts to emulate it, efforts to counter it, and efforts to finesse it. This capability could indeed be emulated by a half dozen of the advanced industrial nations of the world, but at great expense and with a very visible effort; it is unlikely to be emulated by any of the regional powers now considered to be potential aggressors. A more likely strategy for a potential aggressor is to try to finesse this military capability by developing weapons of mass destruction, especially nuclear weapons. Although this response would be essentially suicidal, an aggressor might convince itself that it could succeed in such a bluff. Certainly the self-destructive actions of Iraq suggest that Saddam Hussein was basing much of his strategy on bluffs or gross misconceptions about the resolve of coalition nations. Therefore, a cooperative security regime should place a very high priority on actions designed to prevent the proliferation of weapons of mass destruction, especially nuclear weapons. Another likely strategy for a potential aggressor is to develop countermeasures to a reconnaissance strike force, which can be done to some degree by many nations. Because of this danger United States should probably dedicate a part of its defense effort to appropriate countercountermeasures.

More generally, the United States would require a major restructuring and downsizing of its defense forces under a cooperative security regime. Such restructuring would have three major objectives:

—To effect a significant reduction in the size of U.S. ground and naval forces (with a concomitant reduction in the defense budget). The new ground and naval forces would be sized to deal with credible military threats to U.S. territory, to provide the cadre for a reconstitution of U.S. forces if a new superpower military threat emerged (that is, if the cooperative security regime collapsed), and to supply whatever (minimal) ground and naval support the United States might be requested to provide to multinational military forces.

—To maintain a capability to provide a core contribution to the strategic intelligence evaluations that assess the emergence of new threats to the cooperative security regime, as well as to provide key inputs to the verification of treaties or UN sanctions (such as limits on weapon developments or force deployments).

—To maintain a capability to provide important elements of the reconnaissance strike military forces that would be used in multinational military actions whenever diplomacy and economic sanctions proved to be insufficient.

Other nations belonging to the cooperative security regime would also restructure and downsize their defense forces. Their objectives in restructuring would be conceptually similar to those of the United States, but these objectives would manifest themselves in different ways depending on their circumstances. The first objective would be the same for all members of the regime. For some of these nations, providing for their territorial defense would involve maintaining significant ground forces. For example, Russia, Germany, France, China, and India would require significant ground forces for their territorial defense and would therefore be expected to make up the bulk of the ground forces needed in any multinational expeditionary force. Similarly, the United Kingdom, Italy, and Japan would place a greater emphasis on naval forces for their territorial defense and would therefore make the principal contributions to the naval arm of a multinational force. Only a few nations besides the United States, such as Russia and the United Kingdom, have developed and deployed global strategic intelligence assets that permit them to make a significant contribution to global threat evaluation and verification assessment (the second objective). These nations would be expected to make such a contribution to the appropriate international organization. A handful of nations have military capabilities that would be of special importance to a reconnaissance strike force (the third objective). Russia has a significant capability in airlift, sealift, and air superiority aircraft; France, Germany, and the United Kingdom have a significant capability in air superiority aircraft. Therefore, these nations, along with the United States, would provide the reconnaissance strike elements of any multinational expeditionary force.

Thus, in the interest of maintaining the power projection capability needed when major military actions must be undertaken by the cooperative security regime, some nations will end up with national defense forces larger than those needed for territorial defense. This asymmetry will most likely cause two related political problems. Nations with only territorial defense forces may fear that nations with larger defense forces will apply their military forces to achieve national or hegemonic objectives. Or, alternatively, they may fear that the nations with the larger forces will let this special military capability erode or be reluctant to use it, so that it will not be available when needed for multinational forces. Each of these fears has some historical justification; indeed, both could be realized at the same time. Thus a substantial challenge for a cooperative security regime would be to work out the political measures that minimize these risks. For example, the nations with reconnaissance strike forces could establish dual-command channels (analogous to those established in NATO for nuclear weapons) for these forces. Also, the UN could establish funding to assist in the maintenance of certain of these national forces. Finally, the nations with these special forces could agree not to use them in violation of the UN Charter.

As difficult as it will be to meet these political challenges, the two logical alternatives are even less attractive. One alternative is for the United States, for example, to disband its airlift and reconnaissance strike forces, since arguably they are not needed for territorial defense. But doing so would greatly weaken the ability of any multinational force to decisively defeat a military threat posed by an aggressor nation with sizeable armored forces. The other alternative would be for the United States and other relevant nations to turn over these special forces to the UN, giving the UN a large (several hundred thousand men) permanent military force. For many reasons, such a move would be exceedingly difficult to implement. In any event, the UN would probably be better served by a relatively small permanent military force, designed for peacekeeping duties, as proposed by the present secretary-general. Peacekeeping UN forces would probably be called into action many times; the special expeditionary force would be assembled only on an ad hoc basis, and rarely if the cooperative security regime was effective.

If this rationale for defense restructuring was followed, the United States would have special requirements in its defense modernization to maintain and enhance the reconnaissance strike capability that would be called on by the multinational force. Because the world saw that these units were remarkably effective in operations against the large and well-equipped Iraqi army, any potential aggressor would presumably understand that it would need to develop some plausible way of countering this capability before it could act. But the world also saw certain weaknesses in the reconnaissance strike forces used in Desert Storm. Indeed, the United States has publicly described some of the vulnerabilities of these systems. To be sure, these were "latent" vulnerabilities that the Iraqis failed to exploit, but prudent planning should assume that a future aggressor will try to take full advantage of these vulnerabilities. Therefore, to maintain the effectiveness of this critical capability, the United States should embark on a program to overcome the vulnerabilities of its present systems to countermeasures.

In an article in *Foreign Affairs,* I discussed in detail the U.S. "reconnaissance strike force" as it was used in Desert Storm.[1] I defined that force as consisting of three primary elements: C^3I (command, control, communications, and intelligence), precision-guided munitions, and defense suppression. The first of the critical components is C^3I. In Desert Storm, the United States used reconnaissance satellites, which were developed originally for national intelligence, for combat support. Also, the United States employed an airborne warning and control system (AWACS) to obtain a continuous order-of-battle for all air vehicles and for the first time used a joint surveillance and target attack radar system (JSTARS) for a continuous order-of-battle for all ground vehicles. U.S. forces made extensive use of night vision, as well as global positioning satellites to locate forces on the ground. All this technology gave coalition commanders superb "situation awareness"; that is, they knew precisely where enemy forces were located, where friendly forces were located, and where they themselves were located. At the same time, very early in that campaign, coalition forces essentially destroyed the Iraqi C^3I system. This overwhelming advantage in situation awareness would have given coalition forces a decisive advantage over Iraqi forces, even had they been otherwise comparable.

Precision-guided munitions constituted the second critical component of the reconnaissance strike force. The effectiveness of precision-guided munitions in Desert Storm was demonstrated convincingly by the performance of the F-117 strike aircraft. The F-117 dropped a total of 2,100 one-ton laser-guided bombs; of these, 1,700 landed within ten feet of the designated aim point, thereby destroying the targets they were attacking. There is no precedent for that sort of performance in any previous use of air power, and this remarkable effectiveness played a critical role in the rapid defeat of the Iraqi forces. A significant consequence of this effectiveness in planning future coalition forces is a greatly reduced requirement for numbers of strike aircraft and related logistics support. Another consequence is the ability to attack military forces without endangering nearby civilians.

Defense suppression was a third critical component. The Iraqis had a modern, dense, netted, hardened air defense system, which was especially dense around Baghdad. Historically, air defenses with that capability have inflicted attrition losses of 1 to 2 percent on attacking forces. With the 3,000 sorties a day conducted by coalition air forces, a 1 to 2 percent attrition rate would have resulted in the loss of 30 to 60 airplanes each day, and over a thirty-day campaign, 1,000 to 2,000 airplanes. Instead of losing 30 to 60 airplanes a day, the coalition lost about 1 a day, as a result of the introduction of stealth (the F-117 and the Tomahawk cruise missile) and the use of antiradiation missiles. The combined effectiveness of these three weapon systems essentially destroyed the Iraqi air defense electronics subsystems. As a consequence, that air defense did not have radars or command and control and was left simply with guns that could be fired visually or in a barrage. The result was about one-thirtieth of 1 percent attrition. These defense suppression systems are crucial to conducting military operations with minimum casualties to coalition forces.

Equally important to the effectiveness of the reconnaissance strike force is the synergism among these three components. The effectiveness of defense suppression weapons depends on the use of precision-guided munitions. The effectiveness of precision-guided munitions depends on reconnaissance systems for targeting. The very survivability of reconnaissance systems depends on the effectiveness of defense suppression.

Thus the decisive factor in Desert Storm was the application of this new defense technology, especially the truly extraordinary application of air power deployed in a "system of systems." At present, the United States is the only nation that has this full spectrum of capabilities, and this will continue to be true for the foreseeable future. Therefore, in order for a cooperative security regime to have the military force that can credibly threaten multinational military action if its diplomatic initiatives or economic sanctions fail, the

United States must maintain this capability in the face of plausible countermeasures, and the United States must be willing to make these forces available as its contribution to multinational forces, whenever military action is necessary. The primary objective of having such a military capability, of course, is to make the threat of military force so credible that it will never have to be used. Iraq persisted in its defiance of UN orders, not because it believed it could defeat the coalition forces, but because it believed it could force a long and bloody war on them (as in Vietnam), which would create the conditions for a diplomatic victory.

In my *Foreign Affairs* article, I fully discussed what specific modernization programs are needed for the United States to maintain the effectiveness of its reconnaissance strike complex, even in the face of determined countermeasures by some future aggressor. Briefly, the modernization programs recommended involve

—completing the development and deployment of some of the reconnaissance systems that were rushed into Desert Storm before they were fully ready for deployment;

—"hardening" some of the data links that carry reconnaissance data to tactical commanders so that they are less vulnerable to electronic countermeasures;

—evolving a new generation of precision-guided munitions that have "fire-and-forget" capability, and thus are less vulnerable to counterattack; and

—evolving to the next generation of stealth capability, to stay comfortably ahead of countermeasures that could be introduced in air defense systems.

In sum, a cooperative security regime is designed to create the conditions under which military aggression is not feasible. However, if a nation still persists in aggression, even in the face of political and economic sanctions, a cooperative security regime must be able to threaten military action and, if necessary, invoke it. Thus it must be prepared to assemble a multinational military force that can quickly and decisively defeat any aggressor nation. This military force should be organized around the elements of the reconnaissance strike force that the United States demonstrated in Desert Storm. Such an organization requires that a small number of nations, including the United States, maintain certain elements of their armed forces beyond what is required for territorial defense and make these elements available to multinational forces when needed. This asymmetry in defense forces will cause political problems, but these problems can be mitigated and, in any event, are not as serious as the problems caused by the alternatives to these force asymmetries.

Note

1. William J. Perry, "Desert Storm and Deterrence," *Foreign Affairs,* vol. 70 (Fall 1991), pp. 66–82.

SEVEN

Global Institutions in a Cooperative Order: Does the United Nations Fit In?

James A. Schear

LIKE A DISTANT OASIS, cooperative security offers a very appealing vision for global stability in the twenty-first century. Any fair-minded reading of the concept, as set forth in the introductory chapters, would readily concede its virtuous aspects: it is defensive by inspiration, comprehensive in scope, consensual in application, and pragmatic in terms of seeking to create incentives that favor participation by states of varying sizes and capacities.

The difficult question, of course, is whether this attractive idea can survive the transition that is necessary to achieve it. Governments and not philosopher kings, alas, are the ones that must accept the trade-offs implicit in the concept; and the proposition that armed aggression is becoming outdated as a way to advance national interest does not in itself suggest any particular path to greater cooperation, *even if* that proposition were universally accepted. Furthermore, the incremental application of the concept may require placing uneven amounts of pain and sacrifice on different groupings of states at various stages. Countries that perceive they are being asked to bear unfair burdens will resist joining unless the promoters of the concept can promise an equitable distribution of benefits. Above all, it is the assurance of fairness, credibly conveyed, that will energize progress toward the network of self-restraints and coordinated management of armed forces contemplated by cooperative security. Without this assurance, the prospects for a successful transition look unpromising.

The author is grateful to Ivo Daalder, William J. Durch, Leonard Spector, Jane E. Stromseth, and several members of the UN Secretariat for helpful comments on a draft of this chapter.

Given the need to proceed step by step in implementing the cooperative security design, any strategy for promoting the concept will have to use existing diplomatic mechanisms. That procedure means, unavoidably, some degree of reliance on the United Nations, an institution that was marginal in the eyes of U.S. national security policymakers until recently. It is noteworthy that the cooperative security concept is essentially agnostic on the role of the UN. The concept neither assumes assistance from the organization nor excludes it from participation. The purpose of this chapter is to explore the right "fit" between the concept and the institution: specifically, to what degree can the UN be a vehicle for forging consensus on the basic framework of cooperative security and on its implementation over time?

The Argument

When one surveys the UN from the cooperative security standpoint, three of its traditional functions seem worthy of exploration. *First, the UN is a venue for rule making on security matters,* not for all rules, to be sure, but for those that are global or interregional in scope and that focus on international environments (the high seas, the seabeds, outer space, and so on) as well as on the acquisition or proliferation of weapons.

Second, the organization can be an instrument for managing or resolving conflicts within regions or states. Generally, the activities falling within this category, ranging from "peacekeeping" to "peace-building" operations, involve the implementation of tasks agreed to by parties to a conflict, such as cease-fire monitoring, troop demobilization, or elections management. Although most current conflict zones are found outside the initial geographic frontiers of a prospective cooperative security community, the persistence or spread of such conflicts could act to inhibit the community's enlargement or even to undermine it.

Third, the UN is a legitimizing agent for multilateral responses to armed aggression or other threats to international peace and security—"enforcement," in UN parlance. The cooperative security concept explicitly acknowledges collective security as a residual guarantee to its adherents. In principle, such measures involve a progression of steps ranging from economic or other sanctions to the use of force and could involve coercive modes of disarmament or pacification in postconflict situations.

This chapter begins by examining existing institutions for security related rule making at the UN, assessing their attributes and various problems arising in their performance. Then the chapter explicates four specific applications of UN instruments in order to assess the significance of these tools for the transition to cooperative security. It is the general thesis of this chapter that the UN's rule-making system, which evolved during the cold war but was marginal to the security needs of that era, lends itself rather well to the pursuit of cooperative security. In such areas as weapons transparency, peacekeeping, peace building, and enforcement activity, the organization is generating new or improved modes of operation that could augment the basic cooperative security design. The difficult question at present is how much weight of responsibility can be placed on the UN system without pressuring its current and, as yet, uncorrected weaknesses to a point that would threaten the system's viability.

The UN's "Rule-Making" System: Its Design and Operation

Few institutions have come under greater scrutiny in recent years than the UN. Since the late 1980s, it has moved from the sidelines to the center stage of global security at a time of momentous political upheaval. To be sure, the organization still serves as a kind of global Hyde Park corner where states can voice grievances, proclaim bold visions, and generally play to international and domestic audiences. Beyond this public diplomacy function, however, one also finds a new emphasis on problem solving. Indeed, the array of problems that are now brought before the UN for serious corrective action is unprecedented. Not only are such problems far in excess of the UN's capacity to respond adequately with currently available resources, but they are forcing member states, particularly the larger powers, to face up to an awkward question: just how active or assertive do they want the UN to be?

To understand why the organization has grown in importance, one should consider the current mix of incentives at play among the main constituencies of UN membership. Among the industrialized states, the UN has become a useful means for spreading the costs of collective action and for addressing conflicts in regions where their "reach" was previously sustained by cold war–era alliance structures that are now crumbling.[1] The Persian Gulf War dramatized this trend, but it was evident before August 1990 in the peacekeeping area. Meanwhile, on the opposite end of the spectrum, small and developing states are being drawn to the organization in greater numbers than ever before, partly as a result of the large powers being engaged. Many of these countries see association with the UN as conferring substantial benefits in terms of their own visibility, legitimacy and even security.[2]

Among regional powers, the renaissance of the UN has triggered an ambivalent reaction. The security-related benefits of the UN for this middle group are less compelling than those for small states, and relative to the large powers, it has few opportunities to play a role in shaping UN operations. Within this diverse group, pariah or anti–status quo states usually have no (benign) interest in seeing the organization operate in their own regional backyards. Correspondingly, some nonpariah states that are formally nonaligned are either passive or resistant to UN involvement, since in the post–cold war era, nonalignment has little residual meaning except perhaps in the sense of opposing an activist UN dominated by the Western states. Other, more status quo regional powers evince greater interest in cooperation in the UN framework, at least on some issues.[3]

It is an open question whether this constellation of interests that has galvanized the UN will prove more than short lived. Any number of unhappy developments could quickly undermine its prospects. Great power comity could prove fleeting, middle-range powers could shift from ambivalence to outright hostility, small states could opt out entirely if they sense that global institutions are becoming disinterested in their own security needs, the growing mismatch between ever expanding missions and limited resources could grind the organization to a halt, and the political momentum favoring current reforms could dissipate. Major setbacks in any one of these areas could imperil multilateral security cooperation of the kind that the UN can provide.

Even so, it would be unfortunate to fall prey to excessive pessimism. Much of what the UN can do in the area of international security regime building does not require rigid adherence to the ideal of collective security.[4] Past experience, moreover, may not be a good indicator for the future. The whole idea of cooperative security stems from the view that a sea change among states is occurring, that they see the self-defeating aspects of cross-border aggression more clearly as well as the transcendent benefits of greater integration into a global economy. If this proves true, the UN or something very much like it will prove vital.

The Structure of the System

Though a casual observer might miss it, there is an underlying logic to the structure and rule-making procedures of "security"-related institutions at the UN.[5] The larger system incorporating these institutions, however, is the product less of original inspiration than of incremental fine-tuning. One will find only glimpses of it in the UN Charter, since that document treats international security largely as a problem of disputes between states, to be resolved pacifically, if possible, and only through other means if necessary.

Indeed, the charter is virtually silent on one of the most important tenets of the cooperative security concept, that national military postures have a direct bearing on the incidence and character of international conflict. The charter's predecessor, the Covenant of the League of Nations, by contrast, proclaimed that the maintenance of peace "requires" the reduction of national armaments "to the lowest point consistent with national safety and the enforcement by common action of international obligations."[6] With memories of the interwar years still vivid, and with the nuclear age still unborn, the drafters of the charter discredited the covenant's approach by deliberate omission, opting instead to assign, somewhat taciturnly, certain arms regulatory functions to the General

Assembly (GA) and the Security Council.[7] Unfortunately, the absence of any clear statement in the charter regarding the rightful role of arms regulation in international security has helped to create a mind-set in the UN system that sees this function as somehow separate from the larger collective security agenda.

Generally, the structure of this system is best thought of as having seven discrete elements:[8]

Agenda setting. Traditionally, the *General Assembly* and its subsidiary bodies have set the agenda in this area, either annually or in special sessions. Under the charter, the GA may make recommendations on "principles governing disarmament and the regulation of arms" (Article 11). Resolutions to this end are introduced each fall in the *First Committee* of the GA, while the *UN Disarmament Commission,* also constituted as a committee of the whole, deliberates each spring on selected items in which general guidelines or principles are seen as a tool for consensus building. Recently, the *Security Council* also engaged in agenda setting in its summit meeting of January 1992, when it identified several arms limitation priorities, most notably the nonproliferation of weapons of mass destruction.[9]

Exploratory assessment and analysis. Often, the GA will ask the secretary-general to analyze selected issues, either to examine the appropriateness of an issue for negotiation or to determine potential roles for the UN. For this purpose, the secretary-general appoints *groups of experts* (either governmental or private) to undertake special studies with the assistance of the Secretariat. Typically, these groups include experts from a representative collection of twelve to sixteen states. If a consensus view is reached, these states often act as a caucus group of sorts for subsequent diplomatic initiatives. The *Security Council* also has the power under the charter (Article 26) to "formulate [plans] . . . to be submitted to the Members . . . for the establishment of a system for the regulation of armaments." This authority, however, has never been used.

Negotiation. Formerly comprising forty members, the *Conference on Disarmament (CD)*—now reduced to thirty-eight, with the subtraction of the German Democratic Republic and the former Yugoslavia—is the forum in which multilateral arms regulation and disarmament agreements are negotiated. Based in Geneva, the CD includes all five officially acknowledged nuclear weapon states. The nonnuclear membership is reviewed periodically to ensure that it includes a representative cross section of Western, Eastern, and third world states. Although not subordinate to the General Assembly, the CD develops its own agenda, taking into account GA recommendations. The CD operates by consensus. As a practical matter, however, in situations of near-unanimity, the conference can still report out completed treaty text to the GA as long as dissenters have the opportunity to express contrary views in the CD's report.[10]

Implementation and compliance monitoring. Generally, these functions are "farmed out" to specialized technical agencies. The *International Atomic En-*

ergy Agency (IAEA) in Vienna has supported the Treaty on the Non-Proliferation of Nuclear Weapons (NPT) since 1970, for example, and the long-awaited *Organization for the Prohibition of Chemical Weapons,* which is to be established in The Hague, will support the chemical weapons ban. Another approach, of increasing use recently, has been to seek special services from the office of the *secretary-general.* In the early 1980s the General Assembly gave the secretary-general specific authority to investigate alleged violations of the Geneva Protocol and in 1989 provided specific guidelines for this purpose.[11] There is also the *UN Special Commission (UNSCOM),* created under Security Council Resolution 687 (1991), which, as discussed later, has important roles to play in the implementation of the weapons destruction and control regime in Iraq.

Review and amendment. The process of monitoring the performance of treaties has become more important in recent years. Traditionally, these functions are carried out by periodic *review conferences* that are organized and paid for by states that are parties to the treaty in question, though normally on a scale of assessment used at the United Nations and using UN personnel as executive agents in the servicing aspects.

Enforcement. Although the *Security Council* is assigned the "primary responsibility" for maintaining international peace and security under the charter, and is designated in several treaties as a place to lodge complaints regarding violations, the council, a fifteen-member body, proved incapable of performing any real enforcement role until recently. The council's voting rule for decision requires nine affirmative votes, including the concurrence of the five permanent members (Perm-5). For a council decision to be seen as legitimate, however, requires something closer to a majority of twelve to thirteen members.[12] In the aftermath of the Gulf War, the council issued a high-level declaration in January 1992 that cited the proliferation of all weapons of mass destruction as a threat to international peace and security. If this can be seen as a precedent, the council may take on a more activist role in resolving arms-related security matters in the future. The council has authority and wide latitude to set up subordinate bodies to assist in this task, such as *UNSCOM,* as noted, and the *661 Committee,* an intergovernmental group that is responsible for monitoring multilateral compliance with the comprehensive arms embargo against Iraq.

Training and education. Within the UN system, a time-honored place is reserved for promotional, training, and conference activities in support of treaties or initiatives. The educational-training element is particularly significant in the security area, given that the vast majority of UN members may have no more than two or three civilian government officials who know anything at all about security-related negotiations. The *Secretariat* has sponsored a fellowship training program for young diplomats to prepare them for work in the arms control and disarmament area. Since the late 1980s the Secretariat also has operated three regional centers—in Africa, Asia-Pacific, and Latin America—to encourage regional thinking on arms control problems.

In surveying the UN security system, three design features need to be highlighted in the context of cooperative security. First, the system is structured for inclusiveness. Even in forums in which universal participation is sacrificed in the interests of operational efficiency, as is the case in the Security Council (fifteen members), the CD (thirty-eight members), or governmental expert groups (usually twelve to sixteen members), the system nevertheless imposes a requirement to achieve a judicious cross section of the international community. Broad and representative participation is a legitimizing agent for this process.[13]

Second, there is a fair amount of overlap in terms of functions. Groups of governmental experts, for example, at times take on de facto negotiating roles, most recently in elaborating procedures and criteria for arms transfer registration. By the same token, the CD, when faced with deadlock on whether to start negotiations, has taken the tack of forming ad hoc committees (for outer space, nuclear testing, and so on) to study issues and exchange national viewpoints. Within limits, the system tolerates and sometimes even encourages functional overlap. Problems with this approach could arise, however, if a resurgent Security Council were to begin to play a more central role in the formulation of plans for arms regulation. Although the council's enforcement role is clear to all, the larger memberships of the GA and the CD would most likely resist perceived encroachments on their domains by the council, especially given the widespread perception of its elitist character.

Third, in terms of agenda setting, the substantive purview of these institutions is constrained by the system's bias toward inclusiveness. This bias may seem counterintuitive until one asks what a large group of disparate countries would have in common that could serve as the basis for global negotiations. It is artificial to include issues that affect the security of only a few countries. In the late 1950s the superpowers decided it was inappropriate to conduct their nuclear arms control negotiations within the UN framework, a decision that generated rancor and resentment among the neutral-nonaligned bloc.[14] Similarly, regional groupings—especially (but not only) in Europe—have traditionally had little incentive to invite UN diplomatic initiatives on their arms-related insecurities.

Ultimately, when one pares the global arms control negotiating agenda down to its essentials, three areas have endured: international "domains" regimes (such as outer space, the seabed, Antarctica), regimes to control or eliminate weapons of mass destruction (such as the Chemical Weapons Convention and the Nuclear Non-Proliferation Treaty), and laws of war regimes (such as regulations on "inhumane" weapons).[15] Arms trade registration and transparency may potentially be a fourth area. These are highly significant endeavors, to be sure, but they still represent only a subset of the larger number of bilateral and regional negotiating efforts aimed at arms regulation or disarmament.

The System in Operation

How well does this system "work"? The question invites the flip response: compared with what? The system is terribly cumbersome, slow, and marked by varying amounts of controversy and pie-in-the-sky rhetoric; it is also all we have. In the transition to a cooperative security regime, the task is to look carefully at the system's dysfunctions, both obvious and subtle ones, and think about how to surmount them.

One way to consider the system's performance is to focus on its workings at two levels of activity. The first is the *intergovernmental* level, the domain in which states decide what to do with, for, and to each other within the terms of their association. The second is the *international organizational* level, in which a secretariat performs special technical services (such as disarming Iraq and investigating chemical weapons use) in accordance with a specified mandate from states. Both levels have to operate effectively for the system overall to yield substantive output.

At the intergovernmental level, one can see since the 1950s several types of persistent problems.[16] Most obviously, the system has been largely incapable of producing global agreements that acknowledge existing differentials of power within the international community.[17] It is driven inevitably toward, on the one hand, preclusive agreements (such as nonstationing of nuclear weapons on the seabeds or in the Antarctic) or, on the other hand, comprehensive prohibitions (such as the chemical weapons ban) that impose common rights and obligations on all parties. Control methodologies aimed at stabilizing inequalities, post-NPT, even through the use of offsetting obligations, have been attacked by much of the third world as discriminatory. This global equality litmus test constitutes a strong brake on the rule-making capacity of the system. One can hardly imagine, for example, globalizing the 1987 Soviet-American bilateral ban on intermediate-range missiles, as some have proposed, since that would leave a few states with intercontinental-range missile boosters and the rest of the world with zero.

In part because of this problem, the system has been plagued by excessive amounts of pork barreling. In any bargaining situation, a natural tendency exists to attempt to distribute benefits to all parties as a way of securing broad cooperation; the problem arises when this tactic results in permissive or tortured rule making. Thus the NPT's affirmative promotion of the peaceful uses of nuclear energy (Article 4), subject to safeguarding, may have been a practical necessity to gain adherence among nonnuclear weapon states. But as a consequence, the NPT contains no effective bar against assembling the materials and the manufacturing base for a rapid withdrawal or breakout from the treaty.[18] In a similar fashion, contentious bargaining in the CD over the size and representative character of an "executive" council to oversee implementation of the global chemical weapons ban has yielded a politically correct outcome—the council will seat forty-one states—that may prove to be cumbersome in practical terms.

These tendencies have been reinforced by the system's inability to offer preferential treatment to states that choose to cooperate on security rule making. In principle, these inducements could range from material incentives, to security assurances, to the imposition of sanctions against nonparties that pose threats to members of the regime. And yet none of these approaches has really materialized. It is doubtful that the NPT in practice has offered its members any comparative advantages in terms of gaining assistance for the peaceful uses of atomic energy. Correspondingly, donor countries hitherto have not increased development assistance to countries that participate in arms control regimes, and aid programs in the industrialized states currently lack the excess capacity that would make this approach practical. As for security assurances, large states have generally been leery of offering such commitments to states (especially nonallies) purely on the basis of whether they join arms control agreements.[19]

Beyond this problem, the system has been afflicted to a degree by low participation rates. In certain areas of voluntary cooperative activity, notably in confidence-building measures and transparency, states have simply chosen not to participate, notwithstanding GA endorsement by wide margins. Since the early 1980s, for example, there has been a standardized instrument for military expenditure reporting, stemming from a Swedish initiative, but only about forty or so countries were using it by the early 1990s.[20] Similarly, data-exchange procedures worked out in the wake of the second Biological Weapons Convention review conference in 1986 have been implemented by perhaps no more than one-third of the regime's members. From anecdotal evidence, a wide range of reasons may account for this phenomenon—disinterest, confusion regarding data requirements, a lack of internal coordination with national military authorities, or nonparticipation by regional adversaries.[21] Still, it is likely that participation rates would improve if this issue was a higher political priority within the system at large.

Finally, the system is handicapped by poor connections to national centers of authority. With some exceptions, UN-related work in capitals is a secondary priority for many governments and for the foreign ministries that serve them. Offices with UN responsibilities often carry little weight in, or are even disconnected from, the upper echelons of policymaking, especially in governments in which military elites wield political authority. Furthermore, although the caliber of diplomats posted to the UN is often higher than the national average, one gets a nagging sense that delegations in New York may have more in common with one another than with defense, foreign, or economic policy decisionmakers in their own capitals. That collegiality may facilitate cooperation in New York but possibly at the expense of being able to "deliver" one's government when critical decisions are needed.

At the international organizational level, one also encounters many impediments to performance. Of all the issues on the UN's agenda, few have been more forbidding for international staff than security issues. On certain matters, such as peacekeeping, member states have long accepted a leading role for the Secretariat officials in the planning and implementation of operations. The current shortcomings in logistical support, financing, and execution of peacekeeping operations are due more to rapid increases in the scale of activity than to any fundamental tension in the system.

In the arms limitation area, however, the constraints to Secretariat involvement are more fundamental. Given the national sensitivities involved, this aspect of rule making at the UN clearly lies in the domain of states, not of international staffs. The secretary-general has no formal authority to advise states on arms proposals or to conduct diplomacy,[22] and requests by the General Assembly to the secretary-general to analyze issues always presume that a secretary-general will accept the consensus view of a governmental expert panel that is appointed to "assist" this individual, irrespective of the substance of that consensus. In recent years, the office of the secretary-general has been designated the legal entity with which treaty instruments are deposited. Being a depositary confers modest responsibilities to act as a communications channel among parties. But member states on the whole (especially the larger powers) have been zealous in guarding against perceived encroachments by international staff. The whole idea of "oversight" in the sense of monitoring or coordinating activity, or interpreting results, is not welcomed by states.

In such an atmosphere, international officials have been discouraged from seizing the initiative, even in relatively noncontroversial areas. Member states are always on guard against officials who appear too aggressive in advancing their own priorities or in getting out ahead of the political consensus. Unfortunately, given the political divisiveness surrounding arms control during the cold war, the general requirement of staff to act impartially at all times has bred a degree of passivity. Self-censorship is the tradition. This is not to say that skillful civil servants will always shy away from expressing viewpoints, anticipating problems, or taking affirmative steps to facilitate negotiations. But such behavior is not commonplace in the organizational culture that pervades the present-day UN.

Finally, the presumed impartiality of international organizations makes it extremely difficult in practice to realign programs or resources to meet new requirements. Any such effort can easily be construed by states with vested interests as being pursued for politically motivated reasons. In the 1980s naval security cooperation became an increasingly topical issue for small coastal states with the advent of exclusive economic zones and the growth of "brown-water" navies armed with cruise missiles, but international staff were precluded from pursuing even modest conferencing activity at the time by the flat American refusal to allow any discussion that might raise the taboo subject of naval arms control. Even the IAEA, an organization with an operational arms control mandate, is prone to this problem. Given that the frequency of its routine inspections is determined largely by the quantities and "annual throughput" of materials in civil nuclear power programs, irrespective of the attributes of states that possess these inventories, the agency cannot easily reallocate its inspection assets to states of current proliferation concern.[23] Revealingly, most routine IAEA inspection activity each year is targeted at countries with the largest nuclear power programs—Canada, Japan, and Germany—hardly the best use of the IAEA's safeguards resources.

Implications for Cooperative Security

As the foregoing makes clear, the rule-making system at the UN has many imperfections. Because most of these are inherent in its structure, and indeed in the disparate character of world politics generally, the eclipse of the cold war per se will not magically transform the system. Nevertheless, if current trends toward more intensive cooperation continue, they will help to attenuate some of the system's most pronounced weaknesses. Agenda setting could prove less fractious; participation rates might improve; the system could develop better connections to national levels of authority; and international staff might begin to take greater initiative on matters affecting the interests and resources of the organization, especially as they assume new, more operationally oriented duties.

Perhaps the largest challenge facing the system is substantive. What kinds of rules is it going to produce? It is nearing the end of a cycle with respect to global regimes. With the entry into force of a global chemical weapons prohibition, one of the final foundation stones in the edifice of mass destruction weapons control will have been put into place. In the foreseeable future, there will be much to do in the areas of implementing, verifying, fixing up, conforming, and possibly enforcing regimes, as well as encouraging broad adherence. But global negotiations in fundamentally new areas are unlikely.[24] If so, and if the trend toward regionally based arms control continues, the CD's role as the global system's negotiating mechanism might atrophy while the interregional agenda-setting and enforcement functions of the GA and the Security Council, respectively, would become more important.[25]

Cooperative security, however, could offer the system a new focus. None of the dysfunctions evident in the present system are insurmountable from the cooperative security standpoint. To the contrary, the defining elements of the concept could help energize the system in constructive ways. The approach of equalizing conventional firepower through universally applicable rules on, for example, force density, presumes a sense of balance and fairness that could be very attractive to smaller states. Equally, the notion of offering inclusion into the global economy as a quid for national forbearance and transparency in arms provides in theory a practical arrangement that developing countries could ill afford to pass up. And, indeed, the whole idea of regional cooperation is very much in accord with current trends. For the moment, however, the full-blown version of cooperative security is far too radical by contemporary standards to be achieved quickly. A step-by-step approach toward this goal would endeavor to strengthen those current UN activities that are compatible with the concept. These activities, as will be discussed, fall into four specific areas of innovation. Each faces its own set of problems and challenges. Yet advancements in all these areas, if sustained, could usher in some basic changes in the ways that states view the roles of international organizations in promoting cooperative security arrangements.

Transparency in Conventional Arms

The idea of fostering greater transparency in arms acquisition, which gained popularity in 1991, has been the subject of GA resolutions and expert studies since the mid-1960s. Arguably, such an approach is more in accord with pre-UN traditions than with the UN itself. As a condition of membership, for example, the Covenant of the League of Nations obliged states to "undertake to interchange full and frank information as to the scale of their armaments, their military, naval and air programs and the condition of such of their industries as are adaptable to warlike purposes."[26] The UN Charter imposes no such requirement. In the interwar period, when arms manufacture and trade were largely in private hands, official disclosure was widely seen as an important vehicle for calming international tensions and for strengthening national and interstate control.[27]

Debates about transparency in UN forums in recent years have echoed similar themes. As an international variant of *glasnost* politics, greater transparency has been promoted largely in confidence-building terms: to avoid misperceptions or exaggerated threats to one's security, to communicate benign intentions and the defensive character of one's posture to others, to provide early warning of unsettling flows of arms in various regional settings, and to provide a setting in which nonconforming behavior stands out more clearly. Correspondingly, emphasis has also been given to the beneficial effects of greater transparency on future restraint: to wit, that governments will subject their own export or import decisions to higher scrutiny if they believe that disclosure will generate criticism or that the information gained from disclosures over time will facilitate negotiations on restraints among suppliers and recipients.[28]

Although such propositions are not broadly contested, at least not superficially, their net political impact was nonetheless marginal until 1990. What galvanized the issue was the Persian Gulf War and the discomfiting image of Saddam Hussein's armies outfitted with imported equipment equal or superior to those possessed by forces in the anti-Iraqi coalition. Shortly after the cease-fire, in a flurry of post–Gulf War arms control proposals, major industrial states began to proclaim support for conventional arms transparency via a UN register for transfers.[29] This development dovetailed with ongoing activity inside the UN, including Secretary-General Pérez de Cuéllar's strong personal advocacy for the initiative, and in October 1991 a proposal was formally placed on the table by the European Community states and Japan. Barely two months later, the General Assembly voted in favor of creating a "universal and non-discriminatory" Register of Conventional Arms, which was officially established on January 1, 1992.[30]

The surprisingly wide margin of approval—150 to 0—reflected not only the superficial voguishness of the transparency idea but also some rather frenzied last-minute pork-barrel diplomacy.[31] With few exceptions, industrial and Western countries argued for establishing an arms transfer register at an early stage, limited to select categories of combat equipment with further expansion later on. In contrast, a number of developing states professed skepticism. Some favored outright delay and staunchly backed the idea that a register should also cover national production and stockpiling of weapons as well as transfers. As a Pakistani delegate argued,

> Arms control measures which are partial . . . or unbalanced in the treatment of different elements cannot be implemented successfully. This is particularly true of measures that focus on transparency in international arms transfers while relegating to a different plane equally important issues such as the indigenous armaments production capability of States. . . . The collection of information on military matters concerning all States could create potential problems for smaller and militarily weaker States. . . . While these States may not essentially benefit from the information they receive regarding the military capability of bigger States, information concerning themselves . . . could be used to their disadvantage by bigger States seeking regional or global hegemony.[32]

In the final bargaining, those favoring early creation of a registration scheme essentially got what they wanted, for a price. The register was established in rudimentary form. Participating states are to provide annual submissions by the end of each April of data on the following:

—*The number of items* imported into or exported from their territory during the previous year in seven categories of equipment: battle tanks, armored combat vehicles, large-caliber artillery systems, combat aircraft, attack helicopters, warships with a displacement in excess of 750 metric tons, and missiles or missile systems with ranges in excess of 25 kilometers.[33]

—For items registered in these seven categories, *all imports will specify the supplying state,* and *all exports will specify the recipient state* and the state of origin if not the exporting state.

In addition to these core provisions, however, the transparency resolution went considerably further. It stated that the register would be expanded to include data on military holdings, procurement through national production, and relevant policies pending the recommendations of a panel of governmental experts and a subsequent decision of the General Assembly. States were also encouraged to submit these additional data to the secretary-general, who would make it available for consultation by member states at their request (that is, the data are not public). Additionally, the secretary-general was asked to refine the reporting procedures and categories, to make adjustments deemed necessary to the effective operation of the register, and to prepare a report in 1994 on the register's operation over its first two years and on the feasibility of further expansion. Meanwhile, the resolution requested the CD to elaborate transparency measures that address excessive and destabilizing accumulation of arms, including national military holdings and procurement, and also to address means to increase openness and transparency related to the transfer of high technology with military applications, especially those associated with weapons of mass destruction.

Given this bewildering array of panels, deadlines, and forums, the job of pushing the diplomatic process forward on transparency is going to be arduous. Clearly, there is a strong presumption in favor of expanding the scope of the register to include such things as national holdings, for until this happens, the universality criterion for participation will be very hard to meet. Major arms recipients that perceive security threats from arms-producing neighbors would resist participating until then, even though they may have to "participate" in a practical sense when suppliers identify them as the final destination for exports. Surprisingly, however, by late 1993 it appeared that approximately eighty countries had registered their transfers in the initial round, including initially all arms suppliers and a substantial number of major recipients.

Certainly, in its current design, the register's contribution to transparency will be fairly modest. On the plus side, the retrospective reporting of major end items in the specified categories could provide a measure of early warning, given that large numbers of these systems over time are required to upset regional balances. Yet the acquisition of components and subsystems can greatly enhance existing capability, and these are not currently included.[34] Moreover, it has proved difficult to refine further the seven categories of equipment and to specify the kinds of data required. Having voted for the register, a number of countries, including first-tier suppliers (especially those that also import from other suppliers), have sought to maintain a degree of opacity by resisting disaggregation in certain areas, to a point where the data in some categories may not tell very much.[35] The standardized forms that have been designed for this scheme include columns for "remarks" on the item or its transfer, but the expert panel was unable to reach a consensus on what type of descriptive information would be appropriate or whether it should be considered part of a properly completed submission.[36] There are also some notable exclusions, for example, ground-to-air missiles and patrol boats unless they are outfitted with reportable missiles. And finally, the Secretariat will be sharply constrained in terms of its own actions in regard to the data, their analyses, or ultimate uses.[37]

Overall, then, in terms of both scope and level of specificity, the optimal balance between opacity and openness is still evolving. No one has ever claimed that transparency should be total. A previous UN study on the subject concluded, "Information of major strategic or tactical value, such as performance characteristics of the arms in question, or their precise location might be beyond the reasonable claims of transparency, since transparency measures should in no way increase the vulnerability of states against military operations in general and surprise attack in particular."[38] Outside this core of legitimate secrecy, however, the handling of national force holdings, production, and technology transfers remains controversial.

In a cooperative security regime, transparency would play a pivotal role.[39] One difference between the current UN approach and the cooperative security concept is that, while the former sees transparency mainly as a confidence-building device, the latter also views it as a quid for gaining greater access to advanced dual-use technologies. Efforts to promote this latter view might promote movement toward cooperative security by drawing in developing countries as a major constituency. Transparency as a gateway to access, however, also requires verifiable assurances on the end uses of technologies and equipment; simple disclosure of a transfer is not enough.

Some Western audiences have dismissed the Register of Conventional Arms as little more than a sop to public opinion and a diversion from the real business of limiting arms transfers. This attitude is surprising, for it fails to consider the potential implications of officially sanctioned disclosure for the great majority of countries (including some developed countries) whose military decision-makers operate in the absence of appreciable public scrutiny. Disclosure internationally will sooner or later lead to greater demands at home for internal accountability, monitoring, and control. In the near term, the main priority of the register exercise is fairly modest: to establish the initial parameters of legitimate transparency and to refine commonly accepted definitions of weapons types, mainly in the interest of confidence building without triggering instability. Yet if a modest registry is able to generate pressures favoring greater openness over the long term, both internationally and domestically, larger progressive forces will have been set in motion, forces that would be favorable to cooperative security.

Peacekeeping and Peace-Building Operations

Unlike transparency, peacekeeping has long been a mainstream activity of the UN. In the post–cold war era, peacekeeping operations (PKOs) have become a major growth industry for the organization: of the twenty-six operations undertaken between 1948 and 1992, thirteen were launched after 1987.[40] None of this activity is firmly anchored to any specific part of the charter, but a virtual ironclad consensus has evolved over the years that peacekeeping fits into the basic purposes and principles of the organization.[41] These operations vary enormously in terms of goals, methods, and expectations of success.[42] What concerns us here is the possible role of PKOs, as well as more expansive peace-building operations, in broadening the base of a prospective cooperative security community.

In their initial form, PKOs involved the use of unarmed military observers to monitor truces and cease-fire agreements. Beginning with the UN Emergency Force, which was dispatched during the 1956 Suez Crisis, force separation and buffer zone monitoring functions were added to the repertoire. Generally, military units performing these tasks are lightly armed and mobile and are authorized to use force only to the minimum extent necessary.[43] There are, however, many "neoclassical" variations to PKOs, involving civilian as well as military personnel, which perform multimission roles: elections or human rights monitoring, troop demobilization, public security, or civil administrative oversight. Thus, over time, UN peacekeeping activity has broadened to encompass not only conflict control but also conflict resolution (or "peace building"), and its scope for application includes not only international conflicts but also internal disputes with interstate dimensions.[44]

Rule making for peacekeeping activity is very much a context-specific process and departs from the sequence discussed earlier. Over time, some basic parameters for decision have evolved as a product of interactions between the Secretariat, the Security Council, the General Assembly, and the parties to specific conflicts. The most important rules are those that define the basic requirements for PKOs: that all parties consent to a proposed operation and its mandate, that UN personnel discharge their duties impartially and with maximum restraint, that personnel-contributing member states accept the risks entailed, and that an operation receives adequate backing from the Security Council and the GA.[45] Beyond these preconditions, the character of the operation will vary greatly depending on the route by which a PKO is established, specifically whether it stems from an unprompted request by parties or whether it is brokered by other states.

Both traditional and multimission PKOs perform weapons control and monitoring functions. The classical example in the former category is the UN Disengagement Observation Force (UNDOF), which was established in March 1974 as part of the Israeli-Syrian separation of forces agreement mediated by

Secretary of State Henry Kissinger after the Yom Kippur War. UNDOF controls a series of observation posts along a narrow buffer zone running between Syrian and Israeli forces in the Golan Heights. In addition to monitoring the absence of incursions into this area, UNDOF units (two motorized battalions) conduct routine on-site inspections at least once every two weeks to verify agreed-upon weapons and other restrictions within two wider, equally sized zones occupied by opposing forces on each side of the separation area. UNDOF also conducts challenge inspections at the request of either side, and results are reported to both.[46] The operation has operated successfully without serious incident up to the present.

Within larger, multicomponent PKOs, these cease-fire monitoring and buffer functions have been coupled to more diverse security-related tasks. The UN Angola Verification Mission, for example, monitored the phased withdrawal of Cuban troops. During roughly the same time in Namibia, units of the UN Transitional Assistance Group, among others, supervised the deactivation of military bases along the northern border, monitored movement restrictions on the South West Africa People's Organization and South African Defense Forces and the confinement of arms and ammunition to agreed locations, and verified the withdrawal of South African troops. In Nicaragua, the UN Central America Observer Group, augmented with a Venezuelan infantry battalion, cantoned, disarmed, and demobilized some 20,000 Contra troops during April to June 1990.[47] A joint UN–Organization of American States unit certified the demobilization of troops, and an OAS field mission has undertaken postsettlement weapons disposal and mediation.[48] In the former Yugoslavia, the UN Protection Force (UNPROFOR) was deployed in March 1992 on Croatian territory to expedite the disengagement of the Yugoslav National Army, Sebian irregular units, and the Croatian army. UNPROFOR's basic mission, as originally conceived, was to supervise several demilitarized areas in Croatia, providing a secure environment for local residents and facilitating the return of displaced persons.[49]

The most ambitious step in this progression, to date, is illustrated by the UN operation in Cambodia. Outfitted with twelve infantry battalions, plus additional logistics, engineering, and air support elements, and a corps of several thousand civilians, the UN Transitional Authority in Cambodia (UNTAC) assumed responsibility for implementing a peace settlement among four warring Cambodian factions that was brokered by a group of eighteen countries, consisting of the Perm-5, the Association of South East Asian Nations, and Indochina states.[50] Under these accords, signed in Paris in October 1991, UNTAC was given the tasks of supervising a rapid dissolution of the stalemated civil war and paving the way for nationwide elections. To these ends, in the preparatory phase of the elections process, UNTAC registered 4.7 million Cambodian voters, repatriated 360,000 refugees from border camps in Thailand, conducted civic and human rights education, rebuilt roads and bridges throughout the country, supervised and controlled existing civil administrations, trained more than 50,000 Cambodian polling staff, and coordinated the initial phases of an $880 million program pledged by international donors for Cambodia's future reconstruction and development.

The security-related responsibilities borne by UNTAC were substantial. It was assigned the job of monitoring the nonreturn of foreign (mainly Vietnamese) forces and the cessation of outside military assistance to the four Cambodian factions. It devised plans for regrouping, cantoning, and disarming some 200,000 regular forces of the four warring factions, for disarming an additional 250,000 village militia, and for assuming custody of approximately 300,000 weapons and some 80 million rounds of ammunition. It deployed mobile teams (air-, land-, and water-borne) to investigate alleged violations of the settlement, including breaches of the cease-fire and the illegal return of foreign forces. It established special units to locate and destroy undeclared caches of arms and supplies in the countryside. On top of all this, UNTAC organized programs for training former Cambodian soldiers in mine clearance and pursued its own demining in high-priority areas, including major roads, regroupment areas, and refugee reception centers.[51]

To carry out these tasks, the UN devised procedures that were fairly esoteric by normal peacekeeping standards. The parties were obliged to disclose data on their troop strength; locations; holdings of arms, ammunition, and equipment; and known minefields. Hot lines were set up to link factional commanders to UNTAC and the Cambodian transitional governmental authority (the Supreme National Council). UNTAC established a tactical intelligence capacity in the field to help with monitoring and investigatory functions. Demobilization certifications were prepared as an incentive device (and, indeed, as a public security measure) to channel discharged soldiers into reintegration and vocational training programs.

In the end the UNTAC operation was not able to achieve demilitarization on the vast scale envisaged by the Paris Accords.[52] It did, however, manage to bring the country safely through a highly successful multiparty election in May 1993, despite political violence and an unstable military situation; and it helped to forge a coalition between the two political factions that won the vast majority of seats in the new consituent assembly, the royalist opposition party, led by Prince Norodom Ranariddh, and the Phnom Penh regime, headed by Prime Minister Hun Sen. As of late 1993 UNTAC had turned over authority to the new government formed in 1993 under a new constitution, and had substantially departed from the country, leaving behind a small residual UN presence.[53]

By any measure, UNTAC marks a sharp departure from the UN's traditional approach to peacekeeping. Rather than simply aim for stability in the narrow military sense, UNTAC's goal was to oversee a political transition process, one that would dislodge all the Cambodian factions from their stalemated pattern of confrontation and help to lay a democratic foundation for national reconstruction. In this respect, UNTAC's activities were more characteristic of what Secretary-General Boutros Boutros-Ghali has termed postconflict "peace-building."[54] Yet, whether UNTAC's achievements suggest that it can be a model for future UN operations remains unclear. The enormous size and expense of UNTAC make it very difficult to emulate, and certain key factors favoring a settlement to the Cambodian conflict might be absent elsewhere.[55]

From the UN's standpoint, the Cambodia experience teaches the overriding value of an agreed international legal framework for UNTAC's operations—the Paris Accords—along with a consensus among the large powers and regional states backing up that framework. The comprehensive political settlement provided a strong foundation for UNTAC that many other PKOs clearly lack. It also changed the psychology of the UN operation in a subtle but dramatic way. Although UNTAC was obliged to conduct itself in a neutral and evenhanded mannner, its mandate also required that it act as a "partisan" for the settlement itself, cajoling or pressuring parties to abide by its terms, condemning noncompliance, and not simply withdrawing at the first sign of trouble. Such an approach is not without risks. One party or another, having been pressured into a settlement by outside patrons, might completely withdraw from participation if UN activism constrains its options.[56] But the strength of this approach is that the UN has much greater latitude to engage in "mid-course" adjustments in mission mandates that are responsive to local conditions and to focus outside pressure on noncomplying parties.

In a cooperative security context, peacekeeping and peace-building operations should be viewed in two dimensions. First, they can be a useful vehicle for promoting coordinated activity among major military establishments in areas that (at least to them) are strategically peripheral. Hitherto, PKOs have been dominated by midsize neutral states whose presence was more widely acceptable in many conflicts during the cold war era. In the current climate, however, greater participation of large states can offer a powerful political reinforcement to an operation, not to mention valuable equipment and logistical and intelligence support, and it can have indirect confidence-building effects among the larger states.

Second, since third world regions are the principal beneficiaries of this activity, greater reliance on UN instruments, especially for peace building, could help to build constituencies for cooperative security in these regions. This possibility is especially strong in the disarming, demobilizing, and mine-clearance aspects of UN operations, as well as for humanitarian relief, all of which have important social consequences for countries long plagued by civil disorders and a surfeit of soldiers. These security procedures, coupled with the increasingly common use of elections to establish democratic governance and an international support structure for development assistance, can greatly assist the task of nation building and rebuilding in the eyes of the local population.

Despite these contributions, UN field operations face herculean challenges. Many of the conflicts at issue (for example, Bosnia, Somalia) are so deeply rooted internally that it is difficult to imagine successful transitions, even under agreements that are broadly acceptable internationally. With domestic attitudes often lagging far behind the international consensus, the UN is forced to weigh whether a PKO would risk an open-ended involvement in shoring up weak governments against the ever-present threat of insurgencies or anarchic civil strife. This problem is accentuated by the phenomenon that, as the strongest organizational entity in many of these local contexts, the UN finds its mere presence encourages not so subtle forms of dependency that can complicate a graceful exit from a situation.[57]

Beyond these problems, the organization's wherewithal to conduct effective peacekeeping is being stressed by several institutional constraints. Typically, large-scale operations have been plagued by slow deployment, inadequate logistics support, poor training, the absence of good cohesion among units of different nationalities, and an overreliance on best-case planning. Even with solid international backing and good improvising in the field, it is often difficult for the UN to be agile enough to preempt problems, especially if anticipatory action would tend to show favoritism to one side or another. Moreover, as domestic and ethnic conflicts loom larger on the global agenda, support for an active UN involvement, even with the consent of parties, may ebb among groups of states with traditionally acute concerns over sovereignty.

There is also the dilemma of what happens, in the peacekeeping context, if cease-fires are violated or if a party not only withdraws its consent but seeks to disrupt an operation violently. Hitherto, the UN has not been postured to engage in "peace enforcement," preferring instead to keep a clear distinction between consensual peacekeeping and nonconsensual responses to acts of aggression. The boundary line, however, is becoming blurred, especially as concerns the provision of humanitarian assistance in conflict situations. UN operations in Bosnia-Herzegovina or Somalia are not strictly peacekeeping activities, yet they fall short of full-scale enforcement.[58] States have been reluctant to commit troops under confused and dangerous circumstances, and planners in the Secretariat, sensing qualms among members, have consistently pushed for full agreement among all parties on a cease-fire and on the terms of any UN deployment. The results, very often, have been delay and frustration.[59] None of these problems undermine the essential utility of PKOs, but they do suggest the kinds of challenges that have to be overcome if the full potential of the instrument is to be realized.[60]

Enforcement, Part One: Sanctions and Use of Force

In UN terminology, *enforcement* refers to a range of actions that the organization can take to compel a state to bring its behavior into line with specific demands. The charter defines the kinds of deviant behavior worthy of such treatment only in the broadest terms, as "threats to the peace . . . acts of aggression or other breaches of the peace."[61] It is up to the Security Council to determine the existence of such threats (or acts) in specific cases, and to decide on what measures would be appropriate for maintaining or restoring international peace and security. In principle, the coercive power conveyed by this grant of authority is formidable.[62] In the past, what thwarted the use of this compulsory power were the charter's requirements for unanimity among the permanent council members and the cold war realities that precluded consensus. With these constraints now relaxed, at least to a degree, the council has begun to test its capacity for action.

In a cooperative security community, the members need the means to resist aggressive behavior. For reasons of principle as well as of prudence, however, these means have to be internationalized in the sense that the risks, costs, and decisionmaking associated with such means are broadly supported by the community. Amicable relations among the largest powers is a necessary but certainly not a sufficient condition for effective enforcement action. Indeed, as unconsented UN operations have become commonplace, they have begun to raise a host of difficult questions that were never fully ventilated during the cold war. When does governmental behavior become egregious enough to trigger an international response? Once enforcement is deemed necessary, which tools should be applied in various situations? And to what extent can the council exert control over the application of these tools? Any effort to achieve a cooperative security framework would require a greater degree of international unanimity on these questions than exists today.

When to Intervene?

The first issue—triggering criteria—unavoidably brings into play subjective judgments among UN members on what constitutes a threat to international peace and security. Classic cases of interstate aggression, such as Iraq's invasion of Kuwait, pose relatively few problems from the doctrinal standpoint. Below this threshold, however, the job of individuating cases has been more difficult. Violent overthrows of governments are politically beyond the UN's reach at present. The council, for example, conspicuously avoided taking up the case of Haiti in the immediate aftermath of the 1991 overthrow of the democratically elected Aristide government.[63] On the other hand, the council has shown greater activism in addressing large-scale repression and domestic violence with substantial transborder effects. The flight of Kurdish refugees from Saddam Hussein's armies into Iran and Turkey was deemed by the council to pose a threat to peace and security, prompting it to support a major humanitarian operation preceded by allied military action to protect Kurdish minorities in northern Iraq.[64] In Bosnia-Herzegovina, the council invoked

Chapter 7 to authorize "all measures necessary" to ensure the delivery of humanitarian assistance to beleaguered populations caught up in the fighting.[65] In Somalia, where the threat was anarchy and massive starvation, the council took action to authorize the use of all necessary means to "establish a secure environment" for humanitarian relief, opening the door for the U.S.-led intervention in December 1992.[66]

In the wake of the Persian Gulf War, the council also has begun to scrutinize weapons acquisition behavior by states from the perspective of enforcement. In its widely heralded summit statement of January 1992, the council proclaimed that the "proliferation of all weapons of mass destruction constitutes a threat to international peace and security," and it committed itself to work "to prevent the spread of technology related to the research for or production of such weapons and to take appropriate action to that end."[67] Apart from mandating Iraqi disarmament, discussed in the next section, it has not as yet established any practice in support of its commitment. In another area of concern—state-sponsored terrorism—the council has taken action in one case, imposing an arms and air embargo against Libya to compel it to give up two suspects wanted in the Pam Am 103 bombing, but the council's affirmative vote was politically divisive and efforts to resolve the stalemate have not been successful.[68]

As this pattern of cases suggests, the triggering criteria for UN enforcement are expanding in scope. Domestic conflict and repression are no longer a priori exempt from forcible international action if they have significant spillover effects across borders. At the same time, as the U.S. ambassador to the UN, Thomas Pickering, has intimated, some fundamental constraints have to be recognized: "We are unlikely to see the rapid elaboration of sweeping tenets of international law to provide automatic external guarantees for minority rights, democratically elected governments, or hungry people caught in a civil war. A significant number of UN members do not see such principles as leading to order but as subversive of it, or at least subversive of an order based on firm doctrines of state sovereignty and nonintervention."[69] Differences of this magnitude are bound to have an important braking effect on council action. And they have been a significant factor, though not the only one, in generating criticism of the council's performance in areas where it has acted.

Iraq notwithstanding, the council cannot claim to be a master of decisive and timely action. Its assertion of legal jurisdiction is often firmer than its collective will to act. The major powers, including the United States, have been hesitant to commit resources and lives to operations that were either problematic in terms of success or secondary from the standpoint of engaging core national interests.[70] In the former Yugoslavia, after launching a large peacekeeping operation in Croatia, the council was painfully slow to react to the spread of ethnic conflict into Bosnia, and it has failed to back up its decisions, even those taken under Chapter 7, with real enforcement action.[71] In

Somalia the council was fitful in 1992 in the attention paid to the disintegration of that country, vainly searching for low-cost consensual modes of intervention while between 300,000 and 500,000 Somalis died from the effects of famine and thuggery.[72] These experiences have damaged the council's credibility as a consistent and principled arbiter of collective action.[73]

The council's tendency to tailor enforcement mandates to the securing of humanitarian relief has raised additional complications. To be sure, the impulses to relieve human suffering are understandable, especially if the most likely alternative is to do nothing at all. Television images of violence against civilians have created a sense of obligation to act that few governments are prepared to flout on doctrinal grounds. Still, there are serious drawbacks in making humanitarian relief the *sole* object of enforcement. Politically, the practice tends to remove pressure on states to make hard choices on how to deal with the causes, not merely the symptoms, of conflict.[74] It also tends to convey the misguided notion that force could somehow be applied neutrally, not against someone in particular but against conflict in general. To do their jobs correctly, UN commanders supporting humanitarian missions need a fair amount of local cooperation and restraint from all sides; tactical uses of force may achieve short-term goals, like getting through a road block, but not without giving UN forces a partisan taint that would risk drawing them into the cross fire later on. Faced with this trade-off, local commanders shrink from using force at all, even when the rules of engagement would permit (or require) it. As a result, relief operations such as those in Sarajevo become hostage to the daily whims of the combatants.

This problem is but one illustration of a much larger challenge for the UN and, indeed, for the cooperative security regime as a whole: how to strike a judicious balance between being a neutral mediator of conflicting claims and an enforcer of international judgments. In the abstract, enforcement is mainly about punishing aggressors and restoring the status quo. In practical terms, however, it is mainly about making choices between parties, about validating the claims of one side and condemning the other side. This is a difficult task for a universal membership body like the UN. In the real world most disputes lack the quality of one-sidedness that would automatically pit all against one, and the organization is constitutionally obliged to promote negotiated settlements as a first step.

Even if the arguments favoring enforcement are compelling, it can still be a difficult choice if substantial costs are attached. In the former Yugoslavia, UN peacekeeping in Croatia clearly helped to limit harm to civilians. But any benefits of coercive action against Serbia over the Bosnian civil war would have to be balanced against the risk that the peacekeeping mission in Croatia would further unravel. The trade-offs between mediation and enforcement, and the difficulties of shifting from one posture to the other, may explain in part why the council has tended to structure UN enforcement around ostensibly "nonpartisan" mandates, such as humanitarian relief or arms embargoes on all parties.

Invoking Sanctions

As the enforcement bridge is crossed, the question of appropriate means becomes ever more urgent. Resort to economic and other sanctions is often the preferred point of departure, for several reasons. The charter in Article 41 gives broad authority to the council to impose sanctions;[75] the near universality of UN membership makes the organization a logical place to develop and apply them; they can be tailored to the severity of the circumstances; and, politically, sanctions are an important consensus-building tool for more forcible action if such becomes necessary. During the cold war the council imposed mandatory and comprehensive economic sanctions only once, against Rhodesia in 1965, and an embargo on arms trade with South Africa in 1978. Between 1990 and early 1993, it imposed comprehensive sanctions against Iraq and Serbia-Montenegro, as well as arms embargoes against the warring factions in Somalia, all of the former Yugoslav republics, and Liberia, and an air embargo on Libya.[76]

Although the UN's agility in crafting trade and financial sanctions has clearly improved, more frequent use of these tools has exposed some new challenges. First, sanctions are rarely self-implementing unless the target country has few ties to the outside world. In the Persian Gulf case the United States and coalition allies spent considerable political and diplomatic resources appealing to Iraq's commercial partners to make the necessary internal adjustments in order to uphold the sanctions regime. Second, the implementation of sanctions is rarely self-evident. The council's standard practice when authorizing sanctions is to create an intergovernmental subcommittee to "monitor" the compliance of states and to assess the regime's effectiveness; but this function entails little more than receiving submissions by member states on their own implementation, plus occasional fact-finding missions sponsored by the secretary-general and whatever intelligence data third parties may be willing to supply. Systematic monitoring is lacking.[77]

Another challenge posed by sanctions concerns the difficulties of reliable enforcement. The council on occasion has authorized maritime interdiction of blockade runners, and this technique has proved to be effective, given the ready availability of sufficient naval vessels.[78] Exerting control over commercial routes on land is another matter, however, and neighboring countries whose cooperation would be required are often the most likely suspects from the compliance standpoint. Finally, offsetting the damage inflicted by sanctions on civilian populations and complying states has proved difficult for the UN to handle. Economic strangulation is an ugly and blunt instrument, and it provides no swift or certain leverage against the actions of a ruthless government. On humanitarian grounds the council has routinely exempted the import of medical supplies and foodstuffs into targeted states, but the distribution of these items can become a bone of contention between the local government and the UN, as has been the case in Iraq.

As for the economic hardships borne by countries involved in enforcement, there is a strong prudential case for taking the issue seriously, given the need to maintain multilateral support for sanctions among less developed countries. The charter provides states with the right to consult with the Security Council on "the solution of those problems," and in the Iraqi case, the council specifically authorized its sanctions committee to examine requests for such assistance.[79] One serious problem, however, is to develop ways to assess the diverse impacts of sanctions objectively and to sort out bloated from legitimate claims of hardship.[80]

Military Measures

If multilateral sanctions management is not easy, it nevertheless appears open to improvement through existing decisionmaking procedures. The collective application of military measures is more problematic. Many UN procedures have never been reliably tested and would, if used, raise serious objections by several constituencies in the organization.

The Persian Gulf War case is instructive. As events in Iraq unfolded, the council improvised in ways that seemed logical in light of realities on the ground and its own lack of prior experience. With sanctions in place but not achieving the desired effect, the council approved Resolution 678, authorizing states "cooperating" with Kuwait to use "all necessary means" to secure Iraq's withdrawal from Kuwait and "to restore international peace and security in the area."[81] This delegation of authority, qualified only by a six-week deadline to give Iraq "one final opportunity" to withdraw, provided virtually open-ended flexibility to the anti-Iraq coalition. As Pickering observed, "It gave a UN license for the use of force without restriction as to its manner or extent, or explicit terms for its cessation."[82] In particular, the explicit authorization to restore peace and security in the region validated steps going far beyond simply evicting Iraqi armies from Kuwait.

The action against Iraq turned out to be a swift and unqualified success on the battlefield. But it also created, to use Pickering's phrase, an "uncovered risk" from the political standpoint. Under different circumstances, the deputizing of a coalition to act on behalf of the international community—the "delegated" enforcement approach—could have seriously backfired. The force employed could have been indefensibly excessive. Iraq could have widened the conflict, drawing in states on both sides. The coalition itself could have split apart under the pressures of a lengthy campaign or disagreements over command. None of these unhappy circumstances materialized, and yet any one of them could have greatly strengthened the perception that a few powerful states had abused their UN license in forcing Iraq out of Kuwait. Rather than set a pattern for the future, the Gulf operation inspired new efforts at the UN to find ways of exerting greater multilateral control over military action carried out in the UN's name.

Broadly, the search for a better approach has followed two different paths. The first option is to place military capability at the disposal of the organization itself, by implementing the charter's long-dormant provisions on force contributions for enforcement purposes. In his report, *An Agenda for Peace,* Secretary-General Boutros-Ghali endorsed the idea of negotiating so-called "Article 43 agreements," under which individual states (or groups of states) would commit in advance combat forces to the council for its use in UN enforcement action.[83] Such agreements, once ratified at the national level, would represent the reservoir of capability, not only of troops and equipment but also of facilities and other forms of assistance, from which the council could draw in certain contingencies.

The Article 43 approach could have several beneficial effects. It certainly would provide a degree of legitimacy for enforcement that is not available when the operation has to be delegated to ad hoc coalitions, especially those dominated by a single country.[84] Equally important, the existence of the agreements would create a much greater propensity at the UN for prompt action, something that potential target states would be loath to ignore. On a domestic level the process of reaching these agreements could strengthen the sense of obligation within key states to participate in enforcement operations, while allowing a degree of flexibility on the form of their contribution as well as on the automaticity implied by the commitment.[85] At the same time, Article 43 forces are no panacea. Operations on the scale of a Desert Storm would probably extend well beyond the capabilities that special agreements could collectively provide. Moreover, if non-NATO countries were to participate, which would be desirable politically, the UN would have to make a large investment in the training and exercising of troops and in the development of compatible military doctrines and standards for interoperable equipment, all of which would be necessary to enable various national units to integrate quickly under hostile circumstances.

Finally, the Article 43 approach does not resolve the thorny question of multilateral command. There is little dissent at the UN from the proposition that operational command of forces in the theater should go to a serving officer who has the imprimatur of the largest troop-contributing country, and that this force commander would need a multinational staff broadly reflective of the mix present in the UN-earmarked units. The difficult issue is where the chain of command ascends from there. The council itself is more a forum for decision than an international command authority. Though the secretary-general directs peacekeeping operations, and selects PKO commanders, his subordinate status to the council makes him more akin to a foreign minister than to a commander-in-chief. Nor is there a chairman of a UN joint chiefs-of-staff in an operational sense. The charter deliberately sidesteps this issue. While establishing the Military Staff Committee (MSC), composed of the five permanent members, to play an advisory role to the council, the charter's drafters specifically stated that "questions relating to the command of such forces shall be worked out subsequently."[86]

This ambiguity in what constitutes a "UN command" has prompted a second general approach to strengthening multilateral control, specifically to augment the council's capacity to influence the general pace and extent of enforcement operations, but within the basic framework of a delegated approach.[87] Suggestions along this line have been numerous.[88] Their basic thrust is to improve the capacity of the council to refine the terms of enforcement operations and to make midcourse corrections, while leaving operational command authority with states that provide the disproportionate share of the military capability.

The council's December 1992 authorization of the United Nations Task Force (UNITAF) operation in Somalia reveals some tentative steps in this direction. The council, among other things, enjoined participating states to establish coordination between the UN and their military forces; it appointed an ad hoc commission to monitor the operation; and, finally, it expressly reserved the right to decide on when to shift the operation from an enforcement to a peacekeeping footing.[89] No provisions of this kind were included in the Gulf enforcement mandate. In addition, UNOSOM II, the operation that took over from UNITAF in mid-1993, made special provisions for U.S. control over a "quick reaction force" while establishing an integrated command structure for the peacekeeping force.[90]

From the cooperative security standpoint the precise details of command decisions are less important than the ability of the council over time to act upon, in the words of the secretary-general, its "legitimate interest in the manner in which [enforcement] is carried out."[91] Without this capacity, the quality of the council's imprimatur will come into question. Its decisions are credible only if the international community broadly accepts the legitimacy of its authority.

Enforcement, Part Two: Arms Control Operations

Weapons control is assuming a larger role in Security Council enforcement practice, mainly because of the Persian Gulf War. After Kuwait was liberated, Iraq stood beaten but unbowed. Its mass-destruction weapons capabilities had been bombed but not destroyed, and the full extent of these capabilities remained unclear. As part of its cease-fire demands, the council decided to compel Iraq to relinquish its nuclear, chemical and biological, and missile capability and to impose an arms and technology denial regime as part of the existing sanctions against Iraq.[92] The secretary-general was asked to organize inspection, disposal, and long-term monitoring operations on Iraqi territory and to develop in consultation with states guidelines for implementing arms-related sanctions.[93] Thus was the UN launched suddenly into the forbidding terrain of arms control enforcement.

Coercive disarmament has an important, if unhappy, historical analogue in the post–World War I experience. Under the Treaty of Versailles "Inter-Allied Commissions of Control" were created in 1920 to supervise the demobilization of German naval, land, and air forces; to receive and destroy weapons; and to dismantle fortifications specified in the treaty.[94] Their efforts, though successful in a few areas, were unsuccessful in most, and the commissions were withdrawn from German territory after 1927. Some of the problems encountered by these commissions have sobering parallels in present-day Iraq.[95] To date, however, two of the key differences are the binding power of Security Council actions and the political backing of the UN-sponsored operation by states with the power of decision.

Organizing the Operation

The scope of the Security Council's requirements under Resolution 687 forced UN officials into a period of rapid improvisation. The Secretariat itself had no background in arms control operations, and the specialized agencies called upon to render services (such as the IAEA and World Health Organization) had no weapons-related expertise or experience in operating under adversarial conditions. For the secretary-general, the immediate need was to organize a special commission, which would, subject to the council's approval, inspect and dispose of Iraq's chemical and biological weapons capability, inspect and supervise the destruction by Iraq of its relevant ballistic missile capability, provide assistance to the IAEA in undertaking similar activity in the nuclear field, and designate locations for inspection in addition to those contained in declarations of proscribed capabilities to be supplied by the Iraqis.

Starting from scratch, the Secretariat had to grapple with some fundamental questions. What should be the character and composition of this as yet undefined commission? What level of cooperation should be expected from the Iraqis? How should the UN personnel comport themselves in the field, and how intrusive should inspection activity be? How would the commission determine which additional sites should be inspected? On top of all these questions, the funding of the operation proved nettlesome. There was near-universal agreement that Baghdad should pay for the privilege of being disarmed, but the council was disinclined to seek obligatory assessments for funds to cover the operation pending such payments, preferring instead a pay-as-you-go voluntary approach.

Establishing the new commission and locating it within the Secretariat was a politically delicate task. To be acceptable as a UN entity, it had to be inclusive and collegial; yet to be operationally effective, it had to be hierarchical, small, and technically competent. At some level, these two sets of criteria were bound to clash, and as in a heart transplant operation there is always some risk of the new organ being rejected by the surrounding tissue. Thus the structure and composition of UNSCOM reflected a careful set of choices and trade-offs that, as it turned out, has proved to be reasonably successful.

It was decided that UNSCOM itself would be composed of twenty-one members, a rather large number. It would, however, be for the most part technical rather than diplomatic. Members would divide up into nuclear, chemical and biological, missile, and future compliance subgroups. While individual UNSCOM members might be chosen to lead inspections, the teams of inspecting personnel, of roughly fifteen to thirty-five each, would be recruited separately and assemble at a field office in the region (Bahrain) for deployment into Iraq.

With respect to UNSCOM's composition, several basic guidelines were observed: no two members should come from the same state; leading members of the anti-Iraqi coalition and all the Perm-5 states would be included, with the remainder to be drawn from a balanced group of countries possessing the requisite technical skills and incentives to participate (for example, Indonesia, Japan, Nigeria, Norway, Poland, Venezuela); and UNSCOM's "executive" head would be a national from other than a permanent member state. Finally, in terms of operational routine, while the full commission would assemble in New York only at intervals to provide strategic direction and review findings, a small directing staff comprising the chairman, the deputy chairman, and a cross section of UNSCOM members and technical support staff would work at UN headquarters on a continuing basis. In all these ways the contrasting needs for efficiency and inclusion were satisfied.

Progress and Obstacles

The saga of UNSCOM and IAEA activity in Iraq has been widely reported and need not be recapitulated here.[96] Overall, as of mid-1993, the operation could claim some major achievements in carrying out the Security Council's mandate. First, it assembled a more detailed picture of Iraq's nuclear weapons program than was known anywhere outside the country until the war. Through painstaking investigative work the operation exposed Iraq's extensive uranium-enrichment programs, illegal plutonium-extraction activity, overseas procurement efforts in support of nuclear and missile programs, and, most important, Iraq's development program for a nuclear explosive device (the so-called PC-3 program) and associated surface-to-surface missile delivery system. Second, by mid-1993 the operation had removed or destroyed most of

Iraq's nuclear and missile equipment covered by UN resolutions—far more than allied aircraft had been able to accomplish during the war—and it was well advanced in the hazardous process of disposing of Iraq's large stockpile of chemical munitions and bulk agent.[97] Third, the operation had begun the laborious process of putting in place equipment and personnel to track Iraq's continuing compliance with UN prohibitions under the guise of "interim" monitoring.

Despite these accomplishments, UNSCOM and the IAEA still faced major hurdles more than two years after the Gulf War cease-fire. Field operations were plagued by continued stonewalling, duplicity, and occasional harassment of inspectors on the part of the Iraqis. Interference with UNSCOM flight operations, among other things, triggered an allied bombing raid against a nuclear-industrial site near Baghdad in January 1993. Meanwhile, the Iraqi government remained unyielding in the obligation to provide a "full, final, and complete" disclosure of all of its weapons programs, as called for by the Security Council.[98] It also remained hostile to the council's plan for the long-term monitoring of Iraqi imports, weapons development, and industrial activities, the UN's only real margin of safety against reversals for the foreseeable future. By July 1993 there were some signs that Baghdad might reconsider its opposition to the long-term monitoring requirement, albeit as part of a bargaining strategy designed to coax the council into relaxing its terms for dropping the economic embargo.[99]

Ultimately, whatever judgments are rendered on the operation's performance, UNSCOM and the IAEA will have amassed a wealth of practical experience. One area of learning has been in the design and conduct of multinational inspection operations, not only in handling the nationality mix but also in identifying skill categories, orientation and debriefing procedures, and support requirements (such as air transport, medical, and explosive ordnance disposal). In general, multinational teaming among thirty-five countries has turned out to be less difficult than feared, whereas the logistics requirements have proved somewhat more onerous than expected.[100] Much has also been learned about the sharing, control, and analysis of sensitive information provided by several states, as well as about the operation of reconnaissance aircraft. In addition, a vast amount has been learned about the prerequisites and mechanics of staging challenge inspections at undeclared sites and the optimal methods for coordinating on-site operations with local reconnaissance from rotary- and fixed-wing aircraft.

A less well recognized area of learning concerns the question of achieving "cooperation" between the United Nations and a host country in an adversarial setting. UN planners reckoned early on that the operation could not be effective without Iraqi cooperation, however obtained. Inspectors simply could not shoot their way in; the country was not occupied; and Baghdad would quickly seize upon any pretext for discrediting the operation internationally. In light of these considerations, a working relationship could only be achieved, first, by establishing clear rights and obligations for both sides and, second, by accepting the practical reality of offsetting vulnerabilities. Just as UN teams would be hostage to Iraqi goodwill at the field level, so would Iraq be hostage to the threat of further military action at the strategic level. Despite near-constant disputes with Iraqis over some aspects of the operation, particularly the challenge inspections, this general approach has worked tolerably well, and proposals to apply coercion at the field level (for example, to equip UN teams with armed escorts) as a way to "put teeth" into the operation were seen at UN headquarters as highly counterproductive. Nonetheless, with the ever-present threat of harassment against inspectors, the situation has remained tense throughout.

Larger Implications

How should one assess the implications of the Iraq experience for cooperative security? Clearly, if enforcement is needed to deal with threats to a cooperative security regime, coercive modes of disarmament would logically be a part of such practices. The whole community would benefit from broadly acceptable methods for dealing with major arms acquisitions by states that are clearly bent on aggression. The Iraqi operation has demonstrated that the UN, albeit under special conditions, can act quickly to concentrate technical assets in order to subject a universally acknowledged rogue state to a high level of multilateral scrutiny and control. Indeed, the operation, despite its limitations, has helped to make Iraqi disarmament a legitimate international priority, not simply the narrow obsession of a few states.

The harder questions to answer are what kinds of imposed weapons controls are necessary for international peace and security, and at what cost? In the Iraqi case Baghdad's invasion of Kuwait had been the triggering event for the enforcement action, and its weapons of mass destruction could hardly be ignored in restoring the peace. The risk of failing to deal with these weapons was unacceptably high, and the price to be paid for eliminating them was small in relation to the costs already incurred in evicting Saddam Hussein from Kuwait. Moreover, though it was not fully revealed at the time, Iraq had breached its international legal obligations under the NPT, an objective legal standard whose violation tended only to further stigmatize Iraq's egregious behavior.

In other situations, and with other categories of weaponry, calculations of risks and costs may be less clear-cut. In Somalia the United States initially disclaimed any suggestion that its forces involved in the UNITAF operation should attempt to disarm rival Somali clans, even though doing so would appear vital to the longer-term prospects for UN-authorized humanitarian operations in that country. And even with weapons of mass destruction, which pose the clearest hazards, it remains to be seen what type of balance the

Security Council will attempt to strike between promoting nonproliferation norms through cooperative diplomacy, on the one hand, and enforcing such norms, on the other.[101]

As for consensual forms of arms limitation, the Iraqi operation cannot be a useful model, it is often argued, because the encroachments on sovereignty have been too massive to imagine they could be freely negotiated in a multilateral context. Although this concern, at least at present, has a self-evident validity, it tends to gloss over the larger political and organizational effects of this case for international cooperation.

The shock of the Iraqi disclosures, compelled as they were, has become a driving factor behind efforts to achieve greater transparency. With the inadequacy of existing nuclear safeguards clearly revealed, the IAEA's leadership has now begun to press its membership for more stringent reporting, monitoring, and control procedures, including acceptance of special inspections to clarify the facts in cases in which undeclared nuclear material or installations are suspected.[102] The value of information analysis and assessment for multilateral operations has been more clearly established. On a smaller scale an UNSCOM-like entity, focused solely on information assessment, could be quite valuable to the secretary-general as a tool for the early detection and monitoring of crisis situations, using authority already contained in the charter.[103] Even in the negotiating arena, the UN operation in Iraq has had a considerable impact. A wide array of UNSCOM activities, from sampling and destruction techniques to the long-term monitoring of dual-use facilities, has proved useful in devising plans for the implementation of the recently completed Chemical Weapons Convention.

This is not to say that one can blithely ignore areas of sensitivity. Intelligence sharing is a case in point. Although it has been indispensable in the operation and has created new patterns of cooperation, the multilateral handling of intelligence remains problematic. The cuing of inspections with "input" data provided by the United States and other countries is by no means straightforward, but it has been demonstrated to work, given a basic confidence in the individuals receiving the information and the presence of a clearly defined target country. Problems, however, arise on the "output" side, in the analysis of data collected from these inspections and in the recycling of that data to states that have a compelling national interest in its collection. It is only natural to expect that states providing data to international operations would want something in return. Yet, beyond some threshold, an extended pattern of cooperation between an international monitoring entity and those few states with major intelligence services could be politically corrosive to the UN.[104] The task of reconciling the UN's growing need for information with the political sensitivities that surround intelligence gathering is a major task that has yet to be faced squarely, and one that would be central to the design of a cooperative security regime.

Conclusion

Roused initially by the cold war's demise, the UN has expanded its activities on a scale that seemed unimaginable even a few years ago. The suddenness of this expansion, alas, has shaken the organization to its core. Its uneven performance in some regional conflicts has disappointed those who had hoped that the institution, freed from the cold war's stultifying effect, could suddenly be an effective instrument for international power. Over the longer term, however, there is no inherent reason why the UN could not be very helpful in the pursuit of the cooperative security concept. As argued, in the areas of arms transparency, peacekeeping and peace building, and enforcement operations, the system is generating innovations in goals and procedures that could help in shaping the transition. Slowly and painfully, UN members are developing better habits of cooperation on security matters, and international secretariats are becoming more proficient across a range of operational activities.

The main problem facing the UN is in the medium term. Over five years or so, as the organization begins to shoulder more weight for international decisionmaking on security matters, latent tensions in the system, especially as regards the authority of the Security Council, are likely to escalate to a point that could, if uncorrected, threaten the institution's viability. As noted previously, the charter gives enormous latitude to the council to identify and act upon threats to international peace and security. It can compel states to do things simply by virtue of their membership. Yet, under current conditions, if the enforcement sword is used too frequently or (in the views of some) capriciously, it will hamper cooperative efforts to induce global arms restraint. Correspondingly, if the council overextends the UN or embroils the organization in conflicts that it cannot moderate or resolve, support in member states for the UN could be fatally undermined.

Consequently, the prospects for achieving cooperative security on a global scale will depend considerably on the degree to which the UN system itself can be reformed or restructured. At a minimum, this would mean a Security Council that is more representative of all powers and all regions than the one at present;[105] a greater degree of consensus on the triggering criteria for UN enforcement actions and on the terms and conditions for applying coercive measures; an international Secretariat that is far better equipped and funded to mount major field operations; and, perhaps hardest of all, an abiding sense among a greater number of states that independence of action must at times be balanced by the need for prompt collective effort in dealing with conflicts and in spreading the political, human, and financial risks that such conflicts may pose internationally. In a fundamental sense changes of this kind are as much psychological as institutional, but they will be absolutely necessary in providing a future cooperative security community with the requisite diplomatic tools to meet the challenges of its era.

Notes

1. Since the late 1980s there has been a clear trend in UN diplomacy toward Perm-5 activism in dealing with various trouble spots. Such efforts involve the five permanent members of the Security Council—China, France, the Russian Federation, the United Kingdom, and the United States—working in concert with other key states (Japan and Germany, and regional powers) on specific conflict control or resolution measures. Obviously, this pattern of cooperation is not comprehensive; it excludes some contentious issues that arise directly between the major powers, such as territorial adjustments (for example, Hong Kong, the northern islands off Japan) or human rights (for example, Tibet). But it does include geographic areas that were previously ruled out of bounds to the UN because of spheres of influence sensitivity (for example, Central America, Afghanistan, the horn of Africa). And it diverges sharply from what even seasoned diplomats thought was possible just a few years ago. See Anthony Parsons, "The United Nations and the National Interests of States," in Adam Roberts and Benedict Kingsbury, eds., *United Nations, Divided World* (Oxford: Clarendon Books, 1989), pp. 50–51.

2. The perks of association are more than simply the prestige of having one's delegation seated in the General Assembly in New York. In many smaller states enormous credibility attaches to hosting a UN institutional presence on one's territory or participating in UN-authorized operations; some even see an in-country presence as conferring a kind of international security assurance.

3. Indonesia, for example, has been highly supportive of UN involvement in the Indochina conflict and has played a leading role in shaping that involvement, but it would probably be less well disposed toward UN action on secessionist strife within its own archipelago (that is, East Timor).

4. For further debate over collective security, see Richard K. Betts, "Systems for Peace or Causes for War? Collective Security, Arms Control, and the New Europe," *International Security,* vol. 17 (Summer 1992), pp. 5–43. The framers of the UN Charter probably would not have been blind to the essential correctness of Stanley Hoffmann's understated observation that a "commitment to forcible resistance to aggression independently of the character of the aggressor and of the victim remains not very compatible with the essence of foreign policy behavior." Stanley Hoffmann, "Away from the Past: European Politics and Security 1990," in Aspen Strategy Group, *Facing the Future: American Strategy in the 1990s* (Lanham, Md.: University Press of America, 1991), p. 132. If nothing else, the idea of giving the great powers a veto represented a prior acknowledgement that collective security operations would be constrained to areas in which great power interests did not conflict. In this view, collective security does not require an identity of interests everywhere in general to be very useful in a few places in particular; it does not need to replace alliance structures in order to have some utility, idealist rhetoric notwithstanding; and of course it can (and often does) contemplate punitive measures short of force.

5. I put "security" in quotes here because the word has never fared as well as the politically correct appellation "disarmament" in UN parlance. Somewhat in contrast to the spirit of the UN Charter, "disarmament" has featured prominently in the titles of many relevant UN bodies and offices created since 1945 (such as the UN Disarmament Commission, the Office for Disarmament Affairs), even though disarmament represents only part of the work pursued in these entities. The main reason, interestingly, is bureaucratic: use of the word *security* by the General Assembly or the Secretariat would have tended to confuse jurisdictional boundary lines with the "Security" Council, at a time when the council was deadlocked in the larger cold war stalemate.

6. See the appendix in Leland M. Goodrich, Edvard Hambro, and Anne Patricia Simons, *Charter of the United Nations: Commentary and Documents,* 3d ed. (Columbia University Press, 1969), pp. 655–56.

7. Interestingly, arms regulation (the U.S. term) or disarmament (the Soviet term) is not mentioned in the statement of the organization's objectives. Historical accounts of Dumbarton Oaks suggest that participants were leery of trying to identify any particular objective or principle for arms regulations; a modest British proposal to this effect was rejected. See Ruth B. Russell, *A History of the United Nations Charter: The Role of the United States, 1940–1945* (Brookings, 1958), p. 477. The allies had already agreed on general exhortations for arms regulations in the Atlantic Charter and the Moscow Declaration, and all readily accepted the idea of imposing disarmament on the axis powers. As for the UN design, it was decided to do no more than to provide a basis for states to consider the issue in the future. See Goodrich and others, *Charter of the United Nations,* p. 212. For brief but useful commentary on this point, see Jeffrey Laurenti, *The Common Defense: Peace and Security in a Changing World* (New York: United Nations Association, Global Policy Project, 1992), p. 41.

8. For variations on this general presentation, see Yasushi Akashi, "The Role of the United Nations in Disarmament," *Disarmament: A Periodic Review by the United Nations,* vol. 14, no. 2 (1991), pp. 33–44. See also Kathryn G. Sessions, "Future Roles for the United Nations in Arms Control and Disarmament: Global Norms, Regional Innovations, and Multidisciplinary Frameworks," paper prepared for the Fletcher/UNA-USA Roundtable, January 29–31, 1992.

9. See statement by British prime minister John Major as acting president of the Security Council, in *Note by the President of the Security Council,* S/23500, January 31, 1992 (New York: United Nations, 1992), pp. 4–5.

10. The CD has not been the only body to negotiate agreements with security-related implications. For example, the UN Committee on the Peaceful Uses of Outer Space, established by the GA in 1959, negotiated the Convention on the Registration of Objects Launched into Outer Space in the early 1970s, a transparency measure that obliges participating states to file the orbital parameters and "general function" of satellites. See Coit D. Blacker and Gloria Duffy, *International Arms Control: Issues and Agreements,* 2d ed. (Stanford University Press, 1984), p. 123.

11. UN General Assembly Resolution 37/98D, December 13, 1982, titled "Provisional Procedures to Uphold the Authority of the 1925 Geneva Protocol." Because the eastern bloc had voted against the resolution, the secretary-general undertook an initial investigation of Iranian allegations of Iraqi chemical weapon use in March 1984, using procedures in the resolution but acting under his own authority under Article 99 of the charter. The subsequent guidelines were developed by a group of governmental experts and are found in General Assembly, *Chemical and Bacteriological (Biological) Weapons: Report of the Secretary-General,* A/44/561, October 4, 1989 (United Nations, 1989).

12. Although the charter in Article 27 stipulates "the concurring votes" of the five permanent members as a requirement for affirmative decisions, traditional practice over time has been to treat abstentions as not blocking the required Perm-5 concurrence.

13. For elaboration on this point, see chapter 3 in this volume.

14. Nuclear arms control has always been a contentious diplomatic issue in the UN. Although only a few states engage in nuclear weapons activities, the community at large has a definite stake in the potential security risks posed by nuclear competition. For background on the movement of superpower arms control out of the UN, see Michael Howard, "The United Nations and International Security," in Roberts and Kingsbury, eds., *United Nations, Divided World,* pp. 37–43.

15. One anomaly in this pattern are nuclear weapon–free zones. Although not necessarily negotiated within the UN framework, these zones have occupied an important place on the UN's agenda because of their interregional applicability.

16. For useful historical surveys, see Alan F. Neidle, "The Rise and Fall of Multilateral Arms Control," in Edward C. Luck, ed., *Arms Control: The Multilateral Alternative* (New York University Press, 1983), pp. 7–34; and Blacker and Duffy, eds., *International Arms Control,* especially chap. 7.

17. In retrospect one can make precisely the same criticism of U.S.-Soviet bargaining in the cold war period. As former secretary of state Henry Kissinger discovered in the Strategic Arms Limitation Talks (SALT) negotiations, when he attempted in the face of Pentagon opposition to concede to the Soviets a superiority in "heavy" missiles in return for Soviet concessions to the United States on other issues, it is inherently difficult for governments to accept inequalities de jure that they would otherwise have tolerated de facto. For further discussion of power asymmetries, see chapter 4 in this volume.

18. For discussion on the NPT's weaknesses, see Leonard S. Spector, "Meeting the New Challenges to the NPT," in United Nations Department for Disarmament Affairs, *Disarmament Topical Papers* 8 (United Nations, 1991), pp. 178–81.

19. For elaboration, see Lewis A. Dunn and James A. Schear, *Combatting Chemical Weapons Proliferation: The Role of Sanctions and Assurances,* Occasional Paper 3 (Washington: Henry L. Stimson Center, 1991), pp. 22–26. To a degree, of course, a revitalized Security Council that takes on arms control enforcement could in time be seen as a security assurance to parties threatened by noncompliant neighbors.

20. Report of the Secretary-General, *Study on Ways and Means of Promoting Transparency in International Transfers of Conventional Arms,* A/46/301 (United Nations, 1992), p. 29. This figure, however, is nearly twice the number that participated in the 1980s, so at least the trend line is positive. See *The United Nations Disarmament Yearbook,* vol. 14, 1989 (United Nations, 1991), pp. 342, 353n.

21. Simple lack of official knowledge is particularly acute in some countries. There is also the problem of jurisdiction. For example, the United States had knowledge of several high-level containment facilities for biomedical research in francophone Africa, but these went unreported until recently by host countries because the facilities in question were owned and operated by French companies.

22. It is, however, a common practice for Secretariat staff to offer behind-the-scenes suggestions to delegations, when requested, on the crafting of resolutions, the preparation of position papers, or the drafting of statements, as well as advice on procedures and tactics. In such ways Secretariat staff in whom delegations have confidence can usefully influence details, but this role falls far short of guiding policy.

23. The formula for routine inspections, which is common for all parties, is set forth in International Atomic Energy Agency, *The Structure and Content of Agreements between the Agency and States Required in Connection with the Treaty on the Non-Proliferation of Nuclear Weapons,* INFCIRC/153, June 1972, paragraphs 78–82. The use of so-called special inspections is in theory a potential corrective to this problem, but its practical value remains uncertain.

24. Multilateral negotiations on a comprehensive nuclear test ban or on the cutoff of fissionable materials production could be global in scope but conceptually more in the nature of augmentations to existing regimes than fundamentally new departures.

25. The theme of impending changes in the institutional machinery appears in a report by Secretary-General Boutros Boutros-Ghali, *New Dimensions of Arms Regulation and Disarmament in the Post–Cold War Era,* A/C.1/47/7, October 23, 1992 (United Nations, 1992), p. 12. The secretary-general supports greater involvement by the Secu-

rity Council in arms control matters, in particular the enforcement of nonproliferation treaties, and he has raised the idea of giving the CD unspecified "review and supervisory" functions over some existing multilateral agreements.

26. Article 8(6) of the Covenant of the League of Nations, reproduced in Goodrich and others, *Charter of the United Nations,* p. 656. It was under this authority that the League published an annual Statistical Yearbook from 1925 to 1938 on arms imports and exports based on officially provided data. Andrew Pierre, "How Important Is a UN Register, What Are the Problems Blocking Agreement, and How Might They Be Overcome?" in Oxford Research Group and Saferworld Foundation, *International Control of Weapons Transfers,* Consultative Document (October 1991), p. 5.

27. The covenant proclaimed that the private manufacture of munitions was open to "grave objections" and that the Council of the League should advise on how the "evil effects" of such activity could be prevented. Interestingly, however, in the same breath, it anticipated objections also at play today, by saying that such advice should be made with due regard being paid to the "necessities" of members that are not able "to manufacture the munitions and implements of war necessary for their safety." See Article 8(5). in Goodrich and others, *Charter of the United Nations,* p. 656.

28. For a sketch of these arguments, see United Nations, *Study on Ways and Means of Promoting Transparency,* pp. 23–24. For a useful overview of the transparency issue, see Michael Moodie, "Transparency in Armaments: A New Item for the New Security Agenda," *Washington Quarterly,* vol. 15 (Summer 1992), pp. 75–82.

29. See, for example, "Declaration on Conventional Arms Transfers and Nuclear, Biological, and Chemical Weapons (NBC) Non-proliferation Treaty," Summit of Industrialized Nations (G7), London, July 16, 1991 (New York: British Information Services, July 16, 1991). Virtually all the G-7 states had made individual national proposals on a register before the fall of 1991.

30. UNGA Resolution 46/36L "Transparency in Armaments," passed December 9, 1991.

31. Cuba and Iraq abstained. China, Myanmar, and Sudan did not participate in the vote. Tea-leaf readers at the UN interpreted China's stance as a perceptible improvement over its abstention in the First Committee vote. Three other countries, Pakistan, North Korea, and Oman, switched from abstentions to yes votes in the final GA tally.

32. Statement by Mr. Marker, representative of Pakistan to the United Nations Disarmament Commission, A/CN.10/PV.166 (April 21, 1992), pp. 29–30.

33. In the months after the resolution a UN experts panel recommended adjustments in some of the definitions of the categories of equipment to be reported. See Secretary-General, *General and Complete Disarmament: Transparency in Armaments Report on the Register of Conventional Arms,* A/47/342 (United Nations, 1992), pp. 10–12.

34. Edward J. Laurence, "Enhancing Transparency Related to the Transfer of Military Technology and Weapons of Mass Destruction in Accordance with Existing Legal Instruments," paper presented to the Tokyo Workshop on Transparency in Armaments, June 1–3, 1992, p. 2.

35. One can imagine what the catch-all category of missiles and missile systems would look like if it remains unpacked. Suppose country A exports the following items to country B: ten cruise missiles, two armored box launchers, seven intermediate-range ballistic missiles, and three transporter-erector-launchers. Country A's data submission in this category will read: twenty-two items to country B. Not very revealing. Interestingly, second-tier suppliers and states with newly passed domestic disclosure laws are professing greater interest in openness. Apparently, some second-tier suppliers feel that the scale of their arms exports has long been exaggerated by others and that the register provides a chance for them to be exonerated.

36. The most that the panel could agree upon was some general guidelines to assist states in filling out the forms. Thus: "Member States may wish to enter designation, type or model of equipment, or use various descriptive elements contained in the definitions of categories I to VII, which also serve as guides to describe equipment transferred. Member States may also use this column to clarify, for example, that a transfer is of obsolete equipment, the result of co-production, or for other such explanatory remarks as Member States see fit." Secretary-General, *General and Complete Disarmament,* p. 13.

37. There is a strong view among certain states that the Secretariat must not make any public analysis of the reported information and will not be responsible for clarifying incomplete submissions with individual states or for whistle-blowing in the event of discrepancies between export and import data; these kinds of responsibilities will be left to states or research institutions.

38. United Nations, *Ways and Means of Promoting Transparency,* p. 25.

39. Ashton B. Carter, William J. Perry, and John D. Steinbruner, *A New Concept of Cooperative Security* (Brookings, 1992), pp. 38–41.

40. Boutros Boutros-Ghali, *An Agenda for Peace: Preventive Diplomacy, Peace-making and Peace-Keeping* (United Nations, 1992), p. 28.

41. Dag Hammarskjöld once dubbed peacekeeping a Chapter "six and a half" activity, since it went beyond diplomatic means of conflict mediation as set forth in Chapter 6 of the United Nations Charter but fell short of the kind of military enforcement activity foreseen in Chapter 7. *The Blue Helmets: A Review of United Nations Peace-keeping,* 2d ed. (United Nations, 1990), p. 5.

42. For a typology of peacekeeping activity, see Johan Jorgen Holst, "Enhancing Peacekeeping Operations," *Survival,* vol. 32 (May–June 1990), pp. 265–66.

43. Generally this has been interpreted to mean the use of force only in cases of self-defense. But self-defense nevertheless covers a lot of ground. It is also within UN practice to permit minimum use of force, subject to proper authorization, in order to resist efforts by armed elements to prevent UN forces from carrying out their mandate. Brian Urquhart, "Beyond the 'Sheriff's Posse,'" *Survival,* vol. 32 (May–June 1990), p. 198. In addition, force may be authorized to halt extremely grave acts deemed to be criminal: attacks on refugee columns, prisoners of war, or soldiers who have disarmed. In general, though, there is always a very strong presumption against any use of force, for the obvious reason that it cannot be done impartially and would draw UN forces into a conflict as partisans.

44. Remarks by Marrack Goulding, then UN under-secretary-general for special political affairs, in *The Singapore Symposium: The Changing Roles of the United Nations in Conflict Resolution and Peace-keeping,* March 13–15, 1991 (United Nations, 1991), p. 25.

45. Typically, the Security Council acts as the authorizing body, subject to its usual voting rules, and the GA appropriates the funding. In very rare instances, however, when the council has been deadlocked, the GA has also acted as the authorizing body (for example, UNEF-I).

46. Itshak Lederman, *The Arab-Israeli Experience in Verification and Its Relevance to Conventional Arms Control in Europe,* Occasional Paper 2 (College Park: Center for International Security Studies at Maryland, 1989), p. 5. Interestingly, a former UNDOF force commander has written that each side bars UNDOF from access to certain areas within the two force restriction areas, but this practice is tacitly accepted by both sides because both also receive satellite imagery from the United States at regular intervals. See Gustav Hagglund, "Peace-keeping in a Modern War Zone," *Survival,* vol. 32 (May–June 1990), p. 235.

47. United Nations, *Blue Helmets,* pp. 394–400; for details on southern Africa, see Marjorie Ann Browne, *United Nations Peacekeeping: Historical Overview and Current Issues,* CRS Report 90–96F (Congressional Research Service, January 31, 1990), pp. 65–67.

48. Reportedly, the OAS's so-called International Commission of Support and Verification has received and destroyed some 137,000 weapons, in addition to providing humanitarian services and calming disputes between former Contras and local police. See Shirley Christian, "OAS Goes in Peace (That's What It Came For)," *New York Times,* July 16, 1992, p. A4.

49. Under the initial plan, three so-called UN Protected Areas were established in Croatia. UN personnel were to supervise the withdrawal or disbanding of armed units inside the areas, to control access to the areas, to ensure that local police carry out their duties without prejudice to the population, and to provide for safe custody of weapons if not otherwise withdrawn by the Croatian or the Yugoslav National armies. For this purpose a two-lock system was set up whereby the UN force commander and the president of the local council in the region concerned would both have to give consent to any release of weapons. See Security Council, *Report of the Secretary-General Pursuant to Security Council Resolution 721 (1991),* S/23280, December 11, 1991 (United Nations, 1991), pp. 16–20. For reference to the two-lock system, see Security Council, *Further Report of the Secretary-General Pursuant to Security Council Resolution 721 (1991),* S/23592, February 15, 1992 (United Nations, 1992), p. 3. By early 1993, however, the arrangement had seriously unraveled in the face of provocations by both Serbs and Croats, and UNPROFOR itself was becoming a target of growing local resentment and occasional attacks. See *Report of the Secretary-General Pursuant to Security Council Resolution 815 (1993),* S/25777, May 18, 1993 (United Nations, 1993), pp. 5–6.

50. See *Agreements on a Comprehensive Political Settlement of the Cambodia Conflict,* October 23, 1991 (United Nations, 1992), pp. 17–22.

51. For details on UNTAC's mandate, see Security Council, *Report of the Secretary-General on Cambodia,* S/23613, February 19, 1992 (United Nations, 1992). Under the Paris Accords the four factions pledged to accept a 70 percent reduction in forces and weapons. Although there was no provision for the actual destruction of these weapons, UNTAC had authority from the Security Council, under Resolution 745 (1992), February 28, 1992, to gain agreement with the four parties on the partial disposal of arms, with the rest to be absorbed by a new Cambodian army.

52. This was due mainly to the refusal of the Party of Democratic Kampuchea (PDK)—the so-called Khmer Rouge—to disarm their forces and to permit unrestricted access to areas under its control. The PDK asserted that other parts of the Paris Accords were not being fairly implemented and that it could not cooperate as a result. Thus the other three factions only partially and voluntarily disarmed. In late November 1992 the Security Council decided that UNTAC should proceed with national elections in parts of the country not under PDK control (roughly 85 percent), redeploy its military units to provide protection for the elections process, and tighten up controls around PDK areas. These steps were successfully carried out despite serious threats by the PDK to disrupt the elections by violence. Even so, UNTAC's performance generated some controversy. See William Branigin, "Missteps on the Path to Peace," *Washington Post,* September 22, 1992, p. A1. For more sympathetic treatment, see Nayan Chanda, "Easy Scapegoat," *Far Eastern Economic Review,* October 22, 1992, p. 18; and Elizabeth Becker, "Showdown with the Khmer Rouge," *Washington Post,* November 8, 1992, p. C7. For an overview of UNTAC's operation in the buildup to the elections, see James A. Schear, "The United Nations Operation in Cambodia: A Status Report," in Dick Clark, ed., *The*

Challenge of Indochina: An Examination of the U.S. Role (Queenstown, Md.: Aspen Institute, 1993), pp. 21–26.

53. The electoral outcome is discussed in *Report of the Secretary-General on the Conduct and Results of the Elections in Cambodia,* S/25913, June 10, 1993 (United Nations, 1993); UNTAC's withdrawal and suggestions for a post-UNTAC UN presence are found in *Report of the Secretary-General Pursuant to Paragraph 7 of Resolution 840 (1993),* S/26090, July 16, 1993 (United Nations, 1993). An important aspect of UNTAC's postelection role was to provide budgetary support for the armed forces and civil administrations of the three factions that participated in the elections, in order to promote their loyalty to the new government and facilitate their integration into a unified structure.

54. See Boutros-Ghali, *An Agenda for Peace,* p. 11.

55. These factors include (1) the presence of Prince Norodom Sihanouk as a mediator between the factions and a unifying force in the country; (2) an army that appears pragmatic and nonideological; (3) the economic dynamism of the Southeast Asian region and the influx of private capital to underwrite certain types of local development; and finally (4) a strong international consensus on Cambodia that deprives any of the factions from seeking outside political backing or financial support for going its own way.

56. As William Durch and Barry Blechman perceptively note, settlement "brokerage" that occurs before the conflict can be counterproductive: "Arrangements motivated solely by outside pressure . . . are unlikely to produce durable settlements, as the shifts in the local political calculus that they induce are likely to be expedient and temporary, rather than fundamental." William J. Durch and Barry M. Blechman, *Keeping the Peace: The United Nations in the Emerging World Order* (Washington: Henry L. Stimson Center, 1992), n3, pp. 29–30.

57. In Cambodia, for example, the factions found it extremely difficult to work together, even on fairly technical matters, unless UN officials were present to act as a moderating influence. UNTAC staff conducting civic education in the countryside reported that it was not uncommon for villagers to ask whether they could vote for the "UN party" in the upcoming elections; and when the polling took place, some voters put messages into the ballot boxes imploring the UN to stay. Two U.S. experts have floated the idea of a UN "conservatorship," under which the UN would take over administrative control of "failed" states, such as Somalia, until they are capable of self-government. Although the authors correctly warn that such operations should not devolve into long-term custody arrangements, the phenomenon noted here would tend to make a smooth departure extremely difficult. See Gerald B. Helman and Steven R. Ratner, "Saving Failed States," *Foreign Policy,* no. 89 (Winter 1992–93), pp. 3–20.

58. For a general introduction to this problem, see John Mackinlay and Jarat Chopra, "Second Generation Multilateral Operations," *Washington Quarterly,* vol. 15 (Summer 1992), pp. 114–31.

59. The United Nations Operation in Somalia (UNOSOM) is a case in point. Anarchic conditions frustrated the operation in providing protection for food and other relief supplies based on the UN's standard approach of obtaining prior consent of parties. By late 1992 most of the 3,500 troops authorized for UNOSOM had not been provided by states, and food deliveries had been severely hampered by continuing lawlessness. See Trevor Rowe, "UN Officials Weigh Use of Force in Somalia," *Washington Post,* October 28, 1992, p. A26; and Jane Perlez, "Top UN Relief Official in Somalia Quits in Dispute with Headquarters," *New York Times,* October 31, 1992, p. A1. In December 1992 the Security Council authorized a U.S.-led intervention. This new operation—the United Task Force (UNITAF)—was authorized under Chapter 7 of the

charter as a short-term police action, to reestablish basic order and a secure environment for the provision of humanitarian relief. In May 1993 UNITAF withdrew, handing over responsibility to the follow-on UN operation, UNOSOM II, whose mandate (to continue with humanitarian relief, disarmament, and pacification and to strengthen domestic political institutions, and so on) was also based on Chapter 7 authority. See S/RES/814 (1993), March 26, 1993. UNOSOM II, however, has encountered stiff resistance from clan leader General Mohamed Farah Aideed, and the use of force to subdue Aideed's armed elements triggered tensions within UNOSOM II's military command. See Alan Cowell, "Italy, in U.N. Rift, Threatens Recall of Somalia Troops," *New York Times,* July 16, 1993, p. A1.

It is to deal with such problems, in part, that the secretary-general has called for the creation of peace enforcement units, composed of volunteer troops "on call" to the organization. Peace enforcement units would be more heavily armed than peacekeeping units and undergo extensive training. See Boutros-Ghali, *An Agenda for Peace,* p. 26. They would, however, be distinct from either peacekeepers or combat units assigned to deal with acts of aggression falling fully under Chapter 7 of the charter. In light of the controversy over the handling of enforcement on UNOSOM II, it seems very unlikely that such a proposal would be adopted in the forseeable future.

60. There are, in addition, a number of daunting financial problems associated with UN peacekeeping. For a discussion of some of these and associated problems, and possible solutions, see Boutros-Ghali, *An Agenda for Peace,* pp. 30–31, 41–44.

61. Article 1, paragraph 1 of the charter. This paragraph also provides the best working definition of enforcement in the charter: "collective measures for the prevention and removal of threats" and the "suppression of acts of aggression or other breaches of the peace."

62. Under Article 25 of the charter, decisions (as distinct from recommendations) of the Security Council are binding on member states provided they are taken in accordance with the charter. Yet that largely unused binding power is still light years ahead of political attitudes among states. Thomas Pickering observed candidly: "Most states have absolutely no idea that by joining the United Nations they have given over to the Security Council, under certain formulas, the power to make law for them internationally." Thomas R. Pickering, "The Post–Cold War Security Council: Forging an International Consensus," *Arms Control Today,* vol. 22 (June 1992), p. 8. Moreover, if these decisions are taken under its so-called Chapter 7 authority, the council's actions trump the charter's otherwise robust prohibition against intrusions by the UN into states' domestic affairs.

63. Nevertheless, it is worthy of note that the OAS imposed a hemispheric trade embargo against Haiti, and this action was strongly backed by the UN General Assembly. Subsequently, in June 1993 the Security Council imposed an oil and arms embargo against Haiti after a formal request from the exiled government of President Jean-Betrand Aristide. The measure, astonishingly, was adopted unanimously, with the Chinese representative explaining that his government's support for the resolution did not constitute a change in China's consistent position opposing the council's involvement in the domestic affairs of states. See UN Department of Public Information (DPI) press release, SC/5649 (June 16, 1993), p. 7.

64. S/RES/688 (1991), April 5, 1991. Much has been made of the fact that this resolution did not expressly authorize forcible actions to protect the Iraqi Kurds. The Chinese and others would certainly have voted against this on doctrinal grounds. As a result, the secretary-general had to negotiate terms with the Iraqi government on the deployment of UN personnel (the so-called Blue Guards) to support the humanitarian effort. Still, in the context of ongoing allied humanitarian operations in a country

already subject to Chapter 7 enforcement, it is fair to say that Iraqi consent to the UN presence was less than fully voluntary.

65. S/RES/770 (1992), August 13, 1992.

66. See S/RES/794 (1992), December 3, 1992. Interestingly, although there was a real threat of a Chinese veto on UN efforts to assist the Kurds in the face of a repressive central government, China was more forthcoming in the Somalia situation and voted for the resolution.

67. See *Note by the President of the Security Council,* S/23500, p. 4.

68. S/RES/748 (1992), March 31, 1992. The resolution mustered only ten affirmative votes with five abstentions. Most council members from the developing world abstained—India, Morocco, Zimbabwe—as well as China. Subsequent efforts to strengthen the embargo have been resisted by Russia.

69. Thomas R. Pickering, "The UN Contribution to Future International Security," *Naval War College Review,* Winter 1993, p. 98.

70. In the Balkans conflict it has been not just doctrinal differences of view on the limits of intervention in civil war situations but realpolitik differences among the permanent members. In particular, the Yeltsin government, fearing a right-wing backlash in Russia, made it known that it would not support, and would possibly veto, coercive action against Serbia.

71. Troops to support UN relief efforts were slow to arrive. A ban on non-UN or UN-supported military flights in the air space of Bosnia-Herzegovina was established in S/RES/781 (1992), October 8, 1992, but to date it has not been enforced because of differences in the council. See "Eagleburger Criticizes Allies' Resolve," *Washington Post,* January 15, 1993, p. A29. On the other hand, the council has approved an expansion in UNPROFOR's mandate to include preventive deployment of troops into Macedonia, in hopes of deterring a Serbian move south. See S/RES/795 (1992), December 11, 1992. Some 700 troops have been deployed there.

72. Figures on Somali dead are for 1992 alone, cited in an address by the secretary-general to a summit meeting of the Organization of African Unity, SG/SM/5029, June 28, 1993. p. 2.

73. This point has been amplified by Edward C. Luck, "Making Peace," *Foreign Policy,* no. 89 (Winter 1992–93), pp. 147–49. Inevitably, slow responses by the council invite unfavorable comparisons to instances of quick response, such as in Kuwait, eliciting criticism that council members apply double standards to their decisions. Even Secretary-General Boutros-Ghali on occasion has publicly expressed frustration with the council on its choice of priorities. See *Report of the Secretary-General on the Situation in Bosnia and Herzegovina,* S/24333, July 21, 1992 (United Nations, 1992), p. 4.

74. It is also arguable, however, that enforceable humanitarian protections can be a first step in dealing with conflicts. Without a safe haven zone in northern Iraq, it is doubtful that the Iraqi government would have felt compelled to negotiate with the Kurds over an autonomy agreement or that the Kurds could have held elections. Jane E. Stromseth, "Iraq's Repression of Its Civilian Population: Collective Responses and Continuing Challenges," in Lori Fisler Damrosch, ed., *Enforcing Restraint: Collective Involvement in Internal Conflicts* (New York: Council on Foreign Relations Press, 1993), p. 99.

75. Article 41 of the charter provides that "the Security Council may decide what measures not involving the use of armed force are to be employed to give effect to its decisions, and it may call upon the Members of the United Nations to apply such measures. These may include complete or partial interruption of economic relations and

of rail, sea, air, postal, telegraphic, radio and other means of communication, and the severance of diplomatic relations."

76. *Partners for Peace: Strengthening Collective Security for the 21st Century,* Report of the Global Policy Project of the United Nations Association of the United States of America (New York, 1992), p. 18.

Provisions for comprehensive trade and financial sanctions adopted by the Security Council against Iraq were carried over practically verbatim in those subsequently imposed on the Federal Republic of Yugoslavia (Serbia and Montenegro). Compare S/RES/661 (1990), August 6, 1990, and S/RES/757 (1992), May 30, 1992. The latter resolution also provides for strictures on diplomatic representation in Yugoslavia and the suspension of scientific and technical cooperation and culture exchanges, among other provisions.

Outside the scope of Chapter 7, the UN has sponsored a number of recommendatory sanctions regimes over the years, most notably the economic and other sanctions against South Africa. In 1992 the General Assembly voiced support for the OAS's embargo of Haiti (followed up by mandatory sanctions imposed by the council in June 1993). In late 1992 the council called for limited sanctions against areas of Cambodia controlled by the Party of Democratic Kampuchea (the so-called Khmer Rouge).

77. The UN's high degree of reliance upon information-rich states, such as the United States, for sanctions monitoring has triggered numerous complaints from smaller countries. For discussion and some suggestions on remedies, see *Partners for Peace,* pp. 21–22.

78. In the Iraqi case the council authorized states participating in the maritime operation against Iraq to use "such measures as may be necessary under the authority of the Security Council to halt all inward and outward maritime shipping in order to inspect and verify their cargos and destinations" and to enforce the sanctions contained in Resolution 661. See S/RES/665 (1990), August 25, 1990. Reportedly, in the two months after the passage of Resolution 661, approximately 1,400 vessels were interdicted by coalition warships in the Gulf. Of these, more than 125 vessels were boarded, and in six cases in-bound vessels were prevented from proceeding to port. David J. Scheffer, "The United States in the Gulf Crisis and Options for U.S. Policy," UNA-USA Background Paper, October 1990, p. 12.

79. Article 50 of the charter provides this right to any state, whether a member of the UN or not, in the event that preventive or enforcement measures are taken by the Security Council. The council authorized the examination of economic problems in S/RES/669 (1990), September 24, 1990.

80. In the Iraqi case the council heard claims but provided no compensation. Some bilateral efforts were pursued. Japan and the European Community assisted Jordan, while the United States and Saudi Arabia aided Egypt and Turkey (in part through loan forgiveness). India got nothing. As for inflated claims of losses, there was some skepticism over Syria's submission, which attributed a loss equal to 70 percent of its gross national product. See *Partners for Peace,* pp. 24–25.

81. Arguably, however, the sanctions were having at least one desired effect—to reduce Iraq's ability to respond to the coalition's use of force. The council's authorization is contained in S/RES/678 (1990), November 29, 1990, paragraph 2.

82. Pickering, "UN Contribution to Future International Security," p. 99. The six-week deadline, though termed in the resolution as a "pause of goodwill," also gave time for the coalition to complete preparations for its military operations. The qualifier "necessary" in the authorization of means did introduce the notion of proportionality, and thus it placed some restriction barring the excessive (or "unnecessary") use of force;

at the same time, the resolution did not, and indeed could not, define what "necessary" meant.

83. Article 43 of the charter states in part that "All Members . . . undertake to make available to the Security Council, on its call and in accordance with a special agreement or agreements, armed forces, assistance, and facilities, including rights of passage, necessary for the purpose of maintaining international peace and security." The secretary-general's endorsement is contained in Boutros-Ghali, *Agenda for Peace,* p. 25. There have been proposals in the United States and other countries for such agreements, most notably: Richard N. Gardner, "Collective Security and the 'New World Order': What Role for the United Nations?" in Joseph S. Nye, Jr., and Roger K. Smith, eds., *After the Storm: Lessons from the Gulf War* (Lanham, Md.: Madison Books, 1992), pp. 39–47. Gardner's basic plan calls for some 20 to 30 member states to designate brigade-strength units of 2,000 to 3,000 troops, composed of volunteers, which could be used in a rapid-deployment mode. The basic idea has also received support from Senator David Boren (Democrat of Oklahoma), former cochairman of the Senate Intelligence Committee, in David Boren, "The World Needs an Army on Call," *New York Times,* August 26, 1992, p. A21.

84. Gardner, "Collective Security," p. 44.

85. It would be interesting and possibly beneficial if a state's willingness to enter into an Article 43 agreement were to become a political precondition for membership on the Security Council, not only for new permanent members but also for rotating nonpermanent members. As for automaticity, the UNA-USA report correctly observes: "Though no agreement among sovereign states—not even NATO—can prevent a nation from holding back its forces in a crisis, special agreements create an expectation that the units designated for the Council's call will, in fact, be made available to it." See *Partners for Peace,* p. 33. That very expectation, of course, could make council members more cautious about voting for enforcement measures. Depending on the domestic constitutional structure of a state, the commitment could be fairly automatic or, more likely, subject to some form of legislative approval. In the U.S. case the administration in power could exercise its veto in the Security Council on action of which it did not approve. Congress, for its part, would most likely craft numerical and purpose-based limits into the commitment of U.S. forces under an Article 43 agreement, and if deemed necessary, it would establish statutory authority requiring congressional–executive branch consultation or even modes of fast-track approval in Congress, in advance of dispatching Article 43 forces. For discussion, see Jane E. Stromseth, "Rethinking War Powers: Congress, the President, and the United Nations," *Georgetown Law Journal,* no. 3 (March 1993), pp. 666–73.

86. Article 47, paragraph 3, of the charter. Among other functions, the MSC is supposed to "advise and assist" the Security Council on the military requirements for enforcement, and on the employment and command of armed forces at the council's disposal. It is also responsible for the "strategic direction" of those forces. Article 47, paragraphs 1 and 3. The present membership of the MSC would be a bone of contention, however, in any effort to make it more effective. The presence of Chinese and Russian representatives would raise problems for Western members, while the exclusion of all other states is a problem for nonpermanent members. The charter in Article 47, paragragh 2, does provide for any state to be seated on the committee when "the efficient discharge of the Committee's responsibilities requires the participation of that Member." How workable this procedure would be remains to be seen.

87. Thomas Pickering, among others, has stressed that delegated enforcement is explicitly anticipated in the charter. Pickering, "U.N. Contribution to Future International Security," p. 100. Article 48 of the charter in part provides: "The action required

to carry out the decisions of the Security Council . . . shall be taken by all the Members of the United Nations or by some of them, as the Security Council may determine." Article 53 provides that the council can, if it wishes, use "regional arrangements or agencies for enforcement action."

88. In this vein Pickering has suggested that the council could develop a more explicit articulation of aims in any given enforcement action; it could also specify the minimum terms for a cessation of the action; and it could develop closer consultative links with states involved in the operation. See Pickering, "U.N. Contribution to Future International Security," p. 101. More ambitiously, former secretary-general Pérez de Cuéllar suggested "mechanisms" that would enable the council "to satisfy itself that the rule of proportionality in the employment of armed force is observed and that the rules of humanitarian law applicable in armed conflicts are complied with." *Report of the Secretary-General on the Work of the Organization,* A/46/1, September 6, 1991 (United Nations, 1991), p. 6. The UNA-USA report offers many ideas for strengthening the council's capacity to plan for, and act promptly on, enforcement decisions. See *Partners for Peace,* pp. 36–41.

89. S/RES/794 (1992), December 3, 1992. The resolution passed unanimously. The provisions related to the council's and the secretary-general's involvement in the operation draw on some, though not all, of a series of proposals made by the secretary-general. *Letter of the Secretary-General to the President of the Security Council,* S/24868, November 29, 1992 (United Nations, 1992). The decision on implementing the resolution's requirement for a "prompt transition" from enforcement to peacekeeping in Somalia would depend on a determination that a "secure environment" had been attained in accordance with the resolution's mandate. Unfortunately, the difficulties that UN peacekeeping forces in Somalia encountered from June to October 1993 suggest that the decision on a transition had been premature.

90. For a useful description, see *Resolution Authorizing the Use of United States Armed Forces in Somalia,* Report together with Minority Views, House Foreign Affairs Committee, 103 Cong. 1 sess. (Government Printing Office, 1993), pp. 7–9.

91. S/24868, November 29, 1992, p. 7.

92. Security Council Resolution 687 (1991) established the terms and conditions for the cease-fire. See S/RES/687 (1991), April 3, 1991. The arms limitation, disarmament and sanctions provisions are contained in sections C and F (paragraphs 24 to 27) of the resolution. The core disarmament obligation is that Iraq shall accept unconditionally the destruction, removal, or rendering harmless of its nuclear, chemical, biological, and ballistic missile (above 150 kilometers in range) capabilities, including all weapons-usable materials, subsystems, and components and all research, development, support, and manufacturing facilities.

93. Armaments were already included in the comprehensive sanctions imposed on Iraq after its invasion of Kuwait; what Resolution 687 did, among other things, was to put arms denial on a firmer foundation in the cease-fire and beyond and to introduce additional guidelines for national enforcement. The secretary-general recommended that the so-called 661 committee, established to coordinate the comprehensive sanctions, should be responsible for providing guidance to states on agreed interpretations of proscribed items falling within the scope of Resolution 687. *Report of the Secretary-General Pursuant to Paragraph 26 of Security Council Resolution 687 (1991),* S/22660, June 2, 1991 (United Nations, 1991). This was accepted by the council. Subsequently, in Resolution 715 (1991), the council requested the 661 committee and other UN agencies involved in the Iraqi disarmament operation to develop a mechanism for monitoring "any future sales or supplies" to Iraq of relevant items. S/RES/715 (1991), October 11, 1991, operative paragraph 7. This task extends beyond the coordi-

nation of national enforcement and is to be developed under long-term monitoring plans that remained in dispute between Iraq and the Security Council as of mid-1993. *Report of the Secretary-General: Plan for Future Ongoing Monitoring and Verification of Iraq's Compliance with Relevant Parts of Section C of Security Council Resolution 687 (1991),* S/22871/Rev.1, October 2, 1991 (United Nations, 1991), p. 3.

94. For a detailed history, see Richard Dean Burns and Donald Urquidi, *Disarmament in Perspective: An Analysis of Selected Arms Control and Disarmament Agreements between the World Wars, 1919–1941,* Report RS-55 (Washington: U.S. Arms Control and Disarmament Agency, 1968), vol. 1, chap. 6.

95. Thus Germany undertook unsupervised demobilizations, leaving the commissions incapable of fully verifying the alleged destruction of equipment. Disagreements arose over terms in the treaty that were not self-defining, such as the authority inter alia to "render things useless" or the surrender of "war materials." (As a British general reportedly complained: "Is a field kitchen war material? Or a field ambulance? Or a motor lorry?") Passive resistance was put up by the German peace commissions, which served as liaisons for inspectors. Disputes occurred between the allies over the degree of German compliance with treaty terms. Jurisdictional frictions arose at times between the commissions. See ibid., pp. 154–68.

96. See UNSCOM's progress reports, *Reports by the Executive Chairman of the Special Commission established by the Secretary-General pursuant to paragraph 9 (b) (i) of Security Council resolution 687 (1991),* especially S/23165 (October 25, 1991), S/23268 (December 4, 1991), S/24108 (June 16, 1992), S/25620 (April 21, 1993), and S/25977 (June 21, 1993). See also statements by UNSCOM's Executive Chairman Rolf Ekeus and IAEA Director General Hans Blix to the Security Council of November 23, 1992, in *Provisional Verbatim Record of the Three Thousand One Hundred and Thirty-ninth Meeting* (Resumption 1), S/PV.3139, November 23, 1992, pp. 102–17. For a useful overview of UNSCOM's operations, see Tim Trevan, "UNSCOM Faces Entirely New Verification Challenges in Iraq," *Arms Control Today,* no. 3 (April 1993), pp. 11–15.

97. In the nuclear area, IAEA/UNSCOM inspectors supervised destruction of large portions of the Al Atheer-Al Hatteen nuclear weapons development center, as well as centrifuges, electromagnetic isotope separators, and other nuclear-related equipment at the Tuwaitha, Tarmiya, and Ash Sharqat sites. All known nuclear weapons–usable material had been removed from the country except irradiated reactor fuel that was in the custody of IAEA teams pending final shipment to Russia (its point of origin). In the chemical area a facility built by the Iraqis under UNSCOM's supervision at Al Muthanna was proceeding with the disposal of mustard and nerve gas stockpiles. Earlier, UNSCOM had destroyed in situ hundreds of chemically armed 122-millimeter rockets and thousands of empty munitions casings. Precise figures are found in DPI press release, April 22, 1993. In the ballistic missile area, UNSCOM previously had destroyed or verified the destruction of 151 ballistic missiles, 19 mobile launchers, 122 high-explosive warheads, and scores of associated items of equipment, including 3 long-range superguns, as well as production equipment for the solid rocket motors associated with Iraq's advanced missile programs. For details, see *DPI Update,* United Nations Special Commission, DPI/1239/Rev., June 1, 1992 (UN Department of Public Information, 1992); statements of Blix and Ekeus, in S/PV.3139 (Resumption 1), November 23, 1992; and John Gee, "Security Council Resolution 687 (1991): Problems and Lessons," *Disarmament Topical Papers* 10 (United Nations, 1992), pp. 65–79.

98. See S/RES/707 (1991), August 15, 1991. During 1992 data on Iraq's outside sources and its uses of technology and equipment remained sketchy. Estimates of its ballistic missile inventories also remained contentious, as did the extent of Iraq's prewar

biological weapons program. There were also large gaps in the collected data on the full magnitude of Iraq's centrifuge program and of its array of sources for producing nuclear bomb–grade material, including possibly still-hidden reactor capabilities. See interview with Ambassador Rolf Ekeus, "Unearthing Iraq's Arsenals," *Arms Control Today,* vol. 22 (April 1992), pp. 6–9; and Carnegie Endowment for International Peace, *Nuclear Proliferation Status Report* (Washington, July 1992), p. 5.

99. After a major confrontation, Iraq finally relented to allow the installation of UNSCOM monitoring cameras at a missile test site. It also indicated willingess to meet in New York to discuss all outstanding issues connected with its compliance with the monitoring requirements contained in various council resolutions. UN Department of Public Information press release, August 2, 1993.

100. Early on, some thought was given to the idea of fielding purely national teams, mainly for reasons of efficiency. This approach, however, would have been politically incorrect from the UN's standpoint, and it would certainly have opened the door to mischief making by Baghdad and the ever-present risk that teams would be tempted to ask or receive special directions from national capitals, outside the UN chain of command.

101. As Ambassador Rolf Ekeus, the executive chairman of UNSCOM, noted, the Security Council summit statement of January 31, 1992, lays a foundation for enforcement measures in the future against states that violate international nonproliferation obligations, such as the NPT, or otherwise attempt to acquire mass-destruction weapons. Rolf Ekeus, "The Iraqi Experience and the Future of Nuclear Nonproliferation," *Washington Quarterly,* vol. 15 (Autumn 1992), p. 72. But it is, at best, an open question whether the council could ever gain a consensus or even a working majority on "appropriate actions" for dealing with proliferation problems in any instance short of armed aggression of the kind that characterized the Iraqi case. Indian prime minister P. V. Narasimha Rao foreshadowed this point at the council's summit meeting: "Measures of preventive or punitive action on a selective basis will not achieve the results we are aiming at. . . . The difficulties of monitoring and policing activities in a large number of States, several of them not even accurately identified at any given time, preclude effective results. The Secretary-General cannot, I submit, be expected to be inspecting basements and searching for bombs." S/PV.3046 (January 31, 1992), p. 99.

102. Hans Blix, "Verification of Nuclear Nonproliferation: The Lessons of Iraq," *Washington Quarterly,* vol. 15 (Autumn 1992), pp. 61–62. Whether the agency can achieve such reforms remains a contentious issue. Former IAEA official David Kay, who served as chief inspector on several UN inspections in Iraq, argues that the organizational culture of the agency impedes its ability to be more aggressive in pursuing covert nuclear activities within its member states. David Kay, "The IAEA—How Can It Be Strengthened?" in Robert Litwak and Mitchell Reiss, eds., *Nuclear Proliferation in the 1990s: Challenges and Opportunities* (Washington: Woodrow Wilson International Center for Scholars, forthcoming).

103. Article 99 of the charter states that "the Secretary-General may bring to the attention of the Security Council any matter which in his opinion may threaten the maintenance of international peace and security."

104. Thus, as one former UNSCOM official warned, "A U.N. that developed intelligence capabilities would soon be regarded by many of its member States as a threat to their own national security rather than as avenue of solution to problems of international security." Remarks by Derek Boothby to the American Physical Society General Meeting, Washington, April 20, 1992.

105. Some suggestions on reforming the Security Council are contained in the UNA-USA report. *Partners for Peace,* pp. 56–59.

Part Three

APPLICATIONS OF COOPERATIVE SECURITY

EIGHT

Cooperative Security in Europe

Catherine McArdle Kelleher

IN THE EARLY 1990s, Europe is by every measure the best test bed for cooperative security.[1] In no other region has there been more progress toward mutual regulation of military capabilities and operations, toward mutual reassurance and the avoidance of tension and uncertainty. The core elements of cooperative security have been practiced in Europe, in West but also East, for at least a half decade—including offensive force limitations, defensive restructuring, confidence-building operational measures, overlapping organizational arrangements facilitating transparency and cooperative verification, and joint controls on the proliferation of military technology.[2] Western Europe enjoys in the North Atlantic Treaty Organization (NATO) a functioning collective security guarantee against both external threats and the risk of civil violence; central and eastern European states only aspire to membership in such a system. But there are outlines of an emerging Europe-wide cooperative security system that has the potential to overcome the new violent challenges posed to European security cooperation, including war in the former Yugoslavia and in some parts of the former Soviet Union.

In many senses, cooperative security in Europe represents a fortuitous inheritance from four decades of division and cold war stalemate. The basis for the "long peace" may indeed have been the ultimate risk of nuclear use, but it also involved forty years of effort, in East and West, to overcome the dangers arising from military confrontation and standing alert.[3] Over the years, the

I wish to acknowledge the supportive research assistance of Rachel Epstein, Charlotte Hebebrand, and David Bird in the preparation of this chapter, and the help of Janelle Jameson in its presentation. Of critical importance to the evolution of the argument presented in this chapter have been the comments and critiques of Dorn Crawford, Ivo Daalder, Lee Feinstein, Stephen Flanagan, Natalie Goldring, Ingo Peters, Elizabeth Pond, Judith Reppy, Kori Schake, Jane Sharp, Paul Stares, and Andrew Winner.

proposed alternatives to the NATO–Warsaw Pact offensive standoff differed widely—détente, disengagement, common security, security partnership, constructive engagement, defensive defense, and many more. But the fundamental assumptions were always the same: there would be no peace in Europe so long as the development and deployment of offensive capabilities remained unchecked, as threats and suspicions of hostile intent permitted no grounds for mutual reassurance, and as political division prevented transparency, communication, and cooperation.

The fall of the Berlin Wall released a rush of change and new cooperative initiatives. Some were made easier, and others harder, by the unification of Germany and by the end of communist rule first in eastern Europe and then in the Soviet Union itself. The scope and pace of change, the range of problems that now can and must be resolved, continue to defy easy comprehension or simple solutions. Each of the more than fifty states that define themselves as European is now assessing its security requirements, the scope and expense of its military establishment, and the role of its defense industry in terms of post–cold war political realities. In the West, this is being attempted cooperatively within the joint transatlantic and European frameworks; in the East, often with almost exclusive emphasis on national priorities. But new multilateral security organizations have been created, most particularly the Europe-wide regime of transparent national ceilings for arms and manpower under the Conventional Armed Forces in Europe (CFE and CFE 1A) agreements. Older arrangements, such as the confidence- and security-building measures under the Conference on Security and Cooperation in Europe (CSCE), have been transformed; still others are promised for the future.

Two quite different scenarios can be derived for the future of the cooperative security regime in Europe. The first proffers that the changed character of risks in post–cold war Europe suggests new opportunities to extend and deepen the western European cooperative system to a continentwide regime. Building from the CFE-CSCE regime of weapons limits and transparency, the system would ultimately be based on the NATO model and its fundamental principles of collective defense. Despite what may be a long transition, the new European political environment makes the inclusion of some collective security elements (peacekeeping and peacemaking) in the cooperative security regime more possible than at any time during the cold war. The principal threats to European security are those posed by the possible collapse of Russia into anarchy or neoauthoritarianism, which in turn are avoidable only through the rapid democratic transformation and economic reform of Russia. All other threats—the revival of old tribal wars and the horrors of "civil violence" atrocities, to name only the most obvious elements of the Yugoslav crisis—should prompt Europe to mobilize and to develop new forms of intrusion on sovereignty to preserve human rights.

A contrary argument is that prospects for global or regional cooperation are not at all positive and do not support or encourage the eastward spread of Western security institutions, as was suggested in the first post-Wall euphoria. Some view the CFE limits and the process of agreed inspections and data exchanges as instruments suited only to the cold war stalemate, not adequate for an uncertain future of economic and ethnic instability. The continuing failure to resolve or even mitigate the brutal conflicts in the former Yugoslavia is both a fundamental repudiation of what has been achieved and a warning of ethnic and civil conflicts to come.

There is also debate and confusion about the next steps toward uniting western Europe, with the disputes of 1992 and 1993 casting doubt on the ambitious blueprints for the European political and social union and a common European foreign and security policy as set out in the Maastricht Treaty in 1991. Most European political elites are reassessing the situation, still set on achieving the general goal of a secure, peaceful Europe but less able and willing in hard economic times to sacrifice for the present process. They are also less confident about how to limit the security risks inherent in the transformation of eastern Europe and especially the more violent transitions in the former Soviet Union.

Whatever the final shape and scope of Europe's cooperative security regime, many of its central elements are unlikely to translate easily to other regional contexts. Europe's postwar experience was built on the death and destruction of a century of total war and thus is unique.[4] The transition in postwar western Europe to multiple, interlocking structures that have moved states and peoples away from systems of national compellance and toward converging expectations about security and about "normal" multinational solutions is also striking.

Yet there are partial principles and suggestive models for others to follow. The evolving CFE experience is a critical resource. The development of national equipment ceilings in relation to neighbors under the CFE, the setting of destruction quotas, the steps toward transparency through intrusive inspections, and reliable continuous data exchange could all contribute to regional stability. The cumulative experience under the CSCE also provides some measure of stability through steps devised first for cold war confidence building and now for force stabilization. The military-to-military exchanges and dialogues, and even the rudimentary techniques of fact finding and conflict monitoring, are basic provisions of the CSCE process. And the Open Skies regime, once fully ratified, can easily be adapted to encompass even wider regions and more focused data collection.

Even more important than technique or specific experience will be the importance of cooperative security in Europe as a benchmark, a guide to what is politically possible. Measured against its twentieth-century past, the western and central parts of the European continent will for some time be relatively free from the risks of traditional interstate war. There are, of course, exceptions, such as the 1993 tensions between Russia and Ukraine over nuclear control questions, but it is hard to imagine other interstate contingencies, at least in the next decade. With an established cooperative security framework, Europe—East and West—may now implement the promises made in the Helsinki Declarations almost twenty years ago: that true national security can be achieved only in a Europe without war and only when national programs do not diminish the security of one's neighbors.[5] As the Yugoslav crisis proves, there are still grave risks of civil war, and as the Russian experience illustrates, there are real fears of political fragmentation. There is no common understanding as yet about limits to the right of self-determination or how to ensure the political and human rights of minorities. But progress toward a Europe-wide zone of peace will ultimately mean greater limitation of the military potential of individual states and the legitimation of multilateral processes for conflict avoidance and conflict resolution both between and within states.

This chapter focuses on the challenges and the problems that are involved in building a Europe-wide cooperative security system (including Russia and the former Soviet republics) while simultaneously maintaining and deepening the core western European regime. It begins with a review of the shape and pace of what was achieved during the cold war, both in western Europe and across the East-West divide. It then focuses on the sources of change, positive and negative, in the post–cold war period and outlines the opportunities and the risks in further evolution in a pan-European cooperative security regime.

Cooperative Security in Cold War Europe

How Europe came to develop the foundation for a cooperative security regime seems in retrospect to have been a straightforward and perhaps inevitable process.[6] Traditional analysis, broadly accurate, links the process of building confidence and limiting military capabilities in Europe to the context of the cold war, which allowed for continuous progress toward cooperative control of military establishments within the Western defensive alliance and episodic progress toward East-West conciliation in periods of détente or lowered tension. During the first half of the 1980s, the superpowers loosened control over their respective power blocs. Subsequently, as tensions between Washington and Moscow escalated, many eastern and western European leaders continued the search for agreement, for arms limitations, for the reduction of risk and military confrontation, and for other such measures. With the ascent of Mikhail Gorbachev and then the revolutionary events of 1989, they achieved success.

But these conclusions obscure the complexity of the process through which cooperative security concepts evolved. Indeed, they understate many of the necessary lessons to be learned about the nonlinear progress of these measures.

Still not truly a continentwide system, the European security system has developed in fits and starts, with several different regimes evolving at different rates and with different supporting structures and participants. The key distinctions are of three kinds: (1) the differences between the gains made by western Europe and those under a pan-Europe approach, (2) the varied contribution of formal structures and informal procedures in reinforcing the European zone of peace, and (3) the changing mix of bilateral and multilateral elements as "forcing" factors in cooperation.

Cooperative Security in Western Europe, 1949–89

The United States and Europe face a critical turning point in their security relationships. Beset with new challenges in warring Yugoslavia and the former Soviet bloc, Western leaders must redefine foreign policy objectives and devise innovative cooperative economic and military strategies in order to achieve stability and prosperity. It is instructive to look back on the evolution of European and transatlantic cooperation as these leaders try to determine the ways in which to transform and expand the existing security organizations.

THE ATLANTIC SYSTEM. Evolution toward a cooperative security regime in western Europe constitutes the traditional or benchmark case. Creation of a zone of peace founded within a framework of transatlantic political cooperation and mutual economic prosperity began after World War II with the Marshall Plan. This was primarily achieved through the interactive impacts of two multilateral organizational efforts—NATO and the European Community (EC). Both were associations of states perceived as like minded, if sometimes competitive; and both grew slowly under strict conditions for membership. Begun as a traditional military alliance, by the early 1960s NATO had established a framework for cooperative military action and decisionmaking. The United States took the role of benign hegemon in this alliance—actively engaged as leader, mediator, and guarantor not only against the Soviet Union but also against the reemergence of German militarism or of interstate rivalries of the kind experienced in Europe in the 1920s and the 1930s. Military establishments were bound in a consciously designed, thickening web of equipment and structural constraints, collectively devised and with mutual oversight.

NATO became in effect a collective security system involving sixteen member states, led and presided over by the United States.[7] Other critical elements were the permanent diplomatic conference, the standing military forces in the central region, and supporting cooperative structures for planning, training, and operations.[8] Involved too were hosts of formal and informal networks, primarily bilateral but also multilateral channels for consultation and coordination on a wide-ranging security agenda.

NATO's list of potential members was initially somewhat vague; in the end, membership mixed targets of opportunity, issues of geostrategic necessity, and particular political imperatives. By the end of the 1950s, NATO's scope was set to be the widest possible reach across the European "free world," with the tightest political-military integration and largest number of standing peacetime forces in NATO's central region, the zone considered of maximum danger. The northern and southern flanks, and the seas themselves, saw looser forms of military organization and more traditional interstate cooperation.

In all areas, NATO evolved specific ways of doing business with wide-ranging implications. The general mode was one of U.S. leadership, with formal interstate bargaining, and most often, compromises struck on the trading of specific benefits and risks. But the level and the extent of cooperation seemed to increase yearly with important policy implications even within bilateral channels. At issue were patterns of managed burden-sharing, never as pervasive as the United States insisted but probably more than many national parliaments would have derived independently. There was de facto mutual oversight over all offensive forces in the European theater, given the day-to-day facts of a permanent integrated command structure and the necessity of mutual transparency. There was also the impact of common experience among the military—continuous interaction and confidence building that changed patterns of decisionmaking at home as well as within the multilateral command and planning functions.

NATO developed a number of critical initiatives on economic security as well. These were not the formal efforts toward coordination and the elimination of economic competition foreseen in Article 2 of the North Atlantic Treaty; those duties were left first to the Organization for European Economic Cooperation (the OEEC, which later became the Organization for Economic Co-operation and Development, or OECD), and then to the evolving European Community. Rather it was the impact of defense cooperation on national economies that led to significant integration—the specific calculation of burden-sharing formulas, the economics of weapons development and acquisition, the issues of shared economic stakes in continuing research and development. Indeed by the 1970s and 1980s, NATO sharing meant joint agreement to an infrastructure paid for and maintained with common resources, an annual survey of budget plans and commitments, and far-reaching consultations at every level about military research, force structure changes, and plans for new weapons systems.

THE EUROPEAN COMMUNITY. In light of the lessons drawn from the 1920s and 1930s, the Community was the primary vehicle designed to achieve the economic transparency and eventual integration deemed essential for true security. Even in the initial phase of the Europe of the Six (France, Germany, Italy, Benelux), the EC defined and met the economic requirements of mutual reassurance. It promoted the elimination of economic rivalries and the beggar-thy-neighbor policies that had historically caused interstate tension and war. EC economic initiatives replaced them with cooperative patterns of trade according to comparative advantage and the evolution of a single European market. Transparency and market access were to be the watchwords of governmental cooperation on all levels and the best security guarantees against the politics of fear and the risk of surprise.

More important, the Community established the habits and expectations of cooperative cross-border solutions to problems perceived as being vital to national interests and electorates. The central goal of Community construction was to provide solid ground for peace in Europe by stabilizing the Franco-German relationship and by creating and securing a balanced German-European relationship in which positive economic incentives on all sides encouraged interdependence.

The pace of Community development was slow, with periodic and significant reversals. The dashing of the great hopes attending the European Defense Community (EDC) and the stillborn European Political Community of the mid-1950s led to more limited ambitions, such as the tantalizing Genscher-Colombo initiative on closer security cooperation of the early 1980s.[9] Such limited efforts also failed to find broad political support. Moreover, even though the potential membership of the EC seemed clear, especially in the cold war context, actual entry was sometimes inhibited or prevented altogether by Community disagreement.

But the effort to build Europe continued, and slowly but surely it began to fulfill the dreams of Jean Monnet and the original postwar functionalists that peace would result from ever broader functional integration. It created new ways of doing business across borders, new patterns of governmental and bureaucratic interaction, new sources of confidence and mutual reassurance, and new hopes for the inevitability of a European zone of peace. With the design of a single European economic space by the mid-1980s, there might still have been debate about final goals and structures, but the process of European integration seemed irreversible.

Yet there were other significant aspects to the western European regime that emerged over the four postwar decades. The first was *architectural redundancy:* the evolution of many different organizations with overlapping responsibilities, all moving along the same general path. An ambitious EDC or European Political Community failed to develop in the 1950s, but a looser Western European Union (WEU) and a narrowly focused Independent European Program Group both existed as special caucuses within NATO. The significance of a European Free Trade Association, a European Atomic Energy Community, or a Council of Europe waxed and waned with changing political conditions and changing participation, but did so within an increasingly "normal" European framework.

The second was the *multiplicity of relationships,* key to the establishment of mutual reassurance. Traditional alliance theory proffered that the existence of a common compelling threat—the Soviet Union—would provide sufficient basis for international cohesion. But as Karl Deutsch argued in the 1950s, what was really at stake was the building of a security community rooted as much in shared values, intentions, and attitudes among like-minded states as in effective fighting capabilities positioned against a common enemy.[10]

The central core in almost every collaborative forum was Franco-German rapprochement, the convergence of both national policies and popular perceptions of the past and expectations about the future. There were other critical bilateral ties as well—Anglo-French, Anglo-German, and, most particularly, American ties to Britain, Germany, and France.[11] Although obscured by the more positive experience of later years, European relations involved disputes and irritation, issues of competition and hierarchy, and conflict over who was to be defined as part of "us." All also ultimately turned on what became increasingly irreversible national decisions to embed bilateral relations within a broader multilateral framework. These decisions sought to provide offsetting forces, to allow for greater scope and benefit, and even to promote greater mutual harmony.

Each relationship also focused on how to balance military strength and economic potential in a Europe twice savaged by German expansionism. The special wisdom of postwar European international politics was that security was most easily achieved by making Germany a partner in this balancing process and by enmeshing all states cooperatively in Germany's containment. Germany was always a formal equal in NATO and in the EC no matter what its special obligations were or how it implemented the military constraints required. Avoiding an isolated Germany, vulnerable (as after World War I) to demagogic legends, meant developing mutual security structures in which Germany would both give and receive hostages against the future in the form of mutually binding guarantees.

The treatment of Germany became the core demonstration of how to extend cooperative security guarantees to an erstwhile enemy turned ally and is therefore relevant to present efforts to include Russia and the central European states in the dialogue on European security. For example, Germany accepted stationed forces on its territory for its own security and to help alleviate the fears of other states, but its own forces also interacted and coordinated with foreign forces on an equal footing. Its military arsenal in all but the area of nuclear capability represented an equal (and sometimes greater) share in the collective security apparatus, and its strategy and doctrine were open to the influence of others and also decided in common. Guarding against German "singularization"—allowing for the principles of self-limitation and regulation to gain acceptance—became more and more important for all of Germany's allies as a political foundation for broad areas of European cooperation.

Fundamental to all these structures was a *commitment to transparency,* a variable identified as key to a successful cooperative security regime. In NATO, for example, there was de facto mutual regulation of all offensive forces in the European theater. An integrated command posited continuous operational consultation about interallied forces, regular intrusive inspections and evaluations, and joint assessments of present and future technologies and capabilities.[12]

In the EC, broader functional integration entailed requirements for openness and regular unrestricted access to information about national policies and plans that went even further. Increasingly, the free flow of goods and individuals across European borders meant continuous communication about national economic arrangements and planning, including regular reporting to allow cooperative regulation of national sectors. It demanded the development of common standards and the common assessment of penalties for multiple forms of activities, and a continuing reaffirmation of the costs and the risks associated with a breakdown in cooperation among Community states.

Almost equally important was the development of *broad popular support for multilateral solutions* as at least equal in legitimacy and effectiveness to national decisions. In the military area immediately following the war, this conviction stemmed in part from disillusionment with national capabilities or a pragmatic judgment that cooperation in NATO was the price of security derived from an American guarantee. Even when there were widespread calls by the European Left in the 1970s and 1980s for the elimination of NATO, or its transformation into an independent European security organization more attuned to a diminishing threat, the alternative security framework being promoted was multinational. It always contained a high degree of cross-border cooperation or functional integration, which was believed to provide more benefits than risks and which would encourage trust and continuing cooperation on a more or less equal basis.

In sum, by 1989, primarily through the evolution of the EC and NATO, there had developed the basic framework of a cooperative security regime in Europe with obvious political and economic benefits for participating states, and even for the neutral states outside both NATO and the EC. Some proponents of cooperative security stressed that Europe fell short of the Wilsonian collective security ideal, especially in its lack of cooperative arrangements for global peacekeeping, and there were persistent disputes about coordinating "out-of-area" initiatives, political or military. But all of the important elements were clearly in place for developing such initiatives, and cooperation was already the established, well-practiced norm.

Cooperative Security across Europe, 1975–90

Progress toward a cooperative security regime embracing eastern as well as western Europe has been far more uneven and unpredictable than the evolution in western Europe alone. The first steps emerged in the context of détente in the early 1970s, including especially two, somewhat contradictory, policy initiatives: the linked decisions to begin the thirty-five-member CSCE and to initiate the talks on Mutual and Balanced Force Reductions talks (MBFR) between the twenty-three states of the NATO and Warsaw Treaty Organization (WTO) alliances. The CSCE was the broader and more innovative of the two. Initiated by the Soviet Union but pushed particularly hard by western Europeans, it was an attempt to address the nonmilitary aspects of security and to reduce uncertainty about national intentions and military operations. Fostered largely by the United States, the MBFR, in contrast, was the first of several efforts to use formal arms control negotiations to limit Soviet conventional capabilities and to lessen the risks arising from the massive military concentrations in Europe. At the same time, the initiative represented an effort to outflank domestic critics of growing military budgets in the United States and throughout western Europe. The MBFR was to achieve a binding multilateral scheme aimed at producing reduction in forces and budgets in the East in return for equal reductions in the West.

Particularly at the time, the arms control path seemed to many to be the more legitimate, if not necessarily the more promising, approach to achieving military stability in Europe.[13] The MBFR process itself produced few results, although it opened interesting opportunities for East-West European back-channel interactions. Progress in arms control came only after the Gorbachev revolution. The specific breakthroughs toward agreement for arms reductions came in the late 1980s, with the Intermediate-Range Nuclear Forces (INF) Treaty for asymmetric reductions in Soviet and American nuclear systems leading the way to new approaches to U.S.-Soviet conventional agreements.

The MBFR's successors, the CFE agreements, limited conventional weapons and forces in the Atlantic-to-the-Urals (ATTU) area,[14] and were the capstones of this changed environment. Both the INF and CFE accords still assumed competing alliances and adversarial interests. But both also involved new levels of cooperation, including bold steps toward transparency and verification. For example, it became routine to hold regular and short-notice intrusive inspections on national territories and to seek multilateral approaches to a wide range of issues, from the character of weapons deployment to agreed methods for weapon dismantlement and destruction.

As the political climate changed dramatically in the 1980s, the MBFR stalled and the CSCE gained new momentum. Efforts in the CSCE became focused on changing European military concepts, and operational practices, especially those that raised the risk of surprise attack, heightened uncertainty about intentions, or seemed to lead to automatic crisis escalation. From the outset, the CSCE negotiations reflected the inherent tension between attempts to stabilize the existing confrontational nature of the East-West relationship and a commitment to change the status quo. The Helsinki documents of 1975 were statements of principles and declarations of intent. They did not amount to a binding international treaty or even formal agreements among like-minded states. Still, they reflected some core requisites of cooperative security: the promise to use force only for defensive ends, the commitment not to try to alter borders by force, the use of transparency to eliminate uncertainty and risk, and the legitimacy of an international interest in the way other states treat their own citizens and minorities.

Progress over the course of the CSCE's first decade was slow, and focused largely on increasing communication flows about nonmilitary aspects of security (human rights, transparency) and ensuring the autonomous participation (and thus the independent voice) of the eastern European states. The first truly cooperative steps were the relatively limited confidence-building measures agreed to in Helsinki: the agreement to provide prior notification of military movements involving more than 25,000 personnel and the voluntary exchange of observers at military exercises.[15] After a rocky start, these measures were observed by all parties almost without exception and thus served as a body of experience and a precedent for more far-ranging agreements reached at the review conferences in Stockholm (1986) and Vienna (1990).[16]

The agreement to increasingly intrusive confidence- and security-building measures (CSBMs) had a number of impacts: more stringent restrictions on military exercises and required information about alert procedures; open exchange of data on forces, weapons, and deployments; new rights allowing for challenge inspections; and increased exchanges among high-ranking professional military and civilian officials (for example, the February 1990 Military Doctrine seminar). The CSCE was also the formal convener of the CFE negotiations, beginning with the so-called mandate talks in 1987 that allowed the neutral and nonaligned European states (NNAs) for the first time to have a right of oversight and occasional influence over East-West military arrangements.

Ultimately, the CSCE's critical contributions came less often in the form of disarmament than in the legitimation of a comprehensive political framework for ongoing security cooperation among all European states. Many of the concepts of mutual security and defensive restructuring discussed were unworkable; many of the sessions were only "talk shops" that revealed the degree of division and the influence of superpower competition among participants. But even a weakly organized CSCE created channels and habits of discussion and gave credibility to regular contacts among states on security questions. Moreover, in the domestic politics of many European states, most particularly in eastern Europe, the CSCE locked in patterns of popular expectation about compliance and set goals and standards, at least at the rhetorical level, to which governments could be held accountable at home and abroad.

Post–Cold War Momentum toward Europe-wide Cooperative Security

The collapse of communism and then of the Soviet Union itself gave dramatic stimulus and new urgency to the evolution of cooperative security regimes in Europe. The underpinnings of the postwar era were gone. Uncertainty about possible future threats, however real, proved no substitute for East-West confrontation as an organizing principle or as a justification for large military budgets. Popular sentiment in almost every state supported the drive for drastic reductions in military forces and budgets. Most also supported multilateral solutions for crisis prevention and management rather than the use of force, and emphasized the need for democratic reform and economic marketization to preserve European stability.

To borrow terms from a narrower but related debate in the EC, the challenge to be faced was the need to simultaneously widen and deepen European cooperative security. The extension eastward meant a return to first principles and the promotion of agreement on the core elements of the existing pan-European regime. Acceptance of these principles was promised but never fully implemented by either the central European or eastern European states. Most basic of all was the definition of the borders of Europe—which states had to be involved for cooperative security to survive? Which states should be excluded and on what grounds? How was the question of collective security guarantees to be broached and implemented? Should the regime form a new institution or adapt and link to the western European system?

Preserving what had been accomplished in western Europe posed somewhat different problems. There was the need for adaptation, to transform NATO and related organizations in light of the lower level of military threat, the absence of a central commanding focus for cooperation, and the resulting downsizing of forces and budgets. Other problems involved the political consequence of an emerging western European political union, on terms that encouraged for the first time a more integrated, tightly bound European security and defense policy within the Community. Last but hardly least was the special challenge of the Yugoslavia war and the patent failure of the Community, along with others, to either stop the fighting or bring about a negotiated settlement peacefully.

What is clear is that none of these issues are yet perfectly resolved and that the interim solutions do not have even a fraction of the certainty that pervaded the EC-NATO system before 1989. This is still a system in evolution, in transition. And the greatest challenges may begin only once the shooting war in the former Yugoslavia comes to an end.

New Process, New Transparency

In terms of the goals of cooperative security, the most important development in post–cold war Europe is the new process of transparency and constraint that affects the military forces, equipment, and budgets of more than fifty European states. This process grows out of the intersecting, synergistic effects of three ground-breaking agreements: the CFE treaty and the follow-up CFE 1A agreements acceded to by thirty members of NATO and the former Warsaw

Pact;[17] the Vienna Document 1992, eventually binding fifty-three CSCE participants to new CSBMs and goals for cooperative action; and the Open Skies Treaty, not yet officially in force but already tested in critical trials.[18] The result is the first specific test of cooperative security principles and demonstrates both their logic and their robustness in the face of both dramatic political change and a transformed security environment.

The evolution of the CFE regime is perhaps the most compelling evidence of this effort.[19] Under the impact of the Gorbachev revolution, talks between NATO and the WTO states started in earnest in March 1989 on alliance-to-alliance arms reductions in the ATTU area. The primary aim was to reduce under inspection the most dangerous, frozen concentration of equipment in Europe's central zone, but also with assurance against future buildups on the less confrontational northern and southern flanks. Five categories of equipment were eventually to be reduced: battle tanks, artillery, armored combat vehicles, attack helicopters, and combat aircraft. The NATO goal was to reduce equipment levels by approximately 5 percent below the level of NATO holdings in the ATTU in 1989, although the WTO favored much deeper cuts.[20]

In the twenty-one months that followed, the CFE negotiations were buffeted by momentous changes in Europe; some analysts indeed argued that the CFE treaty represented an approach whose time had passed.[21] In November 1989 the Berlin Wall fell, and less than a year later Germany was unified. The WTO dissolved in 1991; all Soviet forces were to be withdrawn from the eastern German territories by the end of 1994. The Soviet Union disintegrated into Russia and the newly independent states (NIS), and Soviet forces were transformed into the forces of the Commonwealth of Independent States (CIS), which encompassed new national forces and Russian forces stationed both inside Russia and on the territory of other republics.

The CFE emerged, however, as a framework in which to manage change.[22] Under the leadership of both George Bush and Gorbachev, the ongoing negotiations were a forum through which the concepts of force limitation and intrusive inspection moderated and reduced the uncertainty of the post–cold war environment. Equipment limits; destruction quotas and procedures; a range of reporting, monitoring, and inspection requirements; and the manpower limits established by CFE 1A all promoted critical transparency and acceptable levels of security forces to reduce fears of a sudden major conventional attack in Europe. The CFE and CFE 1A outcomes further constituted assurance against a future military expansion of a united Germany. Moreover, although the Soviet Union concluded bilateral withdrawal agreements with each of its former satellite states almost a year before the CFE was signed, the treaty provided an additional enforcement mechanism for those agreements. As the Warsaw Pact and the Soviet Union dissolved, the resulting power vacuum and geopolitical instability might have encouraged eastern states to increase their military equipment holdings. But because of the CFE's international context, incentives for states to comply with treaty obligations were strengthened by the threat of both local and transatlantic retaliation in response to the abrogation of the treaty. Finally, the procedures in place under the CFE treaty provided a mechanism to manage the military aspects of the "velvet divorce" in 1993 of the Czech and Slovak republics.

Perhaps the clearest CFE milestones were reached in the management of the transformation of the Soviet Union. The CFE framework, the quiet diplomacy of both the United States and Germany, and the willingness at critical points of the Gorbachev and Boris Yeltsin regimes to overcome the dogged opposition of the Soviet military were key to the conclusion of the supportive CIS-Tashkent agreement and the reallocation of CFE-limited equipment quotas in 1992.[23] These factors allowed the relatively smooth and clearly peaceful distribution of the equipment ceilings on the territory of the former Soviet Union (FSU), while also enforcing the obligations for destruction and preserving the rights and responsibilities of data access and reporting. Moreover, participation in the ongoing CFE negotiations allowed for the NIS's relatively painless initiation into political-military diplomacy and led them to accept internationally negotiated restraints that addressed the risks of regional conflict and, in some cases, promoted defensive military postures in the context of international controls. The CFE process also permitted the United States and its European allies to quickly open channels of influence to the NIS.

The reallocation of the CFE-limited equipment was not totally successful, however, especially from the perspective of the Russian military and therefore of the growing right-wing and nationalist groups in the Russian parliament. Military opposition to the CFE agreements was long-standing and had resulted in two major controversies that surfaced at the time of the CFE treaty signing in November 1990: (1) the transfer of already counted treaty-limited equipment (TLE) to naval infantry command outside the treaty's scope, and (2) the transfer of thousands of TLE east of the Urals and therefore outside the ATTU area. In the Joint Consultative Group (JCG), designed to resolve disputes, the West denounced both actions as violations of the treaty's intent (even if the second was not a violation, since it predated the effective treaty regime) and threatened not to ratify the CFE. Acceptable resolution came only through final guarantees given to the United States by Gorbachev himself.[24]

Implementation of the accords has led to new military unease and to calls for changes in the CFE regime. There are many complaints, but issues of particular importance are the zonal sublimits on the flanks and the procedures for the assigned destruction responsibilities. Artifacts of cold war zonal construction have left Russia at what some Russian military personnel feel is a relative disadvantage vis-à-vis Ukraine in the number of tanks, and against the warring trans-Caucasus republics in most equipment categories. Zonal sublimits and requirements for equipment storage, particularly on the flanks and especially in the former Leningrad military district, leave Russia, in their view, with insufficient equipment to protect Russian interests in the Caucasus conflicts, and with no opportunity to use sites in the North Caucasus region to station troops and equipment withdrawn from eastern Germany and the former Warsaw Pact states.[25] These complaints have been magnified by nationalist opposition in both Russia and Ukraine to external control over the use or disposition of their respective military forces.

In September 1993 Russia and Ukraine submitted formal requests in the JCG to examine the CFE flank sublimits to allow greater numbers of tanks and heavy weapons to be stationed in the Caucasus.[26] Many observers are sympathetic to the need to deal with these anomalies and the overarching need to provide reassurance of the CFE's fairness and adaptability at a time of growing Russian perceptions of conventional weakness. Although neither state is required to fulfill all the obligations of the CFE accords until the end of 1995, violation of the interim reduction targets or even the movement of troops and equipment contrary to the accords' intent would be cause for alarm.[27] The Western states fear opening up a Pandora's box of requests for further changes but are basically committed to finding cooperative solutions that will preserve the overall treaty regime.

Unquestionably, much of the conceptual flexibility in the CFE regime resulted from initial French insistence that the final agreements reflect more than a bloc-to-bloc approach. France, ever suspicious of arms control and never approving of the division into which Europe had been frozen since World War II, hoped to minimize its association with NATO while simultaneously preventing German neutrality.[28] The multizone formula, for example, allowed the Baltic states at independence to be released from the terms of the treaty with the understanding that Soviet arms within those territories would be counted among the Soviet equipment subject to prescribed ceilings. At the very least, this formula allowed a far more flexible system for the distribution of Soviet obligations and entitlements than either straight alliance ceilings or simple national limits would have done.

From the perspective of 1994, the zones and the sublimits undoubtedly need reconsideration, not to mention extension and deepening. The old Soviet military districts that were the base units for the construction of zones are now less relevant, given the new republican borders, ongoing civil wars, and new threats outside the ATTU. In some cases, these have led to skewed regional balances.[29] The flanks, for example, might be divided into separate northern and southern sublimits, each with specific storage requirements, and still within the general limits set down in the CFE accords. But once brought to JCG agreement, any revisions can be accommodated within the flexible CFE framework.

Perhaps the CFE accords' contributions of greatest present relevance are their advances in transparency. Much like the earlier INF inspection regime, the CFE treaty provided for baseline inspections to verify national holdings, followed by a regime of active, passive, and challenge inspection possibilities.

There is then to be a second baseline round after reductions and destruction, and a second inspection period, all to be completed by November 1995. The number of inspections allowed at declared sites is considerable; in the baseline period that concluded in November 1992, for example, the NATO states conducted 238 inspections and hosted 128. Perhaps the most path-breaking were the 17 additional site inspections conducted by the non-NATO states within their own group during the same period.[30] The JCG has met frequently since the signing of the accords to deal with issues such as modifying destruction procedures, the establishment of a uniform data collection and dissemination system, and disputes over the access for on-site inspectors.

Possible verification techniques allow for a range of transparency options—national and multinational on-site inspection teams, physical presence at destruction facilities and at the recertification of equipment that has been functionally altered. There is also emphasis on both national and multinational satellite observations (formally, national and multinational technical means) and on improved access to national data and to the Russian and French commercial services for the smaller states without access to satellite data.[31] A point of continuing discussion is the possible real-time sharing of satellite images through a CFE-wide system of distribution.

The supplemental CFE 1A agreement setting ceilings for air and ground personnel in the ATTU was completed after the CFE, and entered into force provisionally with it on July 17, 1992. It is not a treaty but a politically binding agreement.[32] It was pursued most energetically by Germany, in large part because the unification Two-Plus-Four Talks had already limited German military personnel as did a politically binding statement concluded in conjunction with the CFE treaty, and Germany, characteristically hoping to avoid singularization, was eager to have its neighbors accept parallel limitations.[33] The limits are set nationally, rather than by zones. Given budgetary pressures and declining support for military establishments generally in the post–cold war era, these ceilings now seem anachronistic and could easily be revised downward—certainly by another 20 to 25 percent for the larger states—to provide further reassurance.

Aerial inspection of the CFE ATTU area, indeed of the larger CSCE Vancouver-to-Vladivostock area, came about through negotiation of the Open Skies Treaty, which was signed by twenty-five states on March 24, 1992.[34] President Dwight D. Eisenhower first introduced the concept of "open skies" in July 1955, and President Bush revisited the idea in May 1989. The treaty, once fully ratified, will allow the systematic inspection of signatory states' military structure, readiness, and strength. The agreement is significant not only for its originality and breadth but also for its symbolic content.[35] As such, the agreement was not negotiated along bloc-to-bloc lines but included the nonaligned and neutral (NNA) states and allowed countries as diverse as Canada, Hungary, and Romania to play pivotal roles in the instigation and negotiation of the treaty.[36]

The final terms of the agreement declare that a country may not conduct more overflights than it accepts on its own territory. The territory encompassing Russia and Belarus must host forty-two flights a year, as must the United States. Most midsize European states will host twelve, while other countries will host and conduct a number of overflights proportionate to their size and population. Each flight requires just seventy-two hours' prior notification, with twenty-four hours' notice of the exact flight path.[37]

European cooperative security has also relied on increasingly sophisticated and intrusive CSBMs. The Vienna Document 1990, adopted by the CSCE participants on November 17, 1990, fostered transparency in military activities and improved communication among CSCE states.[38] The Vienna Document was politically binding; CSCE states had to comply with a wide range of new expanded CSBMs. The document called for the annual exchange of data on military capability, including numbers of troops and equipment inventory, as well as military budget information and notification of large weapon systems deployment. CSCE states were to exchange routine visits of officials to air bases and other military installations. As in the Stockholm Document of 1986, important features of the Vienna Document were measures specifically designed to diminish the fear of surprise attack, including prior notification of major troop movements and exercises and limits on military maneuvers. Finally, there were verification and compliance features, in addition to the commitment to establish a common data base and automatic communication networks among and between CSCE capitals.[39]

In May 1992 the Vienna Document 1992 officially replaced the Vienna Document 1990. It built on and went beyond many of the original provisions and included forty-eight signatories, including ten former Soviet republics. In addition, both the information exchanges and the verification and inspection processes were made more elaborate, including for the first time multinational inspection teams and more detailed restrictions on troop movements, force generation capabilities, and data on and demonstration of major weapon and equipment systems.[40]

The Vienna Document 1992 is the first agreement that places actual limits on military activities. For example, any country or military organization may host only one military exercise involving 40,000 troops or 900 battle tanks every two years. Similar limitations apply to smaller military exercises; no more than six exercises with more than 13,000 but fewer than 40,000 troops may be carried out every year, and of these six exercises, only three can consist of more than 25,000 troops.[41]

Still rooted in cold war assumptions about threat and limited political agreement, the Vienna Document 1992 and its predecessors have not led Europe through the great strategic and political changes of the last four years.

Indeed, both NATO members and the newly democratizing states in central and eastern Europe have had to limit their military activities for budgetary reasons. More important, the Yugoslav crisis proves that the CSCE alone is incapable of crisis management on the Continent. Recent developments in the CSCE appear to be only reactive, but the channels of communication and methods of conflict management and resolution may prove invaluable to cooperative peacekeeping and peacemaking efforts in the future, particularly if economic and security interests in Europe harmonize, and if a greater consensus develops around a Europe-wide security framework. In the near term, existing CSBMs could be further tightened through stricter constraints on troop movements and mobilization, progressively more intensive programs for mediation and conflict resolution, or more thorough inspection and evaluation processes involving new and old member states.

New Architecture, New Process

Perhaps the most dramatic debates have been about the architecture of European security. In the two years following the fall of the Berlin Wall, both the CSCE and NATO, the two principal security organizations, began a process of reassessment and redesign. Governments have tried to adapt these institutions both to the new security environment and to the security requirements of the eastern and central European states. Since 1991 those challenges have increased manyfold: the collapse of the Soviet Union and ensuing civil wars, the breakup of Yugoslavia, and the deceleration of European integration have left Western security strategists wondering which institution, if any, will bring stability to the new Europe. (See table 8-1 for a comprehensive list of the important Atlantic-European organizations and treaties as of mid-1993.)

The widening and deepening of cooperative security in the East were the primary concerns in the hectic first phase of regime adaptation, a period extending roughly from November 1989, the fall of the Wall, to December 1991, the dissolution of the Soviet Union. The goal was to strengthen the channels and patterns of mutual force limitation that had already been established in the 1980s through the CSCE and the CFE negotiations. An equally important goal was to provide support and encouragement for the emerging democracies in central Europe to help them continue to choose policies that would lead to greater cooperation across the range of security issues—force structure, armament, alert rates, border defense, and civil control.

Many, particularly in Europe, placed their initial confidence in a further strengthening of the CSCE, the one institution that already stretched from Vancouver to Vladivostock. More than fifty states, including all of the former Soviet republics, have signed on to its principles, even if some of the newer members are still trying to master all its procedures and informal requirements. All are now to adhere to the earlier CSBM regimes and to the new, even more

Table 8-1. *Membership in Atlantic-European Organizations and Treaties as of December 1993*

Country	*CSCE*	*NACC*	*NATO*	*WEU*	*EC*	*Council of Europe*[a]	*CFE*	*Open Skies*
Albania	✔	✔						
Armenia	✔	✔					✔	
Austria	✔					✔		
Azerbaijan	✔	✔					✔	
Belarus	✔	✔					✔	✔
Belgium	✔	✔	✔	✔	✔	✔	✔	✔
Bosnia	✔							
Bulgaria	✔	✔				✔	✔	✔
Canada	✔	✔	✔				✔	✔
Croatia	✔							
Cyprus	✔					✔		
Czech Republic	✔	✔				✔	✔	✔
Denmark	✔	✔	✔		✔	✔	✔	✔
Estonia	✔	✔				✔		
Finland	✔					✔		
France	✔	✔	✔	✔	✔	✔	✔	✔
Georgia	✔	✔					✔	✔
Germany	✔	✔	✔	✔	✔	✔	✔	✔
Greece	✔	✔	✔	✔	✔	✔	✔	✔
Holy See	✔							
Hungary	✔	✔				✔	✔	✔
Iceland	✔	✔	✔			✔	✔	✔
Ireland	✔				✔	✔		
Italy	✔	✔	✔	✔	✔	✔	✔	✔
Kazakhstan	✔	✔					✔	
Kyrgyzstan	✔	✔						✔
Latvia	✔	✔						
Liechtenstein	✔					✔		
Lithuania	✔	✔				✔		
Luxembourg	✔	✔	✔	✔	✔	✔	✔	✔
Malta	✔					✔		
Moldova	✔	✔					✔	
Monaco	✔							
Netherlands	✔	✔	✔	✔	✔	✔	✔	✔
Norway	✔	✔	✔			✔	✔	✔
Poland	✔	✔				✔	✔	✔
Portugal	✔	✔	✔	✔	✔	✔	✔	✔
Romania	✔	✔					✔	✔
Russia	✔	✔					✔	✔
San Marino	✔					✔		

(*continued*)

Table 8-1 (*continued*)

Country	*CSCE*	*NACC*	*NATO*	*WEU*	*EC*	*Council of Europe*[a]	*CFE*	*Open Skies*
Slovakia	✔	✔				✔	✔	✔
Slovenia	✔					✔		
Spain	✔	✔	✔	✔	✔	✔	✔	✔
Sweden	✔					✔		
Switzerland	✔					✔		
Tajikistan	✔	✔						
Turkey	✔	✔	✔			✔	✔	✔
Turkmenistan	✔	✔						
Ukraine	✔	✔					✔	✔
United Kingdom	✔	✔	✔	✔	✔	✔	✔	✔
United States	✔	✔	✔				✔	✔
Uzbekistan	✔	✔						
Yugoslavia	CSCE participation suspended; succession of Serbia and Montenegro under review							
Total	52	38	16	10	12	31	30	27

Source: Based on data from Dorn Crawford, Arms Control and Disarmament Agency, April 1993.

a. Estonia, Lithuania, and Slovenia acceded to the Council of Europe on May 14, 1993. Council of Europe, *Conventions and Agreements* (Strasbourg, 1993).

encompassing transparency regulations agreed to in Vienna in 1992.[42] It remains a rudimentary formal organization but now has a full-time secretary-general, a Council of Foreign Ministers with a chairman, a Committee of Senior Officials acting as deputies, a troika of chairmen (including the preceding and succeeding ones) to ensure continuity, and a high commissioner on national minorities.

Two additional institutions are slowly emerging: a CSCE Parliamentary Assembly, which met for the first time in July 1992 in Budapest, and a Court of Conciliation and Arbitration, designed to build on the Dispute Settlement Mechanism agreed to at Valletta in February 1991. The CSCE has established several small but permanent centers—a secretariat in Prague, a Conflict Prevention Centre (CPC) in Vienna, an Office of Democratic Institutions and Human Rights in Warsaw, and a hotline and communications network.[43] Even in its rudimentary form, the CSCE has taken on expanded obligations toward cooperative security—notably in the areas of timely warning of impending conflict, dispute resolution, conflict prevention, crisis management, and peacekeeping.[44]

During the period of the CSCE's greatest success, 1989 to 1991, many CSCE enthusiasts hoped that the organization would take on a military role beyond that of an arms control forum for CFE negotiations, perhaps through the deployment of NATO or possibly even its own forces. Departing from the old CSCE rule of absolute consensus, the Berlin conference in June 1991 laid the groundwork for allowing thirteen participants to set an emergency session in motion, without consent of the remaining members.[45] But the central question remains: has the CSCE been able to foster and maintain a broad membership and common values only because it does not use force? In the period between 1991 and the present, the resounding answer to this question has been yes. Despite extensive institutionalization, states have failed to empower the CSCE by neglecting the various crisis prevention and peacekeeping bodies. Moreover, several of the CSCE's conflict prevention procedures have already been severely tested and largely found wanting by the crisis over the former Yugoslavia and the four de facto civil wars raging in the ATTU area of the FSU beginning in 1992—in Nagorno-Karabakh, Moldova, Ossetia, and Abkhazia.

Although there is an encouraging convergence of values embodied in the CSCE, even its strongest advocates concede that many of the principles on which it was founded must now be reexamined and revised, and some discarded.[46] With the dissolution of the Soviet Union and the emergence of states whose identities are deeply tied to ethnicity, nationalism has returned to Europe. Out of this has come new dangers threatening human rights. The strict principle of nonintervention set out in the Helsinki Final Act of 1975 has devastating consequences for the protection of minority and diaspora populations, as the war in Bosnia so brutally demonstrates. Moreover, the principle of unconditional self-determination threatens to legitimate a spiral of new secessionist movements.

The prevailing view is that the CSCE has had some limited success in building a broad consensus on some important values, and has even made progress in shifting the orientation of those values to the post–cold war environment.[47] It provides a forum in which members, rich and poor, from East or West, participate on equal footing. As such, the CSCE still has a role in transforming traditional arms control negotiations into a new broad-ranging security dialogue through the new, relatively untried Forum on Security Cooperation (FSC), based in Vienna.[48] Issues for consideration will include new CSBMs, transparency in military planning, and force restructuring, as well as new provisions for both subregional arrangements and cooperation on global security challenges, such as the proliferation of advanced weapons. All CSCE states participate in the FSC, but potentially with global linkage, since the CSCE is now acting as a regional security organization under the United Nations.[49] Conflict prevention measures and all verification regimes are nominally assigned to the Vienna CPC for integration and elaboration. But fundamentally transforming the CSCE into a cooperative, then a collective, security organization would require a massive redefinition of basic principles as well as a new method of far more timely decisionmaking. Without these changes, new leadership, and new enthusiasm in Europe, the CSCE will not become Europe's principal security organization in the foreseeable future.

NATO has emerged as the most promising security organization that could build on its success over the last forty years and extend its presence into central and eastern Europe and ultimately over the entire CSCE area. In addition to its established credibility, NATO has logistical arrangements in place and has the best-equipped arsenal and backlog of joint experience of any of the existing security organizations. Moreover, continued U.S. membership will be an advantage in whatever develops as the chief European security organization, not only in terms of providing resources but also because the United States will be needed now, as before, to play a balancing role, particularly in terms of German potential and reassurance. The United States, however, will be on more equal footing with its European counterparts in the post–cold war era and may confront far more European agendas and initiatives.

Until 1991 NATO's principal concern was the design of a new political and security strategy. Such a strategy was formally announced in Rome in November 1991 after continuing dispute—particularly between France and the United States—but was quickly overshadowed by the collapse of the Soviet Union. The central concepts still had cold war tinges, and there were problems over concrete issues such as the division of labor between European and NATO institutions in fulfilling what were now designated as NATO's core functions. As defined, NATO's mission was to act as *one* foundation for stability in Europe, to be the forum for transatlantic political consultation, to constitute the primary mechanism to deter and defend against attacks on its members, and to preserve the strategic balance in Europe.[50] Its new missions were to include collective action in peace and crisis as well as in war, particularly preventive diplomacy and crisis management. NATO and the United States explicitly recognized these shared responsibilities, and were to continue to work in concert with other European and multilateral organizations to provide for the "necessary transparency and complementarity."[51]

There was also a mandate to begin an ambitious NATO force restructuring program—then, as now, besieged by domestic budget-cutting imperatives and a general reluctance to make major changes in spending priorities that would exacerbate continuing high unemployment levels in the already shrinking defense industrial sector. Perhaps the greatest question came with the introduction of a newly integrated Allied Command Europe Rapid Reaction Corps (ARRC) for crisis intervention, but still only within the NATO area. Through the existence of the ARRC, NATO will be able to maintain other forces at lower levels, and both will benefit from integrated command structures. More important, the ARRC is a multinational force of high readiness that will be deployable throughout the NATO area. But although the experience gained will be of value for all contingencies, the ARRC is still formally bound to "in-area" defense and to the protection of territory against direct military attacks across borders.

One of NATO's greatest successes came in its response to the expanded geography of the European security system, the North Atlantic Cooperation

Council (NACC), a hybrid institution that came to cover Vancouver-to-Vladivostock. The product of a German-American initiative in the aftermath of the August 1991 coup attempt in the Soviet Union, the NACC was designed initially to reassure the eastern European states (subsequently the NIS states as well) that NATO countries were not indifferent to the formers' security concerns or to the democratic transformation of their societies. The aim was to involve the new states as limited partners in the broad issues of a NATO security dialogue and in narrow areas of practical cooperation without granting them full or even associate alliance membership.[52] But true to French fears at the outset, the existence of an organizational framework and appointed liaison representatives led to increased consultation, and the emergence of the NACC was viewed by some as an attempt to develop a pan-European competitor to the CSCE. Indeed, after their first meeting in December 1991, the new NACC states actively pursued consultation and explored options for a transition to a stronger set of security arrangements for cooperation and mutual guarantees. Moreover, there were some initial steps toward practical cooperation in peacekeeping through training, information sharing, and consultation.

Although NATO strategists have made some progressive changes, the alliance's planning does not yet meet the new challenges of the post–cold war security environment. In the past, the mainstay of NATO's military posture was Article 5, which mandates military action by all NATO signatories in the event that one member's territory is violated. But because the major threat to European security stems largely from domestic turmoil, ethnic conflict, and secessionist movements, a greater number of alliance actions in the future will depend on invigorating Article 4, under which alliance members consult and act politically on security issues beyond their territorial defense.

Since the new sources of instability emanate across almost all of Europe's borders and not from the Soviet Union of old, the notions of "in-area" versus "out-of-area" no longer correspond to NATO's interest in maintaining peace and stability in a potentially turbulent region. NATO faces in this both a political and a conceptual challenge. Should NATO continue to plan and develop the means to act only when the legitimacy of member states or of their borders is in dispute? Or is there surely now sufficient political consensus to anticipate the need for common action against cross-border contingencies? And what will be the long-term impact of SHAPE's (NATO's Supreme Headquarters, Allied Powers Europe) increasingly sophisticated planning on Bosnia? Among the new initiatives have been coordination with the UN, inputs from nonmember states, and even preparations for the first NATO deployment of troops in a region racked by civil war. Unless NATO takes all these issues into account, and indeed considers a Europe-wide framework close to the CSCE boundaries, it is hard to imagine a valid NATO claim to be the primary European security institution.

During the Rome Conference in 1991, military strategists considered only some of these issues, which might be called the safe cases of out-of-area contingencies and the threats arising out of "uncertainties" in the East. They reduced ground troops while maintaining air and naval forces only slightly below cold war levels. While the United States is currently best equipped to project forces quickly and efficiently, an enhanced ability to coordinate French and British projection capabilities will be essential to NATO's competence in maintaining security outside Europe.

In view of the new security environment in which war and conflict will almost certainly originate outside the traditional NATO boundaries, NATO has begun, but not yet completed, new plans preparing for cooperative military ventures and expanding NATO membership, first through informal channels, and then formally. The crisis in former Yugoslavia has provided one opportunity to think through what might be required to undertake Article 4–type operations, including the participation of nonmember states such as Russia and Ukraine. The American initiative dubbed "Partnership for Peace" provides another. As agreed to at the January 1994 summit, the partnership will allow central and eastern European states to conclude bilateral treaties on military cooperation with the alliance.[53] What is needed at a minimum vis-à-vis Russia and the other central and eastern European states and those of the former republics able to participate is to improve projection capabilities, further develop the compatibility of forces, monitor political and geographic areas of tension, and consult on areas of shared military and strategic concern, allowing NATO to provide commitments just short of security guarantees.

Widening NATO membership will no doubt be a long and sometimes arduous process; it is hoped that behavioral tests rather than abstract labels will be the basis for choosing among candidate members. But the first step is deepening the security dialogue that complements Western economic aid and political legitimization. There are also a number of specific "eastward" proposals that might help facilitate the transition. Steps toward effective cooperation and sharing of resources are needed in order to change the political and military orientations of NATO, the former eastern bloc, Russia, and the NIS.

What impact these organizational changes within the European security system will have in the long run is still far from clear. In many ways, for example, the NACC was a creative redefinition of NATO's broader commitment to democratization as the best arms control, and the Partnership for Peace allows for both self-selection and differential evolution among the republics of the former Soviet Union. But thus far, most of NATO's changes do not go to the heart of the post–cold war alliance dilemma—that is, how to define a new overarching purpose that will garner public support and that goes beyond preparing for defense against uncertainty and then transforms the alliance accordingly. For many in the United States and in Europe, particularly in eastern Europe, NATO's principal function is to frame U.S. involvement in

Europe, as well as to demonstrate the United States's continuing commitment to the evolution of a cooperative security system. For others, notably in France, the basic structure of NATO remains rooted in the cold war era and is not susceptible to change, especially given the dominant role assumed by the United States. NATO's continuation, according to some in the French leadership, should therefore be limited to a transitional period—sufficient to allow Europe to absorb the initial impact of German unification and the revolutions in the East.

If NATO is going to fill Europe's chief security role, clearly the attitudes of the larger European nations will be key, and, in particular, France will have to become a more regular participant in all of NATO's operations. Again, the Gulf War and the Yugoslav crisis, as well as the change of leadership in France, have provided new instances of cooperation; these should continue. Just as important, Germany must resolve its own "out-of-area" debate in such a way as to allow Germany's full participation in cooperative military activities. Germany's unconstrained involvement in NATO will be crucial to the United States's continuing commitment to Europe and will be instrumental in coordinating central and eastern European participation in a traditionally Western security organization.

In some instances, overlapping responsibilities have propelled organizational competition as the transformation of the western European security institutions has proceeded. One issue has been the future role of an expanded WEU as the holder of a new European security identity of the EC sanctioned under the Maastricht Treaty. Months of hostile exchanges, both transatlantic and intra-European, focused on the appropriate relation of the WEU to various versions of a redesigned NATO and on the impact that this relationship would have on continuing American commitments to European security.[54] Even more intractable was the question whether there would be separate WEU forces and where and how these forces would be used: within NATO, in "out-of-area" contingencies, under NATO's integrated command, or outside it.

The focus of the most intense transatlantic debates occurred as a result of the Kohl-Mitterrand proposal for a new Franco-German corps, to be created by 1995 outside the NATO (and for a while even outside the WEU) framework. As originally conceived, this corps was to constitute the central element for a new multinational Eurocorps.[55] Other nations were to contribute units either on a continuing basis or for purposes of common training or exercises, and the result was to be a European Rapid Reaction Force, a clear reflection of European commitment and ultimately of an independent European defense policy. It was eventually to function under the common European foreign and security structure that had been hoped for before Maastricht, to be achieved by the end of the decade.[56] Protests and objections to this perceived "anti-NATO" proposal came from Washington as well as from Britain and several of the smaller European NATO members.

In the end, the result has been a compromise, most often making a virtue of the necessity of papering over Franco-American disagreements.[57] But this compromise also resulted in real progress, helping to underscore the important interconnections among all these institutions for a true security regime and to show the advantages of flexibility and redundancy in the new reduced-threat, but still uncertain, political environment.[58] NATO's adoption of the new "Joint Task Force structure" in January 1994 complements and extends this compromise.

The WEU is now formally both an agent of the EC and a critical component of NATO; it is the accepted framework for Europeanization or a European pillar. The Petersburg Declaration of June 1992 called for a WEU reaction force that would include the Eurocorps when created. The units assigned to it by NATO member states, in turn, will wear two hats—one NATO, one WEU—which means that all but the French forces will be subject first to tasking from the NATO command.[59] These forces may be sent on peacekeeping, humanitarian, and other missions around the world, but only in response to requests from the UN or the CSCE. They may also be used in Europe, but most leaders expect that they will be used only when "NATO might not be willing or able to act."[60]

The New Challenges to the Security Regime

The cooperative security regime that is emerging in Europe both reflects and influences the crucial security relationships in the Northern Hemisphere. Once established, a European security regime that firmly embraces cooperative security precepts and practices could become the cornerstone of a new global system, perhaps one operating under the United Nations and forged from linked regional arrangements. But such a regime, even in Europe, is still in a crucial evolutionary phase. Certainly it has a defined direction and a set of newly designed institutional arrangements, but it must still contend with the constant buffeting of regional instabilities and general political uncertainty. The emerging regime also faces a number of fundamental barriers to its implementation, as well as some outright failures, a stalemate that is affecting both its credibility in day-to-day operations and its potential as a model for other regions.

The Yugoslav Crisis and Its Implications

The first of these failures is Europe's inability to contain the crisis and then end the war resulting from the fragmentation of the former Yugoslavia.[61] The resolution of strife in Yugoslavia was a test that western Europe, particularly the states of the EC, set for itself explicitly. But despite continuing efforts since 1991, neither the EC nor any other European or transatlantic security institution has yet found the means to develop an effective program of action to achieve peace or mitigate the consequences of war. The breakdown was not strictly a failure of either cooperative or collective security. Yugoslavia was outside NATO and the EC, and there was no firm pledge under Atlantic or European agreements, or indeed in the CSCE, to preserve unity or to achieve an international assessment of blame and to impose, by force if necessary, a collective solution. The measure of failure in the current case stems from a less binding test—the standards of international behavior that were cooperatively set by the CSCE states for themselves. Moreover, CSCE Europe had proclaimed that it had the ability to invoke conflict resolution mechanisms at an early stage: prompt decisions to intervene on behalf of human rights, including those of minorities; the timely imposition of credible political, economic, and military sanctions; and a commitment to use all possible efforts to ensure a war-free Europe. In Yugoslavia, few of these mechanisms were tried, and those that were enjoyed only limited success.

After more than two years of crisis and conflict in the former Yugoslavia, Europe's response to the outrages in Bosnia appears particularly weak and divided. Despite popular outcries, there have been expressions of grave concern and the imposition of economic sanctions, but great operational diffidence and constant delay. The EC has been most engaged, but only with intermittent success and with marked failures of political agreement. Involved have been conflict resolution efforts, the monitoring of a series of cease-fire attempts, or emergency humanitarian measures. With the UN, the EC was the coconvener of the peace negotiations that produced the Vance-Owen proposal. But this did not receive active support even from all the EC member countries. Nor did it prove a rallying cry to mobilize the additional troops, within the EC or outside it, that would have been needed to allow for implementation of the Vance-Owen peace plan or any other plan requiring significant commitment.

But the EC has not been the only organization to fall short of expectations. The CSCE is the official sponsor of the peace-monitoring force currently stationed in Croatia, Bosnia, and Macedonia. Much of the central organizing role for CSCE-sponsored monitoring and for humanitarian work has indeed come from specially assigned European NATO contingents. And any implementation of a comprehensive peace scheme or of safe havens would have been based essentially on NATO planning, including the inputs of Russia, France, and Ukraine, as well as those of the other NATO members.

NATO itself has taken a limited formal role, reflecting continuing Franco-American disagreements over command and the unwillingness of the Bush administration to become actively involved until essentially its last months in office. NATO's role has increased as the situation in Bosnia has worsened—with the aerial reinforcement of the "no-fly" zone, the humanitarian air drops, the "loan" of a NATO field headquarters and airborne warning and control system (AWACS) capability, and ultimately the threat of air strikes to deter attacks against UN-EC monitors and peacekeepers.

Overall, however, most of the European organizations seem to have decided on actions that were too little too late, partial measures pursued halfheartedly, or previously untried procedures that simply failed. The London-Geneva UN-

EC peace process that produced the Vance-Owen plan included few new cooperative elements for bringing about an end to the hostilities.[62] And the Clinton administration made clear its commitment to consultation and to multilateral action, but wavered on specific actions if any action at all.[63]

Yet the prospects for peaceful resolution or even the mitigation of the war's impact on civilians were never strong. Europe's failure to deal effectively with the Yugoslavian crisis stemmed from multiple sources, including the facts that (1) the crisis occurred before any of the necessary institutional structures and procedures had been fully formed in Europe and at a time when the UN was already overburdened with other peacekeeping missions; (2) the complex politics of Yugoslavia hindered the attempts of any outsiders to influence the situation decisively; (3) parts of the physical terrain of Yugoslavia pose intractable barriers and impede intervention or even selective military sanctions; and (4) the instruments for restraining or punishing incidents of civil war are simply still too rudimentary at this stage to contend with a crisis of the scope and complexity of that in Yugoslavia.

But although all these arguments appear credible, the critical factor, both within Europe and in the United States, appears to be the lack of political will. There has indeed never been a European decision taken within the Community or elsewhere to commit the time and resources—political, economic, and military—to resolve the crisis. The dominant theme has been the stated unwillingness of governments to risk lives in direct intervention and their inability to use political and military incentives to help induce an early end to the fighting and to the horrors of ethnic cleansing.

The Yugoslav crisis has raised questions about two other factors, key to the future of Europe's cooperative security system. First, for most of 1991, fears about the breakup of Yugoslavia were fueled by far greater anxieties concerning the future of the Soviet Union, with dramatic parallels being drawn between the brutal fighting in Yugoslavia and that to come in the Soviet Union. At issue were the degree of ethnic hostility, the role of the conservative ex-communists, and the precedents the international community was setting regarding intervention in the domestic affairs of a state still formally sovereign.

By the end of 1991, with the collapse of the Soviet Union, these fears were replaced with new worries about events in Yugoslavia as the first of an unending string of ethnic conflicts, especially along the periphery of the FSU. There were exaggerated arguments about cascading fragmentation throughout eastern and central Europe. The collapse of the artificial states and the borders constructed after World War I and World War II, like those in Yugoslavia, and the exploitation or manipulation of the potentially explosive diasporas that had been created—Russian, Hungarian, Polish, and Ukrainian, to name only a few—would be involved. The Yugoslav crisis seemed to legitimate once again the right to self-determination for any group, however small, that was able to organize politically. And it flatly contradicted the basic CSCE tenet of no border changes without political agreements satisfactory to all sides.

A State-Based Security System

Moreover, the unfolding of the Yugoslav tragedy revealed the obsolescence of several critical assumptions at the heart of the cold war system. All existing European and transatlantic institutions involved in cooperative security tasks presuppose the existence or emergence of state actors. For the system to "work," member states must be capable of providing for the basic security and human rights of their populations, of ensuring minimal political order, and of ensuring respect for clear state boundaries. The definition of European cooperation under the CSCE accords includes formal equality and inclusion of all states that acknowledge CSCE principles, even for states that clearly bring with them great burdens of instability, such as refugees, ethnic strife, and repressive or undemocratic governments.

Less obviously, western European and transatlantic commitments to NATO's collective security system presupposed strong state organizations, capable of keeping civil violence to a minimum level. The promise of all states to defend one another against civil violence was therefore to be invoked rarely, and the most probable contingency was a communist-led attempt at overthrow or revolution—in the style of Greece in the late 1940s, for example. In its pan-European efforts, the West indeed approached the socialist central European states as illegitimate in their origin and in their exercise of power but as still capable of preserving boundaries and civil order.

The European cooperative security system was therefore state based and not really prepared to deal directly either with emerging civil societies in the cold war period or with nonstate actors such as ethnic or minority groups in the present. Moreover, states experiencing severe problems of economic decline, political disintegration, or an inability to form effective governments pose intractable difficulties for a cooperative framework. The only instrument of censure for the regime against a state that is violating collective norms is exclusion, and this is a limited penalty in weak institutions like the CSCE. For states that have experienced political and economic disintegration, the only formal way to cooperate is to wait until a statelike entity emerges from the current disorder.

In stronger, more powerful cooperative institutions such as NATO and the EC, the response to disintegration or political heterogeneity is simply not to extend equal benefits and guarantees or membership. Turkey, for example, is not "European" enough to be a member of the EC. Similarly, NATO has had difficulties with the NNA countries, as well as with the Baltics. As the Partnership for Peace debate showed, there are gradations seen among candidates to NATO membership—Poland, Hungary, the Czech Republic, and perhaps the

Baltics are perceived as somehow more "European" than the rest. These states are thought to be more likely to share the goals and the core activities of cooperative security, to be able to limit not only military capabilities but also the sources of civil violence in a democratic manner. The rest of eastern Europe and many of the CIS states are, by contrast, still viewed largely as aspirants, which will have looser ties and which will require a substantial transition period before inclusion in the tighter circle is granted by core members.

The unspoken question is whether cooperative security in Europe can be pursued at all among states that have highly unequal levels of economic development, a disparity likely to remain for a significant period in Europe. Proponents of cooperative security tend to argue that the most acute threats to European stability have an economic cause and thus an economic solution, whether these be ethnic conflicts, irredentist border disputes, tensions over the protection of national minorities on the territory of others, or unchecked flows of refugees searching for security and economic prosperity. In the oft-repeated formulation of former German foreign minister Hans-Dietrich Genscher, the primary long-term security task must be economic restructuring in the East to establish, with massive economic assistance from the West, the basic conditions of democracy and stability.[64]

Skeptics are more likely to argue that ethnic conflicts—except, perhaps, those that spill over existing borders or involve clear genocide—are probably beyond settlement through external influence, particularly once fighting has begun. Most ethnic disputes are not amenable to the pressure of economic or political sanctions. These arguments suggest the need to intensify cooperative security actions to stem state disintegration only for "damage limitation," that is, to ensure the security of neighboring states, to redress the problems of refugees, and to design options for long-term resolution of political disputes once the fighting stops.

The Challenge of Inclusion

In the interim, the question is how to devise new instruments and arrangements that reflect and accommodate the differences in power, accountability, and political will among states involved in pan-European arrangements. One concept, for example, comes from Jacques Delors: a European security structure that resembles linked concentric circles, much like a spiderweb, with those most capable and willing to take concerted action at the core, and that would in turn be linked to other states in wider institutional groupings by ties that can be affirmed or loosened at both ends.[65]

NATO has available a set of informal but legitimated arrangements among the major transatlantic partners, called the Quad (the United States, United Kingdom, France, and Germany) and the Quint (the four plus Italy), that allows for special consultation in crisis and for action if appropriate.[66] Similarly, the

CSCE might be strengthened and made more effective if there was an informal "directorate" made up of larger and smaller states. Candidate members would see the NATO Quint supplemented by Russia and Ukraine in the CSCE leadership, and, when desirable, perhaps a Turkey or an engaged neutral such as Sweden or Austria would participate. There might even be opportunity for more ad hoc coalitions—states prepared as in the Gulf War or in Somalia to assume particular tasks or burdens assigned or sanctioned by the UN within the CSCE framework. But this unquestionably would involve a major restructuring of perceptions and practice in the CSCE. The overcoming of even middle-power opposition to a new hierarchy would require major political resources, committed leadership, and unprecedented levels of confidence and permissive consensus.

The specific roles to be played by the United States and Russia in any new European regime are also problematic. To date, this has largely been the result of Washington's ambivalence and uncertainty about its own role in Europe. Until well into 1991, the United States dismissed the CSCE as another collective security folly promoted by the Europeans at the expense of NATO. The Bush administration sparred repeatedly with France and Germany over how a European security identity should be articulated. From 1989 through early 1992, the administration fought a losing battle to preserve the status quo through NATO, stressing the unique and exclusive military responsibilities of U.S. NATO command.[67] U.S. officials embraced the need for a continuing American military commitment to NATO as opposed to a revived WEU, an independent Franco-German corps, or any European security organization that might have the power to involve the United States under NATO's Article 5 or any other cooperative security pledge. Most Europeans still value direct U.S. involvement and presence at some level, and few want NATO disbanded at least in the medium term.[68] But despite the more positive Clinton approach to European integration, some still question whether the United States will accept a truly equal sharing of decisionmaking authority.

How Russia is to be folded into European cooperation poses somewhat different problems. The role that Russia can or should play remains unclear, especially given its political instability and its unresolved internal and regional military and economic crises. Moreover, in the CSCE and elsewhere, Russia has often been second only to France in its unwillingness to support immediate assertive action for crisis prevention or direct crisis management. Its reluctance has stemmed from its own interpretation of the importance of historical ties in eastern Europe, apprehension about military escalation, and, most especially, concerns that precedents could later be used against Russia on its own territory or in crises involving Russian peacekeeping in the former republics or in the interests of the Russian diaspora. The Gorbachev and Yeltsin governments have both preferred to deal directly with the United States on questions of major hardware limitation, a strategy that reaffirms their status as a nuclear superpower but mitigates full involvement in Europe. The Russian government has resisted and resented being treated as anything other than the first among CIS equals in all European forums, a status for which Russia obviously qualifies as the strongest European military nuclear power.

Few Europeans see Yeltsin or his potential successors as capable of making a significant contribution to European stability until Russia's own process of economic reform is well under way and the problems of domestic political balance (especially in the civil-military area) are at least partially resolved. Most believe that a central Russian role in Europe for the foreseeable future would be only a source of continuing discord and enhanced vulnerability. The key concerns are reversibility of democracies, fears of traditional Russian Slavophile ambitions vis-à-vis eastern Europe and the NIS, and Russia's deep commitment to the protection of the Russian diaspora. In the final analysis, European opinion is seriously divided over whether Russian membership would mean that such a radically transformed NATO would have lost all meaning.

Given the current fragile conditions in Russia, many American leaders are seeking to keep open all possible channels for Russian integration, including potential Russian membership in NATO, and are encouraging Russia to agree to at least limited experiments in extending cooperative security, including joint peacekeeping. Such measures are seen as a minimum test of what is operationally possible, of the ways in which the cooperative security regime can help secure a range of beneficial outcomes in Russia and in the NIS. The immediate benefits of having Russia (and perhaps Ukraine and Belarus as well) within the tightest possible European framework would be to ensure full consultation about renewed commitment to nuclear and other forms of nonproliferation. If Russia and the states of the former Soviet Union succeed in their political and economic transformations, keeping the NATO door open can allow for both NATO and the CSCE to begin to merge membership and functions and to pursue both a broader and a deeper security agenda.

The Way Forward

What might be the next steps in the evolution of the European cooperative security regime? The worst case scenario would be a retreat to weakened security systems in both Europe and the North Atlantic area, unable to meet their goals because of high costs, lack of political will, and insufficient public support. In this situation, the EC would continue to endorse the rhetoric of a European defense identity while providing only inadequate planning and few capabilities to make it a reality. The investment in the expeditionary forces required for the out-of-area contingencies would not materialize, nor would the hard political bargaining about a new Europe-wide division of labor resulting in forces, training, research and development (R&D) investment, and far more. In the event of a crisis, Europe may agree to act, but it would find itself without sufficient resources or perhaps even without prepared policies.

Moreover, the United States might find itself unable and unwilling to maintain either troops in Europe or capabilities compatible with European forces. A lessening nuclear threat, shrinking military budgets, and a similarly reduced force structure would provide few incentives to preserve Europe-specific forces in the face of other demands. In addition, a move away from an integrated command even to the most efficient system of joint exercises, periodic staff talks, and compatible equipment would assume that there would be a lengthy period of mobilization and cooperation building once a crisis begins. It might indeed be easier to exercise joint operations outside of the NATO area than within it.

An acceptable outcome in terms of the principles of cooperative security would be a gradual sharpening and incremental extension to emerging democracies in the Vancouver-to-Vladivostock expanse of what has been achieved so far in western Europe. Progress will not necessarily be continuous, and the roster of states and entities that will be core participants may well change over time. Whatever the declaratory commitments, there will continue to be a Europe of several speeds in which various states occupy different levels of economic development and military sophistication. They will therefore enjoy varying degrees of European integration. And success will still be measured by further agreements and cooperative actions on the regulation and reduction of offensive forces, the restructuring of national forces and facilities to ensure their increasingly defensive character, the assurance of increasing mutual transparency and communication, and the further multilateral control of surprise attack capabilities. The institutional framework will eventually be tighter and the assignment of responsibilities and penalties will become a somewhat more automatic process.

A more interesting policy exercise is to specify scenarios to move security cooperation in Europe to higher levels of effectiveness, institutionalization, and political confidence. The assumptions to be made, of course, verge on the heroic—an acceptable solution to the conflicts in the former Yugoslavia, continuing steps toward the nonviolent economic transformation in Russia and the CIS, and reinvigoration of political will among the major European states, which are now so inward-looking and exhausted by the post-Maastricht gloom. And to be of major interest, the analysis would have to posit the states involved to be the present membership of NATO, the EC, and the NNA, along with Poland, the Czech Republic, Slovakia, and Hungary. Russia and the United States would be assumed to be directly participant in and supportive of the step up in cooperative decisionmaking.

There are a number of candidate scenarios, but three would seem to offer the most interesting and dramatic contrasts. The first focuses on ways to extend and thicken the CFE–CSBM–Open Skies regime in the near term, within the general framework already laid out in the CSCE's Forum on Security Cooperation. The second explores the possibilities for foreseeable future success in the cooperative limitation of arms production, development, and export, and the third considers longer-term challenges in creating cooperative structures for all phases of peacekeeping within or outside Europe.

A Near-Term Goal: Extending the Present CFE-CSBM Regime

Clearly, the most straightforward scenarios would involve broadening and deepening the fundamental provisions of the intersecting regimes set in place under the CFE, the CSCE, and the Open Skies agreements in 1992. The goal would be not only to rationalize efforts but also to use these unique frameworks to help shape the short- and longer-term outcomes in Russia and the NIS in ways eventually consistent with NATO-CSCE standards. The next action-forcing deadline to stimulate action is the CSCE Review Conference, to take place in Budapest from October to December 1994. And there is already at least one agreed-upon agenda, the fourteen-point Programme for Immediate Action established in the Helsinki Document of July 1992.[69]

There has, however, been little or no progress beyond the outline of the agenda items and a number of tabled proposals. The reasons for the inaction are clear: the almost total self-absorption of several key actors; the gloom of economic recession and the conflict in the former Yugoslavia; the tendency of bureaucracy to await perfection of the existing regime in all its technical details before embarking on new initiatives; and even what one analyst has called "arms control fatigue" after the rapid changes and simultaneous negotiations of the preceding two years.[70] Yet to build on the present regime requires new strategic concepts and renewed political leadership, spearheaded by the United States but involving at least Russia and Germany in key roles. There also must be widening political awareness throughout Europe and most especially in the United States that the present regime has critical holes and vulnerabilities that may grow in significance in the face of repeated crisis. And without extension and reinforcement of the present regime now, there may be more crises and fewer chances for gradual evolution of the cooperative security regime in the post-Yugoslav environment in Europe.

Broadening the scope of the existing regimes is an obvious first step once the political turmoil, especially in Russia, diminishes. There is already some unofficial broadening—the informal sharing of information, for example, among CFE and non-CFE states in the CSCE context. Far more advantageous for long-lasting transparency, however, would be reporting measures to go beyond the CFE boundaries of the Atlantic to the Urals. Critical to meeting Russian concerns about symbolic equity with the United States would be an immediate global data exchange—reports on all national holdings, Vancouver to Vladivostock, and thus for the first time on all American forces outside of Europe and on all Russian forces east of the Urals.[71] Neither the American nor the Russian military is currently prepared to go beyond data exchange to talk about limitations on or verification of these total holdings or constraints on naval forces and, indeed, may never be prepared to do so without critical strategic changes that convince each side that the other will never harbor military ambitions against it. But there seems little reason not to begin annual data exchanges on selected categories of military equipment, and very soon to include more detailed reporting on equipment, national manpower levels, locations, and general force organization as well. This would provide both a new baseline for the dissemination of information within and outside CFE-CSCE and perhaps a foundation for eventual expansion to reporting on major national holdings in Asia, especially on Chinese forces, of concern to both Russia and the United States.

It would seem at least worthwhile to attempt to expand the CFE treaty regime, with its critical limits and verification provisions, to the non-CFE members of the CSCE—the remaining republics of the FSU, the NNA states, and any emerging states in the CSCE region. Although this alone will not have a major impact on the risks of internal conflict, it would contribute to the further lowering of interstate conflict. The optimal solution would be adaptation and adoption of the full CFE measures: limits in terms of national ceilings, constraints on transfer and force generation, and the full program of monitoring, inspection, and verification. These states so far have offered a number of reasons for delay or for partial implementation, perhaps even for a differing reporting basis. The NNA states have argued, for example, that they have particular problems with full transparency, given their reliance on large numbers of reserve forces and on dispersed equipment stocks for what would be slow, observable mobilization in times of crisis. But immediate steps toward reporting existing stocks would be a critical icebreaker and would provide reassurance and validation to neighboring states, in effect raising the standard of information flows within the CSCE–Vienna Document arrangements to that of the CFE treaty provisions in both scope and level of detail.

Deepening the existing regime involves a greater number of options and is undoubtedly of more importance in the short run to the implementation of cooperative security principles than the territorial extension to any particular non-CFE state. One set of actions falls within the FSC charge to "harmonize" all arms control arrangements. Of clear advantage to the smaller states, but also to the Russian skeptics, would be an integration and consolidation of the regular inspection and reporting requirements of the CFE, the CSCE, and Open Skies when it enters into force. The smaller states have already complained about the economic and manpower burdens; indeed, in the widespread budget-driven cuts, states are sometimes cutting their trained inspection personnel by as much as one-half. The Russians, on the other hand, need evidence to persuade domestic critics, in the military and on the right, that these reflect a coherent, equitable set of rules and obligations that yield information and new instruments of reassurance against all their neighbors.

This integration would require a far more active, politically capable FSC (and by extension a similarly capable JCG), able to deal with a range of present questions about cross-regime integration and new additions or exceptions. These questions might involve issues as large as a temporary stay or cooperative assistance for countries unable to meet their destruction quotas, implementation issues such as the possibility of joint inspection and verification tasking of inspection missions, or perhaps even the substitution of inspection missions under one regime for at least some of those under another.

More difficult will be the task of reopening discussion of national and zonal limits, especially the flank subzonal limits that are of such irritation to the Russian military. There are legitimate concerns in Washington and elsewhere about the perils of reopening agreed provisions of the CFE or even of trying for further formal amendments. But there would seem an urgent need to use the JCG and the FSC, even in their somewhat unwieldy numbers, to extend the CFE's ability to adapt to the dynamics of political change. And the aim should be to rely, when possible, on new politically binding agreements rather than on new or renegotiated treaty language.

An interesting alternative approach would be to acknowledge the lack of a compelling FSC-wide focus and to use, as the first forum for the negotiation of changes in limits or ceilings, regional subgroups, or what are often called "regional tables," to achieve political agreement among the most concerned states. The focus might be on major subzone changes as well as on specific requirements for reassurance or for tighter arms control provisions in critical regions.[72] The first of these groups were, in essence, CSBMs, formed to breach the cold war divide in Europe—the *Pentagonale* (Austria, Czechoslovakia, Hungary, Italy, the former Yugoslavia), for example, to allow central European discussions on environment and information exchange. Now they could function as working groups, charged by the FSC to explore disputes and deficiencies in implementation and verification and to devise solutions, including both changes and new requirements, acceptable to the concerned states. Formal ratification would still be by the FSC, but a more important factor would be the membership in all the tables, which would include the United States and Russia, both for reassurance and for momentum.

Given present controversies, there seems to be a need for tables in four areas. The first and perhaps most urgently needed would focus on reframing the Russian-Ukrainian balance and finding new methods for regional reassurance, with Germany, Belarus, Poland, and the United States as key players as well. Further specification of stabilization and transparency measures might mean the participation as well of Austria and the Visegrad states beyond Poland

(Hungary, Czech Republic, Slovakia). A second would be a northern Europe–Baltic table (with Russia, the United States, the Baltic states, Finland, Poland, and Germany) to deal with issues of Russian troop withdrawals and general adaptation to the changed force balance, given the withdrawals into the St. Petersburg military district of men and equipment from eastern Europe.

A basic but difficult task for both these tables would be to explore directly (1) the question of changes in regional sublimits mandated by the CFE, especially the possibility of allowing new lower ceilings in categories of particular sensitivity for a defined period; and (2) the question of how to deal with the uneven results of national reductions taken for budgetary reasons or because of growing obsolescence and maintenance problems. In the latter case, the CFE limits already agreed to will almost certainly prevent the retention by one state or another of overwhelmingly superior capability. What will be needed is a regional framework and a specified process by which to secure rapid reassurance and compensation and offset without formal invocation of the full, time-consuming treaty process.

The other two tables would focus on regions where conflict is already present, and they will thus have to fit within whatever peacekeeping or peace enforcement measures are in place. One might deal with linked political discussions and peacekeeping options as well as equipment and manpower questions in the Caucasus and would have to include Turkey, Armenia, Azerbaijan, and Georgia as well as the superpowers. And a fourth Balkan table might attempt to anticipate the readjustments needed in southeastern Europe given a settlement in Moldova or a lessening crisis in the former Yugoslavia.

In each case, the aim would be not immediate agreement but at least a continuing multilateral framework for dialogue and the use of transparency measures to confront controversies both directly and at the earliest possible stage. Some of the new arrangements would constitute special CSBMs—more frequent inspections or exchanges, special overflight rights as in the bilateral Romanian-Hungarian Open Skies agreement, and perhaps special provisions for international control of equipment storage or for constraints on further force generation. There might even be further development of the "crisis CBM"—that is, direct measures to dampen conflict or to reinforce cease-fires through, for example, international storage of heavy weapons, as was begun unsuccessfully in the Yugoslav case.

The full FSC is clearly the best arena for discussion for the new operationalization of the CSCE's basic principles into a code of conduct. As the various proposals already tabled suggest, such a code will be a politically binding statement on the full scope of internal and external security relations, one that reflects the widespread agreement to tighten the standards set in the 1980s and the desire to overcome the deficiencies revealed by Europe's crisis experiences since 1989. The goal would be to set norms for intrastate as well as interstate relations in arms control, democratic military decisionmaking and civilian control of the military, the just treatment of national minorities, and even for the "new" security issues like drug traffic, environmental issues, and refugees. Critics, including many in the United States, argue that the code will have no more status than similar pledges made under the UN Charter and in a host of other international and European agreements. But proponents argue that it would provide a new, firmer basis for the CSCE and also the CFE, allowing the formulation of appropriate crisis responses more quickly and with greater cooperative impact in questions of violation and noncompliance.

Cooperative Limitation of Arms Production and Sales: A Short-Term Challenge

What kind of European framework would be needed to ensure cooperative regulation and constraint of European production of major weapons systems? As is argued elsewhere in this volume, the regulation should be imposed on clear end use, not through the tracking of countless applications of particular technologies. The task would be enormous, given the large volume of trade in components and subcomponents, but still manageable. A minimal approach that would promise short-run success would be to place this under the jurisdiction of the strong western European security organizations—the EC or perhaps a revitalized WEU.

Whatever the regime, arms industry consolidation and internationalization have significant implications for cooperative security. The opportunity for arms industry downsizing should be seized at this critical juncture of budgetary constraints in the post–cold war environment in order to maximize standardization of equipment, training, and military planning. Moreover, enhanced internationalization in the arms sector could facilitate harmonization in the development of new arms export control regimes, as is discussed in greater detail below. Eventually, the new provisions could then gradually be spread eastward to incorporate other states in eastern Europe and the CIS. There could also be an immediate effort to increase transparency and information sharing and to establish either an arms register or a continuous Europe-wide monitoring system of arms production plans and the specifics of sales and licensing abroad.

Viewed against European developments since the early 1950s, arms production would seem an unlikely candidate for progress toward cooperative reduction in the short term. The situation in eastern Europe appears most unfavorable. Arms production was a cornerstone of the socialist economies; in the slow economic transformations of the present, it remains a sector with which to earn hard currency and, in the eyes of the hardliners at least, to restore national pride. Initially, just as the cold war was coming to an end, there was a good deal of optimism, which led progressively minded leaders like Czechoslovakian president Václav Havel to declare an end to arms exports.[73] This has now been replaced by a more permissive, if not cynical, attitude to continued sales.

The situation in the former Soviet Union is also discouraging. In particular, Russia has experienced a severe drop-off in orders from cold war clients such as Afghanistan, Angola, and Ethiopia, resulting in a dramatic cut in the value of arms exports. And although the Soviet Union exported more than $20 billion worth of arms annually in the mid-1980s, the former Soviet republics sold only $2.5 billion worth of weapons in 1992,[74] reflecting both shrinking markets and diminished CIS production in most sectors. But as recently as April 1993, the Russian foreign economic relations minister, Sergey Glazyev, announced that Russia would "strive to the maximum to trade in arms," in everything from ships to atomic power engineering equipment, probably scoping out new markets in developing countries, particularly in Asia and the Middle East.[75] Russian production capabilities will almost certainly increase as time passes and economic recovery takes hold. If it has the capacity to profit from arms exports, Russia, like other industrialized powers, will certainly do so in the absence of an expansive and powerful multilateral export control regime.

Yet there are some reasons to try even now for a Europe-wide system, especially given current economic conditions in western and eastern Europe. The collapse of the former socialist economies and the dependence of the emerging democracies on both international funds and external goods for economic reconstruction have meant little continuing investment in military industry. Because of the general post–cold war drop-off in global sales and the inability of the eastern European firms to offer either special trade incentives or high-technology alternatives, many of the previous trading arrangements have collapsed, as in the Russian case. In addition, reform has meant a shrinking domestic market, one that no longer supports even half the previous scale of typical eastern European production. This will limit the former eastern bloc's ability to sustain an arms industry at its previous cold war level.

The task now is to strengthen and multilateralize the decisions of the reform leadership in almost every country to reverse the guns versus butter ratio of the socialist period. For the moment, the opposition of domestic publics to defense spending and the pressure on international and bilateral channels have meant that only the most modern and efficient military production has survived in eastern Europe. These production capacities could well be adapted to the changed requirements of European security; the benefit of standardized equipment on joint peace efforts is just one example. And the opportunities to channel economic activity through overseas investment, to reward conversion efforts and participation in international control regimes, are at an all time high.

The situation in western Europe appears far more favorable. Ever since the revival of the European arms industries in the 1960s, the larger European states at least have pursued traditional national production autonomy or collaboration–cartel creation with selected European partners on the basis of equal return (*juste retour*).[76] But developments over the last decade give new impetus to plans for reductions and to prospects for multilateral cooperative control. Even before the Wall fell, economic forces had led to a remarkable consolidation of western European defense industries. In part, the cause was the small market size aggravated by the high ratio of fixed to variable production costs.[77] Adoption of the Single European Act in February 1986 increased the search for economies of scale and for ways to compete against American production giants in Europe and worldwide through aggressive consolidation. Governments and firms adopted somewhat contradictory two-pronged strategies: greater dependence on Europe-wide cooperation and transnational links among companies along with the selection or creation of large "national champions" or near monopolies structured at the national level in several key sectors.[78]

By the time of the security revolution of the 1990s, the result was a smaller, more visible production community. At most, France, Germany, and the United Kingdom still had independent arms production capabilities, and those were concentrated in a very small number of firms. As the new arms industry sector emerged, companies that survived the changing economic and political environment in Europe had oftentimes used mergers, joint ventures, and takeovers as methods of competing with American giants such as McDonnell Douglas and General Dynamics. In aerospace, for example, DASA of Germany purchased 51 percent of Fokker in 1992.[79] In military electronics comprehensive restructuring was illustrated by the fact that Thomson-CSF purchased seven defense-oriented companies in Europe and the United States from 1988 through 1991.[80]

More recent trends illustrate some striking changes. The number of interfirm agreements on technology transfers among members of the OECD has risen dramatically in the last two decades. Although there were only 156 such agreements in the pre-1972 period, there were nearly 2,000 in the four-year period between 1985 and 1988.[81] The pace of restructuring and internationalization in aerospace and military electronics has also been rapid, whereas in tanks and other military vehicles there has been less movement toward industry concentration. Shipbuilding, having suffered from significant overcapacities and drops in orders as far back as the 1970s, is fairly stagnant in terms of restructuring, but even in this sector international cooperation is common.

Consolidation has five specific benefits that could facilitate cooperative reduction of new weapons production and broader political and military integration in western Europe. First, it makes control easier, since the firms involved are highly visible and highly concentrated. The possibility of hiding production or indeed of secret research undertakings is largely ruled out by the new levels of prominence and transparency required of these firms under present and foreseeable community regulations. Second, except in France, few firms remain national champions in the traditional sense of having an iron claim on national spending or of being susceptible to national direction. These are unquestionably multinational firms with international allies and clienteles, unwilling and by now unable to be tied to purely national objectives or markets. This represents a fundamental change in arms industry–government relations.

Third, national production ambitions should fade in the face of the increasing trends toward more dual-use technologies and fewer government contracts. Internationalization of production necessitates greater cooperation in arms exports and specific arms transfers. As more firms engage in joint ventures in order to defray R&D costs, decisionmaking at the top levels is shared by international partners. Therefore, deciding which technologies to export will become an international activity, demanding ever broader consensus among governments and requiring new export control regimes. Economic forces may propel internationalization, and cooperation on a fundamentally political level will ensue.

The fourth advantage of arms industry consolidation is that as fewer firms are responsible for a greater percentage of European armaments, it will become easier to standardize military equipment and therefore training and exercises, and thus facilitate international cooperation in military ventures when the need arises. Finally, a greater degree of cooperation in Europe will eliminate duplicate production capabilities, thus saving much-needed resources for other uses.

Many of the most fundamental decisions about future European defense production will now be made at the level of these firms, not by national defense ministries. At issue will be which new technologies to exploit, in which markets to sell, and where to produce or pursue export sales. Cooperative multilateral mechanisms are the only means available to concerned governments that will ensure continuous monitoring of these activities and permit assessment of the risks and the benefits that may be involved. They are also the only instruments available to ensure the assignment of responsibility for production and sales decisions and the levying of penalties that will be appropriate to the scale of the activities involved. And they will have to be linked both to regional institutions and ultimately to a global network to permit the widest sharing of information and the earliest warning of armament concentrations and technology applications outside agreed boundaries.

Although cross-border cooperation among EC nations is certainly indicative of converging security interests and deeper political integration, it addresses only one dimension of internationalization. Because international collaboration has too often proved fragile and contentious, with too many teams competing for the same shrinking arms market, businesses are seeking more intense integration than ever before through joint ventures with shared equity and genuine corporate restructuring. Riven with delays, disagreements, cost overruns, and inefficiency, the floundering Eurofighter 2000, formerly known as the European Fighter Aircraft (EFA), is an example of a program that is encouraging other firms to seek cooperation in a manner that circumvents national political channels.[82]

All types of arms industry collaboration, both those initiated for political reasons at the government level and those designed by firms themselves, have sweeping arms export control implications. Not only can internationalization facilitate control as transparency increases, but collaborative production and procurement compel nations to cooperate on arms and technology transfer. The more deeply integrated the European defense community becomes, the more difficult it is to sell arms without a broad consensus among nations participating in any given program. Moreover, as a growing number of commercially available dual-use technologies emerge, and as eastern Europe, the CIS, and other lesser developed countries clamor for freer trade in the interest of economic development, the urgency to create new technology transfer regimes increases. So although the Eurofighter 2000 program illustrates that significant arms procurement decisions are still made on the national level, internationalization in which firms have equal decisionmaking power will propel cooperation not only on an economic level but also on a fundamentally political level.

Western European arms industry consolidation and integration is now at a crucial turning point. The end of the cold war budget cycle is in sight, and the next round of defense appropriations will be far less generous than the last. The question now is whether western and eastern European nations are willing to suffer the short-term costs of moving decisively toward greater international concentration of the arms industry, particularly in aerospace. If so, they will all have to yield some measure of sovereignty in arms procurement and export decisions to achieve meaningful defense conversion and downsizing of current overcapacities.

There are still barriers to be overcome. There is still the danger, for example, that the defense industry will dig in its heels, resist prevailing economic forces, and call for greater government protection in the interest of jobs and research advantages. The pressure is becoming intense. In aerospace, for example, there are now nine producers of medium-distance or regional passenger transport aircraft in the world, but according to experts, this number must be cut to three in a fairly short time, with only one European producer.[83] Although free-market forces may encourage further internationalization and rationalization of the arms industry, there is no guarantee that a reduction in arms production will result. In conspiracy with idiosyncratic and protective governments, arms industries in Europe and the United States may market their products more aggressively both domestically and abroad and, in the worst-case scenario, inadvertently foster regional arms races by facilitating continued arms accumulation.[84]

It is not clear which institution will adopt the responsibility of coordinating arms industry consolidation, but as argued above, in western Europe and perhaps beyond, the EC would be the exemplary locus of such efforts. It would allow comprehensive regulation and cooperation, especially in the thornier aspects of dual-use technologies, and provide the basis for later extension and expansion. Over the last several years, there has also been considerable European Commission and popular support for extending Community oversight into the defense sector, comparable to that which is now in place over purely civilian production. The move toward establishing common export controls for EC members is explained by the fact that "the application of 'export controls' on intra-EC trade in certain goods and technologies that can be used for both civilian and military purposes poses a problem for the completion of the internal market."[85] Such oversight will allow regulation at the firm level, whether the firm is national or multinational in character. The Community has also begun to work on common export control procedures and the training of national and company officials in overseeing declared end use.[86]

Clearly, arms industry consolidation is an area in which greater military security could develop, but only with rational strategic planning and even greater political consensus among European nations. Although economic forces demonstrate a natural trend toward financial and political integration through arms industry internationalization, inward-looking states could still choose to protect their industries rather than to act cooperatively. There would clearly also be a need for parallel constraints on American production and sales, and eventually on eastern Europe and Russia as well, if only to ensure a level playing field. Should sound strategic planning prevail, however, all of Europe stands to benefit from equipment standardization, comprehensive export controls, and a more efficient, less costly defense industry, all of which would contribute to greater cooperation and security.

Cooperation in Peacekeeping: The Long-Term Test

Cooperation in peacekeeping poses far more fundamental and difficult challenges to the emerging European security system. There is substantial planning and development currently under way, but no amount of cooperative strategizing among leaders can create the political will necessary to build a cohesive and credible security regime. The Gulf crisis and the Yugoslav debates show how difficult it is to ensure that even all EC members simultaneously recognize a threat and agree upon a response. The NATO collective security system turns on a direct attack on a member; anything else requires only political consultation. The Community is largely based on the free movement of people, goods, and services and the de facto eradication of political boundaries, but armed conflict inevitably comes back to national interests and borders. The failures in the former Yugoslavia color present assessments of what can be achieved through European interstate cooperation. Politicians need to continually gauge the political climate and public opinion to determine a workable policy. But one can still identify practical reasons why cooperation for intervention in Yugoslavia has not been more successful.

First, there should have been a better exchange of ideas and information across the Atlantic, particularly as the Clinton transition team prepared to take office. Early Eurocentrism succeeded only in shutting the United States out of a process in which it too might have been a more evenhanded peacebroker than Germany or the Community. Moreover, although there was initially a reluctance to use UN forces in the war because of the prevailing sense that Europe should handle the situation, the Europeans should have been more willing to exploit the UN's widely perceived neutrality.[87]

At present, the EC and indeed NATO seem neither prepared politically nor equipped militarily to deal with Yugoslav-like aggression or with the similar conflicts that have erupted within the FSU. Security decisions, particularly those involving the deployment of troops, are still made at a national level, and European populations appear still to want it that way. NATO and WEU have gone the farthest in articulating objectives through political debate and in conducting some preliminary planning for possible contingencies as well as support operations. But even in these interstate organizations, the initiatives consist of hedged guarantees, dependent on circumstance and state action, limited primarily to alliance territory, based on case-by-case decisions, and requiring unanimity. For now, no European state—East or West—is willing to make a binding commitment to future cooperation in peacekeeping in a way that would significantly limit its sovereign decisionmaking. And after the debate on peacekeeping in the fall of 1993, the United States is probably at least as unwilling to undertake noncontingent guarantees.

There are options for change in the future if the EC moves to more coordinated political choices and therefore to a more integrated security and foreign policy. Most recently, Belgium has said it would contribute forces to the Eurocorps, which will now reach 40,000 troops by 1995. Spearheaded by France and Germany, the Eurocorps will operate under NATO command in NATO actions and as a part of the WEU, ultimately subject to EC decisions, as well.[88] The strategic objective is to have specially trained troops that Europe could call upon to react rapidly, to provide humanitarian assistance before and during conflicts, or to ensure high-technology, real-time monitoring of cease-fire and conflict functions.

Progress will also come through a fundamental transformation of NATO structures and procedures. Selective participation will be appropriate under the new NATO Joint Task Force plans. But if the regime is to be credible, military commitments cannot be only crisis-specific but must function according to agreed-upon principles and prior planning and training. Both a negotiated U.S.-European agreement outlining a division of labor and a significant overlap of missions and capabilities between the European and American security pillars would seem appropriate. The new regime might establish separate but also joint priorities for each pillar and make arrangements for national, regional, or cooperative funding of key projects and activities that will be essential to an effective cooperative security organization. Viewed broadly, these indeed have been the tools with which the United States, as the leader of the alliance, worked for the past forty years to guarantee cooperation among states with varying economic and military capabilities, including those with and without nuclear weapons. They must now be reshaped and extended.

A plausible alternative would be to give NATO primary responsibility for the security dialogue with central Europe and the republics of the FSU. The WEU would thus function primarily as NATO's European pillar. In this instance, NATO would provide the decisionmaking forum for both Americans and Europeans on three key issues: (1) laying the groundwork for inclusion of the East in peacekeeping and peacemaking within Europe and in those areas that constitute a direct security threat to a broadened zone of peace; (2) maintaining a military dialogue with and providing technical and financial assistance to the East on central questions such as the democratization of security and defense restructuring; and (3) conducting operational activities on behalf of the CSCE and the UN in situations of direct crisis management.

To do this would require a range of new military links to the East going substantially beyond present plans for unit exchanges, joint training, and joint school preparation for officers. At a minimum, it would mean regular transatlantic political consultation and a permanent European-American policy forum, as well as maintenance of key aspects of NATO's present integrated command and SHAPE's planning functions. In addition, it would probably involve some cross-Atlantic deployments and training, as well as preservation of an American presence on the continent.

Achievement of these outcomes will mark a decisive break with past European military tradition. Few European militaries have been trained for or have participated in UN or other peacekeeping missions in the past.[89] At home such functions have often been assigned to gendarmerie or "third force" units; militaries have been involved in peacekeeping almost exclusively in colonial crises, hardly the best model. In the few exceptions in Europe—as in Northern Ireland—there have been dramatic demonstrations of the need for intensive training of nonconscript, long-serving soldiers and for frequent rotation and political communication. Joint training and continuing cooperation in the acquisition and the development of equipment particularly suited to peacekeeping tasks will also be important new departures.

Some argue that Europe-wide cooperation might be easier if there were a clearer differentiation made between crisis and conflict intervention or at least clearer distinctions established among the quite different functions and risks now loosely defined as "peacekeeping." Only a small number of these actually fit within the framework of the classic, UN-style peacekeeping operation, the monitoring of a negotiated peace or a cease-fire agreement.

The lessons of the Yugoslav crisis suggest that the demands on European states are more likely to be for joint action at an early stage for crisis prevention, and then for conflict management and resolution. As is currently being practiced under the CSCE, the classic peacekeeping instruments are almost all nonmilitary, including fact finding, mediation and arbitration, or helping to press for and negotiate a settlement. Quite separate, the argument runs, would be those political and military functions at the core of a collective security regime: joint action to achieve conflict management or the containment of horizontal or vertical escalation. A more demanding requirement would be for forces and policies to support peacemaking or the enforcement of an international decision against warring parties. This function clearly would involve a NATO-wide commitment to act within a specific region (as in Article 5) and with clear structures for decisions and command. States that are participants in a broader cooperative security regime could and probably would want to take far more limited roles, perhaps involving only attempts to ensure transparency and humanitarian assistance.

From the vantage point of 1994, there seems little reason to expect the rapid evolution of a Europe-wide system that involves joint standing forces dedicated to peacekeeping or procedures for large-scale, automatic cooperative involvement in emerging conflict, either globally or along Europe's borders. As Bosnia has demonstrated, even in the simpler, nonmilitary aspects and in the initial stages of a conflict, cooperative peacekeeping requires the ability to identify and to react jointly to risk on the basis of broad political agreement on goals, outcomes, and deep mutual confidence and trust. Democracies and states with conscript forces require the tolerance, or, better, the political support of populations for action in the present as well as for that which may be needed if the conflict widens or deepens and if the political and military costs mount. Without these elements, cooperation is achieved only through negotiation, often protracted and subject to the distractions and delays of democracies and sometimes disrupted by the demands or intransigencies of several powerful states.

What this means in most cases is that there is a limit to the essentially functionalist integration argument inherent in the present European cooperative security regime—at least for the present. If at all, action will be taken by individual states, perhaps in different coalitions in each case, who decide to act. This may not necessarily ensure timely crisis intervention or effective peacekeeping, given the stringent demands cooperation will impose on the maintenance and performance of interstate coalitions. The Bosnian experience shows that supplying protection for relief aid, especially under attack, involves a myriad of linked or contingent decisions. What is its operational goal—to protect the convoys, the recipients of the convoys, or both? Is this to be done on the ground or with overflights? Within a narrow territorial band or for the long-range identification of attackers (for example, AWACS) and the launching of counterattacks? What about hot pursuit? What is the appropriate level of response—equal to the attack, deterrent, or preemptive? Within what time period? In the face of a further escalatory move?

Moreover, once there is direct conflict, there are few moves to be made at any level without the trust or the exhaustion of the belligerents. Humanitarian aid missions, for example, almost always constitute political intervention on one side. Assistance is rarely neutral, since it clearly involves military benefits (for example, food aid for a besieged population delays surrender) or generally implies an international ascription of blame. And humanitarian missions may become appealing targets for an adversary who sees there is little still to be lost internationally, who is determined to demonstrate resolve, or who inflicts punishment on "outsiders" in order to influence their domestic publics.

Cooperative intervention by only a few self-selected states—that is, without legitimation through the UN, NATO, or the EC—is clearly one solution. Separable (but not separate) forces within a joint framework can function in some cases and for the immediate future. But in terms of constructing and extending eastward a cooperative security regime, intervention à la carte would seem of little lasting political value in the probable and problematic crises in the post–cold war European order: ethnic conflicts that escalate, conflicts that involve the protection of ethnic diasporas outside national boundaries, and border fights or refugee streams. Intervention for the objective protection of minorities from repression may become a more widespread European norm in line with the CSCE principles and the Wilsonesque statements by German officials in the rush of post-Wall euphoria. There must also be an answer for the several states that oppose any early action because they feel vulnerable to the setting of any precedent regarding national policy toward minorities—Britain, Romania, and Slovakia, to name only three present cases. The prospects for success may well be few; all that outside parties and institutions can provide is a framework for settlement and peacekeeping once the fighting stops.

But in those cases for which there is a chance, the key would seem to be organization of the broadest possible cooperative agreement on early nonmilitary intervention. This means early consultation and full information sharing, early offers of mediation and nonmilitary incentives toward peace, and credible cooperative resolve against conflict. These are precisely the steps that require political choice, for which organizational frameworks become relevant and necessary only after the decision to cooperate has been made. Integration of the transformed NATO-CSCE frameworks would seem to be the answer, for they have sufficient capacity if the political will for early action exists.

European leaders should continue developing cooperative security regimes but without raising expectations that go beyond the political mandate established jointly. What is needed is leadership to mobilize support for cooperation within an agreed-upon framework, not automatic or organizational predisposition to a set of fixed responses. Some EC states indeed fear that conditions set out in Maastricht will "compel the reluctant to act against the will of their electorates."[90] Military operations are still inherently national. Without political consensus, risking and possibly losing the lives of a multinational force, even in monitoring or extended humanitarian missions, could undermine the credibility of cooperative security efforts as a whole. Under present conditions, the ultimate challenge in the former Yugoslavia and elsewhere is to take early preventive action in a crisis and, if possible, to build on economic and cooperative military relations to provide options for peaceful conflict resolutions.

Epilogue

As President Clinton ended his first year in office, the cooperative security regime that has evolved in Europe and across the Northern Hemisphere faced challenges and opportunities greater than at any time in the postwar period. From a point of low expectations and even lower public support, there has emerged a complex, interwoven system of institutions and capabilities that might be activated to meet most security requirements in the present era of relative peace in Europe. Short of massive civil unrest in Russia or global conflict, parts of the system now in place can be used to organize the limitation of offensive capabilities, provide mechanisms of reassurance against fears of surprise attack or fast-moving hostile action, and achieve transparency and verification in real time.

What is lacking at present is the political will to take on this task—in its entirety or even in some of its critical dimensions. There are political and economic costs, above all the stretching of consensus among domestic publics weary from cold war burdens. What appears in the wake of the horrors of Bosnia to be the necessary inclusion of some collective security elements is the subject of great debate and even greater reluctance and political resistance. There is no new overarching definition of security that seems adequate to justify actions or prepare publics for contingencies beyond state borders.

Once again, the critical factor is leadership. It is a role, a task, a burden that many believe is now uniquely that of the United States. Events in the Gulf, Somalia, and Bosnia suggest now even more strongly that where the United States does not lead, Europe, East and West, does not follow.[91] And the chance that this allocation of burden will change, at least in the foreseeable future, seems slim.

At the most basic level, the choices to be made are remarkably parallel to those open at the end of another war—the hot conflict of 1939–45. The arguments for action and inaction are the same; the resources, political and economic, needed for success are of comparable magnitude. The preferred instruments are also similar—international and multilateral institution building, cooperation rather than competition, democratization and economic prosperity as the lodestones of security. Few states in history have had the luxury of confronting the same choices twice, and perhaps on even more favorable terms the second time.

There is every reason to support and to extend the present cooperative security regime in Europe. All states involved must take robust action that reflects the belief that the benefits of cooperative security continue to outweigh the risks and that the increasingly sensitive issues of molding unilateral prerogatives with multilateral processes of consultation and decision must be confronted. The available alternatives—the loss of transparency and confidence, the threat of widespread renationalization of security and defense policy, especially in Germany and the East—are hardly attractive. The deadline for developing an extended cooperative security strategy is not fixed, but there seems little reason to suggest that more time will make the tasks smaller or easier. The choice seems clear.

Appendix: Membership in Atlantic and European Security Organizations

WEU: Full members (10): Belgium, France, Germany, Greece, Italy, Luxembourg, the Netherlands, Portugal, Spain, United Kingdom. Associate members (3): Iceland, Norway, Turkey. Observers (2): Denmark, Ireland.

NATO: (16) All full members of WEU and Canada, Denmark, Iceland, Norway, Turkey, United States.

NATO Quad: (4) France, Germany, United Kingdom, United States.

NATO Quint: (5) All members of NATO Quad and Italy.

NACC: (38) All members of NATO; the former Warsaw Pact members and former Soviet republics (Armenia, Azerbaijan, Belarus, Georgia, Kazakhstan, Kyrgyzstan, Moldova, Russia, Tajikistan, Turkmenistan, Ukraine, Uzbekistan [CIS]; Bulgaria, Czech Republic, Estonia, Hungary, Latvia, Lithuania, Poland, Romania, Slovakia); and Albania.

CSCE: (52 active members, 53 counting Serbia or rump Yugoslavia) All 16 members of NATO, those states on the territory of the former Warsaw Pact: Armenia, Azerbaijan, Belarus, Georgia, Kazakhstan, Kyrgyzstan, Moldova, Russia, Tajikistan, Turkmenistan, Ukraine, Uzbekistan [CIS], Bulgaria, Czech Republic, Estonia, Hungary, Latvia, Lithuania, Poland, Romania, Slovakia; and Albania, Austria, Bosnia-Herzegovina, Croatia, Cyprus, Finland, Ireland, Liechtenstein, Malta, Monaco, San Marino, Slovenia, Sweden, Switzerland, Vatican, Serbia or rump Yugoslavia (suspended).

European Community: (12) Belgium, Denmark, France, Germany, Greece, Ireland, Italy, Luxembourg, Netherlands, Portugal, Spain, United Kingdom.

European Free Trade Association: (7) Austria, Finland, Iceland, Liechtenstein, Norway, Sweden, Switzerland.

Group of Seven, or G-7: (7) Canada, France, Germany, Italy, Japan, United Kingdom, United States.

Group of Twenty-four, or G-24: (24) 16 members of NATO and Australia, Austria, Finland, Japan, Ireland, New Zealand, Sweden, Switzerland. Same as Organization for Economic Cooperation and Development (OECD).

Notes

1. See also the related research reported in Catherine McArdle Kelleher, "A Renewed Security Partnership? The United States and the European Community in the 1990s," *Brookings Review,* vol. 11 (Fall 1993) pp. 30–35; and Kelleher, *A New Security Order: The United States and the European Community in the 1990s,* Occasional Paper (Pittsburgh: European Community Studies Association, June 1993).

2. See the related essay by Paul B. Stares and John D. Steinbruner, "Cooperative Security in the New Europe," in Paul B. Stares, ed., *The New Germany and the New Europe* (Brookings, 1992), pp. 218–48.

3. This argument partially disputes the "long peace" argument of John Gaddis: that peace came not in spite of but because of East-West nuclear confrontation in which the stakes were so high (nuclear risks plus the military and political devastation of two world wars) that no one dared go to war. See John Lewis Gaddis, *The Long Peace: Inquiries into the History of the Cold War* (Oxford University Press, 1987), especially pp. 215–45.

4. The judgment is that of Raymond Aron, *The Century of Total War* (Westport, Conn.: Greenwood Press, 1981), p. 302.

5. This construct is, of course, the "nonzero sum" construct that was at the core of the Palme Commission's plan for common security. See Independent Commission on Disarmament and Security Issues, *Common Security: A Blueprint for Survival* (Simon and Schuster, 1982).

6. A sympathetic but nonideological account of the European experience is Derek W. Urwin, *The Community of Europe: A History of European Integration since 1945* (New York: Longman, 1991).

7. Under Article 5, each state pledged to regard attacks on other members as an attack on itself and to take appropriate action. See *North Atlantic Treaty Organization: Facts and Figures,* 11th ed. (Brussels: NATO Information Service, 1989), p. 377.

8. It is worth noting that the only institutional arrangement actually required by the North Atlantic Treaty is the North Atlantic Council. Everything else in NATO was created after treaty ratification to enhance cooperation, interdependence, and multilateral oversight.

9. The Genscher-Colombo proposal was put forth by Hans-Dietrich Genscher and Emilio Colombo in 1981. Although the initiative failed, many analysts view such cooperative efforts as a means through which prospects for a common security and foreign policy have gradually developed in Europe. See Lily Gardner Feldman, "The EC in the International Arena: A New Activism?" *Europe and the United States: Competition and Cooperation in the 1990s,* House Committee on Foreign Affairs, 102 Cong. 2 sess. (Government Printing Office, June 1992), p. 143; and Anne-Marie Le Gloannec, "The Implications of German Unification for Western Europe," in Stares, ed., *New Germany and the New Europe,* p. 257.

10. Karl W. Deutsch and others, *Political Community and the North Atlantic Area: International Organization in Light of Historical Experience* (Greenwood Press, 1969), especially pp. 123ff.

11. On American perceptions of these ties see Catherine McArdle Kelleher, "America Looks at Europe," in Lawrence Freedman, ed., *The Troubled Alliance: Atlantic Relations in the 1980s* (St. Martin's Press, 1983), pp. 44–66.

12. See Paul B. Stares, *Command Performance: The Neglected Dimension of European Security* (Brookings, 1991), pp. 82–125.

13. Catherine McArdle Kelleher, "Arms Control in a Revolutionary Future: Europe," *Daedalus* (special issue, *Arms Control: Thirty Years On*), vol. 120 (Winter 1991), pp. 111–31. The CSCE is best understood in its initial phases as a limited consensus emerging from divergent goals—for the Soviet Union, the political legitimation of the status quo; for the United States, the cost of stabilizing military relationships in the MBFR; for the western Europeans, the humanitarian but also political imperatives to overcome the division of Europe and especially the division of Germany. See the discussion of these continuing divergences in two volumes by Vojtech Mastny: *Helsinki, Human Rights, and European Security: Analysis and Documentation* (Duke University Press, 1986); and *The Helsinki Process and the Reintegration of Europe, 1986–1991: Analysis and Documentation* (New York University Press, 1992).

14. For more on the INF, see the interview with Catherine McArdle Kelleher and others, "Will the Reagan Administration Accept Its Own INF Proposal?" *Arms Control Today*, vol. 17 (April 1987), pp. 2–7. For more on the CFE, see Ivo H. Daalder, *The CFE Treaty: An Overview and an Assessment* (Washington: Johns Hopkins Foreign Policy Institute, 1991); the articles and books of Jonathan Dean, especially Jonathan Dean and Peter Clausen, *The INF Treaty and the Future of Western Security* (Washington: Union of Concerned Scientists, 1988); and the following definitive chapters by Jane M. O. Sharp: "Conventional Arms Control in Europe: Problems and Prospects," in *S[tockholm] I[nternational] P[eace] R[esearch] I[nstitute] Yearbook 1988: World Armaments and Disarmament* (Oxford University Press, 1988), pp. 315–37; "Conventional Arms Control in Europe," *SIPRI Yearbook 1989: World Armaments and Disarmament* (Oxford University Press, 1989), pp. 369–402; "Conventional Arms Control in Europe," *SIPRI Yearbook 1990: World Armaments and Disarmament* (Oxford University Press, 1990), pp. 459–507; "Conventional Arms Control in Europe," *SIPRI Yearbook 1991: World Armaments and Disarmament* (Oxford University Press, 1991), pp. 407–60; "Conventional Arms Control in Europe: Developments and Prospects in 1991," *SIPRI Yearbook 1992: World Armaments and Disarmament* (Oxford University Press, 1992), pp. 459–79; and "Conventional Arms Control in Europe," *SIPRI Yearbook 1993: World Armaments and Disarmament* (Oxford University Press, 1993), pp. 591–617.

15. On the evolution of the CSCE, see John Borawski, ed., *Avoiding War in the Nuclear Age: Confidence-Building Measures for Crisis Stability* (Boulder, Colo.: Westview Press, 1986), especially p. 25; and James E. Goodby, *CSCE: The Diplomacy of Europe Whole and Free,* Occasional Paper (Washington: Atlantic Council of the United States, July 1990). For specifics on what was actually done, see the annual compilation of activities, exercises, and inspections in *Arms Control Reporter* (Cambridge, Mass.: Institute for Defense and Disarmament Studies, 1986–92), sections 402 and 407 from 1988 on.

16. Stockholm indeed represented a decisive blurring of the earlier arms control–CSCE division. Since all other arms control talks were broken off during the INF crisis and because of the coming "second cold war" in the 1980s, it became a primary channel for the East-West security dialogue. On the Stockholm Conference, see Victor-Yves

Ghebali, *Confidence-Building Measures within the CSCE Process: Paragraph-by-Paragraph Analysis of the Helsinki and Stockholm Regimes,* UNIDIR Research Paper 3, UNIDIR/89/14 (New York: United Nations, March 1989), especially pp. 25–98. On the Vienna Conference, see John Borawski, *Security for a New Europe: The Vienna Negotiations on Confidence- and Security-Building Measures 1989–1990, and Beyond* (London: Brassey's, 1992).

17. The CFE treaty has an unusual diplomatic history. The original treaty was signed on November 19, 1990, with certain treaty functions entering into force at signature: data exchanges, notifications, and the Joint Consultative Group for the resolution of implementation questions and difficulties. The collapse of the Warsaw Pact was accompanied by the Budapest agreement of November 1990, which set CFE restrictions and verification procedures for the five non-Soviet Warsaw Treaty Organization states. See Richard Albert Falkenrath, "The Entry into Force of the CFE Treaty," in Lawrence Freedman, Catherine Kelleher, and Jane Sharp, eds., *CFE and the Future of Conventional Arms Control* (forthcoming). The breakup of the Soviet Union led to the Tashkent agreement in May 1992 among eight successor states (Russia, Ukraine, Belarus, Armenia, Azerbaijan, Georgia, Kazakhstan, Moldova), which divided up the CFE limits and the responsibilities agreed to by the Soviet Union. The revised treaty, incorporating the Budapest and Tashkent accords, was signed by all twenty-nine states on July 10, 1992, with provisional entry into force commencing on July 17, 1992. The treaty entered into de jure force on November 9, 1992, and was expanded to thirty signatories in January 1993 to allow accession by the now-divided Czech Republic and Slovakia.

18. According to the U.S. State Department, by October 1993 twenty-seven states had signed the Open Skies Treaty, but only eight states had ratified it (Canada, France, Denmark, the Czech Republic, Slovakia, Hungary, Greece, Norway). "[The] Treaty enters into force after ratification of 20 states [including Canada and Hungary] and all signatories with a passive inspection of quota of more than 8." *Arms Control Reporter 1992,* p. 409.A.4. The duration of the Open Skies Treaty is unlimited; the first review conference will convene three years after initial enactment, and then every five years afterward. For a detailed analysis of ways in which Open Skies agreements may be used to enhance transparency and stability, see Michael Krepon and Amy E. Smithson, eds., *Open Skies, Arms Control and Cooperative Security* (St. Martin's Press for the Henry L. Stimson Center, 1992). For additional information on the development of the CSCE, see Ivo H. Daalder, *Cooperative Arms Control: A New Agenda for the Post–Cold War Era* (College Park, Md.: Center for International Security Studies at Maryland, October 1992); and Adam Daniel Rotfeld, "The CSCE: Towards a Security Organization," *SIPRI Yearbook 1993,* pp. 171–89.

19. On the CFE's evolution see the essays of analysts and practitioners prepared for the Ford Foundation Project on Conventional Arms Control (King's College, London: July 13–14, 1993), and collected in Freedman, Kelleher, and Sharp, eds., *CFE and the Future of Conventional Arms Control.*

20. Interview with Dorn Crawford, August 1993.

21. See the critiques cited in Sharp, "Conventional Arms Control in Europe," *SIPRI Yearbook 1992,* pp. 459–75.

22. For more information on CFE implementation in the CIS, see Falkenrath, "Entry into Force of the CFE Treaty."

23. Increasing problems related to the breakup of the Soviet Union necessitated the Tashkent summit on May 15, 1992. At Tashkent, the CIS states agreed to a revised allocation of treaty-limited equipment (TLE) under the CFE treaty, obfuscating the final

obstacle that until then had prevented some countries from ratifying the CFE. For more information, see *Arms Control Reporter 1993*, p. 407.A.3.

24. The "naval" TLE was eventually counted back against the Russian ceilings. In early June 1991 Gorbachev ordered the military to accept the CFE treaty and, through Foreign Minister Alexander Bessmertnykh, promised that the TLE east of the Urals would be either destroyed, used to replace or repair old equipment, transferred to units in Asia or stored in ways that prevented the creation of a new strategic reserve. However, there was nothing illegal about the transfer of Soviet equipment outside the ATTU before the CFE signature, and, in fact, many of the Russian reductions had been promised on a unilateral basis. See Sharp, "Conventional Arms Control in Europe," *SIPRI Yearbook 1992,* p. 463, and the formal Russian statements on these issues reprinted in *The CFE Treaty,* Hearings before the Senate Subcommittee on European Affairs of the Foreign Relations Committee, 102 Cong. 1 sess. (GPO, March–July 1991), pp. 363ff. For a more recent account of Russian requests to alter the conditions of the CFE treaty, particularly the desire to base higher levels of equipment in Russia and in the Caucasus region, see Daniel Sneider, "Russia Seeks CFE Changes As Warfare Rages at Border," *Defense News,* August 2–8, 1993, p. 4.

25. Other complaints attributed to the Russian military include (1) the unwillingness to assume responsibility for that part of Russian TLE stationed in the NIS that was missing or has been diverted by republican forces; (2) dissatisfaction with the inspection rights on Russian territory that the CFE grants to the former Warsaw Pact and eventually the republics, especially those now engaged in conflict with Russian forces involved; and (3) affront at external controls on the disposition of Russian forces on Russian territory without parallel constraints on the United States.

26. These requests were made at the September 13 meeting of the JCG in Vienna. For more information, see Craig R. Whitney, "From Russia, a Bid to Increase Arms in Caucasus," *New York Times,* October 7, 1993, p. A9; and Barbara Starr, "Russia Still Looking to Amend CFE Treaty," *Jane's Defence Weekly,* September 18, 1993, p. 7.

27. For more information, see Lee Feinstein, "CFE: Off the Endangered List?" *Arms Control Today,* vol. 23 (October 1993), pp. 3–6.

28. Michael J. McNerney and Andrew C. Winner, "The Interaction of Politics and Arms Control: The Turning Points of CFE," in Freedman, Kelleher, and Sharp, eds., *CFE and the Future of Conventional Arms Control.*

29. This is clearly the case in the northern flank zone and especially along the Finno-Russian border, and there are some grounds to accept the Russian military's formula of imbalance along the Caucasus fault lines.

30. See *Arms Control Reporter 1992,* p. 407.B.483. This represents a significant change beyond the CSCE procedures under which members of the same alliance agreed not to inspect one another. Each state is allowed the right to conduct five inspections of members within the same group. Although former WTO states have exercised the new right, NATO has held to the earlier Stockholm Document standard, in part to avoid additional tension between Greece and Turkey but also to maximize the possibility of observing every destruction event within the quota system. They have even invited non-NATO states to become part of the multilateral NATO missions, since intragroup inspections also count against the total number of inspections any country is bound to accept. *Arms Control Reporter 1993,* pp. 407.B.490–91.

31. Involved are the American and Russian satellite systems; the HELIOS system of France, Italy, and Spain; and the commercial, lower-resolution, but still quite adequate services of Russia and the French SPOT system. Critics point out, however, that this still leaves the smaller states at the mercy of the observing nation's interests—for example,

U.S. attention to Iraq in 1990 meant fewer resources devoted to observing the Soviet removal of equipment east of the Urals.

32. *Arms Control Reporter 1993,* p. 407.A.4.

33. Sharp, "Conventional Arms Control in Europe," *SIPRI Yearbook 1992,* p. 476.

34. Signatories include the sixteen NATO members, five former non-Soviet WTO states, and four former Soviet republics (Russia, Belarus, Ukraine, and eventually Georgia). See Richard Kokoski, "The Treaty on Open Skies," *SIPRI Yearbook 1993,* p. 633.

35. Jonathan Tucker points out that this treaty was the first signed by a unified Germany and the newly independent states of the former Soviet Union, thus symbolizing the dramatic transformation of Europe. Jonathan B. Tucker, "Negotiating Open Skies: A Diplomatic History," in Krepon and Smithson, eds., *Open Skies,* pp. 5–50, especially pp. 5, 44.

36. Michael Krepon and Amy E. Smithson, "Introduction," in ibid., p. 3. Hungary was especially receptive to President Bush's proposal in 1989 and consequently initiated the first two major conferences on Open Skies in Ottawa and Budapest. Wanting to enhance their own security and set a precedent for the rest of Europe, Hungary and Romania agreed to a bilateral treaty that provides for four overflights a year per country, each flight lasting three hours or covering 1,200 kilometers, whichever expires first. The agreement is impressive because the Hungarian-Romanian relationship has been acrimonious, and the agreement requires a high degree of openness, sophisticated communication, and close coordination, even down to the level of technical personnel. For more information, see Morton Krasznai, "Cooperative Bilateral Aerial Inspections: The Hungarian-Romanian Experience," in Krepon and Smithson, *Open Skies,* pp. 135–46.

37. Data obtained from Sharp, "Conventional Arms Control in Europe," *SIPRI Yearbook 1992,* p. 479.

38. The Vienna Document 1990 was not a new initiative but rather an extension of the 1986 Stockholm Document, and as the process continued to evolve, first at Helsinki in 1992 and next toward Budapest in 1994, new provisions have been added to enhance openness and stability.

39. For a more detailed analysis of how these provisions were carried out, see Zdzislaw Lachowski, "Implementation of the Vienna Document 1990 in 1991," *SIPRI Yearbook 1992,* p. 481, and the similar chapter of Lachowski, "The Vienna Confidence- and Security-Building Measures in 1992," *SIPRI Yearbook 1993,* pp. 618–31.

40. For a more detailed account of these provisions, see *Arms Control Reporter 1992,* p. 402.B.297–98.

41. Lachowski, "Vienna Confidence- and Security-Building Measures in 1992," pp. 626–27.

42. At the second meeting of the CSCE Council of Ministers in Prague in January 1992, it was set forth that new member states had to accept in their entirety all the "CSCE commitments and responsibilities." See the meeting's "Summary of Conclusions," reprinted in *SIPRI Yearbook 1992,* pp. 584–85.

43. These centers were set forth in the "Charter of Paris for a New Europe of November 21, 1990," and its "Supplementary Document to Give Effect to Certain Provisions Contained in the Charter of Paris for a New Europe," both reprinted in Adam Daniel Rotfeld and Walther Stützle, eds., *Germany and Europe in Transition* (Oxford University Press, 1991), pp. 219–30. They were also taken up at the Prague CSCE Council meeting on January 30–31, 1992; see Adam Daniel Rotfeld, "CSCE: Continuity and Change," in Ian M. Cuthbertson, ed., *Redefining the CSCE: Challenges and Opportunities in the New Europe* (New York: Institute for East West Studies, 1992), pp. 43–68, especially p. 54. The charter also provided for the Parliamentary Assembly, and the Court of Conciliation and Arbitration was based on an earlier Franco-German proposal

to extend the Valletta process formally adopted at the CSCE's Berlin meeting in June 1991.

44. This evolved in a series of moves beginning with the Charter of Paris of November 1990 and culminating in the Helsinki Declaration and Decisions of July 9, 1992. See *Arms Control Reporter* (1990–92), section 402, for sources and specific details. For a reflection on the evolving CSCE norms on the use of force, see Ingo Peters, "Normen- und Institutionenbildung der KSZE im Widerstreit politischer Interessen," in Bernard von Plate (Hrsg.), *Europa auf dem Wege zur kollektiven Sicherheit? konzeptionelle und organisatorische Entwicklungen im Umgang mit der veränderten Sicherheitslage* (Baden-Baden: Nomos-Verlag, 1993).

45. There is now a process by which an emergency meeting can be requested by one state and convened if at least twelve other states support it, decided on at the Berlin CSCE Council Meeting in June 1991. Rotfeld, "The CSCE: Towards a Security Organization," p. 173. At the Prague Council of Ministers Meeting in January 1992, the new decisionmaking process of "consensus minus one" was agreed upon, which allows the council to react to major violations of CSCE commitments in the area of human rights, democracy, and the rule of law without reaching complete consensus. Its actions, however, may be only declarations or steps applicable outside the concerned country, not peacekeeping or peacemaking actions.

46. See the arguments put forth by Rotfeld in "The CSCE: Towards a security organization," pp. 171–72.

47. The Prague Council meeting in January 1992 expanded membership in the CSCE to the republics of the former Soviet Union. They had to sign on to all commitments and responsibilities of the organization, and they "declared their determination to act in accordance with" commitments outlined in the Vienna Documents of 1990 and 1992, including the requirements of CSBMs and ratification of the CFE treaty. Ibid., p. 184.

48. The mandate for the FSC was included as chapter 5 in the decisions section of the CSCE Helsinki Document 1992, adopted at the July 9–10 Helsinki Summit. See *Conference on Security and Cooperation in Europe: The Helsinki Document 1992: The Challenges of Change* (Washington: U.S. Arms Control and Disarmament Agency [1992]), pp. 22–30 (hereafter *Helsinki Document 1992*). It also emphasizes cooperation on questions of nonproliferation, global data exchanges, defense conversion, and regional security issues or "specific security problems for example in relation to border areas" (section B.11).

49. The Helsinki Summit Declaration, July 9–10, 1992, not only provides a formal basis for collective security actions but also will presumably provide political cover for states such as Germany that are tied—formally or informally—to action only within the UN framework. See *Arms Control Reporter 1992*, p. 402.B.308.

50. *Rome Declaration on Peace and Cooperation* (Brussels: NATO Office of Information and Press, November 1991). Just what was to constitute balance among which forces was deliberately left vague.

51. Ibid., p. 3.

52. In the fall of 1993, the NACC included thirty-eight participants—all the NATO, WTO, and CIS states, with some of the neutral and nonaligned nations accorded observer status. It meets regularly in Brussels on the ambassadorial level and through liaison-observer status in NATO subordinate committees, as well as at the highest level of defense and foreign ministers, and through informal consultations and briefings. For insight into the background and evolution of the NACC initiative, see Stephen J. Flanagan, "NATO and Central and Eastern Europe: From Liaison to Security Partnership," *Washington Quarterly,* vol. 15 (Spring 1992), pp. 141–51; and "North Atlantic Cooperation Council Statement on Dialogue, Partnership and Cooperation, Brussels,

20 Dec 1991," in SSI Special Report, *NATO Documents pertaining to European Security, 1991* (Carlisle, Pa.: Strategic Studies Institute of the Army War College, 1992), pp. 53–57. There are, of course, practical limits on the NACC—for example, the problems that some of the easternmost CIS states face, given their lack of hard currency to cover representation costs and the scarcity of trained, expert personnel.

53. For more information on the background, see Daniel Burroughs, "Joining the Club: NATO Debates Terms for Welcoming Former Foes," *Armed Forces Journal,* December 1993, p. 25.

54. For more discussion of these issues see Kelleher, *A New Security Order.*

55. Background on both the original Franco-German proposal to the Dutch president of the European Council of October 14, 1991, and the follow-up proposal announced at La Rochelle on May 22, 1992, are traced in Karen E. Donfried's comprehensive analysis in "The Franco-German Eurocorps: Implications for the U.S. Security Role in Europe," *CRS Report* (Congressional Research Service, October 22, 1992).

56. See the important commentaries on the new European security policy competencies by Lily Gardner Feldman, "The EC in the International Arena: A New Activism?" Roy H. Ginsberg, "Political Union," and Stanley R. Sloan, "U.S.-West European Relations and Europe's Future," in *Europe and the United States: Competition and Cooperation in the 1990s,* Study Papers submitted to the Subcommittee on International Economic Policy and Trade and the Subcommittee on Europe and the Middle East of the House Committee on Foreign Affairs, 102 Cong. 2 sess. (GPO, June 1992), pp. 97–107, 141–76; and the detailed historical account in Anthony Forster, Anand Menon, and William Wallace, "A Common European Defence?" *Survival,* vol. 34 (Autumn 1992), pp. 98–118.

57. France has since agreed that the Franco-German Eurocorps can operate under NATO command. Michael Mecham, "NATO Gets Commitment from Franco-German Corps," *Aviation Week and Space Technology,* vol. 137 (December 7, 1992), p. 27.

58. For a comprehensive review of the recent compromises, see Edward Mortimer, *European Security after the Cold War,* Adelphi Paper 271 (London: International Institute for Strategic Studies, Summer 1992), especially pp. 47–65.

59. For the political background to the declaration, see Robert Mauthner, "WEU to Be Given Military Units for Peacekeeping Role," *Financial Times,* June 20, 1992, p. 3. The December meeting of the NATO Council also received a memo from Germany and France stressing that the Eurocorps can operate under NATO command, thus ending considerable transatlantic irritation. See Mecham, "NATO Gets Commitment." The WEU has also tried to find a niche between the CSCE and the NACC in providing security links to the democratizing East. It allowed for an expanded membership only within Europe (for example, Greece) and created the new mechanism of the WEU Forum of Consultation for association only with eight central and eastern European countries.

60. The argument of German defense minister Volker Rühe, quoted by Steve Vogel in "West European Force to be Formed; Nine Nations Take Step to Establish Common Security System," *Washington Post,* June 20, 1992, p. A18.

61. For brief critical reviews of the role of European institutions in Yugoslavia, see James E. Goodby, "Peacekeeping in the New Europe," *Washington Quarterly,* vol. 15 (Spring 1992), pp. 153–71; and Hugh Miall, *New Conflicts in Europe: Prevention and Resolution,* Current Decisions Report 10 (Oxford Research Group, July 1992), pp. 1–6.

62. The London Conference on the Former Yugoslavia was held August 26–27, 1992. It was cochaired by the secretary-general of the UN and the president of the European Council of Ministers.

63. See Catherine M. Kelleher, "Security in the New Order: Presidents, Polls, and the Use of Force," in Daniel Yankelovich and I. M. Destler, eds., *Beyond the Beltway: Engaging the Public in U.S. Foreign Policy* (Norton, forthcoming).

64. See particularly Foreign Minister Genscher's speech at the opening of the CSCE Follow-Up Meeting in Helsinki, March 24, 1992. It echoes themes that the foreign minister sounded in his February 1987 speech at Davos, reproduced in Hans-Dietrich Genscher, *Unterwegs zur Einheit, Reden und Dokumente aus bewegter Zeit* (Berlin: Siedler Verlag, 1991), pp. 137–50; and the address to a conference of the Tutzing Protestant Academy of January 31, 1990, reproduced in Lawrence Freedman, ed., *Europe Transformed: Documents on the End of the Cold War* (St. Martin's Press, 1990), pp. 436–45.

65. See Alan Riding, "Europeans in Accord to Create Vastly Expanded Trading Bloc," *New York Times*, October 23, 1991, p. A1.

66. I extend my appreciation to Stephen Flanagan for stressing this point.

67. This battle has been evident in formal and informal exchanges in almost every European-American channel since the Berlin Wall fell. Perhaps the sharpest remarks came in two confidential letters: the so-called Bartholomew letter of February 1991, written to the European governments that were both NATO and WEU members, cautioning against the independent evolution of WEU competencies; and the spring 1992 letter of Robert Zoellick, undersecretary of state for economic affairs, to selected German officials cautioning against the evolution of a Franco-German corps outside the NATO command structure. Interview sources in Bonn and Washington; and Kelleher, *A New Security Order.*

68. Polls conducted in August and December 1992 by the U.S. Information Agency's Office of Research show that comfortable majorities in Germany, Britain, and Italy regard NATO as "essential to their national security," and half of those polled in France expressed the same view. The studies also showed that "while there is considerable support for reducing American military presence in Europe, majorities in all countries prefer scenarios other than the complete withdrawal of American forces from the continent." See USIA Opinion Research memoranda: *West European Opinion on NATO Positive, Stable* (August 31, 1992), pp. 1, 3, 8; and *European Opinion on: The United States, NATO and the U.S. Military Presence* (February 1993).

69. *Helsinki Document 1992,* chap. 5. Two of the three general areas are specifically assigned to the Forum on Security and Cooperation: (1) harmonization of arms control, disarmament, and confidence and security building, and (2) security enhancement, encompassing force planning, defense conversion, regional security, and cooperation toward nonproliferation goals. Ibid., p. 25.

70. Stephen J. Flanagan, "Arms Control in the New Europe: From FSC to Peacemaking," in Freedman, Kelleher, and Sharp, eds., *CFE and the Future of Conventional Arms Control.* See also Daalder, *Cooperative Arms Control.*

71. For further details, see Victor-Yves Ghebali, "The CSCE Forum for Security Cooperation: The Opening Gambits," *NATO Review,* vol. 41 (June 1993), pp. 23–27.

72. See Flanagan, "Arms Control in the New Europe," for more detailed proposals on this issue.

73. Sometime after Havel announced a ban on Czech arms imports, some members of the administration argued that, contrary to Havel's hopes, other countries never took the bold step of discontinuing their arms trade but instead have subsumed the Czech Republic's market share, leaving Czech factories idle and Czech workers unemployed. Consequently, the Czech government has since announced that the weapons industry will be reactivated and will in turn be allowed to seek out new markets abroad. In the political and economic climate of the 1990s, in which defense conversion has proved

prohibitively expensive and in which Western aid has not materialized to the extent it was promised, Havel's original pledge to abandon arms exports was regarded as "naïve and costly." See Jane Perlez, "Czechs Gear Up to Resume Weapons Exports," *New York Times,* July 4, 1993, p. F7.

74. Thomas W. Lippman, "Ex-Soviet Arms Exports Plunge," *Washington Post,* June 13, 1993, p. A28. This article summarizes the testimony of William Grundmann, director of combat support of the U.S. Defense Intelligence Agency, before Congress's Joint Economic Committee.

75. Sergey Podyapolskiy, "Glazyev Says Weapons Exports to Remain at 25–30 Percent," *ITAR-TASS,* April 1, 1993, in Foreign Broadcast Information Service, *Daily Report: Central Eurasia,* April 2, 1993, p. 29. See also Lippman, "Ex-Soviet Arms Exports."

76. Technically, *juste retour* suggests "there should be rough equality between the amount of funds a country spends on defense procurement and the amount of defense work which is created in the country." Joel L. Johnson, "The United States: Partnerships with Europe," in Ethan B. Kapstein, ed., *Global Arms Production: Policy Dilemmas for the 1990s* (Lanham, Md.: University Press of America, 1992), pp. 105–33, especially p. 114. But balances can be struck both within a single program and on a multisystem-multiyear basis. Helpful data on this concept and more generally on European arms industries and recent trends are found in David Garnham, *The Politics of European Defense Cooperation: Germany, France, Britain, and America* (Ballinger, 1988); and James B. Steinberg, *The Transformation of the European Defense Industry: Emerging Trends and Prospects for Future U.S.-European Competition and Collaboration,* R-4141-ACQ (Santa Monica, Calif.: RAND, 1992).

77. See Elisabeth Sköns, "Western Europe: Internationalization of the Arms Industry," in Herbert Wulf, ed., *Arms Industry Limited* (Oxford University Press, 1993), pp. 160–90, especially p. 165.

78. For a more detailed discussion, see Steinberg, *Transformation of the European Defense Industry,* pp. 65–74.

79. See Sköns, "Western Europe," p. 168. For good accounts of the changing environment and restructuring of European defense industries, see Michael Brzoska and Peter Lock, eds., *Restructuring of Arms Production in Western Europe* (Oxford University Press, 1992).

80. Sköns, "Western Europe," p. 179.

81. Ibid., p. 166.

82. Nowhere have the interactive effects on industry consolidation and declining public tolerance been clearer than in the case of the EFA. Proposals for the development of a next-generation multinational fighter date back to 1980 and have attracted collaboration from Britain, Germany, Italy, and Spain. In June 1992, near the end of the EFA development phase, Bonn declared that it was unwilling to go ahead to production, claiming that the EFA was no longer appropriate to the needs of the post–cold war era. What was needed was at most a lighter, more affordable, less technologically advanced fighter, and perhaps no new fighter at all, given the foreseeable European security environment. Defense spokespersons stressed the enormous costs involved, the domestic burdens caused by unification, and the political symbolism of proceeding with "West German business as usual," along the old East-West fault lines. Many of the other partners seemed to agree. Only Britain appeared determined to proceed as planned with the EFA program. As of mid-1993 the project was still in turmoil. According to "confidential" figures, the price of the EFA, by this time renamed the Eurofighter 2000, had jumped by 50 percent since the project was initiated in 1988; it will now cost an estimated $49 billion. For more details on these events, see David Marsh and Edward Mortimer, "Fighter Tamed by Friendly Skies," *Financial Times,* July 7, 1992, p. 18;

David White, "Eurofighter Fails to Find Its Wings," *Financial Times,* May 10, 1993, p. 4; and David White, "Eurofighter Costs Jump 50% over First Estimates," *Financial Times,* May 10, 1993, p. 14. Despite Germany's flip-flop and eventual decision to stay with the program, German funding for the project is still uncertain. In April 1993 German defense minister Volker Rühe needed DM 520 million to meet 1993 development costs, but only DM 100 million for the Eurofighter were remaining in the defense budget. Parliament would have to approve additional funding for the project just when public support for military armaments was diminishing. More recently, the first flight of the aircraft has been delayed several more months because the computerized flight-control system is not working properly. For more information, see "Ende Juni ist das Geld für den 'Jäger 90' verbraucht," *Frankfurter Allgemeine Zeitung,* April 21, 1993, p. 4; and David White, "New Setback for Eurofighter," *Financial Times,* October 7, 1993, p. 1.

83. Sköns, "Western Europe," p. 169.

84. Herbert Wulf, "Arms Industry Limited: The Turning-Point in the 1990s," in Wulf, ed., *Arms Industry Limited,* pp. 3–26, especially p. 26.

85. There has now been positive action on "a proposal for a Council Regulation (EEC) on the control of exports of certain dual-use goods and of certain nuclear products and technologies." Commission of the European Communities, COM (92) 317, Brussels, August 31, 1992, p. 2.

86. For more information about recent Community export control efforts, see Wolfgang H. Reinicke, "Arms Sales Abroad: European Community Export Controls beyond 1992," *Brookings Review,* vol. 10 (Summer 1992), pp. 22–25. Brussels has also recently endorsed the assignment of responsibility for end use declarations for arms exports to the company level. This assignment draws on German experience with the KOBRA system, a system much discussed and revised after German firms were implicated in strategic arms exports to Iraq. The KOBRA system has many innovative, computerized tracking and monitoring features. Perhaps the unique feature is that it makes a named company official responsible for the assessment of any export's end use, an official who can later be held accountable for any foreseeable diversion. For a detailed discussion of KOBRA, see chapter 5 in this volume and the narrative account given by Harald Müller, "The Exports Control Debate in the 'New' European Community," *Arms Control Today,* vol. 23 (March 1993), pp. 10–14. For more proposals on European export controls, see Paul Eavis and Owen Green, "Regulating Arms Exports: A Program for the European Community," in Hans Günter Brauch and others, eds., *Controlling the Development and Spread of Military Technology: Lessons from the Past and Challenges for the 1990s* (Amsterdam: VU University Press, 1992), pp. 283–99; and Susan Willett, *Controlling the Arms Trade: Supply and Demand Dynamics,* Faraday Discussion Paper 18 (London: Council for Arms Control, November 1991).

87. See the arguments put forth by Lord David Owen in "The Future of the Balkans: An Interview with David Owen," *Foreign Affairs,* vol. 72 (Spring 1993), pp. 1–9, especially p. 6.

88. David Gardner and Andrew Hill, "Belgium Keen to Contribute to Eurocorps," *Financial Times,* May 24, 1993, p. 2. Spain has also indicated a willingness to contribute.

89. The states that participated were the smaller states, the Netherlands in the UN Transitional Authority in Cambodia, and the NNA.

90. Ian Davidson, "No More Maastrichts," *Financial Times,* May 24, 1993, p. 28.

91. Charles Krauthammer, "The Unipolar Moment," *Foreign Affairs: America and the World, 1990/91,* vol. 70, no. 1 (1991), pp. 23–33, especially p. 24.

NINE

Emerging States and Military Legacies in the Former Soviet Union

Coit D. Blacker

THE FATE of any system for the cooperative management of international security relations will be determined, at least in part, by near- to medium-term political developments within the fifteen newly independent states that until December 1991 constituted the Union of Soviet Socialist Republics. Most influential will be the trajectory of events within the three Slavic republics—the Russian Federation, Ukraine, and Belarus—and Kazakhstan, which together account for about 80 percent of the population, economic activity, and military potential of the former union. What happens in and to the eleven other countries that have emerged from the ruins of the Soviet empire will also have a direct bearing on the possible emergence of a more cooperative global order, although their impact is likely to be both less important than that of the three Slavic republics and Kazakhstan and, given their political volatility, almost entirely negative.[1]

As of late 1993, developments within what used to be the USSR were less than auspicious for the establishment of a cooperative security regime in which the largest and most important of the Soviet successor states might play a constructive role. To a degree that is not well understood in the West even now, what currently exists in place of the former Soviet Union is less a collection of sovereign nation-states struggling within clearly defined parameters to assert their newly won independence and to acquire the trappings of statehood than a manifest political vacuum, within which powerful actors representing virtually every social, economic, and ethnic interest are competing to establish physical

I wish to thank Brian A. Davenport for his valuable assistance in the preparation of this chapter.

control over this or that piece of terrain to which they feel entitled and have asserted claim. This process of political and social disintegration, which began well in advance of the union's actual demise, shows no signs of abating; it is, in fact, likely to accelerate in the near future as economic conditions deteriorate further, and the multiple and reinforcing bonds that once linked the peoples of the world's last great empire continue to dissolve.

Fortunately not all the news is bad. Notwithstanding the political and economic turmoil within the region, most of the fifteen regimes that have assumed the responsibilities of government once exercised by the Soviet Communist party have articulated foreign policy positions that are, in the main, consistent, or at least not inconsistent, with the logic of cooperative security. The pronouncements of the Russian government and of its foreign minister, Andrey Kozyrev, have been particularly consistent in this respect.

During Russia's first year as a fully independent country, Kozyrev advanced a detailed program for the conduct of his country's foreign policy that placed Russia's becoming what he termed a "normal" state at the heart of Moscow's diplomatic agenda. Among other measures, Kozyrev signaled Russia's determination to pursue a nonconfrontational and nonideological foreign policy, to respect the political independence and territorial integrity of all neighboring countries, to renounce the threat or use of force, and to reduce Russian military capabilities to a level adequate for defense but insufficient for aggression. For Kozyrev, bringing Russian foreign policy into line with accepted diplomatic practice and prevailing international legal norms has been a priority, a necessary first step in overcoming the consequences of his country's communist past and in securing Russia's place in a new and more cooperative global order.

Consumed by events closer to home, political leaders in the other fourteen republics of the former union have been noticeably less diligent in outlining the central features of their countries' foreign policies. Even the Ukrainians, next to the Russians those with the strongest incentive to offer up a coherent vision for the conduct of foreign policy, have done less than they might have. Since independence they have spent the bulk of their time, it seems, trying to convince the rest of the world to regard them as a kind of eastern European version of France and to treat them accordingly.

As for the remainder of the new states, especially those in the Caucasus and central Asia, foreign policy constitutes either a distraction (from the more pressing business of neutralizing domestic political opposition and maintaining a firm grip on power) or an extension of domestic politics (for example, a vehicle to enlist outside political support for their irredentist claims against their neighbors and to attract foreign investment). Although there is little in the foreign policy statements that have been issued to which U.S. and Western policymakers might take exception, neither has there been much to celebrate; most are simply bereft of any real content.

In surveying the wreckage of the once mighty Soviet superstate, one is presented, then, with something of a paradox. The collapse of Soviet power, both at home and abroad, offers an unprecedented opportunity for reducing global political and military tensions and for remaking world politics, including the possible establishment of a state-centered system for the cooperative management of international security relations. At the same time, the political and economic chaos that has attended the Soviet Union's sudden disappearance militates against such far-reaching cooperation, at least in the short term, and vastly complicates planning for any international regime based on the logic of cooperative security.

Which of these two legacies of the second Russian revolution—the liberating effect of communism's demise or the limiting impact of state-seeking nationalism—proves to be the more enduring will have enormous consequences for the character and conduct of regional relations (between and among the republics of the former Soviet Union and between individual republics and neighboring states) and for international politics in general. How the political situation evolves within the former USSR will also shape, and perhaps determine, the potential for cooperation on security-related issues among the world's large and medium powers, most of which cannot afford to ignore political change of the magnitude they are witnessing today in Russia and surrounding areas.

This chapter is divided into three parts. The first section explores the potential receptivity of the post-Soviet republics to the concepts of cooperative security, as elaborated in other chapters of this volume. Since the Russian Federation is the largest and most powerful of the Soviet successor states, the policies of its government are accorded special attention. The second section examines existing and prospective obstacles to the creation of a cooperative security regime that spring from conditions within the former union. The third section advances a number of suggestions for overcoming these obstacles and for devising incentives to induce cooperative behavior over the near to medium term.

Foreign Policy and the Soviet Successor States: Implications for Cooperative Security

Political and economic conditions inside the fifteen now-independent republics of the former USSR could be worse from the perspective of those interested in securing their participation in the structuring of a new and more cooperative global order. They could also be much better. The good news is that the most important republics—the Russian Federation, Belarus, Ukraine, and Kazakhstan—have all expressed formal support for democracy, human rights, political pluralism, and the establishment of market-oriented economies. As noted, each has also pledged to become a "normal" state, to use Kozyrev's phrase, and to pursue its legitimate national interests without recourse to force.[2]

The bad news is that most of these commitments remain just that, expressions of intent that have yet to be translated into action. The Russians are the clear exception; the Yeltsin government has been extremely active diplomatically in the period since independence and has made the fostering of a reliable and sustainable partnership with the West the linchpin of its foreign policy. The other states, for whom foreign policy constitutes terra nova, have been less focused than the Russians and also less disciplined.

Worse, none of the governments of the larger republics, with the possible exception of Nursultan Nazarbayev's in Kazakhstan, is in firm control of events. Political instability in Russia, for example, shows no signs of abating, as discussed later. In Ukraine, President Leonid Kravchuk faces continuing opposition, both from ultranationalists, who want him to adopt an even harder line in his dealings with the Russians, and from those who seek to preserve many of the existing bonds with Moscow and who agitate for a greater degree of accommodation. As if this opposition were not enough, the Ukrainian economy is in dire straits, and there has been little progress toward meaningful reform, let alone anything akin to genuine "marketization." To the east, in central Asia, politics has become an intensely personal affair in which bonds of blood and friendship account for more than principle or purpose; running the country for the social good has become a distinctly secondary consideration for those in or contending for power.

Whatever the specific problems arising out of the Soviet collapse that might impinge on the creation of a regime of cooperative security, the more fundamental problem is that many of the region's governments do not determine political outcomes. In a real sense, power, particularly in Russia, has devolved to lower and lower levels within the system, and—although it may not be anyone's for the taking, as Leon Trotsky is reputed to have said in 1917—neither is it securely in the hands of the country's elected and appointed officials. Moreover, the trend toward anarchy is almost certain to accelerate over the next several years as economic conditions worsen and political life, both in Russia and elsewhere, becomes more extreme.

This trend is the real significance of the Soviet Union's inelegant collapse in 1991, the implications of which are only now beginning to be comprehended.

Breaking with the Past: Foreign Policy Trends within the Post-Soviet Republics

The root causes of the Soviet collapse were the country's rapid economic decline during the 1980s and the failure of *perestroika,* Mikhail Gorbachev's largely ad hoc package of reforms, to spark anything resembling a genuine or sustainable recovery. The urgent need to restart the stalled Soviet economy also forced Gorbachev, albeit reluctantly, to embrace the cause of political reform, by which he hoped to restore faith and confidence in the renewability of socialism and, through 1990, salvage the fortunes of the ruling Communist party. In much the same way, domestic economic conditions precipitated the profound changes in foreign and defense policy that the embattled Soviet leader engineered between his election as general secretary of the Communist party in March 1985 and his forced retirement almost seven years later.

Simply put, only by demilitarizing the Soviet system, thereby freeing up resources for new investments in the country's aging industrial, agricultural, scientific, and technological infrastructure, could Gorbachev hope to stave off economic and political disaster. Key to the success of any attempt to curtail military spending and to reduce the size of the armed forces was Gorbachev's ability to neutralize the perceived threat to Soviet security interests said to be posed by the West. Gorbachev sought to reduce this threat in three ways: by demonstrating a willingness to eliminate unilaterally the most provocative features of the Soviet Union's own military posture (thus his advocacy of "reasonable sufficiency" as a guide to the sizing of Soviet armed forces and of "defensive defense");[3] by concluding a series of far-reaching arms control agreements with the United States and its NATO allies (for example, the 1987 treaty on the elimination of intermediate-range nuclear forces, the 1990 agreement on the reduction of conventional forces in Europe, and the 1991 accord on U.S. and Soviet strategic forces); and by elaborating an entirely new basis for the conduct of Soviet foreign policy that he and Foreign Minister Eduard Shevardnadze labeled the new political thinking.

At base the new political thinking was an attempt to conventionalize the country's foreign policy: to set aside such uniquely (and to outsiders incomprehensible) Soviet notions as "proletarian internationalism" and "the correlation of forces"—most of which, according to Shevardnadze, were nonsensical inventions that had done irreparable harm to the foreign policy interests of the Soviet state—and to replace them with concepts more in keeping with existing political realities and, therefore, more recognizable to Moscow's negotiating partners.[4] Chief among these concepts were the admissions that, in the nuclear age, security between the United States and the USSR could only be mutual and that the Soviet tendency in the conduct of its foreign policy to divide the world into economic classes had now to give way to the interests of humanity as a whole (or to what Gorbachev had labeled in 1988 "the supremacy of the common human idea").[5]

Depending on one's perspective, the new political thinking can be judged either a modest success or a catastrophic failure. On the one hand, to the degree that it contributed to the dramatic improvement in Soviet relations with the United States, NATO Europe, and China between 1986 and 1989—three of Gorbachev's central foreign policy objectives—it should be accorded high marks. On the other hand, to the extent that it undermined the foundations of postwar Soviet foreign policy—for example, by making it all but impossible for Moscow to intervene militarily in eastern Europe in 1989 in order to reverse the manifest erosion of its authority—it can be seen as a policy blunder of colossal proportions.

Again, depending on one's point of view, Gorbachev's departures in foreign policy went either too far or not far enough. To the Soviet leader's conservative critics, the "new thinking" led in an almost linear fashion to the breakup of the empire and, ultimately, to the unraveling of the state itself; to his liberal opponents, it amounted to reform at the margins—"nothing more than a substantially liberalized modification of the earlier Soviet foreign policy course"—and was therefore destined to fail.[6]

The Russian Federation

However pointed the criticisms directed against Gorbachev and his foreign policy strategy both at the time and in retrospect, the link between what he started and what the Russian government now seeks to complete is evident. Gorbachev's essential purposes, particularly in the period after the collapse of Moscow's eastern European glacis in 1989, were to achieve the normalization of relations with leading Western countries, especially the United States, and to negotiate the USSR's entry into the full range of international political and economic institutions sponsored by Washington in the aftermath of World War II, to which the Soviet Union had been denied admission. Foremost among these were the World Bank, the International Monetary Fund (IMF), and the General Agreement on Tariffs and Trade.[7]

Only by adopting this approach, the Soviets seemed to believe, could they hope to overcome the disastrous material consequences of more than forty years of isolation, some of which they had imposed upon themselves in the mistaken belief that they were creating an alternative international system and some of which the United States and its allies had forced upon them. As both Gorbachev and Shevardnadze repeatedly insisted, Moscow's new foreign policy was designed to assist—"to positively advance"—the twin processes of domestic economic revitalization and internal political reform.

The Russian political leadership characterizes the purposes of its foreign policy in much the same way. There are, however, important differences, primarily in the way the Russian government conceives of and proposes to resolve the challenges it confronts internationally. To the end, Gorbachev and Shevardnadze sought to preserve the fiction that the Soviet Union remained a superpower and that it could secure entry into the community of Western institutions as Washington's political and economic equal. By contrast, Russian president Boris Yeltsin and Foreign Minister Kozyrev describe their vast but bankrupt country more modestly, as a "great power," and admit that Russia comes to the West in a severely weakened state and in desperate need of massive economic assistance.

Throughout, Gorbachev and Shevardnadze believed it both possible and desirable to retain at least some of the essential features of the Soviet system—the emphasis on social equality, for example—and to borrow from the West selectively. The Russian leadership rejects the Soviet experiment in its entirety. As Kozyrev wrote in early 1992, the actions of the Russian government "are predicated on a conscientious and deliberate policy aimed at pulling out the roots of the fallen tree of totalitarian rule. This is the essence of the entire program of reforms undertaken by the democratic leaders of Russia. . . . The success of reforms will signify precisely the triumph of democracy over the threats of any imperial revival."[8]

But exactly how does Russia—no longer a superpower and no longer communist—gain admission to the international community as a "normal" state? According to its leadership, it does so in two stages. The first requirement is to complete its own democratic transformation: Russia cannot become a normal country, Yeltsin and his allies argue, until the process of democratization is substantially complete (and until the threats to democracy posed by the government's protofascist and neocommunist enemies are defeated). The second step is to organize the country's foreign policy around the same set of principles that allegedly guide interstate relations among all "civilized" states, namely "freedom of movement for people, goods, services, ideas and capital across national state borders,"[9] adherence to and compliance with international law, respect for human rights (including the rights of national minorities), the nonuse of force, and noninterference in the internal affairs of other countries.

What the Yeltsin government proposes, in fact, is that Russia—once and for all—cast its lot with the West. In a January 1992 *Izvestiya* interview, Kozyrev left little doubt that forging a new relationship with Western countries was Moscow's paramount foreign policy goal, saying, "In general, in our relations with the West we will have to take to their logical conclusion the not always consistent steps toward rapprochement [that] started with perestroika. The developed countries of the West are Russia's natural allies. It is time finally to say firmly that we are not adversaries, nor in any way poor kid brothers obediently following the orders of a rich and malevolent West bent on buying up Russia."

The interviewer asked why he expressed willingness to ally Russia with the West after seventy-five years of official hostility, mutual suspicion, and occasional armed conflict. Kozyrev's answer came in two parts. First, he insisted, "We ourselves threaten no one and we proceed from the premise that no developed, democratic, and civilian society, in which a reasonable, rational principle holds sway, can threaten us." Second, only by joining Western-led international economic organizations could Russia rebuild its shattered economy and society. "We must," the foreign minister argued, "become part of the world community. . . . Our active foreign policy and our diplomacy are essential to ensure our economic entry into the world community through international recognition and thereby help satisfy Russia's domestic needs, too."[10]

Russia's leaders sought early on to establish fully normal relations with the United States, both to underscore the complete break with Soviet diplomacy and to facilitate the Russian Federation's entry into the Western community of states. In the statement issued at the conclusion of the hastily called meeting between Presidents George Bush and Yeltsin, held at Camp David in February 1992, the two sides characterized as the "distinguishing feature" of their relationship "friendship and partnership based on mutual trust, respect, and a common commitment to democracy and economic freedom." They also pledged to cooperate to prevent the further proliferation of weapons of mass destruction, to resolve regional conflicts by peaceful means, and to combat jointly international terrorism and trafficking in drugs. To the delight of the Russians, the so-called Camp David Declaration ended with an explicit reference to "a new alliance of partners" to combat "the common dangers which threaten us."[11]

The first full-dress Bush-Yeltsin summit, in June 1992 in Washington, was equally upbeat and, if anything, even more optimistic about the prospective development of U.S.-Russian relations. Among the accords signed during the Russian president's state visit were a joint understanding on reductions in strategic offensive forces that obligates the two sides to undertake force cuts far in excess of those required by the 1991 Strategic Arms Reduction Talks (START) accord, three treaties, ten bilateral agreements, and thirteen joint statements (on issues as diverse as the conversion of military industry and the preservation of Lake Baikal). Bush and Yeltsin also signed "A Charter for American-Russian Partnership and Friendship" that ran more than six single-spaced pages, with sections devoted to "democracy and partnership," "international peace and security," and the development of economic relations.[12] Yeltsin and President Bill Clinton, meeting in April 1993 in Vancouver, British Columbia, reaffirmed the importance to each side of the "partnership" between Moscow and Washington first outlined at the February 1992 meeting in Washington; they pledged, in particular, to complete the negotiations on the reduction of U.S. and Russian strategic nuclear forces and to deepen and extend bilateral economic cooperation.[13]

Early on, the Russians moved on several other fronts to allay suspicions about the sincerity of their commitment to join "civilized" international society. As the "successor state" to the Soviet Union,[14] the Yeltsin government legally assumed all the USSR's existing treaty obligations, including, most important from the West's perspective, those attending the 1963 Limited Test Ban Treaty, the 1968 Nuclear Non-Proliferation Treaty, the 1972 Anti-Ballistic Missile Treaty, and the Intermediate-Range Nuclear Forces, Conventional

Armed Forces in Europe (CFE), and START agreements, concluded between 1987 and 1991. The Russians also signaled their willingness to absorb and service the Soviet government's entire foreign debt—some $75 billion in early 1992—should their partners in the anemic Commonwealth of Independent States (CIS) choose to renege on their fiscal responsibilities.

During its first year of independence, in other words, the Russian government did everything within reason to align its foreign policy with those of other "democratic" states, such as the United States, to which it looked for political support and economic aid. Rhetorically, at least after June 1992, no substantial barriers remained to the kinds of cooperation between Russia and the developed world that both Yeltsin and Kozyrev have made the centerpiece of their diplomacy.

Yet two problems have handicapped the Russian government as it has set out to translate its ambitious vision into reality. The first barrier to cooperation is not of the government's making, at least not entirely. The second and more serious obstacle, however, only Russia can overcome.

The future of cooperative security in its broadest sense hinges on Russia's ability to succeed in its transition to democracy. The future of democracy and of democratic government in Russia, in turn, depends on the ability of the country's leaders to improve the material lot of the Russian people. The economic reforms implemented at the urging of former acting prime minister Yegor Gaidar failed to spur an economic recovery. In fact, they made conditions worse—measurably so—for the vast majority of the population. To date, the policies of Gaidar's successor, Viktor Chernomyrdin, have proved to be equally ineffective. To complicate matters further, opposition to reform by conservatives in the Russian parliament before its violent dissolution in October 1993 required the Yeltsin government either to water down or to postpone the enactment of critical elements of the reform program, further slowing the country's transition from a command-driven to a more market-oriented economic system.

In particular, the decision by Yeltsin during 1992 to heed the warnings of those inside and outside the Russian government who counseled patience and argued for more time undermined the confidence of Russia's would-be partners in the regime's commitment to thoroughgoing reform. As Russia drew back from the logic of economic shock therapy, the West, determined not to throw good money after bad, delayed providing the roughly $24 billion in aid pledged during 1992 and attached various conditions that it wanted satisfied before agreeing to release the funds.[15] In 1993, as Russia edged closer to the economic abyss, the Group of Seven industrialized countries, led by Washington, pledged to revisit the issue of large-scale economic assistance to Russia. As of this writing, however, little has changed, and the amount of Western financial aid that Moscow has actually received remains modest.

Of special concern to both the IMF and Western governments has been Russia's unwillingness to reduce deficit spending and to restrict the growth in the money supply, without which they are reluctant to furnish the $6 billion needed to stabilize the ruble and to ensure its convertibility on world financial markets.[16] With prices inside the country increasing at an annual rate well in excess of 1,000 percent, Western lenders fear the onset of runaway, Weimar-like inflation and a complete breakdown of the economic order. Although not insensitive to such concerns, Russian political leaders argue that to impose the truly draconian measures demanded by the West would force many of the country's gigantic industrial enterprises into outright bankruptcy, deprive millions of workers of their jobs, and place the government at immediate and enormous political risk.

Should this impasse persist and the Russian economy continue to deteriorate, it is doubtful whether Yeltsin, currently scheduled to face the electorate again in 1994, could secure reelection as Russia's president. What might ensue is, of course, anybody's guess. What does seem certain, however, is that Yeltsin's replacement, whoever that person might be, will be less democratic in orientation and, given the latent appeal of the nationalist card in Russian politics, very likely to reject the contention that the United States and its allies constitute Russia's natural allies. Under such conditions, the likelihood that a successor Russian government, insecure in its authority and determined to find an international scapegoat for the country's problems, would participate in a cooperative scheme for the management of regional and international security relations approaches zero.

The second problem could produce the same outcome, although for different reasons. As severe as the economic crisis in Russia has become, the country's political problems may be worse. At stake, it appears, is nothing less than the state's survival as a sovereign entity. Already stripped of two regions—Ukraine and Belarus—that for centuries constituted integral parts of the Russian (and later Soviet) empire, the country continues to fracture along multiple political fault lines, some ancient and some of more recent origin.

Besides the challenges to Moscow's leadership posed by the Kazan Tatars and the Chechen and Ingush republics in southern Russia, considerable indigenous support has emerged for the establishment of an independent Dagestan in the northern Caucasus, a sovereign Yakutiya in western Siberia, and a separate Russian Republic of the Far East. Few of these movements for political independence are likely to bear fruit any time soon (particularly in light of the violent suppression of the parliamentary opposition to Yeltsin in October 1993 and the nascent trend toward the recentralization of political authority that became manifest in the immediate aftermath of the event), but the drama is far from over.

The larger point, in any event, is that political conditions in Russia are much as they were in 1917, when the Czarist autocracy crumbled and the Bolsheviks seized power from the ineffective provisional government of Alexander Kerensky. Although Yeltsin, in the second half of 1993, remained more popular than any other politician in Russia, the same cannot be said for many of those elevated to power by him. Gaidar, forced to resign as acting prime minister in December 1992 by Yeltsin's opponents in the Congress of People's Deputies, staged a partial political comeback in 1993 but remains one of the most unpopular figures in Russian public life. Kozyrev survives but finds himself under constant and withering attack because of his allegedly pro-Western biases. Before his arrest in October 1993, former vice president Aleksandr Rutskoy, the Afghan war hero and fervent Russian nationalist, repeatedly took both Yeltsin and his ministers to task politically for their failure to cure the country's ills, as did Ruslan Khasbulatov, former chairman of the Russian Supreme Soviet, who spearheaded the political opposition to Yeltsin.

It is difficult to exaggerate the seriousness of the political crisis currently besetting Russia. Although the Yeltsin government enjoys considerable legitimacy among the populace, its ability to exercise authority—to get things done—continues to erode. The optimism with which the majority of the Russian people initially greeted the ambitious plans of the reformers is today nowhere in evidence. The mood has turned black. In the caustic judgment of one Russian political commentator, for the second time in seventy-five years, "we [Russians] have burned down our own house in order to light the way for humanity."[17]

Without demonstrable progress toward stabilizing the Russian economy, any hopes for arresting the country's political disintegration are probably misplaced. Without economic stabilization, the outlook is for a further fracturing of the political order. This fracturing could well be accompanied by widespread civil violence, in which "democratic" and liberal forces could find themselves at war with a powerful coalition of "reds and browns" (communists and fascists).

This scenario is not the only, let alone the most probable, outcome. Other, less disturbing, futures for Russia are also conceivable. It is, however, a distinct possibility, and one that Western governments would do well to consider as they begin to plan in earnest for the conduct of international relations in the post-Soviet era.

Ukraine

The foreign policy preferences of the other post-Soviet republics are harder to discern than are those of the Russian Federation, which, as indicated, has been careful in the period since independence to elaborate the foundations of its external relations and to discharge faithfully its international legal obligations as the self-styled continuer-state to the USSR. On balance, the non-Russian successor governments have been much more attentive to relations with neighboring states, and in particular to relations with their former sister republics, than they have been to ties with more distant countries.

Nowhere is this more true than in Ukraine, where the government of President Leonid Kravchuk has been locked in an often tense battle of wills with the Russian political leadership since the rebirth of the Ukrainian state in late 1991. The list of issues about which Ukraine and Russia have quarreled and over which they continue to struggle is a long one; most of the disagreements—over the disposition of the Black Sea fleet, for example—have come over how to divide up the Soviet carcass. The fundamental problem besetting relations, however, is not who gets what, but what is to be the basis for and the character of relations between an independent Ukraine and an independent Russia.

For the most part, the international community readily accepts the proposition that the Russian Federation, for all its current travails, constitutes a sovereign political actor, enjoying all the major attributes of statehood. In one form or another, Russia has been an organized political entity at least since the days of Ivan III and the Grand Principality of Muscovy in the fifteenth century.

Ukraine's political history has been less straightforward. Although it once was the center of Russian civilization, by the fourteenth century much of the Ukraine had fallen under Lithuanian or Mongol suzerainty. Not until late in the eighteenth century, in fact, did Catherine the Great's armies (assisted by her diplomats) reestablish Russia's authority over most of what we now think of as Ukraine, or, as it was known at the time, Little Russia. At no point between the thirteenth century, when the balance of political power between Kiev and Moscow shifted irrevocably to the latter, and the collapse of the Russian empire in 1917 did the Ukrainians enjoy much political independence. Nationalist leaders did declare the establishment of a separate Ukrainian state late in 1917, but the experiment proved to be short-lived. By 1920 the Bolsheviks were firmly in power, and in 1922 the Ukraine was incorporated into the new USSR.

This complex history accounts for much of the behavior of the Kravchuk government vis-à-vis the Russian Federation since the passage on December 1, 1991, of the referendum on Ukrainian independence.[18] Although Russia's leaders have repeatedly assured the government in Kiev that they fully respect Ukraine's political independence and harbor no ambitions to reclaim the region as part of Russia's historical patrimony, the Ukrainians—not without reason, perhaps—remain wary and determined to safeguard what they have achieved. "The main theme of Ukrainian statecraft," wrote an American student of the region, "has thus been to define the contours of sovereignty and to assert and test that sovereignty at every turn."[19]

Ukraine's campaign to discourage Russian (and all other conceivable forms of) irredentism has manifested itself in a variety of ways. Three are particularly noteworthy in the context of cooperative security: a commitment to maintain the country's existing territorial frontiers; the decision to establish national armed forces of sufficient size to protect the republic against would-be aggressors;[20] and a strong disinclination to infuse the CIS with any real power, detecting in such proposals evidence of Russia's continuing interest in areas and issues beyond its immediate political reach.[21] It was for this reason, among others, that when representatives of six CIS governments, including Russia's, gathered in Tashkent in May 1992 to sign an agreement on collective security, the Ukrainians were nowhere to be seen.[22] Kiev seemed to fear that the treaty, whatever its ostensible purpose, could be used at a later time to sanction or otherwise legitimize armed intervention in the internal affairs of one or more of the participating states.

Ukraine's determination to keep the Russian leadership off balance and at arm's length also explains in part the Kiev government's on-again, off-again shipment of Soviet tactical nuclear weapons to Russia during spring 1992, its continuing reluctance to cede formal authority over the strategic nuclear forces deployed on its soil to the CIS joint military command in Moscow, and its insistence that it too be a party to the START treaty. Many Western governments tend reflexively to side with the Russians on these matters and to be sharply critical of the Ukrainian government's conduct. Although such criticisms may be warranted, they overlook the degree to which Kiev's actions are directed primarily against Russia—to remind Moscow that Ukraine is now sovereign and must be dealt with accordingly—rather than against the West or Western interests.

Since mid-1992, relations between Ukraine and Russia have been on an upswing. At a meeting between Kravchuk and Yeltsin in June 1992 in Dagomys, on the Black Sea, the two leaders reached a series of understandings on a number of sensitive political and economic issues. They agreed, for example, to defer discussion of the Crimean peninsula—one of the most divisive and potentially explosive items on the bilateral agenda[23]—to the indefinite future and to base their trade relations on prices set by world markets. They also agreed, at least in principle, on a division of the Black Sea fleet and confirmed an earlier understanding on the disposition of conventional Soviet military assets, as noted later in this section. Command and control arrangements covering strategic nuclear forces remained somewhat confused, but even on this contentious issue the two leaders seemed eager to avoid an open split.[24]

Other problems are certain to develop between Kiev and Moscow over the near to medium term, and no one in either capital expects the road ahead to be free of obstacles. At the same time the concerns expressed by some in the West that the two countries might soon come to blows seem wide of the mark. Despite their political divorce, Ukraine and Russia remain tightly linked; in addition to the economic ties that bind them, they connect to each other through language, culture, and a common ethnic heritage. More like estranged relatives than enemies, Russians and Ukrainians must now learn to coexist, not as constituent parts of a single, multinational empire but as distinct societies, struggling to assert their separate national identities, with a shared stake in the positive development of relations with the West.

To the extent that Kravchuk and his foreign minister, Anatoly Zlenko, have allowed themselves to concentrate on Ukraine's relations with countries other than Russia (and the other CIS republics), their primary focus has been the United States. Washington too has a keen interest in Ukraine, largely because of the latter's possession of some 200 formerly Soviet long-range nuclear systems that the U.S. government wants to see returned to Russia and dismantled.[25] When Kravchuk temporarily suspended the transfer of tactical nuclear weapons to Russia in March 1992,[26] the United States forcefully reminded the Ukrainians that Washington expected Kiev to live up to the commitments it had voluntarily assumed in the nuclear field, including the promise to be rid of all nuclear systems by mid-1994. The United States is also eager for Ukraine to make good on its promise to accede to the Nuclear Non-Proliferation Treaty (NPT) as a non–nuclear weapon state.

For its part, Ukraine has sought to manipulate Washington's nuclear worries to secure the undivided attention of U.S. policymakers and to obtain at least a measure of direct U.S. economic assistance. When Kravchuk, in April 1992, suggested that the United States provide a nuclear guarantee to Ukraine in exchange for the republic's denuclearization, Secretary of State James Baker rejected the suggestion in no uncertain terms.[27] In May 1992, at the conclusion of Kravchuk's visit to Washington to confer with senior Bush administration officials, the United States did agree to extend most favored nation status to and to ensure U.S. commercial investments in the republic, but on balance the results of this first-ever U.S.-Ukrainian summit were meager.[28]

Relations between Kiev and Washington were better during 1993 than they had been at earlier junctures, helped along by the May 23, 1992, agreement among the United States, Russia, and the three other post-Soviet republics with nuclear weapons on their soil to open up the START treaty for the three republics' signatures.[29] Until Ukraine rids itself of all nuclear weapons deployed on its territory and actually ratifies without conditions both the START I treaty and the NPT, however, relations with Washington are unlikely to improve much beyond their current lukewarm state.

Ukraine's diplomacy with other Western countries has been low key and modest in scope. Other than a treaty concluded with France in June 1992 pledging regular high-level consultations and cooperative undertakings in such areas as communications, energy, the environment, space, and health policies,[30] Kiev has failed to establish much of a presence one way or the other in international politics. Its presence will increase, but slowly, given the country's severe domestic economic problems and its preoccupation with regional affairs closer to home.

Ukraine's current intense focus on tasks associated with nation building, combined with the unsettled character of its relations with Russia, will necessarily limit Kiev's interest in any prospective system or systems for the cooperative management of international security relations, as well as its willingness to take part in any institutional arrangements that might be forthcoming. Notwithstanding the government's participation in preliminary multilateral discussions concerning the possible creation of various political groupings and regional free-trade associations,[31] Ukraine will be loath to undertake any commitments that might limit the exercise of its sovereignty or, most especially, interfere with its ability to resort to force in order to safeguard the country's independence. In other words, although Ukraine cannot prevent others from entering into agreements to limit military capabilities and to restrict weapons transfers, it can—and almost certainly would—choose to stand outside them, at least for the time being.

The Central Asian Republics

The foreign policies of the five central Asian republics—Kazakhstan, Kyrgyzstan, Tajikistan, Turkmenistan, and Uzbekistan—share some of the essential features of Ukrainian policy, including a preoccupation with Russia (and with their immediate neighbors) and an interest in establishing good working relations with the United States. At the same time, they are, if anything, even less well developed and more inwardly directed.

From the U.S. perspective, the most important of the republics is Kazakhstan, home to 16.5 million Kazakhs, Russians, Ukrainians, and ethnic Germans and 104 SS-18 ICBMs. Like Kravchuk in Ukraine, Kazakhstan's president, Nursultan Nazarbayev, is a popular "reformed" communist and a strident (if recently converted) nationalist. Also like Kravchuk, Nazarbayev has proved to be a skilled negotiator, particularly on the nuclear issue, alternately threatening to preserve his country's nuclear options and promising to turn over his weapons (to whom, exactly, remains somewhat obscure) at the earliest possible date.

Early on, Nazarbayev gave every indication that Kazakhstan's strategic nuclear weapons were likely to remain where they were, at least for the time being. In an interview published on February 20, 1992, for example, he argued that through no fault of its own Kazakhstan had become a nuclear weapon state. He cautioned that it could take as long as fifteen years for the SS-18s deployed at Derzhavinsk and Zhangiz-Tobe to be dismantled and destroyed and that the disarmament process in Kazakhstan would be helped along if the Chinese, Indian, and Pakistani governments were to join in.[32] An aide to Nazarbayev went considerably further in an interview with a Turkish newspaper in April 1992, in which he declared that Kazakhstan understood the political and military significance of nuclear weapons and that "we never want to enter the ranks of countries which have none." In five short sentences that must have given both Moscow and Washington pause, the presidential aide outlined his reasoning: "Kazakhstan is the only country with atomic bombs in a 1.3 billion people–strong Islamic world. We will destroy these bombs only when Russia destroys its own nuclear and atomic weapons. As a deterrent and a guarantee of peace, our nuclear force is a guarantee for the Turkic world. That force is at its disposal. America, Britain, and France are helping us because we possess atomic bombs."[33]

The Nazarbayev government's seeming interest in an Islamic-Turkic nuclear capability proved to be short-lived and may, in fact, have been nothing more than a device to remind Russia, the United States, and other interested parties that Kazakhstan was not to be trifled with. Nazarbayev himself spoke frequently to the nuclear issue, and although reluctant to abandon the position that Alma Ata could well decide to retain the SS-18 force on its soil, gave progressively stronger hints as the months passed that his country was prepared to do without it.

Following the signing of the May 15, 1992, CIS agreement on collective security and his visit to Washington several days later to confer with President Bush and Secretary of State Baker, Nazarbayev made it explicit. The new treaty on collective security, he declared, made it possible for Kazakhstan to surrender its ICBMs, since under the terms of the accord Russia had agreed to provide Kazakhstan with a nuclear guarantee. In Washington Nazarbayev revealed that the U.S. administration had consented to invite Kazakhstan, as well as Ukraine and Belarus, to join the START ratification process as principals, thus enabling him to reaffirm Alma Ata's commitment to do away with its potent force of long-range ballistic missiles and to accede to the NPT as a non–nuclear weapon state.[34]

Aside from early tensions over the disposition of strategic nuclear forces, relations between Kazakhstan and Russia have been good, for the most part. The transfer of Soviet tactical nuclear weapons from Kazakhstan to Russia proceeded without a hitch. At least as important, in late May 1992 the two countries signed a "treaty on friendship, cooperation and mutual aid" that provides for the "joint use of military installations," the establishment of a common economic space, and regular political consultations at the highest level. They also pledged to regard each other's borders as inviolable.[35]

Doubtless the relatively harmonious state of relations has something to do with the presence within Kazakhstan of some 6 million ethnic Russians (almost 40 percent of the total population), a substantial degree of economic interdependence, and a shared frontier that runs for about 3,500 kilometers. Nationalism in Kazakhstan is also much less developed than the Ukrainian variant and, in general, ethnic Kazakhs view Russians with little of the suspicion and antipathy that constitute the backdrop to relations between Kiev and Moscow. It is perhaps useful to note in this context that the Nazarbayev government was a strong advocate of a renewed federal union during fall 1991 and did not press for complete independence until the Soviet Union's outright collapse at the end of the year.

The other central Asian republics, according to Martha Brill Olcott, "are having trouble defining their 'national interests.'"[36] Washington too seems unsure about how to proceed in its diplomacy with these four new states and how to assess the content and direction of their policies. Nor is there much incentive to do so, given that none of the republics possesses much by way of economic or military potential and that the region's entire population totals less than 35 million. Other Western countries are, if anything, even less attentive to regional affairs than the United States is.

In Kyrgyzstan, Turkmenistan, and Uzbekistan the people are largely Turkic in origin; the Tajiks, for the most part, are ethnically Persian. It should come as no surprise, therefore, that both Turkey and Iran have been politically and economically very active in the region, as have Saudi Arabia and Kuwait to a lesser extent. Moscow remains quite interested in central Asian affairs despite the breakup of the Soviet empire, and Tajikistan, Turkmenistan, and Uzbekistan are members of the May 1992 treaty on collective security that the Russians brought with them in draft to Tashkent. The Russian government also signed a bilateral defense treaty with Turkmenistan in June 1992 that encourages the latter to create its own armed forces but stipulates that they are to be placed under joint command.[37]

Except for Kazakhstan, which besides its latent nuclear potential retains a sophisticated infrastructure for the manufacture of some kinds of advanced conventional weaponry, the central Asian republics pose a military threat to no one but themselves. Many of their immediate neighbors, by contrast, are well armed and capable of mounting military operations throughout the region, should they choose to do so.

In this sense, the four countries constitute a threat to the possible development of a regional security system because of their weakness, not because of their strength. None enjoys much political stability at the moment (Tajikistan is in the midst of a civil war), and change rather than continuity is likely to be a recurring theme in their domestic politics for some time to come. And although they have done nothing in their foreign policy activity to date that would bar their participation in a regime built around the concepts of cooperative security, neither have they done much to advance the cause. In light of their circumstances—small populations, unsettled political conditions, relatively low levels of economic development, and unfortunate geography—the central Asian states are certain to be consumers (or victims, depending on one's point of view) of any system for the multilateral management of security relations, not its architects.[38]

Challenges to Security Arising from the Soviet Demise

A diverse array of concrete challenges to the maintenance of regional and international security have come to the fore as a direct consequence of the breakup of the Soviet state. For purposes of analysis, they are divided into three groups. As of this writing, those in the first group constitute relatively minor threats, although the perception is often otherwise. Those in the second group are of significantly greater importance and will likely prove much harder to manage. Those in the third group present the most serious challenges of all and will require sustained effort, unprecedented levels of cooperation, and more than a little luck if they are to be overcome.

Group 1 Challenges: More Apparent Than Real

In the immediate aftermath of the dissolution of the Soviet state, two issues, both military in character, dominated Western media coverage of events. Such attention was probably warranted, given the possible consequences of a failure to resolve each problem peacefully. In hindsight, however, many of the fears expressed by those reporting on these issues proved to be groundless and the problems that remain are unlikely to constitute a casus belli among the parties.

THE COMMAND AND CONTROL OF NUCLEAR WEAPONS. Reasonably, much of the anxiety in the West over the Soviet collapse centered initially on the issue of the command and control of nuclear forces. Who exactly had authority to launch the country's strategic nuclear weapons, since Gorbachev had stepped down as president and the Soviet Union had ceased to exist? Was the principle of a single, unified strategic command to be preserved, or was authority to be shared among the heads of state (and the militaries) of the four ex-Soviet republics on whose territory long-range nuclear systems had been deployed? Was there to be one finger on the nuclear button or four?

Answers to these questions seemed to depend on who was being asked. According to the Russians, upon Gorbachev's resignation on December 25, 1991, political command of and responsibility for the Soviet Union's nuclear arsenal passed directly and without interruption to Boris Yeltsin, in his capacity as president of the Russian Federation.[39] Gorbachev allegedly confirmed this arrangement in a telephone conversation with President Bush on the day he left office.[40] Earlier in December the four CIS republics with nuclear weapons had agreed that operational control of the nuclear arsenal was to be vested in a "unified command structure" that looked and functioned very much like its Soviet predecessor. At the apex of this military structure, they subsequently announced, stood Marshal Yevgeniy Shaposhnikov as commander-in-chief. Shaposhnikov, former commander-in-chief of Soviet airborne forces, was to report to Yeltsin—but also, and in some ill-defined way, to Kravchuk, Nazarbayev, and Stanislav Shushkevich of Belarus. From the outset, however, Russian political authorities insisted that it was Yeltsin—and Yeltsin alone—to whom CIS military commanders would turn should a decision be required regarding the possible use of nuclear weapons.

At a meeting on December 30, 1991, the member states of the CIS, now numbering eleven, hammered out an agreement on the control of strategic nuclear forces that seemed to confirm Russia's status, in nuclear matters, as first among equals. "Until the complete elimination of nuclear weapons," the document declared, "the decision on the need for their use is made by the president of the Russian Federation in agreement with the heads of the Republic of Belarus, the Republic of Kazakhstan, and Ukraine, and in consultation with the heads of the other member states of the Commonwealth."[41]

The Ukrainians, in particular, took strong exception to the developing Russian position that whatever the rhetoric, *real* authority to launch CIS nuclear weapons had been delegated to Moscow. Early on, Kravchuk argued that Ukraine enjoyed what amounted to a unit veto over any prospective use of CIS nuclear weapons and claimed that Ukrainian authorities had the physical capacity to block any possible launch.[42] Nazarbayev of Kazakhstan also alluded to the existence of a four-key system on at least one occasion, although he was neither as clear nor as forceful as his Ukrainian colleague and seemed much more willing than Kravchuk to accept the reality of Russian dominance.

On several occasions in the period since the Commonwealth's founding, Yeltsin has gone out of his way to assert that dominance, all but declaring that he and senior CIS military commanders can in fact authorize the use of nuclear weapons, arm them, and order their delivery.[43] According to Moscow, the several agreements concluded between Russia and its sister republics on nuclear weapons issues require the Russian president to secure the political consent of his counterparts in Ukraine, Belarus, and Kazakhstan before taking any action; at the same time, again according to the Russians, none of the three has the capacity to prevent the use of these weapons should decisionmakers in Moscow issue orders to employ them.

Although the precise arrangements governing the possible use of CIS nuclear weapons remain obscure, all available evidence points to the essential correctness of the Russian position. No evidence has yet emerged, at least not publicly, to suggest that Ukraine enjoys "positive" control over any of the nuclear weapons deployed on its soil. The same, it appears, holds for Kazakhstan and Belarus. Kiev may have a degree of what it terms administrative control over at least some of these systems, including a small force of nuclear-capable long-range bombers, that may enable Ukraine to defeat any effort to launch these weapons platforms. As of late 1993, however, the three long-range missile complexes on Ukrainian soil remained in the hands of CIS military authorities who, as a practical matter, report to Moscow and not Kiev.

Privately, the Russians contend that by the end of 1994—by which time, according to agreements already concluded, all long-range nuclear systems currently based in Ukraine, Kazakhstan, and Belarus will have been returned to Russia and withdrawn from service—any lingering uncertainties concerning nuclear release and launch authority will be resolved, once and for all. With the removal of these missiles, the government in Moscow insists, Russia will become the Soviet Union's sole nuclear heir (with full authority to dispose of its nuclear forces as it sees fit) and all joint command arrangements will be dissolved.[44] For this to happen, however, the withdrawal of nuclear systems from Russia's three neighboring nuclear republics must first be completed, a scenario that seems possible but far from certain at this juncture.

In the interim, Moscow must remain faithful to the appearance (if not the substance) of the joint command arrangements for nuclear weapons worked out at successive CIS summit sessions if it wishes to preserve at least a semblance of unity within the shaky twelve-member CIS and prevent a dramatic downturn in relations, particularly with the government in Kiev.

THE DIVISION OF MILITARY ASSETS. Settling on an equitable division of Soviet conventional military assets has also proved to be a source of tension between Russia and its sister republics. As in the controversy over the control of nuclear forces, the most intense dispute has been between Russia and Ukraine, which have found themselves at odds over a number of issues, including how to dispose of the Black Sea fleet and, more generally, how to apportion both the military equipment and the uniformed personnel left over from the Soviet collapse. Conflicts of a superficially similar nature have arisen between the Russian Federation and other Commonwealth members as well, but none of these has had either the intensity or the duration of the dispute between the two largest Slavic republics.

For Russia and Ukraine the disposition of Soviet military assets has both a substantive and a symbolic dimension. As the second most populous of the Soviet successor states, with ambitions to become a formidable middle power, Ukraine has moved in a determined fashion since December 1991 to create military forces of sufficient size and capability to secure the country's vital interests. It can do so most expeditiously by nationalizing as much ex-Soviet military equipment as possible and by encouraging the return of ethnic Ukrainians to serve in its armed forces, both of which it has done. These steps also serve to underscore the government's determination to pursue an independent course in foreign and military policy, free of Moscow's tutelage. To obtain the best deal possible in negotiations with the Russians, Ukrainian authorities have advanced claims that by any reasonable standard can only be considered inflated and extreme (for example, insisting that Ukraine is entitled to some 90 percent of the Black Sea fleet).

On balance the Russians have been accommodating. On only two issues has Moscow taken strong exception to Kiev's claims: on military equipment that the Russians deem unambiguously strategic in nature, such as long-range aircraft, and on the Black Sea flotilla. In the first instance, the Russian government argues that aircraft capable of delivering nuclear ordnance—wherever they may be based—should be assigned to the CIS command, in keeping with previous agreements detailing what do and do not constitute strategic nuclear forces. The Ukrainians, who sought in April 1992 to place nuclear-capable bombers within the country directly under their command, contend that the issue is less clear-cut than the Russians allege. Kiev has pressed this particular demand with considerable vigor, but to date at least the aircraft remain under formal CIS command.

The Black Sea flotilla is a different matter. Officially Moscow maintains that the dispute is over what portion of the fleet should be assigned to the Commonwealth and what might rightfully be considered Russian and Ukrainian. At a second level, however, the issue is more parochial: is Russia or Ukraine to receive the lion's share of the Soviet Union's third largest fleet, numbering some 150 ships of various sizes and capabilities? Although the Yeltsin government is prepared to surrender roughly a quarter of the ships to Ukraine—the fleet's home port is Sebastopol, in the Crimea, after all—it insists that the Black Sea fleet has always been Russian, and so it shall remain. Ukraine disputes the Russian charge—how can it be Russian if it is based on Ukrainian territory?—and accuses Moscow of great-power chauvinism. As of this writing, the two sides have tentatively agreed to a division of the assets, although neither side seems particularly pleased with the proposed outcome, and either or both could decide to reopen the discussion at a later time.

Moscow's relatively relaxed posture toward Ukraine's military ambitions has much to do with the realization that the new Russia will be able to support only a fraction of the armed forces once deployed by the Soviet Union. The Russian government has authorized the creation of a military establishment numbering approximately 1.5 million, roughly 40 percent of the size of the armed forces maintained by the Soviet state during the 1980s. Smaller forces mean fewer weapons and less equipment, of course, making the distribution of existing military assets less of an issue from Moscow's perspective than it could be. Moreover, Ukraine, even with armed forces totaling 400,000, is unlikely to pose a serious military threat to Russia, which in addition to its sizeable conventional capabilities seems destined to retain an extremely potent nuclear arsenal for as far into the future as it is possible to predict.

Between Russia and the other CIS republics, the process of dividing up the military spoils has been measurably less contentious. Although all the CIS states have announced plans to field their own militaries, with the exception of Russia and Ukraine few have actually done so, and in most of the countries planning remains at an early stage. With several republic governments—Kazakhstan and Turkmenistan, for example—the Russians are, in fact, working closely in the design and development of appropriate force structures; in these instances, disputes over equipment and personnel have been either minor and transient or absent altogether.

Pressure from the West, and especially from the United States, has played a modestly constructive role in motivating the Commonwealth's often fractious member states to resolve their differences over the allocation of Soviet military equipment. The U.S. and western European governments were particularly eager to obtain the adherence of seven of the republics to the provisions of the

1990 CFE treaty, the status of which was rendered problematic by the collapse of the USSR, and were anything but shy in relaying their anxieties. In response to these concerns, in May 1992 Russia, Ukraine, Belarus, Armenia, Georgia, Azerbaijan, and Moldova informed the other signatories to the CFE that they had agreed on a formula to apportion the seven kinds of military equipment limited by the agreement.[45] They also declared that they would proceed to submit the accord for parliamentary ratification without delay. By February 1993 all seven had done so.

On the narrow issue, then, of who stood to reap what proportion of the Soviet military windfall, most of the major decisions have now been made, although not yet implemented. Of the problems that remain, some, such as the final disposition of the Black Sea fleet, are real; others are contrived. More to the point, none of the disputes, taken individually, is sufficiently grave to ignite armed conflict. Sadly, there is no shortage of flash points between and among the republics, any one of which could lead, or already has led, to the outbreak of war; haggling over leftover military equipment, although it continues to be an irritant to relations among the CIS states, is not one of them.

Group 2 Challenges: Real but Manageable

A second class of problems spawned by the collapse of the Soviet Union constitutes a more serious challenge to regional peace and security than the somewhat opaque arrangements for the command and control of nuclear weapons and the contested division of Soviet military assets. This second group of problems has also proved to be less amenable to resolution.

TO SIGN OR NOT TO SIGN: UKRAINE, KAZAKHSTAN, AND THE NPT. The refusal by several of the Soviet successor states to embrace unequivocally the USSR's international legal commitments, including those contained in a number of important arms control accords, has generated considerable political anxiety in the West. Of special concern to the United States and its allies and to other signatories of the treaty has been the failure of the Ukrainian and Kazakh governments to adhere formally to the NPT.[46]

In the immediate aftermath of the Soviet collapse, three of the four republics with nuclear weapons declared themselves bound by the Soviet Union's international commitments. Russia promised to abide by the treaties concluded by the Soviet government and to ratify all pending accords. At the end of 1991 these commitments included both the 1990 CFE treaty and the 1991 START agreement. The Russian government would do so, it stated, in its capacity as the successor state to the USSR. Ukraine and Belarus undertook similar commitments and pledged to join the NPT as nonnuclear powers at the earliest opportunity. Initially only Kazakhstan equivocated, promising to become a party to all arms control agreements concluded by Moscow, including the NPT, even as it threatened to retain, at least for a time, the strategic nuclear weapons deployed on its territory.

Western relief at the apparent willingness of Ukraine and Kazakhstan, in particular, to confirm their nonnuclear status by acceding to the NPT quickly turned to angst, however, as the months passed and the Kravchuk and Nazarbayev governments declined to make good on their promises. Other troubling news soon followed. In spring 1992 Kiev took issue with Moscow (and Washington) over the right of the Russian government to ratify the START treaty on its behalf, arguing that the presence of several hundred CIS strategic nuclear systems within the country required that Ukraine take part formally in the ratification process. Belarus and Kazakhstan, though less exercised over the matter than the Ukrainians, sided with Kiev.

The issue was not resolved until May 1992, when the United States, with the grudging consent of the Russians, opened up the treaty for multiple signatures (thereby suggesting, at least implicitly, that Ukraine, Kazakhstan, and Belarus were indeed nuclear powers, albeit of a somewhat novel type). In exchange, the U.S. government sought and received assurances that the agreement would be placed before the Ukrainian, Belarussian, and Kazakh parliaments for prompt action. Under U.S. pressure the three republics also reiterated their earlier pledges to join the NPT regime as non–nuclear weapon states.

The refusal, in particular, of the Ukrainian government to sign the NPT—despite repeated assurances that ratification is imminent—represents potentially the most significant medium-term threat to regional and international security that has resulted from the Soviet demise. Should Ukraine decide to retain a manifest (or even an implicit) nuclear capability, other governments, both in the region and beyond, will be inclined either to maintain (and perhaps expand) their existing nuclear arsenals or to redouble attempts to acquire nuclear forces of their own. An expensive and destabilizing series of regional arms races could well result, vastly complicating international efforts to limit membership in the nuclear club and to slow the spread of nuclear weapons technologies.

Ukrainian leaders, it appears, view the proliferation issue in a somewhat different light. For them, the narrow military aspect of the nuclear problem is clearly secondary to the host of political questions that relate to, but are analytically distinct from, the awesome destructive power of the weapons themselves. Whatever else they do, nuclear weapons provide countries in possession of such instruments with enormous political clout. At the same time, the costs, material and otherwise, of sustaining even a rudimentary nuclear capability are considerable. (This cost is especially a burden, of course, for Ukraine, which became a nuclear weapon state by accident and at the present time lacks both the personnel and the infrastructure to maintain the arsenal in anything like its present form.)

As long as the government in Kiev resists pressures to accede to the NPT, for example, it is unlikely to enjoy fully normalized relations with the West or to receive much by way of direct financial and material assistance—two outcomes that would seem to be highly desirable, given the deeply troubled state of its economy and political system. On the other hand, the moment that the Ukrainians ratify the treaty, they will cease being a central focus of the international community, their importance to the West will decline dramatically, and they will lose what modest political leverage they currently enjoy.

Thus, for Ukraine, the strategy with the highest potential payoff is one of linkage: ratification of the NPT and its associated safeguards *in exchange for* Western support on key political issues (vis-à-vis Russia, in particular) and the provision of generous economic assistance. From a Western perspective, such a strategy smacks of blackmail and tends to arouse (or to confirm) deep suspicions about the motivations and purposes of the Ukrainian leadership. Nonetheless, senior political authorities in Kiev appear to have concluded that the risks attending such a posture, though real, are very much worth running.

Assuming that this characterization of Ukrainian motives comes close to the mark,[47] the challenge confronting Western governments is to devise and then implement a policy that facilitates realization of the first-order objective (nuclear nonproliferation), while not losing sight of the goals that are important to the other side (economic development and political stability).

THE SECURITY VACUUM. Not since the early 1920s, in the turbulent aftermath of World War I and the Russian Revolution, has the security environment in east-central Europe and across much of Eurasia been as volatile and unpredictable as it was in 1993. However one interprets the legacy of the communist regime in Moscow, its successes in extending Soviet authority throughout much of the former Russian Empire and later in consolidating "the postwar gains of socialism" in Europe at least ensured that a high degree of regional order would be maintained. With the collapse of Soviet power, first in eastern Europe and then at home, that order evaporated. What we confront in the region today is pervasive insecurity.

Although beset by a collection of seemingly intractable dilemmas, Russia is probably the least vulnerable militarily of the region's political actors and therefore less of a security problem than analysts in the West sometimes suggest. With a population of almost 150 million, the vast majority of the Soviet military establishment, and thousands of nuclear weapons, the Russian Federation has little to fear from its nearest neighbors by way of outright aggression. It also enjoys relatively good relations with the United States, the countries of western and eastern Europe, and China, a marked change in Moscow's geopolitical fortunes since the days of Soviet rule.

Russia could become a threat to security, however, under either of two broad conditions: first, should there come to power in Moscow an aggressive and xenophobic regime, bent on reclaiming the territories lost to Russia since the breakup of the USSR, whatever the costs; or, second, should the Russian state itself disintegrate, providing a once-in-a-millennium opportunity for other countries in the area to gain an advantage at Russia's expense. If either of these scenarios should come to pass, conflict on a massive scale, comparable in scope and intensity to that witnessed during the Russian civil war, would seem to be inevitable.

If, for purposes of argument, it is assumed neither of these two admittedly extreme outcomes occurs in Russia, in terms of regional security the most pressing task confronting the Soviet successor states is how, as independent political actors, to replace the guarantees once provided by the Kremlin. None of the fifteen republics, including Russia, currently belongs to a functioning bilateral or multilateral alliance system; the collective security agreement signed by six of the republics in May 1992 in Tashkent is hardly a reliable instrument at this juncture, although it could become one in the future. Membership in NATO is not immediately an option, and the Conference on Security and Cooperation in Europe lacks a military arm to deter aggression and enforce the peace.

For the moment at least, each of the republics must rely on its own resources as it seeks to protect itself against the appetites of others. The situation is especially acute in central Asia, where the end of Soviet rule instantaneously transformed the region's five republics into geopolitical orphans, and in the Caucasus, where intense fighting along ethnic and religious lines has erupted on a major scale following a seventy-year hiatus. Ukraine, though largely free of the violence that characterizes the process of state building elsewhere in the former union, is nonetheless isolated politically, fearful of the Russian colossus to the north, and without significant allies or friends anywhere in the area.

There is no easy or clear-cut answer to this extraordinarily complex and dangerous problem. The security arrangements that eventually emerge will necessarily reflect, however, underlying power relationships within the region. Russia, weak or strong, is a reality that all states in the area must acknowledge and that most will have to accommodate to one degree or another.

Russia's leadership is also indispensable if sustainable systems for the management of regional security relations are to be built on the ruins of the Soviet empire. The treaties of friendship and cooperation that have already been concluded between Moscow and several of the central Asian republics are important in this regard and indicative of the kinds of arrangements that may come to dominate regional security ties in the near to medium term. Additional agreements will almost certainly follow. Such arrangements cannot be manufactured and then imposed from abroad. Insofar as solutions to these security problems exist, they are, for the most part, to be found within the region itself.

That said, how the West responds to this manifest crisis in security does matter. Moving under clearly specified conditions to integrate the successor states into Western political and economic institutions, thereby reducing their isolation and expediting the transition to democracy and free-market economies, is an obvious first step. Providing forums for the airing and possible mediation and resolution of disputes is another step that could ease regional tensions (where they exist) and promote habits of cooperation. The North Atlantic Cooperation Council is one institution specifically designed with these purposes in mind, and there may be need for others. Punishing republics that resort to force in an effort to settle their regional differences or to expand the amount of territory under their control is also an option, although one that should be exercised as a last resort and with extreme caution.

If the period between the two world wars is any guide, leaving the region entirely on its own to sort out the security challenges it faces is probably a mistake. On the other hand, trying to structure bilateral and multilateral relations from afar, without the direct, intimate, and sustained participation of all regional actors, could be equally disastrous. The task before the West is to develop a viable middle course: one that provides strong incentives for (and conveys the Western commitment to) the creation of a stable regional environment but that leaves the exact nature and timing of security arrangements to the states in the region, recognizing that the systems that develop will be advantageous to some and disadvantageous to others, as well as incomplete, less than fully effective, and subject to radical and unpredictable change.

Group 3 Challenges: Real and Very Dangerous

A third group of challenges came relatively late to the attention of Western policy analysts and government officials, but in the two years that have elapsed since the collapse of Soviet power both the magnitude and potential implications of these problems have become all too evident.

THE TREND TOWARD SOCIAL AND POLITICAL DISINTEGRATION: THE POWER OF RACE, ETHNICITY, AND RELIGION. Reference has already been made to the myriad racial, ethnic, and religious tensions that have surfaced throughout the former Soviet Union since the unraveling of communist authority, many of which have spilled over into violence as the social and economic institutions that once linked the USSR's vast collection of peoples and cultures come apart. It is perhaps sufficient to note here three classes of problems that have their origins in the rich mixture of race, ethnicity, and religion that all but defined the essential character of the multinational Soviet state—and to which, ironically, the country's leaders so often turned as evidence of socialism's superior capacity to accommodate human diversity.

The most visible of the ethnically or religiously inspired conflicts are those *between* various republics, such as the undeclared war between Christian Armenia and Moslem Azerbaijan for control of Nagorno-Karabakh and the simmering dispute between Russia and Georgia over South Ossetia. In the former case, the fighting has already taken several thousand lives. Many more will die or otherwise be victimized as the violence, once confined within the borders of the disputed region, spreads to the homelands of the combatants.

Neither the Armenian nor the Azerbaijani government has acted in a determined fashion to halt the bloodletting; each has become hostage, in fact, to the passions of its people and could not long remain in power were it to abandon the cause. All efforts at mediation have failed abysmally up to this point, and there is no reason to suspect that future initiatives will fare any better. Without massive outside intervention to separate the warring parties—a most unlikely development as of this writing—this ancient and particularly brutal conflict seems destined to continue.

The fighting between Armenia and Azerbaijan is both more extreme and better organized than the violence that has occasionally erupted between the other republics. But ethnic and religious tensions, fueled by economic calamity and social disarray, are on the rise everywhere across the former union, especially in those areas—such as Moldova, Ukraine, parts of the Caucasus, and parts of central Asia—where the lines drawn by Kremlin cartographers during the 1930s and 1940s reflect a combination of administrative convenience and Stalinist whim, corresponding only occasionally to historical patterns of ethnic and religious settlement.

A second major problem within this general category of ills is the existence *within* many of the republics of ethnically distinct populations for whom continued incorporation within the larger polity constitutes, in their judgment, a denial of their basic human rights and a form of political subjugation and cultural repression. The situation is acute in the Russian Federation, home to some fifty separate nationality groups and thirty-two ethnically based administrative zones. Twenty percent of the country's population is ethnically non-Russian. Included in this percentage are roughly 6 million Tatars, whose political leaders have committed themselves to the establishment of a sovereign "Tatarstan," an enclave of several thousand square miles surrounded on all sides by Russian territory.[48] The government in Moscow rejects this declaration of Tatar independence and vows to maintain political control of the region. But the war of words persists and the struggle goes on.

Similar sentiments have been expressed by representatives of at least a dozen other ethnic groups that inhabit historically Russian lands, and although most of these campaigns are unlikely to end in victory for those who would sever all ties to Moscow, they are indicative of just how chaotic and decentralized Russian political life has become since the disintegration of the unitary Soviet state.

Except for the Baltic republics and Belarus, all of Russia's sister republics face comparable challenges. Moreover, few are as well equipped as the Russian republic, either militarily or politically, to contain these movements for greater autonomy or outright independence. It is once again the four smaller central Asian republics, each with sizeable non-Slavic minority populations residing within its borders, that are potentially most at risk in this context, although until now pleas to join various national liberation struggles have gone largely unheeded. For the time being at least, national (and subnational) consciousness in central Asia remains surprisingly underdeveloped.

Russians living outside the territory of the Russian state but within the borders of the old union constitute the third and arguably the most dangerous of the problems that flow from ethnic or religious differences and the tensions these differences produce. The scale of the problem is immense. Between 25 million and 30 million Russians currently reside in areas beyond the reach of the government in Moscow, including 11.3 million in Ukraine and another 6.3 million in Kazakhstan. Collectively, Estonia and Latvia play host to another 1.4 million Russians, constituting over 30 percent of the population in the former country and 34 percent in the latter. Only Armenia, with fewer than 70,000 Russians (out of a total population of 3.3 million), can afford to be fairly complacent about the issue.

Russians living in the near-abroad, as it is termed, have become an extremely potent and sensitive political issue in the Russian Federation. Conservative critics of the current government have made the fate of their fellow countrymen so situated a favorite rallying cry, as well as a potential cause of war between the Russian Federation and a number of neighboring republics.[49] Moldova, which declines to acknowledge the independence of the Russian-inhabited "Trans-Dniester Republic," for example, found itself engaged in a low-level conflict along its eastern frontier with army units (once belonging to the Fourteenth Soviet Army) loyal to Moscow. The treatment of Russians in Ukraine has been a frequent source of contention between the Yeltsin and Kravchuk governments, as it has been between Russia and the Baltic republics. Short of forcing this immense expatriate community to resettle in Russia, a step for which neither the various republic governments nor Moscow has the resources, let alone the desire, to implement, the problem would seem to be intractable. A significant number of Russians will relocate on their own in coming years, particularly those in areas where anti-Russian sentiments run high and violence against them has already occurred. This number is probably no more than a fraction of the total population, however, and under virtually any scenario that one can imagine, many millions of Russians will continue to live in such far-flung reaches of the former Soviet empire as Turkmenistan (9 percent Russian) to the south and Kyrgyzstan (21.5 percent Russian) to the southeast.

If economic conditions continue to deteriorate, relations between local populations and those Russians who elect to stay put will almost certainly take a turn for the worse, as the competition for jobs and resources, already intense, grows furious. This competition could well precipitate a level of civil violence not seen in these regions since the Russian Revolution and comparable in scope to the kind of devastation that has accompanied the political breakup of Yugoslavia.

Like the tragedy in Yugoslavia, such fighting could also produce hundreds of thousands—perhaps millions—of refugees seeking safe passage to more peaceful environs. Well over 1 million people have been displaced since early 1991 as a result of the conflict among the Serbs, the Croats, and the Bosnians; the corresponding figure in the former Soviet Union could be much higher should the barely submerged ethnic and religious tensions that run through the fabric of this shattered society turn violent in a major way.

The human consequences of the war in Yugoslavia are beyond the capacity of the international community to absorb. In Germany alone, more than 200,000 refugees have taken up temporary residence, and more than 100,000 have found their way to Austria, Hungary, and Italy. Events in Bosnia and Herzegovina may be only the warm-up act, however, for what could unfold farther to the east. This is the vision—or the nightmare—that should inform the decisionmaking process in the West as the Group of Seven governments contemplate how much economic assistance to provide to the Russian Federation and the other fourteen Soviet successor states in the years ahead.

THE AUTHORIZED AND UNAUTHORIZED TRANSFER OF WEAPONS AND WEAPONS-RELATED TECHNOLOGIES. One of the most transparent threats to the possible creation of a more cooperative global order is the sale or transfer of Soviet military equipment to any number of interested parties, from countries eager to augment their arsenals at bargain-basement prices to terrorist groups in the market for more sophisticated ways to visit death and destruction on their enemies. A related problem is the outright theft of such equipment, including weapons and ammunition, by military and paramilitary groups inside the former union that have taken up arms, either against one another or against regional governments seeking to suppress them.

The nature of the problem is well illustrated by the conduct of the Russian government, which pursues a policy on weapons transfers that is wholly inconsistent. On the one hand, it has assured the West, and the United States in particular, that it has no intention of becoming the world's leading arms bazaar. On the other hand, reports of major weapons deals between Russia and a host of would-be buyers continue to surface in the Russian and Western press. One such agreement, between Russia and China, is reportedly worth hundreds of millions of dollars. Among the items that the Chinese have purchased (or are about to purchase) are Su-27 fighter aircraft, multiple-rocket launchers, armored vehicles, tanks, and helicopters.[50] In October 1992 the *New York Times* reported that China was also interested in buying various dual-use technologies from the Russians, including advanced guidance systems for use in ballistic missiles and state-of-the-art uranium-enrichment technologies.[51]

A story that appeared in the *Observer* in June 1992 reported that the Russian Federation had decided to sell off approximately one-sixth of the Soviet navy within the next several years. On the list of naval vessels to be sold to the highest bidder were battle cruisers, aircraft carriers, and submarines. In addition to China, potential buyers were said to include Iran, Iraq, Libya, Syria, and the Philippines.[52] India's interest in all manner of Soviet (now Russian) military goods, such as large-lift booster rockets, is well known.

The primary Russian incentive to sell is economic. Russia's state adviser on military conversion, Mikhail Maley, supports plans to boost Russian military exports on the grounds that the monies earned from sales abroad can then be used to convert the majority of the country's defense industry to civilian production—a task, he estimates, that could cost anywhere between $150 billion and $160 billion and take fifteen years to complete.[53] On occasion, even Boris Yeltsin has endorsed calls to sell some of the country's military stockpile to foreign buyers as a way to keep hundreds of thousands of Russian workers in the bloated defense sector gainfully employed until the economy expands enough to provide new sources of jobs. It could be a long wait. With the program to convert Russian military industries hopelessly mired in red tape and going nowhere, government interest in arms exports seems certain to grow rather than diminish, at least in the short run.

Such pressures operate elsewhere in the Commonwealth, of course, but with less force than they do in Russia. The other republics have both less to sell than the Russians and fewer workers who rely on defense-related industries for employment. Also agitating against major weapons sales—in Ukraine, for example—is the need to equip the newly formed republic armies with all kinds of military equipment, from assault rifles to armored personnel carriers to main battle tanks. One of the most urgent security challenges these regimes confront, in fact, is not an excess of military potential but the unauthorized transfer of large numbers of weapons, through sale and theft, to local militias and criminal syndicates with interests to protect, battles to fight, and scores to settle.

The true extent of this particular problem is impossible to assess, given the absence of reliable figures, and no responsible Russian or republic government spokesmen will hazard a guess as to its scope. However, in an off-the-record conversation with me, one Russian Ministry of Foreign Affairs official speculated that the total value of ex-Soviet military goods (primarily small arms, ammunition, and combat vehicles) siphoned off in this way probably exceeded $100 million in the first six months of 1992.

Doubtless, the unauthorized transfer of nuclear weapons (and of the technologies essential to their production) is the single greatest danger in this regard, and much of the attention that Western political leaders and technical experts have devoted to the problem of weapons proliferation and the Soviet collapse has been directed to this vital issue. Although the fears expressed by some in the West that the breakup of the Soviet Union might result in the transfer of some number of nuclear devices to states or other political actors not now in the possession of such weapons appear, in retrospect, to have been exaggerated, the problem of transfer of weapons endures. How the West, together with the governments in the Russian Federation, Belarus, Kazakhstan, and Ukraine, has sought to cope with this challenge to nonproliferation—what has and has not been done and what still requires doing—is discussed in detail in chapter 15 in this volume.

Controlling both the legal and the illicit trade in conventional arms, like most of the challenges that have arisen as a result of the Soviet Union's disintegration, admits of no easy solution. The Russian government's inconsistent position on the issue, though frustrating to those in the West who long for a simple solution to this complex problem, is really a shibboleth. The more important source of the problem is the region's seemingly unchecked descent into a political and economic netherworld, which places the affected governments in an unenviable position: either they can heed the warnings of countries in the developed world, restrict the flow of weapons, and throw a significant number of their citizens out of work, or they can sell off some of the military equipment they no longer want or need, maintain at least some of the existing weapons production runs, and risk the ire (or worse) of much of the international community.

How political leaders in Moscow (and Minsk, Kiev, and Alma Ata) will respond to these conflicting pressures is hard to predict. They will, in all probability, continue to say one thing and do another. The larger point, in any event, is that unless and until (1) political conditions within the former union begin to stabilize and (2) the economies of the successor states bottom out and start to recover, Western policymakers should not expect the Russian (or the Belarussian, the Ukrainian, or the Kazakh) government to impose—let alone enforce—meaningful constraints on the commerce in conventional arms. For them to do so would be political suicide.

Conclusions and Recommendations

Securing the effective participation of the now-sovereign republics of the former Soviet Union in both a regional and an international regime for the cooperative management of security relations is simultaneously necessary and problematic. Too big to be ignored and too unstable to be relied upon, the member states of the CIS collectively constitute the single greatest challenge to security anywhere in Eurasia. At the same time, that very insecurity vastly complicates the development and implementation of a cooperative security regime organized along global lines.

In exploring the relationship between cooperative security regimes and existing and prospective conditions in the former Soviet Union, analysts and policymakers alike might usefully frame their consideration of this complex issue by reference to four central propositions, deduced from the body of the analysis.

First, for the foreseeable future the CIS states are likely to constitute problems for, rather than solutions to, the cooperative management of regional and international security relations. Political developments within the CIS states, including Russia, are highly unpredictable at this juncture because of the interplay of large-scale and extremely powerful economic, social, ethnic, and religious forces that are beyond the ability of governments in the region to control. As a consequence, leaders throughout the region may have the best of intentions but, as a practical matter, may be unable to implement policies that the West deems critically important.

Second, how the West responds to the multiple crises in the former Soviet Union can influence events, developments, and decisions, although to a lesser extent than Western analysts sometimes assume. For example, implementation of the economic assistance package assembled by the World Bank, IMF, and the Group of Seven industrialized states cannot guarantee the triumph of democracy and market economics anywhere in the former Soviet Union. It is equally true, however, that a failure to provide significant Western aid will almost certainly doom efforts to reform the political and economic systems in Russia and elsewhere.

Third, given its size and strategic importance, the primary focus of Western attention and assistance should be Russia (followed by the Baltic states, Ukraine, Belarus, and Kazakhstan). The West can do little for the central Asian republics in light of the region's geographic remoteness, political volatility, and relatively low level of economic development, or for Armenia, Georgia, and Azerbaijan, where the persistence of ethnically and religiously based violence prevents meaningful economic recovery and works at cross-purposes with genuine political reform.

Fourth, in their dealings with the four largest and most important CIS republics, U.S. and Western policymakers should insist on a clear linkage between economic assistance and political support, on the one hand, and responsible conduct in the areas of security, arms control, weapons proliferation, and arms transfers, on the other. Such a policy of conditionality is not only desirable but probably unavoidable because of the political constraints under which leaders within the donor countries must operate.

It is also true, however, that a policy of conditionality, managed poorly, will create more problems than it solves. In dealing with the Russians, in particular, it is essential to understand that, whatever their recent travails, they represent a large, industrially developed, and extremely well-armed country, with vast material resources and one of world's most highly educated work forces. Sensitivity to and an appreciation for Russia's current plight is indispensable. The Russian people must not be patronized or made to feel like hapless recipients of Western largesse.

A realistic strategy for the West to encourage cooperative behavior on the part of the largest and most important of the CIS states might then encompass the following five steps.

—In recognition of its success to date in democratizing the country's political life and in encouraging meaningful economic reform, accelerate the flow of Western economic assistance to the Russian Federation. At the same time and as indicated, the West should continue to specify the conditions that must be met to ensure a continuation of aid and then work together with the Russian government to overcome the remaining obstacles to reform.

—Secure Ukrainian and Kazakh adherence to the NPT and to the Lisbon protocol to the START treaty (Ukraine); once the instruments of ratification are on deposit, increase Western aid and assistance.

—Intensify discussions with the major republics on possible regional security arrangements, both bilateral and multilateral, in which Western governments, including the United States, might undertake certain, limited obligations (including regularized high-level consultations, mediation efforts, and provision of good offices) short of outright security guarantees.

—Redouble efforts to assist the republics in converting their defense industrial facilities to the production of civilian goods, recognizing that initial results will be modest and that the economic and social costs of conversion will be high. Given the scale of the problem, the West should attach priority to the industrial demilitarization of Russia.

—Discourage the sale or transfer of weapons and weapons platforms from CIS republics to third parties by, among other steps, exercising a modicum of Western restraint. U.S. demands that the Russians, in particular, resist the temptation to export armaments for hard currency are likely to fall on deaf ears as long as the leading Western supplier states continue to sell weapons to a variety of buyers when the motivation is clearly economic rather than political (for example, the 1992 sale of U.S. F-16 aircraft to Taiwan).

The collapse of the Soviet empire has transformed both the substance and the conduct of international politics. Regrettably, as of this writing in late 1993, neither those in the West nor those in the East can know precisely what the sudden disappearance of the USSR portends. At a minimum, the Soviet collapse signifies the end of one era in world politics and the start of another. Most of what happens in the fifteen sovereign republics of the former Soviet Union will be determined, of course, by autonomous forces operating with little or no regard for Western preferences. What the West does or does not do, however, can make a difference.

The task confronting the West, as it seeks to elicit behavior on the part of the Soviet successor states that is more cooperative than confrontational, is to devise policies that are simple, consistent, sustainable over the long run, and mutually beneficial. To have the desired effect, such policies must also assist the realization of such *shared* goals as democratization, the creation of markets, regional stability, and nonproliferation.

Notes

1. The twelve non-Slavic republics comprise the three Baltic states (Estonia, Latvia, and Lithuania), five central Asian republics (Kazakhstan, Kyrgyzstan, Tajikistan, Turkmenistan, and Uzbekistan), three Caucasian countries (Armenia, Azerbaijan, and Georgia), and Moldova. Of the twelve, only the Baltic states enjoy a modicum of stability at the moment, and even in this region the potential for upheaval and political violence remains high, given the persistence of ethnically rooted tensions between resident Russians and the local populations.

2. See, for example, Jim Hoagland, "Looking Ahead: At Home and Abroad," *Washington Post,* November 8, 1992, p. A1.

3. See Michael McGuire, *Perestroika and Soviet National Security* (Brookings, 1991), pp. 313–29.

4. See, in particular, "At the USSR Ministry of Foreign Affairs," *Vestnik Ministerstva Inostrannykh Del,* no. 2 (1987), pp. 30–34.

5. See "M. S. Gorbachev Speech at UN Organization," *Pravda,* December 8, 1988, pp. 1–2, in Foreign Broadcast Information Service, *Daily Report: Soviet Union,* December 8, 1988, pp. 11–19. (Hereafter FBIS, *Soviet Union.*)

6. Andrey Kozyrev, "Russia: A Chance for Survival," *Foreign Affairs,* vol. 71 (Spring 1992), p. 14.

7. On Moscow's interest in securing membership in Western-dominated international economic institutions, see Ed A. Hewett with Clifford G. Gaddy, *Open for Business: Russia's Return to the Global Economy* (Brookings, 1992), pp. 4–46.

8. Kozyrev, "Russia," p. 6.

9. Ibid., pp. 12–13.

10. Andrey Kozyrev, "Transformed Russia in a New World," *Izvestiya,* January 2, 1992, p. 3, in FBIS, *Soviet Union,* January 2, 1992, p. 79.

11. "On the Principles of New Mutual Relations: The Camp David Declaration by President Bush and President Yeltsin," *Rossiskaya Gazeta,* February 3, 1992, p. 3, in FBIS, *Daily Report: Central Eurasia,* February 3, 1992, pp. 26–27. (Hereafter FBIS, *Central Eurasia.*)

12. From the packet of materials assembled by the Office of the Press Secretary, the White House, at the conclusion of the Bush-Yeltsin summit meeting, June 17, 1992.

13. See Serge Schmemann, "Yeltsin Leaves Talks with Firm Support and More Aid," *New York Times,* April 5, 1993, p. 1.

14. Upon the Soviet Union's expiration, the Russian government immediately declared itself the "successor state" to the USSR. By so doing, the government prevented Russia's "dropping out" of international relations. This step also enabled the new government in Moscow to appropriate the Soviet Union's embassies and consulates around the world and to lay claim to the USSR's seat in the UN Security Council.

15. Ann Devroy, "U.S., Allies Set $24 Billion in Aid for Ex-Soviet States," *Washington Post,* April 2, 1992, p. A1.

16. On July 5, 1992, the Russian government and the IMF reached tentative agreement on a plan to provide the first $1 billion earmarked for the ruble stabilization fund; they also agreed, in principle, on a two-part program of reform that the Russians promised to implement over the succeeding twelve months that should have resulted in

the phased release of the remaining $23 billion in Western funds already pledged. As of this writing, approximately two-thirds of this amount had been delivered to Russia and a new, larger Western aid package was being assembled.

17. Yuri Glukhov, "The Moles of History Dig Blindly: High-Level Failures of High-Level Politics," *Pravda,* February 24, 1992, in *Current Digest of the Post-Soviet Press,* vol. 44 (March 25, 1992), pp. 8–9.

18. Some 90 percent of those taking part in the referendum voted to establish an independent, sovereign Ukraine. Adrian Karatnycky, "The Ukrainian Factor," *Foreign Affairs,* vol. 71 (Summer 1992), pp. 90–91.

19. Ibid., p. 91.

20. The Ukrainians initially discussed maintaining 400,000 to 450,000 men under arms. Recently they have scaled back their plans and now seem likely to field forces in the range of 150,000 to 250,000. Even this figure may be high, given budgetary constraints.

21. Although Ukraine's fears concerning Russia's regional political ambitions may be exaggerated, they are not groundless. Early in 1992, during the course of a wide-ranging discussion on the future of the Russian Federation and the CIS to which I was a party, one senior Russian official confessed that to him Russia without Ukraine was simply unimaginable. He also observed that the CIS—to the extent that it had any identity at all—existed primarily as a vehicle for advancing the interests of Russia, which, after all, was the only "great power" to emerge from the ruins of the Soviet empire.

22. See "Treaty on Collective Security," *Rossiyskaya Gazeta,* May 23, 1992, p. 2, in FBIS, *Central Eurasia,* May 26, 1992, p. 8.

23. The Crimea, home to an ethnic mix of Russians, Tatars, Ukrainians, and Jews, has emerged as one of the most sensitive issues in Ukrainian-Russian relations. Nikita Khrushchev, in 1954, placed the region under Ukrainian political jurisdiction, despite its having been Russian territory for several centuries. Upon independence, a number of Russian political figures began to agitate for the Crimea's return to the motherland; at one point during spring 1991 the Russian parliament annulled the 1954 decree awarding the peninsula to Ukraine. Kiev retaliated by reaffirming its ownership of the disputed territory. As of this writing, the status of the region has yet to be determined. The most likely solution is that the Crimea will become an autonomous republic within Ukraine. It is also conceivable that Moscow and Kiev will agree to abide by a plebiscite in which those who inhabit the area can determine their own political future.

24. Chrystia Freeland, "Russia, Ukraine to Divide Fleet: Yeltsin, Kravchuk Reach Accord in Principle at Black Sea Talks," *Washington Post,* June 24, 1992, p. A1.

25. Long-range nuclear systems deployed in Ukraine include 46 SS-24 and 130 SS-19 MIRVed ICBMs. Also based on Ukrainian soil are some forty long-range bombers that are capable of delivering nuclear weapons. See "FSU Strategic Nuclear Weapons Outside Russia," Arms Control Association Fact Sheet, Washington, May 1993. In July 1993 Ukrainian authorities began to dismantle SS-19s. See Dunbar Lockwood, "Ukraine's Position Hardens despite Some Positive Signs," *Arms Control Today,* vol. 23 (September 1993), pp. 25, 30.

26. The Kravchuk government resumed the transfer of tactical nuclear weapons to Russia the following month; according to the CIS military command, the last of the weapons left Ukraine in May 1992.

27. Kathy Mihalisko, "Baker: No US Military Commitment to Ukraine, Kazakhstan," *RFE/RL Daily Report,* no. 82 (April 30, 1992), p. 1.

28. Roman Soichanuk, "Bush-Kravchuk Talks," *RFE/RL Daily Report,* no. 87 (May 7, 1992), p. 1.

29. This agreement is known as the Lisbon Protocol. See "Protocol to the Treaty between the United States of America and the Union of Soviet Socialist Republics on the Reduction and Limitation of Strategic Offensive Arms," *Arms Control Today,* vol. 22 (June 1992), pp. 34–35.

30. Yuri Kovalenko, "Ukraine Puts Its Relations with France on a New Basis," *Izvestiya,* June 17, 1992, p. 1.

31. Ukraine has taken part in a number of discussions with other governments concerning the possible establishment of regional political and economic associations; some focus on eastern and central Europe (Poland, the Czech Republic, the Slovak Federal Republic, and Ukraine), others on the Black Sea region (Russia, Romania, Bulgaria, Turkey, and Ukraine, among others). To date, none has progressed much beyond the talking stage.

32. Doug Clarke, "Nazarbaev on Nuclear Threat," *RFE/RL Daily Report,* no. 37 (February 24, 1992), pp. 1–2; and "FSU Strategic Nuclear Weapons outside Russia," Arms Control Association Fact Sheet, May 1993.

33. Interview with Erik Makzumovic Asanbayev, chief assistant to the Kazakhstan president, *Turkiye,* April 10, 1992, p. 11, in FBIS, *Central Eurasia,* April 21, 1992, p. 42.

34. See Don Oberdorfer, "Kazakhstan Agrees to Give Up A-Arms: START Treaty Roadblock Is Cleared," *Washington Post,* May 20, 1992, p. A1. Kazakhstan dutifully ratified the Lisbon Protocol to START in July 1992; it is expected to adhere to the NPT in the near future.

35. Bess Brown, "Russian-Kazakh Friendship Treaty Signed," *RFE/RL Daily Report,* no. 100 (May 26, 1992), pp. 1–2.

36. Martha Brill Olcott, "Central Asia's Catapult to Independence," *Foreign Affairs,* vol. 71 (Summer 1992), p. 129.

37. Stephen Foye, "Russian-Turkmen Defense Accord," *RFE/RL Daily Report,* no. 109 (June 10, 1992), p. 1.

38. The same may be said for Armenia, Georgia, and Azerbaijan in the Caucasus and, for different reasons, also for the three Baltic republics. Simply put, the former have no foreign policies to speak of, except as vehicles to enlist international support in civil conflicts (Georgia) and to secure support for wars of reciprocal annihilation (Armenia and Azerbaijan). Latvia, Lithuania, and Estonia, on the other hand, are very active diplomatically, particularly in northern and western Europe, but have little capacity to influence global or even regional political developments; they are, like other very small countries, the ultimate consumers of the foreign policy decisions made by others.

39. It is less than clear, in fact, that the Russian president, whoever that person might be, is an indispensable part of the nuclear chain of command. In their discussion of Soviet command arrangements, the authors of *Soviet Nuclear Fission: Control of the Nuclear Arsenal in a Disintegrating Soviet Union* argue that "it is doubtful that there exist in the Soviet strategic arsenal, let alone the nuclear arsenal as a whole, safeguards that physically prevent either of the two concerns implied in discussions of command and control at the apex: First, Gorbachev or other political authorities probably cannot prevent the senior military commanders from exercising effective control over nuclear weapons in a leadership crisis, or from launching them. The widely publicized existence of a presidential football, however, probably contributes in a general way to a culture of political, top-down control in the chain of command, even if that control can be physically circumvented at the General Staff level or at lower echelons of the operational chain of command.

"In the second place, it is also unlikely that launch crews would necessarily behave differently depending on whether their orders originated from Gorbachev, from a group of coup plotters, or from their superiors in the military chain of command. . . . [T]here are probably procedural safeguards to guarantee that simple possession of the football does not automatically grant the power to initiate a nuclear strike, but only makes its possessor a potential contributor to a collective procedure by which strike messages could be generated that would be obeyed. Gorbachev's football is probably neither necessary nor sufficient to initiate Soviet nuclear attack."

The same is most likely true for Yeltsin's "football," given the comparability between Soviet and post-Soviet nuclear command and control arrangements. See Kurt M. Campbell, Ashton B. Carter, Steven E. Miller, and Charles A. Zraket, *Soviet Nuclear Fission: Control of the Nuclear Arsenal in a Disintegrating Soviet Union,* CSIA Studies in International Security 1 (Harvard University, Center for Science and International Affairs, November 1991), pp. 10–11.

40. TASS-attributed report, December 25, 1991, in FBIS, *Soviet Union,* December 26, 1991, p. 1.

41. TASS-attributed report, "An Agreement Between the Member States of the Commonwealth of Independent States on Strategic Forces," December 31, 1991, in FBIS, *Soviet Union,* December 31, 1991, p. 17.

42. At a press conference on December 9, 1991, Kravchuk declared that in order for CIS nuclear-tipped missiles to be launched "three buttons must be pressed simultaneously, each of which is under the control of one of the members of the Commonwealth [Russia, Ukraine, and Belarus]. If one of them should press it, the launch will not take place: only three, and three simultaneously." From a TASS-attributed report, December 9, 1991, in FBIS, *Soviet Union,* December 10, 1991, p. 61. Kravchuk subsequently retreated from this particular formula, although he has continued to insist that CIS nuclear forces are under effective joint command; according to Kravchuk, Yeltsin must secure the permission of the heads of government of the three other nuclear weapon–equipped republics before he can order the launch of CIS nuclear forces. This is not to say, of course, that Yeltsin might not choose to ignore the political procedures that have been elaborated and make the decision to launch on his own, following consultations with senior CIS military personnel.

43. See, in particular, the exchange among Yeltsin, Russian Supreme Soviet chairman Ruslan Khasbulatov, and Russian deputy Vladimir Isakov at the December 25 session of the Supreme Soviet of the Russian Soviet Federated Socialist Republic, as relayed in a report carried by the Russian Television Network, December 25, 1991, in FBIS, *Soviet Union,* December 26, 1991, p. 41. See also the interview with Shaposhnikov by Laure Mandeville that appeared in *Le Figaro,* February 8 and 9, 1992, p. 1, in FBIS, *Central Eurasia,* February 11, 1992, p. 1.

44. On the likely dissolution of joint command arrangements after 1994, see Doug Clarke, "Grachev on Nuclear Arms," *RFE/RL Daily Report,* no. 100 (May 26, 1992), p. 1. In a discussion with me in Moscow in September 1992, a very senior official of the Russian Ministry of Defense reiterated Grachev's position.

45. Of the five kinds of military equipment covered by the treaty, the Russian Federation is to receive 54 percent, Ukraine 28 percent, and Belarus 12 percent. The remainder is to be divided among Armenia, Azerbaijan, Georgia, and Moldova. Stockholm International Peace Research Institute, *SIPRI Yearbook 1993* (Oxford University Press, 1993), pp. 611, 762.

46. Although only five of the eleven non–nuclear weapon republics of the former Soviet Union—Azerbaijan, Estonia, Latvia, Lithuania, and Uzbekistan—have as yet acceded to the NPT, the failure of the other six to do so provokes only modest anxiety internationally. None of the six has expressed an interest in acquiring nuclear weapons. More to the point perhaps, none is currently in a position to mount a serious effort to do

so, should political leaders in this or that republic have a sudden change of heart. The expectation is that at least five of the six nonmember states (Armenia being the possible exception) will soon accede to the treaty.

47. Some Western observers contend that both the Kravchuk and Nazarbayev governments are determined to preserve their countries' status as nuclear weapon states for as long as possible and that each will go to considerable lengths to avoid having to surrender the ICBMs deployed on its soil. Such an interpretation of Ukrainian and Kazakh policies is not inconsistent with the version of events offered in this chapter. In acceding to the NPT as non–nuclear weapon states, Ukraine and Kazakhstan could ensure that the aid they so desperately need begins to flow, even as they continue to play host to several hundred SS-18, SS-19, and SS-24 missiles through at least 1994 (if they abide by the commitments they themselves have undertaken) and perhaps to the end of the century (according to the START timetable). In any event, neither country is likely to attain the true mark of a nuclear weapon state—operational control of the forces—without the outright seizure of the missiles from the CIS command, an eventuality that, although not impossible, seems unlikely at present.

48. Ann Sheehy, "Special Status for Tatarstan and Chechnya?" *RFE/RL Daily Report,* no. 101 (May 27, 1992), p. 2; and Fiona Hill, *Report on Ethnic Conflict in the Russian Federation and Transcaucasia* (Harvard University, Kennedy School of Government, Strengthening Democratic Institutions Project, July 1993), pp. i, 3–9.

49. The calls to defend the interests of ethnic Russians in the near-abroad are not limited to the government's conservative critics. Presidential counselor Sergei Stankevich, a political moderate in the Russian context, reportedly assailed the government's policy in a sharply worded article that appeared in *Rossiyskaya gazeta* on June 23, 1992; in the piece, he specifically warned Georgia, Moldova, Latvia, and Estonia that Russia would use force to defend the interests of Russians living in the four former republics should the need arise. See Riina Kionka and Alexander Rahr, "More Calls for Protection of Russians," *RFE/RL Daily Report,* no. 118 (June 24, 1992), p. 2.

50. Sheryl WuDunn, "China Browses for Tanks, Aircraft and Carrier in Ex-Soviet Lands," *New York Times,* June 7, 1992, p. 20. The same report notes China's interest in buying an aircraft carrier, originally intended for the Soviet navy, that is being built in Ukraine.

51. Michael R. Gordon, "Moscow Is Selling Weapons to China, U.S. Officials Say," *New York Times,* October 18, 1992, p. 1.

52. Stephen Foye, "Russian Arms Bazaar Takes Shape," *RFE/RL Daily Report,* no. 117 (June 23, 1992), p. 2. In September 1992 Western press sources reported that the Russians had sold three older model attack submarines to Iran and that at least one of the boats had already set sail for its new destination in the Persian Gulf. The Russians initially denied the reports, then confirmed them, then denied them again. As of this writing, the fate of the three submarines remains unclear.

53. Stephen Foye, "Russian Officials on Defense Conversion," *RFE/RL Daily Report,* no. 99 (May 25, 1992), p. 2; and Jim Hoagland, "An Arms Race in East Asia," *Washington Post,* July 14, 1992, p. 13.

TEN

Cooperative Security in the Middle East

Geoffrey Kemp

THE PARADIGM for cooperative security as a new and potentially important feature of international relations is apparent in western Europe. The concept has evolved in two stages. First, in facing the mutual threat from the Soviet bloc under the framework of collective security, the defense policies of the western European countries became complementary rather than competitive with one another. Second, with the end of the cold war and the defeat of communism, there are hopes that the European members of the former Warsaw Pact will structure their defense capabilities within the framework of European cooperation. Balance of power politics based on competitive military rivalry would not be part of the new Europe. If cooperative security results, it would indeed herald a new era.

Whether cooperative security is actually forthcoming is another matter. Optimists invoke the indisputable logic of why further European security cooperation makes such overwhelming sense. Those less sanguine argue that the shock waves caused by the breakup of the Soviet empire have not yet settled. No one knows whether central and eastern Europe will become part of a larger, more stable Europe or whether the malevolent forces of nationalism and violent disputes about new borders will reignite passions. The breakup of Yugoslavia and the tragedy that has ensued do not portend well for future European stability. Europe, far from being the model for post–cold war cooperation, may be on the brink of chaos and political

This chapter draws heavily on an upcoming study prepared by the Carnegie Endowment's Middle East Arms Control Project: Geoffrey Kemp, *Arab-Israeli Security Agreements: Negotiating Asymmetric Reciprocity.* I would like to give special thanks to Jeremy Pressman, project associate at Carnegie Endowment, for his help with the preparation of this chapter. I would also like to thank Paula Hacopian and Deborah Rivel for their assistance.

unrest (albeit of a very different nature from the conflict witnessed during the past forty years).

In contrast, and with due irony, in the Middle East new realities are at work putting pressure on the regional powers to solve their conflicts peacefully. This chapter argues that strategic, political, and economic changes in the global environment have caused major realignments in Middle East power relationships and have focused attention on the problems facing the region as it tries to compete in the changing world economy. These events bolster the prospects for regional cooperation, including cooperative security. However, to adapt successfully to these changes, Middle Eastern countries must find ways to resolve outstanding political differences.

This resolution will not be easy, nor is it inevitable. Cooperative security will not be possible in the Middle East until there has been a fundamental change in the political behavior and attitudes of the principal adversaries. Two huge constraints stand in the way of positive change: the rejectionist and confrontational ideologies of extremist groups in the Muslim world and in Israel and major strategic asymmetries within the region that create an unstable balance of power and a predilection to resolve conflicts by the use of force.

Nevertheless, the new peace negotiations between Israel and its neighbors, which began in 1991 and reached a climax on September 13, 1993, when the Israeli prime minister, Yitzhak Rabin, and PLO chairman Yasir Arafat shook hands on the White House lawn, are an encouraging sign that a major reassessment is under way. Since the balance of power has not kept the peace, most Middle Eastern leaders are now convinced that the route to stability and long-run economic growth must be a negotiated political settlement. This settlement would ultimately mean that rejectionist states, including Iran, must be pressured to accept Israel's right to exist and that the Palestinian problem must be settled on the basis of territorial compromise.[1]

If the Middle Eastern states fail to exploit these new opportunities, the region risks not only new, more terrifying military confrontation but also economic stagnation and, in all likelihood, political upheaval. Without strong American diplomatic leadership, progress toward conflict resolution, including arms control, will remain elusive and traditional military rivalries will persist.

In this chapter the trends reinforcing the need for regional cooperation, including the impacts of the Gulf War and of the end of the cold war on the region and the economic consequences of continued Middle Eastern conflict, are examined. This examination is followed by a discussion of the obstacles to peace cooperation and the prospects for containing extremism and coping with the consequences of strategic asymmetries.

Trends Reinforcing the Need for Regional Cooperation

Despite ample evidence that the Middle East remains a dangerous place, including radical fundamentalism, a new arms race, and military asymmetries, three phenomena besides the peace process are nudging the region toward conflict resolution. They are the demise of the Soviet Union and the end of the cold war, the Gulf War and its aftermath, and the emerging international economic marketplace, especially the prospects for giant trading blocs dominated by North America, Europe, and East Asia. The impact of the first two events on the Middle East can be reviewed together, since the Gulf coalition and the war would not have been possible without the 180-degree change in Soviet policy, a change that abruptly pulled the rug out from under the Soviet Union's erstwhile radical friends in the region, including Syria, Iraq, and Libya.

The Impact of the Gulf War and the End of the Cold War

The Gulf War demonstrated the effectiveness of modern military forces that have been well trained and well equipped with the latest weapons and are operating in an essentially "permissive" military environment. For the Middle Eastern countries, it demonstrated their own military-technological deficit. Only those countries with oil, such as Saudi Arabia, or generous U.S. aid, such as Israel, can believe they can keep up in the technological race, assuming they are permitted to buy the latest high-technology weapons. The war had a sobering impact on *all* military establishments in the region. None can hope to match the level of military power put together by the United States and its allies during Operation Desert Storm.[2]

The Gulf War also highlighted the dangers of the further proliferation of advanced conventional munitions and weapons of mass destruction to the Middle East. First, introducing such technology into a highly unstable region with unresolved conflicts can only exacerbate existing tensions and lead to an escalating arms race. This situation would be likely to increase the possibility of preemptive war rather than to result in the evolution of stable mutual deterrence, such as that achieved in Europe. A stable balance of terror in the Middle East might be possible if the principal antagonists achieved a nuclear or advanced conventional capability at the same time. However, the evidence suggests that the conditions giving rise to the present very uneven playing fields are almost immutable. One country, Israel, already possesses a formidable nuclear force, whereas others possess significant chemical and missile capabilities or do not acknowledge traditional notions of deterrence and stability. A continuing unchecked arms race is unlikely to lead to mutual equivalence in capabilities. Thus the asymmetric pace of the military buildup itself becomes a source of instability.

Second, the different cultural attitudes of the major contestants in the Middle East suggest that, in extremis, the use of weapons of mass destruction might be contemplated more readily than in many other regions of the world. Although there can be no proof of such an assertion, it is not unreasonable to believe that Ayatollah Khomeini or Muammar Qadaffi might, under certain circumstances, have been tempted to use nuclear weapons either against the West or Israel or, in the case of Khomeini, against Iraq. One can only speculate about what Saddam Hussein would have done during the Gulf crisis if he had had an operational nuclear weapon. Might this weapon have deterred the Western forces from massive military intervention to rescue Kuwait, or alternatively, would he have been prepared to use the weapon against Israel or his Arab neighbors? Fear is also expressed routinely in the Muslim world that as long as Israel is the sole possessor of nuclear weapons, the possibility remains that a maverick Israeli leader, such as Ariel Sharon, might be tempted to flaunt Israel's nuclear monopoly, perhaps to the point of threatening to use it.

The third reason for concern is the special vulnerability of most Middle Eastern countries to attack by advanced conventional munitions and weapons of mass destruction. As the Gulf War demonstrated, it took very few "smart" munitions to cripple Iraq's utility system. The Israeli economy was temporarily paralyzed by small-scale missile attacks using rudimentary Iraqi Scud missiles. The Israeli high-technology industry lost millions of dollars of orders because factories were closed and workers were sitting in basements wearing gas masks over the course of several months. If relatively inefficient Scud technology can cause such a disruption, more advanced missiles could cause untold economic damage to Israel's valuable infrastructure.

Likewise, imagine what F-117-type bombers with smart munitions could do to the oil fields of the Gulf Cooperation Council (GCC) countries if used by a hostile power. It is possible that the entire infrastructure of the Gulf, particularly the oil production, oil loading and unloading facilities, and key water supplies, could be quickly destroyed even in a confrontation of limited scale and duration. In most Middle Eastern countries the general government population and elites are concentrated in one, or at the most two, vulnerable cities. Although a large country, Egypt has all its power structure situated in Cairo. Israel's tiny size suggests that the detonation of one nuclear weapon in Tel Aviv would be catastrophic enough to threaten the very existence of the Jewish state. Syria, Iraq, Saudi Arabia, and Iran are also highly vulnerable. Although the use of a nuclear weapon could be apocalyptic anywhere in the world, it could be argued that other regions such as South or East Asia have more resilience and redundancy in terms of size and population, and that North America and the former Soviet Union also have a more disparate demographic distribution. Geographically and demographically, Europe would be more comparable to the Middle East, together with certain regions in Africa and Latin America.

The proliferation dilemma affects each country in different ways, yet all have an interest in achieving some semblance of stability. The preferred route to stability must be conflict resolution, arms limitation agreements, and more cooperative attitudes toward force procurement and deployment.

The practical problems of moving toward greater cooperation in security, however, are perhaps best illuminated by the case of Israel. Israel's unspoken policy has been that it will use whatever means are necessary to sustain its nuclear monopoly in the region. But is this still a realistic policy? In 1981 Israel destroyed Iraq's major nuclear facilities only to find that ten years later Iraq was once more on the verge of attaining nuclear status. If Israel is unable to deny other countries weapons of mass destruction independently, it will have to depend more on the United States and the international community to help do so. But this dependency would require that Israel itself put limits on its own military programs. Thus the dilemma facing Israel is simple: how to retain a qualitative military edge while at the same time making concessions that would require it to limit this edge. What those limits should be and under what circumstances Israel should negotiate them is the subject of intense domestic and international debate.

The realization that Israel may not be able to ensure its survival by unilateral means has been broached by the senior Israeli military establishment. In the weeks preceding the June 1992 Israeli election, for example, past and present members of the Israeli military publicly aired feelings of uncertainty and concern about the Middle Eastern arms race and the possibility that the Arab states would acquire weapons of mass destruction. On June 15, 1992, the commander of the Israeli Air Force, Major General Herzl Bodinger, explained that "if countries in the region—like Iran, Libya, and other countries—will have nuclear weapons, this can endanger the whole area." Earlier, on June 8, the chief of military intelligence, General Uri Sagi, had said that Iran's nuclear project "might cause us to be concerned about our existence and basic security."[3]

Some have suggested that military trends in the region may force Israel to turn increasingly to the United States for assistance in stopping regional proliferation. In his commentary on the Syrian military and Arab nuclear programs, columnist Ze'ev Schiff noted in *Ha'aretz* that "the American presence in the region constitutes a clear stabilizing factor."[4] Furthermore, *Ha'aretz* cited Israeli defense sources and reported that Israel, the United States, and other countries are already attempting to halt nuclear assistance to Iran and Libya by Western companies.

Clearly, the Arab states and Iran cannot contain the adverse consequences of Israel's weapons of mass destruction unless they too participate in some international or regional arrangement in which Israel is a player. Thus the best interests of the region will be served in the long run if the states cooperate one way or another to achieve limitations on weapons proliferation. Indeed, nonproliferation activities may provide a suitable forum for the growth of cooperative security schemes. Given its already high priority in the region, the effort to control the spread of weapons of mass destruction should take priority over proposals to control other kinds of military activities such as limits on defense expenditures or weapons procurement across the board. In turn, it is unrealistic to expect the regional powers to make progress on limiting the acquisition of weapons of mass destruction in the absence of a breakthrough in the negotiations on a general political settlement between Israel and its neighbors.

THE ECONOMIC GAP. The Gulf War reemphasized the large divide between the rich and poor Middle Eastern states. Saudi Arabia, Kuwait, and the smaller Gulf states have been blessed with vast oil riches. They have been able to support costly domestic programs for education and health care for their populations while purchasing large quantities of military hardware. Though their economies suffered during the Gulf War, they have been able to acquire new weapons—if not necessarily those of the most advanced types—since the end of the conflict. A combination of financial reserves, continuing oil revenue, and loans will permit continued weapons purchases for the forseeable future.

This existing economic order has been reinforced by several postwar policies and events. Poorer countries lost millions in remittances when hundreds of thousands of expatriate workers left or were expelled from Kuwait, Saudi Arabia, and Iraq after Operation Desert Storm. In addition, wealthy Arab supporters of the allied coalition cut or eliminated aid to countries they perceived as having been pro-Iraq, such as Yemen and Jordan. Given currently flat oil prices, a quick and massive revenue infusion is also unlikely, even for the wealthier states. The disparity in wealth and the accompanying resentment that has come to divide rich Arabs from poor ones will probably continue.[5]

Economic assistance to the region is the only other viable equalizer for states that lack accumulated wealth and oil. Israel and Egypt rely heavily on U.S. funds for economic development and military purchases. In the past few years, they have annually received more than $3 billion and $2 billion, respectively. Billions of dollars of Egyptian debt were forgiven in 1992 as a reward for Gulf War support. Other states that do not receive grants and loans still may be given access to certain categories of U.S. military technology on a concessionary basis. Because of U.S. budget constraints, however, even these limited concessionary programs may soon be cut. Japan and Europe are alternative sources of aid, but so far they have proved reluctant to provide significant amounts of new funds.

On one side of this financial and technological divide stand Yemen, Jordan, and Iraq, which lack the ability to acquire advanced weaponry and military technology. On the other side, Saudi Arabia, Kuwait, and the Gulf states stand with U.S.-assisted Egypt and Israel and continue to buy large quantities of arms. With $2 billion in Gulf War rewards, Syria has placed itself in the latter category, at least for the time being.[6]

FEARS OF AMERICAN HEGEMONY OR INDIFFERENCE. Another outcome of the Gulf War is that many Arab states and political groups believe the United States may use its unfettered power to impose its will on the Middle East. Some Arab officials who supported the anti-Saddam coalition now question the extent of U.S. involvement in the region. There is a strong current of anti-U.S. and anti-Western feelings in the Arab media. As one Jordanian journalist put it, "The United States has bullied the entire world with its new world order, which is the order of the law of the jungle."[7]

The April 15, 1992, UN Security Council sanctions imposed against Libya for its refusal to hand over to the United States and United Kingdom two intelligence officers implicated in the 1988 bombing of Pan Am flight 103, for example, generated wide disapproval in the Arab world. The Libyan sanctions were "proof" that the Western countries were intent on "subjugating the Arabs and depriving them of every right to sovereignty and independence."[8] In an editorial the Jordanian newspaper *Al-Dustur* made a similar point: "The West and its protegé, Israel, are aiming to impose a siege on this [entire Arab] nation, humiliate and subjugate it, and plunder all its resources."[9] Unlike in the Iraqi case, in which Cairo's *Al-Akhbar* saw punishing Iraq as just, in the Libyan case it asked, "Is it part of the new world order that the United Nations and the Security Council should become a tool in the hands of the United States and its Western allies?" The article cited Libya's attempts to develop nonconventional weapons as the explanation for the U.S. aggression.[10]

The emergence of new U.S. power also worried the Israeli government of Yitzhak Shamir. Israeli officials expressed their concern over the changing nature of the U.S.-Israeli strategic relationship. The end of the cold war and thus of U.S.-Soviet rivalry for influence in the region removed one of Israel's main cards for soliciting aid, weaponry, and support. Since the end of the Gulf War, Israel's perceptions of a weakening tie to the United States have been seen in light of increasing U.S. military assistance to and alliances with Arab states. Israeli policymakers have watched what they perceive as an erosion of their strategic links with the United States. Although this trend has been checked with the election of the Rabin government, Israelis remain nervous about the degree of U.S. support they can expect in the coming years.

In the last two years the United States has established or explored stronger military ties and security pacts with Saudi Arabia, Kuwait, Qatar, Oman, the United Arab Emirates, and Bahrain. In the most important instance the United States and Saudi Arabia negotiated a "broad expansion of strategic cooperation," according to U.S. and Saudi sources. The agreements often include pre-positioning of U.S. equipment and joint military exercises. These arrangements have left the United States as the unchallenged protector of the Persian Gulf, with much greater military activity and flexibility in the region than before the Gulf War.[11] According to unnamed Pentagon officials, the Pentagon's most urgent Middle Eastern priorities are to build ties with the armed forces of Saudi Arabia and the Persian Gulf states; Israel is, at best, tangential to those ends.[12]

U.S. military sales to Saudi Arabia trigger anxiety in Israel and tend to prompt further Israeli arms requests. According to Ze'ev Schiff, the heads of the Israeli Defense Forces, particularly of the air force, are increasingly concerned about the erosion of Israel's qualitative edge that has resulted from post–Gulf War arms transfers by the United States to other regional powers. Whereas in the past Israel received superior technology and Arab countries like Saudi Arabia struggled to acquire U.S. weapons, more recently Arab states have received better equipment in a more timely fashion, including advanced fighters, Apache helicopters, and Patriot missile batteries.[13] This U.S.-assisted buildup of several Arab military regimes is currently the most troubling factor in Israeli strategic planning.

As a result, Israeli policymakers are "scrambling to find a new basis for the relationship with Washington," according to one commentator.[14] Israelis have been debating the future of the relationship, and many are asking if it is prudent to continue to rely on substantial American political, economic, and military support, calling instead for increasing self-reliance: "the homemade edge."[15] They are unsure if the apparent change in U.S. policy is temporary or permanent. Some policymakers, however, see reliance on the United States as the only alternative.[16] As with any dependent relationship, Israeli security and arms acquisitions may always remain vulnerable to changes in U.S. policy. The call for self-reliance may ring hollow as a consequence of limited Israeli government funds and the apparent absence of economies of scale in Israel's own defense industry. An alternate supplier would be helpful, but oft-mentioned relationships with countries like China and France may be unrealistic options given the political uncertainty of relying on such so-called allies. For these reasons an early task of the new Rabin government has been to improve relations with the United States and to find a way to reformulate the U.S.-Israeli strategic relationship. As Israelis themselves have suggested, Israel is looking "to find strategic relevance" or a "peg on which to hang the strategic relationship" with the United States.[17]

The Clinton administration has reaffirmed strong American support for Israeli security. Supporters of Israel occupy some of the key foreign policy positions in the new administration, and within a few months of taking office President Bill Clinton met with Prime Minister Yitzhak Rabin. Administration officials have publicly defended the current level of U.S. military and economic aid to Israel. Although it is likely that the United States will have to play a larger role in the peace negotiations in an effort to generate progress, there are no signs that the U.S.-Israeli security relationship is endangered.

The Economic Consequences of Middle Eastern Conflict

Continuing conflict hurts Middle Eastern economies in many ways: it creates an unstable environment that discourages outside investment and joint ventures; it encourages boycotts and interregional economic warfare that hurt all participants; it skews spending priorities; it exacerbates competition for scarce resources such as water; most important, it limits the region's ability to compete with the challenge posed by the European Community (EC), Asian, and North American economic blocs. Alternatively, if an Arab-Israeli settlement is reached, all the Middle Eastern countries stand to gain economically. It is interesting to note that since the signing of the Israeli-PLO accord, most of the efforts have been focused on ways to raise foreign capital and economic assistance to rebuild the infrastructure of Gaza and the West Bank. It is clear that unless the fruits of reconciliation have a quick impact on the quality of life of Palestinians in the territories, the peace process may falter and fail.

THE IMPACT OF CONFLICT ON TRADE AND FOREIGN INVESTMENT. Business leaders on all sides of the Middle Eastern conflict have expressed a desire to focus on economic issues instead of on military and strategic ones. In reference to the Middle East, J. R. Abinader, president of the National U.S.-Arab Chamber of Commerce, claimed that "no one is going to put ten cents into that region until it stabilizes. There has to be a sense of security."[18] Dov Frohman, managing director of Intel Israel, said that "to get growth, we really do need the peace process." Most top industrialists and members of the Israeli Manufacturers' Association backed the Labor Party in the election despite Likud's traditional pro-business stance. They believed that Labor's greater commitment to the peace process was now the ultimate pro-business position.[19]

The economic costs of the Arab-Israeli conflict have made their mark at the ballot box in Israel, in particular. In explaining the results of the 1992 Knesset elections, Yaron Ezrahi of Hebrew University noted that "the Israeli middle class increasingly is refusing to pay the bill in blood, sweat and money for the Likud vision [of Greater Israel]."[20] Many Israelis will make greater concessions in the peace process to maintain and enhance this economic life-style. In addition, these changes have had the direct impact of forcing reductions in Israeli defense spending, from 34 percent of gross domestic product in 1975 to 14 percent in 1990, as public services and institutions receive less funding.[21]

Continuing conflict and instability prevent the establishment of a unified trading bloc. Alfred Tovias, senior lecturer at the Department of International Relations at Hebrew University, defined the Israeli dilemma, though the same definition would apply to other Middle Eastern countries' dilemmas as well: "As the world moves away from GATT [General Agreement on Tariffs and Trade] towards major trading blocs, Israel should be asking itself which trading bloc it will belong to."[22] Just as Middle Eastern entrepreneurs are expressing a greater desire to enter the world economy, the growth of trade blocs threatens to shut them out. Since the conflicts of the Middle East prevent a unified approach or economic strategy, most states in the region are left to fend for themselves against the world's most powerful economic players.

Foreign investors are wary of the Middle East, limiting both its potential for involvement in world markets and the level of foreign investment. A European Council official told Israeli correspondents that "your region is not interesting for European investors because it entails political risks. Thailand and eastern European countries seem far more attractive."[23] Even though Thailand has since been swept by protest and violence, the point remains that regions outside the Middle East are viewed by the EC and others as safer economic targets. The Japanese ambassador to Israel, for example, has declared that Japanese commercial banks will not give loan guarantees because of the perceived high financial risk. He explained that lack of progress in the peace talks is one of two factors preventing the issuance of guarantees.[24] Much needed capital, foreign subsidiaries, and other forms of outside investment could give a tremendous boost to countries that are able to overcome the conflict-oriented policies of the past forty years. But until such change comes about, the Middle Eastern countries will continue to risk economic isolation and faltering growth.

DOMESTIC ECONOMIC PROBLEMS: ISRAEL AND THE PALESTINIANS. Israel's economy, which has long needed serious reform, has been forced to cope with hundreds of thousands of new immigrants since 1989. Although it initially boosted home construction and consumer demand, the overall economic impact of immigration has been negative. The absorption of immigrants will require huge amounts of money, though the amounts could decrease if fewer immigrants arrive than expected.[25]

The uncertainty of continued access to American aid is a complicating factor for Israel's economic adjustment. Israel received $29.9 billion from the United States from 1982 to 1991, but some policymakers in both Israel and the United States have called for a reduction in Israeli aid.[26] Growing isolationist tendencies in U.S. politics threaten international aid commitments. In Israel, supporters of aid reduction suggest that Israel must eliminate its great dependence on foreign aid to improve the health of the economy. Heavy reliance on U.S. dollars undermines Israel's autonomy and national security posture. If it is carried out in a gradual manner, proponents of aid reduction argue, the economy would be able to absorb the shock of significant reductions.[27] Since American foreign aid is not as certain as it once was, the Israeli economy could well be subject to such a change in the next few years.[28] Still, adjusting to aid reductions would most likely cause hardship in the short run. As David Levhari of Israel's Hebrew University explained, "As an Israeli, I know how painful it would be to have a reduction of aid. But as an economist, I'm worried that it might take that kind of crisis to push our government to reform."[29]

The structure of the Israeli economy may undergo further structural change as the agricultural sector decreases in relative importance. For several years

Israeli farms have produced excess agricultural goods. In fact, most of Israel's collective farms would have gone bankrupt years ago without government subsidies and protections. To date, government intervention has helped preserve inefficient farmland around Tel Aviv, often at the expense of industrial, commercial, or residential growth. In addition, government agricultural subsidies encourage the overuse of Israel's water supply even though Israeli agriculture is among the most efficient in terms of water use in the world. Some Israelis claim that "Israel's agrarian socialism—especially its water-intensive crops such as cotton and strawberries—fan Mideast tensions by increasing the need for water."[30] In short, government support for Israeli agriculture has led to a distorted allocation of the two resources at the center of the Arab-Israeli dispute, land and water.

Accelerating the development of the high-technology sector of the Israeli economy, by contrast, could replace or complement agricultural growth and allow the state to take advantage of its well-educated and well-trained immigrants. As of mid-1991 about 40 percent of the immigrant workers entering Israel were engineers, architects, scientists, and health workers, compared with about 6 percent in the preexisting Israeli work force or in the United States.[31] With this new concentration of "brainpower," some argue that Israel is poised to develop many small high-technology companies. By establishing relationships with larger, international companies, the Israeli high-technology industry could blossom. Yet as with other schemes that necessitate integration into the world economy, aspirations to diversify further into the high-technology sector are impeded by wary foreign or domestic investors. Both the Arab boycott and the continuing conflict simply scare away many of the needed economic actors.[32]

Israel's goal of being included in the European economic arena that will encompass both the EC and the European Free Trade Association (EFTA) has been frustrated by political issues. The EC is the larger of Israel's two major trading partners—it received 35 percent of Israel's exports and provided 50 percent of its imports in 1990.[33] Although the EC has expressed a willingness to include Israel, it has clearly linked membership to progress at the peace talks. While Europeans disagree on the extent of progress that is necessary for Israeli membership—some argue for it upon completion of the talks, others suggest that it could occur at a stage before complete peace is achieved—all agree that the existing situation precludes Israeli inclusion in the economic partnership. In explaining EC policy, the EC's ambassador to Israel, Gwyn Morgan, stated that "the pace and extent of Israeli integration into the European economic area will depend on the peace process also going along at a certain pace."[34]

Significantly, these economic partnerships are crucial for Israel because of its heavy reliance on the EC market. Israeli policymakers do not believe that the 1975 EC-Israel trade agreement protects Israel's economic interests in post-1992 Europe. Without a new agreement, they argue, Israel could see the end of seventeen years of its prosperous economic relations with western Europe.[35] Discussions have continued, however, with Israel trying to enter through the "back door," by signing a free-trade agreement with EFTA instead of with the EC. The EFTA-Israeli agreement will abolish customs duties and trade barriers for some goods and may serve as this back door.[36]

As for the Palestinians, the economic possibilities for the West Bank and Gaza are limited as long as they remain under Israeli control. Little development took place in the West Bank and Gaza before 1967, and since then, Israel has spent little to develop the economic potential of Arabs in the territories. Hebrew University economist Ephraim Ahiran notes that "the infrastructure is unbelievably neglected" and would require an investment of $10 to $15 billion over the first decade of a new Palestinian economy to achieve even modest progress.[37] In a further blow to the Palestinian work force, Palestinian education has been severely disrupted since 1987 by the Israeli response to the uprisings known as the *intifada,* which have included prolonged closure of schools and universities. As noted, these shortcomings will receive priority attention as a result of the Israeli-PLO agreements.

The multitrack Arab boycott of Israel and of businesses that deal with Israel is another obstacle that impedes the progress of Israeli economic integration and deprives both sides of access to many international firms. The boycott deprives Arab states of trade with the relatively advanced Israeli economy, hurting both sides. Furthermore, the Arab boycott of international companies that deal with Israel forces companies to choose sides rather than enabling them to invest effectively in both the Arab and Israeli economies.

The boycott is directly injurious to the Israeli economy in several ways. First, it limits foreign investment by steering thousands of companies away from Israel. Given the changing world economy, moreover, the boycott also undercuts Israel's international economic structure. As David Weinberg wrote, "This is particularly hurtful at a time when the business world, particularly Israel's largest trading partner—Europe—is increasingly becoming internationalized and integrated. The boycott is an impediment to Israel's integration into these larger markets." The Federation of Israeli Chambers of Commerce estimates that the boycott has reduced Israel's annual exports and foreign investment by 10 percent each. In theory, Israel lost $1.2 billion in exports in 1990. Nearly all Arab countries refuse to buy Israeli products, and many multinational firms sacrifice access to the Israeli market and Israeli goods, especially in the high-technology field, in return for entrance into the larger Arab market.[38]

ECONOMIC BENEFITS FROM PEACE. Geographic proximity is a fundamental economic benefit that is sacrificed by continued regional conflict. "Peace dividends would flow in abundance from combining a patchwork of economically isolated states and territories into a common market," according to one economic observer.[39] Without progress toward peace, these dividends cannot be realized and the opportunity costs are high. By cutting transportation and other transfer costs and using economies of scale, the central states of the Arab-Israeli conflict could gain substantially from bilateral trade. One study estimated that annual trade among Israel, Egypt, Jordan, and Lebanon could amount to $1 billion, not including oil.[40] Indeed, Israel, the West Bank, and Gaza already demonstrate the benefits of border trade. Before the *intifada,* Israeli exports to the West Bank and Gaza totaled $1.1 billion of goods. Since the conflicts began, however, Israeli exports have dropped 50 percent. With the implementation of the proper reforms and the achievement of peace, the West Bank, Gaza, and Israel could "mesh nicely," perhaps returning to the earlier level of trade.[41]

High levels of defense spending have also had a negative impact on some aspects of economic growth and have helped spark renewed interest in placing curbs on defense expenditures. The economic factors supporting the movement toward arms control in the Arab world have been exhaustively reviewed in a book by Yahya Sadowski.[42] Sadowski's thesis is that a new military spending debate in the Arab states has been triggered largely by their faltering economies. For this reason, international economic incentives may be effective in encouraging regional disarmament.

According to Sadowski, the overall weaknesses of the Arab economies are caused by many factors, including lower oil prices, overpopulation, economic mismanagement, foreign policy adventurism, and most recently the Gulf War. The last event destroyed the aid donation system between the rich and the poor countries and drastically changed their labor migration patterns. As refugees flowed into the poorer countries, remittances from their work in wealthier countries ended. Because of these changes and previous policies, the region faces a shortage of capital and a large debt burden, much of which has come from military spending.

At the same time, Sadowski also points to a new antimilitarist sentiment that can be detected in certain Arab countries, particularly among the elites. Along with the desire to cut defense spending, this sentiment suggests that Arab states may be beginning to recognize the opportunity cost of continued military spending and to look for cheaper ways to provide security. In examining alternatives, interest in arms control proposals, such as the Bush or Mubarak plans, or regional security arrangements may be growing. Of particular interest is a Jordanian proposal to trade debt forgiveness for reductions in military expenditures. Jordan has made unilateral force reductions and is actually promoting the arms-debt swap idea.

Sadowski's empirical work reveals new insights into Arab elite thinking and corroborates the overall thesis of this chapter. Economic factors, from broader issues concerning the new structure of the world economy to more specific questions relating to the economic impact of high military spending at home, are now influencing debates in both Arab countries and Israel and are pointing to the need for conflict resolution.

The Obstacles to Peace and Cooperation

The positive trends discussed in this chapter notwithstanding, key obstacles preventing a new political environment in the Middle East remain. These obstacles include the difficulties posed by the major strategic asymmetries between the key parties to the conflict and the negative impact these difficulties have on efforts to institute confidence-building measures and to negotiate arms control regimes and security guarantees.

Perceptions of Deterrence and the Utility of Force

Signed in November 1990, the Conventional Armed Forces in Europe Treaty is the culmination of more than twenty years of negotiations among the United States, the Soviet Union, and the European countries. What relevance, if any, does the European experience of security negotiations and arms control have for the Middle East?[43]

The differences between the two regions remain great. In Europe the notion of security that prevailed for several decades was that the use of force to achieve political ends between the two opposing alliances was an unacceptable risk. The experience of World War II and the dangers posed by the presence of large numbers of nuclear weapons in the European theater undercut the utility of conflict and deterred war. Deterrence was also buttressed by the explicit linkage—codified in military doctrines—between the use of conventional arms and the potential for escalation to the use of nuclear weapons. Much of the cold war debate about military forces primarily concerned prevention of their use or their deterrent value. True, conflict was believed possible in many scenarios, and on certain occasions the Europeans, Americans, and Soviets used military forces for political ends outside the European theater. (In the case of the Soviet Union, it also used them against its own allies.) But a NATO–Warsaw Pact war was implicitly considered a remote possibility because it was difficult to imagine how either side could win decisively without incurring unacceptable costs.

In contrast, Middle Eastern countries have demonstrated that force, at least as a last resort, is a necessary instrument of national policy. Indeed, victory in war has brought rewards, if only in the short run, to the winning side. Israel, for instance, advanced its security objectives, although Arab defeats failed to deter subsequent Arab belligerence and efforts to reverse Israeli gains. The 1973 war against Israel, for example, was perceived by Arab states as a necessary conflict needed to redeem pride and to improve their bargaining position with outside powers. Syria and Iraq have displayed a willingness to use force on many other occasions, and Libya's invasion of Chad indicates that military conflict remains an acceptable, albeit painful, method of diplomacy elsewhere in the region.

The Role of Arms Control

Other differences distinguish the postwar European experience from the Middle East experience. Initial confidence- and security-building measures and arms control agreements were reached in Europe well before the Gorbachev era, even at the height of the cold war. Why was accommodation possible? First, there was a preexisting and durable balance of power. Two organized and offsetting alliances backed up by the nuclear weapons of the respective superpowers ensured that no small country or group of countries within the European arena could fundamentally upset this balance. Although there were border disputes among the European powers, they generally agreed that force would not be used to resolve them.

Diplomatic relations were also actively maintained between the adversaries. Even during the tensest periods of the cold war, American and Soviet diplomats met regularly, as did officials in eastern and western Europe. Despite overt military tensions, the European powers, the Soviet Union, and the United States had had a long history of tacit cooperation on a host of political, economic, and military issues since World War II.

Despite chronic pressures to modernize forces to offset the perceived advantages held by the adversary, a basic stalemate in force levels and types of weaponry existed between the two sides for many years. Finally, the NATO and Warsaw Pact countries came to appreciate the fact that arms and troop reductions could translate directly into enhanced security for all parties. In short, a perception of mutual interest and shared destiny drove the process forward even before decisions were made to implement concrete arms control measures.

In the end, comprehensive progress in arms control can be attributed to the strength of the NATO alliance, to Mikhail Gorbachev's reform policies, and to the subsequent relaxation of East-West tensions. There was political will on both sides to push for reductions. There was a mutual desire for domestic retrenchment. Sources of tension had begun to break down, particularly as *glasnost* and *perestroika* removed many of the fears and misperceptions on both sides. No imminent security threats stemmed from either alliance, nor were there threats to any individual member of either alliance. Finally, the ideological aspects of the cold war ceased to be seen as a zero-sum struggle between the two parties.

Comparable trends are difficult to find in the Middle East today. The ideological struggle among both Muslim and Jewish fundamentalists and moderates is as real as the zero-sum game between communists and Western democrats. Extremist groups, especially those supporting a radical Islamic or Jewish ideology, do not believe it is possible to resolve the basic sources of Middle Eastern conflict by compromise. Radical Islamists want to destroy the state of Israel and overthrow the moderate regimes in the Arab world. Jewish extremists wish to annex all territory captured by Israel in the 1967 war and deny Palestinians any meaningful rights within greater Israel. They point to Jordan as the logical Palestinian homeland. Given such existential threats, it is not surprising that the concept of cooperative security is neither understood nor accepted by most Middle Eastern leaders.

European arms control succeeded because both sides acknowledged its benefits, but to date Middle Eastern governments have manifested only limited recognition that arms control or arms reductions can serve national or mutual interests. Although it is accepted that arms control issues may have some utility (one of the multilateral working groups set up following the Madrid conference is devoted to arms control, for example), so far no movement has been made toward serious negotiations. Arms control is more often perceived by countries in the region as hindering their own military capabilities, including capabilities that regional powers and their outside suppliers believe are necessary for self-defense and stability.

Asymmetries in Threat Perceptions

Unlike European countries, most countries in the Middle East face multiple threats from their neighbors, and no single military standoff between two groups approximates that between the countries of NATO and those of the Warsaw Pact. The infusion, or alternately the withholding, of new arms capabilities from outside the region can rapidly change this volatile balance of power.

Secure and accepted legal boundaries remain another key source of antagonism in the Middle East. The Gulf War highlighted the problems of historical boundaries; some current borders are not recognized, and many still-contested de facto frontiers exist throughout the region. The territorial issue among Israel, Syria, Lebanon, and Jordan remains unresolved. Territorial disputes exist between Syria and Lebanon, with Syria claiming its rights over all of Lebanon. One cause of the Iran-Iraq war, for example, was conflict over the delineation of the boundaries along the Shatt al-Arab waterway, a dispute that had endured without resolution for decades before the open eruption of the conflict.

Thus, unlike in Europe, geopolitical parameters of the region, the basis for security agreements or for political dialogue, are not widely accepted. For example, Turkey has become an important player in the Middle East since the Gulf crisis, but it is also a member of NATO and will most likely be excluded from regional arms restraints. Some view Pakistan as a Middle Eastern player, given its Islamic ties to the Arab states, and often refer to its nuclear weapons as the "Islamic bomb." But Pakistan's military programs are more influenced by its conflict with India, which, in turn, sees China as its enemy. Furthermore, the new Muslim states of central Asia have begun to complicate matters as they develop relationships with countries such as Turkey, Iran, Saudi Arabia, and Pakistan.

To conform to the European model, there must be a shared desire to promote stability and improve relations, with an absence of imminent security threats. These conditions do not currently exist in the Middle East, though the Israel-PLO breakthrough is an encouraging sign. However, it is unlikely that the most radical Middle Eastern countries, especially Iran, Libya, and Iraq, would be part of the process in the foreseeable future. In fact, any regional progress toward peace could stimulate violent protest by radical groups, which could in turn jeopardize or terminate negotiations.

Regional Strategic Asymmetries

Besides interregional differences, very significant asymmetries weaken the appeal of cooperative security in the Middle East. These asymmetries range from the character of weapons inventories to cultural and ideological differences, including the willingness of governments to accept casualties in war in pursuit of political ends and the nature and role of armed forces within society. Also highly relevant are geographic, demographic, and economic asymmetries.

The Gulf War helped highlight asymmetries in the distribution of military power. By reducing the Iraqi military threat, the Gulf War altered the regional power structure. But for many Arab countries, this change was seen as accentuating Israel's role as the regional hegemon. In particular, Israel's nuclear capability is perceived by the Arab states as unilaterally skewing the balance of power and demonstrating the gross asymmetry in military capabilities. It is as if NATO and the Warsaw Pact had existed with only the United States possessing nuclear weapons. This scenario would have produced an entirely different relationship between the two blocs, requiring very different politics, defense doctrines, and force structures.

Geographic vulnerability also varies among states. The absence of depth and the proximity of population centers to enemy forces is one of the key security concerns of Israel, Lebanon, Jordan, the small Gulf states, and Iraq. Other countries, such as Egypt, Syria, and Saudi Arabia, can point to specific elements of their geography that pose acute vulnerabilities (respectively, the Nile river, the Golan Heights, and the Strait of Hormuz).

Economic asymmetries are equally dramatic. The wealthiest countries are those with huge oil reserves and small populations; the poorest ones are those with little or no oil and large populations. If he had not squandered his country's treasures in two disastrous wars, Saddam Hussein might today be in control of the most powerful country in the Middle East, endowed with huge oil reserves and a relatively highly skilled population. Instead, the invasion of Kuwait prompted a wave of support in many Arab quarters for a redistribution of wealth within the Arab world and accentuated tensions between rich and poor states.

Conclusions: Containing Extremism and Promoting Asymmetric Reciprocity

The first condition for Middle East peace is an end to the ideological conflict in which fundamentalist groups continue to deny the rights of others to exist. It applies to Jewish extremists who refuse to recognize the rights of Palestinians to live within their own political entity on the West Bank. Fortunately the power and influence of these extremists have been significantly weakened by the defeat of Likud in the 1992 Israeli elections. However, intra-Israeli political squabbling over the future of the occupied territories could lead to violence if a full-fledged autonomy agreement between the Israeli government and the Palestinians is implemented.

Even more dangerous are the threats from Muslim extremists who refuse to accept Israel's right to exist. To varying degrees, they are using violent tactics and operating in at least six Middle Eastern countries (Iran, Egypt, Lebanon, Sudan, Israel, and Algeria). These groups show no sign of being willing to compromise. On the contrary, efforts to promote Arab-Israeli peace have been met with outright rejection and calls for revolution.

For these reasons, a key challenge for cooperative security will be curbing the ability of extremists to undermine the delicate political structure that is now emerging in the region. This approach will include continued efforts to seek new leadership in Iraq; discriminatory policies to deny radical states, such as Iran, weapons of mass destruction; and the willingness to use force, if necessary, to achieve these goals. Unless and until the military threats and ideological excesses of the radical regimes are curtailed, it will not be possible to redress the problems posed by the various asymmetries in the region, the second condition for progress.

Even if the radical regimes are replaced, the strategic asymmetries among the key Middle Eastern adversaries are sufficiently daunting to make it difficult to envision a stable set of military relationships based on any traditional notions of a balance of power. As long as unresolved geographic disputes and intense nationalist and ethnic rivalries exist, the types of institutional confidence-building measures that have been useful in Europe and between the superpowers will be, at best, limited measures to manage the risks of conflict. Similarly, unilateral arms control and arms limitations initiatives imposed by external powers, though essential for curbing weapons of mass destruction, will do little to address the fundamental sources of instability and hence the probability of continuing military confrontations.

Cooperative security can be implemented only if the regional players are prepared to accept the basic compromises necessary for political conflict resolution and to subscribe to the principle of asymmetric reciprocity. The key adversaries must accept, a priori, the fact that strategic asymmetries cannot be removed and that there can be no neat symmetric formula for reducing military forces and limiting military deployments and technical capabilities.

Here there may be some good news. Asymmetric reciprocity lies behind one of the most successful Middle Eastern agreements in recent years: Israel's withdrawal from the Sinai desert between 1974 and 1982 and the establishment of the Multinational Force and Observers to ensure the demilitarization of the desert. The Israeli-Egyptian agreements required Egypt to accept the condition that much of the Sinai be demilitarized in exchange for the return of control and the acknowledgment of Egypt's sovereignty over the area. So as not to make the arrangement totally one-sided, Israel ultimately agreed to demilitarize a tiny sliver of its own territory in the Negev. Though this move had no practical utility and did not put constraints on Israel's ability to maneuver forces in the Negev, it had important symbolic meaning: Israel was reciprocating, but with asymmetric consequences.

As regards Syria and Israel, a similar formula would probably be necessary. In return for Israeli forfeiture of claims of sovereignty over the Golan Heights, Syria would have to agree to demilitarize the Golan and to allow a limited Israeli presence on the slopes, Mount Hermon, and the plateau. As in the case of the Sinai, Israel might have to accept some limited, token demilitarization in the Finger of Galilee.

Concerning the overall Arab-Israeli strategic balance in the context of peace agreements, parallel agreements on proximate military force levels would be needed. Undoubtedly Israel would have to live with more numerous Arab conventional forces and chemical weapons capabilities, and the Arabs would have to accept an Israeli nuclear monopoly for a time. Lebanon, Jordan, and the Palestinians would probably be required to accept enduring military inferiority and to agree to intrusive verification procedures to ensure their compliance with agreed-upon force levels in exchange for Israeli withdrawal from territory in South Lebanon and the West Bank.

These examples suggest that reaching agreement will require long, complex, and tortuous negotiations, as indeed was true in Europe. All parties will have to make concessions, many of them highly sensitive. Agreement is not likely to be possible until *after* the necessary political groundwork has been laid and will probably be possible only after intensive and intrusive U.S. diplomacy has been exhibited in the region by successive U.S. administrations.

In reality, interest in serious, practical arms control proposals has been greatly stimulated by the American-sponsored peace negotiations. A good deal of analysis and discussion on arms control is currently under way in the key Arab countries and in Israel precisely because arms control is on the agenda for the multilateral talks.[44]

Since the issues fueling the arms race are numerous, and most countries face multiple threats unless all the regional players, including the rejectionist front, accept major arms reductions and limits on defense expenditure, it is difficult to imagine any regional country willingly parting with what it regards as its rightful tools of self-defense. For instance, Israel, the GCC countries, and other Arab allies can hardly be expected to curb their arms programs beyond the limitations already being imposed on them unilaterally by the outside powers, at least not if the problem of Saddam Hussein and his weapons of mass destruction is not fully resolved and not unless Iran is brought into the political process. The chances of these conditions emerging are slender without a change of regime in Baghdad and the abandonment of key tenets of the revolution in Iran. Furthermore, Turkey cannot be excluded from the Middle Eastern power equation in view of its volatile relations with Syria and Iraq and its key geographic position.

For years it was hoped that the central arms race between NATO and the Warsaw Pact could be controlled in spite of the cold war. Yet with the exception of key crisis stability agreements and limitations on certain categories of strategic nuclear weapons systems between the two superpowers, dramatic breakthroughs in nuclear and conventional arms control had to await the ascent of Gorbachev and the end of the cold war. To be sure, there were multilateral arms control talks: they lasted for twenty years on mutual force reductions. But the talks got nowhere and were paralleled by an unprecedented buildup in NATO and Warsaw Pact military capabilities. There was much suspicion that the Soviet Union used arms control talks as a guise for dividing the Western allies while proceeding with its own rearmament program. Furthermore, arms control discussions are not unknown to Middle Eastern countries. Israel and the Arabs have jointly participated for many years at the Geneva Disarmament Conference in the implementation of an array of arms control measures, including the Chemical Weapons Convention. In short, contemporary European history suggests that rapid progress on Middle East arms control and security issues must be preceded by advances in the political realm.

It is also important to clarify the relationship between "arms control" and cuts in defense expenditures. The primary purposes of arms control are to reduce the probability of war and to limit its intensity if it does occur. If these purposes coincide with decreased defense expenditures, well and good. However, the emphasis has historically been on the first two objectives. The extraordinarily successful arms control negotiations between Egypt and Israel that resulted in the establishment of the Multinational Force and Observers in the Sinai were followed by a massive *increase* in defense assistance to both Israel and Egypt as part of the price of achieving peace. Few deny the cost was well worth it. Since the greatest danger in the Middle East is the prospect of a new, major military conflict, the primary goal of arms control has continued to be crisis stability. Reduction of defense expenditure is only a secondary consideration. Determining just what types of confidence-building measures and weapons restrictions are necessary for arms control is not the same as calling for across-the-board cuts in defense expenditures. In fact, such cuts might lead to allocations of resources that promote certain types of weapons over others. That, in turn, may have destabilizing or stabilizing impacts, depending on which particular weapon systems are examined. (See the appendix for a more detailed treatment of this paradox.)

What is the appropriate linkage between measures to reduce defense expenditure or promote arms control and the peace process? I believe that the peace process—the diplomatic efforts aimed at bringing about dialogue and negotiations between Israelis and Arabs and ultimately between Iran and its neighbors—must continue to be the priority of American diplomacy along with very specific initiatives to curb the spread of weapons of mass destruction. The United States' immediate efforts in curtailing weapons of mass destruction *must* be directed against Iraq, Iran, Syria, and Libya, not Israel. Of course, the Israeli nuclear program has to be discussed at some point, but not until there has been much more progress in the peace negotiations. To try to limit Israeli nuclear capabilities beyond a cap on the production of fissile material (the Bush proposal) in the absence of a broader agreement is a recipe for rejection by any Israeli government.

Nevertheless, as has been previously argued, several factors are working in favor of greater cooperation in the Middle East despite the presence of extremism and strategic asymmetry. One can remain hardheaded and practical about the conditions for Middle Eastern peace while concluding that a more cooperative approach makes sense and is the only rational way to resolve disputes that date back thousands of years. However, cooperative security will not be possible in the Middle East until the key parties come to believe what the western Europeans have accepted: that a state may be secure within a system that permits vast asymmetries in power among its members.

From a practical standpoint, what do these conclusions suggest for the Clinton administration as it comes to grips with the complicated and difficult tasks of reducing America's global presence, cutting the defense budget yet retaining U.S. credibility as a guarantor of friends and allies in various regions of the world? The point to reiterate is that any cooperative security regime in the Middle East must have the cooperation of the key regional players. For the first time, Syria, Jordan, Lebanon, Egypt, Israel, most Palestinians, and the Arab Gulf countries all want to see an end to the Arab-Israeli conflict. All recognize that an assertive American role is essential to achieve a political breakthrough. On the other hand, the key rejectionist front—especially Iraq, Iran, and various extremist Muslim groups—is increasingly active and will intensify opposition to the peace process as Israel, the PLO, and Jordan continue to take concrete steps toward peace and a territorial settlement.

The challenge for the United States in the Middle East is therefore twofold: how to sustain and accelerate peace negotiations and at the same time take strong action to curb and contain the behavior of the rejectionists. The first goal requires intense and imaginative diplomacy; the second goal requires a continuing American military presence in the eastern Mediterranean and Persian Gulf with the willingness to use force, if necessary, against adversaries. Achieving these goals could be a risky business, especially since the military component of American policy requires forward deployment of U.S. forces, multiple training exercises with local Arab regimes, and continued military assistance and sales programs that, in turn, help to stimulate further arms transfers by China and Russia to Iran.

The irony is that progress on the peace front may *increase* the risks of conflict in the short run precisely because the rejectionists will feel threatened by the prospects of a political breakthrough, which, in turn, could lead to reduced future conflict and the advent of a cooperative security regime. In this context the role of Syria is critical. If Syria chooses to cooperate with the new peace process and work out a deal with Israel, the forces of rejectionism will suffer a serious setback. On the other hand, if Syria decides to play an obstructionist role and lend greater support to the rejectionists, the delicate tapestry of reconciliation that received such a boost with the Israel-PLO accords could be dealt a fatal blow, and the Middle East could once more be plunged into crisis and possibly war.

Appendix: The Paradox of Arms Control Objectives and Specific Force Limitation Agreements

The three most widely accepted goals of arms control, in order of priority, are to reduce the probability of war, to reduce the intensity of war should it occur, and to reduce the burden of defense expenditure. When these guidelines were applied in the context of NATO–Warsaw Pact military relationships, it was sometimes determined that the most effective way to reduce the probability of war was to introduce a new, more stable weapons system into an inventory. However, to contemplate such a proposition in the Middle East would seem counterintuitive. Not only would it work against the goal of reducing defense expenditure, it would also cause problems for those who believe that arms control is synonymous with arms reductions.

It is against a background of sometimes conflicting arms control objectives that the benefits and costs of different force limitation agreements should be assessed. Table 10A-1 lays out in very general terms some of the considerations

Table 10A-1. *Paradox of Arms Control Objectives and Specific Force Limitation Agreements*

Goal of arms control	*Force limitation agreements (procurement curbs, force cuts)*
1. Reduce the probability of war	+ If specific systems inherently *unstable or provocative*, reductions promote stability.
	– If specific systems part of *effective stable deterrent*, reductions may contribute to instability.
2. Reduce the intensity of war	+ If specific system *only* means of delivering certain weapons, reductions may limit potential for high casualties.
	– If specific system crucial to early war termination, reductions may *prolong war* and casualties.
3. Reduce the defense expenditure	+ If specific systems have high cost and substitutes not needed or less expensive, *goal will be met.*
	– If specific systems are replaced by more expensive substitutes, *goal will not be met.*

that must be taken into account when calculating the relationship between different objectives and force agreements.

A range of force agreements can be envisioned, including procurement curbs, force reductions, and even weapons elimination. Since, by definition, force limitation agreements involve constraint, all force limitation agreements can be lumped together and examined in the context of the three objectives of arms control.

Suppose, for instance, that there was a consensus that the introduction of certain classes of surface-to-surface missiles into Middle Eastern inventories would upset the balance of power between relatively stable adversaries. It would follow that limitations on the deployment of such systems would serve the first objective of arms control: reducing the probability of war. But suppose that surface-to-surface missiles were already in the inventories of these adversaries and that they were in fact contributing to what was considered an effective deterrent system (as Israel would probably argue with respect to its nuclear-armed Jericho missiles). In this case, imposed, or asymmetric, reductions in missile forces might contribute to instability rather than stability. Certainly such anomalies are apparent if one examines combat aircraft. To decide which aircraft are "provocative" and "destabilizing" and which contribute to "deterrence" and "stability" requires taking into account many more factors than the weapons systems themselves.

Consider the second goal of arms control: reducing the intensity of war. If surface-to-surface missiles are the most likely means by which countries in the

Middle East will deliver weapons of mass destruction over long ranges, then reducing the number of missiles will reduce the potential for major attacks with weapons of mass destruction against population centers. On the other hand, there may be situations in which particular weapons systems, including surface-to-surface missiles, are important to the warfighting capability of a particular country. Reductions or asymmetric cuts could prolong wars and therefore intensify casualties. In the case of the Iran-Iraq war, the absence of a sophisticated air force on either side was one factor contributing to the prolongation of the war, with the commensurate rise in casualties. One reason the war came to a rapid end in the summer of 1988 was that Iraq was able to use aircraft, missiles, and chemical weapons more effectively than it did earlier in the war.

The history of conflict in the third world suggests that when certain classes of sophisticated weapons have been denied for one reason or another to conflicting parties, wars have been protracted. During the Nigerian civil war the failure of the federal government to procure a modern air force, in part because of Western arms embargoes, meant that Biafra was able to sustain its rebellion for many years, with increasing casualties on both sides. Hence if an important objective of arms control is to reduce the duration and intensity of war and thereby casualties, reductions in sophisticated weapons systems may in some cases have exactly the reverse effect. One shudders to think what the numbers of Iraqi and allied casualties would have been if U.S. technology had not been so sophisticated. This conclusion may sound paradoxical and somewhat macabre, but "smart weapons" did in fact save lives. Of course this was true because it was U.S. policy to limit collateral damage. Had it been policy to maximize collateral damage, as was the case during the strategic bombing campaigns against Germany and Japan in World War II, high technology would have become the ultimate killer.

A similar dilemma relates to the third objective of arms control: reducing defense expenditures. If particular weapons systems, such as surface-to-surface missiles, have high costs and defensive measures, such as anti–tactical ballistic missile systems, are cheaper to buy as a substitute, then removing or limiting surface-to-surface missiles may reduce defense expenditures. But if the elimination or reduction of surface-to-surface missiles means that countries have to find substitutes, such as combat aircraft, defense expenditures will be likely to rise.

Most important, this analysis suggests that notions about the relationship among arms control objectives, force limitations, and military stability require careful consideration before general statements about the desirability of limiting certain classes of weapons can be made.

What is the empirical evidence linking arms races to war in the Middle East? In the case of the Arab-Israeli wars and near-wars, two occasions can be cited when force was used, or its use was threatened, primarily because of the dynamics of the arms race. Israel's decision to collaborate with Britain and

France in 1956 and the subsequent invasion of the Sinai were, from Israel's point of view, in large part determined by the massive infusions of Soviet arms to Egypt that had begun a year earlier. Israel engaged in a preventive war; it anticipated that if the Egyptians were not stopped in 1956 or soon thereafter, they, together with the other Arabs, might be in a position to threaten Israel's existence.[45]

The second example is Israel's 1981 attack on Iraq's nuclear reactor at Osirak, a move prompted by Israel's fear that once the reactor went critical it would have been impossible to destroy—from a political perspective—owing to the danger of radiation leaks. The reactor would have given Iraq access to nuclear weapons sometime in the 1980s. It was Saddam Hussein's fear that Israel was going to repeat its exercise in coercive arms control in 1990 that prompted his notorious speech of April 2, 1990, in which he threatened to use chemical weapons against Israel if Iraq was attacked. Fear of war between Israel and Iraq in early summer 1990 was real, and these fears were almost entirely driven by the dynamics of the Iraqi military buildup and Israel's doctrine of preventive war.

Notes

1. The two-track Arab-Israeli peace negotiations began in ceremonial fashion in Madrid in October 1991 and continued with a number of more substantive meetings over the following months. Bilateral talks paired Israeli representatives with a joint Jordanian and Palestinian delegation and individual delegations from Syria and Lebanon. Meanwhile a multilateral structure was developed to deal with five areas of concern: arms control and regional security, economic development, the environment, refugees, and water resources. Multilateral talks, under the joint chairmanship of the United States and Russia, began in Moscow in January 1992 and involved Israel, Jordan, Egypt, Saudi Arabia, Kuwait, several other Arab states, Japan, China, European states, and others. Syria and Lebanon boycotted the multilateral talks. It is intended that both bilateral and multilateral negotiations will continue until the major issues of the conflict are resolved.

The first talks began in Madrid on October 30, 1991. At the ceremonial opening, no concessions were made between any parties, although all accepted a public commitment to continue the talks at a later date. Subsequent bilateral talks continued in Washington through late 1991 and throughout 1992, with the sixth round in August and September 1992 producing a flurry of Israeli-Syrian activity. After talks in December 1992, a five-month break occurred as the new U.S. administration settled into office. The year 1993 saw three more rounds of talks, with the secretly negotiated Israel-PLO agreement stealing the thunder from the eleventh round of meetings. By the end of 1993 all five working groups in the multilateral talks were expected to have completed four meetings.

2. For more details on the relative power of the U.S. military establishment vis-à-vis the regional players, see chapter 6 in this volume.

3. In terms of the peace process the nuclear threat also appears noteworthy. In his opening speech to the Knesset, Prime Minister Yitzhak Rabin said that "this [new, nuclear] reality requires us to give additional thought to the urgent need to terminate the

Arab-Israeli conflict and to attain peace with our neighbors." "Rabin Addresses Knesset," *Israel Television Network,* July 13, 1992, in Foreign Broadcast Information Service, *Daily Report: Near East,* July 14, 1992, p. 25. (Hereafter FBIS, *Near East.*) See also "Bodinger—U.S. 'Not Doing Enough,'" *Qol Yisra'el,* June 15, 1992, in ibid., June 16, 1992, pp. 16–17; "Intelligence Official on Iran, 'Arafat Allegation," *IDF Radio,* June 8, 1992, in ibid., June 9, 1992, p. 34; "U.S. Help Needed for Attacks on Nuclear Targets," *Ha'aretz,* June 16, 1992, p. A1, in ibid., June 17, 1992, p. 23; and "Efforts to Halt Iranian Nuclear Program Cited," *Ha'aretz,* June 11, 1992, p. 5, in ibid., June 12, 1992, p. 29.

4. "U.S. Help Needed for Attacks on Nuclear Targets."

5. "A New Arab Order," *Economist,* September 28, 1991, p. 5 of survey section.

6. For a country-by-country analysis of the postwar Middle East economies, see Amy Kaslow and Scott B. MacDonald, "Middle Eastern Economies after the Gulf War," *Middle East Insight,* vol. 8 (March–April 1992), pp. 56–59; and Yahya Sadowski, "Sandstorm with a Silver Lining? Prospects for Arms Control in the Arab World," *Brookings Review,* vol. 10 (Summer 1992), pp. 7–11. (See the appendix to this chapter for more details and critique of Sadowski's thesis.)

7. "U.S. Ambassador's 'Suspect Tours' Denounced," *Al-Ribat,* June 30, 1992, p. 7, in FBIS, *Near East,* July 7, 1992, p. 52. The original column, "Within the Circle of Events: Jordan and America," was written by Bassam al-'Umush.

8. "Commentary: West Seeks to 'Subjugate' Libya," *Syrian Arab Republic Radio Network,* April 15, 1992, in FBIS, *Near East,* April 16, 1992, p. 45.

9. "Editorial Views Arab Stance on Libya, Iraq," *Al-Dustur,* April 20, 1992, in FBIS, *Near East,* April 22, 1992, p. 42.

10. "Reasons for UN Resolution on Libya Discussed," *Al-Akhbar,* April 15, 1992, p. 5, in FBIS, *Near East,* April 23, 1992, p. 14.

11. "Buying Security from the West," *Jane's Defence Weekly,* March 28, 1992, p. 534; "U.S., Qatar to Sign Pact," *Washington Post,* June 5, 1992, p. A45; and Don Oberdorfer, "U.S., Saudis Agree to Use Old Military Pact for Expanding Cooperation," *Washington Post,* May 31, 1992, pp. A10–11. For a brief historical look at U.S.-Saudi ties, see Walter Pincus, "Secret Presidential Pledges over Years Erected U.S. Shield for Saudis," *Washington Post,* February 9, 1992, p. A20.

12. David Hoffman and Barton Gellman, "U.S., Israel Reassess Relations in Painful Time of Adjustment," *Washington Post,* March 23, 1992, p. A1.

13. "Commentary on Need to Keep Local Arms Secret," *Ha'aretz,* January 2, 1992, p. B1, in FBIS, *Near East,* January 8, 1992, p. 35. The commentary by Ze'ev Schiff was called "The Edge Lies in Disparity."

14. Thomas Friedman, "U.S. and Israel at Sea," *New York Times,* March 22, 1992, p. 1.

15. "Commentary on Need to Keep Local Arms Secret."

16. Shibley Telhami, "Israeli Foreign Policy after the Gulf War," *Middle East Policy,* vol. 1, no. 2 (1992), pp. 94–95.

17. David Hoffman, "New Era Forces U.S., Israel to Redefine Alliance," *Washington Post,* July 28, 1992, p. A12.

18. John Rossant and Stanley Reed, "Maybe the Mideast Just Can't Afford to Keep Fighting," *Business Week,* November 11, 1991, p. 39.

19. John Rossant and Neal Sandler, "Why Israeli Business Is So Fed Up," *Business Week,* June 29, 1992, p. 55.

20. Clyde Haberman, "Israel's New Broom: How Much Time to Sweep?" *New York Times,* July 15, 1992, p. A3.

21. Jackson Diehl, "Israeli Quest for 'Normalcy' Reshaping Society," *Washington Post,* June 8, 1992, p. A1.

22. Jonathan Levy, "Israel Wonders Where It Will Fit into Single-Market EC," *Journal of Commerce,* September 30, 1991.

23. "EC Linking Trade, Peace Progress," *Ha'aretz,* March 11, 1992, p. A3, in FBIS, *Near East,* March 12, 1992, pp. 26–27.

24. The ambassador cited the need for agreements that prevent double taxation as the second factor. "Japan to Deny Guarantees until Progress in Talks," *Qol Yisra'el,* June 11, 1992, in FBIS, *Near East,* June 11, 1992, p. 19. From a business perspective, "enticing foreign capital on the scale required [for Israel] could be constricted by geopolitical issues or a market fear that the potential for disruptions could undermine the long-term return on investment." Lisa S. Kaess, "Can Israel Play in the Big League?" *International Economy,* September–October 1991, p. 48.

25. No one knows how much money is needed. Estimates range from $4 billion to $50 billion. What *is* clear is that Israel cannot afford to get loans for these sums without favorable interest rates that would be available only if the United States guaranteed the loans.

26. Carroll J. Doherty, "Where U.S. Aid Has Gone," *Congressional Quarterly,* May 16, 1992, p. 1352. The article is based on figures compiled by the Congressional Research Service. Israel was the top recipient of U.S. aid, followed by Egypt ($23.2 billion) and Turkey ($6.9 billion).

27. Yitzhaq Moda'i, then the Israeli finance minister, said: "One is the fact that the State of Israel's existence and immigration to Israel do not depend solely—not even significantly—on the readiness of our American friends to give us substantial loan guarantees. My other point at the time was a proposal: If the Americans give us the guarantees, we will drop our usual annual aid requests in order to attain finally the only desirable condition for the State of Israel—economic independence." "Moda'i on Alternatives to U.S. Guarantees," *Qol Yisra'el,* March 17, 1992, in FBIS, *Near East,* March 18, 1992, p. 25. For an American perspective on phasing out aid, see Stanley Fischer and Herbert Stein, "Overhaul the Israeli Economy," *New York Times,* October 12, 1991, p. 29.

28. For an article on the changing U.S. perspective on foreign aid, see Carroll J. Doherty, "Support for Foreign Aid Wilting under Glare of Domestic Woes," *Congressional Quarterly,* May 16, 1992, pp. 1351–57.

29. Peter Waldman, "Socialist Mess: Israelis Fail to Deal with a Big Problem: A Troubled Economy," *Wall Street Journal,* June 24, 1992, p. A1.

30. Ibid.

31. Herbert Stein, "Israel Strikes Oil," *Wall Street Journal,* May 21, 1991; and Jackson Diehl, "Immigration Has Israel Awash in Scientists: Country Seeks Ways to Use Soviet Talent," *Washington Post,* June 5, 1991, pp. A21–22.

32. Bernard Avishai, "Israel's Choice: The West Bank or Wealth," *Wall Street Journal,* September 27, 1991, p. 10. For a more detailed account see Bernard Avishai, "Israel's Future: Brainpower, High Tech—and Peace," *Harvard Business Review,* November–December, 1991, pp. 50–64.

33. Patricia A. Wertman, "The Israeli Economy and Its External Economic Relations: An Overview," Congressional Research Service, September 6, 1991, rev. February 28, 1992, p. 21.

34. "EC Envoy on 'Positive' View of Labor," *Qol Yisra'el,* June 25, 1992, in FBIS, *Near East,* June 26, 1992, p. 30.

35. Hugh Carnegy, "EC Links Trade Deal to Israeli Peace Progress," *Financial Times,* July 11, 1991, p. 4; and Levy, "Israel Wonders Where It Will Fit into Single-

Market EC." *Journal of Commerce,* September 30, 1991. The Israeli daily *Ha'aretz* reported, "Israeli sources believe that if the current trade agreements are not adjusted, Israel stands to lose its relative advantage in the EC." "EC Linking Trade, Peace Progress," p. 26.

36. "Israeli Foreign Minister, EC Counterparts Meet," *Qol Yisra'el,* May 12, 1992, in FBIS, *Daily Report: Western Europe,* May 12, 1992, p. 2; "EC Blamed for Trying to 'Torpedo' Accord," *Ha'aretz,* May 6, 1992, p. C3, in FBIS, *Near East,* May 7, 1992, p. 24; and "Israel-EFTA Free Trade Pact," *Financial Times,* July 17, 1992, p. 4.

37. Peter Passell, "What Kind of Economy Would a Palestine Have?" *New York Times,* January 19, 1992, p. D2.

38. David Weinberg, *The Arab Boycott of Israel: 1991 Update* (New York: Anti-Defamation League, 1991), pp. 4–8; quotation on p. 5.

39. Shawn Tully, "The Best Case For Mideast Peace," *Fortune,* vol. 123 (May 20, 1991), p. 129.

40. Gideon Fishelson, ed., *Economic Cooperation in the Middle East* (Boulder, Colo.: Westview Press, 1989), pp. 10–11.

41. Tully, "Best Case for Mideast Peace," pp. 132–33.

42. Yahya M. Sadowski, *Scuds or Butter? The Political Economy of Arms Control in the Arab World* (Brookings, 1992).

43. The following section is based on a revised text initially presented in Geoffrey Kemp, *The Control of the Middle East Arms Race* (Washington: Carnegie Endowment for International Peace, 1991), pp. 124–28.

44. In the past year the author has organized and participated in more than ten workshops and conferences with high-ranking Israelis and Arabs to discuss arms control proposals. Most of these meetings would have been impossible before the Gulf War and the Madrid process.

45. For a highly sophisticated and still relevant treatment of the Arab-Israeli arms race and arms control options between 1948 and 1977, see Yair Evron, *The Role of Arms Control in the Middle East,* Adelphi Paper 138 (London: International Institute for Strategic Studies, Autumn 1977).

ELEVEN

Cooperative Security in the Asia-Pacific Region

Harry Harding

DESPITE MANY remaining uncertainties, today Asia is more stable than at any time in its modern history. In recent years the region has witnessed the end of not just one cold war but two. The confrontation between the Soviet Union and the United States was eased by the moderation of Soviet foreign policy under Mikhail Gorbachev and then ended altogether by the disintegration of the Soviet Union at the end of 1991. At the same time the more accommodative foreign policy of the Soviet Union facilitated the conclusion of the second cold war between Moscow and Beijing, as symbolized by the exchange of summit meetings between Chinese and Soviet leaders in 1989 and 1991. As a result, both Sino-Russian and Russo-American relations are now fully normal and reasonably friendly.

These developments, in turn, have permitted the improvement of subsidiary relationships that had fallen victim to the two cold wars in Asia. The tensions between mainland China and Taiwan, North and South Korea, South Korea and Russia, Russia and Japan, Russia and South Korea, and the United States and Vietnam—all of which were related to the underlying confrontation between the Soviet Union and the United States—have now been ameliorated, at least to a degree. The relationships that were frozen by the Sino-Soviet dispute, including those linking China with Mongolia, Vietnam, and India, are also better today than they have been for many years.

The economic dynamism of the region has further contributed to the amelioration of relations among the major powers and the moderation of most of

I would like to express my gratitude to David Dewitt and Paul Evans, both of York University, and to the other participants in the North Pacific Cooperative Security Dialogue, for introducing me to the process of cooperative security in the Asia-Pacific region. I am also grateful to the participants in the Snowmass Conference on cooperative security for their valuable comments on a draft of this chapter.

East Asia's subregional disputes. With the exceptions of Burma and North Korea, every government in the area has now identified economic development as its central national priority. The emphasis on economics has encouraged a reduction of international tensions, so that each society can gain the greatest possible access to markets, capital, information, and technology from abroad. This economic imperative has been particularly evident in the improvement in China's relations with the rest of the region and in Vietnam's attempts to normalize its ties with its neighbors. It is also helping to stabilize the relationship between China and the United States, counterbalancing the strains produced by Beijing's record on human rights and foreign arms sales.

Although present-day Asia seems relatively prosperous and stable, security concerns have by no means disappeared from the regional agenda. Ethnic disputes spanning international boundaries, controversies over borders on land and at sea, and subregional disputes left over from the cold war could all readily lead to an increase in tension and even to the use of armed force. So could the emerging set of unconventional security problems, including unauthorized migration, environmental pollution, smuggling, piracy, terrorism, and drug trafficking, all of which cross international frontiers. Moreover, the growing national power of some regional actors (such as Japan, China, and India), coupled with the retrenchment of the two superpowers (Russia and the United States), has generated a fluid and potentially imbalanced international strategic environment that is producing considerable unease in capitals across the region.

To a large degree the nations of the Asia-Pacific region are dealing with this new security agenda in very traditional ways. China, Japan, India, Taiwan, and most members of the Association of South East Asian Nations (ASEAN) are all modernizing their armed forces, in some cases through the acquisition of the capability to project force in the air, at sea, and by missile. Indeed, the widespread desire for military modernization in an uncertain environment is producing growing concern about the prospects of an arms race in the Asia-Pacific region.[1]

Besides strengthening their own military establishments, Asian governments are also turning to international alliances to ensure their security. Alliances with the United States remain the cornerstone of the national security policies of Japan, South Korea, and Australia, and residual American security guarantees play a large role in Taiwan's defense posture as well. Singapore and Malaysia continue to rely, at least in part, on the Five-Power Defense Arrangement linking them with Australia, New Zealand, and the United Kingdom.

Nonetheless, even as they depend on these traditional security mechanisms, many governments and policy analysts in the Asia-Pacific region are also showing increased interest in the development of cooperative measures to address challenges to their security. There is a growing awareness that most of the unconventional threats to national safety (such as those posed by piracy, smuggling, emigration, drug trafficking, and pollution) can be dealt with effectively only through international cooperation. In addition, there is an emerging realization that cooperative mechanisms can provide less costly and potentially more fruitful solutions to such conventional security concerns as territorial and ethnic disputes, subregional conflicts, and regional arms races than can either unilateralism or alliances. Calls for "security dialogues" on both regional and subregional issues are now regularly heard in virtually every capital in the Asia-Pacific region, and in recent months there have been welcome signs that several of these proposals are about to be implemented.

This chapter is organized around the three broad areas in which this growing interest in cooperative security is evident. First, it discusses Asia's role in the international regimes that are intended to limit the spread of arms, especially the proliferation of weapons of mass destruction. Most noncommunist Asian nations have long been members of global nonproliferation arrangements, both conventional and nuclear. But two major communist countries, China and North Korea, are more recent and reluctant participants in international nonproliferation efforts. Although China has agreed to ratify the Nuclear Non-Proliferation Treaty (NPT) and to adhere to the Missile Technology Control Regime (MTCR), its willingness and ability to honor these obligations remain in doubt. There is even graver apprehension about North Korean programs to develop nuclear and biochemical weapons and to export ballistic missiles abroad. If the global cooperative security regime is to be effective, then both Beijing and Pyongyang will have to be brought more fully into compliance with the norms of nonproliferation.

Second, the chapter considers attempts to apply the concept of cooperative security to some of the most significant subregional disputes in the Asia-Pacific region. In five of these disputes—those centered on Cambodia, the Korean peninsula, the Sino-Russian border, the Taiwan Strait, and the South China Sea—potential adversaries or former antagonists have been engaging in cooperative efforts to reduce tensions and prevent conflict. To be sure, none of the disputes has been completely resolved. Most discouraging of all, some of the most promising arrangements appear highly fragile: Cambodia's new government is far from secure, tension is growing between Taiwan and mainland China over Taipei's desire for a more visible role in international affairs, and the dialogue on the Korean peninsula has stalled because of Pyongyang's refusal to accept credible inspections of its nuclear facilities. Still, there are more sustained efforts at preventive diplomacy and conflict resolution in Asia today than at any time since World War II.

Finally, the chapter addresses the prospects for a broader multilateral dialogue on security matters, particularly on the emerging conventional arms race in the area. Given substantial skepticism among many major governments, it has not yet been possible to create an intergovernmental security organization with universal membership, comparable to the Conference on Security and

Cooperation in Europe (CSCE). Nor have proposals for formal arms control measures attracted much support. But there is increasing interest in two less ambitious but more realistic mechanisms: unofficial discussions among scholars and policy analysts from all countries in the region and official contact among a somewhat more selective group of Asia-Pacific nations.

Looking ahead, the further pursuit of cooperative security in the Asia-Pacific region will require a multifaceted approach. The collaborative attempts to manage or resolve subregional issues should be intensified, as should the efforts to secure universal compliance with nonproliferation regimes. Unofficial dialogue among knowledgeable scholars and policy analysts should be launched on both a regional and a subregional basis. On the official level government-to-government discussions should be held in both Northeast and Southeast Asia on military strategies and force postures, as well as on the unconventional challenges to regional security. In combination these various mechanisms hold the promise of consolidating the stability that Asia has enjoyed in recent years and of managing the disputes that remain.

The Region's Role in Global Cooperative Security Regimes

The Asia-Pacific region is home to some of the last holdouts from the international regimes that have been created to prevent the spread of weapons of mass destruction. The most notable examples are North Korea and China, whose programs to build nuclear weapons, export nuclear materials, or sell advanced conventional arms are all of considerable concern. But even Japan, in most cases a staunch adherent to international norms, is being criticized for its continued interest in using plutonium as part of the fuel cycle for its nuclear power plants. Other Asian nations have also periodically been accused of flirting with the development of nuclear weapons.

Although most Asia-Pacific nations ratified the Limited Nuclear Test-Ban Treaty of 1963 and the NPT of 1968, for decades China and North Korea remained vociferous critics of the emerging global nonproliferation regime. Both countries regarded the two treaties as an effort by the Soviet Union, the United States, and the other nuclear powers to retain their monopoly over the possession and deployment of nuclear weapons. Both Beijing and Pyongyang continued programs to develop their own atomic arsenals, in defiance of the basic premise of the NPT that no new nations should be permitted to acquire nuclear weapons.

Fortunately, international pressure has subsequently persuaded both countries to adhere, at least nominally, to the norms of nuclear nonproliferation. Since 1980 China has no longer tested nuclear weapons in the atmosphere, thus tacitly abiding by the key provisions of the limited test ban treaty. In 1984, in order to obtain American cooperation in the development of its nuclear power industry, Beijing agreed to join the International Atomic Energy Agency (IAEA) and announced its acceptance of the principle of nonproliferation. In 1992, again under intense pressure from the United States, China signed and ratified the NPT. North Korea signed the NPT somewhat earlier, in 1985. Only after the United States had announced the withdrawal of its own tactical nuclear weapons from South Korea in late 1991, however, did Pyongyang finally agree to accept IAEA inspections of its nuclear facilities.

Despite these signs of progress, major uncertainties remain about both Chinese and North Korean commitment to the norms of nuclear nonproliferation. Beijing has not been drawn into the key elements of the nonproliferation regime other than the NPT and the limited test ban treaty. In 1992 China conducted two underground nuclear tests that were well above the limits specified in the threshold test ban treaty of 1974. Nor is Beijing a member of the London Club of nuclear suppliers, even though it has exported nuclear materials and equipment to such countries as Iran, Algeria, Iraq, and Pakistan. China still refuses to join in strategic arms control negotiations despite the deep cuts that both Russia and the United States have made in their nuclear arsenals. Moreover, past reports of Chinese assistance to the Pakistani nuclear weapons program raise continued concern about Beijing's willingness to fully honor its commitments to nuclear nonproliferation.

There are even graver suspicions about North Korean intentions. During the initial IAEA inspection of its nuclear facilities, Pyongyang acknowledged having processed a small amount of plutonium as part of a program to develop nuclear weapons. But subsequent examination of samples of that plutonium suggested that North Korea had produced more than it had admitted. North Korea refused to permit IAEA inspection of nuclear waste facilities that might shed additional light on this question and refused to develop a program of bilateral inspections with South Korea that might have supplemented the IAEA safeguards. Then, in early 1993, probably out of fear that its violations of the nuclear nonproliferation regime were about to be discovered, Pyongyang gave notice that it was withdrawing from the NPT altogether.

Unless North Korea returns to the nuclear nonproliferation regime and accepts credible inspections of its nuclear facilities, there could be a wave of nuclear proliferation across Northeast Asia. South Korea, Japan, and Taiwan all have the technical capability to develop nuclear weapons. Although they have signed and ratified the NPT, these countries could well decide to renounce their obligations if their security situation demanded it. South Korea's program would most likely be triggered by the deployment of nuclear weapons by the North, Japan's program by the development of nuclear weapons by either of the two Koreas, and Taiwan's efforts by an attempt to bolster its security against a possible attack from mainland China. Such nuclear programs would not necessarily take the form of acknowledged deployments of nuclear weapons. Instead they might involve the overt development of allegedly peaceful atomic explosive devices, the covert deployment of a small number of atomic warheads, or the creation of the capability to assemble nuclear devices on short notice. Still, the destabilizing potential of such programs make it imperative to regain North Korean compliance with the nuclear nonproliferation regime.

How can this best be done? In its negotiations with the United States, North Korea has reportedly demanded a high price for renewing its compliance with the nonproliferation treaty, including the cessation of the annual U.S.–South Korean Team Spirit exercises, an American renunciation of force against the North, and the withdrawal of U.S. forces from the peninsula. Although Washington could reasonably meet some of Pyongyang's terms, the United States does not wish to establish the precedent that governments can successfully demand blackmail as a condition of fulfilling their international obligations. Thus far Washington has been willing to withdraw nuclear weapons from South Korea, to assist North Korea in replacing its present nuclear reactors with less dangerous nuclear technology, and to renounce the use of force against Pyongyang if it adheres to its commitments.[2] It might also be possible to upgrade U.S. diplomatic contacts with North Korea. But it is not feasible to withdraw significant numbers of American troops from South Korea in the absence of an effective agreement on conventional arms control on the peninsula.

Whatever the reluctance to provide North Korea with positive incentives to abide by the nonproliferation regime, it is even more difficult to envision the use of punitive sanctions. A military attack on Pyongyang's nuclear facilities would hold no guarantee of success and could trigger a retaliatory strike against Seoul. Given North Korea's isolation from the international economy, it is not certain that economic sanctions—such as an international trade embargo or a freeze on international financial transactions—would have a quick or decisive impact. Indeed, it is possible that Pyongyang could complete production of a small number of nuclear weapons before the economic sanctions could take full effect.

A complicating factor in bolstering the nuclear nonproliferation regime in Northeast Asia is Japan's continued commitment to a civilian nuclear power program that uses plutonium rather than uranium fuel. The plutonium is currently being produced in Europe, with Japan gradually developing its own reprocessing capabilities domestically. The Japanese government and its supporters say that the use of plutonium is an important element in a national strategy of energy independence and insist that the plutonium fuel could be made into nuclear weapons only with great difficulty. But Japan's critics are concerned about the security of the shipments of plutonium from overseas and the reliability of the mechanisms that monitor Japan's stockpiles of plutonium. They also charge that Tokyo is setting a dangerous precedent by violating the emerging norm against using plutonium as part of the nuclear fuel cycle. Some insist that Japan renounce the use of plutonium fuel altogether. Others propose that it burn plutonium from dismantled Russian and American nuclear weapons, rather than reprocessing additional stocks, and that it place its stockpiles of plutonium under international supervision.[3]

Nuclear nonproliferation aside, there are also worries about Chinese and North Korean compliance with the regimes governing the spread of other weapons systems. Both Beijing and Pyongyang are exporting ballistic missiles to win political influence and to gain foreign exchange. In the mid-1980s China sold Silkworm antiship missiles to Iran and, in one of the most serious challenges to the emerging missile nonproliferation regime to date, exported intermediate-range missiles to Saudi Arabia a few years later. More recently Beijing has been negotiating the sale of medium-range M-9 missiles to Syria and a shorter-range missile, the M-11, to Pakistan.[4] For its part North Korea has been supplying short-range Scud-Cs to Syria and possibly to other nations in the Middle East and has been developing a 600-km missile, the Nodong-1, for export.[5]

Just as they previously opposed the nuclear nonproliferation regime, so too have China and North Korea criticized the more recent international attempts to restrict the sale of ballistic missiles. Both countries charge that the relevant international norms are inequitable, in that they prevent the sale of relatively simple missile technologies that they have been able to master while permitting the United States, Russia, France, and the United Kingdom to export advanced aircraft with comparable capabilities to deliver munitions. Until such aircraft are included in an international nonproliferation regime, it is unlikely that either Beijing or Pyongyang will regard the MTCR as fully legitimate. In addition, although China is expected to adhere to MTCR guidelines, the United States and its allies have thus far refused China the right to participate in the process of drafting them, on the grounds that this would give Beijing access to sensitive intelligence about missile design.

Despite its reservations about the MTCR, in 1991 China agreed to honor its provisions, bowing to intense and sustained pressure from the United States. There has been no subsequent indication that Beijing has consummated the prospective sale of M-9 missiles to Syria or to any other country. But there have been persistent reports that China has been engaging in other activities that either violate or stretch the terms of the MTCR, such as the sale of missile components (including solid fuel, guidance systems, and launchers) to both Syria and Pakistan and the modification of the M-11 missile so that its range would fall just outside the scope of the MTCR. China is also said to be transferring technology to Pakistan, Iran, and Egypt for the production of short-range surface-to-surface and antiship missiles.

After months of internal debate, the U.S. government determined in August 1993 that there was conclusive evidence that China had transferred components of the M-11 missile to Pakistan and that these actions violated the MTCR. Washington therefore imposed a new set of economic sanctions against Peking, particularly affecting the sale of technology to China's space programs and the use of Chinese boosters to launch American-built satellites.[6] It is hoped that these sanctions will be effective in deterring any further Chinese violations of the MTCR. But if violations continue, or if Beijing decides to cease even nominal compliance with the MTCR, then the United States and the rest of the international community will have to determine the steps they will take to uphold the integrity of the nonproliferation regime.[7]

Once again the actions of the rest of the international community are affecting the willingness of nations such as China to adhere scrupulously to the norms of nonproliferation. To a degree, Beijing's willingness to stretch, or even to violate, the terms of the MTCR reflected the importance it assigned to providing Pakistan with a credible, if limited, nuclear deterrent against India. But Beijing's determination may have been increased by the Bush administration's decision, made at the height of the 1992 election campaign, to sell F-16 fighters to Taiwan, a step that Beijing insists violates the 1982 Sino-American communiqué limiting U.S. arms sales to Taipei. If the United States evades its international commitments, Chinese leaders may argue, then Beijing should have the right to do the same.

There has been even less progress in obtaining North Korean subscription to the regimes governing the spread of ballistic missiles. The attention of the international community has been focused almost entirely on ensuring the termination of Pyongyang's nuclear weapons program. The issue of North Korean exports of missiles has not yet been raised in a serious or sustained manner. As a result, Pyongyang has not yet agreed to subscribe to the terms of the MTCR. Given the importance of missile sales to the stagnant North Korean economy, it is unlikely to comply unless it is given significant incentives, positive or negative, to do so.

Although China and North Korea are the principal exporters of advanced conventional weapons in the Asia-Pacific region, they are not the only ones. The United States remains the largest arms merchant in the area, although it steadfastly insists that its provision of military equipment to its friends and allies is a source of stability, not a destabilizing factor. Russia's eagerness to sell arms, largely to earn foreign exchange, is a growing cause for concern. Moscow has already agreed to sell fighters to both China and Malaysia, and there are reports of further negotiations with Beijing over the sale of ballistic missiles, cruise missiles, and even aircraft carriers. Other nations in the area—including Japan, Taiwan, South Korea, Malaysia, and Singapore—are also potential arms exporters, although the volumes of weapons shipped are at this point either nonexistent or slight. Although there has been some discussion of creating a registry of arms transfers in the Asia-Pacific region, there is as yet no effective international mechanism for monitoring, let alone controlling, the sale of advanced weapons in the area.

Chemical and biological weapons are a final cause for alarm. Both China and North Korea are alleged to hold stockpiles of these weapons, and both nations have been accused of exporting precursor components for chemical weapons to such states as Libya, Iran, and Iraq, whose intentions are questionable. Thus far North Korea has refused to sign the Chemical Weapons Convention, which would require it to forgo the deployment or transfer of chemical weapons. As a result, Pyongyang's chemical and biological weapons program, its possible export of chemical precursors to other countries, and its willingness to join the international regime limiting chemical weapons can be expected to be emerging issues in North Korea's relations with Japan, the United States, and the rest of the West. In contrast, China signed the Chemical Weapons Convention in early 1993. As in the case of the MTCR, however, Beijing's compliance with that regime is open to question, as suggested by the American accusations in the summer of 1993 that a Chinese ship, the *Yinhe,* was carrying chemical precursors to Iran.

In short, the image of China and North Korea as "rogue nations," resistant to international nonproliferation efforts, is partially correct. China has joined an increasing number of nonproliferation regimes but does not yet appear to regard them as fully legitimate. In addition, individuals and institutions that profit from arms sales abroad have a powerful incentive to evade or violate the norms of nonproliferation, particularly with regard to conventional weapons and chemical precursors. North Korea's willingness to honor the international nonproliferation regimes is even more problematic.

Securing the full compliance of these two countries with various nonproliferation and arms control regimes will therefore be an important priority for those interested in cooperative security. For China the best strategy is to use various incentives—particularly the level of international economic assistance and the severity of multilateral controls on technology transfer—to persuade Beijing to participate in additional arrangements (including the threshold test ban treaty, strategic arms limitation negotiations, and the London Suppliers Group), as well as to honor the regimes it has already joined. With respect to North Korea, the most appropriate tactic is for both the United States and Japan to make Pyongyang's compliance with conventional nonproliferation regimes, as well as with the NPT, a firm precondition for the extension of diplomatic recognition, trade privileges, or economic assistance.

Applying Cooperative Security to Subregional Disputes

During the last several years there has been notable progress in managing some of the longest-standing subregional issues and territorial disputes in the Asia-Pacific region. In no case has a full-scale cooperative security system been created, in the sense of a formal agreement to regulate the levels and types of military deployments. Nor has any of the controversies in question been fully and finally resolved. But in each instance the parties to the dispute have made some progress toward reducing the chances of armed conflict through varying combinations of military redeployment, diplomatic negotiation, and economic cooperation. Even so, the durability of some of these arrangements (especially in Cambodia and Korea) and the prospects for further progress on others (especially in the Taiwan Strait and the South China Sea) remain in doubt.

Cambodia

For nearly a decade the most recent confrontation in Indochina—caused by Vietnam's intervention in Cambodia in 1978—proceeded according to the classic principles of the balance of power. In opposition to the Vietnamese action a multinational coalition was formed, centering on China and the ASEAN states, which sought to force Hanoi to withdraw. China applied military force directly against Vietnam in the war of 1979. Thereafter, together with the members of ASEAN, Beijing tried to isolate Vietnam diplomatically and economically and provided material assistance to the anti-Vietnamese resistance in Cambodia.

Over time these diplomatic and military pressures laid the groundwork for a negotiated settlement.[8] As part of his plan to normalize relations with China, Mikhail Gorbachev began reducing Soviet military and economic support for Vietnam. That action, in turn, forced Hanoi to scale back its ambitions in Cambodia. In 1989 Vietnam pledged to withdraw all its troops from Cambodia and expressed its willingness to see elections for a new Cambodian government. The following year Hanoi agreed that those elections would be undertaken under UN supervision as part of a comprehensive political settlement. China also softened its position somewhat, withdrawing its call for the complete dismantling of the pro-Hanoi government in Phnom Penh and accepting instead the idea that, pending elections, the UN would take control over the ministries responsible for the most crucial areas of foreign and domestic policy. These concessions by Beijing and Hanoi made it possible for the five permanent members of the UN Security Council to reach an agreement on a solution for Cambodia in August 1990, which was later embodied in the Paris Accords of October 1991.

The Paris Accords called for the creation of an interim coalition government, consisting of representatives of all four Cambodian factions, with administrative powers shared by the existing Phnom Penh authorities and the United Nations. The coalition government was to conduct elections for a national assembly that would first draw up a new constitution and then transform itself into a legislature. In addition, the Paris Accords provided for a cease-fire, the demobilization or cantonment of the military forces of each of the four Cambodian factions, and the cessation of all arms flows to Cambodia from abroad.

The Paris Accords reflected the emergence of an unprecedented concert of powers, all of which agreed on the desirability of a compromise to end the fighting in Cambodia. Nonetheless, the implementation of the agreement has constantly been troubled. The Khmer Rouge, charging that Vietnamese forces remained in Cambodia in the guise of civilian settlers and advisers, refused to cooperate with the military demobilization, honor the cease-fire, or participate in the May 1993 elections. For a brief period after those elections, the pro-Vietnamese faction threatened to ignore the results or else to orchestrate the secession of parts of Cambodia bordering Vietnam. Subsequently, although the Khmer Rouge declared that it would like to participate in the new Cambodian government, it rejected the full merger of its armed forces into a new national army and refused to permit government representatives to enter the areas it controlled. Meanwhile, fighting continued between the Khmer Rouge and the armed forces of the new Phnom Penh government.

The recalcitrant stand of the Khmer Rouge raises the danger of a renewal and intensification of the civil war in Cambodia. But even if this should occur, the likelihood that the outside powers would reenter the Cambodian conflict remains small. Vietnam is preoccupied with its domestic economic and political problems and is loathe to reactivate a confrontation with China, ASEAN, or the United States. China is willing to remain aloof from Cambodia as long as Vietnam remains disengaged. Indeed, once Hanoi announced that it was withdrawing from Cambodia, China halted the flow of arms to the Khmer Rouge, supported international sanctions against its former ally, and endorsed the results of the 1993 elections. Only Thailand appears to be providing any residual support to the Khmer Rouge, largely because powerful Thai economic interests, including some within the military, benefit from trade with the parts of Cambodia that the Khmer Rouge controls. But that support is unlikely to involve any Thai military assistance to the Khmer Rouge.

In short, the progress toward peace in Cambodia represents the successful operation of a regional concert of powers whose members have decided to end their competition over Cambodia and to broker a political settlement among the warring factions. Even if the international community is unable to fully resolve the dispute in Cambodia, and even if civil war resumes there, the concert of powers may be able to prevent the reintroduction of outside forces.

Korea

The Korean War reflected one of the first applications of the collective security regime envisioned in the UN Charter. After the North Korean invasion of South Korea in June 1950, the UN authorized a multinational force, led by the United States, to turn back the aggression. The armistice of 1953 transformed the Korean peninsula into the clearest case of bipolarity in Asia. On one side stood North Korea, linked by military alliance with both the Soviet Union and China. Across the armistice line stood South Korea, allied with the United States and indirectly with Japan. The situation along the demilitarized zone remained tense, with periodic clashes between North Korean and UN forces, occasional North Korean terrorist attacks on South Korean targets, and a significant probability of large-scale conflict.

In the last several years, however, this confrontational situation has begun to ease somewhat and even to assume elements of a cooperative security framework. As in Cambodia the turning point was the end of Asia's two cold wars, which permitted the emergence of an informal concert of powers aimed at preventing the resumption of military hostilities in Korea. Moreover, each participant in this concert of powers began to enlarge its network of diplomatic and, in some cases, economic contacts on the Korean peninsula. China and Russia have had diplomatic relations with South Korea since 1990, and the United States and Japan cautiously expanded their diplomatic dialogue with Pyongyang.

The emergence of this concert of external powers encouraged the two Korean governments to develop their bilateral relations. In 1990 North and South Korea inaugurated a series of talks at the prime ministerial level that led to limited cultural, economic, and humanitarian exchanges. In 1991 both Koreas agreed to enter the UN, as separate and equal political entities. At the end of the same year, North and South Korea signed an "Agreement on Reconciliation, Mutual Non-Aggression, and Exchange and Cooperation," pledging to avoid conflict and to expand bilateral relations.[9] The two sides have also agreed, in principle, to supplement IAEA oversight of their nuclear facilities with independent bilateral inspections.

As in the case of the Paris Accords on Cambodia, however, the fate of this emerging cooperative security regime on the Korean peninsula remains in doubt. As noted, North Korea has not fully met its obligation under the international nuclear nonproliferation regime and has not yet reached agreement with South Korea on a bilateral inspection arrangement. In the meantime South Korea is delaying economic cooperation with the North, and Japan and the United States are holding back diplomatic recognition and economic ties with Pyongyang. Even more dangerous is the possibility that failure to resolve the issue could lead to the imposition of international economic or even military sanctions against North Korea and even to military confrontation on the Korean peninsula. Moreover, if China disagreed with the need for sanctions against its North Korean ally, the regional concert of powers that has helped manage the issue over the last several years could begin to fray or even to fracture.

The immediate imperative is to impose credible safeguards on North Korea's nuclear development program, both through IAEA inspections and through a bilateral challenge inspection program. Once that is done, the most promising directions for further cooperative security arrangements on the Korean peninsula are reasonably clear.[10] The two Koreas could implement traditional confidence-building measures along the armistice line, including the true demilitarization of the demilitarized zone, advance notification of troop rotations and exercises, and restraints on provocative deployments and maneuvers. The two sides could also negotiate a reduction in the level of their conventional forces and the redesign of their military establishments along purely defensive lines. These security arrangements could be encouraged and institutionalized by the expansion of economic ties between the two Koreas.

Although the bilateral North-South dialogue will be central to the resolution of the Korean issue, it should be supplemented by multilateral arrangements. Once North Korea agrees to credible inspections of its nuclear program and joins the international regimes restricting the development and transfer of chemical and biological weapons, the next step would be to construct a fuller network of diplomatic, cultural, and economic ties between Pyongyang and the West, possibly including the creation of the proposed Tumen River development zone spanning portions of North Korea, China, and Russia. In addition, there could be value in a multilateral subregional security dialogue involving the United States, Russia, Japan, China, and the two Koreas, such as both Seoul and Washington have recently proposed. One of the main topics of such discussions would be setting restrictions on the external supply of advanced conventional weapons to both North and South Korea.

In the final analysis, however, the key to resolving the dispute on the Korean peninsula involves neither bilateral negotiation nor multilateral dialogue, but rather the internal situation in North Korea itself. None of the agreements suggested—from nuclear inspections to confidence-building measures along the demilitarized zone—will be fully credible without significant economic reform in North Korea and some preliminary liberalization of its political system. Despite considerable encouragement from both Russia and China, as well as pressure from Japan and the United States, Pyongyang has not yet been willing to take such steps. Most likely, in North Korea internal change of this magnitude will have to await the death of Kim Il-sung and the emergence of a new generation of North Korean leaders.

Yet movement in this direction could, paradoxically, lead to still another set of security problems that would demand a multilateral response. Although South Korean analysts fervently hope that North Korea will start down the road to gradual economic and political reform, they simultaneously acknowledge that gradual progressive change is not the only possible scenario or even the most likely one. Instead, the North Korean economic and political system could very well collapse after the death of Kim Il-sung. Indeed, opening North Korea to the rest of the world could hasten, rather than forestall, the regime's demise.

The disintegration of North Korea would pose enormous difficulties for South Korea, far greater than the problems presented to West Germany by the collapse of the communist regime in the East. Given the dire state of the North Korean economy, vast numbers of refugees would be expected to flood across the demilitarized zone into the South. In such a situation the South Korean government would be under enormous pressure to establish effective political control over the North, a task that would strain its administrative and economic resources to the breaking point. There would be great uncertainty over the fate of North Korea's nuclear installations and concern about the disposition of Pyongyang's conventional military arsenal. Over the longer term the successful reunification of Korea would ultimately reshape, and possibly even disrupt, the balance of power in Northeast Asia.

These issues too require a multilateral response. It is necessary for the interested parties in Northeast Asia to begin cooperative planning for the collapse of the North Korean regime, even if some of them would prefer the gradual reform and liberalization of the northern half of the peninsula. They might also begin informal, unofficial discussions on the implications of Korean reunification for the stability of Northeast Asia. Without better mutual understanding of each other's interests and policies, the disintegration of North Korea could produce considerable suspicion, or even confrontation, among the outside powers.

The Sino-Russian Border

Perhaps the most promising, though still incomplete, set of cooperative security arrangements in East Asia are those being put in place along the Sino-Russian frontier, replacing the military confrontation that prevailed from the mid-1960s through the mid-1980s.[11] The first steps in reducing tensions along the disputed border were taken by Gorbachev, who announced in 1986 that the Soviet Union would withdraw most of its forces from Mongolia and declared two years later that it would unilaterally reduce its troop deployments in Asia by some 200,000 men.[12] These unilateral gestures were supplemented by the agreement that the Soviet Union reached with the United States to ban all intermediate-range ballistic missiles, including the Soviet SS-20s arrayed against China.

The redeployments and force reductions announced by Gorbachev, together with the Soviet withdrawal from Afghanistan and the Vietnamese withdrawal from Cambodia, permitted the full restoration of high-level diplomatic and military contacts between the Soviet Union and China, as symbolized by Gorbachev's visit to Beijing in 1989. They also encouraged a comparable normalization of Sino-Mongolian relations, which had been frozen since the Soviet Union had introduced land and air forces into Mongolia in the mid-1960s. With the diplomatic groundwork set, economic ties across these troubled borders increased rapidly, involving not only the trade conducted under central state plans but also, and even more important, the commercial relations undertaken by neighboring provinces and by private merchants. More disturbing to some, the normalization of Sino-Russian relations has also involved the resumption of military-to-military ties, including the sale of a squadron of SU-27 attack aircraft, reportedly at "friendship prices," from Moscow to Beijing.[13]

The normalization of relations between Moscow and Beijing has also permitted some progress in their bilateral border negotiations, which had been conducted fitfully and inconclusively since the 1960s.[14] In 1991, just before the collapse of the Soviet Union, the two countries had agreed on the demarcation of almost all the eastern border, stretching from Mongolia to near the mouth of the Ussuri River, except for Heixiazi and a few other smaller islands near Khabarovsk.[15] The disintegration of the Soviet Union delayed negotiations on the western portion of the border, which China now shares with Kazakhstan, Kyrgyzstan, and Tajikistan. Finally, at the end of 1992 the parties opened multilateral negotiations on the remaining border issues, with Russian specialists joining with representatives of the three central Asian republics across the table from their Chinese counterparts.

In addition to these border negotiations, Chinese and Russian officials have been conducting discussions, apparently as yet inconclusive, of military confidence-building measures between their two countries. The negotiations are aimed at reducing force levels in Siberia and northern China, demilitarizing the frontier, and allowing for greater transparency in military deployments and exercises. An initial understanding on the guiding principles for the negotiations was apparently reached in 1990. At that time the two sides agreed that their ultimate objective was to reconfigure their forces into defensive deployments and reduce them, through staged reductions, to the minimum level necessary for defense. Unfortunately, subsequent negotiations do not appear to have made much progress toward drafting a more concrete plan for such a reconfiguration, reportedly because the two sides have been unable to agree on the size of a demilitarized zone along the border and because Russia is reluctant to bear the financial cost of redeploying large numbers of troops.[16]

Still, the negotiations over the demarcation of the border and the discussions of military confidence-building measures are promising initiatives that need to be continued and elaborated. The construction of a fuller cooperative security regime would involve resolving the remaining differences between China and Russia on their eastern border, conducting successful negotiations between China and the central Asian republics over the western section of the former Sino-Soviet frontier, and concluding the military confidence-building measures as outlined previously. Economic cooperation between China and the central Asian republics, Mongolia, and Siberia should be expanded, in part by improving the transportation and communications facilities crossing the relevant frontiers. In addition, some kind of security guarantees will have to be constructed for Mongolia, which fears Chinese irredentism but can no longer rely upon Russian protection.

The Taiwan Strait

Like the Korean peninsula and Indochina, the Taiwan Strait is the site of a subregional dispute that contemporary Asia has inherited from the cold war between the United States and the Soviet bloc. Although there were few military clashes after the Quemoy crisis of 1958, the situation in the Taiwan Strait stayed tense and relations between the two sides remained minimal until the mid-1980s.

Under the leadership first of Chiang Ching-kuo and then of Lee Teng-hui, Taiwan has gradually but steadily relaxed its ban on commercial, cultural, and humanitarian contacts with mainland China. Since the government in Taipei began to permit family reunions in 1987, approximately 4 million Taiwanese have visited the People's Republic, many of them more interested in tourism or business than in seeing relatives. Trade has soared, rising from around $300 million a year in the early 1980s to more than $7 billion in 1992.[17] Investment has also increased dramatically, with Taiwanese entrepreneurs attracted by the lower labor costs, looser environmental policies, and rapid growth across the strait. The two sides have established organizations, nominally unofficial, to discuss the practical issues arising from their extensive cultural and commercial interactions. As a result of these developments, tensions between Taiwan and the mainland are now at their lowest point since the communist seizure of power in 1949.[18]

Still, several barriers remain to a further reduction of tensions and to an institutionalization of the new relationships between Taiwan and the mainland. Taipei still restricts commercial and cultural contacts with the People's Republic. Since it does not permit direct communication or transportation links with the mainland, people and goods traveling across the Taiwan Strait must pass through a third port, usually Hong Kong. Although millions of Taiwanese have visited the mainland, Taipei has allowed only a few thousand entry visas to mainland Chinese nationals, and it is particularly reluctant to give members of the Chinese Communist party unhampered access to the island. It insists that it will maintain these restrictions until the People's Republic renounces the use of force against Taiwan, allows Taipei a greater role in the international community, and treats the government of Taiwan as an equal political entity.

Beijing finds all three of these conditions difficult to meet. Although the Chinese Communist party says that it will meet with Taiwan's ruling Nationalist party (the Kuomintang) on equal terms, it continues to portray the government of Taiwan as a subordinate provincial authority rather than as an equal political entity. This attitude, in turn, affects Beijing's position on Taiwan's role in the international community. The mainland has been willing to see Taiwan join nongovernmental organizations (such as the Olympic Games) and some multilateral economic institutions (such as the Asian Development Bank and the General Agreement on Tariffs and Trade), as long as it uses such names as

"Chinese Taipei" or "Taipei, China." But Beijing has broken diplomatic ties with any government that has recognized Taiwan and has steadfastly refused to accept Taiwanese membership in such international political organizations as the UN.

Nor has Beijing been willing to renounce the use of force against Taiwan. Instead it has consistently argued that the potential application of military pressure against the island is the only way to forestall a unilateral declaration of Taiwanese independence and to encourage negotiations on reunification of Taiwan and mainland China. Moreover, several aspects of mainland China's program of military modernization—including its development of a blue-water navy, the creation of an amphibious assault force, the acquisition of in-flight refueling capability, and the above-mentioned purchase of a squadron of advanced attack aircraft from Russia—give an ominous dimension to Beijing's refusal to foreswear the use of force against the island.

The threat of mainland attack is encouraging Taiwan to find ways of increasing its own military capabilities.[19] The disappointing performance of its own indigenous fighter led it to purchase advanced aircraft from abroad, including F-16s from the United States and Mirages from France. Similarly the desire to modernize its navy has caused Taipei to explore purchasing submarines from the Netherlands, buying frigate hulls from Germany and France, and leasing ships from the United States. With its influence in decline, especially in the United States, Beijing can no longer veto such sales as effectively as it did in the 1980s.

But these transactions are not likely to be the end of the story. If mainland China can no longer prevent Taiwan from purchasing advanced weapons from abroad, at least it can acquire its own military hardware as a counterweight. Thus Taipei's recent arms purchases will only accelerate Beijing's efforts to obtain the ability to project force by sea and in the air, both through its own production and by buying arms from the former Soviet Union. As a result, a renewed arms race between Taiwan and the mainland appears highly probable unless preventive measures can be taken.

Several steps would help consolidate and extend the improvements in the relations between Taiwan and the mainland. Since neither reunification nor independence is feasible in the foreseeable future, the best approach for the middle term is for the two sides to negotiate an interim modus vivendi. The mainland should renounce the use of force against Taiwan, except in response to a unilateral declaration of independence by the Taiwanese government. It should also welcome Taiwan's membership in a broader range of international organizations, under formulas that do not suggest that Taiwan is an independent sovereign state. To reciprocate, Taipei should renounce any unilateral declaration of independence, except perhaps in response to a military assault by the mainland. It should relax its restrictions on commercial, cultural, and political relations with the People's Republic, opening direct communications and transportation links across the Taiwan Strait and welcoming visitors and investment from the mainland.

Given the mainland's insistence on maintaining the military capabilities to deter a unilateral declaration of independence, it will be extremely difficult for the two sides to develop the customary military confidence-building measures. However, it might be feasible to construct a multilateral regime that reduces the flow of arms to the two sides, particularly weapons that would give the People's Republic an extensive force projection capability. A first step would be to discourage additional sales of Russian attack aircraft to Beijing, in exchange for restraints on the further provision of advanced Western fighters to Taiwan. Given the widespread nervousness across the region about China's growing military capability, such a regime would have beneficial consequences extending far beyond the Taiwan Strait.

The South China Sea

The fifth subregional dispute to which the principles of cooperative security are being applied is the controversy over the two main island groups of the South China Sea: the Paracels, which are claimed by both China and Vietnam, and the Spratlys, all of which are claimed by China (including Taiwan) and Vietnam, and parts of which are claimed by the Philippines, Malaysia, and Brunei. Although small and barren in themselves, the islands sit astride important sea-lanes of communication and atop undeveloped petroleum and gas reserves. The islands have already occasioned two military clashes between China and Vietnam: first in 1974, when Beijing seized the Paracels from a tottering South Vietnamese government, and again in 1988, when China took some of the Spratlys from Hanoi.

Since 1990 Indonesia has sponsored annual multilateral "workshops" on the South China Sea, attended by representatives from all the countries with claims in the area. The workshops have recommended that the governments concerned pursue their claims through dialogue and negotiation rather than through the use of force. They have also proposed international cooperation in preventing piracy and drug trafficking, ensuring the safety of navigation, promoting research, and protecting marine life. Perhaps most important, the workshops have explored the idea that the claims to sovereignty over the disputed islands could be set aside while the claimants engage in joint exploration and development of seabed resources.[20]

Thus far China's response to these formulas has been ambiguous. Chinese spokesmen have endorsed the concept of joint development of the Spratlys, although not the Paracels. But Beijing has refused to enter into any official negotiations on the conflicting claims to the Spratlys. Nor is it clear whether China is willing to set aside questions of ownership in the meantime or whether it will insist that joint development be conditioned on the acknowledgment of

Chinese sovereignty. Moreover, in 1992 China unilaterally adopted a law on its territorial seas that not only reasserted its claims to the Spratlys and the Paracels but also set out regulations concerning the passage of military and commercial vessels through Chinese territorial waters. Even more disturbing, Beijing signed a contract with an American company to explore for petroleum in parts of the South China Sea claimed by both China and Vietnam, pledging that the Chinese navy would protect the claim by force if necessary.

The concept of joint development is a valuable one that should be vigorously pursued. It could take several different forms. At a minimum it could involve cooperative, government-to-government attempts to exploit the seabed resources in the South China Sea. More ambitiously, the arrangements might supplement joint development with demilitarization or provide for joint development through the creation of a multilateral authority rather than through state-to-state agreements.[21] While the formulas for joint development are being explored, the governments concerned should pledge to pursue their claims peacefully, without resort to force. They must also agree that joint development cannot be conditioned on accepting one party's claims to sovereignty over another's.

The concept of joint development might also be applied to two other groups of islands in the Asia-Pacific region whose sovereignty is in dispute. One group is the Senkaku, or Diaoyutai, Islands, off the northeast corner of Taiwan, which are claimed by both China (including Taiwan) and Japan. These islands have already been the subject of several incidents, including a dozen cases in 1991 amd 1992 in which Chinese naval vessels fired warning shots at passing Japanese cargo ships.[22] The other group comprises the four islands off Hokkaido, known as the Northern Territories, which are occupied by Russia but claimed by Japan. Rising nationalism in both countries is making it more difficult to realize the compromise suggested in the past, by which Russia would gain sovereignty over two of the islands and Japan would take over the others. Instead, joint development, coupled with some form of demilitarization, might be a more feasible approach to the issue in the short to middle term.[23]

Applying Cooperative Security to the Region as a Whole

Besides these efforts to manage or resolve subregional security challenges, there has also been some consideration to applying concepts of cooperative security to the Asia-Pacific region as a whole, through a combination of arms control, confidence-building measures, preventive diplomacy, and dialogue on military issues.[24] Of the three main approaches to cooperative security in the area, this one remains the least well developed as well as the one meeting the most resistance from key governments. Nonetheless, interest in regional cooperative security arrangements is gradually growing.

Initially, many Asia-Pacific governments viewed the prospect of regionwide cooperative security arrangements with considerable skepticism. They were suspicious that the process could be dominated by a few powerful states, acting in their own self-interest; that the agenda would therefore be imbalanced, favoring some nations more than others; that the principles of transparency and verification associated with cooperative security could prove intrusive; or that the creation of a new cooperative security regime might weaken their defense capabilities or erode their existing strategic alliances. As a result, the initial proposals for regionwide cooperative security mechanisms failed to attract much support.

One early idea, for example, envisioned the creation of an official regional dialogue on security matters, to include all governments in the region. In a speech in Vladivostok in 1986, Gorbachev suggested a regionwide meeting on security matters, paralleling the Helsinki process in Europe, a proposal he periodically reiterated until his fall from power at the end of 1991.[25] In 1990 the Australian foreign minister, Gareth Evans, called for a similar kind of official multilateral negotiation, also likening it to the CSCE.[26] The use of such similes led this concept to be labeled as a CSCA: a Conference on Security and Cooperation in Asia.

The idea of a CSCA was viewed with considerable disfavor by many Asia-Pacific governments, particularly Japan and the United States. It was derided as a naive attempt to apply ideas from Europe, where their validity had not yet been demonstrated, to a totally different strategic environment. Critics pointed out that the Asia-Pacific region was bigger, more diverse, and more complex than Europe, and that its member nations were much less experienced in multilateral negotiations on security questions. They also noted that the inclusion of human rights on the cooperative security agenda in Europe made the CSCE an unattractive precedent for many Asian governments. As a result, the skeptics predicted that cooperative security measures in Asia would be difficult to negotiate successfully and that a regionwide dialogue aimed at formulating them would be doomed to failure.[27] Although American and Japanese officials simply evaded the Australian suggestions, they rejected the similar Soviet proposals in the bluntest of terms.[28]

Tokyo and Washington were especially apprehensive that the deliberations of a CSCA would be dominated by a further set of proposals, also put forward primarily by the Soviet Union, for the negotiation of formal arms control and confidence-building measures in the Asia-Pacific region. As originally articulated by Gorbachev between 1986 and 1989, the Soviet arms control agenda included a freeze of naval forces in the western Pacific, limitations on air and naval forces around the Korean peninsula, nuclear-free zones for Korea and for the Indian Ocean, and agreements to prevent incidents at sea and in the air. After the collapse of the Soviet Union, the Russian government repeated many of Gorbachev's proposals. In 1992, for example, Foreign Minister Andrey

Kozyrev suggested limiting the scale of naval exercises and banning them altogether in straits, fishing grounds, and areas of intensive navigation; creating an international naval force to ensure freedom of navigation; and opening discussions of the future of U.S. and Russian bases in the region and of various confidence-building measures.[29]

Washington and Tokyo consistently dismissed such proposals out of hand, charging that they reflected a biased agenda. Because the Soviet Union was a land-based power and the United States was a maritime power, any cooperative security agenda that focused on naval arms control was seen as favoring Soviet over American interests. In the same way Soviet suggestions for nuclear-free zones were also viewed as a canny tactic for weakening American extended deterrence and disrupting the forward deployments of U.S. tactical nuclear weapons. The reaction to the subsequent Russian proposals on naval arms control was equally skeptical, though not as harsh.

Although the idea of regionwide cooperative security arrangements therefore aroused substantial resistance in the late 1980s, more recently it has received a more favorable reception. The reduction of the military deployments of Russia and the United States and the increases in the military budgets of a number of regional and subregional actors, including China, Japan, India, and some of the larger nations of ASEAN, are producing a sense of strategic instability in the area that could conceivably lead to a conventional arms race. Moreover, there is increasing recognition that such a competition cannot be deterred through bilateral or even subregional mechanisms. China's defense planning, for example, is influenced by decisions made in capitals as geographically dispersed as Tokyo, Moscow, Hanoi, and New Delhi. Similarly Japan's security doctrine must take the capabilities and intentions of China, Russia, and the United States into account. Only a regionwide forum on security questions could have any hope of coordinating military deployments to prevent a conventional arms race.

Another reason for the mounting interest in regional cooperative security mechanisms is the growing awareness of the unconventional threats to security in the Asia-Pacific region.[30] One set of such threats includes the various forms of transnational criminal activity, including drug trafficking, piracy, and terrorism. Another set includes such environmental problems as the pollution of the atmosphere and the oceans, excessive fishing in the Pacific Ocean, and the dangers of climatic change. Still other threats could be posed by the uncontrolled movement of peoples across international frontiers, occasioned by civil war, poverty, political repression, or natural disaster. Although governments can still address some of these problems through unilateral means, they cannot fully prevent or resolve them without effective international cooperation.

In addition, the ideas for regionwide cooperative security mechanisms have gradually become more sophisticated and realistic. Compared with the initial concepts introduced in the late 1980s, more recent proposals have placed less emphasis on elaborate arms control agreements than on the development of less ambitious measures to increase confidence among mistrustful governments. The call for formal negotiations among government officials has been supplemented by more modest suggestions for quasi-official discussions among policy analysts and scholars. And there is now a tendency to look to the development of several arenas of dialogue, each with a different set of participants, rather than to the creation of a single regional forum attempting to incorporate everyone. As a result, this new round of suggestions is steadily gaining greater support.

One strand in these recent efforts has been the organization of unofficial multilateral discussions of security issues, involving scholars and policy analysts from universities and research institutions on both sides of the Pacific. Such dialogues began to occur in the mid-1980s, sponsored by such organizations as the Asia Society, the Pacific Forum, and the Malaysian Institute of Strategic and International Studies. Although their agendas often overlapped and there was little sense of progress from one session to another, these meetings did provide the first occasions for academic specialists, some of whom had close connections with their governments, to exchange views on regional strategic developments.

By the early 1990s these unofficial scholarly dialogues began to acquire a somewhat more official standing. Between 1991 and 1993, with support from the Canadian government, York University conducted a North Pacific Cooperative Security Dialogue, with participants drawn from the academic community and the policy planning staffs of Canada, the United States, and six Northeast Asian countries. In 1993 a number of key policy research organizations across the Pacific, most of which have close connections with their governments, agreed to create a Council for Security and Cooperation in the Asia-Pacific (CSCAP), thus forming the first regionwide forum for quasi-official dialogue on security problems in the region. All countries and territories in the region will be invited to send delegations, composed of scholars, policy analysts, and government officials participating in their private capacities, to the annual meetings of the CSCAP. Thus the CSCAP promises to become the equivalent in the security sphere of the Pacific Economic Cooperation Council (PECC).

In 1991 ASEAN put forward still another variant on the proposals for a regional security dialogue. It recommended that its postministerial conference, which had previously been restricted to economic issues, be enlarged to include security questions. The proposal envisioned discussions not only with ASEAN's traditional dialogue partners (the United States, Canada, Japan, Australia, New Zealand, and South Korea) but also with other strategically important states, including Russia, China, Vietnam, and North Korea. Unlike the North Pacific Cooperative Security Dialogue or the CSCAP, the ASEAN concept foresaw formal discussions exclusively among government officials, presumably focusing on strategic issues in Southeast Asia, where ASEAN has special legitimacy as a forum for dialogue.

Although many of the major powers in the region initially had reservations about the proposal, ASEAN's sponsorship made it impossible for them to reject it. In a major breakthrough, Japan, Russia, China, and the United States all assented to participate in a multilateral dialogue with the ASEAN states. After initial meetings in 1992 and 1993, which took the form of a series of bilateral conversations rather than of a single multilateral conference, the parties agreed to create an ASEAN Regional Forum (ARF) on security issues, beginning in 1994. Participants in the forum will include the six ASEAN nations, Vietnam, Papua New Guinea, China, Japan, Russia, the United States, Canada, South Korea, Australia, and New Zealand.

Thus the construction of regionwide cooperative security arrangements is getting under way. Only one official forum has been established, and neither it nor any of a larger number of unofficial forums has yet yielded any concrete results. Indeed, there is as yet no clear consensus on the specific issues that will be discussed at the ARF or the CSCAP, or on the most effective ways of addressing them. In short, so far the application of cooperative security principles to regionwide issues has been less successful than their application to global nonproliferation and to subregional disputes.

Prospects and Recommendations

The application of cooperative security principles to the Asia-Pacific region will necessarily entail a considerable degree of diversity; that is, creating it will require what has variously been called a multilayered or a multifaceted approach. Such a strategy would closely parallel the region's experience in building multilateral economic institutions. That process, which began in the late 1960s, has involved several parallel tracks: creating subregional organizations, such as ASEAN and the South Pacific Forum; convening unofficial dialogues of academics and businesspersons through the Pacific Conference on Trade and Development and the Pacific Basin Economic Council; developing forums such as the PECC, in which officials could participate in their private capacities; and finally creating an official multilateral organization in the form of the Asia-Pacific Economic Cooperation (APEC) group.

By analogy, one should assume that the creation of multilateral security institutions in the Asia-Pacific region will also require patient, sustained, and diversified effort. Drawing on the precedents from the economic realm, as well as on recent experience in the security area, the most feasible approach comprises the following three elements.

First, the nations in the region should continue to address subregional issues in the appropriate ad hoc forums, bolstering those cooperative security arrangements that are currently fragile or incomplete. More specifically, this approach implies full implementation of the Paris Accords on Cambodia, establishment of a nuclear-free zone in Korea, resolution of the disputes involving the Sino-Soviet border and agreement on the reduction and redeployment of forces along it, negotiation of a formal modus vivendi in the Taiwan Strait, and adoption of the principle of joint development of disputed island territories in the western Pacific. The Asian experience suggests that such issues can be managed most effectively when there are economic incentives for the parties directly involved to cooperate with each other, such that there are mechanisms for economic development as well as for cooperative security.

Second, the time has come for a more formal, but still unofficial, dialogue on regionwide security issues. In this connection the formation of the CSCAP is a most welcome development. Its overall aim should be to provide a forum for discussing, more candidly than is possible in official settings, the full range of security issues confronting the Asia-Pacific region. Specifically, the CSCAP could help identify the most feasible ways of managing subregional disputes, recommend the most appropriate methods for addressing unconventional security threats, and begin to formulate the norms that could prevent arms races by regulating national military deployments. It could also consider some of the most central—but also the most abstract and sensitive—issues in Asia-Pacific security, including ways of helping Japan come to terms with its past, harmonizing China's ambitions with those of its neighbors, and coping with the implications of Korean unification.

Finally, it is now possible to launch official multilateral discussions of security problems in the Asia-Pacific region. For the foreseeable future, it is best to envision a reasonable number of overlapping and reinforcing forums, each allowing a different set of actors to address a distinctive set of issues. The new ARF, for example, is clearly the most appropriate forum for a consideration of strategic issues in Southeast Asia, although its deliberations would be more useful if India could be brought into them. Following recent proposals from both the United States and South Korea, a comparable forum should be created in Northeast Asia, to discuss the international dimensions of Korean security and the Russo-Japanese dispute over the Northern Territories. Eventually it may be feasible to create a single regionwide organization, analogous to the CSCE in Europe.

The topics for security dialogue must be chosen with care. One often-mentioned candidate, naval arms control, is highly sensitive for a number of countries in the region and should not be the opening item on the agenda. Other potential issues, such as conventional weapons proliferation and environmental protection, can best be dealt with on a global level. Still other problems, such as smuggling and drug trafficking, are probably too specific to attract and maintain high-level governmental attention.

Instead, without excluding other topics, official regional security dialogues should focus, from the beginning, on what is increasingly acknowledged as the core issue: the emerging arms race in the Asia-Pacific region. The process could start with attempts to increase transparency by exchanging information on national security strategies, defense budgets, and military deployments, in the hope that each nation can reassure its neighbors of its capabilities and intentions. These efforts could then lead to a consideration of multilateral norms to govern those deployments, building on the prior work done at the unofficial level. The ultimate purpose of the dialogue should be to construct what Geoffrey Wiseman has called a "defensive intent regime," in which each country's military forces are clearly configured and deployed for defensive purposes, and in which each nation's military budget can therefore be limited.[31]

Other issues might be referred to APEC for its consideration. Even though APEC should continue to focus primarily on economics, it could usefully devote secondary attention to security issues. It would be a particularly appropriate venue for discussing the intersection of economic and security questions, including the use of economic sanctions to enforce international nonproliferation regimes, and for addressing the unconventional security problems most closely linked to economics, such as smuggling, piracy, unauthorized migration, and environmental pollution. APEC has the advantage of being the only official regional forum to include both Taiwan and mainland China.

Under Presidents Reagan and Bush, the United States adopted a highly skeptical attitude toward cooperative security in the Asia-Pacific region. Fortunately, the Clinton administration has begun to take a more positive approach. During his confirmation hearings before the Senate, Assistant Secretary of State Winston Lord endorsed the multilateral security dialogue organized by ASEAN and proposed that a similar forum be organized to discuss the issues of security in Northeast Asia. During his visit to Korea in July 1993, President Clinton said that such multilateral dialogues, together with existing bilateral alliances, could "function like overlapping plates of armor . . . together covering the full body of our common security concerns."[32]

Now that it has decided to welcome multilateral security dialogues and the first such discussions are getting under way, the Clinton administration must turn its attention to the next issue on the agenda: the specific proposals it will put forward. Many nations in the region, although agreeing to participate in such forums, will do so unenthusiastically and will try to limit discussion to the bland restatement of official security policy. The United States, together with like-minded countries, must insist on something more. A full-fledged cooperative security regime, featuring agreed-upon restrictions on troop deployments and weapons acquisitions, is not yet feasible. But it is reasonable to expect greater transparency about security strategies, defense budgets, and military preparations. Only such transparency can prevent the emergence of an arms race in Asia that could reduce regional stability and even undermine its prosperity.

Notes

1. See Michael T. Klare, "The Next Great Arms Race," *Foreign Affairs,* vol. 72 (Summer 1993), pp. 136–52.

2. The agreements reached between the United States and North Korea are contained in "Joint Statement following U.S.–North Korea Meeting," *US Department of State Dispatch,* vol. 4 (June 14, 1993), p. 440; and "U.S.–North Korea Talks on the Nuclear Issue," *US Department of State Dispatch,* vol. 4 (July 26, 1993), p. 535.

3. For recent analyses, see three articles by David E. Sanger: "Japan Thinks Again about Its Plan to Build Plutonium Stockpile," *New York Times,* August 3, 1992, p. A3; "Japan Shipment of Nuclear Fuel Worries Asians," *New York Times,* November 9, 1992, p. A6; "Japan's Nuclear Fiasco," *New York Times,* December 20, 1992, p. C1; and Jinzaburo Takagi, "Misguided Policy," *Look Japan,* vol. 38 (August 1992), pp. 32–33. For background, see Hiroshi Ogawa, "Nuclear Energy Cooperation: Striking a Delicate Balance," followed by comments by Joseph Nye, in *U.S.-Japan Relations in the 1980's: Towards Burden Sharing,* Annual Report, 1981–82 (Harvard University, Center for International Affairs, Program on U.S.-Japan Relations, 1982), pp. 159–69.

4. On China's sale of conventional arms, see Richard A. Bitzinger, "Arms to Go: Chinese Arms Sales to the Third World," *International Security,* vol. 17 (Fall 1992), pp. 84–111.

5. "North Korea: Joining the World?" Background Brief, Foreign and Commonwealth Office, London, June 1992; and Duncan Lennox, "Clearing the Picture on SRBMs," *Jane's Defence Weekly,* vol. 17 (June 6, 1992), pp. 995–96.

6. Steven Greenhouse, "$1 Billion in Sales of High-Tech Items to China Blocked," *New York Times,* August 26, 1993, p. A1. The United States simultaneously applied sanctions against Pakistan. In each case, however, the impact of the policy was reduced because of economic sanctions already in place: for China because of the Tiananmen Crisis of 1989, for Pakistan because of its nuclear weapons program.

7. On the possibility that China might cease compliance with the MTCR, see the UPI dispatch dated August 27, 1993, citing a statement by Vice Foreign Minister Liu Huaqiu.

8. This discussion of the Cambodian peace process is based on Robert S. Ross, "China and the Cambodian Peace Process: The Value of Coercive Diplomacy," *Asian Survey,* vol. 31 (December 1991), pp. 1170–85; and Michael Leifer, "Power-Sharing and Peacemaking in Cambodia?" *SAIS Review,* vol. 12 (Winter–Spring 1992), pp. 139–53.

9. For the text of the agreement, see "S-N Korean Premiers Reach Agreement on Improved Ties," *Korea News Views* (Washington: Embassy of Korea, Korean Information Office, December 12, 1991).

10. See Tong Whan Park, "Issues of Arms Control between the Two Koreas," *Asian Survey,* vol. 32 (April 1992), pp. 350–65; and Dong-Won Lim, "An Urgent Need for Arms Control on the Korean Peninsula: A Framework for Implementation," *Korean Journal of Defense Analysis,* vol. 3 (Summer 1991), pp. 49–66.

11. A similar set of arrangements is also being negotiated along the Sino-Indian border, an area that falls outside the scope of this chapter.

12. "Gorbachev July 28 Speech in Vladivostok," Moscow Television Service, July 28, 1986, in Foreign Broadcast Information Service (FBIS), *Daily Report: Soviet Union,* July 29, 1986, pp. R1-20; and "M. S. Gorbachev's United Nations Address," *Pravda,* December 8, 1988, in ibid., December 8, 1988, pp. 11–19.

13. Tai Ming Cheung, "Sukhois, Sams, Subs," *Far Eastern Economic Review,* vol. 156 (April 8, 1993), p. 23.

14. Pi Ying-hsien, "China's Boundary Issues with the Former Soviet Union," *Issues and Studies* (Taipei), vol. 28 (July 1992), pp. 63–75.

15. The pact was signed in May 1991 and ratified early the following year. See Michael Dobbs, "Sino-Soviet Pact Signed in Moscow," *Washington Post,* May 17, 1991, p. A21; and "China, Russia, Sign Pact," *Washington Post,* March 17, 1992, p. A11.

16. Tai Ming Cheung, "Quick Response," *Far Eastern Economic Review,* vol. 156 (January 14, 1993), pp. 19–21.

17. *Zhongguo shibao zhoukan* (*China Times Weekly*), May 16–22, 1993, p. 53.

18. See Guocang Huan, "Taipei-Beijing Relations," *World Policy Journal,* vol. 9 (Summer 1992), pp. 569–70.

19. See Julian Baum, "Deprived of Air," *Far Eastern Economic Review,* vol. 155 (June 4, 1992), pp. 18–19.

20. This discussion draws on *Pacific Research* (Canberra), vol. 4 (August 1991), p. 15; and Hurng-yu Chen, "The Prospects for Joint Development in the South China Sea," *Issues and Studies* (Taipei), vol. 27 (December 1991), pp. 112–25.

21. These alternative formulas are explored in Chen, "Prospects for Joint Development." Chen pessimistically concludes, however, that "the case of the South China Sea is just too complicated for any program of joint development to be realized in the near future" (p. 125).

22. Reported by Reuters, July 23, 1992.

23. For an innovative collaborative attempt by American, Japanese, and Russian scholars to address these issues, see Graham Allison, Hiroshi Kimura, and Konstantin Sarkisov, *Beyond Cold War to Trilateral Cooperation in the Asia-Pacific Region: Scenarios for New Relationships between Japan, Russia, and the United States* (Harvard University, Strengthening Democratic Institutions Project, 1992).

24. Some of the best reviews of cooperative security proposals for the Asia-Pacific region have been prepared by Canadian scholars and officials. See, for example, Paul M. Evans, "Emerging Patterns in Asia Pacific Security: The Search for a Regional Framework," paper presented to the Fifth Asia Pacific Roundtable, Kuala Lumpur, June 1991; Stewart Henderson, "Canada and Asia Pacific Security: The North Pacific Cooperative Security Dialogue: Recent Trends," Working Paper 1 (Toronto: York University, North Pacific Cooperative Security Dialogue Research Programme, January 1992); and Peggy Mason, "Asia Pacific Security Forums: Rationale and Options: Canadian Views," paper presented to the Sixth Asia Pacific Roundtable, Kuala Lumpur, June 1992. Useful American accounts include Douglas M. Johnston, "Anticipating Instability in the Asia-Pacific Region," *Washington Quarterly,* vol. 15 (Summer 1992), pp. 103–12; and David Youtz and Paul Midford, *A Northeast Asian Security Regime: Prospects after the Cold War,* Public Policy Paper 5 (New York: Institute for EastWest Studies, 1992).

25. "Gorbachev July 28 Speech in Vladivostok."

26. Henderson, "Canada and Asian Pacific Security," pp. 9–10.

27. Many of the reservations were sympathetically summarized in Richard Fisher, "Why Asia Is Not Ready for Arms Control," Asian Studies Center Backgrounder 113 (Washington: Heritage Foundation, May 25, 1991).

28. See, for example, Gaston J. Sigur and Richard L. Armitage, "To Play in Asia, Moscow Has to Pay," *New York Times,* October 2, 1988, p. E25. At the time Sigur was assistant secretary of state for East Asian and Pacific affairs, while Armitage was assistant secretary of defense for international security affairs. For more on the American and Japanese response to the Soviet proposals, see Youtz and Midford, *Northeast Asian Security Regime,* pp. 18–25.

29. William Branigin, "Russians Offer Asians Naval Cutbacks," *Washington Post,* July 23, 1992, p. A24.

30. See Robert E. Bedeski, "Unconventional Security Threats: An Overview," Working Paper 11 (Toronto: York University, North Pacific Cooperative Security Dialogue Research Programme, May 1992).

31. Geoffrey Wiseman, "Common Security in the Asia-Pacific Region," *Pacific Review,* vol. 5, no. 1 (1992), pp. 42–59.

32. "Remarks to the Korean National Assembly in Seoul," July 10, 1993, in *Weekly Compilation of Presidential Documents,* vol. 29 (July 19, 1993), p. 1312.

TWELVE

Cooperative Security and South Asian Insecurity

Kanti Bajpai and Stephen P. Cohen

ORDER BETWEEN STATES minimally involves security of territory, of sovereignty, and of regime. States seek security through instruments at different levels: unilateral, bilateral or regional, and multilateral. From World War II to the present, states have sought to maintain security unilaterally by means of various strategies of deterrence, defense, and compellence. Bilaterally and regionally, they have resorted to confidence-building measures, arms control and disarmament, no-war agreements, alliances, and economic and political integration. Multilateral efforts have included UN-led or great power–led collective arrangements and regimes. All these putative solutions have been tried in various regions, including South Asia, but none has altogether worked. By South Asia we mean India and its immediate regional neighbors (Pakistan, Nepal, Sri Lanka, Bangladesh, Bhutan, and the Maldives) but, for strategic purposes, also China and Afghanistan. The purpose of this chapter is to ask whether an alternative security model is plausible and might better serve one of the most war-prone and heavily armed regions of the world. This alternative model, *cooperative security,* implies a consensually arrived at commitment on the part of the militarily most significant states in the international system to regulate the size, technical composition, investment patterns, and operational practices of their armed forces such that surprise attack and extended offensive operations are implausible. In short, cooperative security is a strategy of defensive sufficiency.

As policymakers survey the world for examples of cooperative security, they may not linger long on South Asia. The region is perceived as poor and quarrelsome. There appear to be few important interests in the area. Nor are significant threats to international security seen as likely to emanate from the region. Thus it appears unlikely that major outside powers will have occasion to contain either of the major South Asian states or that they will want to ally closely with them. Rather, it would seem outsiders can safely ignore the region and expend their assets on parts of the world seen as more important, threatening, or compatible.

South Asia has ranked so low on the priority lists of most outside powers that it appears difficult to make a case for a strategy of cooperative security involving the region. Prudence suggests that a cooperative security structure be first developed in Europe and then extended to areas of high threat (the Middle East and the Persian Gulf) and to areas where economic and strategic interests are very high and where the costs of conflict could be even higher (Northeast Asia). Strategic "backwaters," such as South Asia, Latin America, and sub-Saharan Africa, could be left to their own devices, their crises to be dealt with on an ad hoc basis.

We challenge this view of South Asia. We argue that, in terms of developing a more effective structure of cooperative security, South Asia is consequential. First, the seven subcontinental states contain about 25 percent of the world's population. They include two near-nuclear states that have fought three wars. Moreover, the region is contiguous to two regions of global importance: the Persian Gulf, with its oil and financial reserves, and Southeast Asia, which is fast emerging as a key cluster within the Asia-Pacific strategic and economic zone. South Asia is not merely contiguous with but in fact linked to neighboring regions. Its professionals, traders, businessmen, workers, and even soldiers have found their way in substantial numbers to the Persian Gulf and historically to central Asia, a movement that may be renewed after the interruption of the Gulf War and the independence of the latter region. Furthermore, South Asia is consequential not only for its size, militarization, war potential, location, and transnational linkages but also for its relative peaceableness over the past twenty years. Without arguing that the lessons to be drawn from South Asia's management of its security dilemmas in this period *will* be applicable elsewhere, this chapter suggests that they may be no less relevant than those drawn from the recent experience of Europe.

Second, there are important policy lessons in the way outsiders have related or have sought to relate to South Asia over the past forty-five years. There were no tight alliances with regional states, yet outsiders cooperated with both India and Pakistan on several important strategic issues. Moreover, they intermittently tried to manage South Asia, sometimes alone, but often in cooperation with each other: thus the United States sought to do so with traditional allies such as the United Kingdom and France, but also by the 1980s tacitly with Moscow, and on one occasion, with Beijing.[1] History suggests that South Asia may offer lessons on how to cooperate with sometime antagonists in a distant and tumultuous region. Cooperative security would seem at least to involve precisely such cooperation.

Third, this is a democratic moment in South Asia. Every one of its major states is under democratic rule, a condition no other region but Europe enjoys.

Thus, like Europe, these states share some basic principles of government and diplomacy with each other, with the United States, and with the growing community of democratic states. This moment may pass, but it is opportune for exploring notions of cooperative security with and in South Asia. Moreover, firmer structures of cooperative security may help preserve democracy in the region.[2]

This discussion of cooperative security and South Asian insecurity is organized into sections considering the following questions: how South Asians and various external powers sought to organize security in the region since 1947; whether on balance the region is "ripe" for cooperative security; how a cooperative security regime to deal with nuclear proliferation might be constructed; how China and various neighboring regions may affect the prospects for cooperative security in South Asia; and finally, what role the United States, as the most powerful military-economic power, could and should play in helping extend a cooperative security regime to include South Asia.

Cooperating before Cooperative Security

It is widely believed that after the British left the subcontinent there was little or no *bilateral* cooperation between the two successor states, India and Pakistan. It is also widely believed that there was no serious effort at forming a *regional* grouping until 1980, when the South Asian Association for Regional Cooperation (SAARC) was formed. This belief is incorrect. Although they rarely reached the levels of economic, political, or strategic cooperation that were too optimistically projected by Lord Louis Mountbatten, the last viceroy and first governor-general of India, there is a remarkable record of efforts at bilateral and regional cooperation—initiated by the regional states themselves—and some notable accomplishments. Finally, there is an impressive record of *external initiatives* aimed at involving India or Pakistan or both in cooperative arrangements.

Bilateral Efforts to Cooperate: India and Pakistan

From 1947 to the early 1980s India and Pakistan were involved again and again in bilateral peacemaking. By our count the two states engaged in bilateral cooperative efforts several times each decade: a series of negotiations on a no-war and joint defense agreement (1949–50, 1953, 1956, 1959, 1968, 1969, 1974, 1977, and 1980–82); Indian interest in some form of confederation (in the 1950s); the Delhi Pact on the treatment of minorities (1950); the settlement of border and territorial claims (1958 and 1960); and the post-1971 war agreements on the normalization of India-Pakistan relations (the Simla Pact, 1972) and the return of Pakistani prisoners of war, as well as Pakistani recognition of Bangladesh (1974) and various Pakistani proposals on a regional nuclear regime (1974, 1980s, and 1991).[3] This section presents these efforts in more or less strict chronological rather than in thematic fashion to emphasize the continuity of cooperative effort.

In November 1949 India proposed a no-war declaration. The two sides negotiated for more than a year without success. Meanwhile, in April 1950 they signed a pact on the treatment of religious minorities in their respective countries. In 1953 Pakistan proposed a joint defense agreement. Indian prime minister Jawaharlal Nehru rejected the idea and renewed his offer of a no-war declaration. In 1956 Pakistan proposed a no-war pact. Nehru welcomed the idea, but both sides stuck to irreconcilable positions. Two years later they agreed on a settlement of the question of the India–East Pakistan border and of enclaves in each other's territories. In April 1959, as India-China relations worsened, Pakistani president Ayub Khan returned to the idea of common defense. Once again New Delhi rejected the idea, fearing that common defense would associate India with the Baghdad Pact or the South East Asia Treaty Organization (SEATO) and thus compromise nonalignment.

A section of Indian opinion now favored some form of regional "confederation." Journalists B. G. Verghese and Frank Moraes justified it in terms of a Chinese threat. Prominent figures, such as former governor-general Rajagopalachari, supported the idea publicly. Jayaprakash Narayan, the Socialist leader and Gandhian, favored common defense. In July 1959 General K. M. Cariappa, retired head of the Indian army, wrote to President Ayub Kahn urging a no-war declaration. Ayub replied that dispute settlement was the key but that Pakistan was not spoiling for war.[4]

At Pakistan's initiative Ayub and Nehru met in September 1959. Once again Pakistan insisted that bilateral disputes be settled, and India proposed a no-war pact. But they agreed to resolve border problems through negotiations or, if this was not possible through negotiations, by arbitration (this formula did not apply to Kashmir). In 1960 the two countries settled five disputed claims along the West Pakistan–India border. In January 1962, when Pakistan brought up Kashmir in the UN Security Council, India offered to enter into bilateral negotiations on all issues.

Thereafter, in August 1968 India's offer of a no-war pact met with the familiar Pakistani response. On January 1, 1969, India proposed joint machinery for all bilateral disputes and the signing of a no-war pact. Pakistan refused unless Kashmir and the Farakka disputes were identified as the basic issues and self-executing machinery for settlement was included. On June 22, 1969, Prime Minister Indira Gandhi suggested that the two countries ease restrictions on commerce, services, and communications and sign a no-war pact. Pakistan once again declined.

The low point in India-Pakistan relations occurred in 1971. Pakistan's response to the crisis in the eastern wing of the country and Indian involvement led to war in December 1971, an Indian victory, and to the creation of Bangladesh. The Simla conference in June 1972 attempted to construct a postwar order for the region. Issues arising out of the war were a focus, but agreements were reached on other issues: normalizing diplomatic relations; resuming trade, communications, and travel; fixing a line of control in Kashmir; and reputedly the elements of a Kashmir settlement. Over the next three years India, Pakistan, and Bangladesh were involved in a series of negotiations, climaxing in Pakistani recognition of Bangladesh in February 1974 and a tripartite agreement on the Pakistani prisoners of war issue in April.

The Indian nuclear explosion of May 1974 raised tensions, but by September talks on communication and travel facilities had resumed. In November the two sides agreed to lift mutual trade embargoes and to extend most favored nation status to each other. Finally, to ease Pakistani fears over its nuclear test, New Delhi offered to sign a nonaggression treaty or to enter into any other security arrangement with Islamabad. Pakistan instead proposed a nuclear weapon–free zone in South Asia (NWFZSA). India rejected the Pakistani idea, but the two sides did sign and implement a hot-line agreement.

The no-war pact idea continued to feature in India-Pakistan relations. In April 1977, anticipating renewed U.S. arms sales to Pakistan, New Delhi once again offered to sign a no-war pact. Also in 1977 Prime Minister Morarji Desai announced that India would not build a nuclear bomb. Desai's Janata government might have done more for regional cooperation, but it fell in 1979 shortly before the Soviet intervention in Afghanistan.

Nevertheless, India-Pakistan cooperation remained on the agenda. Spurred by the Soviet invasion, the two sides traded offers—Pakistan urging negotiations similar to the Mutual and Balanced Force Reductions to lead to a no-war agreement, and India urging a broadened agenda to include increased trade, transport, and cultural contacts, to be codified in a treaty of friendship and cooperation. As before, they failed to agree.

Pakistan proposed various regional nuclear agreements in the 1980s. In addition to NWFZSA Islamabad offered to accede with India to the Nuclear Non-Proliferation Treaty (NPT) and to accept on-site bilateral or multilateral inspections as well as International Atomic Energy Agency full-scope safeguards. New Delhi rejected these alternatives as variants of the NPT. It urged instead an agreement by Pakistan and India not to attack each other's nuclear facilities and not to use nuclear weapons against each other. The no-attack idea was formalized in 1988, and lists of nuclear facilities were finally exchanged in January 1992. In 1990, following up on a U.S. suggestion, India also proposed regional confidence-building measures. This proposal led to agreements by Pakistan and India not to violate each other's airspace and to notify each other of military exercises. Finally, in 1991 Islamabad proposed a five-nation regional nuclear nonproliferation conference consisting of the United States, Russia, China, India, and Pakistan. New Delhi rejected Pakistan's proposal but remains involved in talks aimed at convening some form of regional denuclearization conference, principally with Washington.

In short, since 1947 India and Pakistan have been involved again and again in bilateral peacemaking.[5] This neglected—some might say lost—chapter in history suggests three things. First, leaving aside the sincerity of both sides, over a period of forty-five years the two sides have compiled a surprisingly even record of efforts to cooperate or make peace, a record obscured by conflict and war. Second, this record has been marked by success and failure, the chief successes being the early territorial, border, and riverine settlements and parts of the post-1971 accords, the great failures being Kashmir and nuclearization. Together, these two lessons suggest a third, namely that whereas India and Pakistan have recognized and acted on the need for cooperation, *strictly* bilateral solutions to South Asian insecurity have their limits.

Regional Efforts to Cooperate

Since the 1940s South Asians have been involved in moves toward regional association: in the Asian Relations Conference (1947), a second Asian conference (1949), the Baguio conference (1950), the "Colombo Powers'" conferences (April 1954, December 1954, and December 1956), and the related Afro-Asian conference in Bandung (1955).[6]

Regionally inspired efforts to promote cooperation began in March 1947 when the Indian Council of World Affairs convened the first "Asian Relations Conference." The conference hosted twenty-five Asian and Middle Eastern delegations and dealt with colonialism, racial and migration problems, and cooperation in agriculture and industry. This first conference set in motion a series of conferences in Asia, all of which included India, Pakistan, and Sri Lanka.

In February 1949 Indian representatives met with counterparts from Pakistan, Sri Lanka, and the United Kingdom to help Burma deal with the Karen rebels. New Delhi eventually gave Burma both financial and military assistance.[7] Later in the year India hosted a second Asian conference, this time over the Dutch invasion of Indonesia. Nehru had a permanent regional arrangement in mind, but given the objections of the United States and the United Kingdom and his own doubts about alliances, he retreated from this position.[8] Also in 1949 Taiwan, South Korea, and the Philippines initiated moves for a regional security conference. India rejected the idea of a "Pacific Pact" that would have included Taiwan and South Korea, but along with Pakistan and Sri Lanka, eventually attended a conference in Baguio in May 1950. The result was an agreement to cooperate in cultural matters.[9]

India, Pakistan, Sri Lanka, Burma, and Indonesia continued to be involved in regionalist efforts. In April 1954 they met in Colombo to discuss an agenda that included colonialism, the hydrogen bomb, and communism. There were differences, but eventually an agreement was reached on economic cooperation and an Asian-African conference. The conference was held in Bandung in April 1955. The Sri Lankan and Pakistani insistence on condemning communist expansionism became the focus of discussion and disagreement. Though there was agreement to cooperate in economic and cultural areas, the notion of a regional bloc was rejected. Bandung was effectively the end of the Colombo Powers group. It met for the last time in November 1956, to discuss the Hungarian and Suez crises.[10]

The next serious, "indigenous" effort to launch regional cooperation began in 1977 when Bangladeshi president Ziaur Rahman advanced the idea of a regional organization. Zia produced a formal proposal in May 1980. Official-level talks and modest cooperation in functional areas climaxed in the formation in 1985 of SAARC. SAARC has avoided security and economic cooperation, and its charter prohibits debate on contentious and bilateral issues. However, it has concluded agreements on security-related subjects, such as terrorism and narcotics control, and is slowly moving toward economic cooperation.

Moreover, although bilateral quarrels are beyond formal discussion, they have been the centerpiece of the annual summits and the biannual foreign ministers' meetings at which informal bilateral talks have been convened. These talks would not be possible on a regular basis, given the prevailing norms of diplomatic interaction in the region, and reputedly they have been consequential: the India-Pakistan talks at the 1986 summit apparently played a deescalatory role in the 1986–87 exercises crisis, and the India–Sri Lanka talks at the 1987 foreign ministers' meetings led to their accord on the Tamil problem. In spite of serious bilateral strains, SAARC has survived if not prospered and appears ready to expand its role modestly in the coming decade.

We may abstract the following lessons from these efforts. First, what is striking is how much association has been "in the air" since independence. Second, minimally, the appropriate scope of these efforts was thought initially to be both South and Southeast Asia but shrank over time to encompass only the subcontinent. Third, in most cases the regional effort originated with and was carried through by regional states, either South or Southeast Asian. Fourth, South Asians have been divided among themselves—India versus the others—in these efforts. Finally, though the motivations and deliberations were largely security-related (for example, colonialism, the role of outside powers, and intraregional threats), the conferences usually ended in low-level agreements to cooperate in functional or cultural areas. Put differently, for the most part regional efforts at cooperation were failures. Indeed, so clearly were they failures that South Asians made no further attempt at regional association until the 1980s, when they formed SAARC.[11] Although SAARC has survived and has some accomplishments to its credit, it has avoided an overt security orientation. In sum, South Asia's repeated attempts to cooperate for security within a larger grouping of "local" states have not worked. We now turn to whether efforts sponsored by or involving powerful outsiders have worked better.

Multilaterally Led Efforts at Cooperation: British, Iranian, U.S., and Soviet

South Asia has a virtually continuous history of cooperative or peacemaking efforts led by outside powers. Britain from 1946 to the early 1960s and Iran from 1969 to 1979 attempted to bring India and Pakistan together. The United States (1947 to early 1960s) and the Soviet Union (1964 to 1969) also tried to organize subcontinental cooperation. From 1979 on, the United States tried once again to foster regional security cooperation.

The reactions of New Delhi and Islamabad have been a mixture of disappointment, suspicion, and resentment. Even the successes in functional and economic areas (the Indus Rivers Treaty, the Colombo Plan, and the Economic Commission for Asia and the Far East, later the Economic and Social Commission for Asia and the Pacific) and the Tashkent peace settlement (1966) have been criticized by the supposed beneficiaries. South Asia appears unique in this respect. Nowhere have so many outside powers tried so hard and apparently achieved so little.

BRITAIN. British policies, before and immediately after partition, were directed toward preserving the strategic unity of the subcontinent if possible. In any case, however, the British wanted access to the region's manpower, territory, and industry as a component of Anglo-American security arrangements for the Gulf, central Asia, and even Southeast Asia. The initial British plan involved a joint defense council that was to be chaired by Lord Mountbatten. Mountbatten had hoped that the council would deal with financial and economic matters and eventually with communications and foreign policy. This arrangement would effectively have meant political unity. Beyond this, the British set a minimum goal of some form of defense cooperation between the two successor governments.

Even this plan proved impossible, however, with the outbreak of war over Kashmir (1948). Henceforth Britain's cooperative efforts were restricted to bringing about a UN-sponsored solution to Kashmir (in concert with the United States) and to mediating in the Kutch dispute in 1965. With the outbreak of war between India and Pakistan in 1965, it was clear that even these efforts had failed. Apart from the British-brokered cease-fire in the Rann of Kutch in early 1965, no further serious extraregional effort was made to resolve bilateral disputes until the Tashkent conference in January 1966.[12]

IRAN. Iran, too, has tried to manage regional security in South Asia. From 1969 to 1979 the Shah attempted to bring Pakistan, Afghanistan, and India together in an expanded version of Regional Cooperation for Development

(RCD). After the Shah's overthrow, Tehran continued to be interested in expanding regional economic cooperation beyond the RCD.[13] Iran's primary interest has been the stability and survival of Pakistan, which, it recognizes, is a condition in large part dependent on India. Some form of association with both countries has therefore been an abiding Iranian concern, both before and after the Shah's overthrow. Secondarily, Iran has tried to involve South Asia in its Indian Ocean policy. After British withdrawal from the Gulf in 1968, Iran moved to fill the vacuum. Tehran viewed India *and* Pakistan as part of a consolidated regional response to British withdrawal and to the growing superpower naval presence. Finally, Tehran has sought to balance Arab power by an alliance of Iran, Pakistan, and India.[14]

THE UNITED STATES AND THE SOVIET UNION. Until three years ago the United States had never formulated a South Asia policy outside the context of global struggle. From 1947 to 1990 the United States pursued one direct and one derived strategic policy in South Asia. The direct policy was based on pure cold war calculations. India and Pakistan were courted as allies against the Soviet Union and (after 1949) communist China. This policy led to a formal alliance relationship with Pakistan and treaties in 1952 and 1959. With India there were informal arrangements that served the interests of both sides and a massive economic aid program.[15] At war with China in 1962, New Delhi turned to the United States and the United Kingdom, among others, for arms. Both responded, and the United States carried out military exchanges and training exercises with India from 1963 to 1965. There was also a substantial military assistance program.

The U.S.-Indian relationship that grew out of the 1962 war led to the most concerted American effort to bring the two neighbors into a defensive scheme and to a derived, or secondary, strategic objective. India and Pakistan were seen as important components of a larger containment strategy; to the degree that they canceled each other out by their rivalry, their resources were not available for the larger strategic contest. Furthermore, their conflict was an opportunity for Soviet (and later Chinese) meddling. Thus the United States tried to encourage India and Pakistan to settle their differences and engage in regional cooperation. After the India-China war Washington and London insisted that India and Pakistan enter into negotiations over Kashmir, the source of their major dispute. Both sides resented these pressures and made little attempt to compromise.

As seen from South Asia, U.S. mediations in Kashmir and elsewhere were not disinterested. Indians, in particular, were wary of Washington's geopolitical vision of South Asia's alliance role in containing communism. British rule in India had expanded in a series of alliances with regional rulers and a "divide and rule" strategy of conquest. Postindependence India, and later Pakistan, preferred to maintain a flexible posture. Indian aloofness troubled Washington, but Pakistani membership in a Middle Eastern security structure was seen as an important gain. The United States was increasingly concerned not about South Asian but about Middle Eastern security, in which Pakistan had a political and strategic role that India could or would not play.

At the same time Washington did not want to alienate India altogether or to worsen India-Pakistan relations beyond retrieval. It assured New Delhi that U.S. arms sold to Pakistan would not be used against India and continued to provide economic and technical aid to both countries. Washington's policy affected strategic calculations in New Delhi and Islamabad and gave the United States, whether it sought it or not, a role in shaping the regional balance of power.

After the Soviet intervention in Afghanistan in December 1979, U.S. interest in the region revived. Pakistan had long given up on Washington. Since 1972 it had pursued its own form of multilateral diplomacy, trusting to good relations with China, the Islamic world, and the United States, in that order. Covertly, it had begun a nuclear weapons program designed to reduce its dependence on outside powers and establish nominal equality with New Delhi. The U.S. response to the Soviet invasion was to revive the alliance with Islamabad. Pakistan was projected as critical to stopping the Soviets in Afghanistan and a likely ally in the Persian Gulf. Its close ties to China, once a liability, had become an asset. However, the price Pakistan demanded for an extended strategic relationship was too great: U.S. guarantees against India. This demand forced Washington, in 1983 and 1984, to revert to an earlier policy of balanced relations with New Delhi and Islamabad, now motivated by a desire to protect the latter. The United States once again began to explore ways in which the two states might cooperate. Pakistan's nuclear program, coupled with India's nuclear capability (first demonstrated in 1974), lent urgency to the task. Washington drew up an elaborate program of moving the two regional states down the road of confidence-building measures.

Soviet involvement in the region has been less variable. Until 1955, when Nikita Khrushchev came to power, Moscow's attitude was marked by indifference and contempt: South Asians, though nominally independent, were tied ideologically and economically to the West and possessed little autonomy in the global struggle. After 1955, with Pakistan's formal membership in the U.S.-led Central Treaty Organization (CENTO) and SEATO pacts, Soviet interest focused on India. Nehru's India was now seen as a potential ally in the struggle against the West. Henceforth Moscow tilted toward India in its quarrels with Pakistan and later with China. However, after 1964, with Khrushchev's ouster, Soviet policy shifted. Moscow now attempted to bring greater balance to its approach to South Asia. The Soviet-brokered agreement at Tashkent in 1966 seemed to validate the new approach. Over the next two years Moscow worked to further improve relations with Islamabad, selling arms to Pakistan while reassuring India. In 1969 it aired the idea of Asian collective security. Pakistan immediately rejected the notion, which it saw as anti-Chinese. India equivocated but was not enthusiastic. New Delhi was loath to reject Moscow's venture—it was engaged in secret negotiations over an Indo-Soviet treaty—but like Islamabad it did not want to be identified with an anti-Chinese front.[16] With the outbreak of serious Sino-Soviet clashes in 1969, Moscow's policy swung away from balance and back to a tilt toward India. In large measure, this tilt remained the basis of Soviet policy until the arrival of Mikhail Gorbachev.

Although mutual containment and exclusion were the guiding star for U.S. and Soviet policies in South Asia for more than forty years, there were extended periods when the two states cooperated in the region.[17] This cooperation took four forms.

First, both states "cooperated" by pursuing the same policies for different reasons. For much of the cold war, both competed in South Asia for the favor of India and even of Pakistan. India received substantial amounts of economic aid from both superpowers, and Pakistan received some arms and a steel mill from Moscow. Thus to the degree that this aid helped regional development efforts, it could be said that the two cooperated, although their motives were competitive.

Second, both states "cooperated" strategically in their uncoordinated support of India from 1959 to the late 1960s. Both saw New Delhi as a bulwark against Beijing, and both provided substantial military technology and aid, although some of that equipment was deployed by India against Pakistan.

Third, the two superpowers allowed each other to try to manage regional conflict. After the 1965 India-Pakistan war, the United States withdrew from the subcontinent, disillusioned over its failure to bring about cooperation and its inability to make progress on Kashmir, and annoyed at American arms being used in the conflict. Thus in January 1966 President Ayub of Pakistan and Prime Minister Lal Bahadur Shastri of India met in Tashkent. The Soviets cajoled and coerced and produced a postwar peace agreement.

Finally, in the last phase of the cold war the two superpowers acted in concert to prevent regional conflict. By 1987 the Soviets had begun to recalculate their position in Afghanistan, and their policy during an India-Pakistan border crisis was ambivalent. Three years later they made it clear that they would not support India in a subsequent crisis over Kashmir. Now Russian officials speak openly and critically of the prospect of an India-Pakistan conflict. The United States and Russia engage in regular consultation over South Asia, and officials on both sides have cooperated with a joint American-Russian research project that offered recommendations for resolving the Afghanistan and Kashmir crises.[18]

In sum, we can conclude the following about externally led attempts to forge cooperation in the region or to cooperate for the region. First, the United States tried to balance its relations with India and Pakistan, seeking to avoid too great a tilt toward either side. By contrast, the Soviets tried less often and succeeded less well in balancing their approach to the region. Second, the primary concern of both powers was to enlist India and Pakistan against, or at least to deny them to, each other's camps. Third, for various reasons Washington and Moscow have cooperated in their approaches to South Asia from time to time. Fourth, both outside powers have substantially disengaged from the region since 1971, the exception being the high years of the Afghan war (1980–85). Fifth, neither Washington nor Moscow has been able to prevent war, manage crisis very successfully, or ameliorate underlying and fundamental quarrels. They have done better at terminating hostilities. Most recently, the United States has had success in pushing the two toward confidence-building measures. Finally, India and Pakistan have rarely credited the United States or the former Soviet Union (FSU) with a balanced or consistent approach toward the region, though Moscow has been seen as at least more consistent. Whatever the intentions of the external powers, South Asians have been distrustful of their role.

Cooperative Security and South Asia

Unilateralist means of achieving security, that is, methods resting on the threat or use of force to achieve one's objectives, have three times led to war, caused several "war scares," and sustained at best an uneasy, wary peace in South Asia. At the same time bilateral, regional, and multilateral efforts to organize South Asian security have in large measure run aground. What, then, are the prospects for cooperative security?

On the face of it, the rationale behind cooperative security seems unassailable. Why should states shun the possibility of consensually arrived-at mutual agreements on the size, composition, investment patterns, and operational practices of their armed forces such that surprise and preemptive attacks become difficult if not impossible to contemplate and carry out? Insofar as cooperative security is comprehensive in its inclusion of major military establishments and the agreements are equitable, enforceable, and verifiable, it is an attractive strategy. Not only military stability but also economic payoffs in the form of worldwide "peace dividends" would seem to be plausible goals. Moreover, although cooperative security may not solve fundamental quarrels, it may give rise to political and military habits that can help to resolve such quarrels. Skeptics, on the other hand, would argue that, for a variety of political and technical reasons, cooperative security would not be comprehensive, equitable, enforceable, and verifiable enough to satisfy states that are deeply suspicious of one another.[19] And to the extent that cooperative security does not address the resolution of fundamental quarrels, it will fail to garner interest or commitment.

The plausibility or implausibility of cooperative security at this turning point in international affairs, however, may be better addressed by assessing a number of less abstract themes. A circumstantial case for the plausibility of cooperative security in South Asia at this juncture must take account of conditions and trends on two levels: the global and the regional. At the global level three fundamental motivating conditions can be posited, namely, the end of the cold war, the diffusion of weapons of mass destruction, and growing economic and technological interdependence as well as shrinking national budgets. Together these conditions suggest that states will be increasingly constrained in the use of force in any but a defensive mode. At the regional level South Asia presents a range of impediments to and incentives for cooperation. The impediments are not necessarily fatal to cooperative security arrangements; rather they would seem to be constraints on the character, scope, speed, and intensity of such arrangements. At the same time the incentives will not easily cause South Asians to opt for cooperative security, although incentives may make them more receptive than they would have been in the past.

Motivating Trends and Cooperative Security in South Asia

The end of the cold war, the core of which was the bipolar conflict between the United States and the Soviet Union, has meant a lowering of tensions but also a loss of control over allies and satellites. It has also meant U.S. and FSU disengagement from several regions whose strategic importance depended on the cold war. The new security environment is therefore more fluid and uncertain. Given the relative loss of control of the United States and the FSU and regional disengagement, and in the face of greater fluidity and uncertainty, a new security order must be more consensually derived than before.

Furthermore, the diffusion of military technologies among a whole array of third-level powers below the United States, Russia, China, the United Kingdom, and France implies additional decentralization of the security order and increasingly complicated strategic environments. These environments transcend the usual bilateral and regional arenas, given the reach and dispersal of new delivery systems. Decentralization, complexity, and expanded strategic environments mean that a more inclusive security regime will be required.

Finally, the increasing level of interdependence, especially economic and technological, and the transnationalization of decisions regarding production, investment, and finance raise the costs of any use of force. Patterns of interdependence and transnationalization, moreover, go beyond well-established bilateral and regional networks and are increasingly globally dispersed. And the ability of governments to call forth economic sacrifices from their citizens for military preparations is increasingly under pressure. Budgets are tight and likely to grow tighter, posing further constraints on the use of force. In light of these trends there would seem to be powerful incentives to move toward a structure of negotiated military sufficiency that is primarily defensive in orientation.

The foregoing is a statement of the theology of cooperative security. What are the implications of these trends for South Asia?

First, with the end of the cold war, there has been a general and dramatic reduction of tensions, not just between Moscow and Washington but also between Moscow and Beijing. The Moscow-Washington and Moscow-Beijing relationships no longer intrude into the subcontinent. Moreover, the three outside powers have in large part disengaged from the region, a trend that had started in the mid-1970s, was interrupted by the Soviet invasion of Afghanistan, and was resumed by the mid-1980s. On the part of the United States, the FSU, and China, the competition for allies or the attempt to deny regional states to each other's camps and the willingness to supply military and economic resources have greatly attenuated if not disappeared. At the same time the ability of the small states to appeal to, or maneuver for, external support and resources against India and Indian reliance on external support and resources against Pakistan or China have been much reduced if not eliminated. Thus external interest in South Asia, never very high, has diminished further. External responsibility for South Asia's security troubles has also substantially diminished.

The loss of outside interest in South Asia may harm the security of the smaller states and increase the security of India. If the responsibility for South Asia's troubles can no longer be ascribed to meddlesome outsiders, the smaller states and India must then deal with their mutual security fears directly. In this situation, what are the prospects for cooperative security? One might argue that cooperative security should be attractive to the smaller states: it should be a guarantee to them that India's forces will be configured more defensively and thus in a less interventionary mode. However, any reconfiguration of Indian forces with respect to those of other major powers could still leave it more than adequately capable of intervening against its small neighbors. One might also argue that cooperative security should be attractive to India: it should serve as a guarantee that the capacity of major outside powers to act in an interventionary fashion in South Asia will be reduced, a condition India has long desired. On the other hand, a multilateral reconfiguration of forces toward defensive sufficiency might yet leave powerful outsiders capable of considerable intervention in regional affairs.

This analysis suggests not that cooperative security is irrelevant but that it will have to deal with the formidable task of defining what would constitute a truly defensive sufficiency of forces in a triangle consisting of powerful outsiders, regional powers such as India, and smaller regional states. What is defensively sufficient between India and China may leave a more than adequate capacity for intervention in the hands of New Delhi and Beijing. Implementing a structure of forces that can bridge the asymmetries between powerful outsiders and the regional powers and simultaneously between regional powers and the small states promises to be one of the greatest challenges to achieving cooperative security.

The end of the cold war also led to important nuclear arms control agreements, the most recent of which envisage large-scale cuts in strategic nuclear systems over the next fifteen years. In addition, both American and FSU conventional forces are being drawn down and defense spending is being cut. Thus, although the military asymmetry between outsiders and South Asians will remain substantial, it will be reduced.

This reduction will help the cause of cooperative security. Politically, it will strengthen the hands of those in South Asia who are sympathetic to notions of negotiated defensive sufficiency. These groups will be able to claim that the major powers have shown a willingness to draw down and restructure military forces and that a South Asian move to do so will be consistent with a larger trend. This claim is important. As was seen in the realm of nuclear proliferation, South Asians have in part resisted regulatory efforts by arguing that they were discriminatory—in practice if not in law—because they did little to control the major powers. Those sympathetic to cooperative security notions will be able to make a more positive normative argument; namely, that given the agreements and changes among the major powers, South Asians *should* play their part in enhancing international security through force reductions. It will not be an easy argument to win domestically. Opponents of defensive sufficiency in South Asia will argue that the cuts among the major powers happened after the cold war was called off and that anything remotely comparable in the region must await the end of the local "cold war."

Thus South Asia confronts a "chicken-or-egg" problem: defensive sufficiency requires movement toward fundamental political improvements; political improvements require a stabilization of the military relationship. This suggests that the development of cooperative security will have to move on two tracks simultaneously: a "technical" one of force sufficiency and military regulation but also a "political" one of détente and conflict resolution (as discussed subsequently in this chapter).

Second, the end of the cold war has brought into sharper relief the diffusion of military technologies to third-level powers, the decentralization of the security order, and the rise of security uncertainties. India and Pakistan have near-nuclear capabilities. Both sides are engaged in expanding their missile technologies. And both have the sophistication to turn civilian chemical production to military use. At the same time there has occurred a diffusion of these technologies in their neighborhood over the past several years. The Iranian and Iraqi nuclear programs have advanced, though Baghdad's capability was considerably dismantled after the Gulf War. Saudi Arabia and Iraq have missile capability. Saudi missiles acquired from China can reach parts of India. Iraq used chemical weapons in its long war with Iran. All these developments add up to a more complicated strategic environment for both major South Asian states: the diffusion of military technologies has expanded the security agendas and perimeters of New Delhi and Islamabad. The effects on India and Pakistan are likely to be ambiguous. On the one hand, the proliferation of capability and the denser strategic horizon present an incentive to accelerate South Asian capacities to match regional and extraregional developments. On the other hand, the diffusion of capability and denser environments are also incentives to seek agreements to control the pace, direction, and extent of proliferation. Therefore the effect on South Asia of the diffusion of military technology is indeterminate.

Third, a worldwide deepening of economic interdependence, transnationalization, and financial stringency has been in process. The direct and opportunity costs of war and of the preparation for war are therefore greater. This is an old thesis.[20] Does it bear on South Asia?

Since 1947 South Asians have continued in varying degrees to be involved with outsiders economically. Most recently, Bangladesh, India, and Pakistan have undertaken an array of reforms that recognize their extraregional trade, financial, and technological linkages and the growing need to integrate further with the world economy. Although there exists some domestic opposition to, and doubt about, the character and pace of economic reforms, there is no significant political force committed to reversing the changes. What accounts for South Asia's outward and market strategy after years of autarkic and planned development? Many factors do, but perhaps the most important are the massive internal and external debts, the pressures exerted by external donors, the assertiveness of a burgeoning middle class, and a sense of desperation from watching virtually every region, even those once behind South Asia, move past it. Not surprisingly, India and Pakistan for the first time in decades have cut defense spending. There does exist therefore an economic base on which the idea of cooperative security might be erected. This possibility should not be overstated, however. If purely economic reasoning constrained political decisions, then one might expect that South Asians, more often than others, would have made decisions for military modesty and peace. Yet they have not done so. Indeed, South Asia has been one of the most violent regions in the world.

In sum, the motivating trends present no clear indication of how notions of cooperative security would be received in South Asia. The strongest factor for change in the organization of the region's security appears to be economic. However, even here we would urge caution in reaching definitive conclusions.

Regional Impediments and Incentives to Cooperative Security

A successful strategy of cooperative security will have to be crafted with regional specificities in mind. South Asia presents a number of features that in varying degrees pose impediments to the implementation of cooperative security. Changes in process exist that may ameliorate the worst effects of these impediments. The overall outlook is mixed, suggesting that South Asia may not be altogether ripe for cooperative security. Yet it bears repeating that the impediments are not necessarily fatal to, but rather constraints on, the pace, direction, scope, and intensity of cooperative security development.

The first impediment to the implementation of cooperative security in South Asia is the India-centered structure of the region. India is by far the most powerful state in the region. Moreover, India alone borders the other South Asian states.[21] Not surprisingly, virtually all of South Asia's internal quarrels are between India and the others. At the same time geographic structure prevents the emergence of outright polarization: without common borders India's neighbors cannot organize themselves into an alliance. Together with the power asymmetry the Indocentricity of the region makes this strategic environment particularly brittle. The relative weakness of India's neighbors and their inability to combine among themselves encourage them to seek external friends even as they calculate that outsiders can be unreliable in relation to India, and the Indocentricity of regional disputes as well as the proneness of the smaller states to seek outside support makes New Delhi extremely suspicious about the involvement of extraregional states in South Asian affairs. Insofar as cooperative security means wider participation in South Asian security issues, it will encounter skepticism from the smaller states and India. Will cooperative security help the smaller states "against" India or will it "legitimize" India's predominance? Will it derogate from or support New Delhi's view of its role as a stabilizing influence in the region? Both sides will have to be reassured in the face of structurally engendered suspicions.

Certain structural factors can mitigate the effect of other structural factors. Specifically, high levels of interdependence and deep-rooted similarities in national ideologies or mind-sets can soften the impact of power distributions and geographic configurations. South Asia poses a challenge in this respect, too. Unlike western Europe, East Asia, and now Southeast Asia, South Asia does not feature high levels of intraregional economic interdependence. For instance, only about 2 percent of South Asia's total trade is conducted within the region.[22] Environmentally, the region is much more interdependent: shared hydrological systems and common mountain ranges are sources of opportunities and constraints. South Asia is probably unique in that its patterns of environmental interdependence are not "cross-cutting" but "cumulative." It is different from the Middle East, where, on a crucial resource such as water, all disputes and possibilities do not center on any one actor.[23] In South Asia India is at the center of virtually all the disputes and possibilities arising out of shared environmental problems and resources, mostly as a result of its geographic centrality. These interdependencies demand cooperation, yet the record on cooperation is poor, at least in part because interdependence is asymmetrically in favor of India. The small states fear that Indian preferences will prevail in any cooperative scheme, and India fears a "ganging up" among the smaller states or between the small states and outside powers.[24] Thus interdependence tends not to mitigate but to be assimilated with structural conflict.

Although economic interdependence has been low in South Asia, especially between India and Pakistan, the increasing regionalization of global trading arrangements, the exclusion of both states from these arrangements, the direction of economic reforms in both states, and the pressures within SAARC from the smaller states presage change. South Asians may be moving toward both increasing economic interaction and interdependence. SAARC will probably agree, after ten years of existence, to various measures promoting trade and other economic intercourse. If this happens, South Asians may slowly be constrained to move toward cooperative and away from unilateralist security measures.

A second impediment to implementing cooperative security is that ideological differences between South Asian states exacerbate regional divisions. Broadly, India sees itself as the only democratic, federal, and secular polity in the region. The smaller states, in varying degrees and at various times, have been skeptical of India's claims but in any case question the appropriateness of democracy, federalism, and secularism for their societies. India sees the other states as being ruled by authoritarian and illegitimate governments that remain in power by resorting to fundamentalist (Muslim, Buddhist, or Hindu), praetorian, bonapartist, monarchical, or chauvinist appeals and modes of governance and to depictions of India as a powerful irredentist neighbor. Even when the smaller states see the Indian model as appropriate, they consider India's record flawed. In short, the two sides disagree on the appropriate basis for nation building and regional order.

This divide over nation-building strategies and regional order has implications for cooperative security. The Indian view is that cooperative arrangements with "illegitimate" and "unstable" governments are dangerous and unproductive: authoritarian governments are inherently untrustworthy; any agreements reached with them may not be seen as binding by successor governments; and cooperating with authoritarian governments may help confer a legitimacy on these governments that they do not deserve. Moreover, authoritarian governments in neighboring states are more prone to resort to India bashing as a way of constructing national identities, albeit negative ones, and of distracting attention from their fallibilities. Dictatorial regimes are also prone to oppress their peoples to the point of inciting rebellions that could spill over into India and complicate its security.[25] The smaller states counter with various arguments. They see Indian reluctance to cooperate with undemocratic neighbors as hypocritical (given Indian cooperation with all manner of undemocratic governments) and as New Delhi's way of finessing any serious attempt to negotiate with them. They point to no lack of neighbor bashing in

India's democratic polity. And they suggest that democratic India has its share of rebellions that have spilled over into bordering states.

Ideological tensions notwithstanding, South Asians are closer than they have ever been. Over the past five years Bangladesh, Nepal, and Pakistan have opted for democracy. Moreover, all the major countries of the region are run by political parties that are secularly minded even if fundamentalist forces are at work in their polities. Thus for the first time since 1947, South Asians appear to be converging on the best path to nation building.

A third impediment is that territorial and border problems complicate the prospects for cooperative security in South Asia. Although a number of territorial and border disputes between India and its neighbors have been solved, some remain. The most important is Kashmir, which after twenty years of relative quiescence has become the greatest threat to South Asian peace.

The Kashmir dispute is a problem for cooperative security in at least two ways.[26] First, it is symbolic of different nation-building strategies and is therefore consequential for India and Pakistan beyond the future of the sociopolitical and territorial entity known as Kashmir. Perhaps cooperative security cannot take on the burdens of deep-rooted differences between states; yet if it cannot, it risks irrelevance. Second, even if New Delhi and Islamabad were able to agree on Kashmir, the activities of Kashmiri militant groups, substantially outside the control of *both* governments, would pose a constant threat to any bilateral accords, including cooperative security accords. The problem is that, however independent the militants may be, New Delhi holds Islamabad in large measure responsible for militant activity. Indian leaders worry that during an insurrectionary phase Pakistan may make a grab for Kashmir. They worry at least in part because, in 1948 and 1965, Pakistan in concert with insurgents used force to try to wrest Kashmir away. In 1965 New Delhi responded by expanding hostilities into a generalized war against Pakistan. It reserves the right to do so again and even to initiate hostilities in order to check the insurgency. Defensive sufficiency, however rational it may appear from the outside, is potentially costly to regional actors who want either to maintain or to upset the territorial status quo.[27]

This potential costliness highlights one of the key problems of cooperative security as defensive sufficiency, namely, that it favors the assumption that most international actors can live with the territorial status quo. This assumption was thought to be true for large sections of the globe: the Americas (though even here Quebec has been a problem for Canada) and for Europe, including the Soviet Union. It is clearly no longer true for Europe, and the Quebec problem is by no means settled.

Other territorial and border problems in South Asia may seem minor in comparison with Kashmir, but their symbolism, domestic resonance, and linkage to bigger issues make them important. The most significant of these issues is the India-Pakistan dispute over the Siachen glacier in Kashmir. Siachen has been the site of a miniwar for close to a decade, and there is little prospect that it is about to end. Its strategic importance is questionable, but it has come to be seen as a test of wills over Kashmir. Inevitably, it has become a domestic political issue. The longer and the more costly the involvement of the two sides over Siachen, the more difficult it becomes to resile from it: the human, material, and financial costs must be justified at home to increasingly skeptical publics. Moreover, although the conflict over Siachen has never threatened to escalate into an India-Pakistan war, it has added to the complexity of the Kashmir problem and, more important, to the lack of trust between the two sides, each of which sees the other as trying to overturn the status quo along this remote glacier.[28]

Siachen is not the only territorial and border dispute in South Asia. India-Bangladesh differences remain over the South Moore–Talpatty Islands in the Bay of Bengal and over a possible reopening of the India–Sri Lanka Kachhattivu dispute. Although these appear to be relatively minor quarrels over more or less worthless strips of land or water, they are important for this discussion because of India's involvement in both. New Delhi is wary of even minor disputes and adjustments. The domestic politics of territorial and border issues are particularly hard: most recently, the settlement of the Tin Bigha dispute with Dhaka set off a storm of protest in India. Furthermore, Indian governments worry that concessions on smaller disputes may dispose Pakistan and China to harden their positions in their quarrels with India. In the absence of solutions to its regional border problems, both large and small, New Delhi feels that it must maintain a high level of military capability and readiness.

Territorial and border problems with implications for cooperative security are not just regional in scope; they also extend to neighboring regions. Once again India is involved. For years India and Indonesia have eyed each other warily over various islands in the Indian Ocean. Both keep a close watch on each other's naval forces. The Indonesians have been among the sharpest critics of the expansion of the Indian navy over the past decade. At the same time India, with one of the largest exclusive economic zones (EEZs) in the world, is determined to prevent encroachment into this more extended maritime boundary. India is also a player in the Antarctic and has been alloted an Antarctic zone. The Indian navy is projected to continue expanding to possibly become a three-carrier navy to defend the EEZ and India's Antarctic interest.

Territorial and border problems remain serious, but in this area too there are signs of amelioration. India has been involved in a number of border talks and agreements. The India-China border talks, begun in the early 1980s, continue to be held (even though progress has been very slow). India-Pakistan talks over Siachen have periodically been convened as more people in both countries come to feel that the fight for position on the glacier has been too costly. Most recently, as noted, New Delhi finally ended the Tin Bigha dispute by leasing out a corridor linking Bangladesh to its enclaves in India.

A fourth impediment to the implementation of cooperative security is ethnic conflict. India and Pakistan confront various internal sectarian conflicts. One might argue that these disagreements, by virtue of the distractions and immediate dangers they pose, would serve as an incentive for the development of cooperative security. On balance, however, ethnic conflict would be problematic for cooperative security. Internal security operations have entailed extensive use of the two militaries. Moreover, the herniation of conflict over national boundaries threatens to push the two sides toward war. Pakistan, for instance, must deal with the violence in Sind and the militancy of Azad Kashmiris. Sindhi instability and the activities of Azad Kashmiris impinge on the relationship with India. The presence of Afghan refugees may well complicate Islamabad's relations with Afghanistan. Among other issues, India must deal with Punjab, Kashmir, and the northeastern insurgencies, the demand for a separate state of Gorkhaland in West Bengal, and resurgent separatist feeling in Tamil Nadu, all of which complicate relations with, respectively, Pakistan, Bangladesh, Burma, Nepal, and Sri Lanka. New Delhi must also deal with spillovers from Bangladesh (Chakma separatism and Hindu-Muslim communal troubles), from Bhutan (Nepali settlers increasingly restive under the king's Bhutanization policies are migrating to India), from Nepal (the problems of the Terai Indians), and from Sri Lanka (the Tamils led by the Liberation Tigers of Tamil Eelam).

The movement of people and the attendant internal and external tensions are driven not just by domestic quarrels over political authority but also by economic necessity. Bangladeshis and Nepalis are migrating to India and other South Asian states in search of jobs and land. India's northeast is especially uneasily poised. It is a subregion of fertile land, sparsely populated, relatively rich in natural resources, and contiguous with some of the most densely populated and economically backward areas in the world. The border between India and Nepal and India and Bangladesh is at the same time virtually impossible to police. The so-called ethnic problems of regions such as South Asia are therefore multilayered and driven by a variety of forces: internal dissent and repression leading to separatism, civil war and spillovers across national boundaries, irredentism, and economically motivated migration.

As this list of problems shows, India is central once again. New Delhi has responded with force to ethnic problems both in India (Kashmir, Punjab, and the northeastern states) and in other South Asian countries (East Pakistan in 1971, Sri Lanka from 1987 to 1990, and reportedly Pakistan's Sind province).[29] It expects ethnic challenges and opportunities to continue, necessitating the budgeting of large amounts of military force to deal with them. Any notion of cooperative security will have to engage the demand, especially Indian, for military capability and readiness arising out of the complicated and enduring subnational and transnational ethnic conflicts of the region.[30] Note that this is one regional trend, not only in South Asia, that is not ameliorating and that poses a very serious complication for cooperative security. Cooperative security agreements on force size, structures, and dispositions will have to reflect not only extraregional and regional asymmetries, as suggested earlier, but also the internal demand for force.

Finally, cooperative security may entail significant security and diplomatic, and domestic, political costs. Given the high degree of suspicion between South Asians, various cooperative measures can be viewed ambiguously: they may be seen as stabilizing measures but also maneuvers for unilateral advantage. In part, how they are interpreted will depend on the possibility and reliability of verification measures. Beyond verification, however, there are two other problems. Cooperative security may promise military stability but may also involve certain political and diplomatic costs. For example, if either party suspects that cooperative security is a way of sidetracking or freezing the resolution of a fundamental quarrel such as that over Kashmir, it may balk at such measures. In addition, whereas cooperative security promises to reduce uncertainty in relationships, states may under certain circumstances value uncertainty in prosecuting fundamental quarrels. For instance, as suggested earlier, India may wish to maintain a certain level of uncertainty with respect to its military options in Kashmir and Punjab. The threat of hot pursuit, strikes against Kashmiri and Sikh militants in Pakistan, and even wider military action against Pakistan to persuade it to stop intervening in the two states are coercive options New Delhi may not want to lose. Brinksmanship has its dangers but also its uses.

Cooperative security may also entail domestic political costs. For instance, certain domestic constituencies in India and Pakistan might see cooperative security as appeasement of an adversary or as the thin edge of the wedge in terms of a reconciliation process. There are parties in both countries that will not accept any cooperative moves until fundamental quarrels such as those over Kashmir and Punjab have been settled in their favor and that will brand any other forms of cooperation as appeasement. Some might even favor a certain amount of instability with an external rival as an opportunity for domestic political advantage. Political parties in India or Pakistan as well as the Pakistani military might favor external instabilities as opportunities for political advancement. In a period of financial austerity, for instance, the two militaries might hope for a border incident or two as a reminder to the government and public opinion that defense cuts could be dangerous. The political right wing—Islamic or Hindu—might also be tempted to use instabilities to criticize and to help topple incumbent governments. To avoid these kinds of costs, governments might be reluctant to engage in a cooperative security process.

Whereas cooperative security may entail diplomatic and security and internal political costs, both sides increasingly acknowledge the growing costliness of war. Both appreciate that, notwithstanding the relatively moderate wars they fought in the past, a future war might be far more extensive and damaging. Both understand that, given present trends in warfare and their military capacities—conventional but also nuclear—fighting could be extremely costly in human, economic, and political terms. New Delhi and Islamabad are aware that repetitions of the military exercises crisis of 1986–87 are possible, especially in a complicated disintegrative environment featuring ethnic conflict and spillovers.[31] Although disintegration itself may not be susceptible to control by government-to-government agreements, there is room nevertheless for cooperative agreements to contain the spillovers and enhance the restraints on war. The two sides have therefore begun instituting confidence-building measures.[32] The decline in military preparedness may further dispose them to avoid war and to seek to stabilize their military relationship. The Indian military is in a defensive and introspective phase for many reasons: growing internal policing, reevaluating doctrine in light of the Sri Lanka operation and the Gulf War, equipment problems attendant on the changed relationship with the FSU, and budget cuts. The preparedness of the Pakistani military, though probably superior to that of the Indian military, is limited by similar kinds of constraints.

There are, moreover, the economic costs of the India-Pakistan conflict. Thus, for the first time since the expansion of the military after the China war, Indian defense spending has been cut. Pakistan, under similar pressure, is also cutting defense spending. Under pressure from aid donors and the greater questioning of military spending from domestic critics, the trend toward spending cuts may well be sustained. Both states also increasingly understand the link between their mutual rivalry and the neglect of internal political problems. To deal with these problems will require an allocation of attention and resources away from the perennial issues of war and peace with each other.

Can the regional impediments to cooperative security be limited, or even reduced, and the incentives increased? Some features of regions are not manipulable, whereas others are more pliable. That is, little can be done to change the gross power asymmetry or geographic features of South Asia. Nor can economic interdependence be deepened quickly or ideological compatibility easily enhanced. Contests over territory, borders, ethnic conflict and spillovers, irrendentism, and transnational migration may seem more pliable but on the other hand involve complex legal, political, economic, sociological, and psychological issues.

Cooperative Security in South Asia: Global and Regional Trends

We are cautiously optimistic about the possibility of implementing cooperative security arrangements that seek to include South Asia. Global and regional trends and conditions show some hospitality to the notion of cooperative security extended to this troubled region. At the global level the growing integration of South Asia into the world economy promises to constrain destabilizing unilateralist security measures. At the regional level a number of ameliorating trends seem in process. At the same time there exist serious regional problems—territorial, border, and ethnic—that, strictly speaking, are outside the purview of cooperative security but that strike at the heart of South Asian insecurity. These problems shrink the space of sustained politically rational thought and practice within which cooperative security must be nurtured.

Thus the region may require a cooperative security strategy that goes beyond the pursuit of defensive sufficiency. Cooperative security may have to include regional conflict resolution involving state and nonstate actors and the addressing of an expanded set of issues on the scale of the present Middle East peace talks. Yet it is hard to see the international community led by powerful outsiders—and nothing less than such an approach would seem capable of breaking the deadlock in South Asia—girding itself for another, simultaneous, comprehensive regional peace process. In short, then, cooperative security as defensive sufficiency may be too little for South Asia, and anything more may be infeasible. This conclusion suggests that at the appropriate time the narrower version of cooperative security as well as a more ambitious one may have to be set in motion more or less simultaneously.

Cooperative Security and South Asian Nuclear Proliferation

One security issue, nuclear proliferation, deserves special attention from the point of view of cooperative security. South Asia contains two states that are on the brink of developing a nuclear weapons capability, which could assist others in acquiring nuclear weapons, and which could be said (unlike Brazil, Argentina, and South Africa) to face serious external security threats (from each other but also from outsiders). Furthermore, India and Pakistan find themselves in an environment that contains two known nuclear weapon states (Russia and China) as well as various possible additions to the list (Iraq, Iran, and Kazakhstan). The conjunction of four or five nuclear weapon states, several of them with advanced missile programs and all of them with territorial, ideological, and economic grievances with some or all of their neighbors—in many cases, with each other—would pose a spectacular military conundrum. One attraction of a cooperative security system is that it might *preempt* the development of such a nuclear-armed crowd in an unstable part of the world.

The challenge facing cooperative security is to contain the spread of nuclear weapons, to ensure that existing nuclear weapons states are incorporated into the cooperative framework, and to figure out a way to keep nuclear weapons from becoming the entry ticket to the club. Bringing India and Pakistan into a larger structure might be the most serious challenge to a cooperative security regime. As already discussed, there have been repeated attempts to incorporate one or both states into a larger grouping. In every case the attempt foundered on their rivalry and on the unwillingness of outside powers to provide the kind of ironclad security guarantees that would satisfy regional strategists.

We suggest the following *transitional* strategy as a means of moving toward a cooperative security regime capable of meeting these kinds of nuclear challenges. This strategy does not itself *prescribe* a regime but rather proposes certain preliminary steps that might buy time in the region to enable a more enduring structure to be erected. In outlining those preliminary steps, we are guided by the assumption that neither India nor Pakistan will soon abandon its nuclear program and give up the nuclear option. On the one hand, it is difficult to conceive of credible security guarantees for a nonnuclear Pakistan against a nuclear-armed India (or vice versa), for India against China, or even for Pakistan against Iran. On the other hand, both India and Pakistan have demonstrated conclusively their distrust of such guarantees by their strategy of maintaining a nuclear option. Both have uninspected nuclear programs and either have produced a nuclear explosive device (India in 1974) or, according to a recent Pakistani admission, could do so on short notice. Thus, although elsewhere the world may be moving toward the "demonetization" of the currency of nuclear weapons, in South Asia it is still regarded as *the* currency of great power status. Moreover, nuclear weapons are regarded as the only devices that will deter other nuclear weapons or a massive conventional assault. In short, Indians and Pakistanis see nuclear weapons very much the way Americans, Europeans, and Soviets have seen them for many years.

With this assumption a first step in lowering the pressures for weaponization is to reduce extraregional nuclear threats and influence the India-Pakistan conventional military balance so as to ensure both the stability and survivability of main force units. Although India has been technically capable of doing so for perhaps eighteen years, and Pakistan for four or five years, neither has deployed or announced a nuclear weapons capability. Nuclear threats, in particular, are matters of perception, and statements by the major nuclear powers, especially China, that they will not be the first to use nuclear weapons do affect perceptions. The United States and Russia should be willing to make such statements and agree to a comprehensive test ban in exchange for evidence that the regional dialogue on confidence-building measures has moved forward. Fostering a regional dialogue and introducing verification and stabilizing technologies that would extend the "strategic warning time" of both countries should be another high priority.[33]

A second step, a nuclear cooperative transitional strategy applied to the subcontinent, must be a *coalition* policy involving the nuclear weapon states and important nonnuclear states. The most damning argument encountered in South Asia is that the Nuclear Non-Proliferation Treaty, the Missile Technology Control Regime (MTCR), and various regional restraint schemes are an alliance of the haves against the have-nots. China, a key nuclear state, presents substantial problems for the development of a regional nuclear cooperative regime. It has been alleged that China supported Pakistan's program for many years. Indian nuclear and missile programs are driven in part by fear of and rivalry with China. When the Chinese tested a weapon underground in mid-1992, the Indians responded with a second launch of their intermediate-range ballistic missile, the Agni. In view of the likely instability that may grip China in years to come—and the apparent autonomy of some of its military programs—China cannot be counted on to join a South Asia–oriented cooperative security regime, conventional or otherwise. Indeed, the world may yet see South Asia as an important part of such a regime, with China outside it.

Japan and Germany are important non–nuclear weapon states that should, more visibly, be part of the effort to contain regional proliferation. Non–nuclear weapon regional states, such as Nepal, Bangladesh, and Sri Lanka, though Lilliputian by comparison, also have a role to play. They value cooperation, fear their larger neighbors (especially India), and have expressed their willingness to join outside states in sponsoring a regional nuclear regime that would freeze, contain, or otherwise defer the Indian and Pakistani nuclear and missile programs.

A coalition policy is consistent with the concept of cooperative security as a consensually brokered structure. We favor consensual, facilitating strategies toward the implementation of a cooperative security regime on proliferation because coerced cooperation threatens to unravel once the coercer stops coercing, out of either indifference, distraction, or weakness. Moreover, South Asia's experience shows that coercive strategies aimed at forging subcontinental security cooperation have not worked. India and Pakistan are simply too big to control and, seemingly, too remote both geographically and psychologically to excite and sustain the attention and concerns of the foremost coercive powers.

China, the Neighboring Regions, and South Asia

In the end, if a cooperative security regime is to be extended to South Asia and if it is to last, the desire to join must come from South Asians themselves, a prerequisite that is intrinsic to the notion of cooperative security. However, whether the balance of impediments and incentives is tipped in favor of cooperative security or against it could in part—and we stress in part—depend on the role of outsiders. In this section we examine China and regions neighboring the subcontinent and their possible effect on the prospects for cooperative security in South Asia. Our conclusion turns to the role of the United States in extending cooperative security to South Asia.

China has been and will continue to be a player in South Asian affairs. Beijing's relations with South Asia have gone from partisan to progressively more balanced. From 1949 to 1958 China tilted toward India. As the border quarrel with New Delhi intensified, China tilted toward Pakistan. After the 1962 war with India, the China-Pakistan relationship took on an alliancelike quality, which was matched by a Soviet-Indian entente. Beijing's move toward a more balanced position began in 1976 and, Afghanistan notwithstanding, has proceeded, if slowly. Beginning in 1976 China's position on Kashmir became more neutral, and Chinese leaders encouraged India's neighbors to resolve their differences with New Delhi. Beijing has supported SAARC as a means of narrowing differences. Since 1982 India and China have been involved in a series of border talks and have increased economic and cultural contacts. Most recently they have agreed to various confidence-building measures. With the end of the cold war, India-China relations have warmed further without a deterioration in Beijing's relations with Islamabad. In this sense China should be a force for stability and cooperation in South Asia. Chinese accession to the NPT, to the MTCR, and to the Chemical Weapons Convention, and its long-standing no-first-use pledge would also seem to be reassurances to South Asians and thus encouragements to the development of cooperative security.

Nevertheless, the differing views of China and its role in South Asia are problematic for the implementation of cooperative security. India and Pakistan see China in opposite ways. India will not concede that China is a South Asian power in the sense that it belongs to the region and therefore has a legitimate role to play in the organization of the region's security. Pakistan, on the other hand, is prone to claim that China *does* belong to and has a rightful role in the region. At the same time India insists that Indian and South Asian security cannot be organized without taking into account China's proximity, intrusiveness, and capabilities. So New Delhi argues that India's conventional and nuclear decisions are in part tied to Chinese capabilities and therefore that China (as well as other outsiders) must be part of a larger process of arms control. On the other hand, Pakistan claims that Indian insistence on an expanded arms control regime is a way to deflect attention from the possibility of regional security agreements and that regional arms control is possible. The view of Beijing lies somewhere between these two. It rejects the idea that China is a South Asian power, and it refuses to be involved in South Asian arms control agreements even though it is willing to help facilitate cooperation in the region.[34]

Thus for different reasons and in different ways India and Pakistan want security arrangements that take account of or involve China. China, by contrast, does not want to be too involved in South Asian affairs. It has got most of what it wanted from South Asia, namely, the absence of a serious rival, improved links to Xinjiang and Tibet, and recognition of its position in Tibet. Moreover, its primary security concerns are Japan, Taiwan, the Koreas, Russia, central Asia, and Southeast Asia. Chinese force structuring will be driven by this latter environment rather than by South Asia. To the extent that it is and to the extent that Beijing is unmindful of South Asian insecurities, China will constitute a serious problem for notions of cooperative security in the subcontinent.

Apart from China, South Asians will be watching neighboring regions in Asia. The Gulf and the Middle East consist of many militarily significant and ambitious powers—most prominently, Iran, Iraq, Saudi Arabia, Syria, Egypt, and Israel. How the proliferation of missiles, nuclear capability, and chemical weapons, confidence building, and the broader peace process are handled will either loosen or tighten the pressure on South Asians. The recent Israel-PLO agreement has revived the discussion in South Asia of serious negotiations over the most contentious regional issues, and with the election of Benazir Bhutto, their prospects seem to have improved. But there is still deep resistance in both India and Pakistan over discussions, let alone compromises, on the Kashmir and proliferation issues.[35] Similarly, South Asians, even as they try to deepen their links with central Asia, are mindful of how proliferation, confidence building, and peace are being managed in this new region. If there are delays and hitches, for instance, in asserting complete control over FSU nuclear weapons in the central Asian republics, South Asians will only harden their stand against proliferation efforts aimed at the subcontinent. Developments in Southeast and Northeast Asia will also be consequential. The steady growth of the Japanese defense forces, the North Korean nuclear program, the possibility of Korean unification, and the increasing size and sophistication of the military capabilities of various members of the Association of South East Asian Nations have all been noticed in South Asia and particularly in India.

What this watchfulness within South Asia suggests is that the appropriate scope of cooperative security may already be Asia itself rather than individual Asian regions. The Soviet Union, as early as 1969, had envisaged continent-wide "Asian collective security." The question is, should cooperative security build upward from regional agreements or should it immediately proceed to a continentwide level? Or, indeed, is it conceivable to pursue a parallel and simultaneous process, regional *and* continental? It is beyond the scope of this chapter to attempt an answer, but this is an important procedural matter to be considered in discussions of cooperative security.

Conclusion: The United States, South Asia, and Cooperative Security

Although all the components are in place, the United States still does not have a policy toward South Asia, nor does it have a strategy that would address South Asia's role in the larger regional and global context. Since the end of the cold war, American policy in the region has been made on an issue-by-issue basis. For two years, human rights, nuclear proliferation, economic reform, narcotics, missile and space technology, and a miscellany of other issues have come and gone as the "issue of the week." A number of different bureaucracies, Congress, and some interest groups each press "its" particular cause on a government distracted by events in Europe and more disturbed regions. With the absence of a cold war framework to force compromise and order priorities, American policy has drifted badly. This drift is paradoxical, since American influence in South Asia has never been greater. Both Indian and Pakistani leaders see the United States as the "sole superpower," and both are eager to expand cooperation with Washington. Furthermore, many of the ideas about regional confidence building and arms control that were introduced into the region by American policymakers in the 1980s have begun to take root.

With the end of the cold war the following changes in U.S. policy toward the region could be instituted as preliminary steps toward cooperative security arrangements. These changes relate to policy organization, treaties, dialogue, issues, and attitudes with respect to South Asia.

First, until recently it was clear that the United States was not *organized* to pursue a more active diplomacy of any sort toward South Asia. But in 1991 the Department of State was required to establish a new Bureau of South Asian Affairs, and now three senior officials are available to do the work that one was doing before. It is now possible for the U.S. government to pursue several interests in the region simultaneously (proliferation, human rights, economic reform, and strategic policy, to name only four). In addition to the reorganization of the foreign policy bureaucracy dealing with South Asia, Congress must keep up pressure on the State Department to use the new resources available in formulating and implementing a more comprehensive regional policy.

Second, existing *treaty* arrangements with Pakistan must be recast and new ones developed for India in order to promote a larger framework for cooperative security. America's formal commitments to Pakistan are based on 1954 and 1959 treaties that are anticommunist. They contain no commitments of any sort to India. A new set of treaties, perhaps in the form of "peace and friendship" agreements, would help frame a new policy of cooperative security. Above all, these treaties must formalize what has been American policy for nearly forty-five years: that Washington has an interest in promoting regional strategic cooperation between South Asia's two main powers.

Third, the strategic *dialogue* between the United States and India and Pakistan has been fitful and erratic. A policy of cooperative strategy requires regular, intensive, and serious consultation between American strategists, on the one hand, and Indians and Pakistanis, on the other. At the present time, an irregular series of bilateral U.S.-Indian defense talks are held under the sponsorship of the National Defense University. Pakistanis have expressed an interest in joining these talks. They should be invited, and the dialogue should acquire a more official side by introducing regular policy planning talks among Washington, New Delhi, and Islamabad.

Fourth, the United States must recognize that its relations with the major South Asian states will always be composed of a number of issues, which will assume greater and lesser priority over the years. These include proliferation, the promotion of regional confidence-building and arms control measures, joint action with regard to regional and extraregional threats to American interests, and such nonsecurity issues as narcotics, human rights, and economic reform. Furthermore, Washington must realize that its perception of the rank-order importance of these issues may not match up with New Delhi's or Islamabad's. Thus American policymakers must learn how to better balance and coordinate the country's South Asian interests. Recent history demonstrates vividly that pressing either country too hard on any single issue is counterproductive. In most cases there are Indians and Pakistanis who share American perspectives, even on proliferation, and there are lively national debates over policy choices. In dealing with fellow democracies in South Asia, as in Europe, the United States must guard against hurting its friends. Finally, American policymakers should not be frightened off by the task of tailoring this package of policies to South Asia. Cooperative security must accommodate genuine regional variations and differences. American interests will not be exactly the same in all regions. A South Asia "package" of policies designed to further cooperative security arrangements will look somewhat different from a package of policies designed for Northeast Asia or the Middle East.

Finally, recall the characterization of South Asia at the beginning of this chapter. Because of historical and cultural differences, Americans have unusually distorted perceptions of South Asia—just as South Asians carry around in their minds some bizarre and inaccurate perceptions of the United States. Harold Isaacs wrote of these American misperceptions and distortions nearly thirty years ago.[36] If anything they have since become worse. One could perhaps tolerate these stereotypes at the height of the cold war on the ground that American policy toward South Asia was steered largely by calculations of superpower competition. But now that competition has ended, and the United States finds itself, for the first time in fifty years, in a world made up of many powers, not one made up of close friends and deadly enemies. America is competing with former allies and cooperating with former antagonists. South Asia falls into neither category—but neither does much of the rest of the world. Perhaps the greatest challenge for those who would advocate a global strategy of cooperative security is to understand such regions on their own terms, as neither tight ally nor implacable enemy.

Notes

1. During the Afghan war Washington loosely or tacitly coordinated South Asia policy with China.

2. Democracy and peace are apparently strongly correlated: democractic states seem rarely to fight each other (though they are not so inhibited with respect to nondemocractic states). There are no very convincing explanations of this correlation. Our point simply is that democracy per se is a value that the international community should support as far as possible. The best-known philosophical explanation is Immanuel Kant's, resurrected most recently by Michael W. Doyle, "Liberalism and World Politics," *American Political Science Review,* vol. 80 (December 1986), pp. 1151–69.

3. Most of these episodes in India-Pakistan relations are dealt with in Charles Heimsath and Surjit Mansingh, *A Diplomatic History of Modern India* (Bombay: Allied Publishers, 1971); and Sisir Gupta, *India and Regional Integration in Asia* (London: Asia Publishing House, 1964).

4. Gupta, *India and Regional Integration,* pp. 72–75.

5. This account leaves out several agreements: on the treatment and problems of refugees of "minority communities," on the division of prepartition assets, on the Indus Rivers (1960) and Salal Dam (1978), and on the rationalization of borders. Heimsath and Mansingh, *Diplomatic History of Modern India,* observe that "despite difficulties presented by the Indo-Pakistani disputes arising from the partition, all of them save Kashmir were totally or partially solved by negotiated compromises and, in one case, by arbitration. The achievements thereby recorded leave an impression of constructive diplomatic endeavor less often publicized than the unhappy dealings over Kashmir" (p. 142).

6. The best account of regional efforts to cooperate is Gupta, *India and Regional Integration,* pp. 28–84.

7. Ibid., pp. 75–77.

8. Ibid., pp. 38–45.

9. Ibid., pp. 45–48.

10. Ibid., pp. 51–53, 63–68.

11. The exception was Pakistani involvement in SEATO and CENTO as well its membership with Iran and Turkey in the RCD. After the 1971 war India too seems to have been interested in some form of regional cooperation or "confederation" with at least Bangladesh, Bhutan, Nepal, and Pakistan. However, the assassination of President Mujibur Rahman in Bangladesh and Indira Gandhi's growing domestic problems, among other things, put an end to the idea. On the post-1971 confederal idea, see *Far Eastern Economic Review,* vol. 75 (January 22, 1972), p. 6, and vol. 75 (February 12, 1972), pp. 18–19.

12. H. V. Hodson, *The Great Divide: Britain-India-Pakistan* (London: Hutchinson, 1969), deals with British efforts to maintain some form of defensive unity and cooperation in the subcontinent. After 1965 Britain retreated from the region. Its last cooperative involvement in subcontinental affairs was in 1978 over India-Bangladesh river water problems. See B. M. Abbas, *The Ganges Water Dispute* (New Delhi: Vikas Publishing, 1982), p. 105.

13. The RCD's original membership was—and remained—Iran, Pakistan, and Turkey. After the Shah's overthrow, the RCD was revived as the Economic Cooperation Organization. For more information on Iran's involvement with India and Pakistan, see Sushma Gupta, *Pakistan As a Factor in Indo-Iranian Relations, 1947–78* (New Delhi: S. Chand, 1988); and S. D. Muni and Anuradha Muni, *Regional Cooperation in South Asia* (New Delhi: National Publishing House, 1984), pp. 20–21. For more recent Iranian proposals, see K. P. Nayar, "MoU with Iran Gives India Access to ECO," *Economic Times* (New Delhi), September 23, 1993, 1993, p. 1; and "India, Iran Sign MoU on Gas Pipeline Project," *Hindustan Times* (New Delhi), November 19, 1993, p. 12.

14. Gupta, *Pakistan As a Factor in Indo-Iranian Relations,* chap. 8.

15. In 1951 India signed a mutual defense assistance agreement with the United States, and in 1958 it indicated its acceptance of the terms of the 1954 Mutual Security Act. The two agreements were necessary under U.S. law for purchases of American arms and receipt of American economic assistance, but were apparently of no great political significance. See Heimsath and Mansingh, *Diplomatic History of Modern India,* p. 352.

16. S. Nihal Singh, *The Yogi and the Bear: Story of Indo-Soviet Relations* (Riverdale, Md.: Riverdale, 1986), pp. 76–79.

17. For a fuller exposition of this cooperation, see Stephen P. Cohen, "Superpower Cooperation in South Asia," in Roger E. Kanet and Edward A. Kolodziej, eds., *The Cold War as Cooperation* (Johns Hopkins University Press, 1991), pp. 281–309.

18. The report of this Russian-American study group is available from the Asia Society, New York, or the Oriental Institute, Moscow. A coauthor of this chapter (Cohen) was a member of the study group.

19. The growing literature on international cooperation contains a whole range of arguments about the attractions and possibilities as well as the disadvantages and difficulties of cooperation in political and security areas. See among others, Robert Jervis, "Security Regimes," in Stephen D. Krasner, ed., *International Regimes* (Cornell University Press, 1983), pp. 173–94; Janice Gross Stein, "Detection and Defection: Security 'Regimes' and the Management of International Conflict," *International Journal,* vol. 40 (Autumn 1985), pp. 599–627; the essays in Kenneth A. Oye, ed., *Cooperation under Anarchy* (Princeton University Press, 1986); Joanne Gowa, "Anarchy, Egoism, and Third Images: *The Evolution of Cooperation* and International Relations," *International Organization,* vol. 40 (Winter 1986), pp. 167–86; and Joseph Grieco, "Anarchy and the Limits of Cooperation: A Realist Critique of the Newest Liberal Institutionalism," *International Organization,* vol. 42 (Summer 1988), pp. 485–507.

20. The relationship among interdependence, transnational relations, and the constraints on war is discussed at great length in Norman Angell, *The Great Illusion: A Study of the Relation of Military Power in Nations to Their Economic and Social Advantage* (Putnam, 1911). For a fundamental critique of "idealists" such as Angell, see Edward Hallett Carr, *The Twenty Years' Crisis, 1919–1939* (Harper and Row, 1964).

21. South Asia is unique among regions in this respect. No other region has this geographic structure. Although we present it as an impediment, the Indocentricity of the region also means that a more or less dramatic change in Indian policies or attitudes could at one stroke imply major improvements in South Asian security. The coming to power of the Janata government in 1977 and of the V. P. Singh government in 1989 certainly held out such possibilities.

22. S. K. Modwel and R. K. Pandey, "SAARC-ASEAN Trade: Possibilities of Expansion and Diversification," in Bhabani Sen Gupta, ed., *SAARC-ASEAN: Prospects and Problems of Inter-Regional Cooperation* (New Delhi: South Asian Publishers, 1988), estimate that between 1980 and 1985, for instance, intraregional trade as a proportion of the total volume of the region's trade actually fell from 3.29 to 2.47 percent. A more recent estimate is that intraregional exports are less than 3 percent of total regional exports and intraregional imports amount to 1.8 percent of total regional imports. See Y. P. Pant, *Trade and Cooperation in South Asia: A Nepalese Perspective* (New Delhi: Vikas Publishing, 1991), p. 22.

23. On hydropolitics in the Middle East, see Thomas Naff and Ruth C. Matson, eds., *Water in the Middle East: Conflict or Cooperation* (Boulder, Colo.: Westview Press, 1984). A cross-regional study is Arun P. Elhance, *Hydropolitics in the Third World* (Washington: United States Institute of Peace, forthcoming).

24. On the possibilities for as well as problems of South Asian economic and hydrological cooperation, see Bimal Prasad, ed., *Regional Cooperation in South Asia: Problems and Prospects* (New Delhi: Vikas Publishing, 1989); M. Abdul Hafiz and Iftekharuzzaman, eds., *South Asian Regional Cooperation: A Socio-Economic Approach to Peace and Stability* (Dhaka: Bangladesh Institute of International and Strategic Studies, 1985); and B. G. Verghese, *Waters of Hope: Integrated Water Resource Development and Regional Cooperation within the Himalayan-Ganga-Brahmaputra-Barak Basin* (New Delhi: Oxford and IBH Publishing, 1990).

25. K. Subrahmanyam has made this argument forcefully, for instance, in his "India and Its Neighbors: A Conceptual Framework of Peaceful Coexistence," in U. S. Bajpai, ed., *India and Its Neighborhood* (New Delhi: Lancer International, 1986), pp. 109–39. See also S. D. Muni, "South Asian Relations, Bilateral and Regional," in Leo E. Rose and Eric Gonsalves, eds., *Towards a New World Order: Adjusting India-US Relations* (Berkeley: University of California, Institute of East Asian Studies, 1992), pp. 45–56.

26. The dispute between India and Pakistan over the fate of Kashmir has been ongoing since the British withdrawal from the region in 1947. Under the original British partition plan, princely states like Kashmir were to have the option of joining either India or Pakistan, depending on their location, language, and other factors. Kashmir borders on both India and Pakistan; although its population is predominately Muslim, its army and aristocracy were Hindu. When a Muslim rebellion aimed at uniting Kashmir with Pakistan broke out in 1947, the ruler of Kashmir acceded to India and requested Indian troops to defend against rebel and nomadic Muslim forces. This defense escalated into a major conflict that was ended by a UN-arranged cease-fire in 1949. India maintained that, by virtue of the maharaja's accession, Kashmir was legally Indian, whereas Pakistan contended that, under the terms of the cease-fire, a plebiscite must be held to allow the Kashmiris to determine their own fate. Such a plebiscite was not held, and Kashmir has remained under dispute ever since. For a detailed description of the roots of the Kashmir conflict, see Sisir Gupta, *Kashmir, a Study in India-Pakistan Relations* (Bombay: Asia Publishing House, 1966).

27. Geoffrey Kemp, in his assessment of cooperative security in the Middle East in chapter 10, makes a similar point: In contrast to Europe, "Secure and accepted legal boundaries remain another key source of antagonism in the Middle East." He also argues that "although . . . arms control issues may have some utility . . . so far no movement has been made toward serious negotiations. Arms control is more often perceived by countries in the region as hindering their own military capabilities, including capabilities that regional powers and their outside suppliers believe are necessary for self-defense and stability."

28. W. P. S. Sidhu, "Siachen: The Forgotten War," *India Today,* May 31, 1992, pp. 58–71, is a superb account of the strategic rationale, the fighting, the military difficulties, and the economic and human costs of the glacier war.

29. India also responded to the Sri Lankan government's request for military help in combatting the Jatika Vimukthi Peramuna party insurgents in 1971. More recently Indian troops quelled a coup attempt against the Gayoom government in the Maldives.

30. It has been estimated that in the recent past as much as 60 percent of India's army has been deployed for internal security. This estimate was disclosed by General Gurbir Mansingh, formerly of the Indian army, in a personal conversation with Kanti Bajpai.

31. In December 1986 a massive Indian military exercise along its western border and a smaller Pakistani exercise caused alarm in both capitals. By January 1987 war seemed imminent. It took the two sides three months to agree on how to manage the withdrawal of forces from the border and several months to carry out the withdrawal.

32. In January 1992 they exchanged a list of nuclear facilities and their coordinates as part of an agreement not to attack such facilities. They have also agreed to prior notification of major military exercises and of measures to prevent intrusions into each other's air space. India is also involved in a confidence-building process with China, with which it has agreed to a number of measures.

33. See Stephen P. Cohen, ed., *Nuclear Proliferation in South Asia: The Prospects for Arms Control* (Boulder, Colo.: Westview Press, 1991).

34. The remarks of Professor Luo Renshi of the Beijing Institute of International Strategic Studies at a conference on South Asian nuclear proliferation are revealing. See the conference commentary by Nazir Kamal in *Strategic Studies,* vols. 10 and 11 (Summer and Autumn 1987), p. 156.

35. For a recent discussion of a South Asian peace process, see Stephen P. Cohen, "Solutions for Security," *India Today,* May 15, 1993; for a Pakistani view on the prospects of accommodation in the region, see Moonis Ahmar, "Indo-Pakistan Normalization Process: The Role of CBMs in the Post-Cold War Era," Occasional Paper, University of Illinois at Urbana, Program in Arms Control, Disarmament, and International Security, October, 1993.

36. See Harold Robert Isaacs, *Scratches on Our Minds: American Images of China and India* (New York: John Day, 1958). A more recent set of views on Indian and American relations and images of each other is given in Harold A. Gould and Sumit Ganguly, eds., *The Hope and the Reality: US-Indian Relations from Roosevelt to Reagan* (Boulder, Colo.: Westview Press, 1992).

THIRTEEN

The Collapsing State and International Security

Alex Rondos

THIS CHAPTER focuses on the nonmilitary threats to security that must be taken into account in devising a cooperative security regime in the post–cold war era. The eruptions of ethnic or religious violence in the former Soviet bloc and the Balkans are dramatic variations of a trend, best described as the retreat of the traditional sovereign state, a trend that has been emerging in much of the rest of the third world for well over a decade.[1] The central proposition of this chapter is that some of the greatest threats to international security in the future will result from the absence of legitimate sovereignty, manifested in collapsing central governments and accompanied by the rise of new and previously outlawed forces in politics, such as religion and ethnicity. In many instances these changes will result in civil conflict, more than likely drawing in neighboring states and perhaps the international community as a whole.

Thus far the West has proved unable to reconstitute its operational foreign policy in recognition of this new reality. Western failure to palliate the brutal consequences of war in Yugoslavia or to articulate a well-defined policy on regional wars in the former Soviet Union (concurrent with heightened attention paid to remaining nuclear weapons there) illustrates the fact that, rather than address new threats to security, policymakers have simply reconfigured models from the cold war. Containing the threat of a resurgent Russia, coupled with promoting Western modes of democracy and free market enterprise to foster stability, rank among the highest U.S. priorities.[2] Although the threats of nuclear war or large-scale conventional attack are negligible, U.S. foreign policy planning nevertheless maintains that the chief security threats are largely military. Because of accelerated disintegration in regions that were formerly frozen into cold war totalitarianism, it is still not clear how the West will cope with the ensuing instability.

A major weakness of traditional Western policy in distributing aid has been the continued insistence on funneling resources through heads of state and their attendant organizations even when those institutions and leaders no longer possess the control, ability, or conviction to provide the public with basic services. In other cases, such as in the former Yugoslavia, collective organizations have chosen to deliver aid independently rather than exploit indigenous organizations such as churches that have a more thorough understanding of the political situation on the ground. Finally, when the United States has chosen unofficial channels through which to exercise influence, more often than not it has supported military organizations that have not held humanitarian concerns as a priority. In sum, the West's failure to develop a more nuanced, sophisticated, and ultimately successful approach to deal with political disintegration stems from the inability of leaders to make the intellectual leap from operating in a secular state-based system to developing relief policies appropriate for political systems in the midst of chaos and collapse. Ethnic and religious tensions require solutions designed for a specific social context that maximize the influence of local regimes.[3]

Constructing policy that addresses the new nonmilitary threats to security will require a cooperative effort either to build flexibility into existing institutions or to create new organizations that can provide aid principally through nongovernmental agencies that now inevitably fill the social services void once a government is near or in the midst of collapse. This may mean embracing organizations that have previously been considered inimical to Western ideals of secularism, such as traditional Eastern Orthodox and African churches. Although such an approach will no doubt require a dramatic shift in Western thinking about how to protect what are deemed essential Western values, a more open approach could potentially preserve stability more effectively in many war-torn regions and reduce human suffering in these areas as well.

What will replace the void created by a retreating state-based security system is central to a definition of the kind of new security regime that is sought. There are international instruments and collective experience on which to build coordinated security policy that could perhaps preempt, or at least contain, the consequences of erosion and changing political and economic systems. Collective intervention in states where complete collapse of government has occurred should be characterized by goals of enduring political reconstruction and stability, not just temporary solutions.[4]

Overwhelmed by the burden of their financial commitments and attendant debts, a succession of governments have been forced to withdraw from economic and social roles they had once claimed as their monopoly. In so doing, they have had to relinquish the costly and centralized political patronage that had been the glue of the allegiance upon which they survived. The retreating economic state has also created a vacuum in social services, a vacuum now being readily filled by previously rejected socioeconomic forces—religion, ethnic associations, and privately organized economic interests—that have succeeded in capitalizing politically on the failure of the state.[5] The revival of ethnic solidarity in Africa, for example, has been paralleled by the revival of religious organizations in the Middle East as the purveyor of health, economic subsistence, and education. The former communist states of the eastern bloc live with similar socioeconomic dynamics. Economic and political bankruptcy at the state level, in short, has entailed an unofficial rewriting of the social contract in much of the third world and the former Soviet bloc.[6]

When the transition from autocratic and centralized rule to decentralized, democratic, and pluralistic society fails, civil order typically collapses. Although the similarities between Africa's civil wars and those simmering in the former eastern bloc or the Middle East should not be drawn too closely, the experience of dealing with the threat to international security of imminent social collapse, the nature of feasible intervention, and the eventual reconstruction of these societies will form a central pillar of any new global cooperative security system. The challenge then is to draw on all available experience to elaborate a coordinated system of international cooperation to help societies long asphyxiated by central control, brutalized by war, or militarized for generations to achieve internal cohesion and legitimate government.

The Source and Process of Disintegration

The cycle of debt, decaying government infrastructure, and declining political allegiance has preoccupied the Western donor community in dealing with the third world since the late 1970s. In Africa and the Middle East, the crisis was initially viewed as an economic one, to which macroeconomic policy solutions could be applied. With the intrusion of more purely political dimensions of economic policy reform, the character of reform initiatives was forced to shift, requiring a more nuanced approach able to embrace political and social challenges engendered by the reform process.[7] The economic crisis of the former Soviet Union (FSU) is a chronologically telescoped and politically more potent version of a decade of experience in the third world. In this instance a highly urbanized and educated public is being forced to withstand the shock of economic austerity within an increasingly diffuse and unfamiliar democratic political context.

In the parlance of the World Bank, the changes being prescribed to most debtor nations have become known as "structural adjustment." Any further loans provided by established lending institutions, in other words, are increasingly to be contingent upon evidence of dramatic improvement in government economic and financial management. The 1980s witnessed a rapid multiplication of such structural adjustment loans, and by 1992 these arrangements were being executed in more than fifty countries. For the recipient government, budgets were to be balanced, exchange rates rationalized, and official subsidies for food, transport, and electricity cut to accommodate greater efficiency. Unproductive state sector corporations were to be sold to the private sector or eliminated if it was perceived that there was no potential for profit. New laws to promote this form of economic "liberalization" have as a result given far greater autonomy to fledgling private sectors, enhancing access to credit and other resources.[8]

When it became apparent over time that the effects of these policies, including unemployment and declining access to food and essential commodities, would be a politically unpalatable consequence of the reform programs, safety net mechanisms were introduced. Donors decided to contribute to a "hardship" fund, usually controlled by the government and targeted to assist the affected social groups.

The theory behind these policy changes is that a deregulated economy with well-directed injections of external finance and technical assistance, in conjunction with a willing local government, would be accompanied by the simultaneous expansion of a healthier private sector. Increasing private wealth, in turn, would create more taxable revenue. A regulatory environment that was no longer capricious and disruptive of commerce would attract foreign investors and bring back exported hard currency. Thus governments would be left with only a few of the essential tasks of providing essential services to the marginal and indigent.

In practice, things have not gone entirely according to plan. The local reality among most recipients is that governments are being invited to eliminate the system of patronage that guaranteed political allegiance in otherwise nondemocratic political systems. Bloated state-sector bureaucracies had always meant patronage jobs. Cheap or free education, health services, and subsidized food cemented allegiance to governments among the urban populace.

The violent outbursts of political opposition in various regions, especially the Middle East and Africa, have served as frightening reminders to governments of how perilous their position can become if they are perceived to be serving the wishes of their external creditors too closely. For example, in 1977 when the Egyptian government tried to decrease subsidies for certain agricultural staples, including some kinds of flour, sugar, and rice, in compliance with International Monetary Fund regulations concerning prescribed public deficit limits, major riots broke out all along the Nile Valley, most severely in Cairo and Alexandria.[9] Ever since then, the government of Egypt has found numerous ways to subtly extend subsidies that it acknowledges are financially crippling to the overall economy. The price of bread in Egypt may no longer rise as such, but the size of the loaf continues to diminish. Similar riots broke out in Venezuela when the government tried to impose a draconian austerity program.

Riots over price increases aside, the real political threat to stability lies in the structural detachment of populations from their traditional dependency on government and the attendant increases in various kinds of nongovernmental or private initiative that can prove disruptive to social cohesion. As currently practiced, official economic reform is all about improving government bookkeeping and ensuring that budgets are balanced. But the stark truth is that any government in need of such managerial correctives is likely to be a government that has already undergone the kind of transformation that has marginalized the majority of the population, and one that survives on scant political loyalty. In most societies—and this is now becoming true in significant parts of the FSU—economic survival for most of the population is largely unrelated to any government initiative.

The vacuum of power created by the retreating state role is being filled by alternative forms of social organizations through which an increasingly desperate population has sought recourse. The drug-related coca trade of Latin America, the shift from export crops to household crops in Africa, and the massive default of debts owed to government purchasing agencies in the Russian Federation are economic illustrations of what practitioners of humanitarian relief and economic development refer to as coping or survival mechanisms. Lost in most analyses of the phenomenon are the political consequences for a society that develops its own survival mechanisms independently of government. Survival sought by autonomous means invariably entails alternative political and social organization that, the record suggests, is likely to be provided by religion, ethnic association, or private economic interest groups.

To date the social impact of economic reforms and the retreating state has been insufficiently understood, especially by donors. The explosion of nongovernmental initiatives, bringing communities together to achieve a particular social or economic purpose, is one of the unheralded and so far only anecdotally documented developments of the last decade. These new social groupings are responding spontaneously to the decline in public services, whether they are religious or secular, village communities, other ethnic groups, or particular economic interests. Although the consequences may be similar across regions, the causes of this phenomenon are different in the Middle East—Egypt especially—from those in Africa. The former has suffered from an excess of government even as economic liberalization has been attempted—not unlike that in the eastern bloc—whereas Africa's real crisis has been the relative absence of organized and responsible government.

The rise of the mosque as the provider of essential social services to a growing proportion of the population has been a decisive political factor in Egypt in the last few years. The charitable tradition of Islam has always been strong, but never before has the mosque become so complete an alternative to official political and social organization, providing health services, schooling, and financial assistance. This change is a direct consequence of the government cutting back its previously comprehensive social programs. A similar trend has emerged in the Egyptian Christian community.

To the government, these developments were seen as an unpalatable necessity. Not only did the government, which has always clung to its secular constitutionality, fear the erosion of support in favor of religious groups, but it was equally disturbed over the establishment of philanthropic empires, camouflaged as charity but designed to enhance the message of radical Islam.

It should have come as no surprise in early November 1992 that, after months of clashes between militant Muslim groups and the government, Egyptian security forces shut down most mosque-based charitable activities on the ground that these centers were being used to foment sedition.[10] In the process hundreds of thousands were and will be left without access to essential services; it is likely that they will also be more inclined to lend a favorable ear to the imam than to the minister of the interior. Similar trends have been apparent in Algeria, Tunisia, Jordan, and most strikingly in the Israeli-occupied territories, where the recent signing of the Israel–Palestine Liberation Organization accord has led to heightened tensions and increasing violence between the PLO and the militant Palestinian group Hamas.[11]

Some tentative comparisons of these conditions can be made to those in Russia and the other states of the FSU, where the stability of the government and thus both internal and international security are being threatened by the consequences of a drastic decline in living standards, by the impact of demilitarization and demobilization, and by the impending influx of Russian nationals from the peripheral republics.

As in key states in the Middle East and Africa, price liberalization in Russia has shattered the standard of living and has led to a rapid decline in the availability of social services to which Russians had become accustomed and to rapidly growing unemployment.[12] Since the price liberalization of January 1992 in the Russian Federation, an increasing percentage of household income is spent on food, largely because of the relative rise in the price of goods compared with household income. Between the end of 1991 and the end of 1992, for example, consumer prices increased by more than 2,300 percent, and by March 1993 real wages were only 50 percent of fourth-quarter 1991 levels. The use of hospitals and day care centers (a critical indicator for an urbanized society in which most women work) has declined as these institutions have imposed service charges.[13]

A refugee crisis of massive proportions also beckons. With more than 25 million Russians residing in the central Asian republics, Georgia, Armenia, Ukraine, and the Baltics, the Russian government has had to deal with international pressures to withdraw troops—a condition of outside assistance—while facing a growing threat from domestic political opponents who accuse the government of abandoning its own nationals. Irredentism is an unlikely option in the short term. But the political impact of a vast migration of Russians who feel politically abandoned linking up with legions of demobilized troops who find themselves condemned to life in a civilian sector with few employment opportunities could provide grist for the mill of extreme political opportunists.[14]

However daunting, the statistics still dehumanize the magnitude and character of the crisis and do not fully capture the threat to social stability. In addition to incipient famine and inevitable social disorder, there are other indicators of impending catastrophe that must be tracked. When the financier Jacques Necker warned Louis XVI that "la peur de la disette, crée la disette," he described a reality—that fear of hunger creates hunger, and thus foments political disorder—that is timeless.[15] The fear of a future that holds no viable alternative for families that see budgets shrinking, meals diminishing, and health at risk is present in much of Russia. It is now undeniable that the state—the "victualer of last resort"—is unable to carry out even fundamental obligations to a society accustomed to comprehensive free social care, feeding, shelter, warmth, transportation, and education.

It is the magnitude of the mental leap from comprehensive social security to comprehensive insecurity that may ultimately cause the greatest threats to international security. The cold war may have been won in Western eyes, but to the average citizen of the FSU the current environment simply heralds a grim reality in which both the infrastructure of society and the superstructure of a belief in a social contract have been swept away and not yet replaced by any viable alternative. These conditions engender cynicism, panic, and a potential willingness to succumb to any variety of political and economic panacea peddled by extremists.[16] By contrast, an African farmer, who knows that every year might bring famine, is far better prepared for such conditions. He or she possesses from experience the mental and physical mechanisms with which to attempt to cope. The average Russian simply does not. To evoke Stalingrad during World War II as a precedent inevitably invites the cynical rejoinder that the Great Patriotic War also cost 20 million lives.

Not only does the Russian public face the material reality of rapid impoverishment, it is also being rapidly and dangerously stratified. Already haunted by mass poverty with no safety net, Russians are now being invited to participate in an economic adventure in moving toward free enterprise that will create greater social inequality. To embark on this adventure is an extraordinary leap of faith for a society that had been able to cling to at least the illusion of equal access to the essential services needed for survival. The deprivations of the past aside, the Russian worker will now earn less and enjoy many fewer social amenities than those nuclear scientists who are being targeted for aid by a security-conscious West. Their ranks will be joined by demobilized troops and officers who have no clear alternative employment. A small though growing sector of relatively affluent entrepreneurs will inevitably become visible symbols of the new system. The latter already are heralded in the West as examples of the new success of a liberalized economy. But they will also be held accountable by the masses, who are likely to succumb to the darker politics of resentment nourished by poverty.

Russia has experienced a vastly underreported expansion of nongovernmental initiatives similar to that experienced in other developing regions. Small unofficial organizations attempting to address a myriad of social and economic crises have emerged. Concerns range from coping with the homeless and the destitute to managing hospitals and providing for private medical care to establishing financial schemes to start up small businesses. Many of these groups display traits that are unique to a society with the experience of a highly centralized and oppressive government, including an inbred mistrust of the motives of others and a suspicion of any initiative that is too large and centralized, for fear that it could be co-opted by the state bureaucracy.[17]

The emergence of religion as an organizing force in Russia has also become more evident. The Russian Orthodox Church, though financially weakened, is now seen as one of the main sources of social assistance. The prerevolutionary tradition of brotherhoods and sisterhoods that carried out much of the social work in imperial Russia is being revived. The challenge to the church and to many other social organizations now is to retain financial and political independence in a country where the habit of ubiquitous government control still runs deep.[18]

Russia may not yet be Weimar, but neither should it be considered the latest and largest Lego set in the economist's playpen. Whether countries in the midst of transition from highly centralized economic systems and authoritarian political regimes to deregulated and demilitarized democratic pluralism will achieve this goal will rest to a large extent on the coordinated will of the international system to shepherd so momentous and complex a process. At the very least one could argue that these countries represent a threat of imminent disorder that can be averted. It can only be averted, however, if the structural and political causes of disorder are understood and if in turn this understanding serves as the underpinning for Western economic and political strategies. Such strategies must fully reflect and accommodate the domestic realities of recipient countries. Policies that appear mechanistic or apolitical, by contrast—from economic reform to the promotion of democracy to denuclearization—are bound to fail.

Civil Violence As an International Security Problem

Civil conflicts, the symptom of collapse of civil order, represent a new and particular challenge in the post–cold war era. The demise of the Soviet bloc radically altered the environment in which civil conflicts occur. Neither West nor East now has a reason for competitive intervention in such conflicts, nor a reason to prevent multilateral approaches to their resolution. As such, the ensuing and anticipated outburst of civil conflicts in the former eastern bloc, let alone those that have festered in many other parts of the world, are challenging some of the fundamental assumptions that guided international security policy during the cold war.

There has always been a latent contradiction between the principles of self-determination and the sanctity of frontiers, even those bequeathed by empires.[19] The conflict between the two was contained during the last forty-five years by the adherence of the international system to traditional tenets of sovereignty. Governments, new or old, competent or incompetent, could claim protection behind the veil of sovereignty if at any time their legitimacy was threatened. The calculus of the cold war dictated that such governments could turn to one bloc or another with a fair guarantee of gaining support.

This assumption no longer holds true. The explosion of age-old tensions, incubated during the imposition of imperial or communist order, has undermined many traditional assumptions about sovereignty. Regional politics, ethno-religious influences, international communications, the diffusion of military capabilities globally, and most recently the ascending importance of international humanitarian intervention are influences that transcend national boundaries, help shape the course of civil conflicts, and redefine the scope of international security challenges.

In an international order of increasingly regionalized power blocs, the visceral ties of ethnicity and religion that transcend boundaries are compelling governments to seek new forms of activism when civil conflicts occur. This phenomenon is not new or transitory and should not be underestimated in its consequences for security policies. Unprepared for these transformations, however, the Western policy debate about how to deal with civil conflict has tended to subordinate important regional political imperatives to a limited and quite simplistic discussion of whether the United States should serve in the role of global, muscular humanitarian—in Somalia, for example—or of militarized umpire, as the Europeans would have it in Bosnia.

The international community has a legacy of experience with intervention to stem civil conflict that can be instructive in the current debate. On more than one occasion in the late 1970s and again in the early 1980s the Organization of African Unity created a peacekeeping force to try to preserve stability in Chad.[20] Almost a decade later, when the Liberian government was decimated by internal opposition and a rebel force representing oppressed ethnic groups imposed a siege on the capital, a West African peacekeeping force was dispatched to the country, albeit after much procrastination. In this case the collapse of a state was deemed by more influential countries in the region to be a severe enough threat to the regional security to warrant collective action. The rebellion in Liberia became particularly threatening when the ethnic disintegration led to waves of refugees migrating to and populating frontiers, alarming the government of Sierra Leone.[21] Similarly, the political vacuum in Chad coincided with a period of growing Libyan activism, which was enough to galvanize actions by the Nigerian government, always sensitive to the threat of imported Muslim-Christian antagonisms. In both cases a civil conflict, initiated for reasons cloaked in the language of self-determination, became a justification for a ferocious settling of ethnic accounts domestically and a perceived threat to regional stability.

The many different factors that led to intervention in each case reflect the complexity of those situations at both the domestic and regional levels. In addition to the desire to contain the scope of conflicts, suspicion between francophone and anglophone states proved to be a motive for intervention in both Chad and Liberia. Because France's influence over its former colonies has long antagonized countries such as Nigeria, it was partly to avoid yet another French military intervention that Nigeria was willing to push for an African peacekeeping force for Chad. Similarly, it was because of the perception that francophone states, notably the Ivory Coast and Burkina Faso, had aligned to support the rebellion in Liberia that Nigeria and other anglophone states undertook to set up a peacekeeping operation under the auspices of the Economic Community of West African States.[22] That France had once actively supported the dismemberment of Nigeria by recognizing Biafra and had used surrogate African countries such as the Ivory Coast and Gabon in the exercise has left a profound and lasting suspicion that explains the undercurrent of regional politics in this instance. To ignore these regional dynamics is, as one is discovering in the Balkans, to prescribe responses on the foundations of historical ignorance. Thus the chronological layers of animosity that have lain beneath the surface of Balkan politics during the last century attract concern and involvement.

The most potent ingredients of emerging civil conflicts are ethnicity and religion, two forces that the international security community does not much understand, conceptually and operationally. The two should not be separated, for they almost invariably coincide, constituting for many the basis of cultural identity. Every country that straddles the Sahara and sub-Saharan Africa has known some form of violence caused or fueled by religion and race. In Chad, Sudan, Mali, Mauritania, and even Ethiopia, the racial memory of nonblack Arab slave-raiders is all too recent in societies in which memory is richly and orally transmitted. Sub-Saharan non-Muslim Africans' fear of the imposition of *shari'a* (Islamic law), for example, has hung like the sword of Damocles over Nigerian politics and has been one cause of a bitter and catastrophic civil war in Sudan. President Leopold Senghor once even hinted that Mauritania, where a form of legalized slavery of black Africans exists, should be eliminated and that the territory should be divided between a black Senegalese state and a Muslim, Berber-Arab Morocco. Likewise, many Muslims have chafed under the oppressive rule of black leadership in Chad and Mali, which inherited power from the French at independence.

The disintegration of the former Yugoslavia is equally related to religious and national identity. Whatever the immediate political antecedents, the Croats and Serbs draw their identity from a history dating back to Ottoman and Habsburg rule, both periods that fused the ethnic and religious into one national identity. They represent the fault line between western and eastern Christendom, between Rome and Byzantium. The notion that religious persecution during the communist period bequeathed two secular nationalist forces that are now at war ignores the simple reality that in forging a new postcommunist identity, Serbs and Croats draw from the wellspring of the deep religious roots of their respective national histories.[23]

The potential role of Russia in the Yugoslav conflict is striking testimony to the new power of once outlawed, and all too easily ignored, transnational sentiments of this kind. Russia has deliberately distanced itself from the international condemnations of Serbia, a fellow Slavic and Orthodox Christian country. Given the power of nationalist forces in Russia, and their disappointment with the level of Western support in promoting economic and political transition, it was perhaps inevitable that the nationalist groups would pressure the government in Moscow to show sympathy for the Serbs.[24] For similar historical, religious, and regional reasons, Greece has risked being sanctioned by the West for its continued support of Serbia, and thus also adds to the complication of devising a legitimate multinational resolution to the crisis.[25]

If religion and ethnicity are the forces around which divisions are emerging in post–cold war civil conflicts, the vehicles by which they have effect are modern communications and arms. Muslims throughout the world are presented daily with a picture of Western (read Christian) inaction in the face of an obvious attempt to eliminate a Muslim minority in Bosnia. Beckoning on the Yugoslav horizon as of this writing, moreover, is the strong possibility of a Serbian attempt to "Serbianize" Kosovo, where the vast majority of the population is Albanian Muslim.[26] The pressure on governments of Muslim countries, to say nothing of Western governments, to help arm Bosnian Muslims grows as a consequence. This pressure is especially acute for governments of majority or exclusively Muslim countries that are already under severe pressure from elements of their populations who seek the imposition of a more orthodox Islam in their countries, as in Egypt. Their domestic situations, as such, are complicated by the political demands to demonstrate their concern for a Muslim minority in Europe. Moreover, to the Bosnian tragedy must now be added the trend of Muslim minorities fleeing the central Asian republics as former communist governments restore themselves in some new guise believed to pose a threat to Muslim interests.

Other aspects of civil conflict, including famine and mass migration, must also be considered a part of emerging security challenges. In the course of the last decade, the large-scale famines of Africa that have attracted international attention, such as those in Mozambique, Angola, Liberia, Sudan, Ethiopia, and

Somalia, have been caused by civil conflict. When cast in the international limelight and described by the media, massive deprivation and migration become "humanitarian disasters," usually prompting an explosion of international philanthropic initiatives. These initiatives have tended to be executed by a multitude of nongovernmental organizations, which, although they argue that their intervention is exclusively nonpartisan in purpose, nonetheless have a direct impact on the course of a conflict.

The images of starvation and torture in Bosnia, similarly, provoked an international outcry that is playing an integral part in the course of the conflict. Humanitarian initiatives, precisely because they represent an outpouring of public opinion, have thus come to influence the course of civil conflicts and elevate them to the international level. At issue is whether a relief operation is actually helping to prevent death or to protract war, or perhaps both.

Such operations are not inherently benign or necessarily apolitical. Relief agencies operating from the territory of the Ethiopian government in the 1970s were constantly accused of abetting the survival of the regime in Addis Ababa, for example. In a search for moral equivalency, some organizations opted to work on both sides of the conflict. As far as the course of this conflict was concerned, relief efforts encouraged political fragmentation rather than forced reconciliation, and permitted the two sides to allocate their own material and financial resources to the prosecution of war rather than to the saving of lives.[27]

The extraordinary expansion of nongovernmental initiatives working through local indigenous nongovernmental channels now constitutes a significant new element in civil conflicts. The frustration of these efforts, often because of obstruction by warring parties, has resulted in a gradual redefinition of the role of military force in humanitarian initiatives. Indeed, sovereignty is even being redefined in the face of a massive abuse of human rights in civil conflicts.[28]

Even beyond these difficult questions is the issue of forced migration and the role that plays in the interrelationship among civil conflict, humanitarian initiative, and military intervention. "Ethnic cleansing," by which is meant the removal of populations regarded as antagonistic and inconveniently located, is the current term used in Bosnia. But this phenomenon has existed by other more anodyne names in all the civil conflicts in which there have been major humanitarian efforts in the last few years.

Ethiopia in the mid-1980s, for example, presents a case study of multiple variations of ethnic cleansing. In the midst of a famine, the Ethiopian government tried to "resettle" a significant portion of the population of Tigray in the infested lowlands near the Sudanese frontier, when control of the population was contested between the government and Tigrayan rebel forces. Public outcry over that policy eventually ended the program, though not before many had died. Conversely, in late 1984 tens of thousands of Tigrayans started to arrive on the Sudanese frontier in well-organized waves once it became known that relief supplies were being located at the frontier. Whether the migration to Sudan by those who suffered much worse fates upon their arrival occurred spontaneously or as part of an organized conspiracy by a highly secretive rebel political authority aimed at attracting international attention has never been fully established. The fact that the leadership of the Tigrayan Peoples' Liberation Front never permitted international observers or sustained monitoring by observers of the humanitarian crisis within their territory (a decision to which donors acquiesced) gave cause for concern. In other examples the slaughter of Kurds in Iraq by Saddam Hussein has been amply documented, and for more than ten years the international community has provided relief to the Khmer Rouge camps in Thailand, whose well-controlled population now provides the cannon fodder for a Khmer Rouge insurgence in Cambodia.

Whether it is Sudanese hospitality to Tigrayan or Eritrean refugees, Thai to Cambodians, Malawian to Mozambiquans, Kenyan to southern Somalis, Algerian to the Sahrawi, or Pakistani to Afghan refugees, the fact that populations cross frontiers to establish temporary residence and prepare or arm themselves for a return to their homeland has become a singular characteristic of the regional insecurity generated by these civil conflicts. By crossing a frontier, they are classified as refugees requiring protection and either resettlement or repatriation. But it is clear now that this commitment is being severely tested. In much of western Europe, in particular, the rise of xenophobic attacks on foreigners is prompting a dramatic review of once hospitable immigration laws.[29] And in Yugoslavia not only do Bosnian Muslims find it difficult to move to other western European countries, but they cannot even cross into Croatia, which has now closed its frontiers.

The security dilemma created by migration is the following: refugee programs attract more refugees, and in the context of war these programs can suit the purpose of the aggressor. This dilemma forces the question whether the cause of human rights, international security, and the interests of refugees are served by providing victims with mere protection upon escape. In the absence of simultaneous efforts to (1) prevent forced migrations and (2) protect populations on their own soil and in their own homes, the value of providing temporary refuge on foreign territory is subject to interpretation. More often than not, the victims are never allowed to return.

It would have been unthinkable ten years ago that Western donor governments would seriously consider the dispatch of military forces to protect the delivery of humanitarian supplies to a country undergoing civil strife. Yet this situation has now occurred in northern Iraq, Somalia, and Bosnia. Although the dissolution of the U.S.-Soviet rivalry has removed political impediments to such forms of intervention, there are now new obstacles to such engagements emerging at the multilateral level. Still, the argument that interventions of this sort are a camouflage for some Western "imperialist" assault on smaller nations has given way to the realization that, perhaps, calls to sovereignty are becoming the last refuge of failed and besieged governments.

Implications for a Cooperative Security Regime

The conflict in the former Yugoslavia is perhaps the primary reason that the international community began to recognize civil disorder as a potential international security challenge. But this realization has left many unanswered policy questions. To what degree does intervention in a civil conflict to protect humanitarian efforts become the first step to a protracted military commitment? How costly in money and lives might such a commitment be? What is the degree of public support for such ventures in the countries contemplating intervention?

The ambivalence on the part of industrial countries over intervention in Bosnia is all too indicative of prevailing concerns. Should such initiatives be carried out by the UN, by some other form of coalition, or unilaterally by the largest power, the United States? In Somalia the United States did not act alone, dispatching a substantial force only after a UN force was already present. In northern Iraq U.S.-led coalition forces are in their fourth year of efforts to protect humanitarian assistance for the Kurds from interference from the Iraqi government. What are the rules of engagement for any military force under such circumstances?

One particular problem arises when warring parties possess sophisticated weapons and thus can better disguise the source of an attack on a humanitarian effort or its protector. It is then very easy to retaliate against the wrong party or to play into the wrong hands. Indeed, there is every reason to believe that such attacks on UN relief efforts in Bosnia have been carried out specifically to draw in foreign intervention to a particular side. If the purpose of the intervention is to protect relief supplies, moreover, what policy is there to define the end of the threat to relief? Whether the clans in Somalia, which have not been disarmed, will reemerge after the withdrawal of American forces to carry on their war, for example, remains an open question.

The fundamental issue is whether humanitarian initiatives can be made to constitute part of what now is called preventive diplomacy and thus be rendered far more effective. If so, are there any particular methods by which this can be done? Nowhere is this issue more agonizingly illuminated than in the former Yugoslavia, where diplomatic paralysis has thrust an even greater burden onto humanitarian initiatives in Bosnia. The absence of sufficient relief supplies for Bosnia has aggravated the vulnerability of the respective populations, especially Muslims, and has exacerbated international tensions. The humanitarian challenge is to deliver assistance to several hundred thousand in their besieged homes so as to undermine the very purpose of "ethnic cleansing," which is intended to force victims to flee, succumb to a new authority, or die from privation. These efforts have been conducted by the UN agencies that have tried to organize convoys and to use armed escorts to deliver food or medicines to besieged populations. So far, the results have been far from satisfactory.

In the face of intractability, international policy has leapfrogged from failed UN convoys to calls for military intervention. Most of the debate seems to ignore the fact that this conflict is as much about religion as about secular disputes among old communist apparatchiks. The warring leaders, accompanied by well-armed accomplices, are manipulating divisions over ethnic and religious identity to perpetuate the crisis and gain power. Policymakers in the industrial countries have so assiduously underestimated the religious factor of the war that they have failed not only to understand its dynamics but, more important, to utilize religious forces to support efforts to alleviate suffering, let alone to promote reconciliation.

The intentional evasion of religious networks as an essential and credible indigenous method of delivering assistance in the Yugoslav conflict is a major opportunity cost that has had fatal consequences. It reveals ignorance of the experience of other civil conflicts in which nongovernmental organizations with an indigenous constituency have achieved success. If food and medicine had been pre-positioned in sufficient quantity in Bosnia and made available to church groups, if proper communications among them had been encouraged, if reciprocal deliveries to besieged populations had been carried out, it is almost guaranteed that a level of confidence among the religious communities would have developed, allowing them to play a more active role in negotiating some form of political settlement. Such a policy would have given material weight to the moral authority of the religious bodies that have condemned the conflict. By ignoring them as a material avenue, however, humanitarian policies of governments and multilateral organizations have diminished the strength of those very institutions that might have been able to play a decisive role in alleviating political and religious passions.[30]

Conclusion

A conclusion one must draw from the foregoing discussion is that the present international system is in a state of uncertain transition whose outcome is unpredictable. Governments are further limited in their capacity to influence domestic or international events, a fact mitigated by the increasing influence of forces that have long been ignored and were thought to have been discarded. In some instances state or regional disintegration is a threat that might be averted; in other cases dissolution has such momentum that one can only apply bandages such as humanitarian aid. In all cases, however, the challenge before the international community is to fashion an appropriate form of cooperation through which we can address threats to international security that emanate from predictable disintegration, absolute collapse of civil order, or mismanaged reconstruction.

To make any advance toward such a goal, a number of conceptual and bureaucratic anachronisms should be acknowledged and duly consigned to the past. The first of these is the failure to recognize the important link between disorder arising from social causes such as impoverishment and political disintegration and threats to international security. The sudden elimination of cradle-to-grave social security in former communist countries is inextricably intertwined with a serious security issue, the proliferation of weapons of mass destruction.[31] The dissolution of the Soviet bloc, in turn, is the product of long-ignored social and economic weaknesses inherent in communist governments, the collapse of which has irrevocably altered the nature of international security challenges.

Security must be redefined, in all of its organizational and operational implications, particularly to incorporate the economic and social dimensions of policy along with the purely technical and military. Economic development specialists and military strategists are now forced to sit around the same table more frequently, at least attempting to speak a language of security based on a common lexicon. Those who have devoted themselves to defining international security as entirely driven by the West's relationship with the Soviet bloc and who may have in the process disparaged students of third world issues as regionalists of a lesser order might do well to appreciate that they too have forcibly become regionalists with a functional specialization, but one that has become far too narrow to be adequate for the challenges ahead.

The tendency to think of new political forces such as religion, ethnicity, or economic groupings as essentially static, atavistic phenomena, unchanged by their period in the wilderness, is another misconception. One of the lessons of the rise of ethnic violence in Africa or religious militancy in the Middle East is that both have constantly shifted and reconfigured their character and purpose in response to their status as official outlaws. In the eastern bloc, moreover, we are confronted by a fusion of ethnicity, religion, and economic interest that has been forged by history and has been given added vitality—or virulence, some might argue—by the particular nature of communist oppression and manipulation. Whether a new system of cooperative security will successfully co-opt or be devoured by the former underworld of ethnicity, religion, and transnational economic interests actively depends on how the latter are accommodated in diplomacy as influential actors that have to be engaged.

The new political power of organized religion or ethnic interest is intimately associated with the nature of economic change, and macroeconomic prescriptions for liberalized market economies will have to incorporate a significant reallocation of resources toward nongovernmental organizations and the private sector. As long as programs to finance the market orientation of an economy are funded through the very government bureaucracies that created the crisis, the process of achieving liberalized economies will be totally flawed. Community groups, village associations, women's organizations, and religious associations are mushrooming throughout the world as a spontaneous response to the literal and political bankruptcy of governments. Informal credit schemes, which sidestep the restrictions of the formal banking system, already provide the underpinnings of survival for great numbers of the world's poor. To propose too quickly that these mechanisms will succeed only through externally funded schemes operating through governments is to invite failure.

Strategies abound to strengthen these groups into financially sustainable operations, and there are many efforts to build them, from the bottom up, into confederations, regional associations, or broader representative groupings, serving a purpose not much different from that of broad-based economic and social interest groups in the United States. These efforts, surely, are the stuff of pluralistic democracy in societies within which economy and politics have long stifled that pluralism. International aid, including that of the World Bank, should be significantly reallocated to pass through nongovernmental channels. This reallocation does not mean that more money must be made available. It implies a qualitative reallocation of existing aid funds. The simple fact is that in a deregulated world, the pinstriped donor will have to become more familiar with the grassroots channels for and uses of aid, a subject that has all too often been considered the quaint domain of breast-beating "aid workers." Failure to pursue this course will enhance the immediate destabilizing force of very sudden poverty in the former eastern bloc. Religions, most notably Islam, do not have a monopoly on fanaticism but are nevertheless ignorantly assumed to be darkly atavistic, and such forces are not immune to change if properly engaged.

For societies in danger of collapse, these suggestions may have some merit to the policymaker. However, the question remains: what of the future Bosnias and Somalias—those collapses that have not been prevented and that threaten regional or international security? An assumption of this chapter is that eventually the international community is forced to intervene with varying degrees of vigor in such crises. But the absence of some justifying principles upon which to base a more consistent, and certainly more intrusive, approach feeds the frustrated agitation over intervention in Bosnia (too little and too late) or Somalia (very late and then perhaps too much). It is further aggravated by the absence of any clear vision of what the purpose and, therefore, limit to the intervention should be. How then should the international community be organized and how should it act if it is not to be driven by the belated moral impulse of television cameras and the counterproductive tokenism of parachute drops and televised beach landings by marines?

For the international community to coalesce and for the action to have legitimacy among the parties to the conflict, the intervention must be justified by standards that are immune from prevailing sentiments of local nationalism. Human rights is the obvious principle, though its currency has been severely abused over the years. The simple fact remains that when a government can no longer guarantee food, shelter, clothing, and a modicum of health to its population, it has abdicated the right to sovereignty. When a government permits acts or even perpetrates acts that are a brazen contravention of these most elementary human rights, again in the name of security and sovereignty, that government has effectively eliminated the legitimacy of its security and sovereignty.

In a world where regional security is vulnerable to local social and political collapse, there is an urgent need for timely action. Tired as these principles may seem to a cynical world, they have at least served to propel the international community in the last ten years toward an interpretation of sovereignty that is less benign toward incumbent government and more favorable to those who suffer. Indeed, the coalition intervention in northern Iraq to protect the Kurds, the intervention in Somalia, the provision of very visible U.S. military support for flood relief in Bangladesh, and the loud but vain appeal for military intervention in Bosnia constitute a wave of precedent from which it is unlikely that the international community will shrink. But it will take a commitment to military intervention, by a multilaterally supported force, to disarm and then maintain civil order until such time as the substance of sovereignty is reconstituted to change reactive international policy and ad hoc interventions into a sustained exercise in cooperative security. The mission has two intertwined parts. The first is to actively disarm a population that has broken down into many guerrilla groups. This disarmament should be accompanied by a second, more complex "package" of actions in which policing the restoration of civil order must be combined with the restitution of a legal system, the reestablishment of economic activity and regulations, the reestablishment of the press and electronic media, and the fostering of political parties.

The first part—pacification—must be quick and decisive, carried out by an international force that is adequately equipped, staffed, and informed. As was learned from events in Somalia, there must be one clear command structure, with no second guessing by subordinates who call their own capitals for final confirmation. Finally, the intervention does not need to destroy comprehensively. It must demonstrate sufficient effect and power over a few examples to encourage the others to submit.

Shifting from pacification to the fostering of a functioning civil society is the greatest challenge of all, most successfully met by the Allies in a Germany utterly defeated by war after 1945. The feat involves intervention accompanied by a clear strategy for withdrawal. Drawing on the initial premise of this chapter, a better understanding of what constituted the elements of potential insecurity in the post–cold war era should inform the preparation of a postconflict reconstruction package. This mission must comprise a review of appropriate legal structure, the revival of a market economy, the establishment of a welfare system for people affected by the conflict, the development of media to ensure the dissemination of information, and the development of representative political structures. Failure to incorporate these components into the mission to restore civil order will most likely lead to a resumption of the tensions that brought about social and political collapse. Moreover, it is perfectly possible to engage some of the parties that will inevitably be an element in the political, social, legal, or economic reconstruction, even as the war continues.

One particular lesson learned in southern Africa is that programs for social and economic reintegration must be developed for former guerrillas. The idea that a small donation is enough to launch them happily back into civil society is dangerously erroneous when dealing with ex-fighters who expect rewards for what they believe has been their sacrifice. These guerrillas are the same kinds of people who became the brownshirts of Germany and the blackshirts of Italy. For this reason international efforts to assist Russia's demobilization should be especially commended if they offer long-term security through employment plans to the individuals and their families.

There is a cycle that must be respected if the web of poverty, social collapse, and international insecurity is to be replaced by a system of cooperative security. Improved systems of analysis, relevant to the social, economic, and cultural realities of societies, must be able to trigger cooperative interventions with the versatility to prevent the slide into disorder, to intervene to disarm and pacify, and to remain long enough to reestablish civil order.

Notes

1. A counter argument to this assertion is presented by Stephen D. Krasner in *Structural Conflict: The Third World against Global Liberalism* (University of California Press, 1985). Krasner argues that third world countries strive for power and national sovereignty as assiduously as they strive for material wealth, and in so doing they have promoted regimes that legitimate unilateral exercise of national control. A more recent variation of this theme that discusses the primacy civilizations (characterized by history, language, and religion) as opposed to nation states is Samuel P. Huntington, "The Clash of Civilizations?" *Foreign Affairs,* vol. 72 (Summer 1993), pp. 22–49. Additional discussions of statehood and sovereignty are presented in James N. Rosenau, *Turbulence in World Politics: A Theory of Change and Continuity* (Princeton University Press, 1990); and James N. Rosenau, ed., *International Politics and Foreign Policy: A Reader in Research and Theory,* 2d ed. (Free Press, 1969). For a brief synopsis of recent evidence of the disintegration of the state, see Ewan Anderson, "The Nation State, National Security and Geopolitics," *Jane's Intelligence Review,* vol. 4 (June 1992), pp. 282–83.

2. For a comprehensive view of primary U.S. foreign policy objectives in the Clinton administration, see the four speeches by President Bill Clinton, Secretary of State Warren Christopher, National Security Adviser Anthony Lake, and UN Ambassa-

dor Madeleine Albright in *US Department of State Dispatch,* vol. 4 (September 27, 1993).

3. For a similar view on the U.S. failure to reconstruct foreign policy beyond the cold war paradigms but with a different perspective on how the United States should in turn recast its foreign policy objectives, see Jonathan Clarke, "The Conceptual Poverty of U.S. Foreign Policy," *Atlantic Monthly,* vol. 272 (September 1993), pp. 54–66.

4. For a study on collective military intervention in states where a collapse of government has occurred, see Fred Tanner, ed., *From Versailles to Baghdad: Post-War Armament Control of Defeated States,* UNIDIR/92/70 (New York: United Nations, 1992).

5. For a discussion of the disintegration of the state as a solitary economic entity, see Kenichi Ohmae, "The Rise of the Region State," *Foreign Affairs,* vol. 72 (Spring 1993), pp. 78–87.

6. The "informal sector"—social, economic, religious, or economic entities that are independent of government—most often emerges when government is incapable of providing basic social services. For a discussion of the informal sector in Africa, see Catherine Coquery-Vidrovitch, *Africa: Endurance and Change South of the Sahara,* trans. David Maisel (University of California Press, 1988), pp. 299–308; Donald Rothchild and Naomi Chazan, eds., *The Precarious Balance: State and Society in Africa* (Boulder, Colo.: Westview Press, 1988), pp. 126–27, 160–66, 178–81. For a study on the informal sector's role in one nation, see Jennifer Widner, "Interest Group Structure and Organization in Kenya's Informal Sector: Cultural Despair or a Politics of Multiple Allegiances?" *Comparative Political Studies,* vol. 24 (April 1991), pp. 31–55.

7. Evidence of this shift is presented by the UN Conference on Trade and Development (UNCTD), *Final Review and Appraisal of the United Nations Programme of Action for African Economic Recovery and Development, 1986–1990,* TD/B1280/Add.1/Rev.1 (United Nations, 1991), in which agricultural reforms are the centerpiece of the UN's economic agenda, and in which human resource development, population policies, indigenous entrepreneurial programs, social justice, and refugee programs are all listed as important priorities of the UN's policy in Africa. For additional discussion of prescribed economic policies, see I. G. Patel, ed., *Policies for African Development from the 1980s to the 1990s* (Washington: International Monetary Fund, 1992).

8. UNCTD, *Final Review and Appraisal,* pp. 36–46. See also "Africa: A Continent at Stake," *Financial Times,* September 1, 1993, p. 1.

9. For a more detailed account of these events, see John Waterbury, *The Egypt of Nasser and Sadat: The Political Economy of Two Regimes* (Princeton University Press, 1983), pp. 229–30.

10. All mosques were placed under the direct control of the Egyptian Ministry of Religious Affairs in order to "stymie Islamists." See *Middle East Journal,* vol. 47 (Winter 1993), p. 320. For additional information on increasing tensions between Islamic fundamentalists and the Egyptian government, see three articles by Chris Hedges in the *New York Times:* "Egypt Tightens the Net around Its Militant Opposition," December 10, 1992, p. A3; "Frustrations Blaze a Path for Egypt's Fundamentalists," December 6, 1992, p. D3; and (on Islamic public relief activities) "As Islamic Militants Thunder, Egypt Grows More Nervous," November 12, 1992, p. A1.

11. For an example of recent strife in the occupied territories, see Joel Greenberg, "4 Israelis and 3 Palestinians Killed in Guerrilla Attacks," *New York Times,* September 13, 1993, p. A1.

12. Although official statistics do not show a dramatic increase in reported unemployment in the Russian Federation, the definition of unemployment in the FSU is different than in market economies. For example, citizens without jobs who have

alternative sources of income such as government pensions are not considered unemployed. In addition, state-run enterprises will force unpaid vacations or shorter work weeks on workers in order to meet diminished demand. See *IMF Economic Reviews 1993: Russian Federation* (Washington: International Monetary Fund, 1993), p. 6.

13. Ibid., pp. 1–7.

14. The first signs of such trends are beginning to develop. On November 11, 1993, Russian foreign minister Andrey Kozyrev suggested in an interview broadcast by Radio Mayak that the dangers of a mass migration of the Russian diaspora back to Russia as a result of ethnic conflict throughout the FSU would be reduced if the Russian military became more engaged in peacekeeping activities in the FSU. See Suzanne Crow, "Kozyrev on Immigration, Peacekeeping," *RFE/RL Daily Report,* no. 218 (November 12, 1993). For detailed information on the ethnic and national makeup of the FSU, see *Report on Ethnic Conflict in the Russian Federation and Transcaucasia* (Harvard University, Strengthening Democratic Institutions Project, July 1993).

15. R. C. Cobb, *The Police and The People: French Popular Protest, 1789–1820* (Oxford University Press, 1970).

16. For a similar view on the impact of the rapid pace of current economic reform in eastern Europe since the fall of the Berlin Wall, see Susan L. Woodward, "The Tyranny of Time: Eastern Europe's Race to the Market," *Brookings Review,* vol. 10 (Winter 1992), pp. 6–13; and Daniel N. Nelson, "Democracy, Markets and Security in Eastern Europe," *Survival,* vol. 35 (Summer 1993), pp. 156–71.

17. Because of Soviet disintegration, an informal economy, largely in the form of an elaborate black market, has emerged in the FSU. See Serge Schmemann, "As Soviets Wait Tremulously, Ailing Economy Struggles On," *New York Times,* July 14, 1991, p. A1.

18. For three accounts of the rise of the Russian Orthodox Church in post–cold war Russia, see Serge Schmemann, "An Awakened Church Finds Russia Searching for Its Soul," *New York Times,* April 26, 1992, p. D3; Peter Steinfels, "The Orthodox Church Gains Power in a Post-Marxist World," *New York Times,* November 10, 1991, p. D2; and John Tagliabue, "German Aid to Soviets Begins Journey through Poland," *New York Times,* February 10, 1991, p. A13.

19. As Catherine Kelleher discusses in chapter 8, this contradiction is embodied in the Conference on Security and Cooperation in Europe, and particularly in the 1975 Helsinki Final Act, in which the participating states collectively agreed to abstain from interfering in other states' internal affairs, while simultaneously agreeing to the principle of self-determination. The current crises in the FSU and Yugoslavia demonstrate the inconsistency.

20. For more information on the activities of the Organization of African Unity, see Francis M. Deng and I. William Zartman, eds., *Conflict Resolution in Africa* (Brookings, 1991).

21. For more information on these events, see Kenneth B. Noble, "In Liberia's Illusory Peace, Rebel Leader Rules Empire of His Own Design," *New York Times,* April 14, 1992, p. A1; and Steven A. Holmes, "US Tries to Blunt Harm of Remark on Liberia Peacekeepers," *New York Times,* November 15, 1992, p. A12.

22. The lingering split between the former colonies of France and Britain is not merely a cultural affair. France created a military alliance, invested heavily in the economic structures of each of its former colonies, and went so far as to maintain, at considerable cost, a monetary zone in which all but two states participated.

23. A similar view on the source of modern ethnic conflict in the former Yugoslavia is presented by Cvijeto Job in "Yugoslavia's Ethnic Furies," *Foreign Policy,* no. 92 (Fall 1993), pp. 52–74. In contrast, Paula Franklin Lytle chooses to emphasize more

recent events in analyzing the source of current conflict in the Balkans. See "U.S. Policy toward the Demise of Yugoslavia: The 'Virus of Nationalism,'" *East European Politics and Societies,* vol. 6 (Fall 1992). For an instructive comparison of the respective causes of contemporary ethnic strife in Yugoslavia and India, see Susanne Hoeber Rudolph and Lloyd I. Rudolph, "Modern Hate," *New Republic,* March 22, 1993, pp. 24–29.

24. The UN Security Council vote on Resolution 871, extending the mandate of the more than 20,000 peacekeepers in the former Yugoslavia to restore Croatian authority to Serb-held territories, enable refugees to go home in safety, and disarm Serb insurgents, was postponed until after Russian president Boris Yeltsin successfully led a crackdown on opposition members of the Russian parliament, largely because of the latter's sympathy with Serbia's cause. On October 4, 1993, Russia finally voted for the measure. See Patrick Moore, "Croatia Demands UNPROFOR Carry Out Mandate or Leave," *RFE/RL Daily Report,* no. 187 (September 29, 1993). Additional information is provided by Patrick Moore, "UNPROFOR to Stay Six More Months in Croatia," ibid., no. 191 (October 5, 1993).

25. Greece is suspected of having supplied the Serbs with crucial resources in violation of UN sanctions. See "The Big Leak in Serbia Embargo: Nervous, Needy Macedonia," *New York Times,* July 18, 1993, p. A12.

26. There have been many reports of tension between the Serbian government and the Albanian population in Kosovo. For example, on September 18, 1993, "Serbian police raided several houses of members of the Democratic League of Kosovo (LDK)." Reportedly, the Albanian police forces "demolished furniture and beat people." Evidently, tensions were particularly high in fall 1993 because Albanian children were allegedly prevented from attending privately run Albanian schools. For more information, see Fabian Schmidt, "Kosovo Update," *RFE/RL Daily Report,* no. 180 (September 20, 1993).

27. For more information on factionalism in Ethiopia and the impact of superpower involvement on the horn of Africa, see Robert F. Gorman, *Political Conflict on the Horn of Africa* (Praeger, 1981). Similar arguments have been advanced against the UN arms embargo of Bosnia, where the Muslim population has suffered disproportionately, largely because the Muslims do not have natural allies in neighboring republics and European states as the Croat and Serbian factions do and because they did not control military resources before the war began. For more information, see Stephen Kinzer, "Bosnia Asks World Court to Nullify Peace Accord," *New York Times,* August 26, 1993, p. A13; James Gow, "One Year of War in Bosnia and Herzegovina," *RFE/RL Research Report,* vol. 2 (June 4, 1993), pp. 1–13; and Robert W. Tucker and David C. Hendrickson, "America and Bosnia," *National Interest,* no. 33 (Fall 1993), pp. 14–27.

28. For a detailed discussion of human rights violations of displaced persons around the globe, see Francis M. Deng, *Protecting the Dispossessed: A Challenge for the International Community* (Brookings, 1993).

29. For example, Germany, formerly characterized by the most liberal immigration laws in Europe, has been a reluctant but notorious host to violence against foreigners in recent years. In response, the German leadership initiated a new debate on German asylum laws. In May 1993 the German parliament voted to make it more difficult for foreigners to seek asylum in Germany and composed a list of states in which the German parliament alleges there is no political persecution, thereby preventing anyone from one of those states from applying for asylum in Germany. For a summary of the political debate that took place, see "Wer sagt, Deutschland schotte sich ab, redet falsch Zeugnis," *Frankfurter Allgemeine Zeitung,* May 27, 1993, p. 4. For a summary of the results, including the text of the new law and the list of the so-called safe states, see "Randalierer, Blockaden, Gewalt: Änderung des Asylrechts abschliessend beraten,"

Frankfurter Allgemeine Zeitung, May 27, 1993, p. 1; and "Die alte und die neue Asyl-Regelung im Wortlaut," ibid., p. 2.

30. Anthony Ugolnik argues that the West has so far failed to recognize the legitimacy and potential influence of religious organizations in the former eastern bloc and in the former Yugoslavia. He states that because the United States was unable to capitalize on the emergence of the church as a force for stability and a possible purveyor of social services, it has missed the opportunity to facilitate the East's transition from communism to a system more benign to Western interests. See Anthony Ugolnik, "Living at the Borders: Eastern Orthodoxy and World Disorder," *First Things* (June–July, 1993), pp. 15–23. Another example of an independent institution playing a powerful role in a society characterized by a populace alienated from its government is provided by the former German Democratic Republic. It was only within the walls of Protestant churches that large assemblies were allowed and where "a certain level of dissidence was permitted," including free expression of views concerning peace activism, conscientious objection, and environmental degradation. Later, just before the Berlin Wall fell, the church became a primary motivator and organizing force behind the famous Monday night Leipzig demonstrations protesting communist policies. See Elizabeth Pond, *After the Wall: American Policy toward Germany* (New York: Priority Press, 1990), p. 11; and Pond, *Beyond the Wall: Germany's Road to Unification* (Brookings, 1993), pp. 87, 93–99, 108–10, 114–19.

31. Social disorder and ensuing domestic pressure, particularly from the Russian military, has certainly contributed to the recent promulgation of the new Russian military doctrine in which the Russian government has retracted its earlier pledge of "no first use" of nuclear weapons, further exacerbating the problems of weapons proliferation. For more information, see Daniel Sneider, "New Russian Doctrine Raises Western Suspicions," *Defense News,* vol. 8 (November 8–14, 1993), p. 3; and Fred Hiatt, "Russia Shifts Doctrine on Military Use," *Washington Post,* November 4, 1993, p. A1.

Part Four

NEAR-TERM AND OTHER CHALLENGES

FOURTEEN

Cooperative Security in the United States

Janne E. Nolan

A COOPERATIVE security regime stands little chance of success if the advanced countries do not adapt their national and foreign policies to align with its core principles and precepts. The United States, in particular, would have difficulty championing security cooperation if it engaged in policies that were seen as contributing to global confrontation, unwarranted technical diffusion, or regional tensions. This is not simply a matter of normative or diplomatic sensitivity, but a practical reality. A regime that applies laws and norms selectively, exempting some states according to their relative status or for reasons of expedience, is destined to fail. The only alternative to legitimacy is coercion, hardly a realistic basis for fostering cooperation in a highly diffused world order.

A number of the guiding principles that continue to inform U.S. security policy are the product of an international system whose underpinnings no longer exist. These principles emerged in a world in which state relations were dominated by the military rivalry between the two superpowers and the technological preeminence of the United States went largely unquestioned, and at a time when there was little serious interference in the prerogatives of large powers by less-developed countries. The massive transformations of the international order in recent years are obviously forcing a reevaluation of emerging security conditions and U.S. policy responses.

Comfort in U.S. military superiority, which has served to build support for U.S. defense spending and strategy for decades, is now tempered by the growing realization that its use may be heavily circumscribed and as a practical reality may prove transitory. Because of political and resource constraints, the United States is unlikely to initiate any significant military action in the future without some form of broad international approval. However reluctant some may be to come to the conclusion, there nonetheless is a growing awareness that U.S. military power cannot be used without an internationally supported framework that accords it legitimacy. How this framework will be defined is still a matter of debate and controversy. It is yet to be fully recognized that delays in coming to grips with the demand for an articulated, multinational concept of force projection—one that is widely perceived as legitimate—may undercut U.S. leadership and exacerbate suspicions among smaller powers about long-term U.S. security objectives.

Over time, the global diffusion of advanced technology may preclude an enduring U.S. military superiority unless that superiority is accepted as serving the general international interest. Superior U.S. conventional power projection is derived primarily from the application of dramatic advances in the collection, processing, and transmission of information. The core technologies that support these decisive military functions are being developed in commercial markets, and access to them cannot be denied. Nor can access be denied to the knowledge and materials required to make weapons of mass destruction, which, because of their destructiveness and the fear they engender, could come to be seen by a larger number of states as a way to offset U.S. conventional military power. As such, the ability of the United States to prevent or manage international crises effectively will be affected by decisions made by regional powers, which in turn will be influenced by their perceptions of U.S. intent.

This chapter examines the elements of current U.S. security thinking that may be consonant with a concept of cooperative security and those that may require political or institutional reorientation to support such a regime. The analysis covers the potential influence of several alternative approaches to security on policies guiding military engagement, technical diffusion, and force planning.

The Current Political Climate

Lacking a clear framework within which to define the role of the United States in the world after the cold war, the domestic foreign policy debate in the early 1990s revealed a public mood of partisan divisiveness and general disillusionment. The absence of a foreign policy consensus was evident in the controversies generated in the latter part of the Bush administration by its first draft 1992 defense planning guidance document, in the round of divisive debates set off by the Clinton administration's first defense budget and initial policy statements in early 1993, in the controversies and recriminations surrounding the quest for credible options for intervention in Bosnia, Somalia, and Haiti, and in the isolationist sentiments within Congress and the public, which sought scapegoats to explain declining U.S. competitiveness. The country's perception of its global responsibilities and destiny seemed, in short, conceptually adrift.

In response to the transformation of the strategic landscape, a restructuring of the U.S. defense posture is under way. The adjustments are extensive, affecting nuclear and conventional forces, organizational roles and missions, and the defense industry. Some of this restructuring is prompted by arms control agreements, but much of it is a nearly spontaneous reaction to budget reductions that are themselves the political consequence of a lessened perception of security threats. Most attempts to guide this restructuring have consisted of scenarios under which the United States is called upon to react to redefinitions of a past threat: a reconstituted superpower Russia, for nuclear forces; or one or several implicit replays of the Gulf War, for conventional forces. That U.S. security policy might instead be primarily directed at preventing such threats from arising in the first place is an idea that has not yet fully taken hold. Thus the desirable size of U.S. conventional and nuclear forces, the appropriate rate of modernization, and the degree of combat readiness to be maintained have not been assessed from this perspective.[1]

If the ongoing American security debates could be reduced to three disparate sets of principles, they would include an implicit yearning for American military superiority embodied in a Pax Americana, a strong push to isolationism or disengagement, and a growing trend toward explicit acceptance of multilateralism in the conduct of economic, political, and military affairs. In reality, there are overlapping elements of each of these views in current thinking, but their respective influences are more obvious in some aspects of policy than others.

Competing Definitions of the U.S. Role in the World

The notion of America as the "sole remaining superpower" emerged in the public debate after the demise of the Soviet Union and the success of U.S. forces in the defeat of Iraq. This modern version of a Pax Americana is based on the conviction that the United States can be strong only if it can project decisive power and use force unilaterally as necessary. Sovereign status and military superiority are virtually synonymous in this regard, and multilateralism is seen largely as a needless intrusion on or diversion from the goal of American preeminence. A draft version of the Bush administration's annual defense planning guidance document, leaked to the press in March 1992, reflected some aspects of this line of thinking. The document argued for an American military posture of sufficient capability to prevent any competitors from challenging America's global dominance. Potential competitors included both allies and enemies in a world inexorably destined to face multipolar competition and conflict. U.S. military capabilities and superior technology were depicted as the only reliable guarantors of global stability, to be used to intervene in many kinds of contingencies throughout the world.[2]

Defense officials quickly disavowed the document in the face of public and media criticism, but the incident helped reinforce the view that there may be a substantial body of official opinion that supports such notions. Quite apart from bolstering the case for a large military establishment, a Pax Americana tends to characterize dependence on multilateral institutions, such as the UN, as especially naive and likely to undermine sovereign decisions to bolster the national resources and capabilities needed to defend U.S. interests. International partnerships of this kind cannot help but impose "intolerable limitations on American initiative," as one commentator put it.[3]

At the opposite end of the spectrum, advocates of U.S. global disengagement emerged as a more vocal force in the U.S. political debate in the late 1980s and early 1990s. Evidence of this sentiment was seen in public and congressional opposition to U.S. intervention in the crisis in Bosnia, to the provision of economic assistance to the countries in the former Soviet bloc, and to new trading arrangements, such as the North American Free Trade Agreement, which engendered deep suspicions about its perceived concessions to foreign countries at the expense of American jobs and prosperity.[4] Recessionary domestic economic trends always tend to encourage the perception of foreign policy as an intrusion on the nation's welfare. In both the postwar and current eras, the idea that the United States has an obligation to restore order and to provide for human welfare overseas is pure folly to a member of Congress who cannot secure sufficient funds to extend basic services to constituents.[5] This sentiment has intensified in the current fiscally constrained domestic environment.

Isolationism has strong historical roots in American political culture. It originates with the profound skepticism about foreign entanglements expressed by the founding fathers, perhaps best embodied in George Washington's farewell address warning of the dangers of American involvement in the controversies of European politics. Immediately after World War II, isolationists were unified in their opposition to the Atlanticist view of the world embraced by conservatives, statesmen such as Dean Acheson, George Kennan, and John J. McCloy, Jr. At issue were policies that sought to advance America's sphere of influence by helping to rebuild Europe and forging international partnerships on behalf of containment. The split between Atlanticists and isolationists was about commitments and resources, however, not about the legitimacy of American military intervention.

Only the liberal theory of isolationism advocates true disengagement, at least with regard to the use of military or intelligence operations to coerce foreign governments. Even here its proponents often make exceptions for nonmilitary intervention, such as extending humanitarian assistance to countries in need or on behalf of transnational causes, such as environmental protection. But isolationism has rarely meant the renunciation of American military preeminence. On the contrary, at least conservative isolationists have always believed in the innately superior ability of the United States to influence the values and behavior of other countries, such influence to be achieved by external intervention if necessary.

Advocates of a Pax Americana are certainly distinct in their more overt embrace of America's global role, but conservative isolationists have not usually been opposed to military engagements in the less-developed world, whether in China in the 1950s, Vietnam in the 1960s, or Iraq in the 1990s. The underlying criteria for approving military ventures in both cases are that they be quick and decisive, and require minimal American sacrifice. As expressed by politicians such as conservative commentator Patrick Buchanan, for example, "America First" means opposition to alliances or other forms of international partnerships that imply equality, reciprocity, and obligations to others.[6] Alliances are synonymous with encumbrance. They are bound to impinge on the right of the United States to be self-sufficient and also to act unilaterally should it see fit to do so, especially militarily. A Pax Americana shares the isolationist spirit in its rejection of multilateralism as a credible basis for security. "Going it alone" is the dominant sentiment in both sets of beliefs.

A Pax Americana and conservative isolationism also converge in their belief in the importance of American technological prowess as the ultimate guarantor of U.S. security. The quest for the technological fix to security challenges was perhaps best encapsulated in the notion of a perfect defensive "shield" put forward in the original Strategic Defense Initiative (SDI) in 1983. The SDI, designed to permit the United States to engage globally without the risk of nuclear attack on its own territory, was also intended to unburden the United States from diplomatic obligations to negotiate nuclear agreements with its principal adversary, the Soviet Union. President Ronald Reagan's vision of the SDI was a perfect synthesis of isolationism and a Pax Americana, as such, arguing for American self-sufficiency as the core foundation for unchallenged American global superiority.

Strategic defenses have now been given a barely residual role in U.S. defense planning, but strains of the SDI's philosophical underpinnings still abound in the current discussions of U.S. defense spending and force objectives. U.S. military superiority, manifested in the most advanced weapons deployed for rapid global mobilization, remains the creed justifying many planning decisions. Consistent with this view, the mainstay of U.S. forces is now to be long-range and highly precise weapons that can destroy even distant targets "with little if any loss of U.S. lives and with a minimum of collateral damage and loss of civilian lives on the other side."[7] In other words, the United States can remain the sole superpower by being prepared to engage in decisive, short military engagements that incur minimal risks to Americans and, by implication, pose no risk of vulnerability to the U.S. homeland—a concept that, whatever its merits, is solidly rooted in isolationist philosophy.[8]

The third obvious trend in the current U.S. foreign policy debate is the reemergence of internationalism and multilateralism, manifested in the ascendance of institutions such as the UN and in the growing level of collaboration among countries to deal with crises in Somalia, Bosnia, and elsewhere. At its most extreme, multilateralism reinvokes the spirit of world federalism or the views of other "one-world" advocates that would favor eliminating U.S. capabilities to act alone and subsuming all nations under international authority. As a practical matter, however, multilateralism is currently being pursued for pragmatic, not visionary, ends. Faced with limited resources and waning public support for foreign engagements, the Bush and Clinton administrations have had to seek multilateral backing for many objectives, not least to force Saddam Hussein out of Kuwait or, thus far unsuccessfully, to help bring about a resolution to the conflict over Bosnia.

In its initial phases, the Clinton administration sought to recast the emphasis of U.S. defense planning to include a more open acceptance of multilateralism and explicit limits on the projection of unilateral force. Driven by the momentum to cut U.S. defense spending by more than 20 percent, the administration advanced notions of "limited intervention" and a formulation of U.S. strategy to be tailored explicitly to recognize constraints on U.S. defense resources and according capabilities. This strategy included a shift away from the traditional U.S. commitment to have the capability to fight two significant regional conflicts simultaneously. Popularized in the press as the "win-hold-win" strategy, the new conception of intervention suggested that the United States should be able to mobilize air and sea power to defeat one aggressor while blunting aggression in another part of the world with air power until sufficient forces could be brought to bear to terminate the second conflict.[9]

Conservative critics were quick to blast the Clinton administration for this alleged sign of retrenchment, some referring to the strategy as "lose-hold-lose," while moderates and liberals expressed disappointment that the administration was still clinging to what they perceived as an unrealistic declaratory posture. The debate had a nostalgic quality in which proponents of the necessity of a "two-war" strategy tended to overlook budgetary and political realities in favor of nationalist ideology, while proponents of the new policy tried to depict it as no less of a commitment to American force projection than that of any previous administration's.

Whatever its substantive significance, the controversy highlighted the fact that the attachment to unilateral action is a powerful political undercurrent, prompting the Clinton administration early on to revise its rhetoric accordingly. Within weeks, administration officials reemphasized that the United States had to "be able to fight and win two major regional conflicts, and nearly simultaneously," an objective to be met, despite budget constraints, using advanced technology and the right mix of forces.[10] Similarly, when Undersecretary of State Peter Tarnoff in May 1993 depicted a constrained U.S. global role in a world in which "there will have to be genuine power sharing and responsibility sharing . . . [among allies]," he was promptly and publicly criticized by fellow officials for misrepresenting U.S. policy.[11] After the June 1993 U.S. attack on an Iraqi intelligence facility in retaliation for an Iraqi-sponsored plot to assassinate former president George Bush, unilateralism enjoyed a brief renaissance in the public mind, albeit without affecting force plans in any discernible manner.

No debate has been as contentious as that provoked by the expanding conflict in Bosnia. The failed U.S. effort in early 1993 to elicit European support for various strategies of intervention was among the first stumbling blocks of the new administration, largely seen as a diplomatic catastrophe and a demonstration of the limits of U.S. influence. If nothing else, the experience helped to underscore the inescapable reality that multilateralism was not an option but a necessity, however elusive it has remained in the search for a common and effective policy. In arguing for new criteria for U.S. involvement in peacekeeping operations in June 1993, for example, the U.S. ambassador to the UN called for U.S. commitment to a strategy of "assertive multilateralism," a distinct shift in the rhetoric, if not yet the substance, of U.S. policy.[12]

Obvious limits remain to U.S. willingness to fully embrace multilateralism as an integral principle to guide force planning. Instead, elements of several of the belief systems discussed in this chapter are informing the current security policy framework, if not always consciously. The primary division can be reduced to the tension between a confrontational framework based on the primacy of unilateral uses of force (or international only to the degree that they involve alliances of convenience) and a more multilateral and cooperative approach to security that emphasizes preventive diplomacy, nonmilitary instruments for conflict prevention, mediation in place of war, and collective intervention only when other instruments fail. Despite the success of the coalition war against Iraq and the dismal experience of the lack of any such cooperation in Bosnia, however, joint actions are still unfamiliar instruments in the core of U.S. security planning. The idea of cooperation for preventive actions that could preclude the need for future intervention is even more remote, although it is embodied implicitly in efforts toward the denuclearization of the former Soviet Union and the dismantling of Iraq's arsenal of nonconventional weapons.

What has already occurred on both a national and an international scale, however, is at least an underlying recognition that multilateral security initiatives are likely to enhance rather than constrain legitimate and effective uses of political and military power. In the end, the reality of a resource-constrained and fragmented international system argues persuasively for a policy of selective engagement based on cooperative planning.

With this latter principle as its main premise, cooperative security is obviously distinct from both of the extremes, "one-world" multilateralism and lone superpower unilateralism. The concept of cooperative security does not attempt to reinvent power relations in an effort to assume away conflict in international affairs. Nor does it harken back to a distant past to imagine a world in which the United States can act alone. It is based instead on the recognition that conflicts and military threats are likely to persist, but that the effective use of American power will require political art to sustain support for U.S. international engagements. Eliciting multinational legitimacy for international ventures is not a politically or economically dispensable impulse. Notwithstanding the apparent popularity in the West of limited demonstrations of U.S. power, such as the June 1993 retaliation against Iraq, the choice is increasingly legitimacy or paralysis.

Effects of Alternative Frameworks on Policy

This section examines the potential influence of the three alternative policy frameworks on five areas. The areas are (1) the use of force, (2) the conduct of regional relations, (3) the perceived role of nuclear weapons, (4) efforts to control the proliferation of weapons internationally, and (5) the overall character of U.S. defense investment.

Principles Guiding the Use of Force

With the waning of the Soviet threat, regional aggression had already begun in the Bush administration to be viewed as the most important and demanding threat to U.S. interests, especially by nations armed with nonconventional munitions and long-range delivery systems.[13] The Clinton administration, building on this premise, introduced four new areas of security priorities for the post–cold war environment:

—"Regional threats," the basis for judging the requisite size and character of forces for future military intervention;

—"'New' nuclear threats," including nations in the former Soviet bloc as well as terrorist groups and lawless nations (which, it is believed, cannot be deterred by traditional means);

—The failure of democracy in countries where military coups or the ascendance of authoritarian regimes is thought to be more likely to prompt destabilizing actions and where peacekeeping and humanitarian intervention may be necessary;

—"Economic security," including national and international efforts to convert excess defense production capabilities and resources to civilian uses and to revitalize the U.S. defense technology base.[14]

The current administration's defense policy, like its predecessor's, asserts that "uncertainty" about who future adversaries may be requires a permanently high level of military preparedness for global application. In response to arguments that the United States faces a drastically diminished set of security risks, the former chairman of the Joint Chiefs of Staff, General Colin Powell, for example, argued that the world is far more turbulent than ever before. In presenting the U.S. defense program to Congress in 1992, he stated that "the real threat [to our security] is the unknown, the uncertain. In a very real sense the primary threat to our security is instability."[15] That statement summarizes the prevailing security posture of the United States. The United States is planning for military confrontation against an enemy it does not think it can predict under circumstances whose uncertainty it does not think it can manage.

Countering threats and deterrence through readiness are the traditional bases for defense planning. Yet in both the conventional and the nuclear realms, today's defense policy problems are not anchored in immediate threats. That the world appears to have become more complex to policymakers long preoccupied with a "simpler" paradigm defined by the U.S.-Soviet rivalry is undeniable. But even under Secretary of Defense Les Aspin's initiative to conduct a so-called bottom-up review of budgetary and military needs in mid-1993, wherein new force requirements are supposed to be calibrated with the scale and character of regional threats, uncertainty has come to replace deterrence as the new open-ended rationale for justifying major U.S. military programs. Constraints are being imposed because of budgetary imperatives far more than because of any deliberate reconceptualization of America's future security role.

For advocates of a Pax Americana, the Clinton administration's plan is disappointing not only for its excessively multinational rhetoric but also for its failure to provide adequate forces or a concrete vision for ensuring superior U.S. military power in the future. Specific elements of the proposed force posture, such as cuts in the number of aircraft carriers, the failure to maintain a larger force of B-2 bombers, and the downscaling or outright cancellation of plans to develop and deploy space-based strategic defenses are particularly contentious examples. New elements of the Clinton plan, such as larger allocations for peacekeeping, are also seen as an intrusion on more vital security priorities.[16]

For opponents of military intervention, by contrast, the administration's plan represents a security perspective that is excessively "globalist," out of date, and too expensive. According to both conservative and liberal critics, the administration simply set out to find new rationales for maintaining a military establishment that contains elements which should have become relics of the cold war or which suggest that the United States is recklessly becoming "the world's policeman."[17] Any veneer of multinationalism and calls for collective security is belied by the gross disparities in material and financial burdens being borne by allies and their continued reluctance to rectify this situation with commensurately larger allocations.

The principles that would guide a cooperative approach to security would take issue with elements of the new administration's strategy for different reasons. Cooperative security foresees a security system in which military force is used as a last resort, after other instruments of dissuasion or coercion have been exhausted. The use of force for significant engagement would be unavoidably multinational. In either case, instruments for preventive diplomacy—well before a requirement for conflict mediation, peacekeeping, or intervention emerged—would serve as integral and far more prominent elements of an overall defense strategy. Despite their current salience for eastern Europe, the Middle East, and Africa, new conceptions of conflict prevention are barely mentioned in current Defense Department statements and remain for now a vague diplomatic objective.

A cooperative security regime would also differ by moving far more expeditiously to renounce offensive force configurations and to reduce reliance on nuclear weapons, which would be replaced by an effective conventional deterrent. Residual nuclear forces would be taken off alert and disassembled, and nuclear-based deterrence would be drastically deemphasized (as discussed later in this chapter). This approach is distinct from the current administration's apparent reluctance to explicitly devalue the role and potential utility of nuclear forces in U.S. strategy or to impose significantly higher standards of operational safety, even at the lower levels established in recent agreements.

U.S. conventional forces, in turn, would be subject to restrictions guiding the types of forces developed, the patterns of their deployment, and declaratory and operational doctrines. An explicit objective would be to establish defensive standards for technological development and force deployment, reversing a growing trend toward the acquisition of capabilities for prompt, preemptive operations. Such forces could potentially be placed under multinational control, as William Perry argues in chapter 6, in an institutional arrangement that would adjudicate procedures and criteria for force configurations and judge when just cause exists for launching a major military initiative. The effect of these changes on policies guiding the acquisition and use of force would obviously be profound.

Although everyone agrees that the United States should remain prepared for ongoing instability throughout the world, the means by which threats would be identified and interests defended would be significantly different in a cooperative regime. Assessments of security needs under a cooperative security regime would have to be guided by criteria that are far more empirically rooted than the notion of hedging against the unknown. The U.S. preference for unilateralism would have to yield to a more realistic appreciation of the necessity for both military and nonmilitary intervention organized around politically legitimate coalitions, shared intelligence, and commonly agreed-upon guidelines for intervention.

The ability to act in concert with others, in turn, would require the kind of military investment that gives the United States maximum flexibility and mobility, more than is currently envisioned. As was made clear during Operation Desert Storm, even the NATO allies were not fully prepared for joint military action. Each nation sent its forces to the region individually and then tried to assemble them into a military coalition after the fact. The logistical and command inadequacies were obvious ones, to which the United States contributed by its lack of adequate familiarity with the operational practices of European and other countries' militaries.

As a political message, the character of U.S. force objectives needs to be aligned with new security realities that focus seriously on regional instability as the key risk to U.S. interests. U.S. defense planning priorities are linked to decisions made by other countries to acquire particular military capabilities in several important ways. U.S. force decisions can abet proliferation indirectly, by helping to reify certain military capabilities as key currencies of state power or by suggesting that the technically advanced powers may collude to wield force against lesser powers for self-serving ends. American rhetoric may also inadvertently encourage states to acquire nuclear, chemical, or missile technologies by hyping the current capabilities of and risks posed by third world arsenals. More realistic assessments would avoid actions which suggest that possession of proscribed weapons automatically enhances a country's international status.

Of particular concern are discussions of plans for the conduct of preemptive military operations against countries seen to be violating international nonproliferation standards. There was considerable debate in the United States beginning in 1991 about the possibility of using military measures to stop North Korean nuclear developments, for example. American opinion was divided about the wisdom of this course, with only a few, though vocal, advocates in Congress and the executive branch urging prompt military destruction of suspect nuclear sites. Other U.S. officials, as well as key U.S. allies such as Japan, South Korea, and the members of the Association of South East Asian Nations, stressed the potentially self-defeating nature of military measures at a time when Pyongyang seemed to be moving gradually toward international accommodation or could retaliate with devastating effect against the South.[18] The latter view has prevailed to date, although perhaps more because of operational military constraints than of political convictions.

It is not widely appreciated that a stated intent to manage proliferation largely by coercive means may prove as self-destructive as it is elusive. Coercion need not be only military. Disinterested or simply untutored in the domestic complexities of such a country as Ukraine, for example, the United States initially believed it could use its economic leverage to dictate the terms of Ukraine's denuclearization, demanding instant surrender of nuclear warheads to Russian control and obedience to treaty obligations that the Ukrainian government had had no part in negotiating. What began as a positive interaction with a country eager to join the international community and to rid itself of nuclear risk evolved into a confrontation over injured sovereignty and unheeded security concerns. The fate of Ukraine's nuclear weapons was thrown into doubt, and the weapons themselves transformed from military albatrosses into expensive diplomatic bargaining chips. Despite their obvious disutility for current security, the nuclear weapons on Ukrainian territory became a political vehicle for extracting concessions from the West and heightening Ukraine's political stature internationally.

The inadequacy of the American strategy was only slowly recognized by its architects, but it eventually prompted a reevaluation of policy and tactics. The need to accommodate Ukrainian historic sensitivities about Russian imperialism, to understand the recalcitrance prompted by American heavy-handedness in pressuring the Ukrainian government to accede to its demands, and to try to defuse domestic opposition in a newly activated democracy was more fully appreciated. The United States advanced proposals in June 1993 for dismantling and storing nuclear weapons under multinational safeguards on Ukrainian soil pending ratification of agreements for further constraints, along with discussions of extending security guarantees and additional economic inducements to facilitate Ukrainian accession.

An even more glaring policy deficiency is the continued lack of preparation for and effective response to the violence and political disorder sweeping across former Soviet bloc countries, as well as in other areas, such as Somalia. Traditional security approaches have little to contribute to the question of how to restore or protect stability in states that are fragmenting, where territorial boundaries are not recognized or honored and where massive influxes of displaced persons are becoming a common occurrence.[19]

For now, the UN has assumed responsibility for many crises that exceed the ability or interest of the United States to manage, but it has been forced to do so far out of proportion to its ability to conduct operations effectively. Controversies abound over whether existing peacekeeping mechanisms can or should take on larger security commitments, perhaps to the point of deploying multilateral forces in actual conflicts in the effort to establish cease-fires, a debate that intensified in 1993. The bitter domestic disputes over proposals for intervention in the former Yugoslavia made it clear not only that the U.S. public was not ready to contemplate sending Americans into combat situations in the interest of stability in the former Soviet bloc, but also that institutional arrangements for implementing such actions were wholly inadequate.

Proposals to develop well-equipped, specialized forces to help restore or protect political order under UN authority have foundered on governments' reluctance to commit resources commensurate to these challenges.[20] Nations, including the United States, still look upon investment in preventive actions as a subordinate objective that should not impinge on national plans for military preparedness. Before his resignation even Secretary of Defense Aspin had stressed that funding peacekeeping operations from the operating Pentagon budget could impede military readiness and lead to a "hollow force."[21]

Financial obligations could be redirected under a cooperative security regime to redress many resource and political constraints impinging on such preventive measures. If U.S. forces were organized and equipped so that they could actually be deployed in international coalitions anywhere in the world on short notice, resources could be allocated more equitably and efficiently among allies. The need for overseas basing and troop deployments—and their attendant costs—could also be reduced significantly. Remaining forces forward deployed could and should evolve from national to more fully international obligations in any case, helping to dampen the image that the United States upholds an outmoded, confrontational security order, reducing controversies over burden-sharing, and helping to mitigate potential frictions that can arise in regions where domestic tensions could be exacerbated by an exclusively U.S. military presence.

In the final analysis, the underpinning of a cooperative security regime is transparency and information, maximizing the need for high-quality intelligence and analyses of politicomilitary developments to help anticipate, identify, and prevent conflicts before they occur. The Clinton administration is trying to move in this direction, certainly as compared with its predecessor. In his testimony before Congress in March 1993, for example, the current director of the Central Intelligence Agency, R. James Woolsey, pledged that the intelligence community would redirect its resources and talents to new forms of intelligence and analysis focused on global political and economic developments. In the previous administration, proposals from the Senate and House Select Committees on Intelligence to refocus Defense Intelligence and National Security Agency efforts in this manner encountered outright opposition from Secretary of Defense Richard Cheney, among others. Cheney argued that these agencies were compelled to be "combat support agencies" that must be "especially responsive to the needs of war-fighting commanders."[22] Even today, the latter view has yet to be dispelled among career and some appointed intelligence officials, for whom security may always remain a purely military concept.

Regional Relations

The previous administration's approach to security planning in Europe reflected the traditional U.S. distrust of new security partnerships and a dogged effort to maintain the status quo in the midst of overwhelming change. The belief that NATO was the only credible Western alliance organization overshadowed any serious support for a Europe-wide organization that might better reflect current political realities. Even as European security institutions have multiplied and begun to overwhelm NATO's relevance in key areas, elements of the current policymaking apparatus still try to cling to a NATO-centric approach as the basis for European engagement, though less dogmatically than their predecessors.

Political rigidity toward institution building and the management of relations in Europe could prove especially damaging to U.S. leadership and continue to hinder effective preparation for collective approaches to future crises. Contrary to the beliefs of either isolationists or advocates of a Pax Americana, American participation in European security affairs will be necessary to ensure continued American influence and to secure the victory won in the cold war. Even if the forces of anarchy and civic violence do not spill over into the rest of Europe, these conditions just in the former Soviet bloc hardly signify a triumph for the West. A strong U.S. role is needed to help deter the escalation of regional instabilities, to help NATO countries forge enduring relationships with new democracies, to assist in the demobilization and conversion of the military sectors of former adversaries, and to help express the sense of common purpose between East and West.

A new European cooperative security structure could complement rather than undercut NATO and need not be damaging to American interests. Given the political diversity of Europe, no single institution can carry the weight of providing for European security in any case. American engagement does not mean an extensive American troop presence; the burden of European defense and collective security appropriately rests with the Europeans. But however the Europeans choose to organize themselves, the United States has to be involved as a partner if it intends to maintain a role in determining the region's future.

The United States has long believed itself to be the principal guarantor of stability in other regions, especially in Asia. Recently, however, domestic pressures for U.S. disengagement in this region have intensified. The opposition to U.S. involvement in Asia has focused largely on questions of trade with economic competitors, U.S. troop deployments in Korea and elsewhere, the future military role of Japan, and the desirability of continued U.S.-China ties. The major regional powers, conversely, have made it clear that they want the United States to maintain some level of military presence to prevent dramatic changes in the regional balance, and are typically more concerned about U.S. protectionism or retrenchment than about other potential sources of instability.

The costs of either an isolationist or a Pax Americana approach to security in Asia are fairly easy to discern. Protectionist trade measures and pressures on Japan to dramatically alter its military policies could undermine regional stability and the foundations for a cooperative U.S.-Japanese approach to security. Urging Japan to augment its force posture and to discard the idea of its military as existing only for self-defense would be seen as provocative by other states. A widening divergence between the United States and Japan could even prompt the only major nonnuclear power in Northeast Asia to conclude that it could no longer rely on the American security commitment, and thus to reassess its own military policies. It is much more in the United States' interest to see Japan's security policies evolve in the context of a cooperative relationship, helping thereby to foster adherence to international norms guiding military behavior, defense-related technology exports, and free trade.

Current U.S. policy toward China has been the subject of protracted domestic controversy for several years, recently over the issues of China's human rights violations and its arms and technology export policies. The original rationale for forging a strategic relationship with China—to provide a military counterweight to the Soviet Union—is no longer relevant. The United States is left with a complicated relationship with a recalcitrant government that it often seems not to understand. The perception of China as a rogue state bent on flouting international norms has also grown steadily in the public and in Congress in the last few years. As a metaphor for U.S.-China relations, U.S. failure to persuade China to abide by international human rights and defense technology trade standards reinforces the view among critics that the bilateral relationship is a one-way street, little more than a strategic expedience for the Chinese in which the United States is an unwitting or decidedly inept pawn.

Congressional initiatives calling for punitive measures against Japan, China, or other Asian countries that seem to be violating international standards are perhaps understandable, but for many reasons this strategy is not likely to be effective. Wholesale threats of embargoes or other punitive trade sanctions seem to have little positive impact on the behavior of sovereign powers. For China, frontal assaults seem simply to remind it of its separateness in the international order, or to drive proscribed activities underground. Unaccompanied by incentives and various other face-saving devices, efforts to effect reforms through punitive measures are usually counterproductive, especially if they are not fully supported by the international community as a whole.

It may be obvious that U.S. policy will never be effective as long as it is based on an inadequate appreciation of regional and domestic politics in Asia. But explaining the forces that impel unpopular policies in certain countries, while stressing the need for continued ties with those states, is a hard sell to Congress and to the American public. Controversies over trade or human rights policies are microcosms of the larger challenge of trying to persuade Americans that severing relations or imposing sanctions in response to infractions may not be the best way to promote democratization, military restraint, and overall U.S. interests.

This is a classic foreign policy dilemma in U.S. relations with countries whose governments differ from Western democracies. The question is how far one can stretch international norms to accommodate the domestic imperatives of intransigent states before appearing to be weak willed. Conversely, one has to gauge how stringently to pressure states to abide by norms before antagonizing them and thereby losing all leverage.

In emphasizing a cooperative over a confrontational approach, the United States may be able to gain critical leverage by appealing to the growing interest of China and other regional powers in becoming more equal partners in the international order, on the one hand, while being able to marshal strong international reaction if recalcitrance continues. Integration into the economic system is a potentially powerful form of self-interest to which the United States can appeal in promoting other objectives, especially with industrializing countries such as China or even North Korea. The United States already uses access to technology as an instrument of dissuasion, but a policy that trades critical technology for concessions on the nonproliferation front, for example, could be far more effectively exploited if undertaken in an internationally cooperative manner.

Similarly, decisions to reduce the U.S. force presence in Asia have always prompted controversy because they were seen as a sign of U.S. retrenchment. Even as forces are being drawn down in the current environment, the United States will still rely on maritime power in the western Pacific, some U.S. armed forces in Japan, and a combat-ready presence in South Korea until a peaceful resolution of Korean relations is worked out. Whatever the configuration of U.S. forces, however, the world community's stake in the world's most economically dynamic region has long been and will remain vital. Of all of the regions in the world, it is most obvious in Asia that international interests need not be defined either as unilaterally American or as largely military. A cooperative approach to security in this region, as such, is already unavoidable if the United States is to preserve its own interests and manage controversies arising from desirable or unavoidable alterations in its own commitments.

In mid-1993 the nuclear ambitions of North Korea helped to highlight the profound stakes of the international community in developments on the Korean peninsula. North Korea's refusal to allow adequate inspections of its suspect nuclear facilities and its threat in 1992 to leave the Nuclear Non-Proliferation Treaty (NPT) regime sent a clear message that North Korean intentions had international implications, with especially adverse consequences for the global effort to stop the spread of nuclear weapons. The United States took the lead in helping to dissuade North Korea from terminating its membership in the NPT (a decision reached in June 1993), but any enduring arrangement for North Korean adherence to international agreements clearly will require broader international involvement, including involvement by China, Japan, and Russia. Leaving an issue as sensitive as North Korea's nuclear program to the United States to rectify threatens to narrow the debate to a bilateral or quasi-regional dispute, in which the United States is forced to assume responsibility for unilateral—and potentially controversial and less than decisive— retaliation if the effort fails.

In the Middle East, the proliferation of weapons of mass destruction, especially in Syria, Iran, and Iraq, has been identified by the Clinton administration as the most serious threat to U.S. and allied interests. At the same time, the disappearance of a Soviet threat, the progressive disarmament of Iraq, and the agreement between Israel and the PLO signed in September 1993 have opened new diplomatic opportunities for mediating and reducing hostilities between Israel and its Arab antagonists. The administration has sustained its predecessor's ambitious initiatives to promote peace in the region, including brokering peace talks and pressing for serious concessions from both sides. For the United States to take full advantage of the potential promises for accommodation in the region, diplomatic skill may prove far more important than the substance of U.S. force plans. A preoccupation with force projection, overseas basing, and other traditional indicators of military preparedness may not be relevant to many of the potential catalysts for instabilities in the region. The issue of arms and technology sales, currently being driven in large measure by economic competition among the major industrial suppliers, is especially sensitive. Only a multilateral approach to arms proliferation can redress the potentially adverse security effects of uncontrolled weapon sales pursued for short-term nationalistic interests.

U.S. plans in the early 1990s to sell more than $20 billion in major combat equipment to the region might be construed as inconsistent with an overall policy preaching military restraint and arms limitations.[23] The Bush and Clinton administrations have correctly argued that there is a trade-off between arms sales and the U.S. ability to minimize the size of ground forces deployed in the Gulf, although the tendency is more often to stress the importance of these contracts for U.S. industry. Whatever the wisdom of these arms deals, however, they certainly will not reduce the economic strains in the region, nor will they encourage a political transition away from high levels of military control over government expenditures and economic planning in key states.[24] These latter problems are still relegated to a lower level of importance than force augmentation and modernization.

A more prominent U.S. military presence in certain countries, as is currently envisioned, may also not necessarily improve the prospects for successful management of regional problems. On the contrary, the deployment of troops in countries such as Saudi Arabia may exacerbate local opposition to what is seen as excessive Western influence, as occurred in Iran in the 1970s. To this end, even selective and seemingly justified unilateral punitive attacks on adversarial states such as Iraq may prove to be counterproductive in the long run if U.S. actions are seen by friendly Arab governments and populations as an illegitimate exercise of U.S. power.

In the rest of the world, the United States has exhibited a strong trend toward disengagement or at least indifference in large segments of Africa and even in Central America. Except for Somalia, these regions currently receive relatively little official U.S. attention, a far cry from the days when the Soviet airlift to Ethiopia in the late 1970s or the civil war in Nicaragua in the 1980s dominated the U.S. foreign policy agenda. No longer useful as surrogates in the superpowers' struggle for ascendancy, they loom instead as unwanted burdens on dwindling foreign assistance budgets.

Current U.S. policy in the third world is still predominantly driven by a perception that the future of U.S. security is imperiled by anarchic and aggressive states bent on disrupting global stability. This concept is not new in U.S. relations with the third world. In the 1970s U.S. concerns focused on the threat of economic blackmail from embittered former colonial states that felt disenfranchised from the international economic and political system.[25] Unlike during the 1970s, however, when it was largely conceded that these countries had legitimate grievances, the current view tends to dismiss the importance of root causes of third world aggression and simply seeks to contain or punish its perpetrators. As a basis for eliciting third world participation in a U.S.-led security regime, this notion is not exactly visionary and may not help enfranchise a large number of states on behalf of common goals.

Role and Utility of Nuclear Weapons

The agreement reached in June 1992 by Presidents George Bush and Boris Yeltsin to reduce the two states' nuclear inventories, signed by the two sides in the last days of the Bush administration, was unprecedented in both the scope of its provisions and its potential for further stabilizing actions in the future. Once implemented, the agreement would reduce the two nations' strategic inventories by about 70 percent from the levels established by the 1991 Strategic Arms Reduction Talks. More important, the new agreement calls for the complete elimination of both sides' most destabilizing weapons, land-based missiles with multiple independently targetable warheads.

The new limits on nuclear arsenals have overshadowed the more modest debate about the continued importance ascribed to nuclear weapons in U.S. strategy, or the criteria guiding the size, character, safety, or targeting of remaining nuclear forces. The perceived utility of nuclear weapons in defending U.S. interests is a subject of considerable confusion. The domestic debate about the role of nuclear weapons has never been particularly coherent, but it has now run logically amok. The competing strands of thinking are reflected in proposals as disparate as developing low-yield weapons or arming expeditionary forces with nuclear capabilities for intervention in third world contingencies, retaining a permanently robust nuclear deterrent that must always exceed the collective arsenals of other nuclear powers, encouraging allies to acquire nuclear weapons through a system of "managed proliferation," or proposing that nuclear weapons and warfare be outlawed as a "crime against humanity and the environment."[26]

Current strategy is to retain a triad of nuclear weapons sufficient to counter the Russian strategic force and to provide a secure retaliatory capability to deter the use of nuclear weapons by "hostile and irresponsible countries," as Secretary of Defense Cheney put it in 1992 in a statement that was reiterated in similar terms by Clinton officials.[27] The reasons for retaining a triad, a product of very conservative estimates of what would be required to cope with a disarming Soviet first strike, are not discussed officially. Current force levels and reductions, which have been driven largely by political events of the recent past, are also not necessarily tied to prior assessments of military requirements or efficiency. The assumption is that a floor exists beneath which U.S. forces cannot be allowed to fall, but this minimum level is not necessarily determined by targeting doctrine or by the political goals that the doctrine is meant to uphold.

The question of which countries the United States will target with nuclear weapons in the future and under what circumstances is simply not articulated and certainly not clearly understood, even among planners. According to some officials, this question does not require an a priori answer. The preponderance of U.S. strategic forces remain targeted at the former Soviet nuclear arsenal, considered an immutable imperative. The targeting review conducted during the Bush administration in 1991, moreover, purportedly generated plans that provided for flexible options for global application, including the ability to retarget weapons in "real time" to meet any contingency. This plan is a modern version of a *tout azimuth* nuclear strategy. More recently, plans have been discussed among defense officials to target third world countries with highly accurate conventional forces as well.[28]

The vanishing nuclear order was the product of a need to deter aggression against NATO by superior Warsaw Pact conventional forces. NATO members were unwilling or unable to dedicate sufficient resources or to take the steps necessary to restructure their defense sectors to rectify the disparities in conventional capabilities. Nuclear weapons were thus a cheap way of maintaining a military balance. Outside NATO, nuclear guarantees were extended very selectively to close U.S. allies that confronted proximate enemies allied with or part of the Soviet bloc. Insofar as these arrangements were considered legitimate, it was as part of a bipolar system in which the United States, Europe, and a few other allies were united in a defensive alliance, while the Soviet Union was seen as an expansionist power bent on global hegemony.

With the exception of Russia and China, the current nuclear threat, to the extent that it can be reliably defined, consists of a handful of states with small or fledgling programs or sometimes just immodest ambitions. This definition is not meant to belittle the dangers such states may pose to international or regional stability in the future. But the sudden elevation of third world powers to the status of ruthless enemies on a par with the Soviet Union bears further examination, especially since it is now becoming a principal rationale for retaining a U.S. nuclear deterrent. According to former secretary of defense Aspin, the only remaining nuclear threat to the United States, except for the loss of control over Soviet nuclear assets, will come from a few nuclear-armed rogue states bent on aggression or terrorism. This unspecified group of nuclear thugs, which are untutored in and therefore undaunted by the refined logic of deterrence, may be able to "equalize" U.S. conventional superiority with just a few crude nuclear devices. Had Saddam Hussein had just six nuclear weapons capable of reaching Riyadh or Tel Aviv, according to this view, there is serious doubt that the United States would have succeeded in assembling a political coalition for Operation Desert Storm.

It is obviously not possible to prove or disprove such a premise. But if this argument is correct, it seems to pose immense implications for both the future utility of U.S. nuclear forces and the way in which the legacy of nuclear weapons is judged. NATO was prepared for more than three decades to risk nuclear confrontation with an equal or (according to some in more recent years) superior nuclear adversary. NATO doctrine included the intent to initiate nuclear conflict if necessary, regardless of the certainty that this act could prompt retaliation sufficient to annihilate Western society. That aside, the West today would be paralyzed in the face of a few weapons in the hands of "irrational" and "undeterrable" enemies such as Iraq, according to Aspin and others.

Part of the logic of this argument hinges on the notion that the Soviet Union was rational, valued its survival, and could be targeted effectively, whereas the nuclear powers of the future probably will not share these traits. As Aspin argued in a speech in June 1992, "Will our nuclear adversaries always be rational, or at least operate with the same logic as we do? We can't be sure. Will we always be able to put our adversaries at risk to make deterrence work? Not necessarily, particularly with terrorists whom we may not even be able to find."[29] But if one is going to make the argument that U.S. strategy falls apart in the face of a third world atomic adversary, one has the intellectual responsibility to explain the reasons. What is the basis for the vast differences in U.S. and Western resolve against enemies that are nuclear dwarfs compared to the Soviet Union? What do these differences say for the legacy of flexible response? Was the nuclear competition over Europe between the United States and the Soviet Union merely an abstraction, whereas the Iraqi scenario is serious?

The retroactive depiction of the Soviet Union as an essentially benign adversary that could be counted on to play by the rules certainly runs counter to the volumes written by erudite scholars about the Soviet proclivity for war or the lower value Soviet citizens placed on human life. Without even a decent interval, the Soviets have been strangely redeemed, and emerging or aspiring third world nuclear powers have inherited the Soviets' mantle. They are now the warmongers that have a higher tolerance for death and are driven by causes that supersede rational calculation. It hardly needs mention that this caricature of the third world is rather racist; one also can discern that it is often meant to depict the Islamic world. The notion that there are undeterrable states seems to suggest that the architecture of nuclear-based deterrence has little utility in the modern world. Deterrence has always relied on the demonstrated ability and willingness to use nuclear weapons if necessary and to communicate this intent to potential adversaries. However, officials have proved remarkably squeamish when asked to articulate the way in which targeting and use of residual U.S. nuclear forces will occur in the new world order. The political hazards of discussing such contingencies are obvious, and no agreed-upon procedures exist to even begin discussions about the future role of nuclear forces operating in the third world.

In the haste to define new threats, there has been no opportunity for an adequate evaluation of the legacy of nuclear weapons for American security, let alone time to think about their future. Did nuclear weapons prevent war? What are the lessons to be derived from the history of nuclear deterrence, different operational practices, or the use of nuclear threats? Which among these lessons would the United States want other states to emulate? Unless the nuclear powers are willing to confront the security benefits or dangers of their own policies, it is not possible to craft coherent policy for others. What is decided about the nuclear legacy, in short, has important ramifications for future force planning and, most important, for designing credible nonproliferation policies.

In contrast to the principles guiding cooperative security discussed in preceding chapters, current nuclear plans do not focus adequately on the most critical risk to U.S. security: the possible failure of operational control over nuclear weapons. For now, discussion has been limited about ways to make nuclear weapons less usable (such as the renunciation of practices requiring the prompt launch of nuclear forces, improvements in command and control, significant reductions in alert status, and other restraints on the ability to conduct a surprise attack) or about negative controls (such as permissive action links). Indeed, the rationales driving nuclear planning often seem more intent on preserving at least the edifice of the nuclear status quo, in anticipation of the return of a Soviet-type nuclear adversary.

The traditional objective of deterrence against the Soviet Union required the ability to initiate a large nuclear attack within a few minutes and to complete it within a few hours. The danger of a prior attack on U.S. deterrent forces required in turn that in a crisis it be possible to disperse this capability to a relatively large number of widely separated operational commanders. The commitments to rapid response, dispersed control, and detailed programming for large-scale attack, as such, made operational readiness rather than safety necessarily the preeminent goal of U.S. strategy. As long as the threat of sudden attack was considered the primary security problem, the safe management of weapons was accepted as a subordinate, though certainly vital, consideration. Extensive provisions were developed to protect against the accidental or unauthorized explosion of any nuclear weapon as well as against any compromise of physical custody. Still, these provisions were all designed to preserve a large inventory of weapons in an extremely responsive state of deployment. As best as it can be determined, despite the inherent tensions between operational readiness and control, the record has been a success. No unintended nuclear detonations occurred, and the only known compromises of physical custody have been the result of operational accidents whose frequency seems to have diminished with accumulating experience.[30]

The current risks, however, are different. The internal pressures on the strategic command system of the former Soviet Union are so extensive and of such uncertain consequence that its ability to maintain standards of safety while preserving a highly reactive operational posture cannot prudently be assumed. Moreover, the possibility that the two strategic forces could accidentally trigger each other because of their highly reactive postures is an enduring problem that simply cannot be measured on the basis of past experience.[31]

The various initiatives that have been recently undertaken to reduce nuclear weapons deployments and to relax routine alert procedures will alleviate but not eliminate the internal pressures on the strategic command system in the former Soviet Union. And they will have very little material effect on the underlying problem of crisis interaction. The commitment to rapid reaction has not been altered, and traditional crisis alert procedures remain in effect on both sides, as does the pattern of dispersed control. Even the sharply reduced forces and reconfigured weapons deployments that are to result from the June 1992 framework agreement are capable of inflicting enormous damage on any industrial society. In fact, even at these lower force levels, an inadvertent triggering of the strategic attack plans that are being continued as the basis for deterrence would still be the largest man-made catastrophe in history. Given the inherent inability to determine the probability of such an event, there is strong reason to seek higher standards of safety by removing the commitment to rapid reaction and dispersed control.

Aside from reducing the risk of strategic interaction, reductions in the alert status of U.S., Russian, and other states' nuclear weapons would be an important demonstration of the devaluation of nuclear weapons as instruments of state power. This could be a critical, if not sufficient, foundation for efforts to delegitimize nuclear weapons globally. Although such alterations may not be sufficient to dissuade some regional powers from their own agendas, the diminution of the global status of nuclear forces is an important first step toward the devaluation, reduction, and perhaps eventual elimination of all weapons of mass destruction.

Many officials and establishment experts, however, seem to believe that limits on U.S. nuclear capabilities that go much further than current constraints would weaken the ability of the United States to influence other countries. Rather than promote nuclear restraint, they argue, deeper cuts and operational changes could actually encourage hostile nations to acquire nuclear capabilities to threaten or to actually use such weapons against U.S. forces in a crisis. The United States might even lose the ability to offset superior conventional capabilities of future adversaries. The ultimately ironic argument, advanced by "centrists," is that the United States needs nuclear weapons to retaliate against countries that breach a nonproliferation regime.

Realistically, contradictions in nuclear beliefs and practices are not likely to be resolved soon. In the near term, however, the possibility of further constraints on the development of nuclear weapons has become a more acceptable topic within establishment circles. Long considered the domain of fringe disarmament advocates, a move toward a ban on testing nuclear weapons, for example, has finally won qualified support in the Clinton administration, beginning with a policy to extend the current moratorium on U.S. testing as long as no other nation conducts tests first.[32]

Perhaps for the first time, practical reality coincides with political objectives. The United States ceased production of special nuclear materials and new nuclear warheads in 1991 and announced an intiative for an international fissile material production cut-off for weapons use in 1993. The administration's defense program for fiscal 1993–97 is slated to cancel all major modernization programs for nuclear forces except the Trident II submarine-launched ballistic missile. As early as 1992, the Bush administration announced that in the future any nuclear tests would be limited in number and conducted strictly for safety or reliability, a position widely supported in Congress and by the Clinton administration.

An agreement to halt nuclear testing would not be the decisive element of a U.S. commitment to denuclearization, nor sufficient incentive for other nuclear powers to renounce their own ambitions. But if it is no longer necessary to develop new types of nuclear weapons and it is agreed that the preparation to fight nuclear wars is an unnecessary and counterproductive precaution, clinging to the prerogative to test imposes costs with no discernible benefit. As George Perkovich has argued, "The central requirement of nonproliferation is to convince other countries that nuclear weapons are not usable and therefore not worth trying to acquire. Continued nuclear testing sends just the opposite message. By ceaselessly refining and testing these weapons, we suggest they *are* usable."[33]

Obviously the concern about North-South asymmetries and the belief that a comprehensive test ban might enhance U.S. stature in championing the NPT are not views shared by all defense analysts. For some, testing is needed not just as a way to ensure warhead and stockpile reliability but also to maintain cadres of expert designers, engineers, and other specialists as a hedge against new threats or the return of the strategic threat. The United States may again find it desirable to develop new warhead designs, according to this view. As one commentator summarized the situation, "They must explore every possible technical option that renegade nations might exploit in developing their own versions of atomic bombs . . . and only testing can do that job . . . [The nuclear laboratories] must design, develop and test advanced warhead prototypes for the future to prove out new weapons systems that the United States might eventually need in an uncertain and unstable world."[34]

The rejection of testing limits serves as a useful microcosm of many of the arguments of isolationists, Pax Americana advocates, and those who feel nostalgic about the passing of the cold war. As a statement of isolationist sentiment, the position embraces the idea that the United States has little to gain from trying to influence other countries, and certainly not if this influence imposes undue self-restraint on American security options. For those who tend toward the views of a Pax Americana, a continued commitment to nuclear weapon testing and innovation is a vital element of U.S. military and technological superiority, an objective whose benefits far surpass those of any tertiary diplomatic objective such as strengthening the NPT. For aging cold warriors, continued testing, like nuclear targeting, demonstrates in a concrete way that the United States will always be prepared for the enemy, whoever and wherever it may be.

Controlling Technology Proliferation

The majority of controls on weapons and weapons technologies that have evolved over the past four decades consist of initiatives undertaken by the larger powers to restrict access to proscribed technologies by smaller states, usually while preserving the right to retain these weapons in their own arsenals. That is certainly true for nuclear weapons but also for various conventional armaments and until recently chemical weapons.[35] Although invoking the interests of global security, nonproliferation arrangements ratify the right of the technologically powerful to impinge on the technical sovereignty of lesser states. The various control regimes range from arms embargoes, supplier cartels, and safeguard agreements on sensitive technologies, to threats of attack. They rely on trade barriers, punitive sanctions, and high-minded principle to dissuade or prevent states from attempting to emulate some aspects of the military capabilities of the large powers. The NPT, the Coordinating Committee on Multilateral Export Controls (COCOM), and the Missile Technology Control Regime (MTCR) were unabashedly designed to protect a hierarchical international system in which the United States and some allies would retain certain advantages while encouraging restraint on the part of others.

The United States and other industrial states also reserve the right to promote technology proliferation when it is expedient. They have often abetted proliferation directly, by treating the defense trade at least in the conventional area as almost a standard form of commerce for all but the most sensitive technologies. It is not unusual for officials to discuss the burgeoning threat of third world militarization in one part of a statement and then turn to the importance of U.S. competiveness in the global arms market. There was no intended irony in Secretary of Defense Cheney's statement to Congress in

February 1992, for example, in which he championed the importance of arms sales to partners in the Middle East and shortly after warned of the dangers of a global diffusion of military and dual-use technologies: "[These technologies] will enable a growing number of countries to field highly capable weapons systems, such as ballistic missiles, stealthy cruise missiles, integrated air defenses, submarines, modern command and control systems, and even space-based assets. *Unfortunately, there are both governments and individuals willing to supply proliferating countries with both systems and technical expertise*."[36]

The few periodic attempts to control conventional arms proliferation over the last three decades have essentially failed.[37] Most industrial states believe it is to their advantage to be fairly permissive in the export of conventional arms, though with some restraints on highly advanced weapon systems or technologies.[38] Arms transfers have been a key instrument of efforts by the large powers to gain influence in the third world, and more recently to defray the costs of their own arms industries with export revenues. In the aftermath of the Iraqi war, the five permanent members of the UN Security Council began to discuss broad guidelines to coordinate their respective exports of advanced conventional weaponry, but such guidelines have yet to affect national decisions to export arms in any demonstrable manner.[39]

Not incidentally the apparatus for managing defense technology trade in the U.S. bureaucracy is responsible for both promoting and controlling U.S. exports. U.S. technology transfer policy is fragmented institutionally and intellectually. It cuts across traditional demarcations of economic, military, and diplomatic interests and impinges on such disparate elements of policy as commercial investments and export promotion, management of the domestic defense industrial base, strategic trade controls, development and security assistance, and international trade cartels for controlling particularly sensitive technologies, such as those used in nuclear and chemical weapons. Weaknesses in the U.S. policy apparatus for technology transfers have been accentuated by the rapid changes and growing complexity of the international technology market. Commercially available components of military significance, including guidance and telemetry equipment, satellites, and computer technology, have contributed to developing countries' capacity for independent or quasi-independent weapon production programs. Many countries have proceeded with military production programs with the assistance of an expanding international system of commercial entrepreneurs, in an elaborate pattern of military trade that operates largely outside U.S. control.

The evolution of the international technology market has not been accompanied by commensurate changes in the bureaucratic apparatus. The complex jurisdictional structures established for promoting or restraining technology transactions have evolved into a highly stratified bureaucratic regime, rife with discontinuities and contradictions. To illustrate, a decision in 1986 to sell advanced computers to India through commercial channels, heralded as "a major opportunity to increase American influence in that nation at the expense of the Soviet Union," led in 1989 to serious concerns about India's potential use of supercomputers in its missile and nuclear development programs, which the United States is actively trying to discourage. Similarly, the imposition of congressionally mandated U.S. sanctions on companies that violate the MTCR resulted in serious frictions between the United States and the Indian and Russian governments over a space technology contract at just the time when the United States had embarked on a major effort to expand trade and political relations with both countries.

The disparities in objectives and practices among agencies that oversee different types of technology transfer impede the implementation of coherent export guidelines. A common feature in COCOM discussions of the past, internecine controversies among the Commerce, State, and Defense departments and between Congress and the executive branch have plagued the effort to implement coherent export controls for decades.

In practice, the sheer volume of arms sales requests means that the preponderance of U.S. military licenses granted each year are approved or denied with a minimum of scrutiny or debate. Of the approximately 55,000 license requests or agreements processed annually through the State Department's Office of Defense Trade, for example, less than 20 percent are likely to be referred to other agencies for review, and less than 1 percent to Congress. In turn, most arms sales decisions are approved or denied on the basis of routine recommendations by midlevel officials and are only rarely examined by more senior officials.

In controversial cases, the factors weighed in the review process are a diffuse amalgam of technical, political, and military judgments, deriving as much from transitory political interests and different agencies' interpretations of policy as from any formal statutes or precedents. Although some export guidelines are enduring and clear-cut, such as the prohibitions on the transfer of nuclear weapons, interagency deliberations about significant arms transactions are rarely driven by objective assessments of long-term national security interests.

The recurring patterns of bureaucratic disputes, reflecting long-standing institutional biases, determine policy much more than formal criteria do. Although in theory all agencies are supposed to operate with a coherent and consistent concept of "the national interest," this ideal is far from reality. Insofar as biases can be summarized across cabinet agencies, the State Department will typically be concerned about the adverse political and diplomatic effects of turning down requests for arms, whereas the Department of Defense and its constituent agencies tend to focus on the potential effects on the military capabilities of recipients and the costs or benefits of arms exports for U.S. military planning. The Commerce Department, which has played a more salient policy role as the content of trade has shifted toward a greater emphasis on commercial technologies, tends to protect American economic competitiveness and often opposes export controls on those grounds.

The outcome of deliberations over arms sales is often influenced by such factors as the relative clout of the agencies involved, the perceived importance of the recipient in domestic political terms, and even the expertise or endurance of individual participants involved in evaluating cases. Bureaucratic warfare, rather than analysis, tends to be the modus operandi in what is often a protracted process of plea bargaining and political compromise, which may or may not reflect long-term national objectives. Such a situation is particularly common when there is no unanimity about U.S. objectives at the highest levels of policymaking, as is now true in U.S. conventional arms transfer policy.

The spread of advanced chemical, biological, and conventional weapon manufacturing capabilities exemplifies the inherent weaknesses of supply-side controls for weapons readily produced with dual-use technologies. The maturation of developing countries' economies, coupled with the growing commercialization and internationalization of the technology market, virtually guarantees that countries determined to acquire these capabilities will do so. This certainty argues for a control system that begins to shift the focus away from controls only on the supply of technology to controls on the actual application of technologies. Such arrangements would require far greater levels of transparency in the international trading system and a system of cooperative enforcement among like-minded states to verify compliance and to isolate and penalize violators. Currently governments place blanket prohibitions on technologies that have legitimate uses, such as space launch vehicles, but when forced for political reasons to make exceptions lack the means to monitor the disposition of that technology after sales take place. This situation is the worst of all possible worlds: unenforceable export controls with no ability to monitor the destination or uses of transferred technologies.

Supplier restrictions still have a critical role to play in identifying and targeting a few of the technologies pertinent to weapons development. Many vital inputs for nuclear or missile development, such as advanced guidance needed for missile accuracy, remain in the hands of just a few suppliers. Future proliferation of such items therefore depends in part on policies devised by industrial countries guiding technological cooperation with other countries. Given current trends, however, the pace of international technical diffusion may eventually render controls on supply ineffectual for all but the most highly specialized or advanced products.

Emerging defense technologies may make the difficulty of differentiating among military and civilian exports even more pronounced. New technologies that are at the cutting edge of Western military modernization (including, for example, advanced information processing, composite materials, directed energy systems, and biotechnologies) are to varying degrees equally vital to civilian modernization. Advances in biotechnology enabling the production of superlethal pathogens usable in biological warfare, for instance, could also be used to develop more cost-effective and efficient agricultural techniques and medicines. Although certain biotechnologies could be highly destabilizing in a military sense, they could also have positive effects on political stability in countries where poverty and disease are important catalysts for social unrest.

More recent additions to the instruments for managing proliferation are not diplomatic or trade related but technological. These include the idea of so-called coercive arms control, destroying military installations in countries whose objectives have been deemed problematic. The notion of unilateral military preemption, even on behalf of nonproliferation objectives, is unlikely to be consonant with the politics or operational assumptions of cooperative security. However desirable in theory, a danger exists that countermilitary options could distract attention from the real challenges of nonproliferation. The legitimacy of this instrument aside, the notion that the West can arm itself to remove unwanted military facilities when necessary is probably naive.

As a political message, the notion of coercive arms control is also not consonant with a policy seeking to promote global military restraint. The idea that a few states have the right to eliminate military capabilities in states of which they disapprove will not help Western credibility in its quest for international acceptance of nonproliferation objectives. Although military options will remain one of several instruments that could be used to punish those states that violate treaties, they are not likely to be a long-term or widely applicable solution.

One legacy of the successful Israeli strike on the Osiraq nuclear reactor in Iraq was to drive Iraqi military programs into clandestine, underground installations that could resist destruction. As was discovered after Operation Desert Storm in the effort to implement UN Resolution 687, it is not easy to destroy a military infrastructure of this kind, however superior one's forces. Indeed, as the executive chairman of the UN special commission has repeatedly emphasized, inspection teams, not military strikes, have succeeded in destroying most of Iraq's nonconventional arsenal.[40] The core of Iraq's and other third world countries' military potential is entrenched in a growing industrial capability, human capital, and ability to attract suppliers. These factors are not readily susceptible to change by air strikes.

In turn, the sale of defensive systems and technology to states that have or are trying to develop missile production capabilities could inadvertently contribute to proliferation by granting those countries access to technologies useful for developing offensive systems. These range from guidance and rocket components to testing equipment and expertise about the phenomenology of missiles. Knowledge gained about the operation of antimissile systems is inherently applicable to other kinds of missile activities. South Korea, for example, succeeded in modifying the U.S. Nike-Hercules air defense system into a ballistic missile, a program that it pursued despite strenuous U.S. objections. This potential dilemma is another reason for developing effective safeguards on the end uses of sensitive technology.

A less obvious cost associated with the pursuit of technological fixes and countermilitary responses is that it typically occurs at the expense of effective diplomacy. Nonproliferation has never commanded the attention it deserved from policymakers, usually in the mistaken belief that the third world would never pose a serious military risk that the West could not counter. The effort to develop military solutions to proliferation tends to reinforce such a belief—that diplomacy is not as urgent a priority as the development of new technologies to counter any new threat, even one to which the United States may have contributed. The quest for perpetual innovations to overwhelm potential adversaries, moreover, adds to pressures to develop technologies whose proliferation would be extremely dangerous, including antisatellite capabilities, biotechnologies, and highly accurate conventional weapons.

This threat argues for a new system of regional security consultation arrangements aimed at helping states to develop stable security postures without contributing to proliferation. Supplier policies to constrain the spread of weapons will have to be bolstered with efforts to lessen demand for proscribed military acquisitions. It is in this context that regional confidence- and security-building measures are vitally important. The developed world cannot control demand for weapons technology without simultaneously working to enhance developing states' security perceptions. Regional agreements have played too small a role in the promotion of nonproliferation and conflict resolution regimes in the past. Building on such agreements as the 1968 Treaty of Tlatelolco and 1986 Treaty of Rarotonga establishing nuclear weapon–free zones in Latin America and the South Pacific, initiatives that originate among the governments in the regions are likely to be much more readily supported and enforced.

U.S. Defense Investment

The overarching goal of U.S. defense investment is to preserve an American technological edge. The premise is that the United States will always be able to maintain superior status in a technologically stratified international system. This notion may be tested more severely in coming years, however. If current trends continue, the pace of technological diffusion may eventually vitiate the U.S. reliance on technological superiority to influence international events. By reducing the time between generations of weapons and between the creation of weapons and the development of countermeasures, the rapid passing of state-of-the-art technology into obsolescence may make the quest for technological advantage ever more elusive.

Moreover, the significance of this qualitative edge may be progressively undercut if equipment widely available internationally begins to approximate the capabilities of recent innovations or at least can interfere with the latter's performance. There may be a point of technical exhaustion, in other words, at which the quest for an increment of technological superiority hits unmistakably diminishing military returns. The notion that the industrial world can continue to subsidize its own military preparedness by helping smaller states to prepare for war may hasten the point at which technological superiority ceases to be a decisive determinant of national influence. The sale of weapons and weapons technology cannot be equated with the sale of other commodities, with the developed world simply unburdening its excess products for profit. As developing countries' military capabilities continue to improve, the redistribution of military capability may begin to alter the contours of any remaining international hierarchy.

As defense allocations continue to decline, the Pentagon and defense industries have taken to promoting overseas arms sales more explicitly as a way to preserve the U.S. defense industrial base. Efforts to get Export-Import Bank subsidies for arms export promotion, to use government funds to allow American companies to participate in international weapons trade shows, or to garner congressional votes for controversial arms sales on behalf of American workers are all elements of this new emphasis. Apart from being at odds with official policy statements that proliferation is the current main problem for U.S. national security, these actions are promoting the myth that export markets can significantly forestall recession and contraction in U.S. or other national defense industries.[41]

The current administration seems to be grappling with, and seeking opportunities to help guide American industry through, this difficult transition. The defense market is in free fall, with downsizing of industry occurring randomly and apparently without benefit of a long-term vision. It is only logical that industry would be pressing for fewer restrictions on defense trade, such as lessening restrictions on third country sales, and using unions to lobby for arms exports in a desperate effort to keep jobs. The challenge now is for the government to actively encourage economic adjustment strategies that could promote the twin goals of economic stability and nonproliferation.

A vital security dilemma for the United States is finding the means to preserve superior military technologies and a healthy industrial base without a chronic dependency on exports of the kind that accelerate technical diffusion beyond what is prudent. In many respects proliferation is an economic and industrial issue. The extent to which defense-related technological innovations may require arms exports to defray their cost and the associated risks that highly lethal technologies could proliferate suggest that nonproliferation policy must be crafted before decisions guiding defense investment. The cost of innovations and the dangers of the latter's proliferation need to be integrated into decisions about whether to acquire new capabilities and, if so, the pace at which they should be procured.

Conclusion

The United States is increasingly finding itself mired in multinational endeavors, from the Conference on Security and Cooperation in Europe to the Rio Summit to assistance programs for the former Soviet bloc. It is not largely by choice that this involvement has occurred. The United States still seems reluctant to commit fully to strengthening the international mechanisms on which it currently relies. U.S. payments to the UN are seriously in arrears. Elements in Congress oppose aid to the former Soviet Union to help consolidate its economy or even to dismantle its nuclear forces. Many officials question the wisdom of giving greater resources and authority to the International Atomic Energy Agency, an institution that in the last few years has been given tasks that greatly exceed its current budget. Although the United States is by no means solely responsible, the failure to support the UN has led to chronic underfunding of peacekeeping operations, the UN Special Commission, and other vital activities. Regional conflicts are in competition for resources that are already too scarce, pitting Bosnia against Somalia in a zero-sum game.[42]

The domestic debate about the future of U.S. security is obviously in turmoil, and competing trends both impel and constrain a move to a genuinely cooperative security system. There are now agreements of unprecedented scope for nuclear limitations, but their future is in some doubt. The United States triumphs in the victory over the cold war but is incapable of responding decisively as the fruits of that victory threaten to crumble into chaos and despair. Prevailing domestic skepticism about multilateral involvement has been particularly damaging to U.S. global interests. Much of U.S. official rhetoric invites suspicions among states that think that any notion of cooperation in security may simply be a new cosmetic invented by the industrial powers to dress up old patterns of state behavior.

In the end, the failure to recognize and to adapt successfully to new international imperatives may result from a stubborn reluctance to consider the interests of regional powers as a compelling determinant of U.S. policy and a new international order. Credible international norms cannot be designed by those who are not persuaded that other countries are worthy of equality or that their amity is important in crafting new rules for the international system. In the United States, in particular, this intellectual impediment is especially difficult to dislodge. It is the product of years of studied indifference to all but a narrow set of technical security issues and a proud embrace of ignorance about and rejection of politics, culture, and regional dynamics as legitimate influences on national policy.

Finally, the question is whether the United States will be forced into half-hearted cooperation by domestic constraints and international realities or will seize the opportunities presented to it, taking the lead in crafting a global transition. The core challenge is the degree to which the United States and other countries that are in a position to promote a new security regime will be willing to sacrifice traditional notions of military-based sovereignty on its behalf. Put differently, at what point does the potential cooperative regime infringe on traditional conceptions of national prerogatives to the point that old habits compete and make it no longer possible for states to support the regime? That is the measure of commitment and ultimately of success.

Notes

1. The secretary of defense's 1993 report is revealing in this regard. See Les Aspin, *Report on the Bottom-Up Review* (Office of the Secretary of Defense, 1993).

2. See Patrick E. Tyler, "Lone Superpower Plan: Ammunition for Critics," *New York Times,* March 10, 1992, p. A12; and Patrick E. Tyler, "U.S. Strategy Plan Calls for Insuring No Rivals to Develop," *New York Times,* March 8, 1992, p. A1.

3. Former presidential candidate Patrick Buchanan and Senator Joseph Biden (Democrat of Delaware) were among the more prominent critics of the Pentagon planning document, in a rare coincidence of views between people from opposite poles of the political spectrum. Both decried the notion that the United States should bear the price of being the "world's policeman" in a time of declining resources and an urgent domestic agenda. As Buchanan put it, the strategy is "a formula for endless American intervention in quarrels and war," in which the United States simply extends a "blank check" to other countries in an open-ended pledge to protect their interests. For further discussion see, for instance, Stephen S. Rosenfeld, "The Trouble with Going It Alone," *Washington Post,* March 20, 1992, p. A25.

4. For additional discussion, see David Rosenbaum, "The Nation; Good Economics Meet Protective Politics," *New York Times,* September 19, 1993, p. D5; Paul Krugman, "The Uncomfortable Truth about NAFTA," *Foreign Affairs,* vol. 72 (November–December 1993), pp. 13–19; and William A. Orme, Jr., "NAFTA: Myths versus Facts," ibid., pp. 2–12.

5. See Steven A. Holmes, "Finding Strong Allies for Foreign Aid," *New York Times,* June 23, 1993, p. A19.

6. As Buchanan put it in early 1992, "With a $4 trillion debt, with a U.S. budget chronically out of balance, should the United States be required to carry indefinitely the full burden of defending rich and prosperous allies who take America's generosity for granted as they invade our markets?" Quoted in William Greider, "Buchanan Rethinks the American Empire," *Rolling Stone,* February 6, 1992, p. 39.

7. The quotation is from a speech given by Representative Les Aspin, September 1992. Cited in *Congressional Quarterly,* January 9, 1993, p. 82. See also Barton Gellman, "Pentagon May Seek $20 Billion More; Aspin Outlines Cost of Restructuring," *Washington Post,* August 13, 1993, p. A1.

8. Although obviously not as quixotic as the SDI, some expert analyses of future force contingencies conducted in the early 1990s emphasized the role that air power could play in according the United States clear technological—and thus political and

military—superiority in all conceivable conflicts at a minimum cost. As a RAND report argued in June 1993, for example, "By the turn of the century, if provided with available technology, U.S. airpower will be capable of stopping an attack force of over 8,000 armored vehicles and 1,000 aircraft in little more than a week," and, with some assistance from land and sea forces, could allow the U.S. to manage concurrent crises in the Persian Gulf and Korea. Charles W. Corddry, "Air Power Must Be First in Future, Study Says," *Baltimore Sun*, June 23, 1993, p. 9. The public release version of this study is Christopher Bowie and others, *The New Calculus: Analyzing Airpower's Changing Role in Joint Theater Campaigns*, report prepared for the United States Air Force by the RAND Institution (Santa Monica, Calif., 1993).

9. Barton Gellman and John Lancaster, "U.S. May Drop 2-War Capability," *Washington Post*, June 17, 1993, p. A1.

10. Speech by Secretary of Defense Les Aspin at Andrews Air Force Base, cited in John Lancaster, "Aspin Opts for Winning Two Wars—Not 1½—at Once," *Washington Post*, June 25, 1993, p. A6. For further discussion, see, for instance, Bruce B. Auster, "A High-Tech Cavalry," *U.S. News and World Report*, June 28, 1993, p. 29.

11. See Michael Mandelbaum, "Like It or Not, We Must Lead," *Washington Post*, June 9, 1993, p. A21.

12. R. Jeffrey Smith and Julia Preston, "U.S. Plans Wider Role in U.N. Peace Keeping," *Washington Post*, June 18, 1993, p. A1.

13. Congressional Budget Office, *Structuring U.S. Forces after the Cold War: Costs and Effects of Increased Reliance on the Reserves* (September 1992).

14. Office of Assistant Secretary of Defense (Public Affairs), "FY 1994 Budget Begins New Era," News Release, March 27, 1993. In the Bush administration, defense priorities were expressed in more traditional, confrontational terms, including the position that the United States would rely on four major elements to protect its overseas interests: "strategic deterrence and defense," based on a modified nuclear triad on a lower level of alert, along with missile defenses; "forward presence," including long-range bombers, carriers, and new overseas bases, if necessary; "crisis response," based on the ability to project power instantaneously "in diverse areas of the world," which means globally; and "reconstitution," an ability to provide for "a global warfighting capability" should the need arise. Technological superiority, robust nuclear forces, a more pronounced overseas military presence in the Gulf, and military options for countering proliferation were key elements of this strategy, with research and development and force deployments directed accordingly. See *Department of Defense Annual Report to the President and the Congress, Fiscal Year 1992*. It is too early to predict if the differences with the succeeding administration will be significant in substance as well as in rhetoric.

15. "Statement of General Colin L. Powell, chairman of the Joint Chiefs of Staff, before the Senate Committee on Armed Services," January 31, 1992.

16. Art Pine, "Defense Budget Lists Funds for Peacekeeping," *Los Angeles Times*, March 26, 1993, p. A5.

17. See, for instance, Christopher Layne and Ted Galen Carpenter, "Arabian Nightmares: Washington's Persian Gulf Entanglement," *Policy Analysis* (Cato Institute), no. 142 (November 9, 1990).

18. See, for instance, "DOD Revamps North Korea Contingency Plan to Focus on USAF Preemptive Strikes," *Inside the Air Force*, vol. 2 (November 29, 1991), p. 1; Gwen Ifill, "In Korea, Chilling Reminders of Cold War," *New York Times*, July 18, 1993, p. D1; and David E. Sanger, "Clinton, in Seoul, Tells North Korea to Drop Arms Plan," *New York Times*, July 11, 1993, p. A1.

19. Other regional threats that are not likely to be responsive to enhanced U.S. power projection capabilities include, among others, the increasing concerns in Europe about further emigration from North Africa; the emergence of five new central Asian republics and three new nations in the Caucasus that may not be cohesive and could become the objects of rivalry among regional powers; the continued expansion of intra–Middle East and intra–third world consortiums for the development and production of and trade in armaments, including ballistic missiles and unconventional munitions; and the reemergence of Iran as a major political power in the Gulf.

20. As is analyzed in detail in chapter 7 in this volume, the main donor countries in the UN are in serious arrears just in their payments for existing obligations. In mid-1993, for example, the United States owed an estimated $310 million for peacekeeping operations. See also Richard Bernstein, "Sniping Is Growing at U.N.'s Weakness as a Peacekeeper," *New York Times,* June 21, 1993, p. A1.

21. Pine, "Defense Budget Lists Funds for Peacekeeping."

22. George Lardner, Jr., "Cheney Assails Intelligence Revision Plan," *Washington Post,* March 24, 1992, p. A5.

23. See, for example, Natalie J. Goldring, "Transfer of Advanced Technology and Sophisticated Weapons," paper prepared for the United Nations Conference on Disarmament Issues, entitled "Disarmament and National Security in the Interdependent World," Kyoto, Japan, April 13–16, 1993.

24. For a detailed discussion of the political economy of the region and the link to military expenditures, see Yahya Sadowski, *Scuds or Butter? The Political Economy of Arms Control in the Middle East* (Brookings, 1992).

25. This focus is discussed eloquently in Robert W. Tucker and David C. Hendrickson, *The Imperial Temptation: The New World Order and America's Purpose* (New York: Council on Foreign Relations Press, 1992), pp. 37–39.

26. For discussion of these various points of view, see Thomas C. Reed and Michael O. Wheeler, "The Role of Nuclear Weapons in the New World Order," prepared for the director of the Joint Strategic Targeting and Planning Staff by the Study Group on the Future of Nuclear Weapons, July 1991; John J. Mearsheimer, "Back to the Future: Instability in Europe after the Cold War," in Sean M. Lynn-Jones, ed., *The Cold War and After: Prospects for Peace* (MIT Press, 1991), pp. 141–92; the statement issued by the Preparatory Committee for the UN Conference on Environment and Development Group, cited in *Chemical Weapons Convention Bulletin,* no. 16 (June 1992), p. 13; and Mark Thompson, "A Push for Mini-Nukes Research," *Philadelphia Inquirer,* June 17, 1993, p. 2.

27. See *Department of Defense Annual Report, Fiscal Year 1992,* p. 5. See also the transcript of the second presidential debate, in *Washington Post,* October 16, 1992, p. A36; and Aspin, *Report on the Bottom-Up Review.*

28. Eric Schmitt, "Head of Nuclear Forces Plans for a New World," *New York Times,* February 25, 1993, p. B7.

29. Representative Les Aspin, "Three Propositions for a New Era Nuclear Policy," speech given at the Massachusetts Institute of Technology, Cambridge, Mass., June 1, 1992.

30. For a detailed study on nuclear false alarms and nuclear safety, see Scott D. Sagan, *The Limits of Safety: Organizations, Accidents, and Nuclear Weapons* (Princeton University Press, 1992).

31. In particular, the warning systems that mediate the critical judgment about whether a nuclear attack is or is not in progress have never encountered the unique flows of information and problems of interpretation that a full process of alerting forces would create. It cannot be presumed that the probability of a catastrophic misjudgment would

remain as low in crisis as it certainly has been under the peacetime and mild crisis circumstances encountered to date. The system has not yet been tested under severe stress. For a detailed discussion of these problems, see Bruce G. Blair, *The Logic of Accidental Nuclear War* (Brookings, 1993).

32. For more information on the U.S. decision not to test, see Ann Devroy and R. Jeffrey Smith, "U.S. Drops Nuclear Test Plans; Policy Now Would Be to Resume Blasts Only If Another Nation Does," *Washington Post,* June 30, 1993, p. A1. The former Soviet Union has not tested a nuclear weapon for nearly two years, and Russian production of nuclear forces and materials have been cut back substantially. China, France, and the United Kingdom continue to modernize their much smaller nuclear forces with a small number of tests annually, although France recently imposed a moratorium on its testing program and the U.K.'s tests are performed as part of the U.S. program. That China resumed its nuclear testing program in late 1993 was not seen as sufficient reason for the United States to alter its policy. See the "Statement by the Press Secretary," The White House, Washington, October 5, 1993. For more information on China's most recent nuclear test, see Steven A. Holmes, "World Moratorium on Nuclear Tests Is Broken by China," *New York Times,* October 6, 1993, p. A1.

33. George Perkovich, "Proliferation by Example," *Washington Post,* May 5, 1993, p. A21.

34. David Perlman, "Lab's Weapons Experts Revise Rationale for Tests," *San Francisco Chronicle,* May 26, 1992, p. 4.

35. Until 1991, the United States insisted it had to retain a chemical weapon stockpile until all states had ratified the Chemical Weapon Convention banning the production and use of these weapons.

36. *Department of Defense Annual Report, Fiscal Year 1992,* p. 5. Emphasis added.

37. One example was the Tripartite Agreement of 1950, in which the United Kingdom, France, and the United States agreed to refrain from transferring arms to the Middle East. This pact broke down when the Soviet Union and Czechoslovakia agreed to transfer armaments to Egypt in 1955. Similarly, the Conventional Arms Transfer talks between the United States and the Soviet Union in the 1970s failed in the face of tension between the two superpowers and lagging support from other industrial countries. See, for instance, Janne E. Nolan, "The U.S.-Soviet Conventional Arms Transfer Negotiations," in Alexander L. George, Philip J. Farley, and Alexander Dallin, *U.S.-Soviet Security Cooperation* (Oxford University Press, 1988), pp. 510–24.

38. Aside from COCOM, the only organized regime for controlling conventional weapon and dual-use technology to have endured for more than a few years is the MTCR agreement among industrial countries to restrict trade in ballistic and cruise missile technologies. Announced in April 1987, the regime now has twenty-three members. This voluntary supplier cartel controls ballistic and cruise missiles capable of carrying nuclear, chemical, or biological materials with a range of 300 kilometers, regardless of payload. The MTCR is not reinforced by an accompanying international treaty to support its goals. It is simply a set of export guidelines that a group of industrial countries agreed to incorporate into national export laws or use in judging the appropriateness of transfers of missile or dual-use technologies. The original MTCR members chose explicitly not to involve potential recipient states at the outset, fearing that negotiation of an expanded agreement would be time consuming and ultimately not fruitful.

39. In a series of meetings beginning in July 1991, representatives of the United States, the United Kingdom, France, China, and Russia agreed to refrain from transfers that would "increase regional instability" and to notify the group when transferring certain types of conventional weaponry. The five also agreed to create an international

arms trade registry to be administered by the UN. The reluctance of the permanent five members of the Security Council to seek more serious controls on the arms trade reflects the centrality of this instrument to the foreign policy of those nations. China, moreover, refused to continue participating in the talks in mid-1992 after the United States approved the sale of F-16 fighters to Taiwan.

40. As Rolf Ekeus put it, "What has been destroyed [in Iraq] is through the peaceful means of inspection. I would like to say that arms control has demonstrated that it is that way to destroy weapons, and not through bombings and attacks." Quoted in Seth Faison, "Tracker of Iraqi Arms," *New York Times,* July 28, 1992, p. A8.

41. For a further discussion of the Clinton administration's arms sales policies, see "Meet Bill Clinton, Arms Merchant," *Business Week,* June 28, 1993, p. 32.

42. In July 1992 the UN secretary-general revealed the gravity of the UN's position in a dispute with British officials over the European Community's effort to use UN forces to impose a cease-fire in Bosnia and Herzegovina. Boutros-Ghali accused Lord Carrington, the current head of the EC's peace efforts in the region, of trying to deplete UN resources for a "war of the rich" at the expense of Somalia, whose situation was even more dire. See Seth Faison, "UN Chief Mired in Dispute with Security Council," *New York Times,* July 24, 1991, p. A3.

FIFTEEN

Cooperative Security and the Former Soviet Union: Near-Term Challenges

Ashton B. Carter and Steven E. Miller

IN THE NEAR TERM many of the greatest opportunities and challenges for cooperative approaches to international security will be found within the reaches of the former Soviet Union (FSU). The opportunities derive from the end of the cold war and the collapse of the USSR, which allow serious consideration of international orders predicated on high levels of security cooperation. The new policies emanating from Moscow and the other capitals of the formerly Soviet states have already produced a number of tangible results in arms control, including substantial reductions of nuclear and conventional arms and unprecedented dialogue on security issues of mutual concern. A realistic chance now exists to move further toward the demilitarization of relations among the major powers and toward strengthened global regimes for containing the spread of weapons of mass destruction and other weaponry. A more benign international security order is plausibly within reach, and the movement from bitter confrontation to greater cooperation in relations with the FSU is a large part of the reason.

Even a cursory glance at the newspaper, however, suggests the challenges that may arise to this more hopeful vision. Almost daily, troubling news emerges from somewhere in the FSU and parades through the headlines: "Estonian Troops Exchange Fire with Russian Soldiers," "Hard-Pressed Russia Seeks to Revive Global Arms Sales," "Russia Caught in Republics' Conflict," "Shevardnadze Defeats Coup Attempt in Georgia," "Moldovans Join a Long

We wish to thank the Carnegie Corporation of New York for its support of Harvard University's Center for Science and International Affairs projects on post–cold war reconstruction and cooperative security, from which this chapter is derived.

Line of Refugees Fleeing Fighting," "Yeltsin Declares Emergencies in Caucasus Region," "In Crushing Blow to Georgia, City Falls to Secessionists," "Yeltsin Calls Army to Moscow after Armed Enemies Rampage."[1] Although nothing cataclysmic has yet occurred, considerable potential for disorder, conflict, and violence in this vast area clearly exists. It would be a disappointing setback to hopes for a more cooperative security regime if the positive developments of recent years in the FSU were to be overcome by these negative possibilities.

The problem of designing a more cooperative security relationship with the FSU is therefore not a distant task but an immediate policy concern. Obviously, it is desirable to establish patterns of security cooperation that might exploit the opportunities and minimize the potential disappointments that flow from the changes in the FSU. A near-term strategy of cooperative engagement would have three broad, interrelated objectives: to preserve peace and order in the FSU, to restructure Western security relationships with the FSU, and to cooperate with the FSU on global security issues. The most urgent of these objectives is the first, since the latter two will be more difficult to achieve if the FSU comes to be marked by widespread conflict or disorder. Thus a priority for Western policy is to identify an agenda of security cooperation with the FSU that may contribute to the emergence of a stable and peaceful security order among the fifteen now-independent republics. Achieving this first goal will probably entail considerable progress toward the second goal, restructuring Western security relationships with the FSU.

The purpose of this chapter is to identify those immediate security issues that pose the greatest threat to the positive trends within the FSU and to sketch paths of security cooperation that may contribute to their successful resolution. Four near-term concerns are paramount. First, there is the need to cope with the nuclear legacy of the Soviet Union. Failure to do so could result in multiple nuclear powers within the FSU, increased risks of accidental or unauthorized use of nuclear weapons, and greater likelihood that Soviet nuclear materials or expertise could spread into the international marketplace. North Korea's reported attempt to hire Russian nuclear experts for its nuclear program is a striking example of the potential for this kind of "brain drain."[2] This outcome would be the most dramatic event in the history of nuclear nonproliferation, with unfortunate effects both within the FSU and in the world. Second, there is great potential for hostility and conflict within the FSU, as witnessed by the spreading ethnic and nationalist conflict, particularly in the southern tier. Accordingly, it is necessary to undertake efforts to prevent this region from becoming marked by tension, confrontation, arms racing, and conflict. Europe will not be a continent of peace if its eastern half becomes a security nightmare, and the FSU will not be an attractive partner for security cooperation if it becomes increasingly absorbed in violent internecine conflict. Third, with surpluses of military equipment produced by recent arms control agreements, with rapidly shrinking defense budgets, and with desperate needs for hard currency–earning foreign sales, the states of the FSU will face a strong temptation to engage vigorously in the international export of arms. By exporting arms, the FSU could complicate or undermine hopes to bring the international arms trade under tighter control. Fourth, constraining arms racing within the FSU and limiting arms exports from the FSU will cause enormous problems of conversion for the huge military-industrial complex that was created by the Soviet Union. These measures will have both economic and political implications: economically, a large sector of the economy will have to be reoriented; politically, efforts to accomplish this reorientation could provoke resistance, or even revolt, by the officers and industrialists whose lives and careers will be affected.

We do not mean to suggest that these four issues exhaust the menu of security problems in the former USSR; clearly they do not. We do believe, however, that these issues deserve the highest priority on the immediate policy agenda. This chapter discusses each issue in turn, with a focus on the question of what forms of cooperative engagement might help to facilitate desirable outcomes.

Cooperative Denuclearizaton

The most obviously urgent and fertile field for security cooperation with the FSU is nuclear weapons.[3] In this field, traditions of cooperation are established, in the form of negotiated superpower arms control and the global nonproliferation regime. Both traditions are in need of change, and the direction of change will tend to bring them into greater interrelation and mutual support. The nuclear relationship between the United States and the Soviet Union underwent profound transformation well before the breakup of the USSR, but with its final demise the pace of change has quickened. The reciprocal unilateral pledges of Presidents George Bush and Mikhail Gorbachev in the fall of 1991 led to the withdrawal in a few short months of the forty-year-old deployments of tactical nuclear weapons, which were closely associated with conventional forces and warfighting roles. The Strategic Arms Reduction Talks (START) and START follow-on agreements, if ratified and implemented, would mark a similarly bold demobilization of strategic nuclear forces. But there nevertheless remains a need to deepen, hasten, and make irreversible the progress that is occurring. To do so requires the inauguration of new forms of security cooperation, new forms of involvement on the part of the international community outside the United States and the FSU, and the realization of new linkages between the cold war nuclear demobilization and the global nonproliferation regime.

Since the dawn of the nuclear age, the threat of global war between East and West beginning in Europe defined the roles and established the salience of nuclear weapons in the defense planning of the major powers. Neither bloc could contemplate defeat in such a contest. Neither would depend on its conventional forces alone to prevent such defeat. Thus resort to the use of nuclear weapons seemed probable and preparation for such use essential. The simple possession of nuclear weapons could not alone slake the thirst for ironclad deterrence in the face of such profound distrust of the opponent, and the many possibilities and scenarios for the breakout of war, given the many theaters of confrontation, seemed to require a commensurate elaboration of nuclear doctrines and forces to cover all conceivable eventualities. The result was large, complex, and diverse nuclear forces marbled among the air, naval, and ground forces, a similarly large overlay of intercontinental weapons, and a growth of theories and plans to apply them.

At hand with the ending of East-West confrontation is the prospect of radical deemphasis of nuclear weapons in the security conceptions of the major powers. In this vision, nuclear weapons would stand in the background of the military establishments of the major powers rather than in the foreground. Possession alone would be nine-tenths of deterrence, as it is of the law. Doctrines covering the residual nuclear forces—themselves much shrunk and simplified—would foresee retaliation only, and that only in response to first nuclear use and without any automatic response. Pledges in late 1991 and early 1992 by Washington and Moscow to move their forces to "zero alert" and to remove the target instructions from the memories of the guidance computers atop nuclear missiles are metaphors for this transformation of nuclear doctrine. Motivating this transformation is not only a desire to relax the taut and dangerous cold war standoff but also a recognition that nuclear weapons still hold attractions for aspiring lesser powers, even though they no longer serve compelling needs for the great powers. Deemphasizing nuclear weapons in their own security thinking is a necessary, if not a sufficient, step by the great powers for inducing others to deemphasize them.[4]

This transformation takes place in the midst of an ongoing revolution in the FSU, involving devolution of political authority from the USSR to its fifteen constituent republics and from Moscow and the Communist party to a host of nationalities, factions, and industrial enterprises across Asia. Such political disintegration, and its potential to lead to true chaos, is common enough in the world. But this is the first time it has happened in a nuclear nation, and that fact poses dangers to nuclear safety that are entirely unprecedented. These dangers are of three sorts. The first is that the splintering of the Soviet Union will be accompanied by a splintering of its nuclear arsenal. Ukraine and Kazakhstan, for example, would possess the third and fourth largest nuclear arsenals in the world—larger than those of the United Kingdom, France, and China—if they came into control of the nuclear weapons based on their territory. Although the transfer of tactical nuclear weapons from Belarus, Kazakhstan, and Ukraine to Russia was completed by May 1992, as of November 1993 the status of strategic nuclear weapons deployed outside Russia remained unresolved.[5] The second danger is that there will be loss of control of some fraction of the some 30,000 nuclear weapons of the FSU, through the actions of mutinous military custodians, political factions, opportunists, or terrorists. The third danger is that economic and political chaos will permit the diversion of nuclear materials, expertise, or weapons to parties outside the FSU, thus fueling proliferation.

These dangers can be influenced only by the United States and the international community through cooperative engagement with parties in the FSU. They do not arise from traditional security dilemmas and cannot be addressed through confrontation, deterrence, or adversarial negotiation. Avoiding these dangers depends on the overall economic and political reform and stability of the FSU, but more specifically on three factors upon which the cooperative security concept bears directly. First, the current political crisis in Ukraine over the further withdrawal of former Soviet nuclear forces from its territory, and meanwhile the continued operational control of those weapons from Moscow, will not be resolved unless Ukraine is convinced that its security concerns will be addressed cooperatively, with the participation of the international community. Second, the military and the managers of the nuclear weapons complex in Russia must remain convinced that the terms of the nuclear demobilization are equitable and reciprocal and must furthermore have their material needs met during and after the demobilization. Third, political leaders in the FSU must remain focused on the solemn responsibilities of nuclear custodianship despite the press of the economic and political challenges they face, which might understandably tend to divert their attentions. Being politicians, they must see a political reward in continuing denuclearization.

Thus the process of staving off the nuclear danger inherent in the ongoing revolution in the FSU receives important political cover and sustenance from the nuclear deemphasis and demobilization that had begun before the demise of the USSR. Momentum in denuclearization must therefore be maintained. But more direct forms of cooperative engagement are needed.

A significant start at such engagement was stimulated by the U.S. Congress in the Soviet Nuclear Threat Reduction Act of 1991, known as the Nunn-Lugar amendment because its inspiration came from Senators Sam Nunn (Democrat of Georgia) and Richard G. Lugar (Republican of Indiana). This act authorized the executive branch to finance and assist cooperative programs of denuclearization with funds from the Defense Department. The scope of cooperation authorized in the act included the dismantling of nuclear and chemical warheads and was broadened to include defense conversion and military-to-military contacts when Congress added $400 million to the Nunn-Lugar funds in the 1992 Former Soviet Union Demilitarization Act. Although by early 1993 less than half of the total $800 million Nunn-Lugar funding had been earmarked, with less than one-third of that being formally committed, plans have been laid for assistance in secure storage and transport of nuclear weapons, the dismantling of chemical weapons, research support for weapon scientists and engineers to reorient their efforts to peaceful purposes, and other areas.[6] After some delay the importance of including other states of the FSU besides Russia in the program of cooperation was realized. The Nunn-Lugar amendment succeeded in its principal purpose, which was less to finance specific technical steps than to set an agenda for denuclearization and cooperation and to command attention to this agenda on the part of political leaders in the FSU and leaders of the powerful ministries of defense and atomic power of the former USSR, as well as their counterparts in the West.

If denuclearization is to proceed, cooperative engagement in the style of the Nunn-Lugar amendment must be extended and deepened. In this context the inadequacy of traditional negotiated arms control is evident. The framework for a START follow-on agreement, which was accepted by Presidents Bush and Boris Yeltsin at their Washington summit in June 1992, envisions reductions in strategic arsenals that approach those called for in common notions of "minimal" or "background" deterrence. In this sense the agreement heralds a truly remarkable deemphasis of nuclear weapons. On the other hand, the reductions are not to be completed until 2003. This decade-long timetable is paced by the elaborate procedures for deactivation of nuclear weapon systems worked out in the original START agreement, which was negotiated with the Soviet Union in the 1980s. Such procedures focus on the destruction of launchers rather than on the disposition of nuclear warheads or even of missiles. The destruction of launchers is to be verifiable and irreversible, and thus its accomplishment takes time. It also costs money, and expense is a frequent reason given by parties in the FSU who defend the long timetable. But a decade is several times longer than the probable longevity of at least some of the governments whose cooperation will be necessary to implement the agreement: those of Russia, Ukraine, Kazakhstan, and Belarus. Delay therefore not only fails to capitalize on the opportunity presented by the end of the cold war to reach a new state of nuclear safety quickly but also entails a risk that the process will be derailed. Once again, however, cooperative engagement might achieve results not possible in the traditional arms control framework. Presidents Bush and Yeltsin appear to have recognized this possibility at their June 1992 summit, when they suggested that implementation of the START follow-on agreement might be completed by 2000 rather than 2003 with U.S. assistance.

An example of such a cooperative approach would be to attempt to forge cooperative agreements that focused on warheads instead of on launchers. Important precedents for this approach were the September and October 1991 reciprocal unilateral initiatives covering tactical nuclear weapons, in which the United States and the Soviet Union pledged to withdraw many thousands of tactical warheads from active service and to dismantle many of them. An analogous scheme for strategic weapons would allow the security benefits of the START agreement and the follow-on framework agreement to be achieved well before 2003. The parties could agree to the immediate removal of the warheads from all launchers slated for eventual deactivation under these agreements. Judging from the pace at which tactical nuclear weapons have been removed from active service to central storage depots by both sides since the fall of 1991, the removal of strategic warheads could probably be accomplished in less than a year.[7] Such a bold form of denuclearization would extend the process begun with tactical nuclear weapons to strategic weapons. It would remove the danger of unauthorized or accidental launch of weapons covered by the agreements, since launch would be harmless if the delivery vehicles had no warheads. It would accomplish in one year the removal of all nuclear warheads from Ukraine, Kazakhstan, and Belarus, heading off any possibility of nuclear proliferation in the FSU. It would dramatically underscore the deemphasizing of nuclear weapons that is so much in the interests of the great powers. Though not verifiable by cold war standards, a cooperative scheme could probably be arranged that would give all parties adequate confidence that their security was not being compromised. In any event, warhead removal would be reversible in the short term, and thus warheads could be reloaded if the process bogged down.

A focus on nuclear warheads leads in turn to other fruitful avenues of nuclear cooperation. Both the United States and Russia possess inventories of nuclear weapons almost ten times the size they project for deployment in ten years. The surplus weapons need to be dismantled, plutonium and enriched uranium produced for weapons need to be eliminated or stored, and the nuclear weapon complexes need to be made environmentally safe and restructured for their post–cold war role of supporting smaller and simpler arsenals. All these tasks are appropriate for cooperative effort. Indeed some degree of cooperation is probably a prerequisite for sustaining political support for denuclearization in each country. And in Russia, U.S. assistance might stimulate and hasten actions that would otherwise take place much more slowly, or not at all, both because of lack of money and because they would not otherwise receive high priority amid the many needs of a society in social and economic stress. Finally, an ongoing internationally sanctioned process of nuclear builddown in Russia is probably a prerequisite for Kazakhstan and Belarus to resist any further temptation to try to stake a claim to nuclear weapons based on their territory and may help to encourage Ukraine to abandon its moves toward retaining the nuclear weapons based there.

The needed cooperation does not end with the United States and the states of the FSU. In at least two facets of denuclearization, broader international cooperation is desirable and perhaps necessary. The first is disposing of fissile materials from dismantled weapons and accumulated stocks of weapons-grade plutonium and enriched uranium. Both these materials have half-lives of many thousands of years and no nonweapons use except as fuel for nuclear power reactors. The market for uranium reactor fuels is global, and several states—

notably the United Kingdom, France, and Japan—are involved in actual or planned use of plutonium. These states will inevitably play a role in any use of weapons materials for reactor fuels. It is probably even desirable for the international community to assume long-term custody of weapons-grade materials after denuclearization has taken place in the United States and Russia. Indeed, as already noted, internationalizing the process of denuclearization might be the only way to bring the states of the FSU to agreement on completing it. Finally, broader international participation in denuclearization might prove to be a first exploratory step toward bringing the British, French, and Chinese nuclear arsenals into negotiated arms control, a task that virtually everyone concedes is logically inevitable, but which no one knows quite how to approach.

Efforts to ban further production of fissile material for nuclear weapons might be one way of engaging the other nuclear powers in nuclear arms control. President Bush's July 1992 initiative to halt U.S. production of plutonium or highly enriched uranium (HEU), while simply codifying what had been de facto U.S. policy since 1988, was aimed at persuading other countries to halt or not to begin their own production of these materials. In January 1992 President Yeltsin called for a negotiated agreement with the United States on halting the production of fissile materials but said that even in the absence of such an agreement Russia would cease production of weapons-grade plutonium by the year 2000. In mid-1993 the Clinton administration announced that it would pursue a broad nonproliferation strategy, which includes a call for a global treaty banning the production of HEU and the reprocessing of plutonium, the acceleration of U.S. purchases of HEU from dismantled Soviet weapons, and the opening of fissile material stockpiles to international inspection. Obviously a global cutoff in the supply of fissile materials is impossible without the involvement of other nuclear powers.[8]

If all goes as planned in this historical process of denuclearization, the total inventory of some 55,000 nuclear weapons that was the legacy of cold war with the Soviet Union will have shrunk to some 10,000 weapons in the arsenals of Russia and the United States by the end of the century or soon thereafter. This builddown will accomplish much toward the goal of nuclear safety. But nuclear arsenals need to be made safer as well as smaller. Important steps toward safety, security, and control of nuclear forces can be taken, once again, cooperatively. Traditionally, the cooperative pursuit of nuclear safety has taken place mainly through enhancing "strategic stability," that is, arranging for each side to have the capability for hefty retaliation to a nuclear first strike with high assurance under all conceivable circumstances. This capability is a worthy, indeed indispensable, ingredient of nuclear safety. It was pursued with extraordinary energy by both sides in the cold war, both through unilateral deployments and through cooperation in arms control. Actions by either side that could be interpreted as upsetting retaliatory stability, as with the Soviet SS-18 heavy missile or the U.S. Strategic Defense Initiative, became the bones of contention at the negotiating table. But retaliatory stability was usually pursued much more vigorously than, and sometimes at the price of, what might be called operational stability: not only should retaliation be assured and hefty, but the operations that the nuclear forces must undertake to survive attack and mount retaliation should themselves be safe. Here the cold war record is much poorer. Hasty retaliatory timelines (including provision for retaliation to begin before the provoking attack was even over, and accepting force and command and control configurations that could not accomplish retaliation if orders were delayed too long), dependence on strategic or tactical warning of attack, and subtle interdependencies among legs of the strategic "triad" (as with the supposed dependence of bombers and intercontinental ballistic missiles on each other for launch on tactical warning, or with the dependence of bombers on precursor missile attacks on air defenses to facilitate their penetration of enemy airspace) were accepted in the pursuit of ever more weighty and assured retaliation. Recent allegations about the Soviet "Dead Hand" system, designed to initiate a retaliatory strike automatically if the political and military command structures are destroyed in a nuclear attack, attest to one of the dangerous legacies of the cold war era nuclear structures.[9] The nuclear arsenals after denuclearization should exhibit not only retaliatory stability but also operational stability. The goal should be not only the capability for weighty and assured retaliation but also freedom from dependence on alerting and warning, and above all, reliance on prompt response. Peacetime and alert operations should reemphasize safety and control over readiness—or, in common parlance, negative control over positive control.

Operational stability would be furthered by a number of steps, all of which could be pursued cooperatively. One focus of such cooperation would be the survivability of command and control systems (which have always been the not-so-hidden Achilles heels of the superpower strategic arsenals), emphasizing mutual restraints on capabilities for surprise attack or specialized means of attack on command and control systems, including antisatellites. Another focus would be cooperative restraints covering alerting procedures and nuclear exercises. A third would be cooperative systems for missile warning, such as have been proposed by Russia and the United States. Cooperation in this field could even be taken to the point of permitting each side to install warning sensors in the missile silo fields of the other. Finally, a decisive tip in the direction of negative control would call for installation of the most modern technical safeguards (often called permissive action links, or PALs) on *all* nuclear weapons remaining in the inventory. Such devices should permit physical enabling of weapons only by the highest authorities. Such enabling should also be selective, so that it could be applied to any subset of the arsenal without "unlocking" the rest; contingent, so that unlocked weapons could only be used against intended targets; and reversible, so that unlocked weapons could be locked up again.

With the end of the cold war it is therefore possible to present a vision that dramatically deemphasizes the role of nuclear weapons in security, shrinks and simplifies arsenals, and enhances safety and security—all pursued cooperatively. Although logic might suggest them, these processes will not occur easily on either side unless the other is seen to be undergoing similar change. Furthermore, the ongoing revolution in the FSU poses an entirely new security calculus for the United States: the price of failure to induce a graceful and controlled process of denuclearization would be not just a historic opportunity lost but possibly a true disaster.

It is possible, and highly desirable, that this dramatic denuclearization pending among the great powers will have a salutary effect on thinking about nuclear weapons in other parts of the world and thus on proliferation. Nuclear have-nots and aspirants have always claimed that horizontal proliferation could not be controlled unless vertical proliferation came under control. Among the nuclear haves, many have suspected that this claim merely provided a convenient cover for attitudes toward proliferation that were actually determined by regional security dilemmas and internal politics among the nations considered to be proliferation risks. But the claim was never put to the test. Now it should be. Vertical proliferation is undergoing a dramatic reversal. Though a comprehensive ban on underground nuclear testing, which has frequently been taken to symbolize control over vertical proliferation, is not yet part of the agreed-upon denuclearization agenda between the United States and the FSU, that omission would seem to warrant only a footnote in view of the fivefold or so reductions in warhead inventories and major cutbacks in arsenal modernization planned by the United States and Russia. Deemphasis of nuclear weapons in the military doctrines of the great powers might reinforce abhorrence and rejection of nuclear weapons around the world. Steps to enhance safety, security, and control set an example of sober, responsible custodianship. International control of the disposition of weapons-grade plutonium and enriched uranium would strengthen the global regime of control on nuclear materials. More directly, the failure of denuclearization in the FSU would clearly have a negative effect on nonproliferation if any of the non-Russian successor states fails to carry out its pledge to be nuclear weapon–free, or if sensitive materials, expertise, or weapons are diverted.

Thus the relegation of nuclear weapons to a background role in international security, the reduction of active arsenals and dismantling of the surplus, the enhancement of the safety of remaining weapons, and nonproliferation are all becoming parts of one security problem. Solutions to that problem must be cooperative.

Security Cooperation and the Preservation of Peace in the FSU

An immediate danger of the post-Soviet era is that the fifteen successor states of the FSU will fail to create a stable and peaceful international order in the area. The warning signs are vivid and unmistakable. Already there has been fighting in Moldova, in Georgia, and between Armenia and Azerbaijan in Nagorno-Karabakh. Relations between Russia and the Baltic states are tense and bitter, with occasional eruptions of violence against the continuing Russian presence in the Baltics. Fears of a potential conflict between Russia and Ukraine remain high as disputes over issues ranging from the disposition of the Soviet Black Sea fleet, to the rights of ethnic Russians in eastern Ukraine, to the removal of Soviet nuclear weapons based in Ukraine continue to plague relations between the two states. Moreover, the severe economic difficulties and domestic political instabilities in these new states may create conditions ripe for nationalist demagogues inclined to pursue aggressive policies toward their neighbors. As the U.S.-Russian charter that emerged from the Bush-Yeltsin summit in June 1992 lamented, "Ethnic tensions, territorial disputes, and international rivalries already threaten to turn an opportunity for peace into yet another phase of European turmoil."[10]

Accordingly there is an immediate need to design policies aimed at facilitating a safe transition to a peaceful international order in the FSU. The roots of conflict in the FSU are so many and so deep that, in the end, there may be no successful strategy for attaining this end. But the costs of failure are too high not to try. Stephen Van Evera has written that if this transition is mismanaged, "the world faces the possibility of spreading violence throughout the area—a Yugoslavia on a grand scale, perhaps involving conflict between nuclear-armed adversaries. At best, without a durable peace the region will become a running sore on the international system: a zone of recurrent crises, occasional small wars, and constant worry for nearby powers for many years. At worst the region could eventually spawn a major European war."[11]

A policy of cooperative engagement with the states of the FSU should seek to embed them in international relationships and to commit them to international norms of behavior that remove or dampen likely sources of conflict and inhibit crises and arms races among them. This approach will not necessarily require sharp departures from past policy. Indeed, the tradition of arms control and security cooperation is already so entrenched in Europe that policies of cooperative security need only build on existing arrangements.[12] And not only are many of the ingredients for security cooperation with and within the FSU already in place, but the states of the FSU have already embraced institutions and commitments that might tame the dangers of the transition to a new international order in the region.[13] In Europe, unlike in other regions, the problem is not to create cooperative security structures but rather to render effective those that already exist. Several institutions and treaty regimes deserve particular mention here.

The Conference on Security and Cooperation in Europe

The CSCE occupies center stage in much thinking about a new security framework for Europe. And it is in a number of respects relevant to the consideration of security cooperation with the FSU. First, it is the most inclusive organization in Europe, bridging East and West, aligned and nonaligned, and rich and poor, thereby providing what former secretary of state James A. Baker III called a "comprehensive framework" for the Euro-Atlantic agenda.[14] This inclusiveness may be of particular importance to the new states in the eastern half of the continent, since currently the CSCE is the only European forum in which they can all participate fully.[15]

Second, accession to the CSCE also requires accepting a number of principles that are pertinent to potential security problems in the FSU. The Declaration on Principles Guiding Relations between Participating States, part 1(a) of the Helsinki Final Act of 1975, commits CSCE members to respect the "sovereign equality" of all, to regard frontiers as inviolable and to "respect the territorial integrity" of all members, to refrain from the threat or use of force and to "settle disputes . . . by peaceful means," and to respect the rights of minority peoples.[16] The Charter of Paris for a New Europe, signed at the CSCE summit in Paris on November 21, 1990, reaffirms and in some respects strengthens these commitments, while also pledging member states to practice democracy and to observe individual human rights in their domestic affairs.[17] All the states of the FSU have become members of the CSCE and have thereby pledged their adherence to these principles.

Of course it is true that the existence of signed documents expressing these principles in no way guarantees the application of them in practice. Nevertheless, this collection of principles, if actually applied in the FSU, would do quite well in addressing the dangers of conflict in a region ridden with potential territorial and minority disputes. Furthermore, and more important, these principles, voluntarily accepted by the states in question, can serve as standards of behavior within the FSU, according to which Western states can adjust and calibrate their policies toward the region. There have been a number of calls for the *West* to define standards of conduct for the FSU (and to make its relations with those states conditional on the meeting of those standards),[18] but there is no need for the West to create and impose such standards. The CSCE principles to which the states of the FSU have already pledged to adhere encompass all the main elements of the desired code of conduct.[19]

Third, the past several years have witnessed a spate of institution building within the CSCE, much of it motivated by a desire to strengthen its capacities to play a meaningful role in coping with disputes and conflict in Europe.[20] At the CSCE Paris summit in November 1990, the participants agreed to create a Council of Foreign Ministers to meet at least once annually, to form a Committee of Senior Officials (CSO) to prepare the council's meetings and, most important, to implement its decisions, and to establish a permanent CSCE secretariat, to be based in Prague. These steps represented the transformation of the CSCE from a series of recurring conferences into a standing security institution. For example, the institutional prerogative of the CSO was exercised when it appointed a special envoy to serve as the CSCE mediator in connection with the crisis in Moldova over the fate of the Trans-Dniester.[21] In addition, the Charter of Paris created the Conflict Prevention Centre (CPC), whose permanent secretariat is based in Vienna.[22] Although the CPC's immediate role emphasized support for implementing confidence- and security-building measures (CSBMs), it has an open-ended mandate to perform any task asked of it by the CSCE Council with respect to the conciliation and settlement of disputes.

Prompted by the subsequent inability of the CSCE to play an effective role in the Yugoslav crisis[23] (and, to a lesser extent, in the FSU) despite the existence of these new institutions, the CSCE established still more new institutions and mechanisms at its Helsinki summit in 1992. These included a CSCE high commissioner on national minorities, intended to increase the ability of the CSCE to investigate potential conflicts before they erupt, and a CSCE Court of Arbitration and Conciliation, meant to buttress a dispute settlement mechanism administered by the CPC. The CSCE also declared itself a regional security organization under Chapter 8 of the UN Charter, a stance that enables it to undertake peacekeeping operations.[24] The CSCE itself, of course, lacks military capabilities and hence cannot undertake peacekeeping except in collaboration with member states or with other international organizations. But in June 1992 NATO declared that it would be willing in principle to perform peacekeeping roles asked of it by the CSCE.[25] And at the Helsinki summit the CSCE agreed to set up a Forum on Security Cooperation to facilitate security dialogue and "to co-ordinate all future negotiations on arms control and regional security."[26]

In theory, then, the CSCE provides a substantial base from which to pursue cooperative solutions to security problems in the FSU. It is an inclusive organization that establishes desirable norms of behavior, some of which are particularly apt relative to the potential territorial and minority disputes in the FSU. It has growing institutional capacities and is increasingly oriented toward conflict prevention, crisis management, dispute resolution, and peacekeeping. It would appear to be an ideal instrument of cooperative security with respect to the FSU.

In reality, of course, the CSCE has yet to demonstrate its practical relevance to conflict resolution or prevention in the FSU or anywhere else in Europe; as the *Economist* has commented, it will have "little credibility in the new Europe while the killing goes on."[27] And it may be that an institution that relies on consensual decisionmaking among more than fifty states will never be capable of playing a central role or undertaking decisive action. Nevertheless, to a striking degree, the CSCE embodies norms of cooperative security and is evolving institutional arrangements meant to make it more effective in implementing those norms.

Hence, as part of a near-term strategy of cooperative security, it is probably worth exploring whether ways can be found to allow the CSCE to play a more active and effective role in the FSU. Implementation of at least four ideas might enhance its ability to play a constructive role in managing the transition to a new security order in the FSU. First, the CSCE can play no larger role than its member states wish for it, but some members have been unenthusiastic about expanding and exploiting its capacities.[28] The United States, in particular, was skeptical of the CSCE process from its beginning in the early 1970s and remained a reluctant and grudging participant in more recent efforts to strengthen and institutionalize it.[29] Judging by the rhetoric, this attitude may be changing; former secretary of state Baker has said, for example, that the "CSCE has become a central forum for solving problems and managing crises."[30] To make this genuinely true, however, will require a serious commitment to the CSCE and to multilateral diplomacy in Europe. A sensible step in the direction of incorporating cooperative security into post–cold war American security policy would be to give the CSCE a more prominent and substantial role in American policy toward Europe. Even this step may not permit the CSCE to play the decisive role in the new Europe, but the institution certainly will remain severely handicapped if major actors remain diffident about it.

Second, the United States and its Western allies should more vigorously and explicitly proclaim the Helsinki principles as standards of behavior that the new states of the FSU are expected to meet. And this stance should be conjoined with more disciplined efforts to make Western policy conditional on the fulfillment by the FSU states of their CSCE commitments. It is a self-fulfilling prophesy to treat the Helsinki principles as mere boilerplate. The West should say that they are meaningful and behave accordingly.

Third, serious consideration should be given to moving away from consensual decisionmaking in at least some issue areas. As long as action is subject to universal veto, even by states that might be the object of CSCE diplomatic intervention or peacekeeping efforts in the event of conflict, it is likely to remain crippled.[31]

Fourth, efforts should be made to advance the norm that CSCE peacekeeping and peacemaking efforts should be accepted by parties to conflict.[32] When the CSCE attempted to send one hundred military observers to Nagorno-Karabakh in July 1992, for example, it was unable to do so because those doing the fighting would not agree. Clearly, if CSCE efforts to make peace can be spurned by those violating the peace, it will have a hard time playing a constructive role.

None of these ideas is a panacea, a magic stroke that will transform the CSCE into a central, active, and effective player in the FSU (or in Europe more broadly). Indeed, at least the third and fourth of these notions will probably be very difficult to achieve. But they do offer some prospect of strengthening an organization whose norms and institutions would be very helpful if effectively applied in the FSU.

Three Treaty Regimes

Although the CSCE is a "cooperative security asset" whose potential is not certain to be realized, there are three treaty regimes—CFE, CFE 1A, and the CSBMs regime—that can certainly make tangible contributions to the construction of a new security order in the FSU. And although the CSCE provides norms of behavior and institutions for preventing or resolving conflicts, these agreements create a regime that more directly dampens the likelihood of conventional arms racing in the FSU and establishes procedures that should inhibit the development of spirals of hostility.

Two of these agreements, the Conventional Armed Forces in Europe (CFE) Treaty and the Concluding Act of the Negotiation on Personnel Strength of Conventional Armed Forces in Europe (CFE 1A) are closely related. The CFE, signed in November 1990, establishes numerical limits on five categories of military equipment—battle tanks, armored combat vehicles, artillery, combat aircraft, and attack helicopters—in a zone that stretches from the Atlantic to the Urals (known in the CFE context as the ATTU zone). The CFE 1A, signed at the Helsinki summit in July 1992, supplements the CFE by setting manpower ceilings in the CFE zone of application.

These agreements have produced three desirable effects in the FSU. First, they have compelled explicit security discussions among the newly independent states of the FSU.[33] The CFE treaty did not anticipate the collapse of the Soviet Union into fifteen states, and hence its national ceilings had to be apportioned among the successor states, a process that could be accomplished only by negotiation. Hence in this sense the states of the FSU could not avoid conventional arms control discussions among themselves if they wished to preserve the CFE treaty—as they did.

Their commitment to the perpetuation of the CFE treaty is shown by the fact that even when CFE limitations seemed unsuitable to the post-Soviet period, the FSU states' reaction has been to seek discussion on revision of the treaty rather than to use this as a justification for leaving the treaty regime. For example, the spread of unrest along Russia's southern border, and particularly in the Caucasus, raised concern in Moscow and led to Russia formally requesting in September 1993 that the CFE members consider allowing Moscow to deploy ground forces on its southern flank in excess of those Russia is permitted under the CFE flank allocation. Ukraine, citing similar threats to its security, has also asked for a review of its CFE flank limits.[34]

Second, these intra-FSU negotiations produced mutually agreed-upon caps on the holdings of treaty-limited equipment among the eight participating republics in the CFE zone of application.[35] FSU states accepted the fact that their collective holdings of treaty-limited equipment would not exceed the levels formerly allocated to the Soviet Union. And at a meeting in Tashkent on May 15, 1992, they reached negotiated national subceilings within that collective limit.[36] These subceilings both cap the arms race potential and establish negotiated conventional force ratios among these states. This is surely a desirable attribute to build into the new security order in the FSU.

Third, the CFE–CFE 1A regime institutionalizes a high degree of transparency in the zone of application, including extensive requirements for data exchange and elaborate provisions for on-site inspections. All states are obliged to accept inspections on their territory; this verification regime is intrusive to an unprecedented degree.[37] This scheme is very much in keeping with emphasis in the notion of cooperative security on attempting to build trust and reducing fear and suspicion through mutual transparency; this approach can help to provide values that are likely to be in short supply in the FSU.[38]

The logical next step, from a security vantage point, would be to attempt further negotiations with a more qualitative orientation. Although the CFE had as one of its purposes the reduction of the risk of surprise attack, this purpose was construed in the NATO–Warsaw Pact context and was pursued through quantitative limits. Advocates of cooperative security place emphasis on limiting offensive capabilities and encouraging defensive orientation on the part of all states.[39] Although qualitative conventional arms control is subject to notorious complexities and difficulties, it would be a natural focus of follow-on negotiations, and it would be attractive if only because it might contribute to the creation of a defensively oriented environment within the new international order that is emerging in the FSU. It may be as well that this effort is best undertaken as soon as possible, before further bitter conflicts erupt in the FSU to poison the atmosphere for further arms control and before the states of the region have locked themselves into defensive postures that may or may not conform to the norms of cooperative security.

Buttressing the two CFE treaties is a third treaty regime focused on CSBMs. Starting with the Helsinki Final Act of 1975, which contained some modest CSBMs, an extensive and complex set of CSBMs has evolved, which has been accepted by all CSCE members.[40] These CSBMs too codify attributes that are desirable in the context of the emerging international order in the FSU. Their overarching purpose is to prevent misperception of military activities and deployments and to provide reassurance by reducing fears of surprise attack. They have usually fallen into three categories: transparency about military organization, transparency about military activities, and communications and contacts.[41] This regime, most recently enhanced in the Vienna Document 1992, now incorporates the following elements: extensive annual exchange of information on military forces, weapon capabilities, deployment plans, military budgets, and planned exercises; various risk reduction provisions calling for cooperation and observation in the event of unusual or hazardous military activities; numerous constraints on, requirements for prior notification of, and provisions for, the observation of military exercises; arrangements for contacts among military organizations, including a scheme for visits to air bases; an intrusive verification system including inspections; and an annual implementation meeting. It is important to note that the Vienna Document 1992 was accepted by all the states of the FSU and hence applies throughout the territory that made up the USSR.[42]

Summary

Looking at the CSCE, CFE, CFE 1A, and CSBMs together makes it apparent that a substantial, if incomplete, framework for security cooperation already exists for the FSU by virtue of the inclusion of those states in Europe-wide frameworks whose rules and arrangements already encompass the main attributes that it would be desirable to see emerge in the international order in the FSU. The problem, of course, is that these frameworks have not proved to be reliably effective at either preventing or stopping war, as is tragically demonstrated by the bitter ongoing conflicts in the Balkans (between Bosnia and Serbia) and in the Caucasus (between Armenia and Azerbaijan and between Georgia and Abkhazia). These frameworks seem effective at reinforcing positive trends and developments but appear to be largely impotent in the face of hostility and conflict. This is yet another reason why it is desirable to act now to promote benign tendencies and to prevent wide violent conflagration in the FSU from sweeping away the cooperative frameworks that already exist.

Accordingly, what is required is not the passive hope that European frameworks will keep the peace. Rather, the United States and its industrial allies should act boldly to defend and exploit the structures of security cooperation in Europe. Doing so will necessarily entail not only making clear the high value that the West attaches to these structures but also making Western policies toward the FSU conditional on appropriate behavior within these frameworks, including, as previously noted, observance of the CSCE code of conduct.[43] In other words, Western states should act to increase the likelihood of the effective application of European frameworks of security cooperation in the FSU by linking aid, trade, and political relations to peaceful conduct. While this approach should be applied to all fifteen Soviet successor states, it is inevitable that Russia and Ukraine will play particularly prominent roles in shaping the character of the post-Soviet order, and conditional Western policies ought to be directed above all at them. Although elements of this approach have been evident in U.S. and Western policy so far (as suggested at the Vancouver summit between Presidents Bill Clinton and Boris Yeltsin in April 1993),[44] the West has yet to commit political and financial resources commensurate with the stakes.[45]

Containing FSU Arms Exports and Coping with Defense Conversion

Much narrower but still important near-term policy challenges arise in connection with arms exports from and defense conversion in the FSU. One basic concern is to address the pressure felt in the FSU to export arms abroad. The Soviet Union created an enormous military-industrial complex that involved hundreds of large enterprises and employed more than 4 million people.[46] This military industry met the very large matériel needs of the Soviet military and also supplied billions of dollars in annual arms exports. Throughout the 1980s the USSR exported about $9 billion in arms annually.[47] Now the domestic economy in the FSU is in crisis, internal procurement of weapons is dropping, and conversion cannot possibly happen fast enough to prevent a crisis in the military industry. An obvious solution is to try to export arms, a solution all the more attractive because it might generate much-needed hard currency—potentially $10 billion or more a year despite the steep reduction in international arms sales in the past several years.

This is not merely a hypothetical concern but an immediate reality. The Russian government, for example, is under pressure from the League of Defense Enterprises of Russia to revive arms exports, and the Yeltsin government has not been reluctant to commit itself to so doing.[48] Indeed, it seems clear that Russia, as well as other states in the FSU, will be acting aggressively to maximize arms exports, as attested to by numerous recent arms overtures and deals.[49]

These exports are problematic for at least two reasons. First, exports from the FSU may contribute to arms races and conflict around the world and could cause security problems for the United States and its allies. The pressures to export are so severe that states in the FSU may be willing to sell almost anything to almost anybody. Thus, for example, weapons previously unavailable for export, such as Backfire bombers and certain air-to-surface missiles, are now being actively offered on the international market.[50] Some deals, such as Russia's supplying Iran with submarines, have gone forward despite strong opposition from the United States.[51] Russia has been eager to sell even sensitive technologies to former adversaries, including NATO and the United States; its willingness to offer nuclear-powered submarines and antisubmarine warfare technology to the United States is a case in point.[52] Perhaps even more surprising is Russia's willingness to sell arms in large quantities to an openly expansionist China, with whom Russia shares a long and contested border and a long history of poor relations.[53] A further consideration is that many of Moscow's traditional recipients, who are most dependent on Soviet or Russian arms and who may be most inclined, for reasons of logistics, training, and limited alternative suppliers, to buy from the FSU, are regarded by the United States as international troublemakers—including North Korea, Iraq, Syria, and Libya.

In short, the relatively indiscriminate arms export policy that seems to be emerging in the FSU—particularly in Russia—has the potential to make more, more varied, and, in some cases, better military equipment available to virtually any state willing to pay for it (and often at bargain basement prices). A real potential exists for contributing to regional instabilities and for increasing security problems for the United States and its friends and allies.[54] This scenario is hardly consistent with visions of effective post–cold war security cooperation with Russia and the other states of the FSU.

Second, unrestrained arms exports from Russia and other FSU states will obviously undermine the already fragile prospects for increasing arms trade restraint in the post–cold war era. During the cold war, such efforts always foundered over intractable East-West antagonism. Thus the end of the cold war eliminated an important (although obviously not the only) obstacle to achieving some internationally agreed-upon constraints on international arms transfers. Hopes were raised that it might be possible to establish some rules for arms transfers to try to eliminate or minimize the adverse, destabilizing consequences of selling arms. The willingness of the permanent five members of the UN Security Council (who are also the world's largest arms suppliers) to discuss this issue in 1991 and their modest success in agreeing to a set of broad guidelines for conventional arms transfers suggested that at least some limited progress might be possible.[55] Further evolution of this sort is precisely what is required if a more cooperative security order is to emerge out of strengthened and expanded proliferation control regimes and if there is to be any hope of promoting stable military environments through agreed-upon rules and procedures for selling and buying arms.[56] But there can be no real movement in this direction so long as states in the FSU, Russia and Ukraine above all, face a strong compulsion to sell as much as possible. Hence the arms transfer imperative in the FSU constitutes a significant potential impediment to a more cooperative security order.

Several steps could be taken that might address these concerns. First, the United States and other major industrial suppliers need to recognize the linkage between their own arms export behavior and the incentives for restraint in the FSU. With its own arms exports outnumbering those of the FSU by a factor of four, the United States will be in no position to lecture Russia persuasively on the virtues of restraint.[57] Indeed, if the major Western suppliers are not prepared to check their own conduct, the prospects for enhanced security cooperation in the area of conventional arms transfers will be poor whatever Russia and other

FSU states do. As things now stand, energetic Western pursuit of arms exports is regarded by defense industrialists in the FSU as a threat to their own international markets and as a justification for continuing their own aggressive export efforts.[58] Restraint on conventional arms transfers must begin at home.

Second, the United States and other Western governments that interact with Russia and other FSU states on arms export issues need to be sensitive to the reality that for some time to come a certain level of FSU arms exports will be necessary and desirable to avoid socioeconomic catastrophe in the huge "Soviet" arms industry and to provide a source of urgently needed hard currency. Hence the immediate aim of a more cooperative approach to the arms export issue is not to minimize FSU arms exports but to discourage particularly undesirable sales, such as those to troubling recipients or those involving weapons technologies heretofore restricted. This aim may be hard to achieve if one of the few competitive advantages of FSU arms dealers is their willingness to offer technologies or to sell to recipients that others will not. The implication is that the single-minded pursuit of arms exports by Western governments and defense contractors in relentless competition with FSU exports may be short-sighted and inimical to the prospects for sensible rules of restraint. Governments in Moscow, Kiev, and elsewhere in the FSU can hardly be expected to be enthusiastic about Western arms transfer restraint preferences if one of the largest sectors of their economy is being devastated by Western arms exports.

But in an atmosphere in which the level of security cooperation is rising and in which arms transfers are not fueled by geostrategic rivalry, it ought to be possible to confront this issue directly in bilateral and multilateral discussion with Russia, Ukraine, and other FSU states. Indeed, the Russian foreign minister, Andrey Kozyrev, has already raised this question explicitly in discussions with Secretary of State Warren Christopher in Geneva in February 1993, explaining that economically motivated Russian arms exports should not be regarded as challenges to U.S. regional interests and expressing hope for future dialogue on the issue.[59] Because Western defense industries also face serious difficulties and have strong incentives to export, this subject will not be easy to address in a cooperative manner.[60] But successful cooperation could conceivably lead to some sort of managed competition or market-sharing arrangements, outcomes that have been advocated by some Western scholars.[61] For all the costs and difficulties of this approach, it is hard to see what other outcome as effectively reconciles the need for arms exports from the FSU with the hope for greater restraint in the post–cold war environment.

Third, continued efforts should be undertaken with Russia and the other permanent members of the UN Security Council to discuss and implement constraints on the international arms trade. For reasons noted earlier, only if restraints are observed by all the major suppliers do they have any chance of garnering support and observance by the governments of the FSU.

Fourth, there should be dialogue with the states of the FSU about arms export controls. The collapse of the Soviet Union has left a murky legal legacy, and it is unclear what legal framework, if any, governs the export of arms in many of the newly independent republics. There should also be discussion of, and possible assistance for, enforcement of export control restrictions. It is far from clear that many of these republics can control the flow of arms across their borders.

Finally, the United States and the West should seek to facilitate the process of defense conversion in whatever ways are possible. Ultimately, only a reduction in the defense industrial base in the FSU will reduce the pressure to export. Defense conversion is important for other reasons as well; indeed, even if the linkage to arms exports did not exist, it would deserve a prominent place on the agenda of security cooperation between the West and the FSU. For instance, the defense sector was such a large fraction of the Soviet economy that conversion must inevitably be a serious consideration in terms of economic reform.[62] In this sense, defense conversion must be an urgent priority for internal champions and external supporters of economic reform in Russia. The issue may have domestic political implications as well. The reduction of the military and the contraction of the defense industry are bound to cause some pain and dislocation, no matter how well they are handled. But there is a potential, if things go awry, for catastrophic declines in the well-being of members of the military and defense sectors. It takes little imagination to envision that these problems could cause a political backlash against the political and economic reformers—a backlash that could be very potent, in view of the millions of people in the FSU whose fate is bound up with that of the Soviet military-industrial complex. Finally, there is a security dimension to the conversion issue as well. The Soviet defense industry was geared to producing huge quantities of military equipment every year, thus creating the arsenal that caused such anxiety to the USSR's adversaries and neighbors. Within Russia, at least, this huge defense production capacity is regarded as both surplus to its security requirements in the new era and an impediment to the improvement of the economy and standard of living. Outside Russia, this capacity should be regarded as a latent military threat as well as a source of arms exports. Thus there is a common interest—and a need and opportunity for cooperation—in reducing this defense industrial legacy of the cold war to levels more appropriate to the post–cold war era.

Efforts to facilitate the process of conversion might include, for example, a willingness to offer emergency support to elements of the Soviet defense industrial complex that find themselves in acute socioeconomic crisis; it is in no one's interest to permit "conversion disasters," even recognizing the significant political and economic limits on the ability of the West to provide financial assistance to the FSU.[63] But the United States and its industrial allies could do much else even within their tight political and fiscal constraints.[64]

Assistance could include relaxing trade restrictions that have applied to economic relations with the FSU, providing technical assistance to help create a better climate for Western businesses in the FSU, encouraging Western private investment and joint ventures, and providing training for FSU personnel. No doubt the conversion challenge is large and the bulk of the effort and adaptation will have to come from within the FSU itself, but the West should do what it can to help.

Conclusion

The transformation and eventual demise of the Soviet Union ushered in a new era in international politics and opened up unprecedented opportunities for cooperation on a whole range of East-West and global security issues. If these developments had not occurred, it would not be possible to contemplate building a more cooperative international security system. But potential problems and developments within the FSU also pose the most immediate and urgent threats to prospects for international security cooperation. If hopeful trends are supplanted by negative developments in the FSU, the historic opportunity to move in more cooperative directions will be derailed.

Hence the United States and its allies have a profound interest in helping to promote outcomes in the FSU that are conducive to a world of greater security cooperation. Indeed, a strategy of cooperative engagement with the FSU ought to be regarded as an essential and necessary first step on the road to a more cooperative international order. In this chapter we have tried to outline the immediate priorities for a policy of cooperative engagement and to suggest some steps that may contribute to desired outcomes.

Notes

1. The headlines are randomly chosen from a vast sample. The references are: *Boston Globe,* July 28, 1992, p. 6; *Boston Globe,* July 29, 1992, p. 1; *Financial Times,* June 23, 1992, p. 2; *Financial Times,* June 25, 1992, p. 2; *New York Times,* June 26, 1992, p. A6; *Washington Post,* November 3, 1992, p. A14; *New York Times,* September 28, 1993, p. A10; and *New York Times,* October 4, 1993, p. A1.

2. Evgeniy Tkachenko, "Defense Workers Reportedly Tried to Go to DPKR," Moscow ITAR-TASS, in Foreign Broadcast Information Service, *Daily Report: Central Eurasia,* February 5, 1993, p. 10. (Hereafter FBIS, *Central Eurasia.*)

3. In this section we draw on our earlier work on this subject: Kurt M. Campbell, Ashton B. Carter, Steven E. Miller, and Charles A. Zraket, *Soviet Nuclear Fission: Control of the Nuclear Arsenal in a Disintegrating Soviet Union,* CSIA Studies in International Security 1 (Harvard University, Center for Science and International Affairs, November 1991); Graham Allison, Ashton B. Carter, Steven E. Miller, and Philip Zelikow, eds., *Cooperative Denuclearization: From Pledges to Deeds,* CSIA

Studies in International Security 2 (Harvard University, Center for Science and International Affairs, January 1993); and Ashton B. Carter, William J. Perry, and John D. Steinbruner, *A New Concept of Cooperative Security,* Occasional Papers (Brookings, 1992).

4. However, Russia's new defense doctrine, released in November 1993, shows a continued reliance on nuclear weapons to offset the reduction in conventional military forces and to counter perceived threats to Russia, particularly from Ukraine and China. Daniel Sneider "New Russian Doctrine Raises Western Suspicions," *Defense News,* vol. 8 (November 8–14, 1993), p. 3.

5. Stockholm International Peace Research Institute, *SIPRI Yearbook 1993* (Oxford University Press, 1993), pp. 149, 228.

6. *SIPRI Yearbook 1993,* p. 566; and Dunbar Lockwood, "U.S., Russia Reach Agreement on Sale of Nuclear Weapons Material," *Arms Control Today,* vol. 23 (March 1993), p. 22.

7. The rate of removal of tactical nuclear warheads has indeed been remarkable. President Bush's directive of September 1991 to eliminate all U.S. tactical nuclear weapons and Mikhail Gorbachev's reciprocal announcement on October 5, 1991, covering Soviet tactical weapons were fulfilled by June 1992. See Bush's announcement and Gorbachev's reply in "A New Era of Reciprocal Arms Reductions," *Arms Control Today,* vol. 21 (October 1991), pp. 3–6; and *SIPRI Yearbook 1993,* pp. 224, 228.

8. Jon B. Wolfsthal, "White House Formalizes End to Fissionable Materials Production," *Arms Control Today,* vol. 22 (July–August 1992), p. 25; *SIPRI Yearbook 1993,* p. 571; and R. Jeffrey Smith, "U.S. to Propose New Limits on Materials for Nuclear Weapons," *Washington Post,* September 23, 1993, p. A4.

9. Bruce G. Blair, "Russia's Doomsday Machine," *New York Times,* October 8, 1993, p. A35.

10. "A Charter for American-Russian Partnership and Friendship," *US Department of State Dispatch,* vol. 3 (June 22, 1992), p. 491.

11. Stephen Van Evera, "Managing the Eastern Crisis: Preventing War in the Former Soviet Empire," *Security Studies,* vol. 1 (Spring 1992), p. 361.

12. Our thinking on this point has been influenced by Paul B. Stares and John D. Steinbruner, "Cooperative Security in the New Europe," in Paul B. Stares, ed., *The New Germany and the New Europe* (Brookings, 1992), pp. 218–48.

13. Note, for example, the comment by former secretary of state James Baker: "We have in fact been developing arrangements for cooperative security to meet the needs of the newly emerging democracies [of the former eastern bloc] and to engage a reformed Soviet Union." From his speech, "The Euro-Atlantic Architecture: From West to East," *US Department of State Dispatch,* vol. 2 (June 24, 1991), p. 442.

14. Ibid., pp. 441–42.

15. See, for example, Celeste A. Wallander, "International Institutions and Modern Security Strategies," *Problems of Communism,* vol. 41 (January–April 1992), p. 59, which argues that this was the attitude of the Soviet government through August 1991: "The Soviet government favored CSCE . . . because it was the only institution in which the Soviets could possibly play a role in defining rules and procedures."

16. "Conference on Security and Cooperation in Europe: Final Act," in *Department of State Bulletin,* vol. 73 (September 1, 1975), pp. 324–26.

17. The Charter of Paris and other documents from the Paris summit may be found in Adam Daniel Rotfeld and Walther Stützle, eds., *Germany and Europe in Transition* (Oxford University Press, 1991), pp. 217–30.

18. See, for example, Ted Hopf, "Managing Soviet Disintegration: A Demand for Behavioral Regimes," *International Security,* vol. 17 (Summer 1992), pp. 44–75. See also Van Evera, "Managing the Eastern Crisis," pp. 368–69.

19. On this point see Henning Wegener, "Towards a New Political Order in Europe: Suggestion for a Code of Conduct," in Armand Clesse and Lothar Rühl, eds., *Beyond East-West Confrontation: Searching for a New Security Structure in Europe* (Baden-Baden: Nomos Verlagsgesellschaft, 1990), pp. 162–63.

20. For an extremely useful summary of the evolution of CSCE, see "Post–Cold War Security in and for Europe," SIPRI Fact Sheet, Stockholm International Peace Research Institute, December 1992, pp. 22–23.

21. See, for example, David Shorr, "CSCE Action on Moldova Awaits Envoy's Meeting with Yeltsin," *Basic Reports,* no. 27 (December 23, 1992), pp. 1–2.

22. Details of the CSCE's new institutional arrangements are found in "Supplementary Document to Give Effect to Certain Provisions Contained in the Charter of Paris for a New Europe," Rotfeld and Stützle, eds., *Germany and Europe in Transition,* pp. 226–30; and Adam Daniel Rotfeld, "New Security Structures in Europe: Concepts, Proposals and Decisions," *SIPRI Yearbook 1991: World Armaments and Disarmament* (Oxford University Press, 1991), pp. 585–600.

23. See, for example, the comment of Secretary of State Baker to the CSCE Council meeting in Prague on January 30, 1992: "In light of the tragic events in Yugoslavia, we need to look closely at ways to strengthen CSCE's crisis management and conflict prevention capabilities." Secretary Baker, "CSCE: Our Community of Democratic Values," address at the CSCE Council of Ministers Meeting, Prague, January 30, 1992, *US Department of State Dispatch,* vol. 3 (February 17, 1992), p. 101. (It is ironic to note that the first meeting of the Consultative Committee of the Conflict Prevention Centre in December 1990 was chaired by Yugoslavia.)

24. An extremely useful survey of the results of the 1992 CSCE Helsinki Summit is Jane M. O. Sharp, "New Roles for CSCE," *Bulletin of Arms Control,* no. 7 (August 1992), pp. 14–17. See also "Watch This Space," *Economist,* July 18, 1992, p. 49.

25. Craig R. Whitney, "NATO Sees a Role with Peacekeepers for Eastern Europe," *New York Times,* June 5, 1992, p. A1.

26. Sharp, "New Roles," pp. 15–16; quotation on p. 15.

27. "Watch This Space," p. 49.

28. See, for example, Heinz Vetschera, "The Role of the CSCE in European Conflict Prevention," paper presented at the conference on the Art of Conflict Prevention: Theory and Practice, Helsinki, Finland, June 2, 1992 (revised December 7, 1992), pp. 19–20 and note 244, which mentions the hypocrisy of member states that criticize the ineffectuality of the CSCE even while they are blocking decisions within the CSCE.

29. See, for example, Rotfeld, "New Security Structures in Europe," pp. 598–99.

30. Baker, "CSCE: Our Community of Democratic Values," p. 101.

31. On this point see, for example, Peter Corterier, "Grant CSCE Authority to Act," *Defense News,* vol. 7 (July 6–12, 1992), p. 15.

32. The CSCE already made some movement in this direction at its February 1991 Valletta meeting on the peaceful settlement of disputes. The document produced there declared that "all parties to a dispute will implement meaningfully and in good faith the CSCE Dispute Settlement Procedure." However, most important categories of dispute are excluded from the jurisdiction of the dispute settlement mechanism created at Valletta. See Hugh Miall, *The Peacemakers: Peaceful Settlement of Disputes since 1945* (St. Martin's Press, 1992), pp. 6, 15–16.

33. The discussion that follows draws on Lee Feinstein, "Commonwealth Members Offer Early Support for CFE Treaty," *Arms Control Today,* vol. 22 (January–February 1992), p. 44; Lee Feinstein, "Former Soviet States Agree on CFE Weapons Split," *Arms Control Today,* vol. 22 (June 1992), p. 20; "Former Soviet Republics Announce Inten-

tion to Honor CFE," *Basic Reports,* no. 19 (January 21, 1992), pp. 1–2; and Sharp, "New Roles for CSCE."

34. Lee Feinstein, "Russia Asks CFE Partners to Allow Increase in Arms on Southern Border," *Arms Control Today,* vol. 23 (November 1993), p. 25; and Stephen Foye, "Russia Continues to Ask for CFE Changes," *RFE/RL Daily Report,* no. 221 (November 18, 1993), p. 2.

35. The central Asian republics are outside the CFE zone of application. In addition, it was agreed to exclude the three Baltic republics from this arrangement. See Feinstein, "Former Soviet States Agree."

36. CFE weapon allocations within the FSU can be found in "Weapons in Europe before and after CFE," FACTFILE *Arms Control Today,* vol. 22 (June 1992), p. 32. For a broader discussion of CFE implementation in the FSU, see *SIPRI Yearbook 1993,* pp. 593–606.

37. For a detailed summary, see "The CFE Verification Regime," in Jürgen Altmann, Henny van der Graaf, Patricia M. Lewis, and Peter Markl, eds., *Verification at Vienna: Monitoring Reductions of Conventional Armed Forces* (Philadelphia: Gordon and Breach Science Publishers, 1992), app. 1, pp. 371–77.

38. See, for example, Stares and Steinbruner, "Cooperative Security in the New Europe," p. 225, which identifies mutual transparency as one of the basic design features of a cooperative security system for Europe.

39. See, in particular, ibid., pp. 224–25. See also Jonathan Dean and Randall Watson Forsberg, "CFE and Beyond: The Future of Conventional Arms Control," *International Security,* vol. 17 (Summer 1992), pp. 98–100. For a somewhat different perspective on the qualitative approach, see Keith Krause, "Post-Helsinki Conventional Arms Control: The Qualitative Dimension," *Arms Control,* vol. 12 (September 1991), pp. 211–30.

40. For detailed background on this subject, see John Freeman, *Security and the CSCE Process: The Stockholm Conference and Beyond* (St. Martin's Press, 1991); and Carl C. Krehbiel, *Confidence- and Security-Building Measures in Europe: The Stockholm Conference* (Praeger, 1989).

41. These categories informed NATO's proposal to the Vienna 1990 negotiations, as described in "Gist: Negotiations on Confidence- and Security-Building Measures (CSBMs)," *US Department of State Dispatch,* vol. 2 (July 15, 1991), pp. 507–08.

42. Ibid.; and Michael Z. Wise, "European Security Group Adopts New Rules to Limit Threats," *Washington Post,* March 5, 1992, p. A32.

43. The case for conditional Western policies has been vigorously and persuasively argued by a number of scholars. See, in particular, Graham Allison and Robert Blackwill, "America's Stake in the Soviet Future," *Foreign Affairs,* vol. 70 (Summer 1991), pp. 77–97; Van Evera, "Managing the Eastern Crisis," especially pp. 368–69; and Hopf, "Managing Soviet Disintegration."

44. See, for example, Serge Schmemann, "Yeltsin Leaves Talks with Firm Support and More Aid," *New York Times,* April 5, 1993, p. A1.

45. Van Evera, for example, argues that even a substantially expanded expenditure of financial resources in the FSU will be "a pittance relative to the cosmic stakes at issue, and to the vast wealth Americans expend on far less urgent problems." "Managing the Eastern Crisis," p. 375. See also Allison and Blackwill, "America's Stake in the Soviet Future"; and Graham Allison, Ashton B. Carter, Steven E. Miller, and Philip Zelikow, "Organizing for Denuclearization," in Allison and others, eds., *Cooperative Denuclearization,* pp. 285–86, which notes how small contemplated assistance is relative to even current Western levels of defense expenditure. A very useful summary of U.S. assistance efforts is Barton Kaplan, "U.S. Assistance to the Former Soviet Union:

A Status Report," Occasional Paper 3 (Monterey Institute of International Studies, Center for Russian and Eurasian Studies, March 1993).

46. See Ian Anthony and others, "Arms Production," *SIPRI Yearbook 1990: World Armaments and Disarmament* (Oxford University Press, 1990), pp. 344–58; and Herbert Wulf, "Arms Production," *SIPRI Yearbook 1991: World Armaments and Disarmament* (Oxford University Press, 1991), pp. 298–309.

47. *SIPRI Yearbook 1991,* app. 7A, pp. 230–31.

48. Fred Kaplan, "Hard-Pressed Russia Seeks to Revive Global Arms Sales," *Boston Globe,* July 29, 1992, p. 1.

49. See, for example, Mark Kramer, "The Global Arms Trade after the Persian Gulf War," *Security Studies,* vol. 2 (Winter 1992), pp. 280–82; and Peter Almquist and Edwin Bacon, "Arms Exports in a Post-Soviet Market," *Arms Control Today,* vol. 22 (July–August 1992), pp. 12–17. Also indicative is Philip Finnegan, "Russia Extends Mideast Arms Sale Hunt," *Defense News,* vol. 7 (June 15–21, 1992), p. 1. The Russian government has openly announced its intention to expand arms transfers. See "Government to Increase Sale of Arms Abroad," *Interfax,* February 27, 1993, in FBIS, *Central Eurasia,* March 2, 1993, p. 11; and Serge Schmemann, "Russian Gives U.S. Challenge on Aid," *New York Times,* March 7, 1993, p. A7.

50. See, for example, David R. Markov, "The Fire Sale on Russian Missiles," *Air Force Magazine,* vol. 75 (December 1992), pp. 60–63; and Bill Sweetman, "Backfire Goes to Market," ibid., vol. 76 (February 1993), pp. 42–46.

51. In another case, a Russian effort to supply rocket engines to India was blocked by the United States. On the Indian rocket deal, see Selig S. Harrison and Geoffrey Kemp, *India and America after the Cold War* (Washington: Carnegie Endowment for International Peace, 1993), pp. 38–39; and Greg Koblentz and Jon B. Wolfsthal, "Russia Agrees to Adhere to MTCR, Suspends Rocket Deal with India," *Arms Control Today,* vol. 23 (September 1993), p. 23.

52. Joris Janssen Lok, "'Victor II,' ASW on Offer to the USA," *Jane's Defence Weekly,* vol. 17 (April 25, 1992), p. 685.

53. See, for example, Lena H. Sun, "Russia, China Set Closest Ties in Years: Yeltsin Pledges to Sell Beijing 'The Most Sophisticated' Weapons," *Washington Post,* December 19, 1992, p. A1; Schmemann, "Russian Gives U.S. Challenge"; and Steven Erlanger, "Moscow Insists It Must Sell the Instruments of War to Pay the Costs of Peace," *New York Times,* February 3, 1993, p. A6.

54. Note, as one example, the distress caused in Washington by Russia's arms sales to Iran. See Ruth Sinai, "Iranian Arms Buildup a Threat to U.S., Allies, Director of CIA Warns," *Boston Globe,* November 25, 1992, p. 9; and Michael R. Gordon, "U.S. Sub Checks Gulf's Waters with Iran in Mind," *New York Times,* November 5, 1992, p. A3.

55. For a brief survey, see Ian Anthony and others, "The Trade in Major Conventional Weapons," in *SIPRI Yearbook 1992: World Armaments and Disarmament* (Oxford University Press, 1992), pp. 291–94. The guidelines agreed by the permanent five are found in "Selected Documents relating to Arms Export Control in 1991," *SIPRI Yearbook 1992,* app. 8A, pp. 304–05. By mid-1993, however, China had withdrawn from these talks and had begun to criticize the United States for maintaining a double standard on its own arms export policy. See R. Jeffrey Smith, "China Denounces U.S. Policy on Arms Transfers," *Washington Post,* September 30, 1993, p. A15.

56. Carter and others, "New Concept of Cooperative Security," pp. 7–9, 20–24, 63.

57. *SIPRI Yearbook 1993,* p. 444, reports U.S. exports of major conventional weapons in 1992 at $8.43 billion, USSR-Russia at $2.04 billion.

58. See, for example, Almquist and Bacon, "Arms Exports in a Post-Soviet Market," p. 13. It is worth noting, in this context, that the U.S. share of the global market for

major conventional arms has grown between 1988 and 1992 from less than one-third to nearly one-half, while the Soviet-FSU share has declined from more than one-third to about 10 percent. Based on figures in *SIPRI Yearbook 1993,* p. 444.

59. Maxim Yusin, "Boris Yeltsin and Bill Clinton Will Meet One Week before the Russian Referendum," *Izvestiya,* February 27, 1993, p. 1, in FBIS, *Central Eurasia,* March 1, 1993, pp. 7–8.

60. As indicated by the negative reactions to Kozyrev's comments. See particularly Frank Gaffney, "Russia Hints at Blackmail over Arms," *Defense News,* vol. 8 (March 8–14, 1993), pp. 19–20; and Sergey Svistunov, "The Naive Get 'Left Behind.' The Latest 'Demarche' by Russian Diplomacy Is Prompting a Condescending Smile from the Americans," *Pravda,* February 26, 1993, p. 3, in FBIS, *Central Eurasia,* March 1, 1993, pp. 8–9. Svistunov argues that the "desperate competition" among Western arms manufacturers precludes cooperation between Russia and the West over arms transfers.

61. See, for example, Charles Wolf, Jr., "An Aid Package for Russia—Beyond Clinton's," *Asian Wall Street Journal,* April 19, 1993, which argues that, as part of a more effective Western aid package, the West ought to assure Russia and Ukraine "a reasonable share of the world arms market."

62. See, for example, Julian Cooper, *The Soviet Defence Industry: Conversion and Economic Reform* (New York: Council on Foreign Relations Press for the Royal Institute of International Affairs, 1991), pp. 11–14, for an indication of the scale of the Soviet defense industry. See also David Bernstein and William J. Perry, *Defense Conversion: A Strategic Imperative for Russia* (Stanford University, Center for International Security and Arms Control, August 1992), which suggests (p. 1) that conversion is necessary if economic reforms are to succeed.

63. In this section we draw on Cooper, *Soviet Defence Industry,* pp. 92–95; David Mussington, "Conversion and Demobilization in the CIS Nuclear Weapons Complex," in Allison and others, eds., *Cooperative Denuclearization,* pp. 182–90; and Bernstein and Perry, *Defense Conversion,* pp. 20–21.

64. We have found Bernstein and Perry, *Defense Conversion,* p. 20, to be particularly helpful in identifying constructive measures that do not require much in the way of financial largesse.

Part Five

CONCLUSION

SIXTEEN

A Transition Strategy for the 1990s

Janne E. Nolan and John D. Steinbruner

FUNDAMENTAL SHIFTS in the definition of security begin at the conceptual level and, through a process of interaction with historical circumstances and emerging political perceptions, gradually prompt realignments of practical policy. This process is typically evolutionary, ad hoc, and rarely the result of deliberate or sudden action. New conditions, even those resulting in dramatic change, seldom prompt decisionmakers toward rapid transformations of the premises guiding national planning. In industrial democracies, in particular, the demands of popular consensus, the influence of established institutions, and the reluctance of elites to engender controversy militate against precipitous change. Even major alterations in the security environment, such as the unexpected mutation of the Soviet Union from a formidable adversary into a disintegrating power seeking legitimation and assistance from the West, are not readily understood. As was seen in the slowness of the Bush administration to respond to the demise of the Soviet Union, caution and skepticism are likely to prevail before a process of deliberate accommodation can take place.

In evaluating the prospects for cooperative security to become an accepted framework for security relations, it is important to remember the difficulties involved in prior historical adjustments. The conceptual framework that informed postwar policies resulting from the division of Europe and the ascendancy of a Soviet rival only haltingly evolved into what came to be a predominant ideology of containment. The adoption of containment strategies was not the result of a rejection of alternative approaches based on consensus, nor was it driven by a conscious decision that they were the only suitable framework to guide policy in adjusting to the new balance of power. In the current environment, similarly, the recognition of a strategy that explicitly

William J. Perry and Wolfgang H. Reinicke also contributed to this chapter.

recognizes the limitations of cold war habits, including the preparation for mass conflict as the sacrosanct imperative of security, is no more likely to occur in a logical and comprehensive way.

Cooperative security is only prescriptive to the degree to which it suggests that secular trends in international security are already exceeding the ability of national governments to respond by means of traditional instruments. The choice is between making what appear to be increasingly futile efforts to preserve the trappings of an old security order and harnessing the forces of change for international benefit. For the industrial countries especially, the question is whether they will be forced into halfhearted cooperation by domestic constraints and international realities or if they will seize the opportunities presented and take the lead in crafting a global transition to a more stable international order.

Undoubtedly a regime of the kind analyzed in this volume would evolve in stages, no matter how powerful or compelling may be the forces arguing for more comprehensive change. Were a new conception of security relations to take hold, it would invariably begin with a strategy interweaving existing policy trends already being adapted to current demands for cooperation. As noted in chapter 1, there are already strong foundations for a new security system, based on past and ongoing initiatives, that recognize that most of the more significant security challenges of this decade impel cooperative approaches. These foundations can provide the building blocks for the articulation and expansion of a security regime in which cooperation is explicitly embraced as the driving objective of security.

This concluding chapter provides an initial agenda for implementing such a regime. The purpose is to highlight near-term priorities for security building in areas in which cooperative approaches are already embedded or could benefit from greater emphasis. These include (1) the denuclearization of the former Soviet Union, (2) agreements on conventional force deployments in Europe, (3) new security partnerships, (4) instruments for controlling technology diffusion, (5) the integration of existing control regimes, (6) conflict prevention and mediation, (7) conversion of excess defense capacity, and (8) defining a new leadership role for the United States in promoting nonproliferation and security cooperation.

Denuclearization of the Former Soviet Union

The growing cooperative engagement between the United States and the countries of the former Soviet Union to dismantle and establish control over their nuclear arsenals is one of the most important immediate steps for which a cooperative security approach has been explicitly articulated. The results of this cooperative effort will have a significant influence on subsequent efforts toward joint engagement, in this and other spheres. In just the short time that such initiatives have been undertaken, unanticipated developments have forced alterations in and a redirection of policies. Initially the conception of U.S. assistance to the former Soviet Union consisted of a fairly simple diplomatic trade-off: an offer of U.S. financial and technical assistance in return for agreements to impose strict controls on Soviet nuclear assets. The agreements included decommissioning nuclear weapons, centralizing the command for remaining forces in Russia, and redirecting weapon designers to alternative occupations, including discouraging their migration to other countries that might use their expertise for domestic nuclear weapons development.

The offer of U.S. assistance was made in advance of any specific determination of the actual needs of the states in question and without any offer of reciprocal actions by the United States. It also lacked a political strategy that took into account the underlying political and diplomatic factors involved in such a sensitive undertaking, which would determine its success or failure.

Because Ukraine recognized that there was inherent inequity in American insistence that it relinquish its forces without commensurate concessions from Russia or security assurances from the West, possession of nuclear weapons became a highly politicized issue of nationalistic prerogative for the new government. What began as a promising U.S. venture to help Ukraine rid itself of unwanted nuclear risk evolved into a political controversy about sovereignty and the status thought to be accorded by possession of nuclear weapons. As one Ukrainian general put it in June 1993, "Idiots are people who give up their nuclear weapons."[1]

This experience provided the United States with an object lesson about modern diplomacy. It is a lesson that is particularly relevant for cooperative security: cooperation is not and can never be based on even the appearance of coercion, however benevolent its apparent objective. For the rest of the former Soviet Union, similarly, the larger goal of denuclearization demands a more nuanced political strategy that includes plans for forging full political and economic partnership with the countries in question and easing their transition into the international community.

Denuclearization is only a symptom of a far more complicated political and security agenda, in which reciprocity and legitimacy must be essential elements if American involvement is not to be short-lived or even counterproductive. The near-term objective remains the elimination of nuclear threats from the region. However, it is now more fully understood that this objective is achievable only in a context of broader international accommodation and a commitment to help provide the conditions for peaceful transition and enduring stability.

Still, the immediate steps to be taken to reduce nuclear risk are urgent, and the conditions for advancing this agenda seem promising. Deterrence of deliberate nuclear attack is now accepted as far easier to achieve than it was in the past. Thus even without eliminating the confrontational deployments that remain in the U.S. and Russian force postures, there is much greater scope for improving their operational safety.

The most critical area is the alert status of weapons. If one were to apply standards of safety as exacting as those routinely demanded of nuclear reactors, they would almost certainly require that deployments with high alert status be terminated. It would be an important form of reassurance if nuclear weapons were mutually agreed to be held in a state that required visible and time-consuming preparation before they could actually be used. To ensure adequate protection of forces in such a state of deployment, extensive cooperation in the design and maintenance of operational procedures would also be needed. Thus the greater operational safety and the political benefits that could result from agreements to take nuclear forces off alert provide a strong incentive for cooperation.

Conventional Forces

The process of engagement between the United States and the Commonwealth of Independent States (CIS) to consolidate control over nuclear weapons has provided political impetus and a practical context for working out the details of cooperation. But this initial, narrowly defined objective cannot be achieved unless the process of cooperation is extended to conventional forces. Despite the special organizational arrangements for handling nuclear weapons that developed in both the United States and the former Soviet Union, their operations have been sufficiently integrated into overall military activity so that an effective approach to consolidating control cannot exclude conventional forces.

This condition is especially true for the ground forces that have been the larger part and the organizational core of the traditional Soviet establishment. They are most seriously affected by the impending demobilization, and their fate has a stronger effect on most of the issues endemic to internal security. It is extremely unlikely that secure control of nuclear weapons could be maintained while the Red Army disintegrates.

Neither the CIS itself nor its constituent states can be expected to handle the necessary reconfiguration of their conventional military forces without substantial international collaboration. Without the cover of international restraints on conventional forces, they might not believe themselves able to match the legitimate requirements of territorial defense with their available forces, and they might be driven into primary reliance on nuclear weapons. Such a development would burden the integrated nuclear control that has been agreed upon among the successor states but that cannot be taken for granted. The graceful apportionment of inherited conventional forces by members of the CIS is an issue that could easily trigger internal conflict dangerous to economic and political reform.

It seems both likely and desirable that another form of engagement will be required to deal with the disposition of conventional ground forces in Europe. The process of implementing the Conventional Armed Forces in Europe (CFE) Treaty will require more elaborate international arrangements to guide the distribution of treaty-limited equipment among the CIS states. Additional international assistance will be required to complete the process of removing the forces of the former Soviet Union from their positions in eastern Europe. This process is not just a matter of disposing of military assets. The rapid demobilization of some 195,000 former Soviet military officers, who find themselves suddenly dispossessed and without any assurance of even basic welfare, is a security disaster in the making.

The massive social upheaval resulting from demobilization is a problem that must be embraced as a fully international obligation. The international community, however reluctant to assume new burdens, faces a choice between expanding assistance to ease the difficult social transformations in the region or contending with far graver risks of instability and political disintegration. At a minimum the loss of control over sensitive military technologies and their accompanying transfer to destabilizing countries presents a critical challenge that can be addressed only by cooperative engagement.

Military Contacts and Security Partnerships

Even during the most tendentious periods of U.S.-Soviet rivalry, communication between the two sides' military establishments was considered vital for the management of tensions and the avoidance of war. In the current environment there has been an unprecedented expansion of this form of engagement, now tailored toward finding cooperative solutions to mutual security concerns. The Clinton administration has already initiated a more ambitious agenda for military-to-military contacts and new forms of security dialogue in this regard. This area could benefit from even greater commitment, however, and not just from the United States but from the other major military establishments as well.

It is now not only possible but also essential for the United States and Russia to expand and institutionalize their security engagement for a wide range of objectives, including discussion of desirable force levels, defense budgets and investment decisions, and defense doctrines. It is also imperative that these contacts begin to include all the major military establishments, in recognition of the international community's stakes in the outcome of Russia's political and military transformation.

In both the former Soviet Union and the West, fiscal pressures and competing economic priorities are likely to drive force deployments below the levels embodied in the CFE ceilings. As military establishments on both sides try to protect defense expenditures against draconian cuts, they continue to justify their requirements with traditional rationales of military preparedness against a now unspecified set of potential enemies. Despite the absence of plausible scenarios under which U.S., Russian, or CIS forces would be required to mobilize quickly in large numbers, the outmoded nationalist rhetoric used by military planners is an impediment to the articulation of more realistic and constructive security objectives that reflect current and mutual security dilemmas.

The first task of cooperative engagement in this sphere must be to recast the rationales of military planning from confrontational postures to those that maximize reassurance and nonprovocation. Military planners whose careers were formed during the cold war may never espouse cooperative engagement as a philosophical conviction, but they have tended to do much better in the actual practice of it. Beginning in the Gorbachev years, contact between Soviet military officers and their Western counterparts demonstrated a high degree of responsiveness to notions of security collaboration. Much of the content of this military dialogue has remained at the symbolic and rhetorical level, but it is clear that the dialogue could fairly readily be transformed into more meaningful exchanges and definitions of common purpose.

If military planners of the respective states were authorized to brief one another on their force structure objectives, budget projections, and underlying doctrinal assumptions, this approach would inevitably help foster a sense of mutual interest. Given overriding economic pressures, it should be obvious that states can achieve enhanced security with fewer and more efficiently equipped forces only if they collaborate. If military officials were authorized to experiment with joint operations as well, the foundations for confidence building and the management of joint security initiatives would also be solidified.

In the initial phases of military cooperation initiatives such as the joint conduct of military missions would probably be limited to occasional, experimental exercises until the foundations for trust and reassurance could be developed more fully. In less sensitive areas, however, including military support functions, cooperation is already a serious prospect. For example, official proposals have been made for collaboration in tactical warning of missile launches, a particularly promising area for mutual reassurance. The underlying problem of strategic force interactions is significantly affected by potential vulnerabilities in warning system performance. In fact the control of strategic forces relies heavily on a capacity that has never been tested and is not testable, that is, the ability to prove with high confidence that a strategic attack is not under way when there is heightened suspicion and some evidence that it might be. The inherent fragility in this arrangement must be addressed.

The warning system within the former Soviet Union is particularly susceptible to this potential instability, especially if the control of nuclear assets outside Russia is not ensured. With cooperative efforts a number of technical and operational innovations could alleviate this problem with few, if any, offsetting risks.

A more ambitious cooperative undertaking would be the common management of civil and military air traffic in all of Europe west of the Urals. Since tactical air operations are the most vital element of an offensive military attack and depend on air traffic management, a scheme for joint management of air traffic could eliminate the material conditions that currently allow for preemptive actions. This undertaking would be a powerful and concrete way of extending reassurance about national military objectives. The joint arrangements would have to be terminated well before any aggressive military operation could be undertaken, providing early warning and severely hindering any advantage sought from surprise attack.

As a practical matter the implementation of such an initiative would benefit from past experience. Throughout the period of alliance confrontation, American and Soviet military air traffic was jointly managed in their respective spheres by NATO and the Warsaw Pact. This management required elaborate interactions between the two opposing systems and as such allowed for the development of considerable familiarity with their respective operations. With the demise of military hostility between the two sides, this expertise could be tapped for active collaboration, resulting in the internationalization of a vital element of force planning and operations.

Over time similar cooperative forms of engagement can be contemplated among regional powers. A series of regional consultations is ongoing in various parts of the world, notably the Middle East, East Asia, South Asia, and (although the region is not addressed in detail in this volume) Latin America. Though varied in content and degree of progress, regional confidence- and security-building measures are under active consideration in all of these areas and point to the prospect of greater integration of regional powers into a common system of norms regulating certain forms of military behavior. It is essential that emerging nuclear powers, in particular, be engaged in more active international dialogue about doctrines, operational safety, and other types of nuclear-related activities that could otherwise prove provocative regionally or internationally.

To be credible the rules guiding the regulation of military activity must aspire to universality. There are already serious strains in existing control arrangements arising from the perception of discrimination among smaller states that do not support the extension of a permanently hierarchical international technology and security system. As the larger powers accept limitations on their own military commerce and patterns of force modernization, they must also demonstrate their interest in and commitment to devising equitable controls for regional and global application. As was demonstrated all too clearly in Ukraine, the West can provide assistance and advice to countries seeking to alter their security postures but cannot rely on dictates or threats to promote change.

Monitoring the Flow of Arms and Technology

In December 1991 the UN General Assembly passed a resolution to establish a system of voluntary registration of all arms exports and imports.[2] This resolution is a promising first step in the recognition by the international community of a collective responsibility for monitoring and controlling certain aspects of the arms trade. Even merely as a conceptual achievement, this system is an innovation that could serve as the initial element in a consolidated international management regime for weapons proliferation.

As discussed in preceding chapters, the key objective of international regulation is to promote transparency in the international system. The registry is an example of a transparency instrument, although it obviously would need to be amplified to be a more comprehensive and effective control mechanism. The shift of control regimes from supply-side controls to a more open trading arrangement emphasizing instead requirements for disclosure of technology applications would benefit from a system that recorded and monitored trade flows internationally.

Western enterprises that manufacture and trade dual-use products have long adhered to cumbersome requirements for prior approval under restrictions imposed by national legislation, the Coordinating Committee on Multilateral Trade (COCOM), or more selective cartels such as the Missile Technology Control Regime. Many of these arrangements were directed against the old Soviet Union and its Warsaw Pact allies and have lost much of their original political rationale. But there is still a strong inclination to continue them against newly identified targets such as Iraq. As an improvement over the increasingly futile export control apparatus based on licensing a wide range of dual-use technology transfers, an international registry and a regulating regime founded on the premise of full disclosure of the intended application of the technology could actually reduce the burden of regulation.

At first glance a requirement for reporting, product labeling, and monitoring the disposition of technology would seem to impose added regulatory burdens for industry and for recipients. A new system of end-use monitoring and assurances would have to be devised for sensitive technologies, and it would need to be perceived as reliable. But if such regulations replaced the needless intrusions on legitimate trade that are currently at the core of grievances about existing regimes and still protected credible nonproliferation objectives, they would be likely to be welcomed by participants.

International defense trade controls have typically been imposed by governments without prior consultation with industry. One result in the United States has been antagonism and efforts to undercut unpopular policies through Congress or the media. But industry has a potentially vital role to play in a future restraint regime. As the main source of expertise about technology and usually the party most involved in actual transactions, industry may be the only means by which governments can track and enforce restrictions on exported products. Industry assistance could be used to identify relevant technological inputs for particular proscribed technologies and to help devise safeguards and other end-use restrictions to prevent the diversion of civilian or dual-use equipment to military application.

Clearly developing countries would merit special arrangements. To the extent that large investments in information-processing capability, high-speed communications capacity, and connectivity to global networks are necessary to make the monitoring mechanisms required for a cooperative security approach work, they could be subsidized by richer countries as an incentive to join the system. The computer and communications infrastructure so constructed might even serve as a subsidized core for their advanced network infrastructure development, with spare capacity from the monitoring system used for other national needs. Access to financial resources and development assistance could also be used as a carrot to encourage compliance with the economic and military rules of the game developed by the larger international community. The benefits of access to international markets and greater participation in the advanced global economy by both suppliers and recipients are likely to outweigh by far the relatively modest direct subsidies channeled as incentives for participation.

Constructing an integrated set of cooperative international institutions to monitor and enforce international constraints on military investment and acquisition could thus have tangible benefits for individual nations as well as for the greater international interest. The greatest economic benefits, broadly writ, would be to grant subscribing countries less encumbered access to a global market for high-technology products and services and greater connectivity to a global information infrastructure essential to the functioning of a modern industrial economy. On the other hand, countries that choose not to join may be denied access to these benefits or given access on significantly more restrictive terms, at costs that become more directly calculable by governments and populations.

In sum, by assuming the principle of free trade for all but a few proscribed technologies or renegade states and by providing a clear incentive to suppliers and recipients to abide by monitoring arrangements in return for greater market access, the regime could remove many of the discriminatory and other political impediments currently impeding control agreements.

Cooperative Integration of Control Regimes

An initial step toward a control regime emphasizing disclosure over protectionism would be the rationalization and integration of existing regimes. In the United States alone there are currently at least six distinct control arrangements to restrict nuclear, chemical, and biological weapons; missiles; conventional weapons; and dual-use technologies. They each have had varied histories and political fortunes and prescribe different mechanisms for surveillance, control, enforcement, and administration.

A comprehensive, global cooperative security regime would seek to restructure and consolidate these regimes for their common benefit. Even as they have been operating as separate entities, in practice the regimes face similar legal, regulatory, and administrative challenges. Over time the phenomenon of weapons proliferation has become more synergistic as more countries seek to acquire proscribed weapons, weapons production technology, and material as part of concerted national strategies. Violations experienced within the various regimes often involve the same arms traders and conduits of clandestine transfer and thus pose common intelligence and enforcement challenges as well.

The effort to acquire various types of weapons is typically initiated and controlled by the same military or intelligence institutions within recipient nations. Shared international intelligence, shared procedures for monitoring and inspecting trade flows, joint preparation of lists of controlled items and end users, and a concerted effort to marshal political support for enforcement goals, as such, would obviously benefit from streamlining existing national and multinational enforcement mechanisms. Such measures might be implemented by an International Assessment and Verification Agency, perhaps under the aegis of the UN, that would receive data from national collection systems as well as from its own collection systems (for example, the agency could be associated with the international body responsible for operating an Open Skies collection system). These transparency measures would have to be enacted against the background of an international consensus that would interpret concealment of suspect military facilities and activities as hostile intent, subject to the same penalties as outright violation. The degree of punitive measures imposed for violations would also have to be based on internationally accepted norms.

Currently the rather weak international secretariats that operate control regimes, such as COCOM or the International Atomic Energy Agency (IAEA), have been slow to adapt to current realities, but initiatives are under way to reconsider their missions. The principle of open disclosure and cooperative enforcement is already embedded in the Chemical Weapons Convention, signed by more than 140 nations in early 1993.[3] Similar undertakings include, among others, the U.S. effort to recast the premises and guidelines of the Export Administration Act, negotiations among allies to redirect the focus of

COCOM to include the former Soviet Union and perhaps some industrializing countries, and preparations for more intrusive challenge inspections undertaken as part of the Nuclear Non-Proliferation Treaty (NPT).

A cooperative security system involving extensive constraints on military acquisitions and force preparations would have to require all parties to accept a level of intrusive monitoring of their defense programs. Such transparency would apply to limits on force size and types of equipment, as are already partially provided for in the Strategic Arms Reduction Talks (START) and CFE agreements. It would extend to major exercises and selected military operations, as are covered by the system of European confidence- and security-building measures, in certain superpower agreements covering nuclear accidents and potentially hazardous military activities, and in regional agreements, such as those resulting from the Camp David accords.

Second, transparency would cover certain development, testing, and manufacturing activities, such as those that once again are covered in START and the Intermediate-Range Nuclear Force (INF) and Anti-Ballistic Missile treaties, as well as in the NPT and the Chemical Weapons Convention. Finally it would apply to sales and purchases of military equipment and processes, as stipulated in the nuclear, biological, and chemical weapons regimes. The implementation of these various transparency measures would thus evolve into a more integrated strategy based on the existing arrangements and would be adapted over time to different regional settings according to prevailing political realities.

The underpinnings of a cooperative security regime are transparency and information. Such a regime has a strong need for high-quality intelligence and analyses of political-military developments to help anticipate, identify, and prevent regime violations or the outbreak of conflicts. The ability to monitor agreements and conduct inspections, in particular, would require a greater degree of intelligence cooperation among states than exists currently.

The Clinton administration is trying to redirect the focus of U.S. intelligence agencies, certainly as compared to its predecessor. In his testimony before Congress in March 1993, for example, the director of the Central Intelligence Agency, R. James Woolsey, pledged that the intelligence community would redirect its resources and talents to new forms of intelligence and analysis focused on global political and economic developments.[4] Even today, however, this objective is not universally shared among officials, many of whom believe that intelligence should remain focused on military developments and deployments.

The breakup of the Soviet Union has had the benefit of forcing policymakers to recognize the powerful influence of political, social, and economic variables in determining the foundations of regional and global stability. A preoccupation with quantified force levels, weapons performance characteristics, and technical limitations on arsenals permitted many specialists in the past to dismiss the political and economic dimensions of security. For example, the structural imperatives that in the end forced the Soviet military to collapse were of less concern analytically than force calculations or plans for new weapons requirements. In third world countries, the studied ignorance of the domestic dynamics of regional powers has been even more prevalent.

The unwillingness to take into account political realities in favor of abstract strategic logic has imposed considerable costs on U.S. policy, not just in the Soviet case but also in key client states such as Iran in the 1970s and Iraq in the 1990s. Ignorance of this kind breeds miscalculation and policy reversals. For example, for all of the importance that must be accorded the removal of nuclear weapons from the former Soviet republics, there is the risk that it will again be forgotten that there is no technical fix for the insecurities that could fuel continued regional chaos and eventually reverse any current progress toward denuclearization. Far more sophisticated responses are needed for conflict prevention and mediation, peacekeeping, and strategies to nurture sustained democratization and economic growth.

In the immediate future there is a need for more capable institutions to share intelligence among countries in support of nonproliferation. As the global defense technology market has become truly internationalized, it is increasingly unrealistic to conceive of trade controls and other regulatory measures as national obligations. For the IAEA and the NPT, in particular, proposals are under consideration to pool national intelligence under this international authority, allowing the IAEA to judge more precisely if and when it should conduct challenge inspections or other monitoring functions. The IAEA added an intelligence officer to its staff for the first time in 1991, a step clearly not sufficient to satisfy future intelligence demands but nonetheless an important conceptual evolution for this agency.[5]

There is already considerable intelligence sharing in the area of customs and other export controls, but a more formal commitment among governments to share information about proliferation routinely would help target violators and enforce regimes. In a control system that monitored end users and focused on the flow of a more selective list of proscribed technologies, joint intelligence operations would enable countries to stop proliferation before it had occurred, an easier task than imposing sanctions after the fact. Greater cooperation in the field of satellite and other advanced surveillance, moreover, could give a sense of security to states potentially threatened by aggressors.

Cooperative Regional Security

As discussed earlier, security cooperation is already well developed in Europe. The history of the Conference on Security and Cooperation in Europe (CSCE) reflects the evolution of the basic idea of self-interested security cooperation, and the Paris Charter provides an authoritative statement of its basic principles. The CFE treaty imposes ceilings on major weapons categories for all members of the two historical alliance systems, and the Stockholm Agreement on Confidence and Security Building Measures provides rules for military force operations in the European area. Though these agreements were formulated in the context of the alliance confrontation that has now dissolved, their basic rules, especially their provisions for the exchange of information and direct monitoring of weapons and military activities, can be adapted to the new situation.

The European states have practiced cooperation and have articulated political commitment to the idea well in advance of the clear establishment of cooperative security as the central principle of their defense policies. This experience offers a foundation and possibly a model for the practical evolution of a more comprehensive application of these concepts.

Several challenges lie ahead for articulating and expanding cooperative arrangements both within and beyond Europe. The first and most obvious one is to complete the European transition, especially in the determination of the emerging relationships among NATO countries and the former members of the Warsaw Pact. The North Atlantic Cooperation Council (NACC) was explicitly formed to allow for regular consultations among the states of western and eastern Europe, a conceptual and practical innovation that acknowledges the dissolution of formal confrontation but also demonstrates that residual suspicions and old habits must still be dispelled.

The NACC is a device for giving the eastern European and CIS states observer status in NATO without full membership. Full membership and the necessary redefinition of NATO are clearly the next steps to consider. In their complete form these moves could include all CSCE members, thereby giving the CSCE the institutional and political comprehensiveness that it has previously lacked.

Extending European-type arrangements to other regions is another question. The challenge is to explore the extent to which instruments designed and articulated in the West might be adapted to distinct regional settings. The first candidate region for such initiatives is clearly Asia, where the Russian Federation and the United States are key powers. In fact it may not be possible to fully develop cooperative security arrangements for Europe without including Asia.

One concept has been to consider the extension of CFE-type negotiations or of the CSCE to Asia, with appropriate adjustments to account for its different security and political realities. Since the foundations for such an ambitious undertaking do not yet exist, and the key nations in Asia show a strong disinclination toward any initiatives that appear Eurocentric, future diplomacy will have to be cautious and highly sensitive to the vast differences between the two regions.

The integration of East Asia into international cooperative arrangements would obviously be a powerful impetus for global change. In combination Europe and East Asia represent the largest military establishments and the most capable industrial economies. No international security system can be contemplated, however, unless its rules and procedures are accepted in the developing world, especially in conflict-prone regions such as South Asia and the Middle East. This ambition is more complicated and may come about only as a subsequent development. In articulating and reinforcing a European security design, however, and in contemplating its extension elsewhere, regional understandings must be at the core of the initiative.

In the nuclear area, in particular, a crisis over the extension of the NPT in 1995 could be averted if the established nuclear powers begin to accommodate the demand for greater equity in the regime among regional powers. For example, the renunciation of plans to test nuclear weapons could begin the process of reducing the asymmetries in the international protocol governing nuclear weapons. Even if it were just a matter of removing a pretext used by smaller powers to justify their own actions, a test ban would still lend greater credibility to the effort to discourage the emergence of new nuclear powers. The notion that nuclear weapons can serve as the core of large powers' sovereign interests yet must be denied to others in the interest of peace severely hinders credibility and may have an adverse effect on other nonproliferation initiatives as well. For example, after Iraq broke the taboo on the use of chemical weapons by gassing its Kurdish population, several third world states defended the acquisition of chemical weapons as a counter to the large powers' nuclear arsenals.[6]

Conflict Prevention and Mediation

In a cooperative security regime the importance of preventive operations for security building would be recognized in commensurate contributions. To ensure adequate annual funding, as a first step the U.S. responsibility for peacekeeping should reside in the Defense Department. If future conflicts of the kind occurring in the former Yugoslavia and Somalia are recognized as potentially serious threats to U.S. interests, these security obligations should rightfully be managed by the Pentagon and supported by the intelligence community.

Modernizing peacekeeping operations, including the provision of vitally needed equipment and logistical support, will require additional appropriations. The price of UN peacekeeping has risen tenfold in the last six years, costing 3.7 billion in 1993.[7] Even at this rate, however, the fiscal burden of military preparations for actual conflict will continue to exceed available resources. U.S. participation in the Gulf War alone cost well over the $50 billion pledged by coalition allies.[8] Had the international security system been organized to anticipate potential aggression in the Gulf, preventive measures, including UN peacekeepers stationed on the border of Kuwait, might have averted the immense loss of life and material resources incurred by Iraqi aggression and Operation Desert Storm.[9]

U.S. threat assessments have only recently begun to take seriously the degree to which security problems in much of the third world may be primarily internal and thus unlikely to be addressed by traditional military means. These problems include weak governmental structures, factionalism and religious fundamentalism, and worsening economic circumstances resulting from unsuccessful development strategies and the burden of external indebtedness. They loom as potentially enormous demands on the international community for financial and other forms of assistance and intervention.

Financial priorities could be redirected selectively under a cooperative security regime to redress many resource and political constraints that currently impinge on preventive measures. If U.S. forces were organized and equipped so that they could actually be deployed in international coalitions anywhere in the world on short notice, defense costs could be allocated more equitably and efficiently among allies. The need for overseas basing and troop deployments—and their attendant costs—could also be reduced significantly. The obligations of remaining forward-deployed forces could and should evolve from national to more fully international in any case—helping to soften the image of the United States upholding an outmoded, confrontational security order, reducing controversies over burden sharing, and helping to mitigate potential frictions that can arise in regions where domestic tensions could be exacerbated by an exclusively U.S. military presence.

Defense Conversion

Given the overcapacity of the defense industries of all the industrial and some industrializing nations, it would obviously be helpful to accelerate efforts aimed at rationalizing defense industrial capabilities in Europe, North America, East Asia, and elsewhere. These initiatives have a long and not very successful history. Consolidation could help nonproliferation controls both by coordinating the policies of producers and by reducing pressures for competitive exports.

Interallied economic cooperation will inevitably be accompanied by closer consultation on political and diplomatic issues. At a minimum the working groups and other consultative mechanisms established to implement collaborative economic ventures, by providing the basis for more routine interaction among participating governments, could serve as the basis for consolidating allied interests in export restraint. Collaborative ventures could also help to reduce the costs of technological innovation and thus alleviate some export pressures.

At its core, proliferation is as much an industrial and an economic symptom as a military one. As states' national defense sectors undergo recessionary trends, the urge to export surplus capacity has increased accordingly. This increase is particularly acute in the former Soviet Union, where a large proportion of advanced industrial capacity once resided in the defense establishment.

The United States is in the middle of a ten-year program to decrease its defense spending from 6 percent of the gross national product to about 3 percent of the GNP. That decrease represents a shift of less than one-half percent of the GNP a year from defense spending to civilian spending. Thus, although this shift in the United States is a serious problem for the workers and the companies involved, it is not a serious macroeconomic problem for the country. Until recently the U.S. government's approach was to assume no responsibility for defense conversion, depending on market forces to handle the consolidation of the defense industry. This approach assumed that as the economy grew new jobs would be created by the civilian sector to absorb the excess workers from the defense sector.

In fact this approach has not worked during the last few years because the civilian sector has been in a recession. However, this laissez-faire policy is changing with the advent of a new administration. The Clinton administration has put forward plans to channel resources into the civilian infrastructure in the areas of transportation, communications, and energy and thereby hopes to make maximum use of the excess capacity within the defense industry. This concept raises many questions about the degree to which the defense industry as currently constituted is efficient enough to do the job. In particular, the complex regulations that control defense acquisition create such a large overhead burden that defense companies typically cannot compete with companies relying on more typical commercial procedures. Indeed companies that have significant defense and commercial businesses separate their defense business from its commercial counterpart so as to not "contaminate" their commercial business with overly bureaucratic procedures and associated uncompetitive overhead costs. Beginning in early 1993, several government initiatives got under way to help integrate the U.S. defense industry into the national industrial base by promoting greater efficiency and facilitating defense conversion activities.

A lessened pace of investment in military forces should be reflected in a decreased dedication of scientific and technological resources to weapons research and development. Indeed, the opportunity to address other human needs is itself an important motivation in the quest to achieve cooperative limits on military spending. The significance of such a diversion varies among the Western nations, the countries of the former eastern bloc, and the developing world. But all nations could benefit from new energy, transportation, and telecommunications infrastructures, suitably adapted to local circumstances. In the military sphere, to shift the emphasis from developing new weapons to enhancing the safety and security of existing forces, dismantling the nuclear and chemical weapon surplus of the cold war, and cleaning up production facilities and bases will create new opportunities for technological cooperation, as will developing the technologies of cooperative monitoring and verification.

Leadership, Resources, and a Long-Term Strategy

Traditionally, concerns about proliferation have been subordinate to other foreign policy priorities. Successive U.S. administrations have tended to look the other way in the face of obvious violations by countries that are allies or friends. The United States has been extremely reluctant to question Israel about its nuclear force development, for example.[10] Even in the case of Pakistan, a country with which the United States is far less closely allied, the Reagan and Bush administrations refused for years to confront the country about its nuclear program until forced to do so by U.S. legislation.[11]

The most significant instances of circumvention of NPT controls have involved technology cooperation agreements between third world clients that were perceived as benign and the advanced nuclear powers, including parties to the NPT. For example, the United States, Canada, and the United Kingdom helped India in its nuclear and missile programs. France and the United States assisted Israel in developing nuclear and high-performance missile capabilities, and Germany, France, and the Soviet Union assisted Iraq in chemical, nuclear, and ballistic missile development.

In recent years a number of developing states have chosen to acquire chemical and possibly biological armaments as substitutes for nuclear weapons. However much they may decry it, supplier states have indirectly contributed to this trend by lax export controls or even direct promotion of exports. In the late 1980s it became clear that firms in Germany and other Western nations had assisted Libya, Egypt, Iran, Iraq, and Syria with chemical weapons programs.[12]

If nonproliferation is indeed designated a serious priority, its management will require far more political leadership, accompanied by increases in funding commensurate with the new requirements imposed on existing regimes. At the national level nonproliferation is still the preoccupation of a relatively limited number of mid- to low-level bureaucrats whose influence is diluted by more senior officials who typically are more concerned about "overriding" foreign or defense policy objectives. Unless nonproliferation objectives receive the sustained support of the president and his relevant cabinet secretaries, no amount of dedication by civil servants will prove equal to the forces that are indifferent or even opposed to restraint initiatives.

It seems to be common sense that a serious nonproliferation regime should begin by devaluing the currency that has been so highly valued by its possessors and coveted by others. With the completion of a treaty in 1993 banning their production or use, this devaluation has already occurred with respect to chemical weapons and will be necessary for biological weapons as well. Moreover, if nuclear weapons pose dangers and incur political costs out of proportion to their benefits, this should be stated explicitly, and universal norms should be established accordingly. Depending on judgments about the utility of nuclear forces for guaranteeing U.S. and allied security, it is not totally implausible that a consensus could be reached that nuclear weapons are not very useful and actually impose high costs on their possessors, both politically and operationally.

But if nuclear weapons continue to be perceived as the core guarantor of sovereignty and state security among the established nuclear powers, then it is perhaps a losing proposition to suggest that other states not acquire them. There is great resistance in official circles to the idea that nuclear weapons might one day be included in a global ban on all weapons of mass destruction.

Certainly a proposal to ban nuclear weapons prompts significant practical questions. Would such a ban ever be verifiable? What verification measures and inspection schemes and agencies would be necessary to provide sufficient confidence that all nations had lived up to their commitments? And what about the risk that, after all weapons of mass destruction had been destroyed, a state would decide to rebuild such weapons, since nuclear expertise obviously cannot be disinvented? There are also serious questions about the political feasibility of such an objective. Nations such as Israel and Pakistan are threatened by powerful neighbors. They developed nuclear weapons as a way of countering the larger or superior forces of their rivals. Obviously they would only consider giving up a nuclear capability if the threat of war had receded significantly, and if sufficient time had passed for them to gain confidence in the peaceful intentions of their former enemies.

Of all the various perspectives in the current security debate, only cooperative security begins to address such dilemmas. Although it certainly does not provide a blueprint, cooperative security can provide guidelines for how such an agreement might be sought. A ban on weapons of mass destruction would have to be universal and consensual and based on high levels of transparency agreed to by adherents. It would have to include a system of incentives to elicit support and credible penalties for any breach of the global contract. It would require the massive strengthening of international procedures and organizations to track technology flows, to mediate conflicts, to verify and enforce agreements, and to provide for the security of states that may face potential aggression.

These reflections might be considered premature. But to cling for much longer to the notion that the nuclear "haves" can indefinitely exclude the "have-nots" is surely unrealistic.

Conclusion

If the cold war could be summarized as an era of competition in military development and the quest for military advantage, the emerging era can credibly be projected as a search for reliable control over the results of that competition. The primary security objectives that have guided the major military establishments for decades—the deterrence of nuclear aggression and territorial defense against organized aggression—are no longer the overriding concerns. What has instead been left for resolution is the question of how to manage the secondary consequences of existing deployments, advanced technical developments, excess military production capacity, and the residual effects of large-power decisions on the character and direction of regional security agendas. The need to reconfigure and reliably contain the remains of the Soviet military establishment, to address and reorient the consequences of four decades of strategic force rivalry, to stem what seems now to be the inexorable diffusion of weapons technology, to respond to the challenge of an integrated global economy with its implications for the distribution of potentially new and dangerous technologies, and to counter the continued threat of widespread regional and civil violence are all, in essence, problems of control. These problems might well be solved by concerted international cooperation, but there is no guarantee that this cooperation will either occur or be effective. However, these problems would certainly be worsened by unregulated competition.

The imperatives of control are even more imposing for those countries that have not achieved stable military establishments and that may not have the resources to develop their security postures in a manner that they believe ensures their security. Their perceptions of impending security challenges may invariably be different from the perceptions of the established democracies. Countries without reliable military establishments, particularly those that are vulnerable to potentially hostile states with superior capabilities, are unavoidably dependent on some form of international cooperation for their primary security objectives. But they are also seeking to demonstrate their sovereignty on more equal terms. These competing pressures may raise some states' *objective* stakes in cooperation but will also militate against any proposed form of cooperation that implies new forms of dependency or susceptibility to discrimination.

To achieve a regime that can promote cooperation as well as address the disparities in the distribution of military and technical capacity, the major military establishments will have to demonstrate concretely that they take regional security concerns seriously. They also must understand the potentially provocative effects of their asymmetrically powerful force capabilities if these capabilities are not organized on behalf of collective objectives. As a first step the advanced countries will need to constrain their own military investment and subordinate the projection of their power to matters of international interest rather than national prerogative. They will also have to abide by principles of equity, in substance and procedure, in determining and defining international interests. For their part smaller states that wish to cooperate with larger powers for collective self-interest would also have to align their sovereign aspirations with common standards of military behavior derived from international consensus. Unilateral quests for advantage regionally or to gain leverage over stronger states would have no place in such a security structure.

Notes

1. Cited in Steve Coll and R. Jeffrey Smith, "Is Ukraine Reaching for Control over Nuclear Arms?" *Washington Post,* June 3, 1993, p. 1.

2. One hundred fifty countries approved the resolution, with no dissenting vote and only Cuba and Iraq abstaining. Stockholm International Peace Research Institute, *SIPRI Yearbook 1992* (Oxford University Press, 1992), pp. 299–301.

3. For more information on regulations and procedures, see U.S. Congress, Office of Technology Assessment, *Proliferation of Weapons of Mass Destruction: Assessing the Risks,* OTA-ISC-559 (August 1993).

4. In the previous administration, proposals from the Senate and House Select Committees on Intelligence to refocus Defense Intelligence and National Security Agency efforts in this manner encountered outright opposition from former secretary of defense Cheney, among others. It was argued that these agencies were compelled to be "combat support agencies" that must be "especially responsive to the needs of war-fighting commanders." George Lardner, Jr., "Cheney Assails Intelligence Revision Plan," *Washington Post,* March 24, 1992, p. 5.

5. For further discussion of reform of the IAEA, see, for instance, Anthony Fainberg, *Strengthening IAEA Safeguards: Lessons from Iraq,* Report of the Center for International Security and Arms Control (Stanford University, April 1993).

6. Arab states in particular defended their right to possess chemical weapons as a counter to Israel's nuclear arsenal. See Michael R. Gordon, "Paris Conference Condemns the Use of Chemical Arms," *New York Times,* January 12, 1989, p. A1.

7. Although the price of UN peacekeeping is increasing, members rarely pay their dues on time or in full. By January 31, 1993, for example, only 18 of 180 members had fulfilled their financial obligations. See Paul Lewis, "Panel Sees Growing UN Intervention," *New York Times,* February 27, 1993, p. A4; and Paul Lewis, "UN Is in Arrears on Peace Efforts," *New York Times,* May 16, 1993, p. A9.

8. See David E. Rosenbaum, "War in the Gulf: Financing; U.S. Has Received $50 billion in Pledges for War," *New York Times,* February 11, 1991, p. A13.

9. In addition to the operational and military costs to the United States and its allies, the Arab Monetary Fund reported that the Persian Gulf War has cost the region $676 billion in 1990 and 1991. For more details, see Youssef M. Ibrahim, "Gulf War Is Said to Have Cost the Region $676 Billion in 1990–91," *New York Times,* April 25, 1993, p. A14.

10. Several analysts have tried to document the allegation that the United States lent support to Israel's nuclear ambitions over the course of several administrations, the United States having been motivated in part by the belief that the possession of nuclear weapons by this close ally would prove to be in the U.S. interest in the region. See, for

example, Seymour M. Hersh, *The Samson Option: Israel's Nuclear Arsenal and America's Foreign Policy* (Random House, 1991).

11. With the so-called Pressler amendment, Congress amended the Foreign Assistance Act of 1961 to require suspension of all economic and military aid to Pakistan if the executive branch could not certify that Pakistan was not pursuing nuclear weapons development. After years of formal fiction, even a modified certification proved impossible in 1990, and U.S. aid was terminated. Even so, the Bush administration chose to interpret the aid cut-off as not covering commercial sales and continued to provide dual-use equipment such as spare parts for Pakistan's F-16 (nuclear-capable) fighter aircraft. See, for instance, Steven Greenhouse, "Senators Seek Full Cutoff of Arms to Pakistan," *New York Times,* March 8, 1992, p. A12.

12. Michael R. Gordon, "C.I.A. Sees a Developing World with Developed Arms," *New York Times,* February 10, 1989, p. A3.

Participants

with their affiliations at the time of their project participation

Cooperative Security Consortium Core Group

Kanti Bajpai *Rajiv Gandhi Institute*

Coit D. Blacker *Stanford University*

George Bunn *Stanford University*

Ashton B. Carter *Harvard University*

Abram Chayes *Harvard University*

Antonia Handler Chayes *Consensus Building Institute*

Stephen Cohen *University of Illinois*

Jonathan Dean *Union of Concerned Scientists*

Francis Deng *Brookings Institution*

Kenneth Flamm *Brookings Institution*

Alexander George *Stanford University*

David Hamburg *Carnegie Corporation of New York*

Harry Harding *Brookings Institution*

Catherine McArdle Kelleher *Brookings Institution*

Geoffrey Kemp *Carnegie Endowment for International Peace*

Michael Krepon *Henry L. Stimson Center*

Michael B. Levin *Brookings Institution*

Michael May *Stanford University*

Steven E. Miller *Harvard University*

Frederic Mosher *Carnegie Corporation of New York*

David Mussington *Harvard University*

Janne E. Nolan *Brookings Institution*

William J. Perry *Stanford University*

William Potter *Monterey Institute of International Studies*

Wolfgang H. Reinicke *Brookings Institution*

Condoleezza Rice *Stanford University*

Alex Rondos *International Orthodox Christian Charities*

Yahya M. Sadowski *Brookings Institution*

James A. Schear *Henry L. Stimson Center*

Leonard S. Spector *Carnegie Endowment for International Peace*

Paul B. Stares *Brookings Institution*

John D. Steinbruner *Brookings Institution*

Jane Wales *Carnegie Corporation of New York*

Mitchel Wallerstein *National Academy of Sciences*

Other Workshop Participants

Harvard University: November 7–8, 1991
Brookings Institution: December 5–6, 1991
Stanford University: March 31–April 2, 1992
Carnegie Endowment for International Peace: May 12–13, 1992
Snowmass, Colorado: August 3–7, 1992

Morton Abramowitz *Carnegie Endowment for International Peace*

Herbert Abrams *Stanford University*

Ruth Adams *John D. and Catherine T. MacArthur Foundation*

Bulent Aliriza *Carnegie Endowment for International Peace*

Shaul Bakhash *George Mason University*

Rami Bar-Or *Stanford University*

Robert Bell *Senate Armed Services Committee*

David Bernstein *Stanford University*

Edward Brosh *Harvard University*

Brahma Chellaney *University of Maryland*

Owen Coté *Harvard University*

Sean Coté *Tufts University*

Catharin Dalpino *Asia Foundation*

Brian Davenport *Stanford University*

Mathias Dembenski *Harvard University*

Sidney Drell *Stanford University*

Larry Fabian *Carnegie Endowment for International Peace*

Anthony Fainberg *Stanford University*

Steve Flank *Harvard University*

Mikhail Gerasev *Institute of USA and Canada*

Paul Goble *Carnegie Endowment for International Peace*

Adrianne Goins *Brookings Institution*

Mark Goodman *Harvard University*

Thomas Graham *Rockefeller Foundation*

Morton Halperin *Carnegie Endowment for International Peace*

Robert Hamerton-Kelly *Stanford University*

Rosemary Hamerton-Kelly *Stanford University*

Selig Harrison *Carnegie Endowment for International Peace*

John Harvey *Stanford University*

Ahmed Hashim *International Institute for Strategic Studies*

Laura Holgate *Harvard University*

David Holloway *Stanford University*

Efraim Inbar *Georgetown University*

Mahnaz Ispahani *National Democratic Institute*

John Jenny *Stanford University*

Andrei Kokoshin *Institute of USA and Canada*

Steven Krasner *Stanford University*

John Lewis *Stanford University*

Thomas Longstreth *Department of Defense*

William Martel *Harvard University*

Mathew Meselson *Harvard University*

Kenneth Myers *Office of Senator Richard Lugar*

Ambassador Robert Oakley *U.S. Institute of Peace*

Andrew Pierre *Carnegie Endowment for International Peace*

Daniel Poneman *National Security Council*

Katherine Smith *Stanford University*

Charles Zraket *Harvard University*

Index